MEDITERRANEAN DIET COOKBOOK

1200 Quick & Healthy Recipes That Anyone Can Cook at Home | 30-Days Meal Plan Included |

Jemma Muggs

TABLE OF CONTENTS

MEDITERRANEAN DIET SHOPPING LIST

STAPLES

Oils
- [ ] Olive Oil
- [ ] Extra-virgin olive oil

Vinegar
- [ ] Balsamic
- [ ] Red wine
- [ ] White wine

A variety of dried herbs & spices
- [ ] Basil
- [ ] Parsley
- [ ] Oregano
- [ ] Cayenne pepper
- [ ] Cinnamon
- [ ] Cloves
- [ ] Cumin
- [ ] Coriander
- [ ] Dill
- [ ] Fennel seed
- [ ] Ginger
- [ ] Rosemary
- [ ] Red and white wine
- [ ] Garlic

MEAT & SEAFOOD

- [ ] Clams
- [ ] Cod
- [ ] Crab meat
- [ ] Halibut
- [ ] Mussels
- [ ] Salmon
- [ ] Scallops
- [ ] Shrimp
- [ ] Tilapia
- [ ] Tuna
- [ ] Chicken breast*
- [ ] Chicken thighs*
- [ ] Lean red meat**

CANNED & PACKAGED

- [ ] Olives
- [ ] Canned Tomatoes

Dried & canned beans
- [ ] Cannellini beans
- [ ] Navy beans
- [ ] Chickpeas
- [ ] Black beans
- [ ] Kidney beans
- [ ] Lentils
- [ ] Canned tuna

Whole Grains
- [ ] Whole grain pasta
- [ ] Bulgur
- [ ] Whole wheat couscous
- [ ] Quinoa
- [ ] Brown rice
- [ ] Barley
- [ ] Faro
- [ ] Polenta
- [ ] Oats
- [ ] Whole wheat bread or pita
- [ ] Whole grain crackers

Nuts & seeds
- [ ] Almonds
- [ ] Hazelnuts
- [ ] Pine nuts
- [ ] Walnuts
- [ ] Cashews
- [ ] Sunflower seeds
- [ ] Sesame seeds

REFRIGERATED

Cheese
- [ ] Cream cheese
- [ ] Feta
- [ ] Goat cheese
- [ ] Mozzarella
- [ ] Parmesan
- [ ] Ricotta
- [ ] Low-fat milk
- [ ] Plain or Greek yogurt
- [ ] Eggs

PRODUCE

- [ ] Apples
- [ ] Artichokes
- [ ] Asparagus
- [ ] Avocado
- [ ] Bananas
- [ ] Beets
- [ ] Bell peppers
- [ ] Berries (all types)
- [ ] Broccoli
- [ ] Brussels sprouts
- [ ] Cabbage
- [ ] Carrots
- [ ] Celery
- [ ] Cherries
- [ ] Cucumbers
- [ ] Dates
- [ ] Eggplant
- [ ] Fennel
- [ ] Figs
- [ ] Grapes
- [ ] Green beans
- [ ] Kiwi
- [ ] Leafy greens
- [ ] Lemons
- [ ] Lettuce
- [ ] Limes
- [ ] Melons
- [ ] Mushrooms
- [ ] Nectarines
- [ ] Onions
- [ ] Oranges
- [ ] Peas
- [ ] Peaches
- [ ] Pears
- [ ] Plums
- [ ] Pomegranate
- [ ] Potatoes
- [ ] Shallots
- [ ] Spinach
- [ ] Squash
- [ ] Tomatoes
- [ ] Zucchini

* In moderation, once to twice per week
** On rare occasions, once to twice monthly

INTRODUCTION

"Mediterranean diet" is a generic term based on the traditional eating habits in the countries bordering the Mediterranean Sea. There's not one standard Mediterranean diet. At least 16 countries border the Mediterranean. Eating styles vary among these countries and even among regions within each country because of differences in culture, ethnic background, religion, economy, geography and agricultural production. However, there are some common factors.

Interest in the Mediterranean diet began in the 1960s with the observation that coronary heart disease caused fewer deaths in Mediterranean countries, such as Greece and Italy, than in the U.S. and northern Europe. Subsequent studies found that the Mediterranean diet is associated with reduced risk factors for cardiovascular disease. The Mediterranean diet is a way of eating based on the traditional cuisine of countries bordering the Mediterranean Sea. The foundation of the Mediterranean diet is vegetables, fruits, herbs, nuts, beans and whole grains. Meals are built around these plant-based foods. Moderate amounts of dairy, poultry and eggs are also central to the Mediterranean Diet, as is seafood. In contrast, red meat is eaten only occasionally. Healthy fats are a mainstay of the Mediterranean diet. They're eaten instead of less healthy fats, such as saturated and trans fats, which contribute to heart disease.

Olive oil is the primary source of added fat in the Mediterranean diet. Olive oil provides monounsaturated fat, which has been found to lower total cholesterol and low-density lipoprotein (LDL or "bad") cholesterol levels. The Mediterranean diet typically allows red wine in moderation. Although alcohol has been associated with a reduced risk of heart disease in some studies, it's by no means risk free. Below you can find the shopping list of the most common in the Mediterranean diet. They are divided by category; they are the most used but you will also find recipes with not present in this list.

Chapter 1
The 30-Day Meal Plan

	Breakfast	Lunch	Dinner	Total Calories
DAY 1	Ricotta Toast with Strawberries Calories:274	Black Bean Chili with Mangoes Calories: 430	Roasted Veggies and Brown Rice Bowl Calories: 453	1157
DAY 2	Mediterranean Eggs Calories: 223	Italian Sautéd Cannellini Beans Calories: 435	Asian-Inspired Tuna Lettuce Wraps Calories: 270	928
DAY 3	Breakfast Yogurt Sundae Calories: 236	Turkish Canned Pinto Bean Salad Calories: 402	Roasted Chicken Thighs With Basmati Rice Calories: 400	1038
DAY 4	Savory Breakfast Oatmeal Calories: 197	Bulgur Pilaf with Garbanzo Calories: 462	Quick Chicken Salad Wraps Calories: 428	1087
DAY 5	Tomato and Egg Scramble Calories: 260	Mediterranean Lentils Calories: 426	Mango and Coconut Frozen Pie Calories: 426	1112
DAY 6	Baked Eggs in Avocado Calories: 301	Tomato Basil Pasta Calories: 415	Potato Lamb and Olive Stew Calories: 309	1025
DAY 7	Crustless Tiropita Calories: 181	Ritzy Veggie Chili Calories: 633	Pecan and Carrot Cake Calories: 255	1069
DAY 8	Avocado Toast with Goat Cheese Calories: 136	Caprese Fusilli Calories: 589	Zucchini and Artichokes Bowl with Farro Calories: 366	1091
DAY 9	Berry and Nut Parfait Calories: 507	Walnut and Ricotta Spaghetti Calories: 264	Garlicky Zucchini Cubes with Mint Calories: 146	917
DAY 10	Kale and Apple Smoothie Calories: 177	Chard and Mushroom Risotto Calories: 420	Parsley-Dijon Chicken and Potatoes Calories: 324	921
DAY 11	Calo Cinnamon Oatmeal Calories: 107	Pesto Pasta Calories: 1067	Cauliflower Hash with Carrots Calories: 158	1332
DAY 12	Breakfast Yogurt Sundae Calories: 236	Grana Padano Risotto Calories: 307	Vegetable and Cheese Lavash Pizza Calories: 431	974
DAY 13	Avocado Toast with Goat Cheese Calories: 136	Garlic Shrimp Fettuccine Calories: 615	Sweet Potato and Tomato Curry Calories: 224	975

DAY 14	Banana-Blueberry Breakfast Cookies Calories: 264	Lentil Risotto Calories: 261	Macadamia Pork Calories: 436	**961**
DAY 15	Blackberry-Yogurt Green Smoothie Calories: 201	Cheesy Tomato Linguine Calories: 311	Glazed Mushroom and Vegetable Fajitas Calories: 403	**915**
DAY 16	Spinach Cheese Pie Calories: 417	Chicken and Spaghetti Ragù Bolognese Calories: 477	Spicy Tofu Tacos with Cherry Tomato Salsa Calories: 240	**1134**
DAY 17	Baked Ricotta with Honey Pears Calories: 329 Page:	Black Bean Chili with Mangoes Calories: 430	Roasted Tomato Panini Calories: 323	**1082**
DAY 18	Breakfast Pancakes with Berry Sauce Calories: 275	Italian Sautéd Cannellini Beans Calories: 435	Vegetable and Cheese Lavash Pizza Calories: 431	**1141**
DAY 19	Apple-Tahini Toast Calories: 458	Cumin Quinoa Pilaf Calories: 384	Lamb Tagine with Couscous and Almonds Calories: 447	**1289**
DAY 20	Tomato and Egg Breakfast Pizza Calories: 429	Grana Padano Risotto Calories: 307	Cheesy Sweet Potato Burgers Calories: 290	**1026**
DAY 21	Avocado and Egg Toast Calories: 297	Mint Brown Rice Calories: 514	Cauliflower Rice Risotto with Mushrooms Calories: 167	**978**
DAY 22	Ricotta Toast with Strawberries Calories: 274	Tomato Basil Pasta Calories: 415	Baked Salmon with Basil and Tomato Calories: 403	**1092**
DAY 23	Creamy Vanilla Oatmeal Calories: 117	Ritzy Veggie Chili Calories: 633	Spiced Roast Chicken Calories: 275	**1025**
DAY 24	Mediterranean Eggs (Shakshuka) Calories: 223	Mediterranean Lentils Calories: 426	Lemony Shrimp with Orzo Salad Calories: 565	**1214**
DAY 25	Healthy Chia Pudding Calories: 236	Lentil and Vegetable Curry Stew Calories: 530	Grilled Chicken and Zucchini Kebabs Calories: 283	**1049**
DAY 26	Feta and Spinach Frittata Calories: 529	Wild Rice, Celery, and Cauliflower Pilaf Calories: 214	Roasted Chicken Thighs With Basmati Calories: 400	**1143**
DAY 27	Kale and Apple Smoothie Calories: 177	Pesto Pasta Calories: 1067	Zucchini Fritters Calories: 113	**1357**
DAY 28	Spinach Cheese Pie Calories: 417	Walnut and Ricotta Spaghetti Calories: 264	Brussels Sprouts Linguine Calories: 502	**1183**

DAY 29	Egg Bake Calories: 240	Roasted Ratatouille Pasta Calories: 613	Grilled Vegetable Skewers Calories: 115	**968**
DAY 30	Pumpkin Pie Parfait Calories: 263	Bean and Veggie Pasta Calories: 565	Sauté ed Green Beans with Tomatoes Calories: 219	**1047**

Please note: refer to the index to find the number of the page corresponding to the recipe.

We trust that this 30-day nutritional plan is to your liking!

Chapter 2
Breakfasts

Spinach and Egg Breakfast Wraps

Prep time: 10 minutes | Cook time: 7 minutes | Serves 2

1 tablespoon olive oil	3 large eggs, whisked
¼ cup minced onion	1½ cups packed baby spinach
3 to 4 tablespoons minced sun-dried tomatoes in olive oil and herbs	1 ounce (28 g) crumbled feta cheese
	Salt, to taste
	2 (8-inch) whole-wheat tortillas

1. Heat the olive oil in a large skillet over medium-high heat.
2. Sauté the onion and tomatoes for about 3 minutes, stirring occasionally, until softened.
3. Reduce the heat to medium. Add the whisked eggs and stir-fry for 1 to 2 minutes.
4. Stir in the baby spinach and scatter with the crumbled feta cheese. Season as needed with salt.
5. Remove the egg mixture from the heat to a plate. Set aside.
6. Working in batches, place 2 tortillas on a microwave-safe dish and microwave for about 20 seconds to make them warm.
7. Spoon half of the egg mixture into each tortilla. Fold them in half and roll up, then serve.

Per Serving

calories: 434 | fat: 28.1g | protein: 17.2g | carbs: 30.8g | fiber: 6.0g | sodium: 551mg

Mediterranean Eggs (Shakshuka)

Prep time: 5 minutes | Cook time: 20 minutes | Serves 4

2 tablespoons extra-virgin olive oil	1 (14.5-ounce/ 411-g) can diced tomatoes, drained
1 cup chopped shallots	¼ teaspoon ground cardamom
1 teaspoon garlic powder	
1 cup finely diced potato	¼ teaspoon paprika
1 cup chopped red bell peppers	¼ teaspoon turmeric
	4 large eggs
	¼ cup chopped fresh cilantro

1. Preheat the oven to 350ºF (180ºC).
2. Heat the olive oil in an ovenproof skillet over medium-high heat until it shimmers.
3. Add the shallots and sauté for about 3 minutes, stirring occasionally, until fragrant.
4. Fold in the garlic powder, potato, and bell peppers and stir to combine.
5. Cover and cook for 10 minutes, stirring frequently.
6. Add the tomatoes, cardamon, paprika, and turmeric and mix well.
7. When the mixture begins to bubble, remove from the heat and crack the eggs into the skillet.
8. Transfer the skillet to the preheated oven and bake for 5 to 10 minutes, or until the egg whites are set and the yolks are cooked to your liking.
9. Remove from the oven and garnish with the cilantro before serving.

Per Serving

calories: 223 | fat: 11.8g | protein: 9.1g | carbs: 19.5g | fiber: 3.0g | sodium: 277mg

Ricotta Toast with Strawberries

Prep time: 10 minutes | Cook time: 0 minutes | Serves 2

½ cup crumbled ricotta cheese	4 slices of whole-grain bread, toasted
1 tablespoon honey, plus additional as needed	1 cup sliced fresh strawberries
Pinch of sea salt, plus additional as needed	4 large fresh basil leaves, sliced into thin shreds

1. Mix together the cheese, honey, and salt in a small bowl until well incorporated.
2. Taste and add additional salt and honey as needed.
3. Spoon 2 tablespoons of the cheese mixture onto each slice of bread and spread it all over.
4. Sprinkle the sliced strawberry and basil leaves on top before serving.

Per Serving calories: 274 | fat: 7.9g | protein: 15.1g | carbs: 39.8g | fiber: 5.0g | sodium: 322mg

Egg Bake

Prep time: 10 minutes | Cook time: 30 minutes | Serves 2

1 tablespoon olive oil	½ teaspoon onion powder
1 slice whole-grain bread	¼ teaspoon garlic powder
4 large eggs	¾ cup chopped cherry tomatoes
3 tablespoons unsweetened almond milk	¼ teaspoon salt
	Pinch freshly ground black pepper

1. Preheat the oven to 375ºF (190ºC).
2. Coat two ramekins with the olive oil and transfer to a baking sheet. Line the bottom of each ramekin with ½ of bread slice.
3. In a medium bowl, whisk together the eggs, almond milk, onion powder, garlic powder, tomatoes, salt, and pepper until well combined.
4. Pour the mixture evenly into two ramekins. Bake in the preheated oven for 30 minutes, or until the eggs are completely set.
5. Cool for 5 minutes before serving.

Per Serving

calories: 240 | fat: 17.4g | protein: 9.0g | carbs: 12.2g | fiber: 2.8g | sodium: 396mg

Creamy Peach Smoothie

Prep time: 15 minutes | Cook time: 0 minutes | Serves 2

2 cups packed frozen peaches, partially thawed	2 tablespoons flax meal
	1 tablespoon honey
½ ripe avocado	1 teaspoon orange extract
½ cup plain or vanilla Greek yogurt	1 teaspoon vanilla extract

1. Place all the in a blender and blend until completely mixed and smooth.
2. Divide the mixture into two bowls and serve immediately.

Per Serving

calories: 212 | fat: 13.1g | protein: 6.0g | carbs: 22.5g | fiber: 7.2g | sodium: 40mg

Blueberry Smoothie

Prep time: 5 minutes | Cook time: 0 minutes | Serves 1

1 cup unsweetened almond milk, plus additional as needed

¼ cup frozen blueberries

2 tablespoons unsweetened almond butter

1 tablespoon extra-virgin olive oil

1 tablespoon ground flaxseed or chia seeds

1 to 2 teaspoons maple syrup

½ teaspoon vanilla extract

¼ teaspoon ground cinnamon

1. Blend all the in a blender until smooth and creamy.
2. You can add additional almond milk to reach your preferred consistency as needed. Serve immediately.

Per Serving

calories: 459 | fat: 40.1g | protein: 8.9g | carbs: 20.0g | fiber: 10.1g | sodium: 147mg

Pumpkin Pie Parfait

Prep time: 5 minutes | Cook time: 0 minutes | Serves 4

1 (15-ounce / 425-g) can pure pumpkin purée

4 teaspoons honey

1 teaspoon pumpkin pie spice

¼ teaspoon ground cinnamon

2 cups plain Greek yogurt

1 cup honey granola

1. Combine the pumpkin purée, honey, pumpkin pie spice, and cinnamon in a large bowl and stir to mix well.
2. Cover the bowl with plastic wrap and chill in the refrigerator for at least 2 hours.
3. Make the parfaits: Layer each parfait glass with ¼ cup pumpkin mixture in the bottom. Top with ¼ cup of yogurt and scatter each top with ¼ cup of honey granola. Repeat the layers until the glasses are full.
4. Serve immediately.

Per Serving

calories: 263 | fat: 8.9g | protein: 15.3g | carbs: 34.6g | fiber: 6.0g | sodium: 91mg

Cauliflower Breakfast Porridge

Prep time: 5 minutes | Cook time: 5 minutes | Serves 2

2 cups riced cauliflower

¾ cup unsweetened almond milk

4 tablespoons extra-virgin olive oil, divided

2 teaspoons grated fresh orange peel (from ½ orange)

½ teaspoon almond extract or vanilla extract

½ teaspoon ground cinnamon

⅛ teaspoon salt

4 tablespoons chopped walnuts, divided

1 to 2 teaspoons maple syrup (optional)

1. Place the riced cauliflower, almond milk, 2 tablespoons of olive oil, orange peel, almond extract, cinnamon, and salt in a medium saucepan. Stir to incorporate and bring the mixture to a boil over medium-high heat, stirring.
2. Remove from the heat and add 2 tablespoons of chopped walnuts and maple syrup (if desired).Stir again and divide the porridge into bowls. Sprinkle each bowl evenly with remaining 2 tablespoons of walnuts and olive oil.

Per Serving calories: 381 | fat: 37.8g | protein: 5.2g | carbs: 10.9g | fiber: 4.0g | sodium: 228mg

Morning Overnight Oats with Raspberries

Prep time: 5 minutes | Cook time: 0 minutes | Serves 2

⅔ cup unsweetened almond milk

¼ cup raspberries

⅓ cup rolled oats

1 teaspoon honey

¼ teaspoon turmeric

⅛ teaspoon ground cinnamon

Pinch ground cloves

1. Place the almond milk, raspberries, rolled oats, honey, turmeric, cinnamon, and cloves in a mason jar. Cover and shake to combine. Transfer to the refrigerator for at least 8 hours, preferably 24 hours. Serve chilled.

Per Serving calories: 81 | fat: 1.9g | protein: 2.1g | carbs: 13.8g | fiber: 3.0g | sodium: 97mg

Tomato and Egg Scramble

Prep time: 10 minutes | Cook time: 20 minutes | Serves 4

2 tablespoons extra-virgin olive oil

¼ cup finely minced red onion

1½ cups chopped fresh tomatoes

2 garlic cloves, minced

½ teaspoon dried thyme

½ teaspoon dried oregano

8 large eggs

½ teaspoon salt

¼ teaspoon freshly ground black pepper

¾ cup crumbled feta cheese

¼ cup chopped fresh mint leaves

1. Heat the olive oil in a large skillet over medium heat.
2. Sauté the red onion and tomatoes in the hot skillet for 10 to 12 minutes, or until the tomatoes are softened. Stir in the garlic, thyme, and oregano and sauté for 2 to 4 minutes, or until the garlic is fragrant. Meanwhile, beat the eggs with the salt and pepper in a medium bowl until frothy. Pour the beaten eggs into the skillet and reduce the heat to low. Scramble for 3 to 4 minutes, stirring constantly, or until the eggs are set. Remove from the heat and scatter with the feta cheese and mint. Serve warm.

Per Serving calories: 260 | fat: 21.9g | protein: 10.2g | carbs: 5.8g | fiber: 1.0g | sodium: 571mg

Baked Eggs in Avocado

Prep time: 5 minutes | Cook time: 10 to 15 minutes | Serves 2

1 ripe large avocado

2 large eggs

Salt and freshly ground black pepper, to taste

4 tablespoons jarred pesto, for serving

2 tablespoons chopped tomato, for serving

2 tablespoons crumbled feta cheese, for serving (optional)

1. Preheat the oven to 425ºF (220ºC).
2. Slice the avocado in half, remove the pit and scoop out a generous tablespoon of flesh from each half to create a hole big enough to fit an egg.
3. Transfer the avocado halves (cut-side up) to a baking sheet.
4. Crack 1 egg into each avocado half and sprinkle with salt and pepper.
5. Bake in the preheated oven for 10 to 15 minutes, or until the eggs are cooked to your preferred doneness.
6. Remove the avocado halves from the oven. Scatter each avocado half evenly with the jarred pesto, chopped tomato, and crumbled feta cheese (if desired). Serve immediately.

Per Serving

calories: 301 | fat: 25.9g | protein: 8.1g | carbs: 9.8g | fiber: 5.0g | sodium: 435mg

Crustless Tiropita (Greek Cheese Pie)

Prep time: 10 minutes | Cook time: 35 to 40 minutes | Serves 6

4 tablespoons extra-virgin olive oil, divided	½ teaspoon lemon zest
½ cup whole-milk ricotta cheese	¼ teaspoon freshly ground black pepper
1¼ cups crumbled feta cheese	2 large eggs
1 tablespoon chopped fresh dill	½ teaspoon baking powder
2 tablespoons chopped fresh mint	

1. Preheat the oven to 350°F (180°C). Coat the bottom and sides of a baking dish with 2 tablespoons of olive oil. Set aside.
2. Mix together the ricotta and feta cheese in a medium bowl and stir with a fork until well combined. Add the dill, mint, lemon zest, and black pepper and mix well.
3. In a separate bowl, whisk together the eggs and baking powder. Pour the whisked eggs into the bowl of cheese mixture. Blend well.
4. Slowly pour the mixture into the coated baking dish and drizzle with the remaining 2 tablespoons of olive oil.
5. Bake in the preheated oven for about 35 to 40 minutes, or until the pie is browned around the edges and cooked through.
6. Cool for 5 minutes before slicing into wedges.

Per Serving

calories: 181 | fat: 16.6g | protein: 7.0g | carbs: 1.8g | fiber: 0g | sodium: 321mg

Fluffy Almond Flour Pancakes with Strawberries

Prep time: 5 minutes | Cook time: 15 minutes | Serves 4

1 cup plus 2 tablespoons unsweetened almond milk	1 teaspoon baking soda
1 cup almond flour	¼ teaspoon salt
2 large eggs, whisked ⅓ cup honey	2 tablespoons extra-virgin olive oil
	1 cup sliced strawberries

1. Combine the almond milk, almond flour, whisked eggs, honey, baking soda, and salt in a large bowl and whisk to incorporate.
2. Heat the olive oil in a large skillet over medium-high heat.
3. Make the pancakes: Pour ⅓ cup of batter into the hot skillet and swirl the pan so the batter covers the bottom evenly. Cook for 2 to 3 minutes until the pancake turns golden brown around the edges. Gently flip the pancake with a spatula and cook for 2 to 3 minutes until cooked through. Repeat with the remaining batter.
4. Serve the pancakes with the sliced strawberries on top.

Per Serving

calories: 298 | fat: 11.7g | protein: 11.8g | carbs: 34.8g | fiber: 3.9g | sodium: 195mg

Breakfast Yogurt Sundae

Prep time: 5 minutes | Cook time: 0 minutes | Serves 1

¾ cup plain Greek yogurt	2 tablespoons walnut pieces
¼ cup fresh mixed berries (blueberries, strawberries, blackberries)	1 tablespoon ground flaxseed
	2 fresh mint leaves, shredded

1. Pour the yogurt into a tall parfait glass and sprinkle with the mixed berries, walnut pieces, and flaxseed.
2. Garnish with the shredded mint leaves and serve immediately.

Per Serving

calories: 236 | fat: 10.8g | protein: 21.1g | carbs: 15.9g | fiber: 4.1g | sodium: 63mg

Avocado Toast with Goat Cheese

Prep time: 5 minutes | Cook time: 2 to 3 minutes | Serves 2

2 slices whole-wheat thin-sliced bread	2 tablespoons crumbled goat cheese
½ avocado	Salt, to taste

1. Toast the bread slices in a toaster for 2 to 3 minutes on each side until browned.
2. Scoop out the flesh from the avocado into a medium bowl and mash it with a fork to desired consistency. Spread the mash onto each piece of toast.
3. Scatter the crumbled goat cheese on top and season as needed with salt.
4. Serve immediately.

Per Serving

calories: 136 | fat: 5.9g | protein: 5.0g | carbs: 17.5g | fiber: 5.1g | sodium: 194mg

Banana-Blueberry Breakfast Cookies

Prep time: 10 minutes | Cook time: 13 minutes | Serves 4

2 medium bananas, sliced	1 teaspoon vanilla extract
4 tablespoons almond butter	⅔ cup coconut flour
4 large eggs, lightly beaten	¼ teaspoon salt
½ cup unsweetened applesauce	1 cup fresh or frozen blueberries

1. Preheat the oven to 375°F (190°C). Line a baking sheet with parchment paper.
2. Stir together the bananas and almond butter in a medium bowl until well incorporated.
3. Fold in the beaten eggs, applesauce, and vanilla and blend well.
4. Add the coconut flour and salt and mix well. Add the blueberries and stir to just incorporate.
5. Drop about 2 tablespoons of dough onto the parchment paper-lined baking sheet for each cookie. Using your clean hand, flatten each into a rounded biscuit shape, until it is 1 inch thick.
6. Bake in the preheated oven for about 13 minutes, or until the top is golden brown and a toothpick inserted in the center comes out clean.
7. Let the cookies cool for 5 to 10 minutes before serving.

Per Serving (3 cookies)

calories: 264 | fat: 13.9g | protein: 7.3g | carbs: 27.6g | fiber: 5.2g | sodium: 219mg

Blackberry-Yogurt Green Smoothie

Prep time: 5 minutes | Cook time: 0 minutes | Serves 2

1 cup plain Greek yogurt	½ cup unsweetened almond
1 cup baby spinach	milk
½ cup frozen blackberries	½ teaspoon peeled and grated fresh ginger
	¼ cup chopped pecans

1. Process the yogurt, baby spinach, blackberries, almond milk, and ginger in a food processor until smoothly blended.
2. Divide the mixture into two bowls and serve topped with the chopped pecans.

Per Serving

calories: 201 | fat: 14.5g | protein: 7.1g | carbs: 14.9g | fiber: 4.3g | sodium: 103mg

Buckwheat Porridge

Prep time: 5 minutes | Cook time: 40 minutes | Serves 4

3 cups water	Pinch sea salt
2 cups raw buckwheat groats	1 cup unsweetened almond milk

1. In a medium saucepan, add the water, buckwheat groats, and sea salt and bring to a boil over medium-high heat.
2. Once it starts to boil, reduce the heat to low. Cook for about 20 minutes, stirring occasionally, or until most of the water is absorbed.
3. Fold in the almond milk and whisk well. Continue cooking for about 15 minutes, or until the buckwheat groats are very softened. Ladle the porridge into bowls and serve warm.

Per Serving calories: 121 | fat: 1.0g | protein: 6.3g | carbs: 21.5g | fiber: 3.0g | sodium: 47mg

Healthy Chia Pudding

Prep time: 5 minutes | Cook time: 0 minutes | Serves 4

4 cups unsweetened almond milk	1 teaspoon ground cinnamon
¾ cup chia seeds	Pinch sea salt

1. In a medium bowl, whisk together the almond milk, chia seeds, cinnamon, and sea salt until well incorporated.
2. Cover and transfer to the refrigerator to thicken for about 1 hour, or until a pudding-like texture is achieved.
3. Serve chilled.

Per Serving calories: 236 | fat: 9.8g | protein: 13.1g | carbs: 24.8g | fiber: 11.0g | sodium: 133mg

Creamy Vanilla Oatmeal

Prep time: 5 minutes | Cook time: 40 minutes | Serves 4

4 cups water	¾ cup unsweetened almond milk
Pinch sea salt	
1 cup steel-cut oats	2 teaspoons pure vanilla extract

1. Add the water and salt to a large saucepan over high heat and bring to a boil.
2. Once boiling, reduce the heat to low and add the oats. Mix well and cook for 30 minutes, stirring occasionally.
3. Fold in the almond milk and vanilla and whisk to combine. Continue cooking for about 10 minutes, or until the oats are thick and creamy.
4. Ladle the oatmeal into bowls and serve warm.

Per Serving calories: 117 | fat: 2.2g | protein: 4.3g | carbs: 20.0g | fiber: 3.8g | sodium: 38mg

Cheesy Broccoli and Mushroom Egg Casserole

Prep time: 10 minutes | Cook time: 40 minutes | Serves 4

2 tablespoons extra-virgin olive oil	¼ cup unsweetened almond milk
½ sweet onion, chopped	1 tablespoon chopped fresh
1 teaspoon minced garlic	basil
1 cup sliced button mushrooms	1 cup shredded Cheddar cheese
1 cup chopped broccoli	Sea salt and freshly ground
8 large eggs	black pepper, to taste

1. Preheat the oven to 375°F (190°C).
2. Heat the olive oil in a large ovenproof skillet over medium-high heat.
3. Add the onion, garlic, and mushrooms to the skillet and sauté for about 5 minutes, stirring occasionally.
4. Stir in the broccoli and sauté for 5 minutes until the vegetables start to soften.
5. Meanwhile, beat the eggs with the almond milk and basil in a small bowl until well mixed.
6. Remove the skillet from the heat and pour the egg mixture over the top. Scatter the Cheddar cheese all over.
7. Bake uncovered in the preheated oven for about 30 minutes, or until the top of the casserole is golden brown and a fork inserted in the center comes out clean.
8. Remove from the oven and sprinkle with the sea salt and pepper. Serve hot.

Per Serving

calories: 326 | fat: 27.2g | protein: 14.1g | carbs: 6.7g | fiber: 0.7g | sodium: 246mg

Warm Bulgur Breakfast Bowls with Fruits

Prep time: 5 minutes | Cook time: 15 minutes | Serves 6

2 cups unsweetened almond milk	2 cups frozen (or fresh, pitted) dark sweet cherries
1½ cups uncooked bulgur	8 dried (or fresh) figs, chopped
1 cup water	
½ teaspoon ground cinnamon	½ cup chopped almonds
	¼ cup loosely packed fresh mint, chopped

1. Combine the milk, bulgur, water, and cinnamon in a medium saucepan, stirring, and bring just to a boil.
2. Cover, reduce the heat to medium-low, and allow to simmer for 10 minutes, or until the liquid is absorbed.
3. Turn off the heat, but keep the pan on the stove, and stir in the frozen cherries (no need to thaw), figs, and almonds. Cover and let the hot bulgur thaw the cherries and partially hydrate the figs, about 1 minute.
4. Fold in the mint and stir to combine, then serve.

Per Serving

calories: 207 | fat: 6.0g | protein: 8.0g | carbs: 32.0g | fiber: 4.0g | sodium: 82mg

Avocado Smoothie

Prep time: 2 minutes | Cook time: 0 minutes | Serves 2

1 large avocado	2 tablespoons honey
1½ cups unsweetened coconut milk	

1. Place all in a blender and blend until smooth and creamy.
2. Serve immediately.

Per Serving

calories: 686 | fat: 57.6g | protein: 6.2g | carbs: 35.8g | fiber: 10.7g | sodium: 35mg

Cinnamon Pistachio Smoothie

Prep time: 5 minutes | Cook time: 0 minutes | Serves 1

½ cup unsweetened almond milk, plus more as needed

1 tablespoon shelled pistachios, coarsely chopped

½ cup plain Greek yogurt

¼ to ½ teaspoon ground allspice

Zest and juice of ½ orange

1 tablespoon extra-virgin olive oil

¼ teaspoon vanilla extract

¼ teaspoon ground cinnamon

1. In a blender, combine ½ cup almond milk, yogurt, orange zest and juice, olive oil, pistachios, allspice, vanilla, and cinnamon. Blend until smooth and creamy, adding more almond milk to achieve your desired consistency.
2. Serve chilled.

Per Serving calories: 264 | fat: 22.0g | protein: 6.0g | carbs: 12.0g | fiber: 2.0g | sodium: 127mg

Spinach Cheese Pie

Prep time: 5 minutes | Cook time: 25 minutes | Serves 8

2 tablespoons extra-virgin olive oil

4 large eggs, divided

1 onion, chopped

1 cup grated Parmesan cheese, divided

1 pound (454 g) frozen spinach, thawed

2 puff pastry doughs, at room temperature

¼ teaspoon ground nutmeg

4 hard-boiled eggs, halved

¼ teaspoon garlic salt

Nonstick cooking spray

¼ teaspoon freshly ground black pepper

1. Preheat the oven to 350°F (180°C). Spritz a baking sheet with nonstick cooking spray and set aside.
2. Heat a large skillet over medium-high heat. Add the olive oil and onion and sauté for about 5 minutes, stirring occasionally, or until translucent. Squeeze the excess water from the spinach, then add to the skillet and cook, uncovered, so that any excess water from the spinach can evaporate.
3. Season with the nutmeg, garlic salt, and black pepper. Remove from heat and set aside to cool.
4. Beat 3 eggs in a small bowl. Add the beaten eggs and ½ cup of Parmesan cheese to the spinach mixture, stirring well. Roll out the pastry dough on the prepared baking sheet. Layer the spinach mixture on top of the dough, leaving 2 inches around each edge.
5. Once the spinach is spread onto the pastry dough, evenly place the hard-boiled egg halves throughout the pie, then cover with the second pastry dough. Pinch the edges closed. Beat the remaining 1 egg in the bowl. Brush the egg wash over the pastry dough. Bake in the preheated oven for 15 to 20 minutes until golden brown. Sprinkle with the remaining ½ cup of Parmesan cheese. Cool for 5 minutes before cutting and serving.

Per Serving

calories: 417 | fat: 28.0g | protein: 17.0g | carbs: 25.0g | fiber: 3.0g | sodium: 490mg

Baked Ricotta with Honey Pears

Prep time: 5 minutes | Cook time: 22 to 25 minutes | Serves 4

1 (1-pound / 454-g) container whole-milk ricotta cheese

¼ teaspoon ground nutmeg

1 pear, cored and diced

2 large eggs

2 tablespoons water

¼ cup whole-wheat pastry flour

1 tablespoon honey

1 tablespoon sugar

Nonstick cooking spray

1 teaspoon vanilla extract

1. Preheat the oven to 400°F (205°C). Spray four ramekins with nonstick cooking spray.
2. Beat together the ricotta, eggs, flour, sugar, vanilla, and nutmeg in a large bowl until combined. Spoon the mixture into the ramekins.Bake in the preheated oven for 22 to 25 minutes, or until the ricotta is just set.
3. Meanwhile, in a small saucepan over medium heat, simmer the pear in the water for 10 minutes, or until slightly softened. Remove from the heat, and stir in the honey.
4. Remove the ramekins from the oven and cool slightly on a wire rack. Top the ricotta ramekins with the pear and serve.

Per Serving calories: 329 | fat: 19.0g | protein: 17.0g | carbs: 23.0g | fiber: 3.0g | sodium: 109mg

Quinoa Breakfast Bowls

Prep time: 5 minutes | Cook time: 17 minutes | Serves 1

¼ cup quinoa, rinsed

½ small broccoli head, finely chopped

¾ cup water, plus additional as needed

¼ teaspoon salt

1 carrot, grated

1 tablespoon chopped fresh dill

1. Add the quinoa and water to a small pot over high heat and bring to a boil. Once boiling, reduce the heat to low. Cover and cook for 5 minutes, stirring occasionally.
2. Stir in the carrot, broccoli, and salt and continue cooking for 1o to 12 minutes, or until the quinoa is cooked though and the vegetables are fork- tender. If the mixture gets too thick, you can add additional water as needed.
3. Add the dill and serve warm.

Per Serving calories: 219 | fat: 2.9g | protein: 10.0g | carbs: 40.8g | fiber: 7.1g | sodium: 666mg

Apple-Tahini Toast

Prep time: 5 minutes | Cook time: 0 minutes | Serves 1

2 slices whole-wheat bread, toasted

1 small apple of your choice, cored and thinly sliced

2 tablespoons tahini

1 teaspoon honey

1. Spread the tahini on the toasted bread.
2. Place the apple slices on the bread and drizzle with the honey. Serve immediately.

Per Serving

calories: 458 | fat: 17.8g | protein: 11.0g | carbs: 63.5g | fiber: 10.5g | sodium: 285mg

Breakfast Pancakes with Berry Sauce

Prep time: 5 minutes | Cook time: 10 minutes | Serves 4

Pancakes:
1 cup almond flour
1 teaspoon baking powder
¼ teaspoon salt
6 tablespoon extra-virgin olive oil, divided
2 large eggs, beaten

Zest and juice of 1 lemon
½ teaspoon vanilla extract
Berry Sauce:
1 cup frozen mixed berries
1 tablespoon water, plus more as needed
½ teaspoon vanilla extract

Make the Pancakes

1. In a large bowl, combine the almond flour, baking powder, and salt and stir to break up any clumps.
2. Add 4 tablespoons olive oil, beaten eggs, lemon zest and juice, and vanilla extract and stir until well mixed.
3. Heat 1 tablespoon of olive oil in a large skillet. Spoon about 2 tablespoons of batter for each pancake. Cook until bubbles begin to form, 4 to 5 minutes. Flip and cook for another 2 to 3 minutes. Repeat with the remaining 1 tablespoon of olive oil and batter.

Make the Berry Sauce

4. Combine the frozen berries, water, and vanilla extract in a small saucepan and heat over medium-high heat for 3 to 4 minutes until bubbly, adding more water as needed. Using the back of a spoon or fork, mash the berries and whisk until smooth. Serve the pancakes with the berry sauce.

Per Serving calories: 275 | fat: 26.0g | protein: 4.0g | carbs: 8.0g | fiber: 2.0g | sodium: 271mg

Feta and Spinach Frittata

Prep time: 10 minutes | Cook time: 15 minutes | Serves 2

4 large eggs, beaten
2 tablespoons fresh chopped herbs, such as rosemary, thyme, oregano, basil or 1 teaspoon dried herbs
¼ teaspoon salt
Freshly ground black pepper, to taste
4 tablespoons extra-virgin olive oil, divided

1 cup fresh spinach, arugula, kale, or other leafy greens
4 ounces (113 g) quartered artichoke hearts, rinsed, drained, and thoroughly dried
8 cherry tomatoes, halved
½ cup crumbled soft goat cheese

1. Preheat the broiler to Low.
2. In a small bowl, combine the beaten eggs, herbs, salt, and pepper and whisk well with a fork. Set aside.
3. In an ovenproof skillet, heat 2 tablespoons of olive oil over medium heat. Add the spinach, artichoke hearts, and cherry tomatoes and sauté until just wilted, 1 to 2 minutes.
4. Pour in the egg mixture and let it cook undisturbed over medium heat for 3 to 4 minutes, until the eggs begin to set on the bottom.
5. Sprinkle the goat cheese across the top of the egg mixture and transfer the skillet to the oven.
6. Broil for 4 to 5 minutes, or until the frittata is firm in the center and golden brown on top.
7. Remove from the oven and run a rubber spatula around the edge to loosen the sides. Slice the frittata in half and serve drizzled with the remaining 2 tablespoons of olive oil.

Per Serving

calories: 529 | fat: 46.5g | protein: 21.4g | carbs: 7.1g | fiber: 3.1g | sodium: 762mg

Marinara Poached Eggs

Prep time: 5 minutes | Cook time: 15 minutes | Serves 6

1 tablespoon extra-virgin olive oil
1 cup chopped onion
2 garlic cloves, minced
2 (14.5-ounce / 411-g) cans no-salt-added

Italian diced tomatoes, undrained
6 large eggs
½ cup chopped fresh flat-leaf parsley

1. Heat the olive oil in a large skillet over medium-high heat.
2. Add the onion and sauté for 5 minutes, stirring occasionally. Add the garlic and cook for 1 minute more.
3. Pour the tomatoes with their juices over the onion mixture and cook for 2 to 3 minutes until bubbling.
4. Reduce the heat to medium and use a large spoon to make six indentations in the tomato mixture. Crack the eggs, one at a time, into each indentation.
5. Cover and simmer for 6 to 7 minutes, or until the eggs are cooked to your preference.
6. Serve with the parsley sprinkled on top.

Per Serving

calories: 89 | fat: 6.0g | protein: 4.0g | carbs: 4.0g | fiber: 1.0g | sodium: 77mg

Savory Breakfast Oatmeal

Prep time: 5 minutes | Cook time: 15 minutes | Serves 2

½ cup steel-cut oats
1 cup water
1 medium cucumber, chopped
1 large tomato, chopped
1 tablespoon olive oil

Pinch freshly grated Parmesan cheese
Sea salt and freshly ground pepper, to taste
Flat-leaf parsley or mint, chopped, for garnish

1. Combine the oats and water in a medium saucepan and bring to a boil over high heat, stirring continuously, or until the water is absorbed, about 15 minutes.
2. Divide the oatmeal between 2 bowls and scatter the tomato and cucumber on top. Drizzle with the olive oil and sprinkle with the Parmesan cheese.
3. Season with salt and pepper to taste. Serve garnished with the parsley.

Per Serving

calories: 197 | fat: 8.9g | protein: 6.3g | carbs: 23.1g | fiber: 6.4g | sodium: 27mg

Basil Scrambled Eggs

Prep time: 5 minutes | Cook time: 8 minutes | Serves 2

4 large eggs
2 tablespoons grated Gruyère cheese
2 tablespoons finely chopped fresh basil

1 tablespoon plain Greek yogurt
1 tablespoon olive oil
2 cloves garlic, minced
Sea salt and freshly ground pepper, to taste

1. In a large bowl, beat together the eggs, cheese, basil, and yogurt with a whisk until just combined.
2. Heat the oil in a large, heavy nonstick skillet over medium-low heat. Add the garlic and cook until golden, about 1 minute.
3. Pour the egg mixture into the skillet over the garlic. Work the eggs continuously and cook until fluffy and soft.
4. Season with sea salt and freshly ground pepper to taste. Divide between 2 plates and serve immediately.

Per Serving

Calories: 243 | fat: 19.7g | protein: 15.6g | carbs: 3.4g | fiber: 0.1g | sodium: 568mg

Feta and Olive Scrambled Eggs

Prep time: 5 minutes | Cook time: 5 minutes | Serves 2

4 large eggs	¼ cup crumbled feta cheese
1 tablespoon unsweetened almond milk	10 Kalamata olives, pitted and sliced
Sea salt and freshly ground pepper, to taste	Small bunch fresh mint, chopped, for garnish
1 tablespoon olive oil	

1. Beat the eggs in a bowl until just combined. Add the milk and a pinch of sea salt and whisk well.
2. Heat a medium nonstick skillet over medium-high heat and add the olive oil.
3. Pour in the egg mixture and stir constantly, or until they just begin to curd and firm up, about 2 minutes. Add the feta cheese and olive slices, and stir until evenly combined. Season to taste with salt and pepper.
4. Divide the mixture between 2 plates and serve garnished with the fresh chopped mint.

Per Serving

calories: 244 | fat: 21.9g | protein: 8.4g | carbs:3.5g | fiber: 0.6g | sodium: 339mg

Classic Shakshuka

Prep time: 15 minutes | Cook time: 30 minutes | Serves 2

1 tablespoon olive oil	1 (14.5-ounce / 411-g) can fire-roasted tomatoes
½ red pepper, diced	
½ medium onion, diced	¼ teaspoon salt
2 small garlic cloves, minced	Pinch freshly ground black pepper
½ teaspoon smoked paprika	
½ teaspoon cumin	1 ounce (28 g) crumbled feta cheese (about ¼ cup)
Pinch red pepper flakes'	
3 tablespoons minced fresh parsley	3 large eggs

1. Heat the olive oil in a skillet over medium-high heat and add the pepper, onion, and garlic. Sauté until the vegetables start to turn golden.
2. Add the paprika, cumin, and red pepper flakes and stir to toast the spices for about 30 seconds. Add the tomatoes with their juices.
3. Reduce the heat and let the sauce simmer for 10 minutes, or until it starts to thicken. Add the salt and pepper. Taste the sauce and adjust seasonings as necessary.
4. Scatter the feta cheese on top. Make 3 wells in the sauce and crack one egg into each well.
5. Cover and let the eggs cook for about 7 minutes. Remove the lid and continue cooking for 5 minutes more, or until the yolks are cooked to desired doneness.
6. Garnish with fresh parsley and serve.

Per Serving

calories: 289 | fat: 18.2g | protein: 15.1g | carbs: 18.5g | fiber: 4.9g | sodium: 432mg

Avocado and Egg Toast

Prep time: 5 minutes | Cook time: 8 minutes | Serves 2

2 tablespoons ground flaxseed	½ teaspoon garlic powder, sesame seed, caraway seed, or other dried herbs (optional)
½ teaspoon baking powder	
2 large eggs, beaten	
1 teaspoon salt, plus additional for serving	3 tablespoons extra-virgin olive oil, divided
½ teaspoon freshly ground black pepper, plus additional for serving	1 medium ripe avocado, peeled, pitted, and sliced
	2 tablespoons chopped ripe tomato

1. In a small bowl, combine the flaxseed and baking powder, breaking up any lumps in the baking powder.
2. Add the beaten eggs, salt, pepper, and garlic powder (if desired) and whisk well. Let sit for 2 minutes.
3. In a small nonstick skillet, heat 1 tablespoon of olive oil over medium heat. Pour the egg mixture into the skillet and let cook undisturbed until the egg begins to set on bottom, 2 to 3 minutes.
4. Using a rubber spatula, scrape down the sides to allow uncooked egg to reach the bottom. Cook for an additional 2 to 3 minutes.
5. Once almost set, flip like a pancake and allow the top to fully cook, another 1 to 2 minutes.
6. Remove from the skillet and allow to cool slightly, then slice into 2 pieces.
7. Top each piece with avocado slices, additional salt and pepper, chopped tomato, and drizzle with the remaining 2 tablespoons of olive oil. Serve immediately.

Per Serving

calories: 297 | fat: 26.1g | protein: 8.9g | carbs: 12.0g | fiber: 7.1g | sodium: 1132mg

Tomato and Egg Breakfast Pizza

Prep time: 5 minutes | Cook time: 15 minutes | Serves 2

2 (6- to 8-inch-long) slices of whole-wheat naan bread	1 medium tomato, sliced
	2 large eggs
2 tablespoons prepared pesto	

1. Heat a large nonstick skillet over medium-high heat. Place the naan bread in the skillet and let warm for about 2 minutes on each side, or until softened.
2. Spread 1 tablespoon of the pesto on one side of each slice and top with tomato slices.
3. Remove from the skillet and place each one on its own plate.
4. Crack the eggs into the skillet, keeping them separated, and cook until the whites are no longer translucent and the yolk is cooked to desired doneness.
5. Using a spatula, spoon one egg onto each bread slice. Serve warm.

Per Serving

calories: 429 | fat: 16.8g | protein: 18.1g | carbs: 12.0g | fiber: 4.8g | sodium: 682mg

Parmesan Oatmeal with Greens

Prep time: 10 minutes | Cook time: 18 minutes | Serves 2

1 tablespoon olive oil	1½ cups water, or low-sodium chicken stock
¼ cup minced onion	
2 cups greens (arugula, baby spinach, chopped kale, or Swiss chard)	2 tablespoons Parmesan cheese
	Salt, to taste
¾ cup gluten-free old-fashioned oats	Pinch freshly ground black pepper

1. Heat the olive oil in a saucepan over medium-high heat. Add the minced onion and sauté for 2 minutes, or until softened.
2. Add the greens and stir until they begin to wilt. Transfer this mixture to a bowl and set aside.
3. Add the oats to the pan and let them toast for about 2 minutes. Add the water and bring the oats to a boil.
4. Reduce the heat to low, cover, and let the oats cook for 10 minutes, or until the liquid is absorbed and the oats are tender.
5. Stir the Parmesan cheese into the oats, and add the onion and greens back to the pan. Add additional water if needed, so the oats are creamy and not dry.
6. Stir well and season with salt and black pepper to taste. Serve warm.

Per Serving

calories: 257 | fat: 14.0g | protein: 12.2g | carbs: 30.2g | fiber: 6.1g | sodium: 262mg

Mediterranean Omelet

Prep time: 8 minutes | Cook time: 15 minutes | Serves 2

2 teaspoons extra-virgin olive oil, divided	2 tablespoons chopped fresh parsley, plus extra for garnish
1 garlic clove, minced	
½ yellow bell pepper, thinly sliced	2 tablespoons chopped fresh basil
½ red bell pepper, thinly sliced	½ teaspoon salt
¼ cup thinly sliced red onion	½ teaspoon freshly ground black pepper
	4 large eggs, beaten

1. In a large, heavy skillet, heat 1 teaspoon of the olive oil over medium heat. Add the garlic, peppers, and onion to the skillet and sauté, stirring frequently, for 5 minutes.
2. Add the parsley, basil, salt, and pepper, increase the heat to medium-high, and sauté for 2 minutes. Slide the vegetable mixture onto a plate and return the skillet to the heat.
3. Heat the remaining 1 teaspoon of olive oil in the skillet and pour in the beaten eggs, tilting the pan to coat evenly. Cook the eggs just until the edges are bubbly and all but the center is dry, 3 to 5 minutes.
4. Spoon the vegetable mixture onto one-half of the omelet and use a spatula to fold the empty side over the top. Slide the omelet onto a platter or cutting board.
5. To serve, cut the omelet in half and garnish with extra fresh parsley.

Per Serving

calories: 206 | fat: 14.2g | protein: 13.7g | carbs: 7.2g | fiber: 1.2g | sodium: 729mg

Creamy Breakfast Bulgur with Berries

Prep time: 2 minutes | Cook time: 10 minutes | Serves 2

½ cup medium-grain bulgur wheat	1 teaspoon pure vanilla extract
1 cup water	¼ teaspoon ground cinnamon
Pinch sea salt	
¼ cup unsweetened almond milk	1 cup fresh berries of your choice

1. Put the bulgur in a medium saucepan with the water and sea salt, and bring to a boil.
2. Cover, remove from heat, and let stand for 10 minutes until water is absorbed.
3. Stir in the milk, vanilla, and cinnamon until fully incorporated. Divide between 2 bowls and top with the fresh berries to serve.

Per Serving calories: 173 | fat: 1.6g | protein: 5.7g | carbs: 34.0g | fiber: 6.0g | sodium: 197mg

Banana Corn Fritters

Prep time: 5 minutes | Cook time: 10 minutes | Serves 2

½ cup yellow cornmeal	½ teaspoon baking powder
¼ cup flour	¼ to ½ teaspoon ground chipotle chili
2 small ripe bananas, peeled and mashed	
2 tablespoons unsweetened almond milk	¼ teaspoon ground cinnamon
1 large egg, beaten	¼ teaspoon sea salt
	1 tablespoon olive oil

1. Stir together all except for the olive oil in a large bowl until smooth.
2. Heat a nonstick skillet over medium-high heat. Add the olive oil and drop about 2 tablespoons of batter for each fritter. Cook for 2 to 3 minutes until the bottoms are golden brown, then flip. Continue cooking for 1 to 2 minutes more, until cooked through. Repeat with the remaining batter. Serve warm.

Per Serving calories: 396 | fat: 10.6g | protein: 7.3g | carbs: 68.0g | fiber: 4.8g | sodium: 307mg

Brekky Egg-Potato Hash (Spanish)

Preparation time: 8 minutes | Cooking time: 25 minutes | Servings: 2

1 zucchini, diced	½ cup chicken broth
½ lb. (220 g.) cooked chicken 1 tbsp. olive oil	4 oz. (113 g.) shrimp Salt and black pepper 1 sweet potato, diced 2 eggs
¼ tsp. cayenne pepper 2 tsps. garlic powder 1 cup fresh spinach	

1. In a skillet, add olive oil.
2. Fry the shrimp, cooked chicken, and sweet potato for 2 minutes.
3. Add the cayenne pepper, garlic powder and toss for 4 minutes.
4. Add the zucchini and toss for another 3 minutes.
5. Whisk the eggs in a bowl and add to the skillet.
6. Season using salt and pepper. Cover with the lid.
7. Cook for 1 more minute and mix in the chicken broth.
8. Cover and cook for another 8 minutes on high heat.
9. Add the spinach, toss for 2 more minutes and serve.

Nutrition:

Calories: 198 Fat: 0.7 g. Protein: 4 g.

Breakfast Tostadas (Spanish)

Preparation time: 15 minutes | Cooking time: 16 minutes | Servings: 6

½ white onion, diced 1 tomato, chopped	1 cucumber, chopped
1 tbsp. fresh cilantro, chopped	½ jalapeño pepper, chopped 1 tbsp. lime juice
6 corn tortillas	1tbsp. canola oil
2oz. Cheddar cheese, shredded	½ cup white beans, canned, drained 6 eggs
½ tsp. butter	½ tsp. Sea salt

1. Make the Pico de Gallo:
2. In the salad bowl combine the diced white onion, tomato, cucumber, fresh cilantro, and jalapeño pepper.
3. Then add the lime juice and a ½ tbsp. canola oil. Mix up the mixture well. Pico de Gallo is ready.
4. After this, preheat the oven to 390°F.
5. Line the tray with baking paper.
6. Arrange the corn tortillas on the baking paper and brush with the remaining canola oil from both sides.
7. Bake for 10 minutes.
8. Chill the cooked crunchy tortillas well.
9. Meanwhile, toss the butter in the skillet.
10. Crack the eggs in the melted butter and sprinkle them with sea salt.
11. Fry the eggs for 3–5 minutes over medium heat.
12. After this, mash the beans until you get a puree texture.
13. Spread the bean puree on the corn tortillas.
14. Add the fried eggs.
15. Then top the eggs with the Pico de Gallo and shredded Cheddar cheese.

Nutrition:
Calories: 246 Fat: 11 g. Protein: 14 g.

Butternut Squash Hummus (Greek)

Preparation time: 16 minutes | Cooking time: 15 minutes | Servings: 4

2 lbs. (900 g.) seeded butternut squash, peeled 1 tbsp. olive oil	¼ cup tahini
2 tbsps. lemon juice	2 garlic cloves, minced Salt and pepper

1. Heat the oven to 300°F/148°C.
2. Coat the butternut squash with olive oil.
3. Set in a baking dish to bake for 15 minutes in the oven.
4. Once the squash is cooked, place it in a food processor together with the rest of the .
5. Pulse until smooth.
6. Serve with carrots and celery sticks.
7. For further use of place in individual containers, put a label and store it in the fridge.
8. Allow warming at room temperature before heating in the microwave oven.

Nutrition:
Calories: 115 Fat: 5.8 g. Protein: 2.5 g.

Berry and Nut Parfait

Prep time: 10 minutes | Cook time: 0 minutes | Serves 2

2 cups plain Greek yogurt	1 cup fresh blueberries
2 tablespoons honey	½ cup walnut pieces
1 cup fresh raspberries	

1. In a medium bowl, whisk the yogurt and honey. Spoon into 2 serving bowls.
2. Top each with ½ cup blueberries, ½ cup raspberries, and ¼ cup walnut pieces. Serve immediately.

Per Serving calories: 507 | fat: 23.0g | protein: 24.1g | carbs: 57.0g | fiber: 8.2g | sodium: 172mg

Basil and Tomato Soup (Spanish)

Preparation time: 7 minutes | Cooking time: 25 minutes | Servings: 2

2 tbsps. vegetable broth 1 garlic clove, minced	½ cup white onion
1 celery stalk, chopped 1 carrot, chopped	3 cup tomatoes, chopped Salt and pepper
2 bay leaves	1 ½ cup unsweetened almond milk 1/3 cup basil leaves

1. Cook the vegetable broth in a large saucepan over medium heat.
2. Add in the garlic and onions and cook for 4 minutes.
3. Add in the carrots and celery. Cook for 1 more minute.
4. Mix in the tomatoes and bring to a boil. Simmer for 15 minutes.
5. Add the almond milk, basil, and bay leaves.
6. Season and serve.

Nutrition:
Calories: 213 Fat: 3.9 g. Protein: 6.9 g.

Parmesan Omelet (Italian)

Preparation time: 5 minutes | Cooking time: 10 minutes | Servings: 2

1 tbsp. cream cheese 2 eggs, beaten	¼ tsp. paprika
½ tsp. dried oregano	¼ tsp. dried dill
1 oz. Parmesan, grated 1 tsp. coconut oil	

1. Mix up together the cream cheese with eggs, dried oregano, and dill.
2. Preheat the coconut oil in the skillet.
3. Place the egg mixture in the skillet and flatten it.
4. Add the grated Parmesan and close the lid.
5. Cook omelet for 10 minutes over low heat.
6. Then transfer the cooked omelet to the serving plate and sprinkle with paprika.

Nutrition:
Calories: 148 Fat: 12 g. Protein: 11 g.

Cheesy Amish Breakfast Casserole (Italian)

Prep Time: 10 minutes | Cooking time: 50 minutes | Servings: 12

1-pound sliced bacon, diced, 1 sweet onion, minced meat	4 cups grated and frozen potatoes, thawed
9 lightly beaten eggs	2 cups of grated cheddar cheese
1 1/2 cup of cottage cheese	1 1/4 cups of grated Swiss cheese

1. Preheat the oven to 175 ° C (350 ° F). Grease a 9 x 13-inch baking dish.
2. Heat a large frying pan over medium heat; cook and stir the bacon and onion until the bacon is evenly browned about 10 minutes. Drain. Stir in potatoes, eggs, cheddar cheese, cottage cheese, and Swiss cheese. Pour the mixture into a prepared baking dish.
3. Bake in the preheated oven until the eggs are cooked and the cheese is melted 45 to 50 minutes. Let stand for 10 minutes before cutting and serving.

Nutrition:

314 calories 22.8 g of fat 12.1 g carbohydrates 21.7 g of protein 188 mg cholesterol 609 mg of sodium.

Cinnamon Porridge (Italian)

Prep Time: 10 minutes | Cooking time: 30 minutes | Servings: 4

4 ½ oz. jumbo porridge oats. 20 oz. semi-skimmed milk. 1 tsp. lemon juice.	½ tsp. ground cinnamon + extra to garnish. 2 ripe medium pears, peeled, cored, grated.

1. Add oats, milk, and cinnamon into a nonstick saucepan. Place the saucepan over medium-low heat. Cook until creamy. Stir constantly.
2. Divide into bowls. Scatter pear on top. Drizzle lemon juice on top. Garnish with cinnamon and serve.

Nutrition:

Calories: 383 g. Fat: 14 g. Fiber: 4 g. Carbs: 3 g. Protein: 8 g.

Mediterranean Pasta with Basil (Italian)

Prep time: 12 minutes | Cooking time: 19 minutes | Servings: 4

2 red bell peppers	2 chili peppers
2 red onions	
3 garlic cloves	1 tsp. brown sugar
2 lbs. tomatoes 2/3 lb. pasta	1 tbsp. fresh basil leaves
2 tbsps. Parmesan cheese, grated	2 tbsps. olive oil

1. Preheat the oven to 390ºF. Put the pepper, onion, chili, and garlic in a deep pan. Sprinkle with the sugar, drizzle with olive oil, and season with salt and ground black pepper to taste.
2. Bake in the oven for 15 minutes, add the chopped tomatoes and cook for another 15 minutes.
3. While the vegetables are baking, prepare the pasta following the instructions on the package.
4. Take out the vegetables from the oven and mix the pasta with them. Sprinkle top with parmesan and basil leaves.

Nutrition:

Calories: 136 Fat: 3.2 g. Protein: 4 g.

Cinnamon Oatmeal with Dried Cranberries

Prep time: 5 minutes | Cook time: 8 minutes | Serves 2

1 cup almond milk	1 cup old-fashioned oats
1 cup water	½ cup dried cranberries
Pinch sea salt	1 teaspoon ground cinnamon

1. In a medium saucepan over high heat, bring the almond milk, water, and salt to a boil.
2. Stir in the oats, cranberries, and cinnamon. Reduce the heat to medium and cook for 5 minutes, stirring occasionally.
3. Remove the oatmeal from the heat. Cover and let it stand for 3 minutes.
4. Stir before serving.

Per Serving

calories: 107 | fat: 2.1g | protein: 3.2g | carbs: 18.2g | fiber: 4.1g | sodium: 122mg

Sausage Quiche with Tomatoes (Spanish)

Preparation Time: 15 minutes | Cooking time: 10 minutes | Servings: 6

6 eggs.	12 oz. raw sausage rolls. 10 cherry tomatoes halved
2 tbsps. heavy cream.	
2 tbsps. Parmesan, grated.	5 eggplant slices.
Salt and black pepper, to taste	. 2 tbsps. parsley, chopped.

1. Preheat the oven to 370º F. Press the sausage rolls onto the bottom of a greased pie dish. On top of the sausage, carefully arrange the eggplant slices.
2. Top with cherry tomatoes. Whisk together the eggs along with the heavy cream, Parmesan cheese, salt, and pepper.
3. Spoon the egg mixture over the sausage and bake for about 40 minutes. Serve with parsley.

Nutrition:

Calories: 340 g. Fats: 28 g. Protein: 1.7 g.

Breakfast Couscous (Italian)

Preparation time: 9 minutes | Cooking time: 5 minutes | Servings: 4

3 cup low-fat milk	1 cup whole-wheat couscous, uncooked
1 cinnamon stick	
½ apricot, chopped, dried	¼ cup currants, dried 6 tsps. brown sugar
¼ tsp. salt	4 tsps. melted butter

1. Take a large saucepan and combine the milk and cinnamon stick and heat over medium.
2. Heat for 3 minutes or until micro bubbles forms around the edges of the pan. Do not boil.
3. Remove from heat, stir in the couscous, apricots, currants, salt, and 4 tsps. of brown sugar.
4. Wrap mixture and allow it to sit for 15 minutes. Remove and throw away the cinnamon stick.
5. Divide couscous among 4 bowls, and top each with 1 tsp. melted butter and ½ tsp. brown sugar. Ready to serve.

Nutrition:

Calories: 306 Fat: 6 g. Protein: 11 g.

Delicious Shakshuka (Italian)

Preparation Time: 10 minutes | Cooking time: 30 minutes | Servings: 4

½ cup feta cheese crumbled. 2 tbsps. olive oil extra virgin 8 eggs.	1 onion sliced.
1 tsp. black pepper powder	1 large red bell pepper, sliced.
¼ tsp. salt	3 garlic cloves, minced.
½ tsp. flakes of red pepper. 3 tomatoes blended.	½ tsp. coriander
2 tsps. cumin powder 1 tsp. paprika	1 tsp. fresh parsley chopped.
4 Pieces of almond bread for serving	

1. Heat your oven in advance at 375 ° c.
2. Heat the olive oil in a large frying pan over medium heat.
3. Add the sliced onion and let it fry until it is a nice golden color. Top it off with the red bell pepper pieces and let this cook until the bell peppers are soft.
4. Add the minced garlic cloves to this mixture as well and let it cook until the garlic is nice and fragrant.
5. Add the sliced tomato, cumin powder, coriander, paprika, and flakes of red pepper. Also, add the salt and black pepper powder as well. Let this mix cook for 10 minutes until it thickens.
6. Get a large baking tin and pour in the cooked sauce. Using a spoon, create eight holes in the sauce and each crack an egg and pour it in.
7. Sprinkle a little salt and pepper over the eggs for seasoning. Using aluminum foil, cover the baking tin and transfer it into the oven you heated in advance for 15 minutes until the eggs are well cooked.
8. When they are ready, sprinkle the feta cheese that has been crumbled on top together with the fresh parsley as well.
9. Cut out slices and serve with the almond bread.

Nutrition:
Calories: 122 g. Fat: 5.4 g. Fiber: 2 g. Carbs: 9.7 g. Protein: 8 g

Healthy Breakfast Smoothie (Greek)

Preparation Time: 5 minutes | Cooking time: 1 minute | Servings: 1

1 ¼ cups coconut milk, or almond or regular dairy milk.	½ cup kale or spinach, or both (¼ cup each) if you prefer.
½ avocado, sliced into smaller pieces.	¾ cup cucumber, cut into smaller pieces.
1 cup green grapes.	¼ tsp. ginger, peeled,grated.
1scoop plant-based protein powder. Honey, to taste.	

1. Orderly, mix all the in a small bowl.
2. Blend them until the mixture is smooth.
3. Taste the mixture and add as much honey as you desire.
4. Pour into a glass and serve.

Nutrition:
Calories: 117 g. Fats: 15 g. Protein: 20 g.

Breakfast Sandwich (Greek)

Preparation time: 3 minutes | Cooking time: 20 minutes | Servings: 4

4 multigrain sandwich thins	4 eggs
4 tsps. olive oil	
1tbsp. rosemary, fresh	2cup baby spinach leaves, fresh 1 tomato, sliced
1 tbsp. Feta cheese Pinch of kosher salt Ground black pepper	

1. Set oven to 375°F/190°C.
2. Brush the thins sides with 2 tsps. olive oil and set on a baking sheet.
3. Set in the oven and toast for 5 minutes or until the edges are lightly brown.
4. In a skillet, add in the rest of the olive oil and rosemary to heat over high heat.
5. Break and place the whole eggs one at a time into the skillet.
6. Break the yolks up with a spatula. Flip the egg and cook on another side until done. Remove the eggs from heat.
7. Place the toasted sandwich thins on 4 separate plates. Divine spinach among the thins.
8. Top each thin with 2 tomato slices, the cooked egg, and 1 tbsp. Feta cheese.
9. Lightly sprinkle with salt and pepper for flavoring.
10. Place the remaining sandwich thin halves over the top and they are ready to serve.

Nutrition:
Calories: 241 Fat: 12.2 g. Protein: 13 g.

Summer Day Fruit Salad (Greek)

Preparation time: 16 minutes | Cooking time: 0 minute | Servings: 8

1cups honeydew melon, cubed 2 cups cantaloupe, cubed	2 cups red seedless grapes
1 cup fresh strawberries, sliced 1 cup fresh blueberries	1 large lime zest and juice
½ cup unsweetened toasted coconut flakes	¼ cup honey
¼ tsp. salt	½ cup extra-virgin olive oil

1. Combine all of the fruits, the lime zest, and the coconut flakes in a large bowl and stir well to blend. Set aside.
2. In a blender, mix the lime juice, honey, and salt and blend on low. Once the honey is incorporated, slowly add the olive oil and blend until opaque.
3. Drizzle dressing over the fruit and mix well. Cover and chill for at least 4 hours before serving.

Nutrition:
Calories: 196 Fat: 16 g. Protein: 3 g.

Banana Oats (Greek)

Preparation time: 5 minutes | Cooking time: 0 minute | Servings: 2

1 banana, peeled and sliced	¾ cup almond milk
½ cup cold-brewed coffee 2 pitted dates	2 tbsps. cocoa powder 1 cup rolled oats
1 ½ tbsps. chia seeds	

1. Using a blender, add in all the.
2. Process well for 5 minutes and serve.

Nutrition:

Calories: 288 Fat: 4.4 g. Protein: 7.7 g.

Savory Muffins (Greek)

Preparation time: 9 minutes | Cooking time: 15 minutes | Servings: 6

9 ham slices	1/3 cup spinach, chopped
¼ cup Feta cheese, crumbled	½ cup roasted red peppers, chopped Salt and black pepper
1 ½ tbsps. basil pesto 5 whisked eggs	

1. Grease a muffin tin. Use 1 ½ ham slices to line each of the muffin molds.
2. Except for black pepper, salt, pesto, and eggs, divide the rest of the into your ham cups.
3. Using a bowl, whisk together the pepper, salt, pesto, and eggs. Pour the pepper mixture on top.
4. Set oven to 400°F/204°C and bake for about 15 minutes.
5. Serve immediately.

Nutrition:

Calories: 109 Fat: 6.7 g. Protein: 9.3 g.

Dill and Tomato Frittata (Italian)

Preparation Time: 10 minutes | Cooking time: 35 minutes | Servings: 6

Pepper and salt to taste	1teaspoon red pepper flakes 2 garlic cloves, minced
½ cup crumbled goat cheese – optional 2 tablespoon fresh chives,chopped	2tablespoon fresh dill, chopped 4 tomatoes, diced
8 eggs, whisked	1 teaspoon coconut oil

1. Grease a 9-inch round baking pan and preheat oven to 325oF.
2. In a large bowl, mix well all and pour into prepped pan.
3. Pop into the oven and bake until middle is cooked through around 30-35 minutes.
4. Remove from oven and garnish with more chives and dill.

Nutrition:

Calories per serving: 149 Protein: 13.26g Carbs: 9.93g Fat: 10.28g

Healthy Chia and Oats Smoothie (Greek)

Preparation Time: 10 minutes | Cooking time: 0 minutes | Servings: 2

6 tbsps. oats.	2 tbsps. chia seeds.
2 tbsps. hemp powder.	4 Medjool dates, pitted (optional). 2 bananas, chopped.
1cup almond milk. 1 cup frozen berries.	2big handful's spinach, torn.

1. Add all the to a blender and blend until smooth.
2. Pour in glasses and serve.

Nutrition:

Calories: 140. Fat: 7 g. Fiber: 4 g. Carbs: 12 g. Protein: 12 g.

Paleo Almond Banana Pancakes (Greek)

Prep Time: 10 minutes | Cooking time: 10 minutes | Servings: 3

¼ cup almond flour	½ teaspoon ground cinnamon 3 eggs
1 banana, mashed 1 teaspoon olive oil	1 tablespoon almond butter 1 teaspoon vanilla extract
Sliced banana to serve	

1. Whisk the eggs in a mixing bowl until they become fluffy.
2. In another bowl, mash the banana using a fork and add to the egg mixture.
3. Add the vanilla, almond butter, cinnamon and almond flour.
4. Mix into a smooth batter.
5. Heat the olive oil in a skillet.
6. Add one spoonful of the batter and fry them on both sides.
7. Keep doing these steps until you are done with all the batter.
8. Add some sliced banana on top before serving.

Nutrition:

Calories per serving: 306 Protein: 14.4g Carbs: 3.6g Fat: 26.0g

Zucchini with Egg (Italian)

Prep time: 5 minutes | Cooking time: 10 minutes | Servings: 2

1 1/2 tablespoons olive oil salt and ground black pepper to taste	2 large zucchinis, cut into large chunks
2 large eggs	1 teaspoon water, or as desired

1. Heat the oil in a frying pan over medium heat; sauté zucchini until soft, about 10 minutes. Season the zucchini with salt and black pepper.
2. Beat the eggs with a fork in a bowl. Add water and beat until everything is well mixed. Pour the eggs over the zucchini; boil and stir until scrambled eggs and no more flowing, about 5 minutes. Season zucchini and eggs with salt and black pepper.

Nutrition:

213 calories15.7 grams of fat11.2 g carbohydrates 10.2 g of protein 186 mg of cholesterol 180 mg of sodium.

Sesame-Seared Salmon (Italian)

Prep Time: 5 minutes | Cooking time: 10 minutes | Servings: 4

4 wild salmon fillets (about 1lb.)	2 tbsps. toasted sesame oil.
1 tsp. sea salt.	1 ½ tbsps. sesame seeds.
	1½ tbsps. avocado oil.

1. Using a paper towel or a clean kitchen towel, pat the fillets to dry. Brush each with a tbsp. of sesame oil and season with a ½ tsp. of salt.
2. Place a large skillet over medium-high heat and drizzle with avocado oil. Once the oil is hot, add the salmon fillets with the flesh side down. Cook for about 3 minutes and flip. Cook the skin side for an additional 3–4 minutes, without overcooking it.
3. Remove the pan from the heat and brush with the remaining sesame oil. Season with the remaining salt and sprinkle with sesame seeds. Best served with a green salad.

Nutrition:

Calories: 291 g. Fat: 14 g. Fiber: 6 g. Carbs: 3 g. Protein: 8 g.

Breakfast Egg on Avocado (Italian)

Preparation time: 9 minutes | Cooking time: 15 minutes | Servings: 6

1 tsp. garlic powder	½ tsp. sea salt
¼ cup Parmesan cheese, shredded	¼ tsp. black pepper

3 avocados, pitted, halved 6 eggs

1. Prep muffin tins and preheat the oven to 350ºF/176ºC.
2. Split the avocado. To ensure that the egg would fit inside the cavity of the avocado, lightly scrape off 1/3 of the meat.
3. Place avocado on a muffin tin to ensure that it faces the top-up. Evenly season each avocado with pepper, salt, and garlic powder.
4. Add 1 egg to each avocado cavity and garnish tops with cheese. Set in your oven to bake until the egg white is set, about 15 minutes. Serve and enjoy.

Nutrition:

Calories: 252 Fat: 20 g. Protein: 14 g.

Tuna Sandwich (Spanish)

Preparation time: 9 minutes | Cooking time: 0 minutes | Servings: 2

6 oz. canned tuna, drained and flaked	1 avocado, pitted, peeled, and mashed
4 whole-wheat bread slices	Pinch salt and black pepper
1 tbsp. Feta cheese, crumbled	1 cup baby spinach

1. Using a bowl, stir in the pepper, salt, tuna, and cheese to mix.
2. To the bread slices, apply a spread of the mashed avocado.
3. Equally, divide the tuna mixture and spinach onto 2 of the slices. Top with the remaining 2 slices. Serve.

Nutrition:

Calories: 283 Fat: 11.2 g. Protein: 4.5 g.

Pita Chicken Salad (Greek)

Preparation time: 18 minutes | Cooking time: 4 minutes | Servings: 4

1 tbsp. olive oil	1 piece of chicken breast 2 pieces pita
Dried basil to taste	3 tbsps. natural yogurt 1 tbsp. lemon juice
1 garlic clove	1 bunch (7 oz.) green salad
1 tomato	2 chives
1 cucumber Salt to taste	Ground black pepper to taste

1. Rub the chicken slices with salt, pepper, and dried basil, fry in a pan until cooked.
2. Put the chicken, slices of tomato, cucumber, and onion in half the pits.
3. Mix the yogurt with lemon juice and garlic, add to the salad in Pita. Garnish with chives then serve.

Nutrition:

Calories: 94 Fat: 1.8 g. Protein: 6 g.

Chorizo & Cheese Omelet (Italian)

Preparation Time: 10 minutes | Cooking time: 10 minutes | Servings: 2

4 eggs, beaten	4 oz. mozzarella, grated 1 tbsp. butter
8 chorizo slices, thin 1 tomato, sliced	Salt and black pepper to taste

1. Whisk the eggs with salt and pepper.
2. In a cast-iron skillet, add the butter and cook the eggs for 30 seconds. Create a layer with the chorizo slices.
3. Arrange the sliced tomato and mozzarella over the chorizo and cook for about 3 minutes. Cover the skillet and continue cooking for 3 more minutes, or until the omelet is completely set.
4. With a spatula, run around the edges of the omelet and flip it onto a plate folded-side down. Serve.

Nutrition:

Calories: 451 g. Fats: 36.5 g. Protein: 30g.

Cheesy Yogurt (Greek)

Preparation time: 4 hours and 5 minutes | Cooking time: 0 minutes | Servings: 4

1 cup Greek yogurt	1 tablespoon honey
½ cup feta cheese, crumbled	

1. In a blender, combine the yogurt with the honey and the cheese and pulse well.
2. Divide into bowls and freeze for 4 hours before serving for breakfast.

Nutrition:

Calories 161, fat 10, fiber 0, carbs 11.8, protein 6.6

Kale and Apple Smoothie

Prep time: 5 minutes | Cook time: 0 minutes | Serves 2

2 cups shredded kale	½ Granny Smith apple, unpeeled, cored and chopped
1 cup unsweetened almond milk	
¼ cup 2 percent plain Greek yogurt	½ avocado, diced 3 ice cubes

1. Put all in a blender and blend until smooth and thick.
2. Pour into two glasses and serve immediately.

Per Serving

calories: 177 | fat: 6.8g | protein: 8.2g | carbs: 22.0g | fiber: 4.1g | sodium: 112mg

Salad with Spinach, Tomatoes, and Poached Egg (Italian)

Prep time: 13 minutes | Cooking time: 5 minutes | Servings: 2

3 oz. spinach	2 tomatoes
2 chicken egg	2 oz. Feta cheese 2 tsps. lemon juice
1 tbsp. vegetable oil 2 tbsps. agave syrup	1 ½ tsp. sour cream 15%
1 tbsp. dill	1 ½ oz. red onion
Salt and pepper to taste	

1. Pour the vegetable oil onto the cling film.
2. Gently break the egg so that the yolk remains intact.
3. Collect the film with the egg in a bag, squeeze out the air, tie and cook for 5 minutes.
4. Mix the lemon juice, agave syrup (1 tbsp.), and vegetable oil, let the dressing rest.
5. Cut the tomatoes into a cube and the onion into strips, fill with salt and pepper dressing.
6. Add the spinach leaves, mix.
7. Top with Feta cheese and poached egg.
8. Mix the sour cream with the chopped dill and syrup (1 tbsp.).
9. Pour over the salad dressing with the prepared sauce.

Nutrition:

Calories: 200 Fat: 12 g. Protein: 7.5 g.

Potato Scallops with Truffle Oil (Spanish)

Prep time: 8 minutes | Cooking time: 24 minutes | Servings: 1

4 oz. scallops	3 oz. potato
½ oz. Parmesan cheese	½ tsp. lime zest
½ oz. butter	1 tbsp. olive oil
1 ½ tsp. truffle oil 1 tsp. arugula	2/3 oz. cherry tomatoes 1 chive
½ tsp. thyme Sea salt to taste	Ground black pepper to taste

1. Fry the scallops on both sides in olive oil with thyme, salt, and pepper.
2. Separately, boil the potatoes and rub them through a sieve. Add the zest of lime, grated Parmesan cheese, butter, salt, and pepper.
3. Lightly warm the arugula and cherry tomatoes in olive oil.
4. Put the mashed potatoes through the ring on a plate, scallops symmetrically put on it, arugula and cherry on the scallops, garnish with the thyme and onion, and pour with the truffle oil.

Nutrition:

Calories: 279 Fat: 59.8 g. Protein: 24.5 g.

Healthy Chia and Oats Smoothie (Greek)

Preparation Time: 10 minutes | Cooking time: 0 minutes | Servings: 2

6 tbsps. oats.	2 tbsps. chia seeds.
2 tbsps. hemp powder.	4 Medjool dates, pitted (optional). 2 bananas, chopped.
1cup almond milk. 1 cup frozen berries.	2big handful's spinach, torn.

1. Add all the to a blender and blend until smooth.
2. Pour in glasses and serve.

Nutrition:

Calories: 140. Fat: 7 g. Fiber: 4 g. Carbs: 12 g. Protein: 12 g.

Eggs and Salsa (Italian)

Prep Time: 5 minutes | Cooking time: 5 minutes | Servings: 2

1 cups tomatoes.	1 green onion (bunch).
1 bunch of cilantros, chopped. 1 cup red onion, chopped.	Juice from 1 lime.
2 small habanero chilies, chopped.	8 eggs, whisked.
A drizzle of olive oil. Sea salt.	2 garlic cloves, minced.

1. Mix tomatoes, green onions, red onion, habaneros, garlic, cilantro, and lime juice and toss well.
2. Add a pinch of salt, toss again and keep this in the fridge until you serve it.
3. Heat up a pan with a drizzle of oil, add eggs, and scramble them for 4–5 minutes.
4. Divide scrambled eggs on plates, add salsa on top and serve.

Nutrition:

Calories: 383 g. Fat: 14 g. Fiber: 4 g. Carbs: 3 g. Protein: 8 g.

Bacon & Cream Cheese Mug Muffins (Italian)

Preparation Time: 15 minutes | Cooking time: 15 minutes | Servings: 2

¼ cup flaxseed meal. 1 egg.	1tbsps. heavy cream. 2 tbsps. pesto.
¼ cup almond flour.	¼ tsp. baking soda.
Salt and black pepper, to taste.	4 bacon slices.
½ medium avocado, sliced.	2 tbsps. cream cheese.

1. Mix the flaxseed meal, almond flour, and baking soda in a bowl. Add the egg, heavy cream, and pesto. Then whisk well. Season with salt and pepper.
2. Divide the mixture between 2 ramekins. Microwave for 60–90 seconds. Let cool slightly before filling.
3. Put the bacon in a nonstick skillet and cook until crispy, then set aside.
4. Transfer the muffins onto a plate and cut them in half crosswise. Assemble the sandwiches by spreading the cream cheese and topping with the bacon and avocado slices.

Nutrition:

Calories: 511 g. Fats: 38 g. Protein: 16 g. 31 mg of cholesterol 387 mg of sodium

Spring Ramen Bowl (Italian)

Preparation Time: 15 minutes | Cooking time: 20 minutes | Servings: 4

oz. (100g) soba noodles. 4 eggs.	1 medium zucchini, julienned or grated. 4 cups chicken stock.
2 cups watercress.	½ cup snap peas.
1 cup mushrooms, finely sliced.	1 leek (white part only), finely sliced. 2 cloves garlic, minced.
1 long red chili, seeded and finely chopped. 1.6-inch ginger, minced.	1 tsp. sesame oil.
2 nori sheets, crumbled. 1 lemon, cut into wedges.	1 tbsp. olive oil.

1. To boil the eggs, fill a saucepan with enough water to cover the eggs and set them over medium heat. Bring water to a gentle boil. Add the eggs and cook for 7 minutes. Drain and transfer the eggs into cold water. Set aside.
2. Place a medium-sized saucepan over medium-low heat. Heat the olive oil and sauté the garlic, ginger, leek, and chili for 5 minutes. Add the stock, noodles, and sesame oil. Cook for another 8 minutes or until noodles are cooked according to your desired doneness. During the last minute, add the zucchini, mushroom, and watercress.
3. Divide the ramen between four bowls and top with nori. Serve with eggs and lemon wedges.

Nutrition:

Calories: 300 g. Fat: 12 g. Fiber: 1 g. Carbs: 3 g. Protein: 9 g.

Cherry Smoothie Bowl (Greek)

Preparation Time: 15 minutes | Cooking time: 0 minutes | Servings: 1

½ cup organic rolled oats.	½ cup almond milk, unsweetened. 1 tbsp. chia seeds.
1 tsp. hemp seeds.	2 tsps. almonds, sliced. 1 tbsp. almond butter. 1 tsp. vanilla extract.
½ cup berries, fresh. 1 cup cherries, frozen.	1 cup plain Greek yogurt.

1. Soak the organic rolled oats in almond milk.
2. Prepare a smooth blend with the soaked oats, frozen cherries, yogurt, chia seeds, almond butter, and vanilla extract. Pour the mixture into 2 bowls.
3. To each bowl, add equal parts of the hemp seeds, sliced almonds, and fresh cherries.

Nutrition:

Calories: 130 g. Fats: 0 g. Protein: 1 g.

Spring Ramen Bowl (Italian)

Preparation Time: 15 minutes | Cooking time: 20 minutes | Servings: 4

oz. (100g) soba noodles. 4 eggs.	1 medium zucchini, julienned or grated. 4 cups chicken stock.
2 cups watercress.	½ cup snap peas.
1 cup mushrooms, finely sliced.	1 leek (white part only), finely sliced. 2 cloves garlic, minced.
1 long red chili, seeded and finely chopped. 1.6-inch ginger, minced.	1 tsp. sesame oil.
2 nori sheets, crumbled. 1 lemon, cut into wedges.	1 tbsp. olive oil.

1. To boil the eggs, fill a saucepan with enough water to cover the eggs and set them over medium heat. Bring water to a gentle boil. Add the eggs and cook for 7 minutes. Drain and transfer the eggs into cold water. Set aside.
2. Place a medium-sized saucepan over medium-low heat. Heat the olive oil and sauté the garlic, ginger, leek, and chili for 5 minutes. Add the stock, noodles, and sesame oil. Cook for another 8 minutes or until noodles are cooked according to your desired doneness. During the last minute, add the zucchini, mushroom, and watercress.
3. Divide the ramen between four bowls and top with nori. Serve with eggs and lemon wedges.

Nutrition:

Calories: 300 g. Fat: 12 g. Fiber: 1 g. Carbs: 3 g. Protein: 9 g.

Pepperoni Eggs (Italian)

Preparation Time: 10 minutes | Cooking time: 20 minutes | Servings: 2 Servings

1 cup of egg substitute	1 egg
3 green onions	minced meat
8 slices of pepperoni	diced 1/2 teaspoon of garlic powder
1 teaspoon melted butter 1/4 cup grated Romano cheese	1 pinch of salt and ground black pepper to taste

1. Combine the egg substitute, the egg, the green onions, the pepperoni slices, and the garlic powder in a bowl.
2. Heat the butter in a non-stick frying pan over low heat; Add the egg mixture, cover the pan and cook until the eggs are set, 10 to 15 minutes. Sprinkle Romano's eggs and season with salt and pepper.

Nutrition:

266 calories16.2 g fat 3.7 grams of carbohydrates 25.3 g of protein 124 mg of cholesterol 586 mg of sodium

Avocado-Egg Bowls (Italian)

Preparation Time: 10 minutes | Cooking time: 40 minutes | Servings: 3

1 tsp. coconut oil.	2 organic eggs, free-range. Salt and pepper, to sprinkle. 1 avocado, large and ripe.

For garnishing:

Chopped walnuts, as many as you like. Balsamic pearls to taste.	Fresh thyme to taste.

1. Slice the avocado in 2, then take out the pit and remove enough of the inside so that there is enough space inside to accommodate an entire egg.
2. Cut off a little bit of the bottom of the avocado so that the avocado will sit upright as you place it on a stable surface.
3. Pen the eggs and put each of the yolks in a separate bowl or container. Place the egg whites in the same small bowl. Sprinkle some pepper and salt into the whites according to your taste, then mix them well.
4. Melt the coconut oil in a pan that has a lid that fits, and place it over medium-high heat.
5. Put the avocado "boats" meaty-side down and skin-side up in the pan, and sauté them for approx. 35 seconds, or when they become darker.
6. Turn them over, then add to the spaces inside, almost filling the inside with the egg whites.
7. Then lower the temperature and cover the pan. Let them sit covered for approx. 16–20 minutes, or until the whites are just about fully cooked.
8. Gently, add 1 yolk onto each of the avocados and keep cooking them for 4–5 minutes, or just until they get to the point of cooking you want them to.
9. Move the avocados to a dish and add toppings to each of them using the walnuts, the balsamic pearls, or/and thyme.

Nutrition:
Calories: 215 g. Fats: 18 g. Protein: 9 g.

Citrus-Kissed Melon (Spanish)

Preparation time: 11 minutes | Cooking time: 0 minute | Servings: 4

2 cups melon, cubed	2 cups cantaloupe, cubed
½ cup freshly squeezed orange juice	¼ cup freshly squeezed lime juice 1 tbsp. orange

Zest

1. In a large bowl, incorporate the melon cubes.
2. In a bowl, blend the orange juice, lime juice, and orange zest and pour over the fruit.
3. Cover and chill for at least 4 hours, stirring occasionally.
4. Serve chilled.

Nutrition:
Calories: 101 Fat: 11 g. Protein: 2 g

Eggs With Cauliflower (Italian)

Preparation Time: 10 minutes | Cooking time: 20 minutes | Servings: 4

½ cauliflower head.	1 tbsp. olive oil extra virgin. 3 eggs.
¼ tsp. black pepper freshly ground.	¼ tsp. salt.
¼ tsp. cornstarch.	1 cup cheddar cheese shredded. 2 slices bacon.
2 tsps. paprika	1 tsp. fresh chives.

1. Get a box grater, and with it, grate the half head of cauliflower until it is well grated.
2. Place the grated cauliflower into a mixing container and add an egg to it together with the cheddar cheese that has been shredded, cornstarch, and salt. Mix them all well.
3. Get a large frying pan and heat the olive oil over medium heat. Using a serving spoon, scoop the cauliflower mix into the frying pan and shape it into patties.
4. Cook these patties for five minutes until they are crispy and done. Ensure to flip both sides.
5. Get a saucepan and poach the remaining 2 eggs over medium heat using boiling water.
6. Get another pan for frying and over a medium flame, let the olive oil become hot. Follow this by adding in bacon pieces and allow them to cook until they are crispy.
7. Crack the eggs and remove them from the shell. Slice them into circles.
8. Place the cooked cauliflower patties on a plate and add the sliced eggs together with the slices of crispy bacon. Sprinkle the paprika and chives and serve.

Nutrition:
Calories: 40 g. Fat: 1 g. Fiber: 2 g. Carbs: 8 g. Protein: 2 g.

Mushrooms with a Soy Sauce Glaze (Italian)

Preparation time: 5 minutes Cooking time:10 minutes Servings: 2

2 tablespoons butter	1(8 ounces) package sliced white mushrooms 2 cloves garlic, minced
2 teaspoons soy sauce ground black pepper to taste	

1. Melt the butter in a frying pan over medium heat; add the mushrooms; cook and stir until the mushrooms are soft and released about 5 minutes. Stir in the garlic; keep cooking and stir for 1 minute. Pour the soy sauce; cook the mushrooms in the soy sauce until the liquid has evaporated, about 4 minutes.

Nutrition: 135 calories 11.9 g of fat 5.4 g carbohydrates 4.2 g of protein 31 mg of cholesterol 387 mg of sodium

Ken's Hard-Boiled Egg (Italian)

Preparation Time: 5 minutes Cooking Time:15 minutes | Servings: 8

1 tablespoon of salt	1/4 cup distilled white vinegar
6 cups of water	8 eggs

1. Mix the salt, vinegar, and water in a large saucepan and bring to a boil over high heat. Add the eggs one by one, and be careful not to split them. Lower the heat and cook over low heat and cook for 14 minutes.
2. Remove the eggs from the hot water and place them in a container filled with ice water or cold water. Cool completely, approximately 15 minutes.

Nutrition:

72 calories 5 grams of fat 0.4 g carbohydrates 6.3 g protein 186 mg of cholesterol 947 mg of sodium.

Low Carb Bagels (Italian)

Preparation Time: 10 minutes | Cooking time: 20 minutes | Servings: 4

1 cups almond flour	2 tbsps. bagel seasoning 1 tbsp. powder for baking 3 eggs.
3 cups mozzarella cheese, shredded.	¼ cup cream cheese.

1. Heat your oven in advance at 400 ° c.
2. Get 2 baking sheets and line them well with paper made from parchment.
3. Get a large mixing container and in it, mix the almond flour with the powder for baking.
4. Mix the mozzarella cheese and the cream cheese in a bowl that can be used in a microwave. Place the bowl in a microwave for 2 minutes when the cheese melts and combines.
5. Get the mixture of cheese from the bowl once out of the microwave and pour it into the mixing container with the flour from almonds and the powder for baking. Mix all the until well mixed.
6. Take the dough when done and divide it into eight parts that are equal in measure. Using your palms, take each of the eight dough parts and roll them into balls.
7. Using your fingers, create a hole in each of the balls, and gently stretch the dough to form the shape of a bagel.
8. Take one egg and beat it in a bowl. Brush the eggs on top of each made bagel following this by sprinkling the bagel seasoning at the top as well.
9. Place the bagel dough in the oven on its rack, which is in the middle for 25 minutes when they are nice and golden in color.
10. Remove the bagels from the oven and let them get cold for about 10 minutes before serving them.

Nutrition:

Calories: 275 g. Fat: 20 g. Fiber: 2 g. Carbs: 8 g. Protein: 20 g.

Avocado-Egg Bowls (Italian)

Prep Time: 10 minutes Cooking Time: 40 minutes Servings: 3

1tsp. coconut oil.	2organic eggs, free-range.
	Salt and pepper, to sprinkle.
	1 avocado, large and ripe.
For garnishing:	Chopped walnuts, as many as you like. Balsamic pearls, to taste.

Fresh thyme, to taste.

1. Slice the avocado in 2, then take out the pit and remove enough of the inside so that there is enough space inside to accommodate an entire egg.
2. Cut off a little bit of the bottom of the avocado so that the avocado will sit upright as you place it on a stable surface.
3. Open the eggs and put each of the yolks in a separate bowl or container. Place the egg whites in the same small bowl. Sprinkle some pepper and salt into the whites according to your taste, then mix them well.
4. Melt the coconut oil in a pan that has a lid that fits, and place it over medium-high heat.
5. Put the avocado "boats" meaty-side down and skin-side up in the pan, and sauté them for approx. 35 seconds, or when they become darker.
6. Turn them over, then add to the spaces inside, almost filling the inside with the egg whites.
7. Then lower the temperature and cover the pan. Let them sit covered for approx. 16–20 minutes, or until the whites are just about fully cooked.
8. Gently, add 1 yolk onto each of the avocados and keep cooking them for 4–5 minutes, or just until they get to the point of cooking you want them to.
9. Move the avocados to a dish and add toppings to each of them using the walnuts, the balsamic pearls, or/and thyme.

Nutrition: Calories: 215 g. Fats: 18 g. Protein: 9 g.

Ken's Hard-Boiled Egg (Italian)

Preparation Time: 5 minutes Cooking Time:15 minutes Servings: 8

1 tablespoon of salt	1/4 cup distilled white vinegar 6 cups of water
8 eggs	

1. Mix the salt, vinegar, and water in a large saucepan and bring to a boil over high heat. Add the eggs one by one, and be careful not to split them. Lower the heat and cook over low heat and cook for 14 minutes.
2. Remove the eggs from the hot water and place them in a container filled with ice water or cold water. Cool completely, approximately 15 minutes.

Nutrition: 72 calories 5 grams of fat 0.4 g carbohydrates 6.3 g protein 186 mg of cholesterol 947 mg of sodium

Eggs With Cauliflower (Italian)

Preparation Time: 10 minutes Cooking Time: 20 minutes
Servings: 4

½ cauliflower head.	1 tbsp. olive oil extra virgin. 3 eggs.
¼ tsp. black pepper freshly ground.	¼ tsp. salt.
¼ tsp. cornstarch.	1cup cheddar cheese shredded. 2 slices bacon.
2tsps. paprika	1 tsp. fresh chives.

1. Get a box grater, and with it, grate the half head of cauliflower until it is well grated.
2. Place the grated cauliflower into a mixing container and add an egg to it together with the cheddar cheese that has been shredded, cornstarch, and salt. Mix them all well.
3. Get a large frying pan and heat the olive oil over medium heat. Using a serving spoon, scoop the cauliflower mix into the frying pan and shape it into patties.
4. Cook these patties for five minutes until they are crispy and done. Ensure to flip both sides.
5. Get a saucepan and poach the remaining 2 eggs over medium heat using boiling water.
6. Get another pan for frying and over a medium flame, let the olive oil become hot. Follow this by adding in bacon pieces and allow them to cook until they are crispy.
7. Crack the eggs and remove them from the shell. Slice them into circles.
8. Place the cooked cauliflower patties on a plate and add the sliced eggs together with the slices of crispy bacon. Sprinkle the paprika and chives and serve.

Nutrition: Calories: 40 g. Fat: 1 g. Fiber: 2 g. Carbs: 8 g. Protein: 2 g.

Heart-Healthful Trail Mix (Spanish)

Preparation time: 8 minutes | Cooking time: 32 minutes | Servings: 12

1 cup raw almonds 1 cup walnut halves	1 cup pumpkin seeds
1 cup dried apricots, cut into thin strips 1 cup dried cherries, roughly chopped 1 cup golden raisins	2 tbsps. extra-virgin olive oil 1 tsp. salt

1. Preheat the oven to 300°F. Line a baking sheet with aluminum foil.
2. In a large bowl, mix the almonds, walnuts, pumpkin seeds, apricots, cherries, and raisins. Pour the olive oil over all and toss well with clean hands. Add the salt and toss again to distribute.
3. Pour the nut mixture onto the baking sheet in a single layer and bake until the fruits begin to brown, for 30 minutes. Chill on the baking sheet to room temperature.
4. Store in a large airtight container or zipper-top plastic bag.

Nutrition:
Calories: 109 Fat: 7 g. Protein: 1 g.

Egg Cupcakes (Italian)

Preparation time: 15 minutes Cooking time: 20 minutes
Servings: 6 servings

1 pack of bacon (12 ounces) 6 eggs, 2 tablespoons of milk 1/4 teaspoon salt, 1/4 teaspoon ground black pepper	1c. Melted butter, 1/4 teaspoon. Dried parsley 1/2 cup diced ham
1/4 cup grated mozzarella cheese6 slices gouda	

1. Preheat the oven to 175 ° C (350 ° F).
2. Place the bacon in a large frying pan and cook over medium heat, occasionally turning until brown starts to brown, about 5 minutes. Drain the bacon slices on kitchen paper.
3. Cover 6 cups of the non-stick muffin pan with slices of bacon. Cut the remaining bacon slices and sprinkle the bottom of each cup.
4. In a large bowl, beat eggs, milk, butter, parsley, salt, and pepper. Stir in the ham and mozzarella cheese.
5. Pour the egg mixture into cups filled with bacon; garnish with Gouda cheese.
6. Bake in the preheated oven until Gouda cheese is melted and the eggs are tender about 15 minutes.

Nutrition: 310 calories 22.9 g of fat 2.1 g carbohydrates 23.1 g of protein 249 mg of cholesterol 988 mg of sodium.

Mushrooms with a Soy Sauce Glaze (Italian)

Preparation time: 5 minutes Cooking time:10 minutes |
Servings: 2

2 tablespoons butter	1(8 ounces) package sliced white mushrooms 2 cloves garlic, minced
2 teaspoons soy sauce	ground black pepper to taste

1. Melt the butter in a frying pan over medium heat; add the mushrooms; cook and stir until the mushrooms are soft and released about 5 minutes. Stir in the garlic; keep cooking and stir for 1 minute. Pour the soy sauce; cook the mushrooms in the soy sauce until the liquid has evaporated, about 4 minutes.

Nutrition:
135 calories 11.9 g of fat 5.4 g carbohydrates 4.2 g of protein

Healthy Chia and Oats Smoothie (Greek)

Prep Time: 10 minutes Cooking Time: 0 minutes Servings: 2

6 tbsps. oats.	2 tbsps. chia seeds.
2 tbsps. hemp powder.	4 Medjool dates, pitted (optional). 2 bananas, chopped.
1cup almond milk. 1 cup frozen berries.	2big handful's spinach, torn.

1. Add all the to a blender and blend until smooth.
2. Pour in glasses and serve.

Nutrition: Calories: 140. Fat: 7 g. Fiber: 4 g. Carbs: 12 g. Protein: 12 g.

Low Carb Bagels (Italian)

Preparation Time: 10 minutes Cooking Time: 20 minutes
Servings: 4

1cups almond flour	2tbsps. bagel seasoning 1 tbsp. powder for baking 3 eggs.
3 cups mozzarella cheese, shredded.	¼ cup cream cheese.

1. Heat your oven in advance at 400 ° c.
2. Get 2 baking sheets and line them well with paper made from parchment.
3. Get a large mixing container and in it, mix the almond flour with the powder for baking.
4. Mix the mozzarella cheese and the cream cheese in a bowl that can be used in a microwave. Place the bowl in a microwave for 2 minutes when the cheese melts and combines.
5. Get the mixture of cheese from the bowl once out of the microwave and pour it into the mixing container with the flour from almonds and the powder for baking. Mix all the until well mixed.
6. Take the dough when done and divide it into eight parts that are equal in measure. Using your palms, take each of the eight dough parts and roll them into balls.
7. Using your fingers, create a hole in each of the balls, and gently stretch the dough to form the shape of a bagel.
8. Take one egg and beat it in a bowl. Brush the eggs on top of each made bagel following this by sprinkling the bagel seasoning at the top as well.
9. Place the bagel dough in the oven on its rack, which is in the middle for 25 minutes when they are nice and golden in color.
10. Remove the bagels from the oven and let them get cold for about 10 minutes before serving them.

Nutrition: Calories: 275 g. Fat: 20 g. Fiber: 2 g. Carbs: 8 g. Protein: 20 g.

Pepperoni Eggs (Italian)

Prep Time: 10 minutes Cooking Time: 20 minutes Servings: 2

1 cup of egg substitute	1 egg
3 green onions	minced meat
8 slices of pepperoni	diced 1/2 teaspoon of garlic powder
1 teaspoon melted butter	1/4 cup grated Romano cheese 1 pinch of salt and ground black pepper to taste

1. Combine the egg substitute, the egg, the green onions, the pepperoni slices, and the garlic powder in a bowl.
2. Heat the butter in a non-stick frying pan over low heat; Add the egg mixture, cover the pan and cook until the eggs are set, 10 to 15 minutes. Sprinkle Romano's eggs and season with salt and pepper.

Nutrition: 266 calories16.2 g fat 3.7 grams of carbohydrates 25.3 g of protein 124 mg of cholesterol 586 mg of sodium

Citrus-Kissed Melon (Spanish)

Preparation time: 11 minutes Cooking time: 0 minute
Servings: 4

2 cups melon, cubed	2 cups cantaloupe, cubed
½ cup freshly squeezed orange juice	¼ cup freshly squeezed lime juice 1 tbsp. orange zest

1. In a large bowl, incorporate the melon cubes.
2. In a bowl, blend the orange juice, lime juice, and orange zest and pour over the fruit.
3. Cover and chill for at least 4 hours, stirring occasionally.
4. Serve chilled.

Nutrition: Calories: 101 Fat: 11 g. Protein: 2 g.

Poached Eggs Caprese (Italian)

Preparation time: 5 minutes Cooking time: 15 minutes
Servings: 2

Distilled white vinegar: 1 tbsp. Salt: 2 tsp.	4 eggs
2 English muffin, cut in half	4 slices of mozzarella cheese
Salt, to taste	1 tomato, sliced thick
Pesto: 4 tsp.	

1. In a saucepan, add 2-3" of water and let it boil.
2. Turn the heat low and add salt, vinegar and let it simmer.
3. On each half of the muffin, add cheese and tomato slices. Toast for five minutes in the oven.
4. In a small cup, break an egg and slip gently in the simmering water.
5. Cook for 3 minutes or until the whites set, take the eggs out on tissue paper.
6. Place on top of tomato slices, serve with black pepper, pesto on top.

Nutrition: 428 Cal | 24.9 g Fat |31.7 g Carbs |33 g Protein

Baked Eggs with Avocado & Feta (Greek)

Preparation time: 5 minutes Cooking time: 30 minutes
Servings: 2

Crumbled feta cheese: 2 tbsp. 4 eggs	Salt & black pepper, to taste 1 avocado, cut into 6 slices

1. Let the oven preheat to 400F
2. Place 2 ramekins in the oven for ten minutes and later spray with oil.
3. Put avocado slices in each ramekin with 2 eggs.
4. Add crumbled feta, salt and pepper on top.
5. Bake for 12 to 15 minutes until the yolks are done the way you prefer.
6. Serve right away

Nutrition: 391 Cal |33 g Fat |9.5 g Carbs |16 g Protein

Green Vegetable Eggs (Greek)

Preparation time: 10 minutes Cooking time: 30 minutes
Servings: 4

Kale: 8 oz., chopped without veins & stems	Olive oil: ¼ cup
Kosher salt, to taste	
Brussels sprouts: 8 oz.	1 green onion, chopped
Sliced thin 3 minced garlic cloves	Half lemon's juice
Half red onion, chopped	Baby spinach: 2 cups
Cumin: ¾ tsp.	Aleppo pepper: 1 tsp.
	Coriander: 1 tsp.

4 eggs

1. In a skillet, add olive oil on medium flame. Add sprouts and salt, cook for 5-6 minutes.
2. Turn the heat low and add garlic, onion and cook for 3-4 minutes, till softened.
3. Add kale and cook for five minutes, add spinach and mix well. Season with salt.
4. Add the rest of the spices and mix. Add half a cup of water and turn heat to medium.
5. Cover and cook for 8-10minutes, then add lemon juice.
6. Make four wells in the pan, put one egg in each well and cover it.
7. Cook for four minutes till the eggs are set.
8. Turn off the heat serve with crumbled feta on top.

Nutrition: 229 Cal | 18.2 g Fat | 9 g Carbs | 9.8 g Protein

Spinach Artichoke Frittata (Spanish)

Preparation time: 5 minutes Cooking time: 25 minutes
Servings: 4-6

Full-fat sour cream half cup	Marinated artichoke hearts 2 cups, quartered 10 eggs
Dijon mustard 1 tbsp. Olive oil: 2 tbsp.	Kosher salt: 1 tsp. Black pepper: 1/4 tsp. 2 minced garlic cloves
Grated parmesan cheese 1 cup Baby spinach 5 cups	

1. Let the oven preheat to 400 F, with a rack in the middle.
2. In a bowl, add eggs, salt, parmesan (half cup), mustard, pepper, and sour cream. Whisk and set it aside.
3. In a skillet, add oil on medium flame. Add artichokes in hot oil in an even layer and cook for 6-8 minutes. Add garlic, spinach, and cook for two minutes.
4. Set this mixture into an even layer and pour eggs on top. Add the rest of the cheese on top.
5. Do not stir; let it cook for 2-3 minutes, then bake for 12-15 minutes.
6. Let it cool for five minutes, slice and serve.

Nutrition: 316 Cal | 25.9 g Fat | 6.4 g Carbs | 17.9 g Protein

Sautéed Dandelion Toast (Italian)

Preparation time: 5 minutes Cooking time: 10 minutes
Servings: 4

1 red onion, sliced	Red pepper flakes: 1/8 tsp. Olive oil: 2 tbsp.
Lemon juice: 2 tbsp. Plain yogurt: 1/4 cup Salt: 1/4 tsp.	Black pepper: 1/4 tsp.
1 bunch of dandelion greens	Feta cheese: half cup
Mint leaves: 2 tbsp.	Grated lemon zest: 1 tsp.
1loaf of ciabatta, cut & toasted	

1. 1.In a skillet, add oil on medium flame. Add onion and pepper flakes cook for 4-5 minutes.
2. Add lemon juice and cook for 30 seconds. Turn off the heat and add dandelion greens, season with salt and pepper, toss well.
3. In a food processor, add crumbled feta cheese, and the rest of the except for bread, until smooth and creamy.
4. Spread this mixture on toasted ciabatta and serve with greens and mint leaves on top.

Nutrition: 300 Cal | 14.5 g Fat | 34 g Carbs | 10 g Protein

Banana Walnut Bread (Spanish)

Preparation time: 15 minutes Cooking time: 55 minutes
Servings: 1 loaf

Honey: half cup 2 eggs	Olive oil: 1/3 cup
1ripe bananas, mashed	Ground cardamom: ½-¾
Chopped walnut: 1/3 cup	tsp. Baking soda: 1 tsp.
Low-fat milk: ¼ cup Plain yogurt: 2 tbsp.	
All-purpose/wheat flour: 1 1/3 cup Vanilla extract: 1 tsp.	Ground cinnamon: half tsp. Ground nutmeg: half tsp.
Chopped dates: half cup	

1. Let the oven preheat to 325 F.
2. In a bowl, whisk honey and olive oil. Add eggs and whisk well.
3. Add the rest of the , except for flour, walnuts and dates. Mix well.
4. Add flour and mix lightly; fold in walnuts and dates until just combined.
5. Oil spray a 9 by 5 loaf pan and pour in the batter.
6. Bake for 50 minutes at 350 F until inserted toothpick comes out clean.
7. Let it rest for ten minutes. Slice and serve.

Nutrition: 200 Cal | 6.9 g Fat | 33.6 g Carbs | 2.8 g Protein

Café Cooler (Italian)

Preparation time: 16 minutes Cooking time: 0 minute
Servings: 4

Ice cubes as needed 2 cups low-fat milk	½ tsp. ground cinnamon
½ tsp. pure vanilla extract	1 cup espresso, cooled to room temperature 4 tsps. sugar (optional)

1. Fill 4 tall glasses with ice cubes.
2. In a blender, combine the milk, cinnamon, and vanilla and blend until frothy.
3. Pour the milk over the ice cubes and top each drink with one-quarter of the espresso. If using sugar, stir it into the espresso until it has dissolved.
4. Serve immediately, with a chilled teaspoon for stirring.

Nutrition: Calories: 93 Fat: 7 g. Protein: 1 g.

Egg Breakfast Sandwich with Roasted Tomatoes(Greek)

Prep time: 5 minutes Cooking time: 15 minutes Servings: 1

Olive oil: 1 tsp. Pesto: 1 tbsp.	Egg whites: 1/4 cup Roasted tomatoes: half cup Salt & black pepper, to taste Chopped fresh herbs: 1 tsp.
Provolone cheese: 1 to 2 slices 1 whole ciabatta roll	

1. In a skillet, add oil on medium flame. Add egg whites and salt, pepper.
2. Sprinkle fresh herbs on top. Cook for 3 to 4 minutes.
3. Flip only once and toast the ciabatta bread. Spread pesto on both sides and place egg whites on top with cheese.
4. Add roasted tomatoes on top, sprinkle salt and pepper.
5. Serve right away.

Nutrition: 458 Cal | 24 g Fat | 51 g Carbs | 21 g Protein

Breakfast Pita Pizza (Italian)

Preparation time: 10 minutes Cooking time: 45 minutes
Servings: 2

Extra-virgin olive oil: 2 tbsp. 4 eggs, whisked	1 round pita breads Half tomato, diced
Chopped mushrooms: ¼ cup Pesto: 2 tbsp.	Chopped spinach: half cup Shredded cheddar cheese

1. Let the oven preheat to 350 F, and place parchment paper on a baking sheet.
2. In a skillet, add bacon on medium flame, and cook for ten minutes. Take out on a paper towel.
3. Add onion and cook for five minutes, take them out on a plate.
4. Add oil in the skillet, and add eggs and cook for 3-5 minutes.
5. On the prepared baking sheet, place pita pieces of bread. Spread pesto and top with the rest of the , including bacon and eggs. Sprinkle cheese on top.
6. Bake for ten minutes and serve right away.

Nutrition: 873 Cal | 43.5 g Fat | 43.5 g Carbs | 36.8 g Protein

Spinach & Goat Cheese Egg Muffins (Greek)

Preparation time: 10 minutes
Cooking time: 35 minutes Servings: 12

Olive oil: 1 tbsp. Milk: half cup	1 red pepper, sliced into ¼" pieces Salt & black pepper, to taste
Fresh goat cheese: 1/4 cup, crumbled 6 eggs	2 scallions, diced
Baby spinach: 1 5-oz., chopped	

1. Let the oven preheat to 350 F. oil spray a 12-cup muffin tin.
1. 2.In a skillet, add oil on medium flame. Add red pepper, spinach and season with salt and pepper cook for 6-8 minutes.
2. Turn off the heat and add in scallions.
3. In a bowl, whisk eggs with salt, pepper and milk. Add spinach mixture and mix.
4. Pour this mixture into the muffin cups and add goat cheese on top.
5. Bake for 20-25 minutes until eggs are set.
6. Cool for five minutes and serve right away

Nutrition: 65 Cal | 4.5 g Fat | 2 g Carbs | 4 g Protein

Gingerbread Sweet Quinoa Breakfast Bake(Greek)

Preparation time: 10 minutes + overnight Cooking time: 75 minutes
Servings: 12

Molasses: 1/4 cup Ground ginger: 1 tsp. Pure maple syrup: 1/4 cup	Mashed bananas: 1 ½ cups Vanilla extract: 2 tsp.
Ground cloves: 1 tsp.	Salt: half tsp.
Quinoa uncooked: 1 cup Ground allspice: half tsp. Slivered almonds: 1/4 cup Cinnamon: 1 tbsp. Almond milk, Unsweetened: 2 1/2 Cups	

1. In a casserole dish (2 ½ to 3 qt.), add all except for quinoa, sliced almonds and almond milk. Mix well and add quinoa and combine well.
2. Add almond milk, mix and keep in the fridge overnight.
3. The next day, let the oven preheat to 350 F, and whisk the quinoa mix.
4. Bake the mixture, covered with aluminum foil, for 60-75 minutes.
5. Switch on the broil to high, take the foil off and sprinkle almonds slices on top.
6. Broil for 2 to 4 minutes; make sure not to burn it.
7. Rest for ten minutes, then serve.

Nutrition: 211 Cal | 4.2 g Fat | 40 g Carbs | 4.7 g Protein

Smoked Salmon & Poached Eggs on Toast (Italian)

Prep time: 7 minutes Cooking time: 7 minutes Servings: 1

Smoked salmon: 3.5 oz.	Thinly sliced scallions: 1
Bread toasted: 2 slices	tbsp. Half avocado, smashed Lemon juice: 1/4 tsp.

Salt & black pepper, to taste

2 poached eggs

1. In a bowl, add smashed avocado. Add salt and lemon juice mix well.
2. Poach the eggs if you have not already.
3. Spread the avocado mixture on toast and place smoked salmon on top.
4. Top with poached eggs and serve with black pepper on top.

Nutrition: 178 Cal | 4 g Fat | 16.9 g Carbs | 7 g Protein

Mediterranean Breakfast Quinoa (Greek)

Prep time: 10 minutes Cooking time: 15 minutes Servings: 4

Ground cinnamon: 1 tsp.	Quinoa: 1 cup
Honey: 2 tbsp.	
Chopped toasted almonds:	Sea salt: 1 tsp.
¼ cup Milk: 2 cups	

5 dried apricots, diced

Vanilla extract: 1 tsp. 2 dried dates, diced

1. In a pan, add the quinoa, cinnamon on medium flame.
2. Add salt, milk, mix well and let it come to a boil.
3. Turn the heat low and cover the pan. Let it simmer for 15 minutes.
4. Add apricots, vanilla, dates, honey, and half of the almond slices; mix well.
5. Serve with the rest of the almond slices on top.

Nutrition: 327 Cal | 7.9 g Fat | 50 g Carbs | 11.5 g Protein

Greek Yogurt Pumpkin Parfait (Greek)

Preparation time: 35 minutes

Cooking time: 0 minutes Servings: 6

Low-fat Greek yogurt: 1 ¼ cup Mascarpone cheese: 3 to 4 tbsp. Brown sugar: 2 ½ tbsp.	Vanilla extract: 1 tsp. Pinch of nutmeg Pumpkin puree: 2 cups Molasses: 2 tbsp.
Ground cinnamon: 1 ½ to 2 tsp.	

1. In a bowl, add all except for nuts and chocolate chips, whisk with an electric mixer until smooth.
2. Adjust seasonings to taste and mix well.
3. In small mason jars, divide the mixture and keep it in the fridge for half an hour.
4. Serve with nuts and chocolate chips on top.

Nutrition: 102 Cal | 1.5 g Fat | 15.6 g Carbs | 0.8 g Protein

Balsamic Berries with Honey Yogurt (Greek)

Preparation time: 15 minutes

Cooking time: 0 minutes Servings: 4

Blueberries: 1 cup	Honey: 2 tsp.
Raspberries: 1 cup	Strawberries: 1 ½ cups, cut in halves Balsamic vinegar: 1 tbsp.

Plain Greek yogurt: 2/3 cup

1. In a bowl, toss all berries in balsamic vinegar. Let them rest for ten minutes.
2. Add honey, yogurt to a separate bowl, and whisk.
3. In serving cups, add berries and top with yogurt mixture and serve.

Nutrition: 151 Cal | 6.1 g Fat | 12.6 g Carbs | 2.8 g Protein

Spinach Feta Breakfast Wraps (Italian)

Preparation time: 5 minutes Cooking time: 10 minutes Servings: 4

Baby spinach: 5 cups	1 cup cherry tomatoes, halved 4 ounces feta cheese, crumbled 10 eggs
4 whole-wheat tortillas	Salt & black pepper, to taste

1. In a bowl, whisk eggs well.
2. Place a skillet on medium flame, spray the pan with oil.
3. Add eggs and stir occasionally until cooked.
4. Add black pepper and salt, take out on a plate.
5. Oil spray the pan again and sauté spinach until wilted. Take out on a plate.
6. Place tortilla on a surface, add eggs, feta and spinach. Wrap it tightly.
7. Serve right away.

Nutrition: 521 Cal | 27 g Fat | 45 g Carbs | 28.1 g Protein

Chard Breakfast Skillet (Greek)

Preparation time: 10 minutes Cooking time: 20 minutes Servings: 4

Cherry tomatoes: 1 1/4 cups, quartered Olive oil: 3 tbsp.	Red wine vinegar: 1 tbsp. 2 bunches of Swiss chard
Chopped yellow onion: 2 cups 4 minced garlic cloves	Black pepper: half tsp. Sea salt: half tsp.

4 eggs

1. In a bowl, toss tomatoes with vinegar.
2. Remove the stems off of chard leaves and chop the leaves and rinse them. Let them dry in a colander.
3. Slice the stems thinly.
4. In a skillet, add oil and sauté the stems and onion for ten minutes.
5. Turn the heat low and add garlic; cook for 60 seconds.
6. Add leaves and season with salt and pepper.
7. Toss on high heat until it wilts.
8. Make for wells in the pan and put one egg in each nest.
9. Cook for four minutes until yolks are set.
10. Add tomatoes to the skillet and serve.

Nutrition: 245 Cal | 11 g Fat | 17 g Carbs | 15 g Protein

Greek Omelet Casserole (Greek)

Prep time: 10 minutes Cooking time: 35-40 minutes Servings: 12

12 eggs	Fresh spinach: 1 ½ cups
	Lemon pepper: 1 tsp.
Whole milk: 2 cups	2 minced garlic cloves Dried oregano: 1 tsp.
Artichoke with olives, peppers, chopped without liquid Tomato (sun dried) feta cheese: ¾ cup, crumbled Olive oil: 4 tsp.	Fresh chopped dill: 1 tbsp. Salt: 1 tsp.

1. Let the oven preheat to 350 F.
2. In a skillet, add oil (1 tbsp.), add garlic and spinach, sauté for three minutes.
3. Take a baking dish (9 by 13") and oil spray it.
4. Spread the spinach mixture on the bottom evenly.
5. In a bowl, whisk eggs with the rest of the except for feta cheese.
6. Pour the mixture over spinach mixture, and spread feta cheese on top.
7. Bake for 35 to 40 minutes until set.

Nutrition: 186 Cal | 13 g Fat | 5 g Carbs | 10 g Protein

Easy Breakfast Stuffed Peppers (Greek)

Prep time: 10 minutes Cooking time: 30 minutes Servings: 5-6

Olive oil, as needed	3 bell peppers, halved lengthwise and emptied Water, as needed
Chopped yellow onion: 1 cup Peeled potatoes: 10-12 oz., diced 3 minced garlic cloves Mushrooms: 6 oz., chopped	Salt & black pepper, to taste Chopped cherry tomatoes: half cup Aleppo pepper: ¾ tsp.
Coriander: ¾ tsp. 6 eggs	Organic cumin: ¾ tsp. Turmeric: half tsp.
Chopped fresh parsley, packed: half cup	

1. Let the oven preheat to 350 F.
2. Place the half peppers in the baking dish. Add water (1 cup) in the baking dish, cover with aluminum foil and bake for 10-15 minutes.
3. Place a cast-iron skillet on high flame, add mushrooms, salt and cook until browned. Take them out on a plate.
4. Add olive oil to the skillet (2 tbsp.) add potatoes and onion in hot oil.
5. Season with salt, pepper and other spices. Cook for five minutes and add garlic cook for 5-7 minutes on medium flame until potatoes become tender.
6. Add mushrooms, parsley and tomatoes. Mix well and turn off the heat.
7. Take peppers out from the oven, discard the water and stuff the mixture into the peppers, 3/4 of the way. Put one egg on top of the stuffing.
8. Cover with foil and bake for 18-20 minutes.
9. Serve right away.

Nutrition: 224 Cal 20 g Fat | 15.9 g Carbs | 17 g Protein

Mediterranean Breakfast Salad (Greek)

Preparation time: 15 minutes Cooking time: 10 minutes Servings: 4

Arugula: 10 cups	Halved cherry tomatoes: 2 cups 4 eggs
Mixed herbs: half cup, chopped	Half cucumber, chopped without seeds 1 avocado
Salt & black pepper, to taste	1 lemon
Almonds: 1 cup, chopped	
Cooked cooled quinoa: 1 cup Olive oil, as required	

1. Boil eggs to your desired doneness. (soft-boiled is preferred).
2. In a bowl, mix quinoa, arugula, cucumber, and tomatoes. Toss and drizzle olive oil, season with salt and pepper. Toss to combine.
3. Divide this mixture into four plates and serve with eggs (cut in half), avocado slices and almonds.
4. Squeeze lemon juice on top and serve.

Nutrition: 171 Cal | 12 g Fat | 12 g Carbs | 16 g Protein

Eggs Florentine (Spanish)

Preparation time: 10 minutes Cooking time: 10 minutes Servings: 3

Butter: 2 tbsp.	6 eggs, whisked Mushrooms: half cup, sliced 2 minced garlic cloves
Cream cheese: 3 tbsp., cut into small pieces Half pack of fresh spinach	Salt & black pepper, to taste

1. In a skillet, add butter and sauté garlic, mushrooms for one minute.
2. Add spinach and cook for 2-3 minutes until spinach wilts.
3. Add eggs into the mixture and add salt, pepper. Cook until they set, flip and cook on the other side.
4. Spread cream cheese on top and cook for five minutes on low-medium flame until cheese melts.

Nutrition: 212 Cal | 18.1 g Fat | 13.5 g Carbs | 17 g Protein

Snow Pea & Ricotta Toasts (Greek)

Preparation time: 10 minutes

Cooking time: 0 minutes Servings: 4

Snow peas: 4 oz. Salt: half tsp.	White wine vinegar: 1 tbsp. Olive oil: 1 tbsp.
Ricotta: 4 oz.	Prepared horseradish: 2 tsp. Honey: half tsp.

4 slices of toasted bread

1. Cut peas in ¼ inch thick crosswise. In a bowl, whisk the rest of the with snow peas except for bread and ricotta.
2. On each toast slice, spread one oz. of ricotta and serve with snow peas mixture on top.

Nutrition: 131 Cal | 5.5 g Fat | 17 g Carbs | 8.5 g Protein

Easy Muesli (Italian)

Preparation time: 10 minutes Cooking time: 20 minutes
Servings: 8

Wheat bran: half cup	Coconut flakes,
Kosher salt: half tsp.	unsweetened: half cup
	Ground cinnamon: half tsp.
Dried cherries: 1/4 cup	Raw pecans: 1/4 cup,
Rolled oats: 3 1/2 cups	roughly chopped Dried
Sliced almonds: half cup	apricots: 1/4 cup, coarsely
Raw pepitas: 1/4 cup	chopped

1. Let the oven preheat to 350 F with 2 racks.
2. Place wheat bran, salt, cinnamon and oats on a baking sheet and toss well, make into one even layer.
3. In another baking sheet, add pepitas, almonds, and pecans. Toss and make into an even layer. Roast for 10-12 minutes by placing oats on the top rack and the nuts on the lower rack.
4. Take the nuts' baking sheet out and let it cool.
5. Sprinkle coconuts over oats, and bake again for five minutes. Take out and let it cool for ten minutes.
6. In large bowls, add all contents of both baking sheets.
7. Add cherries and apricot; toss well.
8. Store in an airtight jar and use for 1 month.

Nutrition: 275 Cal | 13.0 g Fat |36.4 g Carbs |8.5 g Protein

White Beans with Greens & Poached Egg(Greek)

Preparation time: 10 minutes Cooking time: 0 minutes
Servings: 4

Za'atar: 2 tsp.	3 tablespoons olive oil 4 eggs, poached
2 minced garlic cloves	Swiss chard: ~10 oz., stems
Kosher salt: 1 tsp.	removed & leaves sliced 1 can of (15-oz.) cannellini beans, rinsed

Red pepper flakes: 1/4 tsp.
Lemon juice: 1 tbsp

1. In a pan, add oil (2 tbsp.) on medium flame until hot.
2. Add beans and cook for 2-4 minutes.
3. Add za'atar (1 tsp.) and salt (half tsp.), mix well.
4. Cook for 3-5 minutes, until beans are golden brown, take them out on a plate.
5. Add oil (1 tbsp.) to the pan, add chard and season with the rest of the za'atar, salt, cook for 3-5 minutes.
6. Turn off the heat and add lemon juice and toss well.
7. In four bowls, add beans and place a poached egg on top with red pepper flakes. Serve right away.

Nutrition: 301 Cal | 15.5 g Fat |26.5 g Carbs |15 g Protein

Zucchini with Eggs (Greek)

Preparation time: 10 minutes Cooking time: 5-7 minutes
Servings: 2

Salt & black pepper, to taste	Water: 1 tsp.
Olive oil: 1 ½ tbsp.	
2 zucchinis, sliced into large	
chunks 2 eggs	

1. In a skillet, add oil and sauté zucchini for ten minutes until tender. Season with salt and black pepper.
2. Whisk eggs in a bowl with water. Pour eggs over zucchini, cook until eggs are scrambled and sprinkle salt and pepper on top.
3. Serve right away.

Nutrition: 111 Cal | 12 g Fat |21 g Carbs |16 g Protein

Easy, Fluffy Lemon Pancakes (Greek)

Preparation time: 10 minutes Cooking time: 20 minutes
Servings: 4

Baking powder: 1 tsp. 4 eggs	Ricotta cheese: 1 cup 2% milk: half cup Granulated sugar: 1 tbsp.
All-purpose flour: 1 cup	1 lemon
Kosher salt: 1/4 tsp	

1. In different bowls, separate whites and yolks.
2. In the egg yolk, add lemon zest and lemon juice.
3. Add milk and ricotta cheese whisk well.
4. Add the rest of the mix until just combined.
5. With a stand mixer, whisk the egg whites for 2-3 minutes until stiff peaks form.
6. Fold the egg whites into the yolk mixture.
7. In a skillet, add enough butter to coat the pan and add ¼ cup of batter.
8. Cook for 2-3 minutes on each side and serve with maple syrup.

Nutrition: 344 Cal | 15.9 g Fat |32.1 g Carbs |17.1 g Protein

Grain Bowl with Sautéed Spinach (Spanish)

Preparation time: 5 minutes Cooking time: 5 minutes Servings: 2

Spinach: 4 cups, roughly chopped Cooked grains: 2 cups	1 minced garlic clove 2 eggs
Olive oil: 1 tbsp. Kosher salt: 1/4 tsp. Half avocado, diced Pepper: 1/4 tsp.	1 tomato, cut into small pieces

1. In bowls, add warmed grains.
2. In a skillet, add oil, garlic and cook for 1 minute.
3. Add spinach and season with salt and pepper, cook for 1-2 minutes.
4. Put on top of grains with avocado and tomato.
5. Cook egg to your desired doneness. Serve the bowls with eggs on top.

Nutrition: 458 Cal | 21 g Fat |52 g Carbs |14 g Protein

Cauliflower Fritters with Hummus (Greek)

Preparation time: 10 minutes Cooking time: 50 minutes
Servings: 4

Cauliflower: 2 cups	broken into smaller pieces 1 can of (15 oz.) Chickpeas to taste Minced garlic: 2 tbsp. Olive Oil: 2 1/2 tbsp. Salt: half tsp.
Chopped Onion: 1 cup	
Black Pepper	

1. Let the oven preheat to 400 F.
2. Dry the chickpeas (half of the can) well, put them in a large bowl, and toss with olive oil (1 tbsp.).
3. Spread on a baking tray, season with salt and black pepper. Bake for 20- 35 minutes until crispy. Take chickpeas out on a plate
4. Place roasted chickpeas in a food processor, and pulse until crumbly and broken down. Do not make it into powder.
5. In a skillet, add the oil and sauté garlic, onion for 2 minutes.
6. Add cauliflower and cook for 2 minutes more until it is golden.
7. Cover the pan and turn the heat low; cook for 3 to 5 minutes, until fork- tender.
8. Put this cauliflower in the food processor, add the rest of the chickpeas and blend until smooth and becomes one.
9. Take out in a bowl and half cup of the crumbly chickpeas. Mix well.
10. Make into patties and cook these patties in a pan for 2 to 3 minutes on each side.
11. Serve with hummus and enjoy.

Nutrition: 251 Cal | 20 g Fat | 24 g Carbs | 17 g Protein

Baked Eggs in Avocado (Greek)

Preparation time: 10 minutes Cooking time: 15 minutes
Servings: 2

Chopped fresh chives: 2 tsp.	1 avocado, halved and emptied Dried parsley, to taste
2 eggs	
Cooked bacon: 2 slices, crumbled Salt & black pepper, to taste	

1. Let the oven preheat to 425 F.
2. In a bowl, add eggs, do no break the yolks.
3. In a baking dish, arrange avocado halves, add one yolk in each half, and pour enough white to fill the shell.
4. Season with salt, chives, parsley and pepper.
5. Put the baking dish in the oven and cook for 15 minutes, serve with bacon on top.
6. Gently place the baking dish in the preheated oven and bake until eggs are cooked about 15 minutes. Sprinkle bacon over avocado.

Nutrition: 251 Cal | 20 g Fat | 24 g Carbs | 17 g Protein

Loaded Mediterranean Omelette (Greek)

Preparation time: 5 minutes Cooking time: 10 minutes
Servings: 2

Milk: 2 tbsp.	Salt & black pepper, to taste Baking powder: ¼ tsp.
4 eggs	Spanish paprika: half tsp. Tzatziki sauce, as required Ground allspice: ¼ tsp.
Olive oil: 1 ½ tsp Toppings:	Artichoke hearts (marinated): ¼-1/3 cup, drained & quartered Cherry tomatoes: half cup, halved
Fresh mint: 2 tbsp., chopped Sliced Kalamata olives: 2 tbsp.	Fresh parsley: 2 tbsp., chopped

1. In a bowl, whisk eggs with baking powder, salt, spices, milk and pepper.
2. In a skillet, add oil and pour the egg mixture (some of it) when it gets hot.
3. Immediately stir the eggs and pour more, repeat the mixture until eggs are cooked.
4. Turn off the heat and add your preferred toppings in the lower part; fold the omelet around the toppings.
5. Cut in half and serve with fresh herbs on top and with tzatziki sauce.

Nutrition: 109 Cal | 12 g Fat | 23 g Carbs | 16.9 g Protein

Persian Baked Omelet (Greek)

Preparation time: 10 minutes Cooking time: 30 minutes
Servings: 6

Parsley leaves: 2 cups	Ground cardamom: ¾ tsp.
Cilantro: 2 cups	Olive oil: 5 tbsp.
Fresh dill: 1 cup, chopped	Baking powder: 1 ½ tsp.
Ground black pepper: ¼ tsp. 6 scallions, chopped	Ground cumin: half tsp. Kosher salt: 1 tsp.
Toasted walnuts: half cup, chopped Ground cinnamon: ¾ tsp.	6 eggs

1. Let the oven preheat to 375 F with the rack in the upper-middle.
2. Cut the parchment paper to fit the 9" round cake pan.
3. Coat both sides of parchment paper, and sides, the bottom of the cake pan with oil (2 tbsp.).
4. Add scallions, parsley, cilantro and dill to a food processor with 3 tbsp. of oil. Pulse until your desired texture is achieved.
5. In a bowl, whisk cumin, baking powder, cinnamon, salt, pepper, cumin, and cardamom. Add two eggs and whisk well.
6. Add herb mixture and walnuts. Mix and pour in the pan.
7. Bake for 20-25 minutes at 375 F.
8. Let it cool for ten minutes. Take out from pan, slice and serve.

Nutrition: 184 Cal | 16.4 g Fat | 3.1 g Carbs | 7.1 g Protein

Veggie Quiche (Greek)

Preparation time: 6 minutes Cooking time: 55 minutes
Servings: 8

½ cup sun-dried tomatoes, chopped 1 prepared pie crust	2 tablespoons avocado oil 1 yellow onion, chopped 2 garlic cloves, minced
2 cups spinach, chopped	1 red bell pepper, chopped
¼ cup kalamata olives, pitted and sliced 1 teaspoon parsley flakes	1 teaspoon oregano, dried
1/3 cup feta cheese, crumbled 4 eggs, whisked	1 and ½ cups almond milk
1cup cheddar cheese, shredded	Salt and black pepper to the taste

1. Heat up a pan with the oil over medium-high heat, add the garlic and onion and sauté for 3 minutes.
2. Add the bell pepper and sauté for 3 minutes more.
3. Add the olives, parsley, spinach, oregano, salt and pepper and cook everything for 5 minutes.
4. Add tomatoes and the cheese, toss and take off the heat.
5. Arrange the pie crust in a pie plate, pour the spinach and tomatoes mix inside and spread.
6. In a bowl, mix the eggs with salt, pepper, the milk and half of the cheese, whisk and pour over the mixture in the pie crust.
7. Sprinkle the remaining cheese on top and bake at 375 degrees F for 40 minutes.
8. Cool the quiche down, slice and serve for breakfast.

Nutrition: calories 211, fat 14.4, fiber 1.4, carbs 12.5, protein 8.6

Potato Hash (Spanish)

Preparation time: 10 minutes Cooking time: 15 minutes
Servings: 4

A drizzle of olive oil 2 gold potatoes	cubed
1garlic cloves chopped	minced 1 yellow onion
1 cup canned chickpeas	drained Salt and black pepper to the taste 1 and ½ teaspoon allspice
ground	
1-pound baby asparagus	trimmed and chopped 1 teaspoon sweet paprika
1 teaspoon oregano	dried
1 teaspoon coriander cubed	ground 2 tomatoes
1 cup parsley	chopped
½ cup feta cheese	crumbled

1. Heat a pan with a drizzle of oil over medium-high heat, add the potatoes, onion, garlic, salt and pepper and cook for 7 minutes.
2. Add the rest of the except the tomatoes, parsley and cheese, toss, cook for 7 more minutes and transfer to a bowl.
3. Add the remaining , toss and serve for breakfast.

Nutrition: calories 535, fat 20.8, fiber 6.6, carbs 34.5, protein 26.6

Chapter 3
Sides, Salads, and Soups

Sumptuous Greek Vegetable Salad

Prep time: 20 minutes | Cook time: 0 minutes | Serves 6

Salad:

1 (15-ounce / 425-g) can chickpeas, drained and rinsed

1 (14-ounce / 397-g) can artichoke hearts, drained and halved

1 head Bibb lettuce, chopped (about 2½ cups)

1 cucumber, peeled deseeded, and chopped (about 1½ cups)

1½ cups grape tomatoes, halved

¼ cup chopped basil leaves

½ cup sliced black olives

½ cup cubed feta cheese

Dressing:

1 tablespoon freshly squeezed lemon juice (from about ½ small lemon)

¼ teaspoon freshly ground black pepper

1 tablespoon chopped fresh oregano

2 tablespoons extra-virgin olive oil

1 tablespoon red wine vinegar

1 teaspoon honey

1. Combine the for the salad in a large salad bowl, then toss to combine well.
2. Combine the for the dressing in a small bowl, then stir to mix well.
3. Dress the salad and serve immediately.

Per Serving

calories: 165 | fat: 8.1g | protein: 7.2g | carbs: 17.9g | fiber: 7.0g | sodium: 337mg

Brussels Sprout and Apple Slaw

Prep time: 15 minutes | Cook time: 0 minutes | Serves 4

Salad:

1 pound (454 g) Brussels sprouts, stem ends removed and sliced thinly

1 apple, cored and sliced thinly

½ red onion, sliced thinly

Dressing:

1 teaspoon Dijon mustard

2 teaspoons apple cider vinegar

1 tablespoon raw honey

1 cup plain coconut yogurt

1 teaspoon sea salt

For Garnish:

½ cup pomegranate seeds

½ cup chopped toasted hazelnuts

1. Combine the for the salad in a large salad bowl, then toss to combine well.
2. Combine the for the dressing in a small bowl, then stir to mix well.
3. Dress the salad let sit for 10 minutes. Serve with pomegranate seeds and toasted hazelnuts on top.

Per Serving

calories: 248 | fat: 11.2g | protein: 12.7g | carbs: 29.9g | fiber: 8.0g | sodium: 645mg

Butternut Squash and Cauliflower Soup

Prep time: 15 minutes | Cook time: 4 hours | Serves 4 to 6

1 pound (454 g) butternut squash, peeled and cut into 1-inch cubes

1 small head cauliflower, cut into 1-inch pieces

1 onion, sliced

2 cups unsweetened coconut milk

1 tablespoon curry powder

½ cup no-added-sugar apple juice

4 cups low-sodium vegetable soup

2 tablespoons coconut oil

1 teaspoon sea salt

¼ teaspoon freshly ground white pepper

¼ cup chopped fresh cilantro, divided

1. Combine all the , except for the cilantro, in the slow cooker. Stir to mix well.
2. Cook on high heat for 4 hours or until the vegetables are tender.
3. Pour the soup in a food processor, then pulse until creamy and smooth.
4. Pour the puréed soup in a large serving bowl and garnish with cilantro before serving.

Per Serving

calories: 415 | fat: 30.8g | protein: 10.1g | carbs: 29.9g | fiber: 7.0g | sodium: 1386mg

Artichoke and Arugula Salad

Prep time: 10 minutes | Cook time: 0 minutes | Serves 6

Salad:

6 canned oil-packed artichoke hearts, sliced

6 cups baby arugula leaves

6 fresh olives, pitted and chopped

1 cup cherry tomatoes, sliced in half

Dressing:

1 teaspoon Dijon mustard

2 tablespoons balsamic vinegar

1 clove garlic, minced

2 tablespoons extra-virgin olive oil

For Garnish:

4 fresh basil leaves, thinly sliced

1. Combine the for the salad in a large salad bowl, then toss to combine well. Combine the for the dressing in a small bowl, then stir to mix well.
2. Dress the salad, then serve with basil leaves on top.

Per Serving calories: 134 | fat: 12.1g | protein: 1.6g | carbs: 6.2g | fiber: 3.0g| sodium: 65mg

Baby Potato and Olive Salad

Prep time: 10 minutes | Cook time: 20 minutes | Serves 6

2 pounds (907 g) baby potatoes, cut into 1-inch cubes
1 tablespoon low-sodium olive brine
3 tablespoons freshly squeezed lemon juice (from about 1 medium lemon)
¼ teaspoon kosher salt
3 tablespoons extra-virgin olive oil
½ cup sliced olives
2 tablespoons torn fresh mint
1 cup sliced celery (about 2 stalks)
2 tablespoons chopped fresh oregano

1. Put the tomatoes in a saucepan, then pour in enough water to submerge the tomatoes about 1 inch. Bring to a boil over high heat, then reduce the heat to medium-low. Simmer for 14 minutes or until the potatoes are soft. Meanwhile, combine the olive brine, lemon juice, salt, and olive oil in a small bow. Stir to mix well.
2. Transfer the cooked tomatoes in a colander, then rinse with running cold water. Pat dry with paper towels. Transfer the tomatoes in a large salad bowl, then drizzle with olive brine mixture. Spread with remaining and toss to combine well. Serve immediately.

Per Serving calories: 220 | fat: 6.1g | protein: 4.3g | carbs: 39.2g | fiber: 5.0g | sodium: 231mg

Barley, Parsley, and Pea Salad

Prep time: 10 minutes | Cook time: 10 minutes | Serves 4

2 cups water
1 cup quick-cooking barley
1 small bunch flat-leaf parsley, chopped (about 1 to 1½ cups)
2 cups sugar snap pea pods
Juice of 1 lemon
½ small red onion, diced
2 tablespoons extra-virgin olive oil
Sea salt and freshly ground pepper, to taste

1. Pour the water in a saucepan. Bring to a boil. Add the barley to the saucepan, then put the lid on.
2. Reduce the heat to low. Simmer the barley for 10 minutes or until the liquid is absorbed, then let sit for 5 minutes.
3. Open the lid, then transfer the barley in a colander and rinse under cold running water.
4. Pour the barley in a large salad bowl and add the remaining . Toss to combine well.
5. Serve immediately.

Per Serving calories: 152 | fat: 7.4g | protein: 3.7g | carbs: 19.3g | fiber: 4.7g | sodium: 20mg

Cheesy Peach and Walnut Salad

Prep time: 10 minutes | Cook time: 0 minutes | Serves 1

1 ripe peach, pitted and sliced
¼ cup chopped walnuts, toasted
¼ cup shredded Parmesan cheese
1 teaspoon raw honey
Zest of 1 lemon
1 tablespoon chopped fresh mint

1. Combine the peach, walnut, and cheese in a medium bowl, then drizzle with honey. Spread the lemon zest and mint on top. Toss to combine everything well. Serve immediately.

Per Serving calories: 373 | fat: 26.4g | protein: 12.9g | carbs: 27.0g | fiber: 4.7g | sodium: 453mg

Greek Chicken, Tomato, and Olive Salad

Prep time: 10 minutes | Cook time: 0 minutes | Serves 2

Salad:
2 grilled boneless, skinless chicken breasts, sliced (about 1 cup)
10 cherry tomatoes, halved
8 pitted Kalamata olives, halved
½ cup thinly sliced red onion
Dressing:
¼ cup balsamic vinegar
1 teaspoon freshly squeezed lemon juice
¼ teaspoon sea salt
¼ teaspoon freshly ground black pepper
2 teaspoons extra-virgin olive oil
For Serving:
2 cups roughly chopped romaine lettuce
½ cup crumbled feta cheese

1. Combine the for the salad in a large bowl. Toss to combine well. Combine the for the dressing in a small bowl. Stir to mix well. Pour the dressing the bowl of salad, then toss to coat well. Wrap the bowl in plastic and refrigerate for at least 2 hours.
2. Remove the bowl from the refrigerator. Spread the lettuce on a large plate, then top with marinated salad. Scatter the salad with feta cheese and serve immediately.

Per Serving calories: 328 | fat: 16.9g | protein: 27.6g | carbs: 15.9g | fiber: 3.1g | sodium: 1102mg

Cherry, Plum, Artichoke, and Cheese Board

Prep time: 15 minutes | Cook time: 0 minutes | Serves 4

2 cups rinsed cherries
2 cups rinsed and sliced plums
2 cups rinsed carrots, cut into sticks
1 cup canned low-sodium artichoke hearts, rinsed and drained
1 cup cubed feta cheese

1. Arrange all the in separated portions on a clean board or a large tray, then serve with spoons, knife, and forks.

Per Serving
calories: 417 | fat: 13.8g | protein: 20.1g | carbs: 56.2g | fiber: 3.0g | sodium: 715mg

Ritzy Summer Fruit Salad

Prep time: 10 minutes | Cook time: 0 minutes | Serves 8

Salad:
1 cup fresh blueberries
2 cups cubed cantaloupe
2 cups red seedless grapes
1 cup sliced fresh strawberries
2 cups cubed honeydew melon
Zest of 1 large lime
½ cup unsweetened toasted coconut flakes
Dressing:
¼ cup raw honey
Juice of 1 large lime
¼ teaspoon sea salt
½ cup extra-virgin olive oil

1. Combine the for the salad in a large salad bowl, then toss to combine well. Combine the for the dressing in a small bowl, then stir to mix well.
2. Dress the salad and serve immediately.

Per Serving calories: 242 | fat: 15.5g | protein: 1.3g | carbs: 28.0g | fiber: 2.4g | sodium: 90mg

Roasted Broccoli and Tomato Panzanella

Prep time: 10 minutes | Cook time: 20 minutes | Serves 4

1 pound (454 g) broccoli (about 3 medium stalks), trimmed, cut into 1- inch florets and ½-inch stem slices
2 tablespoons extra-virgin olive oil, divided
1½ cups cherry tomatoes
1½ teaspoons honey, divided
3 cups cubed whole-grain crusty bread
1 tablespoon balsamic vinegar
¼ teaspoon kosher salt
½ teaspoon freshly ground black pepper
¼ cup grated Parmesan cheese, for serving (optional)
¼ cup chopped fresh oregano leaves, for serving (optional)

1. Preheat the oven to 450ºF (235ºC).
2. Toss the broccoli with 1 tablespoon of olive oil in a large bowl to coat well.
3. Arrange the broccoli on a baking sheet, then add the tomatoes to the same bowl and toss with the remaining olive oil. Add 1 teaspoon of honey and toss again to coat well. Transfer the tomatoes on the baking sheet beside the broccoli.
4. Place the baking sheet in the preheated oven and roast for 15 minutes, then add the bread cubes and flip the vegetables. Roast for an additional 3 minutes or until the broccoli is lightly charred and the bread cubes are golden brown.
5. Meanwhile, combine the remaining , except for the Parmesan and oregano, in a small bowl. Stir to mix well.
6. Transfer the roasted vegetables and bread cubes to the large salad bowl, then dress them and spread with Parmesan and oregano leaves. Toss and serve immediately.

Per Serving

calories: 162 | fat: 6.8g | protein: 8.2g | carbs: 18.9g | fiber: 6.0g | sodium: 397mg

Grilled Bell Pepper and Anchovy Antipasto

Prep time: 15 minutes | Cook time: 8 minutes | Serves 4

2 tablespoons extra-virgin olive oil, divided
4 medium red bell peppers, quartered, stem and seeds removed
6 ounces (170 g) anchovies in oil, chopped
2 tablespoons capers, rinsed and drained
1 cup Kalamata olives, pitted
1 small shallot, chopped
Sea salt and freshly ground pepper, to taste

1. Heat the grill to medium-high heat. Grease the grill grates with 1 tablespoon of olive oil.
2. Arrange the red bell peppers on the preheated grill grates, then grill for 8 minutes or until charred.
3. Turn off the grill and allow the pepper to cool for 10 minutes.
4. Transfer the charred pepper in a colander. Rinse and peel the peppers under running cold water, then pat dry with paper towels.
5. Cut the peppers into chunks and combine with remaining in a large bowl. Toss to mix well.
6. Serve immediately.

Per Serving calories: 227 | fat: 14.9g | protein: 13.9g | carbs: 9.9g | fiber: 3.8g| sodium: 1913mg

Marinated Mushrooms and Olives

Prep time: 1 hour 10 minutes | Cook time: 0 minutes | Serves 8

1 pound (454 g) white button mushrooms, rinsed and drained
1 pound (454 g) fresh olives
½ tablespoon crushed fennel seeds
1 tablespoon white wine vinegar
2 tablespoons fresh thyme leaves
Pinch chili flakes
Sea salt and freshly ground pepper, to taste
2 tablespoons extra-virgin olive oil

1. Combine all the in a large bowl. Toss to mix well.
2. Wrap the bowl in plastic and refrigerate for at least 1 hour to marinate.
3. Remove the bowl from the refrigerate and let sit under room temperature for 10 minutes, then serve.

Per Serving

calories: 111 | fat: 9.7g | protein: 2.4g | carbs: 5.9g | fiber: 2.7g | sodium: 449mg

Root Vegetable Roast

Prep time: 15 minutes | Cook time: 25 minutes | Serves 4 to 6

1 bunch beets, peeled and cut into 1-inch cubes
2 small sweet potatoes, peeled and cut into 1-inch cubes
3 parsnips, peeled and cut into 1-inch rounds
4 carrots, peeled and cut into 1-inch rounds
1 tablespoon raw honey
1 teaspoon sea salt
½ teaspoon freshly ground black pepper
1 tablespoon extra-virgin olive oil
2 tablespoons coconut oil, melted

1. Preheat the oven to 400ºF (205ºC). Line a baking sheet with parchment paper.
2. Combine all the in a large bowl. Toss to coat the vegetables well.
3. Pour the mixture in the baking sheet, then place the sheet in the preheated oven.
4. Roast for 25 minutes or until the vegetables are lightly browned and soft. Flip the vegetables halfway through the cooking time.
5. Remove the vegetables from the oven and allow to cool before serving.

Per Serving

calories: 461 | fat: 18.1g | protein: 5.9g | carbs: 74.2g | fiber: 14.0g | sodium: 759mg

Arugula and Fig Salad

Prep time: 15 minutes | Cook time: 0 minutes | Serves 2

3 cups arugula
4 fresh, ripe figs (or 4 to 6 dried figs), stemmed and sliced
2 tablespoons olive oil
¼ cup lightly toasted pecan halves
2 tablespoons crumbled blue cheese
1 to 2 tablespoons balsamic glaze

1. Toss the arugula and figs with the olive oil in a large bowl until evenly coated. Add the pecans and blue cheese to the bowl. Toss the salad lightly.
2. Drizzle with the balsamic glaze and serve immediately.

Per Serving calories: 517 | fat: 36.2g | protein: 18.9g | carbs: 30.2g | fiber: 6.1g | sodium: 481mg

Sardines with Lemony Tomato Sauce

Prep time: 10 minutes | Cook time: 40 minutes | Serves 4

2 tablespoons olive oil, divided
4 Roma tomatoes, peeled and chopped, reserve the juice
1 small onion, sliced thinly
Zest of 1 orange
Sea salt and freshly ground pepper, to taste

1 pound (454 g) fresh sardines, rinsed, spine removed, butterflied
½ cup white wine
2 tablespoons whole-wheat breadcrumbs

1. Preheat the oven to 425°F (220°C). Grease a baking dish with 1 tablespoon of olive oil.
2. Heath the remaining olive oil in a nonstick skillet over medium-low heat until shimmering.
3. Add the tomatoes with juice, onion, orange zest, salt, and ground pepper to the skillet and simmer for 20 minutes or until it thickens.
4. Pour half of the mixture on the bottom of the baking dish, then top with the butterflied sardines. Pour the remaining mixture and white wine over the sardines.
5. Spread the breadcrumbs on top, then place the baking dish in the preheated oven. Bake for 20 minutes or until the fish is opaque.
6. Remove the baking sheet from the oven and serve the sardines warm.

Per Serving

calories: 363 | fat: 20.2g | protein: 29.7g | carbs: 9.7g | fiber: 2.0g | sodium: 381mg

Greens, Fennel, and Pear Soup with Cashews

Prep time: 15 minutes | Cook time: 15 minutes | Serves 4 to 6

2 tablespoons olive oil
1 fennel bulb, cut into ¼-inch-thick slices
2 leeks, white part only, sliced
2 pears, peeled, cored, and cut into ½-inch cubes

1 teaspoon sea salt
¼ teaspoon freshly ground black pepper
½ cup cashews
2 cups packed blanched spinach
3 cups low-sodium vegetable soup

1. Heat the olive oil in a stockpot over high heat until shimmering.
2. Add the fennel and leeks, then sauté for 5 minutes or until tender.
3. Add the pears and sprinkle with salt and pepper, then sauté for another 3 minutes or until the pears are soft.
4. Add the cashews, spinach, and vegetable soup. Bring to a boil. Reduce the heat to low. Cover and simmer for 5 minutes.
5. Pour the soup in a food processor, then pulse until creamy and smooth.
6. Pour the soup back to the pot and heat over low heat until heated through.
7. Transfer the soup to a large serving bowl and serve immediately.

Per Serving

calories: 266 | fat: 15.1g | protein: 5.2g | carbs: 32.9g | fiber: 7.0g | sodium: 628mg

Veggie Slaw

Prep time: 20 minutes | Cook time: 0 minutes | Serves 4 to 6

Salad:
2 large broccoli stems, peeled and shredded
½ celery root bulb, peeled and shredded
¼ cup chopped fresh Italian parsley
1 large beet, peeled and shredded
2 carrots, peeled and shredded
1 small red onion, sliced thin
2 zucchinis, shredded

Dressing:
1 teaspoon Dijon mustard
½ cup apple cider vinegar
1 tablespoon raw honey
1 teaspoon sea salt
¼ teaspoon freshly ground black pepper
2 tablespoons extra-virgin olive oil

Topping:
½ cup crumbled feta cheese

1. Combine the for the salad in a large salad bowl, then toss to combine well.
2. Combine the for the dressing in a small bowl, then stir to mix well.
3. Dress the salad, then serve with feta cheese on top.

Per Serving

calories: 387 | fat: 30.2g | protein: 8.1g | carbs: 25.9g | fiber: 6.0g | sodium: 980mg

Moroccan Lentil, Tomato, and Cauliflower Soup

Prep time: 15 minutes | Cook time: 4 hours | Serves 6

1 cup chopped carrots
1 cup chopped onions
3 cloves garlic, minced
½ teaspoon ground coriander
1 teaspoon ground cumin
1 teaspoon ground turmeric
¼ teaspoon ground cinnamon
¼ teaspoon freshly ground black pepper
1 cup dry lentils
1 tablespoon red wine vinegar (optional)

28 ounces (794 g) tomatoes, diced, reserve the juice
1½ cups chopped cauliflower
4 cups low-sodium vegetable soup
1 tablespoon no-salt-added tomato paste
1 teaspoon extra-virgin olive oil
1 cup chopped fresh spinach
¼ cup chopped fresh cilantro

1. Put the carrots and onions in the slow cooker, then sprinkle with minced garlic, coriander, cumin, turmeric, cinnamon, and black pepper. Stir to combine well.
2. Add the lentils, tomatoes, and cauliflower, then pour in the vegetable soup and tomato paste. Drizzle with olive oil. Stir to combine well.
3. Put the slow cooker lid on and cook on high for 4 hours or until the vegetables are tender.
4. In the last 30 minutes during the cooking time, open the lid and stir the soup, then fold in the spinach.
5. Pour the cooked soup in a large serving bowl, then spread with cilantro and drizzle with vinegar. Serve immediately.

Per Serving

calories: 131 | fat: 2.1g | protein: 5.6g | carbs: 25.0g | fiber: 5.5g | sodium: 364mg

Mushroom and Soba Noodle Soup

Prep time: 15 minutes | Cook time: 10 minutes | Serves 4

2 tablespoons coconut oil	1 teaspoon sea salt
8 ounces (227 g) shiitake mushrooms, stemmed and sliced thin	4 cups low-sodium vegetable broth
	3 cups water
1 tablespoon minced fresh ginger	4 ounces (113 g) soba noodles
4 scallions, sliced thin	1 bunch spinach, blanched, rinsed and cut into strips
1 garlic clove, minced	1 tablespoon freshly squeezed lemon juice

1. Heat the coconut oil in a stockpot over medium heat until melted.
2. Add the mushrooms, ginger, scallions, garlic, and salt. Sauté for 5 minutes or until fragrant and the mushrooms are tender. Pour in the vegetable broth and water. Bring to a boil, then add the soba noodles and cook for 5 minutes or until al dente.
3. Turn off the heat and add the spinach and lemon juice. Stir to mix well.
4. Pour the soup in a large bowl and serve immediately.

Per Serving

calories: 254 | fat: 9.2g | protein: 13.1g | carbs: 33.9g | fiber: 4.0g | sodium: 1773mg

Pumpkin Soup with Crispy Sage Leaves

Prep time: 15 minutes | Cook time: 10 minutes | Serves 4

1 tablespoon olive oil	2 teaspoons chipotle powder
2 garlic cloves, cut into ⅛-inch-thick slices	1 teaspoon sea salt
1 onion, chopped	½ teaspoon freshly ground black pepper
2 cups freshly puréed pumpkin	½ cup vegetable oil
4 cups low-sodium vegetable soup	12 sage leaves, stemmed

1. Heat the olive oil in a stockpot over high heat until shimmering.
2. Add the garlic and onion, then sauté for 5 minutes or until the onion is translucent.
3. Pour in the puréed pumpkin and vegetable soup in the pot, then sprinkle with chipotle powder, salt, and ground black pepper. Stir to mix well.
4. Bring to a boil. Reduce the heat to low and simmer for 5 minutes.
5. Meanwhile, heat the vegetable oil in a nonstick skillet over high heat.
6. Add the sage leaf to the skillet and sauté for a minute or until crispy. Transfer the sage on paper towels to soak the excess oil.
7. Gently pour the soup in three serving bowls, then divide the crispy sage leaves in bowls for garnish. Serve immediately.

Per Serving

calories: 380 | fat: 20.1g | protein: 8.9g | carbs: 45.2g | fiber: 18.0g | sodium: 1364mg

Mushroom Barley Soup

Prep time: 5 minutes | Cook time: 20 to 23 minutes | Serves 6

2 tablespoons extra-virgin olive oil	¼ cup red wine
	2 tablespoons tomato paste
1 cup chopped carrots	4 sprigs fresh thyme or ½ teaspoon dried thyme
1 cup chopped onion	
5½ cups chopped mushrooms	1 dried bay leaf
	6 tablespoons grated Parmesan cheese
6 cups no-salt-added vegetable broth	
1 cup uncooked pearled barley	

1. In a large stockpot over medium heat, heat the oil. Add the onion and carrots and cook for 5 minutes, stirring frequently. Turn up the heat to medium-high and add the mushrooms. Cook for 3 minutes, stirring frequently.
2. Add the broth, barley, wine, tomato paste, thyme, and bay leaf. Stir, cover, and bring the soup to a boil. Once it's boiling, stir a few times, reduce the heat to medium-low, cover, and cook for another 12 to 15 minutes, until the barley is cooked through.
3. Remove the bay leaf and serve the soup in bowls with 1 tablespoon of cheese sprinkled on top of each.

Per Serving

calories: 195 | fat: 4.0g | protein: 7.0g | carbs: 34.0g | fiber: 6.0g | sodium: 173mg

Paella Soup

Prep time: 6 minutes | Cook time: 24 minutes | Serves 6

2 tablespoons extra-virgin olive oil	2½ cups uncooked instant brown rice
1 cup chopped onion	2 cups low-sodium or no-salt-added chicken broth
1½ cups coarsely chopped green bell pepper	2½ cups water
1½ cups coarsely chopped red bell pepper	1 cup frozen green peas, thawed
2 garlic cloves, chopped	1 (28-ounce / 794-g) can low-sodium or no-salt-added crushed tomatoes
1 teaspoon ground turmeric	
1 teaspoon dried thyme	
2 teaspoons smoked paprika	1 pound (454 g) fresh raw medium shrimp, shells and tails removed

1. In a large stockpot over medium-high heat, heat the oil. Add the onion, bell peppers, and garlic. Cook for 8 minutes, stirring occasionally. Add the turmeric, thyme, and smoked paprika, and cook for 2 minutes more, stirring often. Stir in the rice, broth, and water. Bring to a boil over high heat. Cover, reduce the heat to medium-low, and cook for 10 minutes.
2. Stir the peas, tomatoes, and shrimp into the soup. Cook for 4 minutes, until the shrimp is cooked, turning from gray to pink and white. The soup will be very thick, almost like stew, when ready to serve.
3. Ladle the soup into bowls and serve hot.

Per Serving

calories: 431 | fat: 5.7g | protein: 26.0g | carbs: 69.1g | fiber: 7.4g | sodium: 203mg

Parmesan Roasted Red Potatoes

Prep time: 10 minutes | Cook time: 55 minutes | Serves 2

12 ounces (340 g) red potatoes (3 to 4 small potatoes), scrubbed and diced into 1-inch pieces
1 tablespoon olive oil
½ teaspoon garlic powder
¼ teaspoon salt
1 tablespoon grated Parmesan cheese
1 teaspoon minced fresh rosemary (from 1 sprig)

1. Preheat the oven to 425ºF (220ºC). Line a baking sheet with parchment paper. In a mixing bowl, combine the potatoes, olive oil, garlic powder, and salt. Toss well to coat. Lay the potatoes on the parchment paper and roast for 10 minutes. Flip the potatoes over and roast for another 10 minutes. Check the potatoes to make sure they are golden brown on the top and bottom. Toss them again, turn the heat down to 350ºF (180ºC), and roast for 30 minutes more. When the potatoes are golden brown, scatter the Parmesan cheese over them and toss again. Return to the oven for 3 minutes to melt the cheese.
2. Remove from the oven and sprinkle with the fresh rosemary before serving.

Per Serving calories: 200 | fat: 8.2g | protein: 5.1g | carbs: 30.0g | fiber: 3.2g | sodium: 332mg

Garlic Wilted Greens

Prep time: 10 minutes | Cook time: 5 minutes | Serves 2

1 tablespoon olive oil
2 garlic cloves, minced
3 cups sliced greens (spinach, chard, beet greens, dandelion greens, or a combination)
Pinch salt
Pinch red pepper flakes (or more to taste)

1. Heat the olive oil in a skillet over medium-high heat.
2. Add garlic and sauté for 30 seconds, or just until fragrant.
3. Add the greens, salt, and pepper flakes and stir to combine. Let the greens wilt, but do not overcook.
4. Remove from the skillet and serve on a plate.

Per Serving calories: 93 | fat: 6.8g | protein: 1.2g | carbs: 7.3g | fiber: 3.1g | sodium: 112mg

Sautéed Kale with Olives

Prep time: 10 minutes | Cook time: 10 minutes | Serves 2

1 bunch kale, leaves chopped and stems minced
½ cup celery leaves, roughly chopped, or additional parsley
½ bunch flat-leaf parsley, stems and leaves roughly chopped
4 garlic cloves, chopped
2 teaspoons olive oil
¼ cup pitted Kalamata olives, chopped
Grated zest and juice of 1 lemon
Salt and pepper, to taste

1. Place the kale, celery leaves, parsley, and garlic in a steamer basket set over a medium saucepan. Steam over medium-high heat, covered, for 15 minutes. Remove from the heat and squeeze out any excess moisture. Place a large skillet over medium heat. Add the oil, then add the kale mixture to the skillet. Cook, stirring often, for 5 minutes. Remove from the heat and add the olives and lemon zest and juice. Season with salt and pepper and serve.

Per Serving calories: 86 | fat: 6.4g | protein: 1.8g | carbs: 7.5g | fiber: 2.1g | sodium: 276mg

Balsamic Brussels Sprouts and Delicata Squash

Prep time: 10 minutes | Cook time: 30 minutes | Serves 2

½ pound (227 g) Brussels sprouts, ends trimmed and outer leaves removed
1 medium delicata squash, halved lengthwise, seeded, and cut into 1-inch pieces
1 cup fresh cranberries
2 teaspoons olive oil
Salt and freshly ground black pepper, to taste
½ cup balsamic vinegar
2 tablespoons roasted pumpkin seeds
2 tablespoons fresh pomegranate arils (seeds)

1. Preheat oven to 400ºF (205ºC). Line a sheet pan with parchment paper. Combine the Brussels sprouts, squash, and cranberries in a large bowl. Drizzle with olive oil, and season lightly with salt and pepper. Toss well to coat and arrange in a single layer on the sheet pan.
2. Roast in the preheated oven for 30 minutes, turning vegetables halfway through, or until Brussels sprouts turn brown and crisp in spots. Meanwhile, make the balsamic glaze by simmering the vinegar for 10 to 12 minutes, or until mixture has reduced to about ¼ cup and turns a syrupy consistency. Remove the vegetables from the oven, drizzle with balsamic syrup, and sprinkle with pumpkin seeds and pomegranate arils before serving.

Per Serving calories: 203 | fat: 6.8g | protein: 6.2g | carbs: 22.0g | fiber: 8.2g | sodium: 32mg

Rich Chicken and Small Pasta Broth

Prep time: 10 minutes | Cook time: 4 hours | Serves 6

6 boneless, skinless chicken thighs
4 stalks celery, cut into ½-inch pieces
4 carrots, cut into 1-inch pieces
1 medium yellow onion, halved
2 garlic cloves, minced
2 bay leaves
Sea salt and freshly ground black pepper, to taste
6 cups low-sodium chicken stock
½ cup stelline pasta
¼ cup chopped fresh flat-leaf parsley

1. Combine the chicken thighs, celery, carrots, onion, and garlic in the slow cooker. Spread with bay leaves and sprinkle with salt and pepper. Toss to mix well.
2. Pour in the chicken stock. Put the lid on and cook on high for 4 hours or until the internal temperature of chicken reaches at least 165ºF (74ºC).
3. In the last 20 minutes of the cooking, remove the chicken from the slow cooker and transfer to a bowl to cool until ready to reserve.
4. Discard the bay leaves and add the pasta to the slow cooker. Put the lid on and cook for 15 minutes or until al dente. Meanwhile, slice the chicken, then put the chicken and parsley in the slow cooker and cook for 5 minutes or until well combined. Pour the soup in a large bowl and serve immediately.

Per Serving calories: 285 | fat: 10.8g | protein: 27.4g | carbs: 18.8g | fiber: 2.6g | sodium: 815mg

Cucumber Gazpacho

Prep time: 10 minutes | Cook time: 0 minutes | Serves 4

2 cucumbers, peeled, deseeded, and cut into chunks	2 cups low-sodium vegetable soup
½ cup mint, finely chopped	1 tablespoon no-salt-added tomato paste
2 cups plain Greek yogurt	3 teaspoons fresh dill
2 garlic cloves, minced	Sea salt and freshly ground pepper, to taste

1. Put the cucumber, mint, yogurt, and garlic in a food processor, then pulse until creamy and smooth.
2. Transfer the puréed mixture in a large serving bowl, then add the vegetable soup, tomato paste, dill, salt, and ground black pepper. Stir to mix well.
3. Keep the soup in the refrigerator for at least 2 hours, then serve chilled.

Per Serving

calories: 133 | fat: 1.5g | protein: 14.2g | carbs: 16.5g | fiber: 2.9g | sodium: 331mg

Mixed Salad With Balsamic Honey Dressing

Prep time: 15 minutes | Cook time: 0 minutes | Serves 2

Dressing:

¼ cup balsamic vinegar	½ cup cherry or grape tomatoes, halved
¼ cup olive oil	½ English cucumber, sliced in quarters lengthwise and then cut into bite-size pieces
1 tablespoon honey	
1 teaspoon Dijon mustard	
¼ teaspoon garlic powder	Any combination fresh, torn herbs (parsley, oregano, basil, or chives)
¼ teaspoon salt, or more to taste	
Pinch freshly ground black pepper	1 tablespoon roasted sunflower seeds

Salad:

4 cups chopped red leaf lettuce

Make the Dressing

1. Combine the vinegar, olive oil, honey, mustard, garlic powder, salt, and pepper in a jar with a lid. Shake well.

Make the Salad

2. In a large bowl, combine the lettuce, tomatoes, cucumber, and herbs. Toss well. Pour all or as much dressing as desired over the tossed salad and toss again to coat the salad with dressing. Top with the sunflower seeds before serving.

Per Serving calories: 337 | fat: 26.1g | protein: 4.2g | carbs: 22.2g | fiber: 3.1g | sodium: 172mg

Tricolor Summer Salad

Prep time: 10 minutes | Cook time: 0 minutes | Serves 3 to 4

¼ cup while balsamic vinegar	¼ cup extra-virgin olive oil
2 tablespoons Dijon mustard	1½ cups chopped orange, yellow, and red tomatoes
1 tablespoon sugar	
½ teaspoon garlic salt	½ cucumber, peeled and diced
½ teaspoon freshly ground black pepper	1 small red onion, thinly sliced
	¼ cup crumbled feta (optional)

1. In a small bowl, whisk the vinegar, mustard, sugar, pepper, and garlic salt. Then slowly whisk in the olive oil. In a large bowl, add the tomatoes, cucumber, and red onion. Add the dressing. Toss once or twice, and serve with the feta crumbles (if desired) sprinkled on top.

Per Serving calories: 246 | fat: 18.0g | protein: 1.0g | carbs: 19.0g | fiber: 2.0g | sodium: 483mg

Roasted Root Vegetable Soup

Prep time: 10 minutes | Cook time: 35 minutes | Serves 6

2 parsnips, peeled and sliced	½ teaspoon freshly ground black pepper
2 carrots, peeled and sliced	
2 sweet potatoes, peeled and sliced	2 tablespoons extra-virgin olive oil
1 tps chopped fresh rosemary	4 cups low-sodium vegetable soup
1 teaspoon chopped fresh thyme	
1 teaspoon sea salt	½ cup grated Parmesan cheese, for garnish (optional)

1. Preheat the oven to 400°F (205°C). Line a baking sheet with aluminum foil.
2. Combine the parsnips, carrots, and sweet potatoes in a large bowl, then sprinkle with rosemary, thyme, salt, and pepper, and drizzle with olive oil. Toss to coat the vegetables well.
3. Arrange the vegetables on the baking sheet, then roast in the preheated oven for 30 minutes or until lightly browned and soft. Flip the vegetables halfway through the roasting.
4. Pour the roasted vegetables with vegetable broth in a food processor, then pulse until creamy and smooth.
5. Pour the puréed vegetables in a saucepan, then warm over low heat until heated through. Spoon the soup in a large serving bowl, then scatter with Parmesan cheese. Serve immediately.

Per Serving calories: 192 | fat: 5.7g | protein: 4.8g | carbs: 31.5g | fiber: 5.7g | sodium: 797mg

Super Mushroom and Red Wine Soup

Prep time: 40 minutes | Cook time: 35 minutes | Serves 6

2 ounces (57 g) dried morels	1 teaspoon finely chopped fresh thyme
2 ounces (57 g) dried porcini	
1 tablespoon extra-virgin olive oil	Sea salt and freshly ground pepper, to taste
8 ounces (227 g) button mushrooms, chopped	⅓ cup dry red wine
8 ounces (227 g) portobello mushrooms, chopped	4 cups low-sodium chicken broth
3 shallots, finely chopped	½ cup heavy cream
2 cloves garlic, minced	1 small bunch flat-leaf parsley, chopped

1. Put the dried mushrooms in a large bowl and pour in enough water to submerge the mushrooms. Soak for 30 minutes and drain.
2. Heat the olive oil in a stockpot over medium-high heat until shimmering.
3. Add the mushrooms and shallots to the pot and sauté for 10 minutes or until the mushrooms are tender.
4. Add the garlic and sauté for an additional 1 minute or until fragrant. Sprinkle with thyme, salt, and pepper.
5. Pour in the dry red wine and chicken broth. Bring to a boil over high heat.
6. Reduce the heat to low. Simmer for 20 minutes.
7. After simmering, pour half of the soup in a food processor, then pulse until creamy and smooth.
8. Pour the puréed soup back to the pot, then mix in the cream and heat over low heat until heated through.
9. Pour the soup in a large serving bowl and spread with chopped parsley before serving.

Per Serving

calories: 139 | fat: 7.4g | protein: 7.1g | carbs: 14.4g | fiber: 2.8g | sodium: 94mg

Green Beans with Tahini-Lemon Sauce

Prep time: 5 minutes | Cook time: 10 minutes | Serves 2

1 pound (454 g) green beans, washed and trimmed
2 tablespoons tahini
1 garlic clove, minced
Grated zest and juice of 1 lemon
Salt and black pepper, to taste
1 teaspoon toasted black or white sesame seeds (optional)

1. Steam the beans in a medium saucepan fitted with a steamer basket (or by adding ¼ cup water to a covered saucepan) over medium-high heat. Drain, reserving the cooking water. Mix the tahini, garlic, lemon zest and juice, and salt and pepper to taste. Use the reserved cooking water to thin the sauce as desired.
2. Toss the green beans with the sauce and garnish with the sesame seeds, if desired. Serve immediately.

Per Serving calories: 188 | fat: 8.4g | protein: 7.2g | carbs: 22.2g | fiber: 7.9g | sodium: 200mg

Cheesy Roasted Broccolini

Prep time: 5 minutes | Cook time: 10 minutes | Serves 2

1 bunch broccolini (about 5 ounces / 142 g)
1 tablespoon olive oil
½ teaspoon garlic powder
¼ teaspoon salt
2 tablespoons grated Romano cheese

1. Preheat the oven to 400ºF (205ºC). Line a sheet pan with parchment paper.
2. Slice the tough ends off the broccolini and put in a medium bowl. Add the olive oil, garlic powder, and salt and toss to coat well. Arrange the broccolini on the prepared sheet pan.
3. Roast in the preheated oven for 7 minutes, flipping halfway through the cooking time.
4. Remove the pan from the oven and sprinkle the cheese over the broccolini. Using tongs, carefully flip the broccolini over to coat all sides.
5. Return to the oven and cook for an additional 2 to 3 minutes, or until the cheese melts and starts to turn golden. Serve warm.

Per Serving

calories: 114 | fat: 9.0g | protein: 4.0g | carbs: 5.0g | fiber: 2.0g | sodium: 400mg

Orange-Honey Glazed Carrots

Prep time: 10 minutes | Cook time: 15 to 20 minutes | Serves 2

½ pound (227 g) rainbow carrots, peeled
2 tablespoons fresh orange juice
1 tablespoon honey
½ teaspoon coriander
Pinch salt

1. Preheat the oven to 400ºF (205ºC).
2. Cut the carrots lengthwise into slices of even thickness and place in a large bowl. Stir together the orange juice, honey, coriander, and salt in a small bowl. Pour the orange juice mixture over the carrots and toss until well coated.
3. Spread the carrots in a baking dish in a single layer. Roast for 15 to 20 minutes until fork-tender.
4. Let cool for 5 minutes before serving.

Per Serving

calories: 85 | fat: 0g | protein: 1.0g | carbs: 21.0g | fiber: 3.0g | sodium: 156mg

Roasted Cauliflower

Prep time: 10 minutes | Cook time: 20 minutes | Serves 2

½ large head cauliflower, stemmed and broken into florets (about 3 cups)
1 tablespoon olive oil
2 tablespoons freshly squeezed lemon juice
2 tablespoons tahini
1 tps harissa paste Pinch salt

1. Preheat the oven to 400ºF (205ºC). Line a sheet pan with parchment paper. Toss the cauliflower florets with the olive oil in a large bowl and transfer to the sheet pan.
2. Roast in the preheated oven for 15 minutes, flipping the cauliflower once or twice, or until it starts to become golden. Meanwhile, in a separate bowl, combine the lemon juice, tahini, harissa, and salt and stir to mix well.
3. Remove the pan from the oven and toss the cauliflower with the lemon tahini sauce. Return to the oven and roast for another 5 minutes. Serve hot.

Per Serving calories: 205 | fat: 15.0g | protein: 4.0g | carbs: 15.0g | fiber: 7.0g | sodium: 161mg

Sautéed White Beans with Rosemary

Prep time: 10 minutes | Cook time: 12 minutes | Serves 2

1 tablespoon olive oil
2 garlic cloves, minced
1 (15-ounce / 425-g) can white cannellini beans, drained and rinsed
1 teaspoon minced fresh rosemary plus 1 whole fresh rosemary sprig
¼ teaspoon dried sage
½ cup low-sodium chicken stock
Salt, to taste

1. Heat the olive oil in a saucepan over medium-high heat.
2. Add the garlic and sauté for 30 seconds until fragrant.
3. Add the beans, minced and whole rosemary, sage, and chicken stock and bring the mixture to a boil.
4. Reduce the heat to medium and allow to simmer for 10 minutes, or until most of the liquid is evaporated. If desired, mash some of the beans with a fork to thicken them. Season with salt to taste. Remove the rosemary sprig before serving.

Per Serving calories: 155 | fat: 7.0g | protein: 6.0g | carbs: 17.0g | fiber: 8.0g | sodium: 153mg

Moroccan Spiced Couscous

Prep time: 10 minutes | Cook time: 8 minutes | Serves 2

1 tablespoon olive oil
¾ cup couscous
¼ teaspoon cinnamon
¼ teaspoon garlic powder
¼ teaspoon salt, plus more as needed
1 cup water
2 tablespoons minced dried apricots
2 tablespoons raisins
2 teaspoons minced fresh parsley

1. Heat the olive oil in a saucepan over medium-high heat until it shimmers. Add the couscous, cinnamon, garlic powder, and salt. Stir for 1 minute to toast the couscous and spices. Add the water, apricots, and raisins and bring the mixture to a boil.
2. Cover and turn off the heat. Allow the couscous to sit for 4 to 5 minutes and then fluff it with a fork. Sprinkle with the fresh parsley. Season with more salt as needed and serve.

Per Serving

calories: 338 | fat: 8.0g | protein: 9.0g | carbs: 59.0g | fiber: 4.0g | sodium: 299mg

Lemon-Tahini Hummus

Prep time: 15 minutes | Cook time: 0 minutes | Serves 6

1 (15-ounce / 425-g) can chickpeas, drained and rinsed	2 lemons, juiced
4 tablespoons extra-virgin olive oil, divided	1 lemon, zested, divided
4 to 5 tablespoons tahini (sesame seed paste)	1 tablespoon minced garlic
	Pinch salt

1. In a food processor, combine the chickpeas, 2 tablespoons of olive oil, tahini, lemon juice, half of the lemon zest, and garlic and pulse for up to 1 minute, scraping down the sides of the food processor bowl as necessary.
2. Taste and add salt as needed. Feel free to add 1 teaspoon of water at a time to thin the hummus to a better consistency. Transfer the hummus to a serving bowl. Serve drizzled with the remaining 2 tablespoons of olive oil and remaining half of the lemon zest.

Per Serving calories: 216 | fat: 15.0g | protein: 5.0g | carbs: 17.0g | fiber: 5.0g | sodium: 12mg

Lemon and Spinach Orzo

Prep time: 5 minutes | Cook time: 10 minutes | Makes 2 cups

1 cup dry orzo	¼ teaspoon salt
1 (6-ounce / 170-g) bag baby spinach	Freshly ground black pepper
1 cup halved grape tomatoes	¾ cup crumbled feta cheese
2 tablespoons extra-virgin olive oil	1 lemon, juiced and zested

1. Bring a medium pot of water to a boil. Stir in the orzo and cook uncovered for 8 minutes. Drain the water, then return the orzo to medium heat. Add the spinach and tomatoes and cook until the spinach is wilted. Sprinkle with the olive oil, salt, and pepper and mix well. Top with the feta cheese, lemon juice and zest, then toss one or two more times and serve.

Per Serving (1 cup) calories: 610 | fat: 27.0g | protein: 21.0g | carbs: 74.0g | fiber: 6.0g | sodium: 990mg

Zesty Spanish Potato Salad

Prep time: 10 minutes | Cook time: 5 to 7 minutes | Serves 6 to 8

4 russet potatoes, peeled and chopped	5 tablespoons pitted Spanish olives
3 large hard-boiled eggs, chopped	½ teaspoon freshly ground black pepper
1 cup frozen mixed vegetables, thawed	½ teaspoon dried mustard seed
½ cup plain, unsweetened, full-fat Greek yogurt	½ tablespoon freshly squeezed lemon juice
	½ teaspoon dried dill Salt, to taste

1. Place the potatoes in a large pot of water and boil for 5 to 7 minutes, until just fork-tender, checking periodically for doneness. You don't have to overcook them. Meanwhile, in a large bowl, mix the eggs, vegetables, yogurt, olives, pepper, mustard, lemon juice, and dill. Season with salt to taste.
2. Once the potatoes are cooled somewhat, add them to the large bowl, then toss well and serve.

Per Serving

calories: 192 | fat: 5.0g | protein: 9.0g | carbs: 30.0g | fiber: 2.0g | sodium: 59mg

Greek Salad with Dressing

Prep time: 10 minutes | Cook time: 0 minutes | Serves 4 to 6

1 head iceberg lettuce	1 teaspoon salt
2 cups cherry tomatoes	1 clove garlic, minced
1 large cucumber	1 cup Kalamata olives, pitted
1 medium onion	1 (6-ounce / 170-g) package feta cheese, crumbled
¼ cup lemon juice	
½ cup extra-virgin olive oil	

1. Cut the lettuce into 1-inch pieces and put them in a large salad bowl. Cut the tomatoes in half and add them to the salad bowl. Slice the cucumber into bite-sized pieces and add them to the salad bowl.
2. Thinly slice the onion and add it to the salad bowl. In a separate bowl, whisk together the olive oil, lemon juice, salt, and garlic. Pour the dressing over the salad and gently toss to evenly coat.
3. Top the salad with the Kalamata olives and feta cheese and serve.

Per Serving calories: 539 | fat: 50.0g | protein: 9.0g | carbs: 18.0g | fiber: 4.0g | sodium: 1758mg

Chicken and Pastina Soup

Prep time: 5 minutes | Cook time: 20 minutes | Serves 6

1 tablespoon extra-virgin olive oil	¼ teaspoon freshly ground black pepper
2 garlic cloves, minced	¾ cup uncooked acini de pepe or pastina pasta
3 cups packed chopped kale; center ribs removed	2 cups shredded cooked chicken (about 12 ounces / 340 g)
1 cup minced carrots	
8 cups no-salt-added chicken or vegetable broth	3 tablespoons grated Parmesan cheese
¼ teaspoon kosher or sea salt	

1. In a large stockpot over medium heat, heat the oil. Add the garlic and cook for 30 seconds, stirring frequently. Add the kale and carrots and cook for 5 minutes, stirring occasionally. Add the broth, salt, and pepper, and turn the heat to high. Bring the broth to a boil, and add the pasta. Reduce the heat to medium and cook for 10 minutes, or until the pasta is cooked through, stirring every few minutes so the pasta doesn't stick to the bottom. Add the chicken, and cook for another 2 minutes to warm through.
2. Ladle the soup into six bowls. Top each with ½ tablespoon of cheese and serve.

Per Serving calories: 275 | fat: 19.0g | protein: 16.0g | carbs: 11.0g | fiber: 2.0g | sodium: 298mg

Mediterranean Tomato Hummus Soup

Prep time: 10 minutes | Cook time: 10 minutes | Serves 2

1 (14.5-ounce / 411-g) can crushed tomatoes with basil	Salt, to taste
2 cups low-sodium chicken stock	¼ cup thinly sliced fresh basil leaves, for garnish (optional)
1 cup roasted red pepper hummus	

1. Combine the canned tomatoes, hummus, and chicken stock in a blender and blend until smooth. Pour the mixture into a saucepan and bring it to a boil. Season with salt to taste. Serve garnished with the fresh basil, if desired.

Per Serving

calories: 147 | fat: 6.2g | protein: 5.2g | carbs: 20.1g | fiber: 4.1g | sodium: 682mg

Green Bean and Halloumi Salad

Prep time: 20 minutes | Cook time: 5 minutes | Serves 2

Dressing:
¼ cup unsweetened coconut milk
1 tablespoon olive oil
2 teaspoons freshly squeezed lemon juice
¼ teaspoon garlic powder
¼ teaspoon onion powder
Pinch salt
Pinch freshly ground black pepper

Salad:
½ pound (227 g) fresh green beans, trimmed
2 ounces (57 g) Halloumi cheese, sliced into 2 (½-inch-thick) slices
½ cup halved cherry or grape tomatoes
¼ cup thinly sliced sweet onion

Make the Dressing
1. Combine the coconut milk, olive oil, lemon juice, onion powder, garlic powder, salt, and pepper in a small bowl and whisk well. Set aside.

Make the Salad
2. Fill a medium-size pot with about 1 inch of water and add the green beans. Cover and steam them for about 3 to 4 minutes, or just until beans are tender. Do not overcook. Drain beans, rinse them immediately with cold water, and set them aside to cool.
3. Heat a nonstick skillet over medium-high heat and place the slices of Halloumi in the hot pan. After about 2 minutes, check to see if the cheese is golden on the bottom. If it is, flip the slices and cook for another minute or until the second side is golden. Remove cheese from the pan and cut each piece into cubes (about 1-inch square).
4. Place the green beans, halloumi slices, tomatoes, and onion in a large bowl and toss to combine.
5. Drizzle the dressing over the salad and toss well to combine. Serve immediately.

Per Serving calories: 274 | fat: 18.1g | protein: 8.0g | carbs: 16.8g | fiber: 5.1g | sodium: 499mg

Citrus Salad with Kale and Fennel

Prep time: 15 minutes | Cook time: 0 minutes | Serves 2

Dressing:
3 tablespoons olive oil
2 tablespoons fresh orange juice
1 tablespoon blood orange vinegar, other orange vinegar, or cider vinegar
1 tablespoon honey
Salt and freshly ground black pepper, to taste

Salad:
2 cups packed baby kale
1 medium navel or blood orange, segmented
½ small fennel bulb, stems and leaves removed, sliced into matchsticks
3 tablespoons toasted pecans, chopped
2 ounces (57 g) goat cheese, crumbled

Make the Dressing
1. Mix the olive oil, orange juice, vinegar, and honey in a small bowl and whisk to combine. Season with salt and pepper to taste. Set aside.

Make the Salad
2. Divide the baby kale, orange segments, fennel, pecans, and goat cheese evenly between two plates.
3. Drizzle half of the dressing over each salad and serve.

Per Serving calories: 503 | fat: 39.1g | protein: 13.2g | carbs: 31.2g | fiber: 6.1g | sodium: 156mg

Arugula, Watermelon, and Feta Salad

Prep time: 10 minutes | Cook time: 0 minutes | Serves 2

3 cups packed arugula
2½ cups watermelon, cut into bite-size cubes
2 ounces (57 g) feta cheese, crumbled
2 tablespoons balsamic glaze

1. Divide the arugula between two plates.
2. Divide the watermelon cubes between the beds of arugula.
3. Scatter half of the feta cheese over each salad.
4. Drizzle about 1 tablespoon of the glaze (or more if desired) over each salad. Serve immediately.

Per Serving
calories: 157 | fat: 6.9g | protein: 6.1g | carbs: 22.0g | fiber: 1.1g | sodium: 328mg

Vegetable Fagioli Soup

Prep time: 30 minutes | Cook time: 60 minutes | Serves 2

1 tablespoon olive oil
2 medium carrots, diced
2 medium celery stalks, diced
½ medium onion, diced
1 large garlic clove, minced
3 tablespoons tomato paste
4 cups low-sodium vegetable broth
1 cup packed kale, stemmed and chopped
1 (15-ounce / 425-g) can red kidney beans, drained and rinsed
1 (15-ounce / 425-g) can cannellini beans, drained and rinsed
½ cup chopped fresh basil
Salt and freshly ground black pepper, to taste

1. Heat the olive oil in a stockpot over medium-high heat. Add the carrots, celery, onion, and garlic and sauté for 10 minutes, or until the vegetables start to turn golden.
2. Stir in the tomato paste and cook for about 30 seconds.
3. Add the vegetable broth and bring the soup to a boil. Cover and reduce the heat to low. Cook the soup for 45 minutes, or until the carrots are tender.
4. Using an immersion blender, purée the soup so that it's partly smooth, but with some chunks of vegetables.
5. Add the kale, beans, and basil. Season with salt and pepper to taste, then serve.

Per Serving
calories: 217 | fat: 4.2g | protein: 10.0g | carbs: 36.2g | fiber: 10.2g | sodium: 482mg

Spicy Wilted Greens (Greek)

Preparation time: 10 minutes Cooking time: 5 minutes Serving: 2

1 tablespoon olive oil 2 garlic cloves, minced
Pinch salt
3 cups sliced greens (kale, spinach, chard, beet greens, dandelion greens, or a combination)
Pinch red pepper flakes (or more to taste)

1. Heat the olive oil in a sauté pan over medium-high heat. Add garlic and sauté for 30 seconds, or just until it's fragrant.
2. Add the greens, salt, and pepper flakes and stir to combine. Let the greens wilt, but do not overcook. Remove the pan from the heat and serve.

Nutrition: calories: 91 fats: 7g protein: 1g carbs: 7g fiber: 3g sodium: 111mg

Avgolemono (Lemon Chicken Soup)

Prep time: 15 minutes | Cook time: 60 minutes | Serves 2

½ large onion	3 tablespoons freshly squeezed lemon juice
2 medium carrots	
1 celery stalk	1 egg yolk
1 garlic clove	2 tablespoons chopped fresh dill
5 cups low-sodium chicken stock	
¼ cup brown rice	2 tablespoons chopped fresh parsley
1½ cups (about 5 ounces / 142 g) shredded rotisserie chicken	Salt, to taste

1. Put the onion, carrots, celery, and garlic in a food processor and pulse until the vegetables are minced.
2. Add the vegetables and chicken stock to a stockpot and bring it to a boil over high heat.
3. Reduce the heat to medium-low and add the rice, shredded chicken and lemon juice. Cover and let the soup simmer for 40 minutes, or until the rice is cooked.
4. In a small bowl, whisk the egg yolk lightly. Slowly, while whisking with one hand, pour about ½ of a ladle of the broth into the egg yolk to warm, or temper, the yolk. Slowly add another ladle of broth and continue to whisk.
5. Remove the soup from the heat and pour the whisked egg yolk–broth mixture into the pot. Stir well to combine.
6. Add the fresh dill and parsley. Season with salt to taste and serve.

Per Serving

calories: 172 | fat: 4.2g | protein: 18.2g | carbs: 16.1g | fiber: 2.1g | sodium: 232mg

Herb-Roasted Vegetables (Italian)

Preparation time: 15 minutes Cooking time: 45 minutes Serving: 6

Nonstick cooking spray	1eggplants, peeled and sliced 1/8 inch thick 1 zucchini, sliced ¼ inch thick
1yellow summer squash, sliced ¼ inch thick 2 Roma tomatoes, sliced 1/8 inch thick	¼ cup, plus 2 tablespoons extra-virgin olive oil, divided 1 tablespoon garlic powder
¼ teaspoon dried oregano	¼ teaspoon dried basil
¼ teaspoon salt	Freshly ground black pepper, to taste

1. Preheat the oven to 400°F (205°C).
2. Spray a 9-by-13-inch baking dish with cooking spray. In the dish, toss the eggplant, zucchini, squash, and tomatoes with 2 tablespoons oil, garlic powder, oregano, basil, salt, and pepper.
3. Standing the vegetables up (like little soldiers), alternate layers of eggplant, zucchini, squash, and Roma tomato.
4. Drizzle the top with the remaining ¼ cup of olive oil.
5. Bake, uncovered, for 40 to 45 minutes, or until vegetables are golden brown.

Nutrition: calories: 186 fats: 14g protein: 3g carbs: 15g fiber: 5g sodium: 110mg

Mediterranean Bruschetta Hummus Platter(Greek)

Preparation time: 15 minutes Cooking time: 0 minutes Serving: 6

1/3 cup finely diced seedless English cucumber	½ cup finely diced fresh tomato
4 warmed pitas, cut into wedges, for serving	1 tablespoon fresh chopped parsley or basil
1 (10-ounce / 283-g) container plain hummus	1 teaspoon extra-virgin olive oil
Carrot sticks, for serving	¼ cup Herbed Olive Oil
2 tablespoons crumbled feta cheese	2 tablespoons balsamic glaze
Celery sticks, for serving	Sliced bell peppers, for serving
Purple cauliflower, for serving	Broccoli, for serving

1. In a small bowl, mix the tomato and cucumber and toss with the olive oil. Pile the cucumber mixture over a fresh container of hummus. Drizzle the hummus and vegetables with the balsamic glaze. Top with crumbled feta and fresh parsley.
2. Put the hummus on a large cutting board. Pour the Herbed Olive Oil in a small bowl and put it on the cutting board. Surround the bowls with the pita wedges and cut carrot sticks, celery sticks, sliced bell peppers, broccoli, and cauliflower.

Nutrition: calories: 345 fats: 19g protein: 9g carbs: 32g fiber: 3g sodium: 473mg

Garlic Broccoli with Artichoke Hearts (Greek)

Prep time: 5 minutes Cooking time: 10 minutes Serving: 4

1pounds (907 g) fresh broccoli rabe	½ cup extra-virgin olive oil, divided 3 garlic cloves, finely minced
1 teaspoon salt	1 teaspoon red pepper flakes
1(13 3/4-ounce / 390-g) can artichoke hearts, drained and quartered 1 tablespoon water	2tablespoons red wine vinegar Freshly ground black pepper, to taste

1. Trim away any thick lower stems and yellow leaves from the broccoli rabe and discard. Cut into individual florets with a couple inches of thin stem attached.
2. In a large skillet, heat ¼ cup olive oil over medium-high heat. Add the trimmed broccoli, garlic, salt, and red pepper flakes and sauté for 5 minutes, until the broccoli begins to soften. Add the artichoke hearts and sauté for another 2 minutes.
3. Add the water and reduce the heat to low. Cover and simmer until the broccoli stems are tender, 3 to 5 minutes.
4. In a small bowl, whisk together remaining ¼ cup olive oil and the vinegar. Drizzle over the broccoli and artichokes. Season with ground black pepper, if desired.

Nutrition: calories: 358 fats: 35g protein: 11g carbs: 18g fiber: 10g sodium: 918mg

Roasted Parmesan Rosemary Potatoes (Italian)

Preparation time: 10 minutes
Cooking time: 55 minutes Serving: 2

12 ounces (340 g) red potatoes (3 to 4 small potatoes) 1 tablespoon olive oil

½ teaspoon garlic powder

¼ teaspoon salt

1 tablespoon grated Parmesan cheese

1 teaspoon minced fresh rosemary (from 1 sprig)

1. Preheat the oven to 425ºF (220ºC) and set the rack to the bottom position. Line a baking sheet with parchment paper. (Do not use foil, as the potatoes will stick.)
2. Scrub the potatoes and dry them well. Dice into 1-inch pieces.
3. In a mixing bowl, combine the potatoes, olive oil, garlic powder, and salt. Toss well to coat.
4. Lay the potatoes on the parchment paper and roast for 10 minutes. Flip the potatoes over and return to the oven for 10 more minutes.
5. Check the potatoes to make sure they are golden brown on the top and bottom. Toss them again, turn the heat down to 350ºF (180ºC), and roast for 30 minutes more.
6. When the potatoes are golden, crispy, and cooked through, sprinkle the Parmesan cheese over them and toss again. Return to the oven for 3 minutes to let the cheese melt a bit.
7. Remove from the oven and sprinkle with the fresh rosemary.

Nutrition: calories: 193 | fat: 8g | protein: 5g | carbs: 28g | fiber: 3g | sodium: 334mg

Romano Broccolini (Italian)

Prep time: 5 minutes Cooking time: 10 minutes Serving: 2

1bunch broccolini (about 5 ounces / 142 g) 1 tablespoon olive oil

½ teaspoon garlic powder

¼ teaspoon salt

2tablespoons grated Romano cheese

1. Preheat the oven to 400ºF (205ºC) and set the oven rack to the middle position. Line a sheet pan with parchment paper or foil.
2. Slice the tough ends off the broccolini and place in a medium bowl. Add the olive oil, garlic powder, and salt and toss to combine. Arrange broccolini on the lined sheet pan.
3. Roast for 7 minutes, flipping pieces over halfway through the roasting time.
4. Remove the pan from the oven and sprinkle the cheese over the broccolini. With a pair of tongs, carefully flip the pieces over to coat all sides. Return to the oven for another 2 to 3 minutes, or until the cheese melts and starts to turn golden.

Nutrition: calories: 114 fats: 9g protein: 4g carbs: 5g fiber: 2g sodium: 400mg

Balsamic Brussels Sprouts and Delicata Squash(Spanish)

Preparation time: 10 minutes Cooking time: 30 minutes
Serving: 2

½ pound (227 g) Brussels sprouts, ends trimmed and outer leaves removed
1cup fresh cranberries 2 teaspoons olive oil
½ cup balsamic vinegar

1 medium delicata squash, halved lengthwise, seeded, and cut into 1- inch pieces
Salt and freshly ground black pepper, to taste
2tablespoons roasted pumpkin seeds

2 tablespoons fresh pomegranate arils (seeds)

1. Preheat oven to 400ºF (205ºC) and set the rack to the middle position. Line a sheet pan with parchment paper.
2. Combine the Brussels sprouts, squash, and cranberries in a large bowl. Drizzle with olive oil, and season liberally with salt and pepper. Toss well to coat and arrange in a single layer on the sheet pan.
3. Roast for 30 minutes, turning vegetables halfway through, or until Brussels sprouts turn brown and crisp in spots and squash has golden- brown spots.
4. While vegetables are roasting, prepare the balsamic glaze by simmering the vinegar for 10 to 12 minutes, or until mixture has reduced to about
1. ¼ cup and turns a syrupy consistency.
5. Remove the vegetables from the oven, drizzle with balsamic syrup, and sprinkle with pumpkin seeds and pomegranate arils before serving.

Nutrition: calories: 201 fats: 7g protein: 6g carbs: 21g fiber: 8g sodium: 34mg

Roasted Lemon Tahini Cauliflower (Italian)

Preparation time: 10 minutes Cooking time: 20 minutes
Serving: 2

½ large head cauliflower, stemmed and broken into florets (about 3 cups)
2tablespoons freshly squeezed lemon juice 1 teaspoon harissa paste

1tablespoon olive oil 2 tablespoons tahini

Pinch salt

1. Preheat the oven to 400ºF (205ºC) and set the rack to the lowest position. Line a sheet pan with parchment paper or foil.
2. Toss the cauliflower florets with the olive oil in a large bowl and transfer to the sheet pan. Reserve the bowl to make the tahini sauce.
3. Roast the cauliflower for 15 minutes, turning it once or twice, until it starts to turn golden.
4. In the same bowl, combine the tahini, lemon juice, harissa, and salt.
5. When the cauliflower is tender, remove it from the oven and toss it with the tahini sauce. Return to the sheet pan and roast for 5 minutes more.

Nutrition: calories: 205 fats: 15g protein: 7g carbs: 15g fiber: 7g sodium: 161mg

Honey Roasted Rainbow Carrots (Spanish)

Prep time: 10 minutes Cooking time: 20 minutes Serving: 2

½ pound (227 g) rainbow carrots (about 4) 1 tablespoon honey

½ teaspoon coriander Pinch salt 2 tablespoons fresh orange juice

1. Preheat oven to 400ºF (205ºC) and set the oven rack to the middle position.
2. Peel the carrots and cut them lengthwise into slices of even thickness. Place them in a large bowl.
3. In a small bowl, mix together the orange juice, honey, coriander, and salt.
4. Pour the orange juice mixture over the carrots and toss well to coat.
5. Spread carrots onto a baking dish in a single layer.
6. Roast for 15 to 20 minutes, or until fork-tender.

Nutrition: calories: 85 fats: 0g protein: 1g carbs: 21g fiber: 3g sodium: 156mg

Lemon and Thyme Roasted Vegetables (Greek)

Preparation time: 20 minutes Cooking time: 50 minutes Serving: 2

1head garlic, cloves split apart, unpeeled 2 tablespoons olive oil, divided	2medium carrots
¼ pound (113 g) asparagus 6 Brussels sprouts	2cups cauliflower florets
½ pint cherry or grape tomatoes	½ fresh lemon, sliced
Salt and freshly ground black pepper, to taste	3sprigs fresh thyme or ½ teaspoon dried thyme Freshly squeezed lemon juice

1. Preheat oven to 375ºF (190ºC) and set the rack to the middle position. Line a sheet pan with parchment paper or foil.
2. Place the garlic cloves in a small piece of foil and wrap lightly to enclose them, but don't seal the package. Drizzle with 1 teaspoon of olive oil. Place the foil packet on the sheet pan and roast for 30 minutes while you prepare the remaining vegetables.
3. While garlic is roasting, clean, peel, and trim vegetables: Cut carrots into strips, ½-inch wide and 3 to 4 inches long; snap tough end off asparagus; trim tough end of the Brussels sprouts and cut in half if they are large; trim cauliflower into 2-inch florets; keep tomatoes whole. The vegetables should be cut into pieces of similar size for even roasting.
4. Place all vegetables and the lemon slices into a large mixing bowl. Drizzle with the remaining 5 teaspoons of olive oil and season generously with salt and pepper.
5. Increase the oven temperature to 400ºF (205ºC).
6. Arrange the vegetables on the sheet pan in a single layer, leaving the packet of garlic cloves on the pan. Roast for 20 minutes, turning occasionally, until tender.
7. When the vegetables are tender, remove from the oven and sprinkle with thyme leaves. Let the garlic cloves sit until cool enough to handle, and then remove the skins. Leave them whole, or gently mash.
8. Toss garlic with the vegetables and an additional squeeze of fresh lemon juice.

Nutrition: calories: 256 fats: 15g protein: 7g carbs: 31g fiber: 9g sodium: 168mg

Garlicky Roasted Grape Tomatoes (Spanish)

Prep time: 10 minutes Cooking time: 45 minutes Serving: 2

1-pint grape tomatoes 10 whole garlic cloves, skins removed

¼ cup olive oil ½ teaspoon salt

1 fresh rosemary sprig 1 fresh thyme sprig

1. Preheat oven to 350ºF (180ºC).
2. Toss tomatoes, garlic cloves, oil, salt, and herb sprigs in a baking dish.
3. Roast tomatoes until they are soft and begin to caramelize, about 45 minutes.
4. Remove herbs before serving.

Nutrition: calories: 271 fats: 26g protein: 3g carbs: 12g fiber: 3g sodium: 593mg

Spinach and Zucchini Lasagna (Italian)

Preparation time: 15 minutes Cooking time: 1 hour Serving: 8

½ cup extra-virgin olive oil, divided 4 to 5 medium zucchini squashes	1 teaspoon salt
8 ounces (227 g) frozen spinach, thawed and well drained (about 1 cup) 2 cups whole-milk ricotta cheese	¼ cup chopped fresh basil or 2 teaspoons dried basil 1 teaspoon garlic powder
½ teaspoon freshly ground black pepper	2 cups shredded fresh whole-milk Mozzarella cheese 1 3/4 cups shredded Parmesan cheese
½ (24-ounce / 680-g) jar low-sugar marinara sauce (less than 5 grams sugar)	

1. Preheat the oven to 425ºF (220ºC).
2. Line two baking sheets with parchment paper or aluminum foil and drizzle each with 2 tablespoons olive oil, spreading evenly.
3. Slice the zucchini lengthwise into ¼-inch-thick long slices and place on the prepared baking sheet in a single layer. Sprinkle with ½ teaspoon salt per sheet. Bake until softened, but not mushy, 15 to 18 minutes. Remove from the oven and allow to cool slightly before assembling the lasagna.
4. Reduce the oven temperature to 375ºF (190ºC).
5. While the zucchini cooks, prep the filling. In a large bowl, combine the spinach, ricotta, basil, garlic powder, and pepper. In a small bowl, mix together the Mozzarella and Parmesan cheeses. In a medium bowl, combine the marinara sauce and remaining ¼ cup olive oil and stir to fully incorporate the oil into sauce.
6. To assemble the lasagna, spoon a third of the marinara sauce mixture into the bottom of a 9-by-13-inch glass baking dish and spread evenly.
7. Place 1 layer of softened zucchini slices to fully cover the sauce, then add a third of the ricotta-spinach mixture and spread evenly on top of the zucchini. Sprinkle a third of the Mozzarella-Parmesan mixture on top of the ricotta. Repeat with 2 more cycles of these layers: marinara, zucchini, ricotta-spinach, then cheese blend.
8. Bake until the cheese is bubbly and melted, 30 to 35 minutes. Turn the broiler to low and broil until the top is golden brown, about 5 minutes. Remove from the oven and allow to cool slightly before slicing.

Nutrition: calories: 521 fats: 41g protein: 25g carbs: 13g fiber: 3g sodium: 712mg

Pistachio Citrus Asparagus (Italian)

Preparation time: 10 minutes Cooking time: 15 minutes Serving: 4

5 tablespoons extra-virgin olive oil, divided	Zest and juice of 2 clementine's or 1 orange (about ¼ cup juice and 1 tablespoon zest)
Zest and juice of 1 lemon	1 tablespoon red wine vinegar 1 teaspoon salt, divided
¼ teaspoon freshly ground black pepper	½ cup shelled pistachios
1 pound (454 g) fresh asparagus	1 tablespoon water

1. In a small bowl, whisk together 4 tablespoons olive oil, the clementine and lemon juices and zests, vinegar, ½ teaspoon salt, and pepper. Set aside.
2. In a medium dry skillet, toast the pistachios over medium-high heat until lightly browned, 2 to 3 minutes, being careful not to let them burn. Transfer to a cutting board and coarsely chop. Set aside.
3. Trim the rough ends off the asparagus, usually the last 1 to 2 inches of each spear. In a skillet, heat the remaining 1 tablespoon olive oil over medium-high heat. Add the asparagus and sauté for 2 to 3 minutes. Sprinkle with the remaining ½ teaspoon salt and add the water. Reduce the heat to medium-low, cover, and cook until tender, another 2 to 4 minutes, depending on the thickness of the spears.
4. Transfer the cooked asparagus to a serving dish. Add the pistachios to the dressing and whisk to combine. Pour the dressing over the warm asparagus and toss to coat.

Nutrition: calories: 284 | fat: 24g | protein: 6g | carbs: 11g | fiber: 4g | sodium: 594mg

Sautéed Riced Cauliflower (Spanish)

Preparation time: 5 minutes Cooking time: 5 minutes Serving: 6 to 8

1 small head cauliflower, broken into florets	¼ cup extra-virgin olive oil
2 garlic cloves, finely minced	½ teaspoon freshly ground black pepper
1½ teaspoons salt	

1. Place the florets in a food processor and pulse several times, until the cauliflower is the consistency of rice or couscous.
2. In a large skillet, heat the olive oil over medium-high heat. Add the cauliflower, garlic, salt, and pepper and sauté for 5 minutes, just to take the crunch out but not enough to let the cauliflower become soggy.
3. Remove the cauliflower from the skillet and place in a bowl until ready to use. Toss with chopped herbs and additional olive oil for a simple side, top with sautéed veggies and protein, or use in your favorite recipe.

Nutrition: calories: 92 | fat: 8g | protein: 1g | carbs: 3g | fiber: 0g | sodium: 595mg

Chickpea, Parsley, and Dill Dip (Spanish)

Preparation Time: 11 minutes Cooking time: 22 minutes Servings: 6

8 cups water	1 cup dried chickpeas 3 tablespoons olive oil 2 garlic cloves
2 tablespoons fresh parsley 2 tablespoons fresh dill	1 tablespoon lemon juice
¼ teaspoon salt	

1. Add 4 cups water and chickpeas to the Instant Pot®. Cover, place steam release to Sealing. Set Manual, and time to 1 minute. When the timer beeps, quick-release the pressure until the float valve drops, press the Cancel button, and open the lid.
2. Drain water, rinse the chickpeas, and return to the pot with 4 cups of freshwater. Set aside to soak for 1 hour.
3. Add 1 tablespoon of oil to the pot. Close, adjust steam release to Sealing, click Manual, and the time to 20 minutes. When the alarm beeps, let the pressure release for 20 minutes. Click the Cancel, open, and drain chickpeas.
4. Place chickpeas in a food processor or blender, and add garlic, parsley, dill, lemon juice, and remaining 2 tablespoons water. Blend for about 30 seconds.
5. With the processor or blender lid still in place, slowly add the remaining 2 tablespoons oil while still blending, then add salt. Serve warm or at room temperature.

Nutrition: 76 Calories 4g Fat 2g Protein

Yogurt Dip (Greek)

Prep Time: 5 minutes Cooking time: 10 minutes Servings: 4

½ Lemon	Juiced & Zested 1 cup Greek Yogurt, Plain
1 Tablespoon Chives, Fresh & Chopped	Fine 2 Teaspoons Dill, Fresh & Chopped
2 Teaspoons Thyme, Fresh & Chopped	1 Teaspoon Parsley, Fresh & Chopped
½ Teaspoon Garlic, Minced	¼ Teaspoon Sea Salt, Fine

1. Get out a bowl and mix all your until they're well blended. Season with salt before refrigerating. Serve chilled.

Nutrition: Calories: 59 Protein: 2 Grams Fat: 4 Grams Carbs: 5 Grams

Sage Barley Mix (Greek)

Preparation Time: 10 minutes Cooking time: 45 minutes Servings: 4

1 tablespoon olive oil 1 red onion, chopped	1 tablespoon leaves, chopped 1 garlic clove, minced
14 ounces barley	½ tablespoon parmesan, grated 6 cups veggie stock
Salt and black pepper to the taste	

1. Heat a pan with the oil over medium heat, add the onion and garlic, stir and sauté for 5 minutes.
2. Add the sage, barley, and the rest of the except the parmesan, stir, bring to a simmer, and cook for 40 minutes. Add the parmesan, stir, divide between plates.

Nutrition: 210 Calories 6.5g Fat 3.4g Fiber 8.6g Carbs 3.4g protein

Chickpeas and Beets Mix (Spanish)

Preparation Time: 10 minutes Cooking time: 25 minutes Servings: 4

3 tablespoons capers, drained and chopped Juice of 1 lemon	Zest of 1 lemon, grated 1 red onion, chopped
3 tablespoons olive oil	14 ounces canned chickpeas, drained 8 ounces beets, peeled and cubed
1 tablespoon parsley, chopped Salt and pepper to the taste	

1. Heat a pan with the oil over medium heat, add the onion, lemon zest, lemon juice, and the capers and sauté for 5 minutes.
2. Add the rest of the , stir, and cook over medium-low heat for 20 minutes more. Divide the mix between plates and serve as a side dish.

Nutrition: 199 Calories 4.5g Fat 2.3g Fiber 6.5g Carbs 3.3g protein

Creamy Sweet Potatoes Mix (Spanish)

Preparation Time: 10 minutes
Cooking time: 1 hour Servings: 4

4 tablespoons olive oil 1 garlic clove, minced	4 medium sweet potatoes, pricked with a fork 1 red onion, sliced
3 ounces baby spinach Zest and juice of 1 lemon	A small bunch of dill, chopped
1 and ½ tablespoons Greek yogurt 2 tablespoons tahini paste	Salt and black pepper to the taste

1. Put the potatoes on a baking sheet lined with parchment paper, introduce them in the oven at 350 degrees and cook them for 1 hour.
2. Peel the potatoes then cut them into wedges and put them in a bowl. Add the garlic, the oil, and the rest of the , toss, divide the mix between plates and serve.

Nutrition: 214 Calories 5.6g Fat 3.4g Fiber 6.5g Carbs 3.1g protein

Cabbage and Mushrooms Mix (Greek)

Preparation Time: 10 minutes Cooking time: 15 minutes Servings: 2

1 yellow onion, sliced 2 tablespoons olive oil	1 tablespoon balsamic vinegar
½ pound white mushrooms, sliced 1 green cabbage head, shredded	4 spring onions, chopped Salt and black pepper to the taste

1. Heat a pan with the oil over medium heat, add the yellow onion and the spring onions and cook for 5 minutes.
2. Add the rest of the , cook everything for 10 minutes, divide between plates and serve.

Nutrition: 199 Calories 4.5g Fat 2.4g Fiber 5.6g Carbs 2.2g protein

Lemon Mushroom Rice (Spanish)

Preparation Time: 10 minutes Cooking time: 30 minutes Servings: 4

2 cups chicken stock	1 yellow onion, chopped
½ pound white mushrooms, sliced 2 garlic cloves, minced	8 ounces wild rice
Juice and zest of 1 lemon	1 tablespoon chives, chopped
6 tablespoons goat cheese, crumbled	Salt and black pepper to the taste

1. Heat a pot with the stock over medium heat, add the rice, onion, and the rest of the except the chives and the cheese, bring to a simmer and cook for 25 minutes.
2. Add the remaining , cook everything for 5 minutes, divide between plates, and serve as a side dish.

Nutrition: 222 Calories 5.5g Fat 5.4g Fiber 12.3g Carbs 5.6g protein

Paprika and Chives Potatoes (Spanish)

Preparation Time: 10 minutes
Cooking time: 1 hour and 8 minutes Servings: 4

4 potatoes, scrubbed and pricked with a fork 1 tablespoon olive oil	1 celery stalk, chopped 2 tomatoes, chopped
1 teaspoon sweet paprika 2 tablespoons chives, chopped	Salt and black pepper to the taste

1. Arrange the potatoes on a baking sheet lined with parchment paper, introduce them in the oven and bake at 350 degrees F for 1 hour.
2. Cool the potatoes down, peel, and cut them into larger cubes. Heat a pan with the oil over medium heat, add the celery and the tomatoes and sauté for 2 minutes.
3. Add the potatoes and the rest of the , toss, cook everything for 6 minutes, divide the mix between plates and serve as a side dish.

Nutrition: 233 Calories 8.7g Fat 4.5g Fiber 14.4g Carbs 6.4g protein

Bulgur, Kale and Cheese Mix (Italian)

Preparation Time: 10 minutes
Cooking time: 10 minutes Servings: 6

4 ounces bulgur	4 ounces kale, chopped
1 tablespoon mint, chopped	1 cucumber, chopped
3 spring onions, chopped	
A pinch of allspice, ground 2 tablespoons olive oil Zest and juice of ½ lemon	4 ounces feta cheese, crumbled

1. Put bulgur in a bowl, cover with hot water, aside for 10 minutes, and fluff with a fork. Heat a pan with the oil over medium heat, add the onions and the allspice and cook for 3 minutes.
2. Add the bulgur and the rest of the , cook everything for 5-6 minutes more, divide between plates, and serve.

Nutrition: 200 Calories 6.7g Fat 3.4g Fiber 15.4g Carbs 4.5g protein

Spicy Green Beans Mix (Greek)

Preparation Time: 5 minutes Cooking time: 15 minutes
Servings: 4

4 teaspoons olive oil 1 garlic clove, minced	½ teaspoon hot paprika
¾ cup veggie stock	1 yellow onion, sliced
1-pound green beans, trimmed and halved	½ cup goat cheese, shredded 2 teaspoon balsamic vinegar

1. Heat a pan with the oil over medium heat, add the garlic, stir, and cook for 1 minute.
2. Add the green beans and the rest of the , toss, cook everything for 15 minutes more, divide between plates, and serve as a side dish.

Nutrition: 188 Calories 4g Fat 3g Fiber 12.4g Carbs 4.4g protein

Beans and Rice (Spanish)

Preparation Time: 10 minutes Cooking time: 55 minutes
Servings: 6

1 tablespoon olive oil	1 yellow onion, chopped 2 celery stalks, chopped 2 garlic cloves, minced 2 cups brown rice
1 and ½ cup canned black beans, rinsed and drained 4 cups water	Salt and black pepper to the taste

1. Heat a pan with the oil over medium heat, add the celery, garlic, and onion, stir, and cook for 10 minutes.
2. Add the rest of the , stir, bring to a simmer, and cook over medium heat for 45 minutes. Divide between plates and serve.

Nutrition: 224 Calories 8.4g Fat 3.4g Fiber 15.3g Carbs 6.2g protein

Lime Cucumber Mix (Greek)

Preparation Time: 10 minutes
Cooking time: 0 minute Servings: 8

4 cucumbers, chopped	½ cup green bell pepper, chopped 1 yellow onion, chopped
1 chili pepper, chopped 1 garlic clove, minced	1 teaspoon parsley, chopped 2 tablespoons lime juice
1 tablespoon dill, chopped	Salt and black pepper to the taste 1 tablespoon olive oil

1. In a large bowl, mix the cucumber with the bell peppers and the rest of the , toss, and serve as a side dish.

Nutrition: 123 Calories 4.3g Fat 2.3g Fiber 5.6g Carbs 2g protein

Walnuts Cucumber Mix (Greek)

Prep Time: 5 minutes Cooking time: 0 minute Servings: 2

1 cucumbers, chopped 1 tablespoon olive oil	Salt and black pepper to the taste 1 red chili pepper, dried
1 tablespoon lemon juice	1 tablespoon balsamic
3 tablespoons walnuts, chopped	vinegar 1 teaspoon chives, chopped

1. In a bowl, mix the cucumbers with the oil and the rest of the , toss, and serve as a side dish.

Nutrition: 121 Calories 2.3g Fat 2g Fiber 6.7g Carbs 2.4g protein

Artichoke ala Romana (Greek)

Preparation Time: 10 minutes Cooking time: 50 minutes
Servings: 3

3 artichokes (ideal would be the "Mammole" variety), 1 bunch of mint	1 clove of garlic Salt to taste
Black pepper to taste	7 tablespoons of extra virgin olive oil 1 lemon

1. Start by cutting the lemon in half. Then fill a rather large bowl with water and squeeze half a lemon inside.
2. Take your artichokes and start removing the outer leaves by tearing them with your hands. Then cut the end of the stem and the tip of the artichoke. Once again, with your hands, spread the artichoke, and use a small knife cut into the central part to eliminate the inner beard.
3. Peel away the stem as well and round the end using a sharp knife. Place the artichoke in the water from step 1 and repeat this process for the others. Cover the bowl with paper towels which will keep the artichokes immersed in the water, set aside, and take care of the filling in the meantime.
4. Take the mint and mince it. Switch to the garlic, peel it, and mince it as well, adding it to the mint along with a pinch of salt and black pepper. Mix everything.
5. Drain the artichokes and beat them lightly to remove excess water, then use the mixture prepared in step 4 to stuff them. Season with salt and pepper and transfer them into a pan upside down, keeping them rather close together. Then pour in both the oil and the water: the artichokes must be covered up to the beginning of their stems.
6. Cover with a lid and cook for about 30 minutes on low heat. After that, you can serve your warm artichokes ala Romana!

Nutrition: 515 Calories 8g Carbs 5.1g Protein 10.4g Fiber

Balsamic Asparagus (Greek)

Preparation Time: 10 minutes Cooking time: 15 minutes
Servings: 4

3 tablespoons olive oil 3 garlic cloves minced	Salt and black pepper to the taste
2 tablespoons shallot chopped	2 teaspoons balsamic vinegar
1 and ½ pound asparagus trimmed	

1. Heat a pan with the oil over medium-high heat, add the garlic and the shallot and sauté for 3 minutes.
2. Add the rest of the , cook for 12 minutes more, divide between plates, and serve as a side dish.

Nutrition: 100 Calories 10.5g Fat 1.2g Fiber 2.3g Carbs 2.1g protein

Squash and Tomatoes Mix (Greek)

Preparation Time: 10 minutes
Cooking time: 20 minutes Servings: 6

5 medium squashes, cubed	A pinch of salt and black pepper 3 tablespoons olive oil
1cup pine nuts, toasted	¼ cup goat cheese, crumbled 6 tomatoes, cubed
½ yellow onion, chopped	2tablespoons cilantro, chopped 2 tablespoons lemon juice

1. Heat a pan with the oil over medium heat, add the onion and pine nuts and cook for 3 minutes.
2. Add the squash and the rest of the , cook everything for 15 minutes, divide between plates and serve as a side dish.

Nutrition: 200 Calories 4.5g Fat 3.4g Fiber 6.7g Carbs 4g protein

Eggplant Carpaccio (Spanish)

Preparation Time: 10 minutes
Cooking time: 6 minutes Servings: 4

pounds Eggplant	3/4 cup extra virgin olive oil Lemon juice to taste
6 basil leaves	1 clove of garlic Salt to taste
Black pepper to taste	

1. Start by washing the eggplants under running water and drying them well. Cut them lengthwise into thin slices, using a mandolin to obtain slices of the same thickness.
2. Heat a stovetop grill, put the slices of eggplants on it, salt, and turn them over to cook on both sides (cook for a couple of minutes or until they are well colored with the typical dark streaks that result from grilling). After cooking, place the eggplants on a plate and let them cool.
3. Now take care of the marinade: take an ovenproof dish (make sure that the dish allows for the eggplants to always be covered with the marinade so that they absorb the aromatic seasoning) and pour in the oil, the garlic, the salt, the pepper, and the basil. The marinade is ready.
4. Now dip the eggplants in the marinade, cover the dish with plastic wrap and leave to marinate in the refrigerator for a couple of hours. Before serving, season with lemon to taste. Serve the cold eggplant carpaccio as an appetizer or side dish.

Nutrition: 376 Calories 5.5g Carbs 2.5g Protein 4.5g Fiber

Tomatoes and Endives Mix (Greek)

Preparation time: 10 minutes Cooking time: 20 minutes Servings: 4

4 endives shredded	14 ounces canned tomatoes chopped
Salt and black pepper to the taste	2 garlic cloves minced
½ teaspoon red pepper crushed	3 tablespoons olive oil
1tablespoon oregano chopped	2 tablespoons parmesan grated
1 tablespoon cilantro chopped	

1. Heat up a pan with the oil over medium heat, add the garlic and the red pepper and cook for 2-3 minutes.
2. Add the endives, tomatoes, salt, pepper and the oregano, stir and sauté for 15 minutes more.
3. Add the remaining , toss, cook for 2 minutes, divide the mix between plates and serve as a side dish.

Nutrition: calories 232, fat 7.5, fiber 3.5, carbs 14.3, protein 4.5

Yogurt Peppers Mix (Greek)

Preparation time: 10 minutes Cooking time: 15 minutes Servings: 4

1red bell peppers, cut into thick strips 2 tablespoons olive oil	2shallots, chopped
3 garlic cloves, minced	Salt and black pepper to the taste
½ cup Greek yogurt	1 tablespoon cilantro, chopped

1. Heat up a pan with the oil over medium heat, add the shallots and garlic, stir and cook for 5 minutes.
2. Add the rest of the , toss, cook for 10 minutes more, divide the mix between plates and serve as a side dish.

Nutrition: calories 274, fat 11, fiber 3.5, protein 13.3, carbs 6.5

Basil Artichokes (Italian)

Preparation time: 10 minutes Cooking time: 12 minutes Servings: 4

1red onion, chopped	2garlic cloves, minced
Salt and black pepper to the taste	½ cup veggie stock
10 ounces canned artichoke hearts, drained	1teaspoon lemon juice
2tablespoons basil, chopped	1 tablespoon olive oil

1. Heat up a pan with the oil over medium high heat, add the onion and the garlic, stir and sauté for 2 minutes.
2. Add the artichokes and the rest of the , toss, cook for 10 minutes more, divide between plates and serve as a side dish.

Nutrition: calories 105, fat 7.6, fiber 3, carbs 6.7, protein 2.5

Broccoli and Roasted Peppers (Greek)

Preparation time: 10 minutes Cooking time: 10 minutes Servings: 4

1 pound broccoli florets.	2 garlic cloves, minced.
1 tablespoon olive oil	¼ cup roasted peppers, chopped.
2 tablespoons balsamic vinegar.	Salt and black pepper to the taste.
1 tablespoon cilantro, chopped	

1. Heat up a pan with the oil over medium high heat, add the garlic and the peppers and cook for 2 minutes.
2. Add the broccoli and the rest of the , toss, cook over medium heat for 8 minutes more, divide between plates and serve as a side dish.

Nutrition: calories 193, fat 5.6, fiber 3.45, carbs 8.6, protein 4.5

Cauliflower Quinoa (Greek)

Prep time: 5 minutes Cooking time: 10 minutes Servings: 4

1 and ½ cups quinoa	coked 3 tablespoons olive oil
3 cups cauliflower florets 2 spring onions	chopped Salt and pepper to the taste
1 tablespoon red wine vinegar 1 tablespoon parsley	chopped 1 tablespoon chives chopped

1. Heat up a pan with the oil over medium-high heat, add the spring onions and cook for 2 minutes.
2. Add the cauliflower, quinoa and the rest of the , toss, cook over medium heat for 8-9 minutes, divide between plates and serve as a side dish.

Nutrition: calories 220, fat 16.7, fiber 5.6, carbs 6.8, protein 5.4

Mixed Veggies and Chard (Greek)

Preparation time: 10 minutes Cooking time: 20 minutes
Servings: 4

½ cup celery, chopped	½ cup carrot, chopped
½ cup red onion, chopped	½ cup red bell pepper, chopped 1 tablespoon olive oil
1 cup veggie stock	½ cup black olives, pitted and chopped 10 ounces ruby chard, torn
Salt and black pepper to the taste 1 teaspoon balsamic vinegar	

1. Heat up a pan with the oil over medium-high heat, add the celery, carrot, onion, bell pepper, salt and pepper, stir and sauté for 5 minutes.
2. Add the rest of the , toss, cook over medium heat for 15 minutes more, divide between plates and serve as a side dish.

Nutrition: calories 150, fat 6.7, fiber 2.6, carbs 6.8, protein 5.4

Spicy Broccoli and Almonds (Greek)

Preparation time: 10 minutes Cooking time: 30 minutes
Servings: 4

1 broccoli head, florets separated 2 garlic cloves, minced	1 tablespoon olive oil
1 tablespoon chili powder	Salt and black pepper to the taste
2 tablespoons almonds, toasted and chopped	1 tablespoon mint, chopped

1. In a roasting pan, combine the broccoli with the garlic, oil and the rest of the , toss, introduce in the oven and cook at 390 degrees F for 30 minutes.
2. Divide the mix between plates and serve as a side dish.

Nutrition: calories 156, fat 5.4, fiber 1.2, carbs 4.3, protein 2

Lemony Carrots (Italian)

Preparation time: 10 minutes Cooking time: 40 minutes
Servings: 4

1 tablespoons olive oil	2 pounds baby carrots, trimmed Salt and black pepper to the taste
½ teaspoon lemon zest, grated 1 tablespoon lemon juice	1/3 cup Greek yogurt 1 garlic clove, minced
1 teaspoon cumin, ground 1 tablespoon dill, chopped	

1. In a roasting pan, combine the carrots with the oil, salt, pepper and the rest of the except the dill, toss and bake at 400 degrees F for 20 minutes.
2. Reduce the temperature to 375 degrees F and cook for 20 minutes more.
3. Divide the mix between plates, sprinkle the dill on top and serve.

Nutrition: calories 192, fat 5.4, fiber 3.4, carbs 7.3, protein 5.6

Oregano Potatoes (Spanish)

Preparation time: 10 minutes Cooking time: 40 minutes
Servings: 4

6 red potatoes, peeled and cut into wedges Salt and black pepper to the taste	2 tablespoons olive oil ½ cup chicken stock
1 teaspoon lemon zest, grated 1 teaspoon oregano, dried	1 tablespoon chives, chopped

1. In a roasting pan, combine the potatoes with salt, pepper, the oil and the rest of the except the chives, toss, introduce in the oven and cook at 425 degrees F for 40 minutes.
2. Divide the mix between plates, sprinkle the chives on top and serve as a side dish.

Nutrition: calories 245, fat 4.5, fiber 2.8, carbs 7.1, protein 6.4

Baby Squash and Lentils Mix (Greek)

Preparation time: 10 minutes Cooking time: 10 minutes
Servings: 4

1 tablespoons olive oil	½ teaspoon sweet paprika
10 ounces baby squash, sliced 1 tablespoon balsamic vinegar	15 ounces canned lentils, drained and rinsed Salt and black pepper to the taste
1 tablespoon dill, chopped	

1. Heat up a pan with the oil over medium heat, add the squash, lentils and the rest of the , toss and cook over medium heat for 10 minutes.
2. Divide the mix between plates and serve as a side dish.

Nutrition: calories 438, fat 8.4, fiber 32.4, carbs 65.5, protein 22.4

Parmesan Quinoa and Mushrooms (Spanish)

Preparation time: 10 minutes Cooking time: 20 minutes
Servings: 4

1 cup quinoa, cooked	½ cup chicken stock
2 tablespoons olive oil	6 ounces white mushrooms, sliced 1 teaspoon garlic, minced
Salt and black pepper to the taste	½ cup parmesan, grated
2 tablespoons cilantro, chopped	

1. Heat up a pan with the oil over medium heat, add the garlic and mushrooms, stir and sauté for 10 minutes.
2. Add the quinoa and the rest of the , toss, cook over medium heat for 10 minutes more, divide between plates and serve as a side dish.

Nutrition: calories 233, fat 9.5, fiber 6.4, carbs 27.4, protein 12.5

Chives Rice Mix (Spanish)

Preparation time: 5 minutes Cooking time: 5 minutes Servings: 4

2 tablespoons avocado oil	1 cup Arborio rice cooked
2 tablespoons chives, chopped	Salt and black pepper to the taste 2 teaspoons lemon juice

1. Heat up a pan with the avocado oil over medium high heat, add the rice and the rest of the , toss, cook for 5 minutes, divide the mix between plates and serve as a side dish.

Nutrition: calories 236, fat 9, fiber 12.4, carbs 17.5, protein 4.5

Green Beans and Peppers Mix (Greek)

Preparation time: 10 minutes Cooking time: 10 minutes Servings: 4

2 tablespoons olive oil	1and ½ pounds green beans, trimmed and halved Salt and black pepper to the taste
2red bell peppers, cut into strips 1 tablespoon lime juice	2 tablespoons rosemary, chopped 1 tablespoon dill, chopped

1. Heat up a pan with the oil over medium heat, add the bell peppers and the green beans, toss and cook for 5 minutes.
2. Add the rest of the , toss, cook for 5 minutes more, divide between plates and serve as a side dish.

Nutrition: calories 222, fat 8.6, fiber 3.4, carbs 8.6, protein 3.4

Garlic Snap Peas Mix (Greek)

Preparation time: 10 minutes Cooking time: 10 minutes Servings: 4

½ cup walnuts, chopped 2 teaspoons lime juice	¼ cup olive oil
1 and ½ teaspoons garlic, minced	½ cup veggie stock
1 pound sugar snap peas	Salt and black pepper to the taste 1 tablespoon chives, chopped

1. Heat up a pan with the stock over medium heat, add the snap peas and cook for 5 minutes.
2. Add the rest of the except the chives, cook for 5 minutes more and divide between plates.
3. Sprinkle the chives on top and serve as a side dish.

Nutrition: calories 200, fat 7.6, fiber 3.5, carbs 8.5, protein 4.3

Corn and Olives (Spanish)

Preparation time: 5 minutes Cooking time: 0 minutes Servings: 4

2 cups corn	4 ounces green olives, pitted and halved
½ teaspoon balsamic vinegar Salt and black pepper to the taste 2 tablespoons extra virgin olive oil	1 tablespoon oregano, chopped 1 teaspoon thyme, chopped

1. In a bowl, combine the corn with the olives and the rest of the , toss and serve as a side dish.

Nutrition: calories 154, fat 10, fiber 3.4, carbs 17, protein 9.3

Rosemary Red Quinoa (Greek)

Preparation time: 10 minutes Cooking time: 25 minutes Servings: 6

4 cups chicken stock	2 cups red quinoa, rinsed 1 red onion, chopped
2 tablespoons olive oil	1 tablespoon garlic, minced
1 teaspoon lemon zest, grated 2 tablespoons lemon juice	Salt and black pepper to the taste 2 tablespoons rosemary, chopped

1. Heat up a pan with the oil over medium heat, add the onion and the garlic and sauté for 5 minutes.
2. Add the quinoa, the stock and the rest of the , bring to a simmer and cook for 20 minutes stirring from time to time.
3. Divide the mix between plates and serve.

Nutrition: calories 193, fat 7.9, fiber 1.4, carbs 5.4, protein 1.3

Thyme Corn and Cheese Mix (Greek)

Preparation time: 5 minutes Cooking time: 0 minutes Servings: 4

1 tablespoon olive oil	1teaspoon thyme, chopped 1 cup scallions, sliced
2cups corn	Salt and black pepper to the taste
2 tablespoons blue cheese, crumbled 1 tablespoon chives, chopped	

1. In a salad bowl, combine the corn with scallions, thyme and the rest of the , toss, divide between plates and serve.

Nutrition: calories 183, fat 5.5, fiber 7.5, carbs 14.5

Olives and Carrots Sauté (Greek)

Preparation time: 10 minutes Cooking time: 20 minutes Servings: 4

1tablespoon green olives, pitted and sliced 3 tablespoons olive oil	2teaspoons capers, drained and chopped
½ teaspoon lemon zest, grated	1and ½ teaspoons balsamic vinegar
¼ teaspoon rosemary, dried Salt and black pepper to the taste 2 pounds carrots, sliced 1 tablespoon parsley, chopped	¼ cup veggie stock 2spring onions, chopped

1. Heat up a pan with the oil over medium heat, add the carrots and brown for 5 minutes.
2. Add green olives, capers and the rest of the except the parsley and the chives, stir and cook over medium heat for 15 minutes.
3. Add the chives and parsley, toss, divide the mix between plates and serve as a side dish.

Nutrition: calories 244, fat 11, fiber 3.5, carbs 5.6, protein 6.3

Lemon Endives (Greek)

Preparation time: 10 minutes Cooking time: 35 minutes Servings: 4

Juice of 1 and ½ lemons	Salt and black pepper to the taste 3 tablespoons olive oil
¼ cup veggie stock	4 endives, halved lengthwise 1 tablespoon dill, chopped

1. In a roasting pan, combine the endives with the rest of the, introduce in the oven and cook at 375 degrees F for 35 minutes.
2. Divide the endives between plates and serve as a side dish.

Nutrition: calories 221, fat 5.4, fiber 6.4, carbs 15.4, protein 14.3

Leeks Sauté (Greek)

Preparation time: 10 minutes Cooking time: 15 minutes Servings: 4

2 pounds leeks, sliced	2 tablespoons chicken stock
Salt and black pepper to the taste	2 tablespoons tomato paste 1 tablespoon olive oil

1. Heat up a pan with the oil over medium heat, add the leeks and brown for 5 minutes.
2. Add the rest of the , toss, increase the heat to medium-high and cook for 10 minutes more.
3. Divide everything between plates and serve as a side dish.

Nutrition: calories 200, fat 11.4, fiber 5.6, carbs 16.4, protein 3.6

.Cauliflower Tabbouleh Salad (Italian)

Preparation time: 15 minutes Cooking time: 5 minutes Serving: 6

6 tablespoons extra-virgin olive oil, divided 4 cups riced cauliflower	3 garlic cloves, finely minced 1½ teaspoons salt
½ teaspoon freshly ground black pepper	½ large cucumber, peeled, seeded, and chopped
½ cup chopped mint leaves	½ cup chopped Italian parsley
½ cup chopped pitted Kalamata olives 2 tablespoons minced red onion	Juice of 1 lemon (about 2 tablespoons) 2 cups baby arugula or spinach leaves
2 medium avocados, peeled, pitted, and diced 1 cup quartered cherry tomatoes	

1. In a large skillet, heat 2 tablespoons of olive oil over medium-high heat. Add the rice cauliflower, garlic, salt, and pepper and sauté until just tender but not mushy, 3 to 4 minutes. Remove from the heat and place in a large bowl.
2. Add the cucumber, mint, parsley, olives, red onion, lemon juice, and remaining 4 tablespoons olive oil and toss well. Place in the refrigerator, uncovered, and refrigerate for at least 30 minutes, or up to 2 hours.
3. Before serving, add the arugula, avocado, and tomatoes and toss to combine well. Season to taste with salt and pepper and serve cold or at room temperature.

Nutrition: calories: 235 fat: 21g protein: 4g carbs: 12g fiber: 6g sodium: 623mg

.Beet Summer Salad (Italian)

Preparation time: 20 minutes Cooking time: 40 minutes Serving: 4 to 6

6 mediums to large fresh red or yellow beets	1/3 cup plus 1 tablespoon extra-virgin olive oil, divided 4 heads of Treviso radicchio
2 shallots, peeled and sliced	¼ cup lemon juice
½ teaspoon salt	6 ounces (170 g) feta cheese, crumbled

1. Preheat the oven to 400°F (205°C).
2. Cut off the stems and roots of the beets. Wash the beets thoroughly and dry them off with a paper towel.
3. Peel the beets using a vegetable peeler. Cut into ½-inch pieces and put them into a large bowl.
4. Add 1 tablespoon of olive oil to the bowl and toss to coat, then pour the beets out onto a baking sheet. Spread the beets so that they are evenly distributed.
5. Bake for 35 to 40 minutes until the beets are tender, turning once or twice with a spatula.
6. When the beets are done cooking, set them aside and let cool for 10 minutes.
7. While the beets are cooling, cut the radicchio into 1-inch pieces and place on a serving dish.
8. Once the beets have cooled, spoon them over the radicchio, then evenly distribute the shallots over the beets.
9. In a small bowl, whisk together the remaining 1/3 cup of olive oil, lemon juice, and salt. Drizzle the layered salad with dressing. Finish off the salad with feta cheese on top.

Nutrition: calories: 389 fat: 31g protein: 10g carbs: 22g fiber: 5g sodium: 893mg

.Tomato and Lentil Salad with Feta (Greek)

Preparation time: 10 minutes Cooking time: 30 minutes Serving: 4

3 cups water	1cup brown or green lentils, picked over and rinsed 1½ teaspoons salt, divided
2large ripe tomatoes 2 Persian cucumbers 1/3 cup lemon juice	½ cup extra-virgin olive oil 1 cup crumbled feta cheese

1. In a large pot over medium heat, bring the water, lentils, and 1 teaspoon of salt to a simmer, then reduce heat to low. Cover the pot and continue to cook, stirring occasionally, for 30 minutes. (The lentils should be cooked so that they no longer have a crunch, but still hold their form. You should be able to smooth the lentil between your two fingers when pinched.)
2. Once the lentils are done cooking, strain them to remove any excess water and put them into a large bowl. Let cool.
3. Dice the tomatoes and cucumbers, then add them to the lentils.
4. In a small bowl, whisk together the lemon juice, olive oil, and remaining ½ teaspoon salt.
5. Pour the dressing over the lentils and vegetables. Add the feta cheese to the bowl, and gently toss all of the together.

Nutrition: calories: 521 fat: 36g protein: 18g carbs: 35g fiber: 15g sodium: 1304mg

.Quinoa and Garbanzo Salad (Spanish)

Preparation time: 10 minutes Cooking time: 30 minutes Serving: 8

4 cups water	2 cups red or yellow quinoa 2 teaspoons salt, divided
1 cup thinly sliced onions (red or white)	1 (16-ounce / 454-g) can garbanzo beans, rinsed and drained 1/3 cup extra-virgin olive oil
¼ cup lemon juice	1 teaspoon freshly ground black pepper

1. In a 3-quart pot over medium heat, bring the water to a boil.
2. Add the quinoa and 1 teaspoon of salt to the pot. Stir, cover, and let cook over low heat for 15 to 20 minutes.
3. Turn off the heat, fluff the quinoa with a fork, cover again, and let stand for 5 to 10 more minutes.
4. Put the cooked quinoa, onions, and garbanzo beans in a large bowl.
5. In a separate small bowl, whisk together the olive oil, lemon juice, remaining 1 teaspoon of salt, and black pepper.
6. Add the dressing to the quinoa mixture and gently toss everything together. Serve warm or cold.

Nutrition: calories: 318 fat: 6g protein: 9g carbs: 43g fiber: 13g sodium: 585mg

.Mediterranean Salad with Peppers and Tomatoes(Greek)

Prep Time: 35 minutes Cooking Time: 30 minutes Servings: 2

1 eggplant	1 zucchini
1 bell pepper	4 tomatoes
1 onion	4 sprigs of rosemary 6 sprigs of thyme
4 stalks of sage 3 tbsp olive oil	3 tbsp balsamic vinegar salt and pepper

1. Quarter tomatoes. Cut the remaining vegetables into bite-sized pieces, halve the onion and chop it into small pieces. Line a baking sheet with parchment paper, place the vegetables on top, drizzle with olive oil and mix well.
2. Season with salt and pepper. Scatter the herbs over the vegetables. Put the vegetables in the oven and bake at 200 degrees for about 30 minutes.
3. Remove and transfer to a large bowl and mix with olive oil with balsamic vinegar. Season with salt and pepper.
4. Let it draw covered. When the salad is still lukewarm, add the tomato quarters and mix well.
5. Serve the salad lukewarm.

Nutrition: Calories: 355 Carbohydrates: 39.43g Protein: 6.51g Fat: 21.43g

.Israeli Salad (Greek)

Preparation time: 15 minutes Cooking time: 6 minutes Serving: 4

¼ cup pine nuts	¼ cup shelled pistachios
¼ cup coarsely chopped walnuts	¼ cup shelled pumpkin seeds
¼ cup shelled sunflower seeds	2 large English cucumbers, unpeeled and finely chopped 1 pint cherry tomatoes, finely chopped
½ small red onion, finely chopped	½ cup finely chopped fresh flat-leaf Italian parsley
¼ cup extra-virgin olive oil	2 to 3 tablespoons freshly squeezed lemon juice (from 1 lemon) 1 teaspoon salt
¼ teaspoon freshly ground black pepper 4 cups baby arugula	

1. In a large dry skillet, toast the pine nuts, pistachios, walnuts, pumpkin seeds, and sunflower seeds over medium-low heat until golden and fragrant, 5 to 6 minutes, being careful not to burn them. Remove from the heat and set aside.
2. In a large bowl, combine the cucumber, tomatoes, red onion, and parsley.
3. In a small bowl, whisk together olive oil, lemon juice, salt, and pepper. Pour over the chopped vegetables and toss to coat.
4. Add the toasted nuts and seeds and arugula and toss with the salad to blend well. Serve at room temperature or chilled.

Nutrition: calories: 414 fat: 34g protein: 10g carbs: 17g fiber: 6g sodium: 642mg

.Tahini Barley Salad (Italian)

Preparation time: 20 minutes Cooking time: 8 minutes
Serving: 4 to 6

1½ cups pearl barley	5 tablespoons extra-virgin olive oil, divided 1½ teaspoons table salt, for cooking barley
¼ cup tahini	1 teaspoon grated lemon zest plus ¼ cup juice (2 lemons) 1 tablespoon sumac, divided
1 garlic clove, minced 3/4 teaspoon table salt	1 English cucumber, cut into ½-inch pieces 1 carrot, peeled and shredded
1red bell pepper, stemmed, seeded, and chopped 4 scallions, thinly sliced	2tablespoons finely chopped jarred hot cherry peppers
¼ cup coarsely chopped fresh mint	

1. Combine 6 cups water, barley, 1 tablespoon oil, and 1½ teaspoons salt in Instant Pot. Lock lid in place and close pressure release valve. Select high pressure cook function and cook for 8 minutes. Turn off Instant Pot and let pressure release naturally for 15 minutes. Quick-release any remaining pressure, then carefully remove lid, allowing steam to escape away from you. Drain barley, spread onto rimmed baking sheet, and let cool completely, about 15 minutes.
2. Meanwhile, whisk remaining ¼ cup oil, tahini, 2 tablespoons water, lemon zest and juice, 1 teaspoon sumac, garlic, and ¾ teaspoon salt in large bowl until combined; let sit for 15 minutes.
3. Measure out and reserve ½ cup dressing for serving. Add barley, cucumber, carrot, bell pepper, scallions, and cherry peppers to bowl with dressing and gently toss to combine. Season with salt and pepper to taste. Transfer salad to serving dish and sprinkle with mint and remaining 2 teaspoons sumac. Serve, passing reserved dressing separately.

Nutrition: calories: 370 fat: 18g protein: 8g carbs: 47g fiber: 10g sodium: 510mg

.Healthy Detox Salad (Italian)

Preparation Time: 5 minutes Cooking Time: 0 minutes
Servings: 4

4 cups mixed greens 2 tbsp lemon juice	2 tbsp pumpkin seed oil 1 tbsp chia seeds
2 tbsp almonds, chopped 1 large apple, diced	1 large carrot, coarsely grated 1 large beet, coarsely grated

1. In a medium salad bowl, except for mixed greens, combine all thoroughly.
2. Into 4 salad plates, divide the mixed greens.
3. Evenly top mixed greens with the salad bowl mixture.
4. Serve and enjoy.

Nutrition: Calories: 141; Protein: 2.1g; Carbs: 14.7g; Fat: 8.2g

.Herbed Chicken Salad Greek Style (Greek)

Prep Time: 5 minutes Cooking Time: 0 minutes Servings: 6

¼ cup or 1 oz crumbled feta cheese

½ tsp garlic powder

½ tsp salt

¾ tsp black pepper, divided 1 cup grape tomatoes, halved

1 cup peeled and chopped English cucumbers 1 cup plain fat-free yogurt

1-pound skinless, boneless chicken breast, cut into 1-inch cubes 1 tsp bottled minced garlic

1tsp ground oregano

2tsp sesame seed paste or tahini 5 tsp fresh lemon juice, divided 6 pitted kalamata olives, halved 8 cups chopped romaine lettuce Cooking spray

1. In a bowl, mix together ¼ tsp salt, ½ tsp pepper, garlic powder and oregano. Then on medium-high heat, place a skillet and coat with cooking spray and sauté the spice mixture and chicken until chicken is cooked. Before transferring to bowl, drizzle with juice.
2. In a small bowl, mix thoroughly the following: garlic, tahini, yogurt, ¼ tsp pepper, ¼ tsp salt, and 2 tsp juice.
3. In another bowl, mix olives, tomatoes, cucumber and lettuce.
4. To serve salad, place 2 ½ cups of lettuce mixture on a plate, topped with
1. ½ cup chicken mixture, 3 tbsp yogurt mixture and 1 tbsp of cheese.

Nutrition: Calories: 170.1; Fat: 3.7g; Protein: 20.7g; Carbs: 13.5g

.Mediterranean Potato Salad with Beans (Greek)

Preparation Time: 30 minutes Cooking Time: 15 minutes Servings: 4

500g potatoes 300g green beans 1 tbsp rosemary

8 sun-dried tomatoes 40g bacon

3 tbsp red wine vinegar 200g olives

1 egg yolk

salt and pepper

1. Wash green beans, break into short pieces and boil in salted water for about 10 minutes, then drain in a colander. Collect some boiled bean water.
2. Drain the tomatoes and cut into small pieces. Collect some tomato oil. Chop the rosemary and cut the bacon into thin strips. Fry bacon with chopped rosemary in olive oil and tomato oil in a pan. Pour in the vinegar and the bean water and add the tomato pieces. Heat the potatoes and beans, let them steep and wait until they have cooled down. Then pour off using a sieve and collect the vinaigrette. Mix the potato salad with the olives.
3. Whisk the vinaigrette with egg yolk and then heat gently, stirring constantly, until the sauce thickens. Season with salt and pepper and pour over the salad. Let it steep for an hour. Finished! Serve and enjoy.

Nutrition: Calories: 237 Carbohydrates: 29.02g Protein: 5.81g Fat: 12.26g

.Vegetable Patch Salad (Spanish)

Preparation Time: 10 minutes Cooking Time: 30 minutes Servings: 6

1 bunch cauliflower, cut into florets 1 zucchini, sliced

1sweet potato, peeled and cubed 1/2 pounds baby carrots

Salt and pepper to taste 1 teaspoon dried basil 2 red onions, sliced

2eggplants, cubed

1 endive, sliced

3 tablespoons extra-virgin olive oil 1 lemon, juiced

1tablespoon balsamic vinegar

1. Preheat oven to 350°F. Mix together all vegetables, basil, salt, pepper, and oil in a baking dish and cook for 25-30 minutes.
2. After cooked, pour into a salad bowl and stir in vinegar and lemon juice.
3. Dish up and serve.

Nutrition: Calories: 115 Fat: 9 g Fiber: 85 g Carbs: 11 g Protein: 15 g

.Cashews and Red Cabbage Salad (Greek)

Preparation Time: 10 minutes
Cooking Time: 0 minutes Servings: 4

1-pound red cabbage, shredded

1tablespoons coriander, chopped 1/2 cup cashews halved

2 tablespoons olive oil 1 tomato, cubed

A pinch of salt and black pepper 1 tablespoon white vinegar

1. Mix the cabbage with the coriander and the rest of the in a salad bowl, toss, and serve cold.

Nutrition: Calories: 210 Fat: 6.3 g Protein: 8g

.Authentic Greek Salad (Greek)

Preparation time: 10 minutes Cooking time: 0 minutes Serving: 4

2 large English cucumbers 4 Roma tomatoes, quartered

1 green bell pepper, cut into 1- to 1½-inch chunks

¼ small red onion, thinly sliced

4 ounces (113 g) pitted Kalamata olives

¼ cup extra-virgin olive oil

2 tablespoons freshly squeezed lemon juice 1 tablespoon red wine vinegar

1 tablespoon chopped fresh oregano or 1 teaspoon dried oregano

¼ teaspoon freshly ground black pepper

4 ounces (113 g) crumbled traditional feta cheese

1. Cut the cucumbers in half lengthwise and then into ½-inch-thick half- moons. Place in a large bowl.
2. Add the quartered tomatoes, bell pepper, red onion, and olives.
3. In a small bowl, whisk together the olive oil, lemon juice, vinegar, oregano, and pepper. Drizzle over the vegetables and toss to coat.
4. Divide between salad plates and top each with 1 ounce (28 g) of feta.

Nutrition: calories: 278 fat: 22g protein: 8g carbs: 12g fiber: 4g sodium: 572mg

.Mediterranean Chicken Salad (Greek)

Preparation Time: 5 minutes Cooking Time: 25 minutes Servings: 4

For Chicken:

1 ¾ lb. boneless, skinless chicken breast	¼ teaspoon each of pepper and salt (or as desired) 1 ½ tablespoon of butter, melted
For Mediterranean salad:	1 cup of sliced cucumber
6 cups of romaine lettuce that is torn or roughly chopped 10 pitted Kalamata olives	1 pint of cherry tomatoes
1/3 cup of reduced-fat feta cheese	¼ teaspoon each of pepper and salt (or lesser)
1 small lemon juice (it should be about 2 tablespoons)	

1. Preheat your oven or grill to about 350F. Season the chicken with salt, butter, and black pepper. Roast or grill chicken until it reaches an internal temperature of 1650F in about 25 minutes.
2. Once your chicken breasts are cooked, remove them and keep aside to rest for about 5 minutes before you slice them.
3. Combine all the salad you have and toss everything together very well. Serve the chicken with Mediterranean salad.

Nutrition: Calories: 340 Protein: 45g Carbohydrate: 9g Fat: 4 g

.Minty Olives and Tomatoes Salad (Italian)

Preparation Time: 10 minutes Cooking Time: 0 minutes Servings: 4

1 cup kalamata olives 1 cup black olives	1 cup cherry tomatoes 4 tomatoes
1 red onion, chopped	2 tablespoons oregano, chopped 1 tablespoon mint, chopped
2 tablespoons balsamic vinegar	¼ cup olive oil
2 teaspoons Italian herbs, dried	

1. In a salad bowl, mix the olives with the tomatoes and the rest of the , toss, and serve cold.

Nutrition: 190 Calories 8.1g Fat 4.6g Protein

.Beans and Cucumber Salad (Italian)

Preparation Time: 10 minutes Cooking Time: 0 minutes Servings: 4

15 oz canned great northern beans 2 tablespoons olive oil	½ cup baby arugula 1 cup cucumber
1 tablespoon parsley	2 tomatoes, cubed
2 tablespoon balsamic vinegar	

1. Mix the beans with the cucumber and the rest of the in a large bowl, toss and serve cold.

Nutrition: 233 Calories 9g Fat 8g protein

.Lentil Salmon Salad (Greek)

Preparation Time: 25 minutes Cooking Time: 25 minutes Servings: 4

2 cups vegetable stock 1 rinsed green lentil	1 chopped red onion
1/2 cup chopped parsley	4 ounces shredded smoked salmon 2 tablespoons chopped cilantro
1 chopped red pepper 1 lemon, juiced	Salt and pepper to taste

1. Cook vegetable stock and lentils in a saucepan for 15 to 20 minutes, on low heat. Ensure all liquid has been absorbed and then remove from heat.
2. Pour into a salad bowl and top with red pepper, parsley, cilantro, salt and pepper (to suit your taste) and mix.
3. Mix in lemon juice and shredded salmon.
4. This salad should be served fresh.

Nutrition: Calories: 260 Fat: 2 g Fiber: 8 g Carbs: 17 g Protein: 11 g

.Peppy Pepper Tomato Salad (Greek)

Preparation Time: 20 minutes Cooking Time: 20 minutes Servings: 4

1 yellow bell pepper, cored and diced 4 cucumbers, diced	1 red onion, chopped
1 tablespoon balsamic vinegar	2 tablespoons extra-virgin olive oil 4 diced tomatoes
2 cored and diced red bell peppers 1 pinch chili flakes	Salt and pepper to taste

1. Merge all the above in a salad bowl, except salt and pepper.
2. Season with salt and pepper to suit your taste and mix well.
3. Eat while fresh.

Nutrition: Calories: 260 Fat: 2 g Fiber: 8 g Carbs: 17 g Protein: 11 g

.Chopped Israeli Mediterranean Pasta Salad(Greek)

Preparation Time: 15 minutes Cooking Time: 2 minutes Servings: 8

Small bow tie or other small pasta (.5 lb.) 1/3 cup Cucumber	1/3 cup Radish 1/3 cup Tomato
1/3 cup yellow bell pepper	1/3 cup green olives 1/3 cup red onions 1/3 cup Pepperoncini 1/3 cup Feta cheese
1/3 cup orange bell pepper	
1/3 cup Black olives	
1/3 cup Fresh thyme leaves Dried oregano (1 tsp.) Dressing:	0.25 cup + more, olive oil juice of 1 lemon

1. Slice the green olives into halves. Dice the feta and pepperoncini. Finely dice the remainder of the veggies.
2. Prepare a pot of water with the salt, and simmer the pasta until it's al dente (checking at two minutes under the listed time). Rinse and drain in cold water.
3. Combine a small amount of oil with the pasta. Add the salt, pepper, oregano, thyme, and veggies. Pour in the rest of the oil, lemon juice, mix and fold in the grated feta.
4. Pop it into the fridge within two hours, best if overnight. Taste test and adjust the seasonings to your liking; add fresh thyme.

Nutrition: 65 Calories 5.6g Fats 0.8g Protein

.Feta Tomato Salad (Spanish)

Preparation Time: 5 minutes Cooking Time: 0 minutes
Servings: 4

Balsamic vinegar (2 tbsp.)	Freshly minced basil (1.5 tsp.) or Dried (.5 tsp.) Salt (.5 tsp.)
Coarsely chopped sweet onion (.5 cup) Olive oil (2 tbsp.)	Cherry or grape tomatoes (1 lb.) Crumbled feta cheese (.25 cup.)

1. Whisk the salt, basil, and vinegar. Toss the onion into the vinegar mixture for 5 minutes
2. Slice the tomatoes into halves and stir in the tomatoes, feta cheese, and oil to serve.

Nutrition: 121 Calories 9g Fats 3g Protein

.Greek Pasta Salad (Greek)

Preparation Time: 5 minutes Cooking Time: 11 minutes
Servings: 4

Penne pasta (1 cup) Lemon juice (1.5 tsp.) Red wine vinegar (2 tbsp.) Garlic (1 clove)	Dried oregano (1 tsp.)
Black pepper and sea salt (as desired) Olive oil (.33 cup)	Halved cherry tomatoes (5) Red onion (half of 1 small)
Green & red bell pepper (half of 1 - each) Cucumber (¼ of 1)	Black olives (.25 cup) Crumbled feta cheese (.25 cup)

1. Slice the cucumber and olives. Chop/dice the onion, peppers, and garlic. Slice the tomatoes into halves.
2. Arrange a large pot with water and salt using the high-temperature setting. Once it's boiling, add the pasta and cook for 11 minutes. Rinse it using cold water and drain in a colander.
3. Whisk the oil, juice, salt, pepper, vinegar, oregano, and garlic. Combine the cucumber, cheese, olives, peppers, pasta, onions, and tomatoes in a large salad dish.
4. Add the vinaigrette over the pasta and toss. Chill in the fridge (covered) for about three hours and serve as desired.

Nutrition: 307 Calories 23.6g Fat 5.4g Protein

.Pork and Greens Salad (Greek)

Preparation Time: 10 minutes Cooking Time: 15 minutes
Servings: 4

1-pound pork chops	8 ounces white mushrooms, sliced
½ cup Italian dressing	6 cups mixed salad greens
6 ounces jarred artichoke hearts, drained Salt and black pepper to the taste	½ cup basil, chopped 1 tablespoon olive oil

1. Heat a pan with the oil over medium-high heat, add the pork, and brown for 5 minutes.
2. Add the mushrooms, stir, and sauté for 5 minutes more.
3. Add the dressing, artichokes, salad greens, salt, pepper, and basil, cook for 4-5 minutes, divide everything into bowls and serve.

Nutrition: 235 Calories 6g Fat 11g Protein

.Mediterranean Tortellini Salad (Italian)

Preparation Time: 30 minutes Cooking Time: 12 minutes
Servings: 6

500g tortellini	300g dried tomatoes 2 onions
3 tbsp olive oil	3 tbsp white wine vinegar 1 teaspoon thyme

salt and pepper 200g rocket

1. Cook the tortellini, drain and set aside.
2. Chop the onions and sauté them in olive oil with the thyme. Add the chopped sun-dried tomatoes and fry for about 2 minutes. Then add the tortellini and remove the pan from the heat.
3. Season to taste with salt, pepper and white wine vinegar. Finally add the tomatoes and rocket. Finished! Serve and enjoy.

Nutrition: Calories: 343 Carbohydrates: 45.03g Protein: 12.35g Fat: 12.93g

.Arugula Salad (Greek)

Preparation Time: 5 minutes Cooking Time: 0 minutes
Servings: 4

Arugula leaves (4 cups) Cherry tomatoes (1 cup) Pine nuts (.25 cup)	Rice vinegar (1 tbsp.) Olive/grapeseed oil (2 tbsp.) Grated parmesan cheese (.25 cup) Black pepper & salt (as desired) Large sliced avocado (1)

1. Peel and slice the avocado. Rinse and dry the arugula leaves, grate the cheese, and slice the cherry tomatoes into halves.
2. Combine the arugula, pine nuts, tomatoes, oil, vinegar, salt, pepper, and cheese.
3. Toss the salad to mix and portion it onto plates with the avocado slices to serve.

Nutrition: 257 Calories 23g Fats 6.1g Protein

.Orzo Olive Salad (Italian)

Preparation Time: 180 minutes Cooking Time: 10 minutes
Servings: 4

250g orzo	100g cocktail tomatoes 100g olives
onion	½ bunch of parsley 250g feta cheese For the dressing
1lemon, squeezed salt and pepper 30ml olive oil	2cloves of garlic

1. Cook the pasta for about 10 minutes according to the instructions on the packet. Wash and halve cocktail tomatoes, core the olives, peel and chop the onion, crumble the feta.
2. For the dressing: lemon juice, olive oil, garlic, salt and pepper mixed together.
3. Mix the Orzo together with the dressing and finally add the remaining. Finished. Serve and enjoy.

Nutrition: Calories: 302 Carbohydrates: 25.76g Protein: 13.3g Fat: 17.63g

.Bean and Toasted Pita Salad (Spanish)

Prep Time: 15 minutes Cooking Time: 10 minutes Servings: 4

1tbsp chopped fresh mint	3 tbsp chopped fresh parsley 1 cup crumbled feta cheese 1 cup sliced romaine lettuce
½ cucumber, peeled and sliced 1 cup diced plum tomatoes	2cups cooked pinto beans, well-drained and slightly warmed Pepper to taste
3tbsp extra virgin olive oil	2 tbsp ground toasted cumin seeds 2 tbsp fresh lemon juice
1/8 tsp salt 2 6-inch whole-wheat pita bread, cut or torn into bite-sized pieces	2 cloves garlic, peeled

1. In a large baking sheet, spread torn pita bread and bake in a preheated 400oF oven for 6 minutes.
2. With the back of a knife, mash garlic and salt until paste-like. Add into a medium bowl.
3. Whisk in ground cumin and lemon juice. In a steady and slow stream, pour oil as you whisk continuously. Season with pepper.
4. In a large salad bowl, mix cucumber, tomatoes, and beans. Pour in dressing, toss to coat well.
5. Add mint, parsley, feta, lettuce, and toasted pita, toss to mix once again, and serve.

Nutrition: Calories: 427 Carbohydrates: 47.3g Protein: 17.7g Fat: 20.4g

.Salad With Pine Nuts and Mozzarella (Greek)

Prep Time: 20 minutes Cooking Time: 0 minutes Servings: 2

300g mini mozzarella 100g cocktail tomatoes 40g pine nuts	80g rocket
150g mixed salad	2 teaspoons of olive oil
2 teaspoons of red wine vinegar	1 teaspoon mustard
2 teaspoons of balsamic vinegar	
4 tbsp olive oil	
1tbsp yogurt salt and pepper	

1. Drain the mozzarella. Thoroughly clean and spin lettuce and rocket. Quarter the cherry tomatoes and put everything in a salad bowl.
2. For the dressing: Mix the red wine vinegar, balsamic vinegar, olive oil, mustard and yogurt together. Season with salt and pepper and mix everything with the salad.
3. Then add the pine nuts. Finished! Serve and enjoy.

Nutrition: Calories: 1324 Carbohydrates: 43.69g Protein: 21.88g Fat: 120.18g

.One Bowl Spinach Salad (Spanish)

Prep Time: 10 minutes Cooking Time: 20 minutes Servings: 4

2 red beets, cooked and diced	1 tablespoon apple cider vinegar 3 cups baby spinach
1/4 cup Greek yogurt	1 tablespoon horseradish Salt and pepper to taste

1. Mix beets and spinach in a salad bowl.
2. Add in yogurt, horseradish, and vinegar. You can also add salt and pepper if you wish.
3. Serve the salad as soon as mixed.

Nutrition: Calories: 112 Fat: 11 g Fiber: 8 g Carbs: 10 g Protein: 12 g

.Olive and Red Bean Salad (Italian)

Preparation Time: 10 minutes Cooking Time: 20 minutes Servings: 4

1red onions, sliced	2 garlic cloves, minced
2 tablespoons balsamic vinegar 1/4 cup green olives, sliced Salt and pepper to taste	2 cups mixed greens
1can red beans, drained 1 pinch chili flakes	2tablespoons extra-virgin olive oil 2 tablespoons parsley, chopped

1. In a salad bowl, mix all
2. Season with salt and pepper, if desired, and serve right away.

Nutrition: Calories: 112 Fat: 11 g Fiber: 8 g Carbs: 10 g Protein: 12g

.Fresh and Light Cabbage Salad (Italian)

Preparation Time: 10 minutes Cooking Time: 25 minutes Servings: 4

1tablespoon mint, chopped 1/2 teaspoon ground coriander 1 savoy cabbage, shredded 1/2 cup Greek yogurt	1/4 teaspoon cumin seeds
2tablespoons extra-virgin olive oil 1 carrot, grated	1 red onion, sliced 1 teaspoon honey
1teaspoon lemon zest	2tablespoons lemon juice Salt and pepper to taste

1. In a salad bowl, mix all .
2. You can add salt and pepper to suit your taste and then mix again.
3. This salad is best when cool and freshly made.

Nutrition: Calories: 112 Fat: 11 g Fiber: 8 g Carbs: 10 g Protein: 12g

.Mediterranean Salad with Feta (Spanish)

Preparation Time: 15 minutes Cooking Time: 0 minutes Servings: 2

200g feta cheese	200g cocktail tomatoes 50g almond slivers 100g mixed salad
2tbsp red wine vinegar 1 tbsp raspberry vinegar 1 tbsp green pesto	3tbsp olive oil
1teaspoon mustard salt and pepper	

1. Drain and dice the feta. Clean the lettuce and spin dry. Quarter the cherry tomatoes and place everything in a salad bowl.
2. Mix red wine vinegar, raspberry vinegar, olive oil, mustard and pesto. Season with salt and pepper and pour over the salad.
3. Finally add the almond slivers. Finished! Serve and enjoy.

Nutrition: Calories:959Carbohydrates:15.44gProtein:21.45g Fat: 91.88g

.Tomato and Cucumber Salad with Feta (Spanish)

Preparation Time: 10 minutes Cooking Time: 0 minutes
Servings: 4

1tomatoes	½ cucumber
½ bunch of spring onions	6 tbsp olive oil
200g feta	
3 tbsp balsamic vinegar salt and pepper	

1. Thoroughly clean the tomatoes and cucumber. Eight tomatoes. Cut the cucumber into thin slices. Cut the spring onion into thin rings. Chop the herbs. Dice the feta.
2. Put all in a salad bowl. Add oil and balsamic vinegar, season with salt and pepper and mix well. Done! Serve and enjoy.

Nutrition: Calories: 341 Carbohydrates: 8.28g Protein: 8.-6g Fat: 31.09g

.Couscous Arugula Salad (Greek)

Preparation Time: 15 minutes Cooking Time: 20 minutes
Servings: 4

1/2 cup couscous	1 cup vegetable stock
1 bunch, peeled asparagus 1 lemon, juiced	1 teaspoon dried tarragon 2 cups arugula
Salt and pepper to taste	

1. Heat the vegetable stock in a pot until hot. Remove from heat and add in the couscous. Cover until the couscous has absorbed all the stock.
2. Pour in a bowl and fluff with a fork and then set aside to cool.
3. Peel asparagus with a vegetable peeler, making them into ribbons and put into a bowl with couscous.
4. Merge the remaining and add salt and pepper to suit your taste.
5. Serve the salad immediately.

Nutrition: Calories: 100 Fat: 6 g Fiber: 13 g Carbs: 25 g Protein: 10g

.Spinach and Grilled Feta Salad (Spanish)

Preparation Time: 10 minutes Cooking Time: 25 minutes
Servings: 4

8 ounces feta cheese, sliced	2 garlic cloves, minced
1/4 cup black olives, sliced	
1/4 cup green olives, sliced 4 cups baby spinach	
1teaspoon capers, chopped	2tablespoons extra-virgin olive oil 1 tablespoon red wine vinegar

1. Grill feta cheese slices over medium to high flame until brown on both sides.
2. In a salad bowl, mix green olives, black olives, and spinach.
3. In a separate bowl, mix vinegar, capers, and oil together to make a dressing.
4. Top salad with the dressing and cheese, and it is ready to serve.

Nutrition: Calories: 100 Fat: 6 g Fiber: 13 g Carbs: 25 g Protein: 10g

.Creamy Cool Salad (Greek)

Preparation Time: 10 minutes Cooking Time: 25 minutes
Servings: 4

1/2 cup Greek yogurt	2 tablespoons dill, chopped 1 teaspoon lemon juice
4 cucumbers, diced	2garlic cloves, minced Salt and pepper to taste

1. Mix all in a salad bowl.
2. Season with salt and pepper to suit your taste and eat.

Nutrition: Calories: 115 Fat: 9 g Fiber: 10 g Carbs: 21 g Protein: 9 g

.Apples and Pomegranate Salad (Greek)

Preparation Time: 10 minutes Cooking Time: 0 minutes
Servings: 4

2big apples, cored and cubed	3 cups baby arugula
1 cup pomegranate seeds	
1 cup walnuts, chopped 1 tablespoon olive oil	1teaspoon white sesame seeds
2tablespoons apple cider vinegar	

1. Mix the apples with the arugula and the rest of the in a bowl, toss, and serve cold.

Nutrition: Calories: 160 Fat: 4.3 g Protein: 10 g

.Cranberry Bulgur Mix (Greek)

Preparation Time: 10 minutes Cooking Time: 0 minutes
Servings: 4

1 1/2 cups hot water 1 cup bulgur	Juice of 1/2 lemon
4 tablespoons cilantro, chopped 1/2 cup cranberries	1 1/2 teaspoons curry powder 1/4 cup green onions
1/2 cup red bell peppers 1/2 cup carrots, grated 1 tablespoon olive oil	

1. Put bulgur into a bowl, add the water, stir, cover, leave aside for 10 minutes, fluff, and transfer to a bowl. Merge the rest of the , toss, and serve cold.

Nutrition: Calories: 300 Fat: 6.4 g Protein: 13 g

.Chickpeas Corn and Black Beans Salad (Greek)

Preparation Time: 10 minutes Cooking Time: 0 minutes
Servings: 4

1 1/2 cups black beans	1/2 teaspoon garlic powder 2 teaspoons chili powder
1 1/2 cups canned chickpeas 1 cup baby spinach	1avocado, pitted, peeled, and chopped 1 cup corn kernels, chopped
2tablespoons lemon juice 1 tablespoon olive oil	1tablespoon apple cider vinegar 1 teaspoon chives, chopped

1. Mix the black beans with the garlic powder, chili powder, and the rest of the in a bowl, toss and serve cold.

Nutrition: Calories: 300 Fat: 13.4 g Protein: 13 g

.Lime Spinach and Chickpeas Salad (Italian)

Prep Time: 10 minutes Cooking Time: 0 minutes Servings: 4

16 ounces canned chickpeas   2 tablespoons olive oil
2 cups baby spinach leaves
1/2 tablespoon lime juice
1 teaspoon cumin, ground
1/2 teaspoon chili flakes

1. Mix the chickpeas with the spinach and the rest of the in a large bowl, toss, and serve cold.

Nutrition: Calories: 240 Fat: 8.2 g Protein: 12 g

.Grilled Vegetable Salad (Greek)

Prep Time: 5 minutes Cooking Time: 7 minutes Servings: 3

¼ cup extra virgin olive oil, for brushing	¼ cup fresh basil leaves
¼ lb. feta cheese	½ bunch asparagus, trimmed and cut into bite-size pieces 1 medium onion, cut into ½ inch rings
1-pint cherry tomatoes	1 red bell pepper, quartered, seeds and ribs removed

1yellow bell pepper, quartered, seeds and ribs removed Pepper and salt to taste

1. Toss olive oil and vegetables in a big bowl. Season with salt and pepper.
2. Frill vegetables in a preheated griller for 5-7 minutes or until charred and tender.
3. Transfer veggies to a platter, add feta and basil.
4. In a separate small bowl, mix olive oil, balsamic vinegar, garlic seasoned with pepper and salt.
5. Drizzle dressing over vegetables and serve.

Nutrition: Calories: 147.6; Protein: 3.8g; Fat: 19.2g; Carbs: 13.9 g

.Mediterranean Salad with Parsnips and Peppers(Greek)

Preparation Time: 15 minutes Cooking Time: 1 hour Servings: 2

1 parsnips	1 bell pepper
1 clove of garlic 50g dried tomatoes	1tbsp balsamic vinegar Basil and chili flakes salt and pepper

olive oil

1. Peel the parsnips and cut into thin slices and cook in a saucepan with a little water for about 5 minutes.
2. Clean, core and dice the peppers.
3. Heat olive oil in a pan and fry the chopped peppers and parsnip slices.
4. Peel and chop the garlic and add to the vegetables in the pan. Season to taste with chili flakes, basil, pepper and salt. As soon as the pepper cubes and the parsnip slices are golden brown, put all the in a bowl and mix the whole thing with the balsamic vinegar.
5. Finished! Serve and enjoy.

Nutrition: Calories: 32 Carbohydrates: 7.01g Protein: 1.21g Fat: 0.17g

.Grilled Salmon Summer Salad (Greek)

Preparation Time: 10 minutes Cooking Time: 30 minutes Servings: 4

1salmon fillets	Salt and pepper to taste 2 cups vegetable stock 1/2 cup bulgur
1 cup cherry tomatoes, halved 1/2 cup sweet corn	1 lemon, juiced
1/2 cup green olives, sliced 1 cucumber, cubed	1 green onion, chopped 1 red pepper, chopped
1 red bell pepper, cored and diced	

1. Heat a grill pan on medium and then place salmon on, seasoning with salt and pepper. Grill, both sides of the salmon, until brown and set aside.
2. Heat stock in a saucepan until hot and then add in bulgur and cook until liquid is completely soaked into bulgur.
3. Mix salmon, bulgur, and all other in a salad bowl, and again add salt and pepper, if desired, to suit your taste.
4. Serve the salad as soon as completed.

Nutrition: Calories: 110 Fat: 13 g Fiber: 7 g Carbs: 13 g Protein: 18g

.Broccoli Salad with Caramelized Onions (Italian)

Preparation Time: 10 minutes Cooking Time: 25 minutes Servings: 4

3 tablespoons extra-virgin olive oil 2 red onions, sliced 2tablespoons balsamic vinegar 1-pound broccoli, cut into florets Salt and pepper to taste	1teaspoon dried thyme

1. Heat the oil and add in sliced onions. Cook until the onions are caramelized. Stir in vinegar and thyme, and then remove from the stove.
2. Mix together the broccoli and onion mixture in a bowl, adding salt and pepper if desired. Serve and eat salad as soon as possible.

Nutrition: Calories: 113 Fat: 9 g Fiber: 8 g Carbs: 13 g Protein: 18 g

.Olives and Lentils Salad (Greek)

Preparation Time: 10 minutes Cooking Time: 0 minutes Servings: 2

1/3 cup canned green lentils 1 tablespoon olive oil	1cups baby spinach 1 cup black olives
2 tablespoons sunflower seeds 1 tablespoon Dijon mustard	2 tablespoons balsamic vinegar 2 tablespoons olive oil

1. Mix the lentils with the spinach, olives, and the rest of the in a salad bowl, toss and serve cold.

Nutrition: Calories: 279 Fat: 6.5 g Protein: 12 g

.Chicken and Cabbage Salad (Italian)

Prep Time: 10 minutes Cooking Time: 6 minutes Servings: 4

1medium chicken breasts 4 ounces green cabbage	5 tablespoon extra-virgin olive oil Salt and black pepper to taste
2 tablespoons sherry vinegar tablespoon chives	¼ cup feta cheese, crumbled
¼ cup barbeque sauce	Bacon slices, cooked and crumbled

1. In a bowl, mix 4 tablespoon oils with vinegar, salt and pepper to taste and stir well.
2. Add the shredded cabbage, toss to coat, and leave aside for now.
3. Season chicken with salt and pepper, heat a pan with remaining oil over medium-high heat, add chicken, cook for 6 minutes, take off heat, transfer to a bowl and mix well with barbeque sauce.
4. Arrange salad on serving plates, add chicken strips, sprinkle cheese, chives, and crumbled bacon, and serve right away.

Nutrition: 200 Calories 15g Fat 33g Protein

.Roasted Broccoli Salad (Italian)

Preparation Time: 9 minutes Cooking Time: 17 minutes Servings: 4

1 lb. broccoli	3 tablespoons olive oil, divided 1-pint cherry tomatoes
1 ½ teaspoons honey	3 cups cubed bread, whole grain 1 tablespoon balsamic vinegar
½ teaspoon black pepper	¼ teaspoon sea salt, fine grated parmesan for serving

1. Set the oven to 450, and then place a rimmed baking sheet.
2. Drizzle your broccoli with a tablespoon of oil, and toss to coat.
3. Take out from the oven, and spoon the broccoli. Leave oil at the bottom of the bowl and add in your tomatoes, toss to coat, then mix tomatoes with a tablespoon of honey. place on the same baking sheet.
4. Roast for fifteen minutes, and stir halfway through your cooking time.
5. Add in your bread, and then roast for three more minutes.
6. Whisk two tablespoons of oil, vinegar, and remaining honey. Season. Pour this over your broccoli mix to serve.

Nutrition: 226 Calories 7g Protein 12g Fat

.Tomato Salad (Spanish)

Preparation Time: 22 minutes Cooking Time: 0 minute Servings: 4

1 cucumber, sliced	¼ cup sun-dried tomatoes, chopped 1 lb. tomatoes, cubed
½ cup black olives 1 red onion, sliced	1 tablespoon balsamic vinegar
¼ cup parsley, fresh & chopped 2 tablespoons olive oil	

1. Get out a bowl and combine all your vegetables. To make your dressing mix all your seasoning, olive oil, and vinegar.
2. Toss with your salad and serve fresh.

Nutrition: 126 Calories 2.1g Protein 9.2g Fat

.Feta Beet Salad (Spanish)

Preparation Time: 16 minutes Cooking Time: 0 minute Servings: 4

6 Red Beets, Cooked & Peeled 3 Ounces Feta Cheese, Cubed 2 Tablespoons Olive Oil	2 Tablespoons Balsamic Vinegar

1. Combine everything, and then serve.

Nutrition: 230 Calories 7.3g Protein 12g Fat

.Chickpea Salad (Greek)

Preparation Time: 15 minutes
Cooking Time: 0 minutes Servings: 4

Cooked chickpeas (15 oz.) Diced Roma tomato (1)	Diced green medium bell pepper (half of 1) Fresh parsley (1 tbsp.)
Small white onion (1) Minced garlic (.5 tsp.) Lemon (1 juiced)	

1. Chop the tomato, green pepper, and onion. Mince the garlic. Combine each of the fixings into a salad bowl and toss well.
2. Cover the salad to chill for at least 15 minutes in the fridge. Serve when ready.

Nutrition: 163 Calories 7g Fats 4g Protein

.Baked Cauliflower Mixed Salad (Greek)

Preparation Time: 10 minutes Cooking Time: 30 minutes Servings: 4

2 tablespoons extra-virgin olive oil 1 teaspoon dried mint	1teaspoon dried oregano
2tablespoons chopped parsley 1 red pepper, chopped	1 lemon, juiced
1green onion, chopped	2tablespoons chopped cilantro Salt and pepper to taste

1. Heat oven to 350°F.
2. In a deep baking pan, combine olive oil, mint, cauliflower, and oregano, then bake for 15 minutes.
3. Once cooked, pour into a salad bowl, and add the remaining, stirring together.
4. Plate the salad and eat fresh and warm.

Nutrition: Calories: 123 Fat: 13 g Fiber: 9 g Carbs: 10 g Protein: 12.5 g

Chapter 4
Sandwiches, Pizzas, and Wraps

Falafel Balls with Tahini Sauce

Prep time: 2 hours 20 minutes | Cook time: 20 minutes | Serves 4

Tahini Sauce:
½ cup tahini
2 tablespoons lemon juice
¼ cup finely chopped flat-leaf parsley
2 cloves garlic, minced
½ cup cold water, as needed
Falafel:
1 cup dried chickpeas, soaked overnight, drained
¼ cup chopped flat-leaf parsley
¼ cup chopped cilantro
1 large onion, chopped
1 teaspoon cumin
½ teaspoon chili flakes
4 cloves garlic
1 teaspoon sea salt
5 tablespoons almond flour
1½ teaspoons baking soda, dissolved in 1 teaspoon water
2 cups peanut oil
1 medium bell pepper, chopped
1 medium tomato, chopped
4 whole-wheat pita breads

Make the Tahini Sauce
1. Combine the for the tahini sauce in a small bowl. Stir to mix well until smooth.
2. Wrap the bowl in plastic and refrigerate until ready to serve.

Make the Falafel
3. Put the chickpeas, parsley, cilantro, onion, cumin, chili flakes, garlic, and salt in a food processor. Pulse to mix well but not puréed.
4. Add the flour and baking soda to the food processor, then pulse to form a smooth and tight dough.
5. Put the dough in a large bowl and wrap in plastic. Refrigerate for at least 2 hours to let it rise.
6. Divide and shape the dough into walnut-sized small balls.
7. Pour the peanut oil in a large pot and heat over high heat until the temperature of the oil reaches 375°F (190°C).
8. Drop 6 balls into the oil each time, and fry for 5 minutes or until golden brown and crispy. Turn the balls with a strainer to make them fried evenly.
9. Transfer the balls on paper towels with the strainer, then drain the oil from the balls.
10. Roast the pita breads in the oven for 5 minutes or until golden brown, if needed, then stuff the pitas with falafel balls and top with bell peppers and tomatoes. Drizzle with tahini sauce and serve immediately.

Per Serving
calories: 574 | fat: 27.1g | protein: 19.8g | carbs: 69.7g | fiber: 13.4g | sodium: 1246mg

Glazed Mushroom and Vegetable Fajitas

Prep time: 20 minutes | Cook time: 20 minutes | Makes 6

Spicy Glazed Mushrooms:
1 teaspoon olive oil
1 (10- to 12-ounce / 284- to 340-g) package cremini mushrooms, rinsed and drained, cut into thin slices
to 1 teaspoon chili powder
Sea salt and freshly ground black pepper, to taste
1 teaspoon maple syrup
Fajitas:
2 teaspoons olive oil
1 onion, chopped
Sea salt, to taste
1 bell pepper, any color, deseeded and sliced into long strips
1 zucchini, cut into large matchsticks
6 whole-grain tortilla
2 carrots, grated
3 to 4 scallions, sliced
½ cup fresh cilantro, finely chopped

Make the Spicy Glazed Mushrooms
1. Heat the olive oil in a nonstick skillet over medium heat until shimmering.
2. Add the mushrooms and sauté for 10 minutes or until tender.
3. Sprinkle the mushrooms with chili powder, salt, and ground black pepper. Drizzle with maple syrup. Stir to mix well and cook for 5 to 7 minutes or until the mushrooms are glazed. Set aside until ready to use.

Make the Fajitas
4. Heat the olive oil in the same skillet over medium heat until shimmering.
5. Add the onion and sauté for 5 minutes or until translucent. Sprinkle with salt.
6. Add the bell pepper and zucchini and sauté for 7 minutes or until tender.
7. Meanwhile, toast the tortilla in the oven for 5 minutes or until golden brown.
8. Allow the tortilla to cool for a few minutes until they can be handled, then assemble the tortilla with glazed mushrooms, sautéed vegetables and remaining vegetables to make the fajitas. Serve immediately.

Per Serving
calories: 403 | fat: 14.8g | protein: 11.2g | carbs: 7.9g | fiber: 7.0g | sodium: 230mg

Cheesy Fig Pizzas with Garlic Oil

Prep time: 1 day 40 minutes | Cook time: 10 minutes | Makes 2 pizzas

Dough:
1 cup almond flour
1½ cups whole-wheat flour
¾ teaspoon instant or rapid-rise yeast
2 teaspoons raw honey
1¼ cups ice water
2 tablespoons extra-virgin olive oil
1¾ teaspoons sea salt

Garlic Oil:
4 tablespoons extra-virgin olive oil, divided

½ teaspoon dried thyme
2 garlic cloves, minced
⅛ teaspoon sea salt
½ teaspoon freshly ground pepper

Topping:
1 cup fresh basil leaves
1 cup crumbled feta cheese
8 ounces (227 g) fresh figs, stemmed and quartered lengthwise
2 tablespoons raw honey

Make the Dough
1. Combine the flours, yeast, and honey in a food processor, pulse to combine well. Gently add water while pulsing. Let the dough sit for 10 minutes.
2. Mix the olive oil and salt in the dough and knead the dough until smooth. Wrap in plastic and refrigerate for at least 1 day.

Make the Garlic Oil
3. Heat 2 tablespoons of olive oil in a nonstick skillet over medium-low heat until shimmering.
4. Add the thyme, garlic, salt, and pepper and sauté for 30 seconds or until fragrant. Set them aside until ready to use.

Make the Pizzas
5. Preheat the oven to 500ºF (260ºC). Grease two baking sheets with 2 tablespoons of olive oil.
6. Divide the dough in half and shape into two balls. Press the balls into 13- inch rounds. Sprinkle the rounds with a tough of flour if they are sticky.
7. Top the rounds with the garlic oil and basil leaves, then arrange the rounds on the baking sheets. Scatter with feta cheese and figs.
8. Put the sheets in the preheated oven and bake for 9 minutes or until lightly browned. Rotate the pizza halfway through. Remove the pizzas from the oven, then discard the bay leaves. Drizzle with honey. Let sit for 5 minutes and serve immediately.

Per Serving (1 pizza)
calories: 1350 | fat: 46.5g | protein: 27.5g | carbs: 221.9g | fiber: 23.7g | sodium: 2898mg

Mashed Grape Tomato Pizzas

Prep time: 10 minutes | Cook time: 20 minutes | Serves 6

3 cups grape tomatoes, halved
1 teaspoon chopped fresh thyme leaves
2 garlic cloves, minced
¼ teaspoon kosher salt

¼ teaspoon freshly ground black pepper
1 tablespoon extra-virgin olive oil
¾ cup shredded Parmesan cheese
6 whole-wheat pita breads

1. Preheat the oven to 425ºF (220ºC).
2. Combine the tomatoes, thyme, garlic, salt, ground black pepper, and olive oil in a baking pan.
3. Roast in the preheated oven for 20 minutes. Remove the pan from the oven, mash the tomatoes with a spatula and stir to mix well halfway through the cooking time.
4. Meanwhile, divide and spread the cheese over each pita bread, then place the bread in a separate baking pan and roast in the oven for 5 minutes or until golden brown and the cheese melts.
5. Transfer the pita bread onto a large plate, then top with the roasted mashed tomatoes. Serve immediately.

Per Serving calories: 140 | fat: 5.1g | protein: 6.2g | carbs: 16.9g | fiber: 2.0g | sodium: 466mg

Vegetable and Cheese Lavash Pizza

Prep time: 15 minutes | Cook time: 11 minutes | Serves 4

2 (12 by 9-inch) lavash breads
2 tablespoons extra-virgin olive oil
10 ounces (284 g) frozen spinach, thawed and squeezed dry
1 cup shredded fontina cheese
1 tomato, cored and cut into ½-inch pieces

½ cup pitted large green olives, chopped
¼ teaspoon red pepper flakes
3 garlic cloves, minced
¼ teaspoon sea salt
¼ teaspoon ground black pepper
½ cup grated Parmesan cheese

1. Preheat oven to 475ºF (246ºC).
2. Brush the lavash breads with olive oil, then place them on two baking sheet. Heat in the preheated oven for 4 minutes or until lightly browned. Flip the breads halfway through the cooking time.
3. Meanwhile, combine the spinach, fontina cheese, tomato pieces, olives, red pepper flakes, garlic, salt, and black pepper in a large bowl. Stir to mix well.
4. Remove the lavash bread from the oven and sit them on two large plates, spread them with the spinach mixture, then scatter with the Parmesan cheese on top.
5. Bake in the oven for 7 minutes or until the cheese melts and well browned. Slice and serve warm.

Per Serving calories: 431 | fat: 21.5g | protein: 20.0g | carbs: 38.4g | fiber: 2.5g | sodium: 854mg

Dulse, Avocado, and Tomato Pitas

Prep time: 10 minutes | Cook time: 30 minutes | Makes 4 pitas

2 teaspoons coconut oil
½ cup dulse, picked through and separated
Ground black pepper, to taste
2 avocados, sliced
2 tablespoons lime juice
¼ cup chopped cilantro
2 scallions, white and light green parts, sliced
Sea salt, to taste
4 (8-inch) whole wheat pitas, sliced in half
4 cups chopped romaine
4 plum tomatoes, sliced

1. Heat the coconut oil in a nonstick skillet over medium heat until melted. Add the dulse and sauté for 5 minutes or until crispy. Sprinkle with ground black pepper and turn off the heat. Set aside. Put the avocado, lime juice, cilantro, and scallions in a food processor and sprinkle with salt and ground black pepper. Pulse to combine well until smooth.
2. Toast the pitas in a baking pan in the oven for 1 minute until soft.
3. Transfer the pitas to a clean work surface and open. Spread the avocado mixture over the pitas, then top with dulse, romaine, and tomato slices. Serve immediately.

Per Serving (1 pita) calories: 412 | fat: 18.7g | protein: 9.1g | carbs: 56.1g | fiber: 12.5g | sodium: 695mg

Artichoke and Cucumber Hoagies

Prep time: 10 minutes | Cook time: 15 minutes | Makes 1

1 (12-ounce / 340-g) whole grain baguette, sliced in half horizontally
1 cup frozen and thawed artichoke hearts, roughly chopped
1 cucumber, sliced
2 tomatoes, sliced
1 red bell pepper, sliced
⅓ cup Kalamata olives, pitted and chopped
¼ small red onion, thinly sliced
Sea salt and ground black pepper, to taste
2 tablespoons pesto
Balsamic vinegar, to taste

1. rrange the baguette halves on a clean work surface, then cut off the top third from each half. Scoop some insides of the bottom half out and reserve as breadcrumbs.
2. Toast the baguette in a baking pan in the oven for 1 minute to brown lightly. Put the artichokes, cucumber, tomatoes, bell pepper, olives, and onion in a large bowl. Sprinkle with salt and ground black pepper. Toss to combine well.
3. Spread the bottom half of the baguette with the vegetable mixture and drizzle with balsamic vinegar, then smear the cut side of the baguette top with pesto. Assemble the two baguette halves. Wrap the hoagies in parchment paper and let sit for at least an hour before serving.

Per Serving (1 hoagies) calories: 1263 | fat: 37.7g | protein: 56.3g | carbs: 180.1g | fiber: 37.8g | sodium: 2137mg

Brown Rice and Black Bean Burgers

Prep time: 20 minutes | Cook time: 40 minutes | Makes 8 burgers

1 cup cooked brown rice
1 (15-ounce / 425-g) can black beans, drained and rinsed
1 tablespoon olive oil
2 tablespoons taco or Harissa seasoning
½ yellow onion, finely diced
1 beet, peeled and grated
1 carrot, peeled and grated
2 tablespoons no-salt-added tomato paste
2 tablespoons apple cider vinegar
3 garlic cloves, minced
¼ teaspoon sea salt
Ground black pepper, to taste
8 whole-wheat hamburger buns
Toppings:
16 lettuce leaves, rinsed well
8 tomato slices, rinsed well
Whole-grain mustard, to taste

1. Line a baking sheet with parchment paper. Put the brown rice and black beans in a food processor and pulse until mix well. Pour the mixture in a large bowl and set aside. Heat the olive oil in a nonstick skillet over medium heat until shimmering. Add the taco seasoning and stir for 1 minute or until fragrant. Add the onion, beet, and carrot and sauté for 5 minutes or until the onion is translucent and beet and carrot are tender. Pour in the tomato paste and vinegar, then add the garlic and cook for 3 minutes or until the sauce is thickened. Sprinkle with salt and ground black pepper. Transfer the vegetable mixture to the bowl of rice mixture, then stir to mix well until smooth. Divide and shape the mixture into 8 patties, then arrange the patties on the baking sheet and refrigerate for at least 1 hour. Preheat the oven to 400°F (205°C).
2. Remove the baking sheet from the refrigerator and allow to sit under room temperature for 10 minutes.
3. Bake in the preheated oven for 40 minutes or until golden brown on both sides. Flip the patties halfway through the cooking time. Remove the patties from the oven and allow to cool for 10 minutes. Assemble the buns with patties, lettuce, and tomato slices. Top the filling with mustard and serve immediately.
4. **Per Serving (1 burger)** calories: 544 | fat: 20.0g | protein: 15.8g | carbs: 76.0g | fiber: 10.6g | sodium: 446mg

Greek Vegetable Salad Pita

Prep time: 10 minutes | Cook time: 0 minutes | Serves 4

½ cup baby spinach leaves
½ small red onion, thinly sliced
½ small cucumber, deseeded and chopped
1 tomato, chopped
1 cup chopped romaine lettuce
1 tablespoon extra-virgin olive oil
½ tablespoon red wine vinegar
1 teaspoon Dijon mustard
1 tablespoon crumbled feta cheese
Sea salt and freshly ground pepper, to taste
1 whole-wheat pita

1. Combine all the , except for the pita, in a large bowl. Toss to mix well. Stuff the pita with the salad, then serve immediately. **Per Serving** calories: 137 | fat: 8.1g | protein: 3.1g | carbs: 14.3g | fiber: 2.4g | sodium: 166mg

81

Classic Socca

Prep time: 10 minutes | Cook time: 10 minutes | Serves 4

1½ cups chickpea flour
½ teaspoon ground turmeric
½ teaspoon sea salt
½ teaspoon ground black pepper
2 tablespoons plus 2 teaspoons extra-virgin olive oil
1½ cups water

1. Combine the chickpea flour, turmeric, salt, and black pepper in a bowl. Stir to mix well, then gently mix in 2 tablespoons of olive oil and water. Stir to mix until smooth.
2. Heat 2 teaspoons of olive oil in an 8-inch nonstick skillet over medium- high heat until shimmering. Add half cup of the mixture into the skillet and swirl the skillet so the mixture coat the bottom evenly. Cook for 5 minutes or until lightly browned and crispy. Flip the socca halfway through the cooking time. Repeat with the remaining mixture. Slice and serve warm.

Per Serving calories: 207 | fat: 10.2g | protein: 7.9g | carbs: 20.7g | fiber: 3.9g | sodium: 315mg

Alfalfa Sprout and Nut Rolls

Prep time: 40 minutes | Cook time: 0 minutes | Makes 16 bite-size pieces

1 cup alfalfa sprouts
2 tablespoons Brazil nuts
½ cup chopped fresh cilantro
2 tablespoons flaked coconut
1 garlic clove, minced
2 tablespoons ground flaxseeds
Zest and juice of 1 lemon
Pinch cayenne pepper
Sea salt and freshly ground black pepper, to taste
1 tablespoon melted coconut oil
2 tablespoons water
2 whole-grain wraps

1. Combine all , except for the wraps, in a food processor, then pulse to combine well until smooth.
2. Unfold the wraps on a clean work surface, then spread the mixture over the wraps.
3. Roll the wraps up and refrigerate for 30 minutes until set.
4. Remove the rolls from the refrigerator and slice into 16 bite-sized pieces, if desired, and serve.

Per Serving (1 piece)

calories: 67 | fat: 7.1g | protein: 2.2g | carbs: 2.9g | fiber: 1.0g | sodium: 61mg

Mini Pork and Cucumber Lettuce Wraps

Prep time: 20 minutes | Cook time: 0 minutes | Makes 12 wraps

8 ounces (227 g) cooked ground pork
1 cucumber, diced
1 tomato, diced
1 red onion, sliced
1 ounce (28 g) low-fat feta cheese, crumbled
Juice of 1 lemon
1 tablespoon extra-virgin olive oil
Sea salt and freshly ground pepper, to taste
12 small, intact iceberg lettuce leaves

1. Combine the ground pork, cucumber, tomato, and onion in a large bowl, then scatter with feta cheese.
2. Drizzle with lemon juice and olive oil, and sprinkle with salt and pepper. Toss to mix well.
3. Unfold the small lettuce leaves on a large plate or several small plates, then divide and top with the pork mixture.
4. Wrap and serve immediately.

Per Serving (1 warp)

calories: 78 | fat: 5.6g | protein: 5.5g | carbs: 1.4g | fiber: 0.3g | sodium: 50mg

Mushroom and Caramelized Onion Musakhan

Prep time: 20 minutes | Cook time: 1 hour 5 minutes | Serves 4

2 tablespoons sumac, plus more for sprinkling
1 teaspoon ground allspice
½ teaspoon ground cardamom
½ teaspoon ground cumin
3 tablespoons extra-virgin olive oil, divided
2 pounds (907 g) portobello mushroom caps, gills removed, caps halved and sliced ½ inch thick
3 medium white onions, coarsely chopped
¼ cup water
Kosher salt, to taste
1 whole-wheat Turkish flatbread
¼ cup pine nuts
1 lemon, wedged

1. Preheat the oven to 350ºF (180ºC).
2. Combine 2 tablespoons of sumac, allspice, cardamom, and cumin in a small bowl. Stir to mix well.
3. Heat 2 tablespoons of olive oil in an oven-proof skillet over medium-high heat until shimmering.
4. Add the mushroom to the skillet and sprinkle with half of sumac mixture. Sauté for 8 minutes or until the mushrooms are tender. You may need to work in batches to avoid overcrowding. Transfer the mushrooms to a plate and set side.
5. Heat 1 tablespoon of olive oil in the skillet over medium-high heat until shimmering.
6. Add the onion and sauté for 20 minutes or until caramelized. Sprinkle with remaining sumac mixture, then cook for 1 more minute.
7. Pour in the water and sprinkle with salt. Bring to a simmer.
8. Turn off the heat and put the mushroom back to the skillet.
9. Place the skillet in the preheated oven and bake for 30 minutes.
10. Remove the skillet from the oven and let the mushroom sit for 10 minutes until cooled down.
11. Heat the Turkish flatbread in a baking dish in the oven for 5 minutes or until warmed through.
12. Arrange the bread on a large plate and top with mushrooms, onions, and roasted pine nuts. Squeeze the lemon wedges over and sprinkle with more sumac. Serve immediately.

Per Serving

calories: 336 | fat: 18.7g | protein: 11.5g | carbs: 34.3g | fiber: 6.9g | sodium: 369mg

Red Pepper Coques with Pine Nuts

Prep time: 1 day 40 minutes | Cook time: 45 minutes | Makes 4 coques

Dough:
3 cups almond flour
½ teaspoon instant or rapid-rise yeast
2 teaspoons raw honey
1⅓ cups ice water
3 tablespoons extra-virgin olive oil
1½ teaspoons sea salt

Red Pepper Topping:
4 tablespoons extra-virgin olive oil, divided
2 cups jarred roasted red peppers, patted dry and sliced thinly

2 large onions, halved and sliced thin
3 garlic cloves, minced
¼ teaspoon red pepper flakes
2 bay leaves
3 tablespoons maple syrup
1½ teaspoons sea salt
3 tablespoons red whine vinegar

For Garnish:
¼ cup pine nuts (optional)
1 tablespoon minced fresh parsley

Make the Dough

1. Combine the flour, yeast, and honey in a food processor, pulse to combine well. Gently add water while pulsing. Let the dough sit for 10 minutes.
2. Mix the olive oil and salt in the dough and knead the dough until smooth. Wrap in plastic and refrigerate for at least 1 day.

Make the Topping

3. Heat 1 tablespoon of olive oil in a nonstick skillet over medium heat until shimmering.
4. Add the red peppers, onions, garlic, red pepper flakes, bay leaves, maple syrup, and salt. Sauté for 20 minutes or until the onion is caramelized.
5. Turn off the heat and discard the bay leaves. Remove the onion from the skillet and baste with wine vinegar. Let them sit until ready to use.

Make the Coques

6. Preheat the oven to 500°F (260°C). Grease two baking sheets with 1 tablespoon of olive oil.
7. Divide the dough ball into four balls, then press and shape them into equal-sized oval. Arrange the ovals on the baking sheets and pierce each dough about 12 times.
8. Rub the ovals with 2 tablespoons of olive oil and bake for 7 minutes or until puffed. Flip the ovals halfway through the cooking time.
9. Spread the ovals with the topping and pine nuts, then bake for an additional 15 minutes or until well browned.
10. Remove the coques from the oven and spread with parsley. Allow to cool for 10 minutes before serving.

Per Serving (1 coque)
calories: 658 | fat: 23.1g | protein: 3.4g | carbs: 112.0g | fiber: 6.2g | sodium: 1757mg

Ritzy Garden Burgers

Prep time: 1 hour 30 minutes | Cook time: 30 minutes | Serves 6

1 tablespoon avocado oil
1 yellow onion, diced
½ cup shredded carrots
4 garlic cloves, halved
1 (15 ounces / 425 g) can black beans, rinsed and drained
1 cup gluten-free rolled oats
¼ cup oil-packed sun-dried tomatoes, drained and chopped
½ cup sunflower seeds, toasted
1 teaspoon chili powder
1 teaspoon paprika
1 teaspoon ground cumin
½ cup fresh parsley, stems removed

¼ teaspoon ground red pepper flakes
¾ teaspoon sea salt
¼ teaspoon ground black pepper
¼ cup olive oil

For Serving:
6 whole-wheat buns, split in half and toasted
2 ripe avocados, sliced
1 cup kaiware sprouts or mung bean sprouts
1 ripe tomato, sliced

1. Line a baking sheet with parchment paper.
2. Heat 1 tablespoon of avocado oil in a nonstick skillet over medium heat.
3. Add the onion and carrots and sauté for 10 minutes or until the onion is caramelized.
4. Add the garlic and sauté for 30 seconds or until fragrant.
5. Transfer them into a food processor, then add the remaining , except for the olive oil. Pulse until chopped fine and the mixture holds together. Make sure not to purée the mixture.
6. Divide and form the mixture into six 4-inch diameter and ½-inch thick patties.
7. Arrange the patties on the baking sheet and wrap the sheet in plastic. Put the baking sheet in the refrigerator and freeze for at least an hour until firm.
8. Remove the baking sheet from the refrigerator, let them sit under room temperature for 10 minutes.
9. Heat the olive oil in a nonstick skillet over medium-high heat until shimmering.
10. Fry the patties in the skillet for 15 minutes or until lightly browned and crispy. Flip the patties halfway through the cooking time. You may need to work in batches to avoid overcrowding.
11. Assemble the buns with patties, avocados, sprouts, and tomato slices to make the burgers.

Per Serving
calories: 613 | fat: 23.1g | protein: 26.2g | carbs: 88.3g | fiber: 22.9g | sodium: 456mg

Roasted Tomato Panini

Prep time: 15 minutes | Cook time: 3 hours 6 minutes | Serves 2

2 teaspoons olive oil	Sea salt and freshly ground pepper, to taste
4 Roma tomatoes, halved	
4 cloves garlic	4 slices whole-grain bread
1 tablespoon Italian seasoning	4 basil leaves
	2 slices fresh Mozzarella cheese

1. Preheat the oven to 250ºF (121ºC). Grease a baking pan with olive oil.
2. Place the tomatoes and garlic in the baking pan, then sprinkle with Italian seasoning, salt, and ground pepper. Toss to coat well.
3. Roast in the preheated oven for 3 hours or until the tomatoes are lightly wilted.
4. Preheat the panini press.
5. Make the panini: Place two slices of bread on a clean work surface, then top them with wilted tomatoes. Sprinkle with basil and spread with Mozzarella cheese. Top them with remaining two slices of bread.
6. Cook the panini for 6 minutes or until lightly browned and the cheese melts. Flip the panini halfway through the cooking. Serve immediately.

Per Serving

calories: 323 | fat: 12.0g | protein: 17.4g | carbs: 37.5g | fiber: 7.5g | sodium: 603mg

Samosas in Potatoes

Prep time: 20 minutes | Cook time: 30 minutes | Makes 8

4 small potatoes	Sea salt and freshly ground black pepper, to taste
1 teaspoon coconut oil	
1 small onion, finely chopped	¼ cup frozen peas, thawed
	2 carrots, grated
1 small piece ginger, minced	¼ cup chopped fresh cilantro
2 garlic cloves, minced	
2 to 3 teaspoons curry powder	

1. Preheat the oven to 350ºF (180ºC).
2. Poke small holes into potatoes with a fork, then wrap with aluminum foil.
3. Bake in the preheated oven for 30 minutes until tender.
4. Meanwhile, heat the coconut oil in a nonstick skillet over medium-high heat until melted.
5. Add the onion and sauté for 5 minutes or until translucent.
6. Add the ginger and garlic to the skillet and sauté for 3 minutes or until fragrant.
7. Add the curry powder, salt, and ground black pepper, then stir to coat the onion. Remove them from the heat.
8. When the cooking of potatoes is complete, remove the potatoes from the foil and slice in half.
9. Hollow to potato halves with a spoon, then combine the potato fresh with sautéed onion, peas, carrots, and cilantro in a large bowl. Stir to mix well.
10. Spoon the mixture back to the tomato skins and serve immediately.

Per Serving (1 samosa)

calories: 131 | fat: 13.9g | protein: 3.2g | carbs: 8.8g | fiber: 3.0g | sodium: 111mg

Super Cheeses and Mushroom Tart

Prep time: 30 minutes | Cook time: 1 hour 30 minutes | Serves 4 to 6

Crust:

1¾ cups almond flour	1 pound (454 g) white mushrooms, trimmed and sliced thinly
1 tablespoon raw honey	
¾ teaspoon sea salt	Sea salt, to taste
¼ cup extra-virgin olive oil	1 garlic clove, minced
⅓ cup water	2 teaspoons minced fresh thyme
Filling:	
2 tablespoons extra-virgin olive oil, divided	¼ cup shredded Mozzarella cheese
	½ cup grated Parmesan cheese
	4 ounces (113 g) part-skim ricotta cheese
	Ground black pepper, to taste
	2 tablespoons ground basil

Make the Crust

1. Preheat the oven to 350ºF (180ºC).
2. Combine the flour, honey, salt and olive oil in a large bowl. Stir to mix well. Gently mix in the water until a smooth dough forms.
3. Drop walnut-size clumps from the dough in the single layer on a tart pan. Press the clumps to coat the bottom of the pan.
4. Bake the crust in the preheated oven for 50 minutes or until firm and browned. Rotate the pan halfway through.

Make the Filling

5. While baking the crust, heat 1 tablespoon of olive oil in a nonstick skillet over medium-high heat until shimmering.
6. Add the mushrooms and sprinkle with ½ teaspoon of salt. Sauté for 15 minutes or until tender.
7. Add the garlic and thyme and sauté for 30 seconds or until fragrant.

Make the Tart

8. Meanwhile, combine the cheeses, salt, ground black pepper, and 1 tablespoon of olive oil in a bowl. Stir to mix well.
9. Spread the cheese mixture over the crust, then top with the mushroom mixture.
10. Bake in the oven for 20 minutes or until the cheeses are frothy and the tart is heated through. Rotate the pan halfway through the baking time.
11. Remove the tart from the oven. Allow to cool for at least 10 minutes, then sprinkle with basil. Slice to serve.

Per Serving

calories: 530 | fat: 26.6g | protein: 11.7g | carbs: 63.5g | fiber: 4.6g | sodium: 785mg

Mediterranean Greek Salad Wraps

Prep time: 15 minutes | Cook time: 0 minutes | Serves 4

1½ cups seedless cucumber, peeled and chopped
1 cup chopped tomato
½ cup finely chopped fresh mint
¼ cup diced red onion
1 (2.25-ounce / 64-g) can sliced black olives, drained
2 tablespoons extra-virgin olive oil
1 tablespoon red wine vinegar
¼ teaspoon kosher salt
¼ teaspoon freshly ground black pepper
½ cup crumbled goat cheese
4 whole-wheat flatbread wraps or soft whole-wheat tortillas

1. In a large bowl, stir together the cucumber, tomato, mint, onion and olives.
2. In a small bowl, whisk together the oil, vinegar, salt, and pepper. Spread the dressing over the salad. Toss gently to combine.
3. On a clean work surface, lay the wraps. Divide the goat cheese evenly among the wraps. Scoop a quarter of the salad filling down the center of each wrap.
4. Fold up each wrap: Start by folding up the bottom, then fold one side over and fold the other side over the top. Repeat with the remaining wraps.
5. Serve immediately.

Per Serving

calories: 225 | fat: 12.0g | protein: 12.0g | carbs: 18.0g | fiber: 4.0g | sodium: 349mg

Salmon Salad Wraps

Prep time: 10 minutes | Cook time: 0 minutes | Serves 6

1 pound (454 g) salmon fillets, cooked and flaked
½ cup diced carrots
½ cup diced celery
3 tablespoons diced red onion
3 tablespoons chopped fresh dill
2 tablespoons capers
1½ tablespoons extra-virgin olive oil
1 tablespoon aged balsamic vinegar
¼ teaspoon kosher or sea salt
½ teaspoon freshly ground black pepper
4 whole-wheat flatbread wraps or soft whole-wheat tortillas

1. In a large bowl, stir together all the , except for the wraps.
2. On a clean work surface, lay the wraps. Divide the salmon mixture evenly among the wraps. Fold up the bottom of the wraps, then roll up the wrap.
3. Serve immediately.

Per Serving

calories: 194 | fat: 8.0g | protein: 18.0g | carbs: 13.0g | fiber: 3.0g | sodium: 536mg

Baked Parmesan Chicken Wraps

Prep time: 10 minutes | Cook time: 18 minutes | Serves 6

1 pound (454 g) boneless, skinless chicken breasts
1 large egg
¼ cup unsweetened almond milk
⅔ cup whole-wheat bread crumbs
½ cup grated Parmesan cheese
¾ teaspoon garlic powder, divided
1 cup canned low-sodium or no-salt-added crushed tomatoes
1 teaspoon dried oregano
6 (8-inch) whole-wheat tortillas, or whole-grain spinach wraps
1 cup fresh Mozzarella cheese, sliced
1½ cups loosely packed fresh flat-leaf (Italian) parsley, chopped
Cooking spray

1. Preheat the oven to 425°F (220°C). Line a large, rimmed baking sheet with aluminum foil. Place a wire rack on the aluminum foil, and spritz the rack with nonstick cooking spray. Set aside.
2. Place the chicken breasts into a large plastic bag. With a rolling pin, pound the chicken so it is evenly flattened, about ¼ inch thick. Slice the chicken into six portions.
3. In a bowl, whisk together the egg and milk. In another bowl, stir together the bread crumbs, Parmesan cheese and ½ teaspoon of the garlic powder.
4. Dredge each chicken breast portion into the egg mixture, and then into the Parmesan crumb mixture, pressing the crumbs into the chicken so they stick. Arrange the chicken on the prepared wire rack.
5. Bake in the preheated oven for 15 to 18 minutes, or until the internal temperature of the chicken reads 165°F (74°C) on a meat thermometer and any juices run clear.
6. Transfer the chicken to a cutting board, and cut each portion diagonally into ½-inch pieces.
7. In a small, microwave-safe bowl, stir together the tomatoes, oregano, and the remaining ¼ teaspoon of the garlic powder. Cover the bowl with a paper towel and microwave for about 1 minute on high, until very hot. Set aside.
8. Wrap the tortillas in a damp paper towel and microwave for 30 to 45 seconds on high, or until warmed through.
9. Assemble the wraps: Divide the chicken slices evenly among the six tortillas and top with the sliced Mozzarella cheese. Spread 1 tablespoon of the warm tomato sauce over the cheese on each tortilla, and top each with about ¼ cup of the parsley.
10. Wrap the tortilla: Fold up the bottom of the tortilla, then fold one side over and fold the other side over the top.
11. Serve the wraps warm with the remaining sauce for dipping.

Per Serving

calories: 358 | fat: 12.0g | protein: 21.0g | carbs: 41.0g | fiber: 7.0g | sodium: 755mg

Eggplant, Spinach, and Feta Sandwiches

Prep time: 10 minutes | Cook time: 6 to 8 minutes | Serves 2

1 medium eggplant, sliced into ½-inch-thick slices
2 tablespoons olive oil
Sea salt and freshly ground pepper, to taste
5 to 6 tablespoons hummus
4 slices whole-wheat bread, toasted
1 cup baby spinach leaves
2 ounces (57 g) feta cheese, softened

1. Preheat the grill to medium-high heat.
2. Salt both sides of the sliced eggplant, and let sit for 20 minutes to draw out the bitter juices.
3. Rinse the eggplant and pat dry with a paper towel.
4. Brush the eggplant slices with olive oil and season with sea salt and freshly ground pepper to taste.
5. Grill the eggplant until lightly charred on both sides but still slightly firm in the middle, about 3 to 4 minutes per side.
6. Spread the hummus on the bread slices and top with the spinach leaves, feta cheese, and grilled eggplant. Top with the other slice of bread and serve immediately.

Per Serving

calories: 493 | fat: 25.3g | protein: 17.1g | carbs: 50.9g | fiber: 14.7g | sodium: 789mg

Grilled Caesar Salad Sandwiches

Prep time: 5 minutes | Cook time: 5 minutes | Serves 2

¾ cup olive oil, divided
2 romaine lettuce hearts, left intact
3 to 4 anchovy fillets
Juice of 1 lemon
2 to 3 cloves garlic, peeled
1 teaspoon Dijon mustard
¼ teaspoon Worcestershire sauce
Sea salt and freshly ground pepper, to taste
2 slices whole-wheat bread, toasted
Freshly grated Parmesan cheese, for serving

1. Preheat the grill to medium-high heat and oil the grates.
2. On a cutting board, drizzle the lettuce with 1 to 2 tablespoons of olive oil and place on the grates.
3. Grill for 5 minutes, turning until lettuce is slightly charred on all sides. Let lettuce cool enough to handle.
4. In a food processor, combine the remaining olive oil with the anchovies, lemon juice, garlic, mustard, and Worcestershire sauce.
5. Pulse the until you have a smooth emulsion. Season with sea salt and freshly ground pepper to taste. Chop the lettuce in half and place on the bread.
6. Drizzle with the dressing and serve with a sprinkle of Parmesan cheese.

Per Serving

calories: 949 | fat: 85.6g | protein: 12.9g | carbs: 34.1g | fiber: 13.9g | sodium: 786mg

Green Veggie Sandwiches

Prep time: 20 minutes | Cook time: 0 minutes | Serves 2

Spread:
1 (15-ounce / 425-g) can cannellini beans, drained and rinsed
⅓ cup packed fresh basil leaves
⅓ cup packed fresh parsley
⅓ cup chopped fresh chives
2 garlic cloves, chopped
Zest and juice of ½ lemon
1 tablespoon apple cider vinegar

Sandwiches:
4 whole-grain bread slices, toasted
8 English cucumber slices
1 large beefsteak tomato, cut into slices
1 large avocado, halved, pitted, and cut into slices
1 small yellow bell pepper, cut into slices
2 handfuls broccoli sprouts
2 handfuls fresh spinach

Make the Spread

1. In a food processor, combine the cannellini beans, basil, parsley, chives, garlic, lemon zest and juice, and vinegar. Pulse a few times, scrape down the sides, and purée until smooth. You may need to scrape down the sides again to incorporate all the basil and parsley. Refrigerate for at least 1 hour to allow the flavors to blend.
1. Assemble the Sandwiches
2. Build your sandwiches by spreading several tablespoons of spread on each slice of bread. Layer two slices of bread with the cucumber, tomato, avocado, bell pepper, broccoli sprouts, and spinach. Top with the remaining bread slices and press down lightly.
3. Serve immediately.

Per Serving

calories: 617 | fat: 21.1g | protein: 28.1g | carbs: 86.1g | fiber: 25.6g | sodium: 593mg

Pizza Pockets

Prep time: 10 minutes | Cook time: 0 minutes | Serves 2

½ cup tomato sauce
½ teaspoon oregano
½ teaspoon garlic powder
½ cup chopped black olives
2 canned artichoke hearts, drained and chopped
2 ounces (57 g) pepperoni, chopped
½ cup shredded Mozzarella cheese
1 whole-wheat pita, halved

1. In a medium bowl, stir together the tomato sauce, oregano, and garlic powder.
2. Add the olives, artichoke hearts, pepperoni, and cheese. Stir to mix.
3. Spoon the mixture into the pita halves and serve.

Per Serving

calories: 375 | fat: 23.5g | protein: 17.1g | carbs: 27.1g | fiber: 6.1g | sodium: 1080mg

Mushroom-Pesto Baked Pizza

Prep time: 5 minutes | Cook time: 15 minutes | Serves 2

1 teaspoon extra-virgin olive oil

½ cup sliced mushrooms

½ red onion, sliced

Salt and freshly ground black pepper

¼ cup store-bought pesto sauce

2 whole-wheat flatbreads

¼ cup shredded Mozzarella cheese

1. Preheat the oven to 350ºF (180ºC). In a small skillet, heat the oil over medium heat. Add the mushrooms and onion, and season with salt and pepper. Sauté for 3 to 5 minutes until the onion and mushrooms begin to soften. Spread 2 tablespoons of pesto on each flatbread. Divide the mushroom-onion mixture between the two flatbreads. Top each with 2 tablespoons of cheese. Place the flatbreads on a baking sheet and bake for 10 to 12 minutes until the cheese is melted and bubbly. Serve warm.

Per Serving calories: 348 | fat: 23.5g | protein: 14.2g | carbs: 28.1g | fiber: 7.1g | sodium: 792mg

Tuna and Hummus Wraps

Prep time: 10 minutes | Cook time: 0 minutes | Serves 2

Hummus:

1 cup from 1 (15-ounce / 425-g) can low-sodium chickpeas, drained and rinsed

2 tablespoons tahini

1 tablespoon extra-virgin olive oil

1 garlic clove

Juice of ½ lemon

¼ teaspoon salt

2 tablespoons water

Wraps:

4 large lettuce leaves

1 (5-ounce / 142-g) can chunk light tuna packed in water, drained

1 red bell pepper, seeded and cut into strips

1 cucumber, sliced

Make the Hummus

1. In a blender jar, combine the chickpeas, tahini, olive oil, garlic, lemon juice, salt, and water. Process until smooth. Taste and adjust with additional lemon juice or salt, as needed.

Make the Wraps

2. On each lettuce leaf, spread 1 tablespoon of hummus, and divide the tuna among the leaves. Top each with several strips of red pepper and cucumber slices.

3. Roll up the lettuce leaves, folding in the two shorter sides and rolling away from you, like a burrito. Serve immediately.

Per Serving calories: 192 | fat: 5.1g | protein: 26.1g | carbs: 15.1g | fiber: 4.1g | sodium: 352mg

Turkish Eggplant and Tomatoes Pide with Mint

Prep time: 1 day 40 minutes | Cook time: 20 minutes | Makes 6 pides

Dough:

3 cups almond flour

2 teaspoons raw honey

½ teaspoon instant or rapid-rise yeast

1⅓ cups ice water

1 tablespoon extra-virgin olive oil

1½ teaspoons sea salt

Eggplant and Tomato Toppings:

28 ounces (794 g) whole tomatoes, peeled and puréed

5 tablespoons extra-virgin olive oil, divided

1 pound (454 g) eggplant, cut into ½-inch pieces

½ red bell pepper, chopped

Sea salt and ground black pepper, to taste

3 garlic cloves, minced

¼ teaspoon red pepper flakes

½ teaspoon smoked paprika

6 tablespoons minced fresh mint, divided

1½ cups crumbled feta cheese

Make the Dough

1. Combine the flour, yeast, and honey in a food processor, pulse to combine well. Gently add water while pulsing. Let the dough sit for 10 minutes.

2. Mix the olive oil and salt in the dough and knead the dough until smooth. Wrap in plastic and refrigerate for at least 1 day.

Make the Toppings

3. Heat 2 tablespoons of olive oil in a nonstick skillet over medium-high heat until shimmering.

4. Add the bell pepper, eggplant, and ½ teaspoon of salt. Sauté for 6 minutes or until the eggplant is lightly browned.

5. Add the red pepper flakes, paprika, and garlic. Sauté for 1 minute or until fragrant. Pour in the puréed tomatoes. Bring to a simmer, then cook for 10 minutes or until the mixture is thickened into about 3½ cups. Turn off the heat and mix in 4 tablespoons of mint, salt, and ground black pepper. Set them aside until ready to use.

Make the Turkish Pide

6. Preheat the oven to 500ºF (260ºC). Line three baking sheets with parchment papers.

7. On a clean work surface, divide and shape the dough into six 14 by 5- inch ovals. Transfer the dough to the baking sheets. Brush them with 3 tablespoons of olive oil and spread the eggplant mixture and feta cheese on top.

8. Bake in the preheated oven for 12 minutes or until golden brown. Rotate the pide halfway through the baking time.

9. Remove the pide from the oven and spread with remaining mint and serve immediately.

Per Serving (1 pide) calories: 500 | fat: 22.1g | protein: 8.0g | carbs: 69.7g | fiber: 5.8g | sodium: 1001mg

Veg Mix and Blackeye Pea Burritos

Prep time: 15 minutes | Cook time: 40 minutes | Makes 6 burritos

1 teaspoon olive oil	1 (14-ounce / 397-g) can
1 red onion, diced	blackeye peas
2 garlic cloves, minced	2 teaspoons chili powder
1 zucchini, chopped	Sea salt, to taste
1 tomato, diced	6 whole-grain tortillas
1 bell pepper, any color, deseeded and diced	

1. Preheat the oven to 325°F (160°C).
2. Heat the olive oil in a nonstick skillet over medium heat or until shimmering.
3. Add the onion and sauté for 5 minutes or until translucent.
4. Add the garlic and sauté for 30 seconds or until fragrant.
5. Add the zucchini and sauté for 5 minutes or until tender.
6. Add the tomato and bell pepper and sauté for 2 minutes or until soft.
7. Fold in the black peas and sprinkle them with chili powder and salt. Stir to mix well.
8. Place the tortillas on a clean work surface, then top them with sautéed vegetables mix.
9. Fold one ends of tortillas over the vegetable mix, then tuck and roll them into burritos.
10. Arrange the burritos in a baking dish, seam side down, then pour the juice remains in the skillet over the burritos.
11. Bake in the preheated oven for 25 minutes or until golden brown.
12. Serve immediately.

Per Serving

calories: 335 | fat: 16.2g | protein: 12.1g | carbs: 8.3g | fiber: 8.0g | sodium: 214mg

Tuna and Olive Salad Sandwiches

Prep time: 10 minutes | Cook time: 0 minutes | Serves 4

3 tablespoons freshly squeezed lemon juice	2 (5-ounce / 142-g) cans tuna, drained
2 tablespoons extra-virgin olive oil	1 (2.25-ounce / 64-g) can sliced olives, any green or black variety
1 garlic clove, minced	½ cup chopped fresh fennel, including fronds
½ teaspoon freshly ground black pepper	8 slices whole-grain crusty bread

1. In a medium bowl, whisk together the lemon juice, oil, garlic, and pepper. Add the tuna, olives and fennel to the bowl. Using a fork, separate the tuna into chunks and stir to incorporate all the .
2. Divide the tuna salad equally among 4 slices of bread. Top each with the remaining bread slices.
3. Let the sandwiches sit for at least 5 minutes so the zesty filling can soak into the bread before serving.

Per Serving

calories: 952 | fat: 17.0g | protein: 165.0g | carbs: 37.0g | fiber: 7.0g | sodium: 2572mg

Spicy Black Bean and Poblano Dippers

Prep time: 20 minutes | Cook time: 21 minutes | Serves 8

2 tablespoons avocado oil, plus more for brushing the dippers	1 yellow onion, quartered
	2 garlic cloves
1 (15 ounces / 425 g) can black beans, drained and rinsed	1 teaspoon chili powder
	1 teaspoon ground cumin
	1 teaspoon sea salt
1 poblano, deseeded and quartered	24 organic corn tortillas
1 jalapeño, halved and deseeded	
½ cup fresh cilantro, leaves and tender stems	

1. Preheat the oven to 400°F (205°C). Line a baking sheet with parchment paper and grease with avocado oil.
2. Combine the remaining , except for the tortillas, in a food processor, then pulse until chopped finely and the mixture holds together. Make sure not to purée the mixture.
3. Warm the tortillas on the baking sheet in the preheated oven for 1 minute or until softened.
4. Add a tablespoon of the mixture in the middle of each tortilla. Fold one side of the tortillas over the mixture and tuck to roll them up tightly to make the dippers.
5. Arrange the dippers on the baking sheet and brush them with avocado oil.
1. Bake in the oven for 20 minutes or until well browned. Flip the dippers halfway through the cooking time.
6. Serve immediately.

Per Serving

calories: 388 | fat: 6.5g | protein: 16.2g | carbs: 69.6g | fiber: 13.5g | sodium: 340mg

Chickpea Lettuce Wraps

Prep time: 15 minutes | Cook time: 0 minutes | Serves 2

1 (15-ounce / 425-g) can chickpeas, drained and rinsed well	2 teaspoons freshly squeezed lemon juice
	1 teaspoon raw honey
1 celery stalk, diced	1 teaspoon Dijon mustard
½ shallot, minced	Dash salt
1 green apple, cored and diced	Filtered water, to thin
3 tablespoons tahini (sesame paste)	4 romaine lettuce leaves

1. In a medium bowl, stir together the chickpeas, celery, shallot, apple, tahini, lemon juice, honey, mustard, and salt. If needed, add some water to thin the mixture.
2. Place the romaine lettuce leaves on a plate. Fill each with the chickpea filling, using it all. Wrap the leaves around the filling. Serve immediately.

Per Serving calories: 397 | fat: 15.1g | protein: 15.1g | carbs: 53.1g | fiber: 15.3g | sodium: 409mg

Spicy Tofu Tacos with Cherry Tomato Salsa

Prep time: 20 minutes | Cook time: 11 minutes | Makes 4 tacos

Cherry Tomato Salsa:
¼ cup sliced cherry tomatoes
½ jalapeño, deseeded and sliced
Juice of 1 lime
1 garlic clove, minced
Sea salt and freshly ground black pepper, to taste
2 teaspoons extra-virgin olive oil

Spicy Tofu Taco Filling:
4 tablespoons water, divided
½ cup canned black beans, rinsed and drained

2 teaspoons fresh chopped chives, divided
¾ teaspoon ground cumin, divided
¾ teaspoon smoked paprika, divided
Dash cayenne pepper (optional)
¼ teaspoon sea salt
¼ teaspoon freshly ground black pepper
1 teaspoon extra-virgin olive oil
6 ounces (170 g) firm tofu, drained, rinsed, and pressed
4 corn tortillas
¼ avocado, sliced
¼ cup fresh cilantro

Make the Cherry Tomato Salsa

1. Combine the for the salsa in a small bowl. Stir to mix well. Set aside until ready to use.

Make the Spicy Tofu Taco Filling

2. Add 2 tablespoons of water into a saucepan, then add the black beans and sprinkle with 1 teaspoon of chives, ½ teaspoon of cumin, ¼ teaspoon of smoked paprika, and cayenne. Stir to mix well.

3. Cook for 5 minutes over medium heat until heated through, then mash the black beans with the back of a spoon. Turn off the heat and set aside.

4. Add remaining water into a bowl, then add the remaining chives, cumin, and paprika. Sprinkle with cayenne, salt, and black pepper. Stir to mix well. Set aside.

5. Heat the olive oil in a nonstick skillet over medium heat until shimmering.

6. Add the tofu and drizzle with taco sauce, then sauté for 5 minutes or until the seasoning is absorbed. Remove the tofu from the skillet and set aside.

7. Warm the tortillas in the skillet for 1 minutes or until heated through.

8. Transfer the tortillas onto a large plate and top with tofu, mashed black beans, avocado, cilantro, then drizzle the tomato salsa over. Serve immediately.

Per Serving (1 taco)

calories: 240 | fat: 9.0g | protein: 11.6g | carbs: 31.6g | fiber: 6.7g | sodium: 195mg

Open-Faced Margherita Sandwiches

Prep time: 10 minutes | Cook time: 5 minutes | Serves 4

2 (6- to 7-inch) whole-wheat submarine or hoagie rolls, sliced open horizontally
1 tablespoon extra-virgin olive oil
1 garlic clove, halved
1 large ripe tomato, cut into 8 slices

¼ teaspoon dried oregano
1 cup fresh Mozzarella, sliced
¼ cup lightly packed fresh basil leaves, torn into small pieces
¼ teaspoon freshly ground black pepper

1. Preheat the broiler to High with the rack 4 inches under the heating element. Put the sliced bread on a large, rimmed baking sheet and broil for 1 minute, or until the bread is just lightly toasted. Remove from the oven.

2. Brush each piece of the toasted bread with the oil, and rub a garlic half over each piece. Put the toasted bread back on the baking sheet. Evenly divide the tomato slices on each piece. Sprinkle with the oregano and top with the cheese.

3. Place the baking sheet under the broiler. Set the timer for 1½ minutes, but check after 1 minute. When the cheese is melted and the edges are just starting to get dark brown, remove the sandwiches from the oven. Top each sandwich with the fresh basil and pepper before serving.

Per Serving calories: 93 | fat: 2.0g | protein: 10.0g | carbs: 8.0g | fiber: 2.0g | sodium: 313mg

Zucchini Hummus Wraps

Prep time: 15 minutes | Cook time: 6 minutes | Serves 2

1 zucchini, ends removed, thinly sliced lengthwise
½ teaspoon dried oregano
¼ teaspoon freshly ground black pepper
¼ teaspoon garlic powder
¼ cup hummus
2 whole wheat tortillas
2 Roma tomatoes, cut lengthwise into slices
1 cup chopped kale
2 tablespoons chopped red onion
½ teaspoon ground cumin

1. In a skillet over medium heat, add the zucchini slices and cook for 3 minutes per side. Sprinkle with the oregano, pepper, and garlic powder and remove from the heat.

2. Spread 2 tablespoons of hummus on each tortilla. Lay half the zucchini in the center of each tortilla. Top with tomato slices, kale, red onion, and ¼ teaspoon of cumin. Wrap tightly and serve.

Per Serving

calories: 248 | fat: 8.1g | protein: 9.1g | carbs: 37.1g | fiber: 8.1g | sodium: mg

Roasted Vegetable Panini

Prep time: 10 minutes | Cook time: 15 minutes | Serves 4

2 tablespoons extra-virgin olive oil, divided
1½ cups diced broccoli
1 cup diced zucchini
¼ cup diced onion
¼ teaspoon dried oregano
⅛ teaspoon kosher or sea salt
⅛ teaspoon freshly ground black pepper
1 (12-ounce / 340-g) jar roasted red peppers, drained and finely chopped
2 tablespoons grated Parmesan or Asiago cheese
1 cup fresh Mozzarella (about 4 ounces / 113 g), sliced
1 (2-foot-long) whole-grain Italian loaf, cut into 4 equal lengths Cooking spray

1. Place a large, rimmed baking sheet in the oven. Preheat the oven to 450°F (235°C) with the baking sheet inside.
2. In a large bowl, stir together 1 tablespoon of the oil, broccoli, zucchini, onion, oregano, salt and pepper.
3. Remove the baking sheet from the oven and spritz the baking sheet with cooking spray. Spread the vegetable mixture on the baking sheet and roast for 5 minutes, stirring once halfway through cooking. Remove the baking sheet from the oven. Stir in the red peppers and Parmesan cheese. In a large skillet over medium-high heat, heat the remaining 1 tablespoon of the oil.
4. Cut open each section of bread horizontally, but don't cut all the way through. Fill each with the vegetable mix (about ½ cup), and layer 1 ounce (28 g) of sliced Mozzarella cheese on top. Close the sandwiches, and place two of them on the skillet. Place a heavy object on top and grill for 2½ minutes. Flip the sandwiches and grill for another 2½ minutes. Repeat the grilling process with the remaining two sandwiches. Serve hot.

Per Serving calories: 116 | fat: 4.0g | protein: 12.0g | carbs: 9.0g | fiber: 3.0g | sodium: 569mg

Za'atar Pizza

Prep time: 10 minutes | Cook time: 1o to 12 minutes | Serves 4 to 6

1 sheet puff pastry
¼ cup extra-virgin olive oil
⅓ cup za'atar seasoning

1. Preheat the oven to 350°F (180°C). Line a baking sheet with parchment paper.
2. Place the puff pastry on the prepared baking sheet. Cut the pastry into desired slices.
3. Brush the pastry with the olive oil. Sprinkle with the za'atar seasoning.
4. Put the pastry in the oven and bake for 10 to 12 minutes, or until edges are lightly browned and puffed up.
5. Serve warm.

Per Serving
calories: 374 | fat: 30.0g | protein: 3.0g | carbs: 20.0g | fiber: 1.0g | sodium: 166mg

White Pizzas with Arugula and Spinach

Prep time: 10 minutes | Cook time: 20 minutes | Serves 4

1 pound (454 g) refrigerated fresh pizza dough
2 tablespoons extra-virgin olive oil, divided
½ cup thinly sliced onion
2 garlic cloves, minced
3 cups baby spinach
3 cups arugula
1 tablespoon water
¼ teaspoon freshly ground black pepper
1 tablespoon freshly squeezed lemon juice
½ cup shredded Parmesan cheese
½ cup crumbled goat cheese Cooking spray

1. Preheat the oven to 500°F (260°C). Spritz a large, rimmed baking sheet with cooking spray.
2. Take the pizza dough out of the refrigerator.
3. Heat 1 tablespoon of the oil in a large skillet over medium heat. Add the onion to the skillet and cook for 4 minutes, stirring constantly. Add the garlic and cook for 1 minute, stirring constantly.
4. Stir in the spinach, arugula, water and pepper. Cook for about 2 minutes, stirring constantly, or until all the greens are coated with oil and they start to cook down. Remove the skillet from the heat and drizzle with the lemon juice.
5. On a lightly floured work surface, form the pizza dough into a 12-inch circle or a 10-by-12-inch rectangle, using a rolling pin or by stretching with your hands.
6. Place the dough on the prepared baking sheet. Brush the dough with the remaining 1 tablespoon of the oil. Spread the cooked greens on top of the dough to within ½ inch of the edge. Top with the Parmesan cheese and goat cheese.
7. Bake in the preheated oven for 10 to 12 minutes, or until the crust starts to brown around the edges.
8. Remove from the oven and transfer the pizza to a cutting board. Cut into eight pieces before serving.

Per Serving
calories: 521 | fat: 31.0g | protein: 23.0g | carbs: 38.0g | fiber: 4.0g | sodium: 1073mg

Chapter 5
Beans, Grains, and Pastas

Baked Rolled Oat with Pears and Pecans

Prep time: 15 minutes | Cook time: 30 minutes | Serves 6

2 tablespoons coconut oil, melted, plus more for greasing the pan
3 ripe pears, cored and diced
2 cups unsweetened almond milk
1 tablespoon pure vanilla extract
¼ cup pure maple syrup
2 cups gluten-free rolled oats
½ cup raisins
¾ cup chopped pecans
¼ teaspoon ground nutmeg
1 teaspoon ground cinnamon
½ teaspoon ground ginger
¼ teaspoon sea salt

1. Preheat the oven to 350°F (180°C). Grease a baking dish with melted coconut oil, then spread the pears in a single layer on the baking dish evenly.
2. Combine the almond milk, vanilla extract, maple syrup, and coconut oil in a bowl. Stir to mix well.
3. Combine the remaining in a separate large bowl. Stir to mix well. Fold the almond milk mixture in the bowl, then pour the mixture over the pears.
4. Place the baking dish in the preheated oven and bake for 30 minutes or until lightly browned and set.
5. Serve immediately.

Per Serving

calories: 479 | fat: 34.9g | protein: 8.8g | carbs: 50.1g | fiber: 10.8g | sodium: 113mg

Brown Rice Pilaf with Pistachios and Raisins

Prep time: 5 minutes | Cook time: 15 minutes | Serves 6

1 tablespoon extra-virgin olive oil
1 cup chopped onion
½ cup shredded carrot
½ teaspoon ground cinnamon
1 teaspoon ground cumin
2 cups brown rice
1¾ cups pure orange juice
¼ cup water
½ cup shelled pistachios
1 cup golden raisins
½ cup chopped fresh chives

1. Heat the olive oil in a saucepan over medium-high heat until shimmering.
2. Add the onion and sauté for 5 minutes or until translucent.
3. Add the carrots, cinnamon, and cumin, then sauté for 1 minutes or until aromatic.
4. Pour int the brown rice, orange juice, and water. Bring to a boil. Reduce the heat to medium-low and simmer for 7 minutes or until the liquid is almost absorbed.
5. Transfer the rice mixture in a large serving bowl, then spread with pistachios, raisins, and chives. Serve immediately.

Per Serving

calories: 264 | fat: 7.1g | protein: 5.2g | carbs: 48.9g | fiber: 4.0g | sodium: 86mg

Cherry, Apricot, and Pecan Brown Rice Bowl

Prep time: 15 minutes | Cook time: 1 hour 1 minutes | Serves 2

2 tablespoons olive oil
2 green onions, sliced
½ cup brown rice
1 cup low -sodium chicken stock
2 tablespoons dried cherries
4 dried apricots, chopped
2 tablespoons pecans, toasted and chopped
Sea salt and freshly ground pepper, to taste

1. Heat the olive oil in a medium saucepan over medium-high heat until shimmering.
2. Add the green onions and sauté for 1 minutes or until fragrant.
3. Add the rice. Stir to mix well, then pour in the chicken stock.
4. Bring to a boil. Reduce the heat to low. Cover and simmer for 50 minutes or until the brown rice is soft.
5. Add the cherries, apricots, and pecans, and simmer for 10 more minutes or until the fruits are tender.
6. Pour them in a large serving bowl. Fluff with a fork. Sprinkle with sea salt and freshly ground pepper. Serve immediately.

Per Serving

calories: 451 | fat: 25.9g | protein: 8.2g | carbs: 50.4g | fiber: 4.6g | sodium: 122mg

Curry Apple Couscous with Leeks and Pecans

Prep time: 10 minutes | Cook time: 8 minutes | Serves 4

2 teaspoons extra-virgin olive oil
2 leeks, white parts only, sliced
1 apple, diced
2 cups cooked couscous
2 tablespoons curry powder
½ cup chopped pecans

1. Heat the olive oil in a skillet over medium heat until shimmering.
2. Add the leeks and sauté for 5 minutes or until soft.
3. Add the diced apple and cook for 3 more minutes until tender.
4. Add the couscous and curry powder. Stir to combine.
5. Transfer them in a large serving bowl, then mix in the pecans and serve.

Per Serving

calories: 254 | fat: 11.9g | protein: 5.4g | carbs: 34.3g | fiber: 5.9g | sodium: 15mg

Lebanese Flavor Broken Thin Noodles

Prep time: 10 minutes | Cook time: 25 minutes | Serves 6

1 tablespoon extra-virgin olive oil	½ cup water
1 (3-ounce / 85-g) cup vermicelli, broken into 1- to 1½-inch pieces	2 garlic cloves, mashed
	¼ teaspoon sea salt
	⅛ teaspoon crushed red pepper flakes
3 cups shredded cabbage	½ cup coarsely chopped cilantro
1 cup brown rice	
3 cups low-sodium vegetable soup	Fresh lemon slices, for serving

1. Heat the olive oil in a saucepan over medium-high heat until shimmering.
2. Add the vermicelli and sauté for 3 minutes or until toasted.
3. Add the cabbage and sauté for 4 minutes or until tender.
4. Pour in the brown rice, vegetable soup, and water. Add the garlic and sprinkle with salt and red pepper flakes.
5. Bring to a boil over high heat. Reduce the heat to medium low. Put the lid on and simmer for another 10 minutes.
6. Turn off the heat, then let sit for 5 minutes without opening the lid.
7. Pour them on a large serving platter and spread with cilantro. Squeeze the lemon slices over and serve warm.

Per Serving

calories: 127 | fat: 3.1g | protein: 4.2g | carbs: 22.9g | fiber: 3.0g | sodium: 224mg

Lemony Farro and Avocado Bowl

Prep time: 5 minutes | Cook time: 25 minutes | Serves 4

1 tablespoon plus 2 teaspoons extra-virgin olive oil, divided	2 cups low-sodium vegetable soup
½ medium onion, chopped	2 avocados, peeled, pitted, and sliced
1 carrot, shredded	
2 garlic cloves, minced	Zest and juice of 1 small lemon
1 (6-ounce / 170-g) cup pearled farro	¼ teaspoon sea salt

1. Heat 1 tablespoon of olive oil in a saucepan over medium-high heat until shimmering.
2. Add the onion and sauté for 5 minutes or until translucent.
3. Add the carrot and garlic and sauté for 1 minute or until fragrant.
4. Add the farro and pour in the vegetable soup. Bring to a boil over high heat. Reduce the heat to low. Put the lid on and simmer for 20 minutes or until the farro is al dente.
5. Transfer the farro in a large serving bowl, then fold in the avocado slices. Sprinkle with lemon zest and salt, then drizzle with lemon juice and 2 teaspoons of olive oil.
6. Stir to mix well and serve immediately.

Per Serving calories: 210 | fat: 11.1g | protein: 4.2g | carbs: 27.9g | fiber: 7.0g | sodium: 152mg

Rice and Blueberry Stuffed Sweet Potatoes

Prep time: 15 minutes | Cook time: 20 minutes | Serves 4

2 cups cooked wild rice	1 scallion, white and green parts, peeled and thinly sliced
½ cup dried blueberries	
½ cup chopped hazelnuts	
½ cup shredded Swiss chard	Sea salt and freshly ground black pepper, to taste
1 teaspoon chopped fresh thyme	
	4 sweet potatoes, baked in the skin until tender

1. Preheat the oven to 400°F (205°C).
2. Combine all the , except for the sweet potatoes, in a large bowl. Stir to mix well.
3. Cut the top third of the sweet potato off length wire, then scoop most of the sweet potato flesh out.
4. Fill the potato with the wild rice mixture, then set the sweet potato on a greased baking sheet.
5. Bake in the preheated oven for 20 minutes or until the sweet potato skin is lightly charred.
6. Serve immediately.

Per Serving

calories: 393 | fat: 7.1g | protein: 10.2g | carbs: 76.9g | fiber: 10.0g | sodium: 93mg

Slow Cooked Turkey and Brown Rice

Prep time: 20 minutes | Cook time: 3 hours 10 minutes | Serves 6

1 tablespoon extra-virgin olive oil	¼ cup pitted and sliced Kalamata olives
1½ pounds (680 g) ground turkey	3 medium zucchini, sliced thinly
2 tablespoons chopped fresh sage, divided	¼ cup chopped fresh flat-leaf parsley
2 tablespoons chopped fresh thyme, divided	1 medium yellow onion, chopped
1 teaspoon sea salt	1 tablespoon plus 1 teaspoon balsamic vinegar
½ teaspoon ground black pepper	
2 cups brown rice	2 cups low-sodium chicken stock
1 (14-ounce / 397-g) can stewed tomatoes, with the juice	2 garlic cloves, minced
	½ cup grated Parmesan cheese, for serving

1. Heat the olive oil in a nonstick skillet over medium-high heat until shimmering.
2. Add the ground turkey and sprinkle with 1 tablespoon of sage, 1 tablespoon of thyme, salt and ground black pepper.
3. Sauté for 10 minutes or until the ground turkey is lightly browned.
4. Pour them in the slow cooker, then pour in the remaining , except for the Parmesan. Stir to mix well.
5. Put the lid on and cook on high for 3 hours or until the rice and vegetables are tender.
6. Pour them in a large serving bowl, then spread with Parmesan cheese before serving.

Per Serving

calories: 499 | fat: 16.4g | protein: 32.4g | carbs: 56.5g | fiber: 4.7g | sodium: 758mg

Papaya, Jicama, and Peas Rice Bowl

Prep time: 20 minutes | Cook time: 45 minutes | Serves 4

Sauce:

Juice of ¼ lemon
2 teaspoons chopped fresh basil
1 tablespoon raw honey
1 tablespoon extra-virgin olive oil
Sea salt, to taste

Rice:

1½ cups wild rice
2 papayas, peeled, seeded, and diced
1 jicama, peeled and shredded
1 cup snow peas, julienned
2 cups shredded cabbage
1 scallion, white and green parts, chopped

1. Combine the for the sauce in a bowl. Stir to mix well. Set aside until ready to use.
2. Pour the wild rice in a saucepan, then pour in enough water to cover. Bring to a boil.
3. Reduce the heat to low, then simmer for 45 minutes or until the wild rice is soft and plump. Drain and transfer to a large serving bowl.
4. Top the rice with papayas, jicama, peas, cabbage, and scallion. Pour the sauce over and stir to mix well before serving.

Per Serving

calories: 446 | fat: 7.9g | protein: 13.1g | carbs: 85.8g | fiber: 16.0g | sodium: 70mg

Black Bean Chili with Mangoes

Prep time: 10 minutes | Cook time: 10 minutes | Serves 4

2 tablespoons coconut oil
1 onion, chopped
2 (15-ounce / 425-g) cans black beans, drained and rinsed
1 tablespoon chili powder
1 teaspoon sea salt
¼ teaspoon freshly ground black pepper
1 cup water
2 ripe mangoes, sliced thinly
¼ cup chopped fresh cilantro, divided
¼ cup sliced scallions, divided

1. Heat the coconut oil in a pot over high heat until melted.
2. Put the onion in the pot and sauté for 5 minutes or until translucent. Add the black beans to the pot. Sprinkle with chili powder, salt, and ground black pepper. Pour in the water. Stir to mix well.
3. Bring to a boil. Reduce the heat to low, then simmering for 5 minutes or until the beans are tender.
4. Turn off the heat and mix in the mangoes, then garnish with scallions and cilantro before serving.

Per Serving

calories: 430 | fat: 9.1g | protein: 20.2g | carbs: 71.9g | fiber: 22.0g | sodium: 608mg

Israeli Style Eggplant and Chickpea Salad

Prep time: 5 minutes | Cook time: 20 minutes | Serves 6

2 tablespoons freshly squeezed lemon juice
1 teaspoon ground cumin
¼ teaspoon sea salt
2 tablespoons olive oil, divided
1 (1-pound / 454-g) medium globe eggplant, stem removed, cut into flat cubes (about ½ inch thick)
2 tablespoons balsamic vinegar
1 (15-ounce / 425-g) can chickpeas, drained and rinsed
¼ cup chopped mint leaves
1 cup sliced sweet onion
1 garlic clove, finely minced
1 tablespoon sesame seeds, toasted

1. Preheat the oven to 550°F (288°C) or the highest level of your oven or broiler. Grease a baking sheet with 1 tablespoon of olive oil.
2. Combine the balsamic vinegar, lemon juice, cumin, salt, and 1 tablespoon of olive oil in a small bowl. Stir to mix well.
3. Arrange the eggplant cubes on the baking sheet, then brush with 2 tablespoons of the balsamic vinegar mixture on both sides.
4. Broil in the preheated oven for 8 minutes or until lightly browned. Flip the cubes halfway through the cooking time.
5. Meanwhile, combine the chickpeas, mint, onion, garlic, and sesame seeds in a large serving bowl. Drizzle with remaining balsamic vinegar mixture. Stir to mix well.
6. Remove the eggplant from the oven. Allow to cool for 5 minutes, then slice them into ½-inch strips on a clean work surface.
7. Add the eggplant strips in the serving bowl, then toss to combine well before serving.

Per Serving

calories: 125 | fat: 2.9g | protein: 5.2g | carbs: 20.9g | fiber: 6.0g | sodium: 222mg

Italian Sautéd Cannellini Beans

Prep time: 10 minutes | Cook time: 15 minutes | Serves 6

2 teaspoons extra-virgin olive oil
½ cup minced onion
¼ cup red wine vinegar
1 (12-ounce / 340-g) can no-salt-added tomato paste
2 tablespoons raw honey
½ cup water
¼ teaspoon ground cinnamon

1. 2(15-ounce / 425-g) cans cannellini beans
1. Heat the olive oil in a saucepan over medium heat until shimmering.
2. Add the onion and sauté for 5 minutes or until translucent.
3. Pour in the red wine vinegar, tomato paste, honey, and water. Sprinkle with cinnamon. Stir to mix well.
4. Reduce the heat to low, then pour all the beans into the saucepan. Cook for 10 more minutes. Stir constantly.
5. Serve immediately.

Per Serving

calories: 435 | fat: 2.1g | protein: 26.2g | carbs: 80.3g | fiber: 24.0g | sodium: 72mg

Lentil and Vegetable Curry Stew

Prep time: 20 minutes | Cook time: 4 hours 7 minutes | Serves 8

1 tablespoon coconut oil	2 carrots, peeled and diced
1 yellow onion, diced	8 cups low-sodium vegetable soup, divided
¼ cup yellow Thai curry paste	1 bunch kale, stems removed and roughly chopped
2 cups unsweetened coconut milk	
2 cups dry red lentils, rinsed well and drained	Sea salt, to taste
3 cups bite-sized cauliflower florets	½ cup fresh cilantro, chopped
2 golden potatoes, cut into chunks	Pinch crushed red pepper flakes

1. Heat the coconut oil in a nonstick skillet over medium-high heat until melted. Add the onion and sauté for 5 minutes or until translucent. Pour in the curry paste and sauté for another 2 minutes, then fold in the coconut milk and stir to combine well. Bring to a simmer and turn off the heat.
2. Put the lentils, cauliflower, potatoes, and carrot in the slow cooker. Pour in 6 cups of vegetable soup and the curry mixture. Stir to combine well.
3. Cover and cook on high for 4 hours or until the lentils and vegetables are soft. Stir periodically.
4. During the last 30 minutes, fold the kale in the slow cooker and pour in the remaining vegetable soup. Sprinkle with salt. Pour the stew in a large serving bowl and spread the cilantro and red pepper flakes on top before serving hot.

Per Serving calories: 530 | fat: 19.2g | protein: 20.3g | carbs: 75.2g | fiber: 15.5g | sodium: 562mg

Ritzy Veggie Chili

Prep time: 15 minutes | Cook time: 5 hours | Serves 4

1 (28-ounce / 794-g) can chopped tomatoes, with the juice	1 tablespoon onion powder
	1 teaspoon paprika
1 (15-ounce / 425-g) can black beans, drained and rinsed	1 teaspoon cayenne pepper
	1 teaspoon garlic powder
1 (15-ounce / 425-g) can redly beans, drained and rinsed	½ teaspoon sea salt
	½ teaspoon ground black pepper
1 medium green bell pepper, chopped	1 tablespoon olive oil
	1 large hass avocado, pitted, peeled, and chopped, for garnish
1 yellow onion, chopped	

1. Combine all the , except for the avocado, in the slow cooker. Stir to mix well.
2. Put the slow cooker lid on and cook on high for 5 hours or until the vegetables are tender and the mixture has a thick consistency.
3. Pour the chili in a large serving bowl. Allow to cool for 30 minutes, then spread with chopped avocado and serve.

Per Serving calories: 633 | fat: 16.3g | protein: 31.7g | carbs: 97.0g | fiber: 28.9g | sodium: 792mg

Chickpea, Vegetable, and Fruit Stew

Prep time: 20 minutes | Cook time: 6 hours 4 minutes | Serves 6

1 large bell pepper, any color, chopped	1 teaspoon grated fresh ginger
	2 garlic cloves, minced
6 ounces (170 g) green beans, trimmed and cut into bite-size pieces	1¾ cups low-sodium vegetable soup
3 cups canned chickpeas, rinsed and drained	1 teaspoon ground cumin
	1 tablespoon ground coriander
1 (15-ounce / 425-g) can diced tomatoes, with the juice	¼ tps ground red pepper flakes
	Sea salt and ground black pepper, to taste
1 large carrot, cut into ¼-inch rounds	8 ounces (227 g) fresh baby spinach
2 large potatoes, peeled and cubed	¼ cup diced dried figs
	¼ cup diced dried apricots
1 large yellow onion, chopped	1 cup plain Greek yogurt

1. Place the bell peppers, green beans, chicken peas, tomatoes and juice, carrot, potatoes, onion, ginger, and garlic in the slow cooker. Pour in the vegetable soup and sprinkle with cumin, coriander, red pepper flakes, salt, and ground black pepper. Stir to mix well.
2. Put the slow cooker lid on and cook on high for 6 hours or until the vegetables are soft. Stir periodically.
3. Open the lid and fold in the spinach, figs, apricots, and yogurt. Stir to mix well.
4. Cook for 4 minutes or until the spinach is wilted. Pour them in a large serving bowl. Allow to cool for at least 20 minutes, then serve warm.

Per Serving
calories: 611 | fat: 9.0g | protein: 30.7g | carbs: 107.4g | fiber: 20.8g | sodium: 344mg

Quinoa and Chickpea Vegetable Bowls

Prep time: 20 minutes | Cook time: 15 minutes | Serves 4

1 cup red dry quinoa, rinsed and drained	**Mango Sauce:**
	1 mango, diced
2 cups low-sodium vegetable soup	¼ cup fresh lime juice
	½ teaspoon ground turmeric
2 cups fresh spinach	1 teaspoon finely minced fresh ginger
2 cups finely shredded red cabbage	
	¼ teaspoon sea salt
1 (15-ounce / 425-g) can chickpeas, drained and rinsed	Pinch of ground red pepper
	1 teaspoon pure maple syrup
1 ripe avocado, thinly sliced	2 tablespoons extra-virgin olive oil
1 cup shredded carrots	
1 red bell pepper, thinly sliced	
4 tablespoons Mango Sauce	
½ cup fresh cilantro, chopped	

1. Pour the quinoa and vegetable soup in a saucepan. Bring to a boil. Reduce the heat to low. Cover and cook for 15 minutes or until tender. Fluffy with a fork.
2. Meanwhile, combine the for the mango sauce in a food processor. Pulse until smooth.
3. Divide the quinoa, spinach, and cabbage into 4 serving bowls, then top with chickpeas, avocado, carrots, and bell pepper. Dress them with the mango sauce and spread with cilantro. Serve immediately.

Per Serving calories: 366 | fat: 11.1g | protein: 15.5g | carbs: 55.6g | fiber: 17.7g | sodium: 746mg

Spicy Italian Bean Balls with Marinara

Prep time: 20 minutes | Cook time: 30 minutes | Serves 2 to 4

Bean Balls:
1 tablespoon extra-virgin olive oil
½ yellow onion, minced
1 teaspoon fennel seeds
2 teaspoons dried oregano
½ teaspoon crushed red pepper flakes
1 teaspoon garlic powder
1 (15-ounce / 425-g) can white beans (cannellini or navy), drained and rinsed
½ cup whole-grain bread crumbs
Sea salt and ground black pepper, to taste

Marinara:
1 tablespoon extra-virgin olive oil
3 garlic cloves, minced
Handful basil leaves
1 (28-ounce / 794-g) can chopped tomatoes with juice reserved
Sea salt, to taste

Make the Bean Balls

1. Preheat the oven to 350°F (180°C). Line a baking sheet with parchment paper.
2. Heat the olive oil in a nonstick skillet over medium heat until shimmering.
3. Add the onion and sauté for 5 minutes or until translucent.
4. Sprinkle with fennel seeds, oregano, red pepper flakes, and garlic powder, then cook for 1 minute or until aromatic.
5. Pour the sautéed mixture in a food processor and add the beans and bread crumbs. Sprinkle with salt and ground black pepper, then pulse to combine well and the mixture holds together.
6. Shape the mixture into balls with a 2-ounce (57-g) cookie scoop, then arrange the balls on the baking sheet.
7. Bake in the preheated oven for 30 minutes or until lightly browned. Flip the balls halfway through the cooking time.

Make the Marinara

8. While baking the bean balls, heat the olive oil in a saucepan over medium-high heat until shimmering.
9. Add the garlic and basil and sauté for 2 minutes or until fragrant. Fold in the tomatoes and juice. Bring to a boil. Reduce the heat to low. Put the lid on and simmer for 15 minutes. Sprinkle with salt. Transfer the bean balls on a large plate and baste with marinara before serving.

Per Serving calories: 351 | fat: 16.4g | protein: 11.5g | carbs: 42.9g | fiber: 10.3g | sodium: 377mg

Black-Eyed Peas Salad with Walnuts

Prep time: 10 minutes | Cook time: 0 minutes | Serves 4 to 6

3 tablespoons extra-virgin olive oil
3 tablespoons dukkah, divided
2 tablespoons lemon juice
2 tablespoons pomegranate molasses
¼ tbs salt, or more to taste
⅛ teaspoon pepper, or more to taste
2 (15-ounce / 425-g) cans black-eyed peas, rinsed
½ cup pomegranate seeds
½ cup minced fresh parsley
½ cup walnuts, toasted and chopped
4 scallions, sliced thinly

1. In a large bowl, whisk together the olive oil, 2 tablespoons of the dukkah, lemon juice, pomegranate molasses, salt and pepper. Stir in the remaining . Season with salt and pepper. Sprinkle with the remaining 1 tablespoon of the dukkah before serving.

Per Serving calories: 155 | fat: 11.5g | protein: 2.0g | carbs: 12.5g | fiber: 2.1g | sodium: 105mg

Wild Rice, Celery, and Cauliflower Pilaf

Prep time: 10 minutes | Cook time: 45 minutes | Serves 4

1 tablespoon olive oil, plus more for greasing the baking dish
1 cup wild rice
2 cups low-sodium chicken broth
1 sweet onion, chopped
2 stalks celery, chopped
1 teaspoon minced garlic
2 carrots, peeled, halved lengthwise, and sliced
½ cauliflower head, cut into small florets
1 teaspoon chopped fresh thyme
Sea salt, to taste

1. Preheat the oven to 350°F (180°C). Line a baking sheet with parchment paper and grease with olive oil.
2. Put the wild rice in a saucepan, then pour in the chicken broth. Bring to a boil. Reduce the heat to low and simmer for 30 minutes or until the rice is plump.
3. Meanwhile, heat the remaining olive oil in an oven-proof skillet over medium-high heat until shimmering.
4. Add the onion, celery, and garlic to the skillet and sauté for 3 minutes or until the onion is translucent.
5. Add the carrots and cauliflower to the skillet and sauté for 5 minutes. Turn off the heat and set aside.
6. Pour the cooked rice in the skillet with the vegetables. Sprinkle with thyme and salt.
7. Set the skillet in the preheated oven and bake for 15 minutes or until the vegetables are soft. Serve immediately.

Per Serving calories: 214 | fat: 3.9g | protein: 7.2g | carbs: 37.9g | fiber: 5.0g | sodium: 122mg

Walnut and Ricotta Spaghetti

Prep time: 15 minutes | Cook time: 10 minutes | Serves 6

1 pound (454 g) cooked whole-wheat spaghetti
2 tablespoons extra-virgin olive oil
4 cloves garlic, minced
¾ cup walnuts, toasted and finely chopped
2 tablespoons ricotta cheese
¼ cup flat-leaf parsley, chopped
½ cup grated Parmesan cheese
Sea salt and freshly ground pepper, to taste

1. Reserve a cup of spaghetti water while cooking the spaghetti.
2. Heat the olive oil in a nonstick skillet over medium-low heat or until shimmering.
3. Add the garlic and sauté for a minute or until fragrant.
4. Pour the spaghetti water into the skillet and cook for 8 more minutes.
5. Turn off the heat and mix in the walnuts and ricotta cheese.
6. Put the cooked spaghetti on a large serving plate, then pour the walnut sauce over. Spread with parsley and Parmesan, then sprinkle with salt and ground pepper. Toss to serve.

Per Serving
calories: 264 | fat: 16.8g | protein: 8.6g | carbs: 22.8g | fiber: 4.0g | sodium: 336mg

Butternut Squash, Spinach, and Cheeses Lasagna

Prep time: 30 minutes | Cook time: 3 hours 45 minutes | Serves 4 to 6

2 tablespoons extra-virgin olive oil, divided	½ cup unsweetened almond milk
1 butternut squash, halved lengthwise and deseeded	5 layers whole-wheat lasagna noodles (about 12 ounces / 340 g in total)
½ teaspoon sage	4 ounces (113 g) fresh spinach leaves, divided
½ teaspoon sea salt	
¼ tbs ground black pepper	½ cup shredded part skim Mozzarella, for garnish
¼ cup grated Parmesan cheese	
2 cups ricotta cheese	

1. Preheat the oven to 400°F (205°C). Line a baking sheet with parchment paper. Brush 1 tablespoon of olive oil on the cut side of the butternut squash, then place the squash on the baking sheet. Bake in the preheated oven for 45 minutes or until the squash is tender. Allow to cool until you can handle it, then scoop the flesh out and put the flesh in a food processor to purée. Combine the puréed butternut squash flesh with sage, salt, and ground black pepper in a large bowl. Stir to mix well.
2. Combine the cheeses and milk in a separate bowl, then sprinkle with salt and pepper, to taste.
3. Grease the slow cooker with 1 tablespoon of olive oil, then add a layer of lasagna noodles to coat the bottom of the slow cooker. Spread half of the squash mixture on top of the noodles, then top the squash mixture with another layer of lasagna noodles. Spread half of the spinach over the noodles, then top the spinach with half of cheese mixture. Repeat with remaining 3 layers of lasagna noodles, squash mixture, spinach, and cheese mixture. Top the cheese mixture with Mozzarella, then put the lid on and cook on low for 3 hours or until the lasagna noodles are al dente. Serve immediately.

Per Serving calories: 657 | fat: 37.1g | protein: 30.9g | carbs: 57.2g | fiber: 8.3g | sodium: 918mg

Pesto Pasta

Prep time: 10 minutes | Cook time: 8 minutes | Serves 4 to 6

1 pound (454 g) spaghetti	½ teaspoon freshly ground black pepper
4 cups fresh basil leaves, stems removed	
3 cloves garlic	½ cup toasted pine nuts
1 teaspoon salt	¼ cup lemon juice
	½ cup grated Parmesan cheese
	1 cup extra-virgin olive oil

1. Bring a large pot of salted water to a boil. Add the spaghetti to the pot and cook for 8 minutes.
2. In a food processor, place the remaining , except for the olive oil, and pulse.
3. While the processor is running, slowly drizzle the olive oil through the top opening. Process until all the olive oil has been added.
4. Reserve ½ cup of the cooking liquid. Drain the pasta and put it into a large bowl. Add the pesto and cooking liquid to the bowl of pasta and toss everything together.
5. Serve immediately.

Per Serving
calories: 1067 | fat: 72.0g | protein: 23.0g | carbs: 91..0g | fiber: 6.0g | sodium: 817mg

Minestrone Chickpeas and Macaroni Casserole

Prep time: 20 minutes | Cook time: 7 hours 20 minutes | Serves 5

1 (15-ounce / 425-g) can chickpeas, drained and rinsed	1 teaspoon dried oregano
	2 teaspoons maple syrup
1 (28-ounce / 794-g) can diced tomatoes, with the juice	½ teaspoon sea salt
	¼ teaspoon ground black pepper
1 (6-ounce / 170-g) can no-salt-added tomato paste	½ pound (227-g) fresh green beans, trimmed and cut into bite-size pieces
3 medium carrots, sliced	
3 cloves garlic, minced	1 cup macaroni pasta
1 medium yellow onion, chopped	2 ounces (57 g) Parmesan cheese, grated
1 cup low-sodium vegetable soup	
½ teaspoon dried rosemary	

1. Except for the green beans, pasta, and Parmesan cheese, combine all the in the slow cooker and stir to mix well. Put the slow cooker lid on and cook on low for 7 hours. Fold in the pasta and green beans. Put the lid on and cook on high for 20 minutes or until the vegetable are soft and the pasta is al dente.
2. Pour them in a large serving bowl and spread with Parmesan cheese before serving.

Per Serving calories: 349 | fat: 6.7g | protein: 16.5g | carbs: 59.9g | fiber: 12.9g | sodium: 937mg

Garlic and Parsley Chickpeas

Prep time: 10 minutes | Cook time: 18 to 20 minutes | Serves 4 to 6

¼ cup extra-virgin olive oil, divided	Black pepper, to taste
	2 (15-ounce / 425-g) cans chickpeas, rinsed
4 garlic cloves, sliced thinly	
⅛ teaspoon red pepper flakes	1 cup vegetable broth
	2 tablespoons minced fresh parsley
1 onion, chopped finely	
¼ teaspoon salt, plus more to taste	2 teaspoons lemon juice

1. Add 3 tablespoons of the olive oil, garlic, and pepper flakes to a skillet over medium heat. Cook for about 3 minutes, stirring constantly, or until the garlic turns golden but not brown. Stir in the onion and ¼ teaspoon salt and cook for 5 to 7 minutes, or until softened and lightly browned.
2. Add the chickpeas and broth to the skillet and bring to a simmer. Reduce the heat to medium-low, cover, and cook for about 7 minutes, or until the chickpeas are cooked through and flavors meld. Uncover, increase the heat to high and continue to cook for about 3 minutes more, or until nearly all liquid has evaporated.
3. Turn off the heat, stir in the parsley and lemon juice. Season to taste with salt and pepper and drizzle with remaining 1 tablespoon of the olive oil. Serve warm.

Per Serving calories: 220 | fat: 11.4g | protein: 6.5g | carbs: 24.6g | fiber: 6.0g | sodium: 467mg

Mashed Beans with Cumin

Prep time: 10 minutes | Cook time: 10 to 12 minutes | Serves 4 to 6

1 tablespoon extra-virgin olive oil, plus extra for serving
4 garlic cloves, minced
1 teaspoon ground cumin
2 (15-ounce / 425-g) cans fava beans
3 tablespoons tahini
2 tablespoons lemon juice, plus lemon wedges for serving
Salt and pepper, to taste
1 tomato, cored and cut into ½-inch pieces
1 small onion, chopped finely
2 hard-cooked large eggs, chopped
2 tablespoons minced fresh parsley

1. Add the olive oil, garlic and cumin to a medium saucepan over medium heat. Cook for about 2 minutes, or until fragrant. Stir in the beans with their liquid and tahini. Bring to a simmer and cook for 8 to 10 minutes, or until the liquid thickens slightly.
2. Turn off the heat, mash the beans to a coarse consistency with a potato masher. Stir in the lemon juice and 1 teaspoon pepper. Season with salt and pepper.
3. Transfer the mashed beans to a serving dish. Top with the tomato, onion, eggs and parsley. Drizzle with the extra olive oil. Serve with the lemon wedges.

Per Serving

calories: 125 | fat: 8.6g | protein: 4.9g | carbs: 9.1g | fiber: 2.9g | sodium: 131mg

Turkish Canned Pinto Bean Salad

Prep time: 10 minutes | Cook time: 3 minutes | Serves 4 to 6

¼ cup extra-virgin olive oil, divided
3 garlic cloves, lightly crushed and peeled
2 (15-ounce / 425-g) cans pinto beans, rinsed 2 cups plus
1 tablespoon water
Salt and pepper, to taste
¼ cup tahini
3 tablespoons lemon juice
1 tablespoon ground dried Aleppo pepper, plus extra for serving
8 ounces (227 g) cherry tomatoes, halved
¼ red onion, sliced thinly
½ cup fresh parsley leaves
2 hard-cooked large eggs, quartered
1 tablespoon toasted sesame seeds

1. Add 1 tablespoon of the olive oil and garlic to a medium saucepan over medium heat. Cook for about 3 minutes, stirring constantly, or until the garlic turns golden but not brown.
2. Add the beans, 2 cups of the water and 1 teaspoon salt and bring to a simmer. Remove from the heat, cover and let sit for 20 minutes. Drain the beans and discard the garlic.
3. In a large bowl, whisk together the remaining 3 tablespoons of the oil, tahini, lemon juice, Aleppo, the remaining 1 tablespoon of the water and ¼ teaspoon salt. Stir in the beans, tomatoes, onion and parsley. Season with salt and pepper to taste.
4. Transfer to a serving platter and top with the eggs. Sprinkle with the sesame seeds and extra Aleppo before serving.

Per Serving calories: 402 | fat: 18.9g | protein: 16.2g | carbs: 44.4g | fiber: 11.2g | sodium: 456mg

Fava and Garbanzo Bean Ful

Prep time: 10 minutes | Cook time: 10 minutes | Serves 6

1 (15-ounce / 425-g) can fava beans, rinsed and drained
1 (1-pound / 454-g) can garbanzo beans, rinsed and drained
3 cups water
½ cup lemon juice
3 cloves garlic, peeled and minced
1 teaspoon salt
3 tablespoons extra-virgin olive oil

1. In a pot over medium heat, cook the beans and water for 10 minutes.
2. Drain the beans and transfer to a bowl. Reserve 1 cup of the liquid from the cooked beans.
3. Add the reserved liquid, lemon juice, minced garlic and salt to the bowl with the beans. Mix to combine well. Using a potato masher, mash up about half the beans in the bowl.
4. Give the mixture one more stir to make sure the beans are evenly mixed.
5. Drizzle with the olive oil and serve.

Per Serving

calories: 199 | fat: 9.0g | protein: 10.0g | carbs: 25.0g | fiber: 9.0g | sodium: 395mg

Triple-Green Pasta with Cheese

Prep time: 5 minutes | Cook time: 14 to 16 minutes | Serves 4

8 ounces (227 g) uncooked penne
1 tablespoon extra-virgin olive oil
2 garlic cloves, minced
¼ teaspoon crushed red pepper
2 cups chopped fresh flat-leaf parsley, including stems
5 cups loosely packed baby spinach
¼ teaspoon ground nutmeg
¼ teaspoon kosher salt
¼ teaspoon freshly ground black pepper
⅓ cup Castelvetrano olives, pitted and sliced
⅓ cup grated Parmesan cheese

1. In a large stockpot of salted water, cook the pasta for about 8 to 10 minutes. Drain the pasta and reserve ¼ cup of the cooking liquid.
2. Meanwhile, heat the olive oil in a large skillet over medium heat. Add the garlic and red pepper and cook for 30 seconds, stirring constantly.
3. Add the parsley and cook for 1 minute, stirring constantly. Add the spinach, nutmeg, salt, and pepper, and cook for 3 minutes, stirring occasionally, or until the spinach is wilted.
4. Add the cooked pasta and the reserved ¼ cup cooking liquid to the skillet. Stir in the olives and cook for about 2 minutes, or until most of the pasta water has been absorbed.
5. Remove from the heat and stir in the cheese before serving.

Per Serving

calories: 262 | fat: 4.0g | protein: 15.0g | carbs: 51.0g | fiber: 13.0g | sodium: 1180mg

Caprese Pasta with Roasted Asparagus

Prep time: 5 minutes | Cook time: 25 minutes | Serves 6

8 ounces (227 g) uncooked small pasta, like orecchiette (little ears) or farfalle (bow ties)

1½ pounds (680 g) fresh asparagus, ends trimmed and stalks chopped into 1- inch pieces

1½ cups grape tomatoes, halved

2 tablespoons extra-virgin olive oil

¼ teaspoon kosher salt

¼ teaspoon freshly ground black pepper

2 cups fresh Mozzarella, drained and cut into bite-size pieces (about 8 ounces / 227 g)

⅓ cup torn fresh basil leaves

2 tablespoons balsamic vinegar

1. Preheat the oven to 400ºF (205ºC).
2. In a large stockpot of salted water, cook the pasta for about 8 to 10 minutes. Drain and reserve about ¼ cup of the cooking liquid.
3. Meanwhile, in a large bowl, toss together the asparagus, tomatoes, oil, salt and pepper. Spread the mixture onto a large, rimmed baking sheet and bake in the oven for 15 minutes, stirring twice during cooking.
4. Remove the vegetables from the oven and add the cooked pasta to the baking sheet. Mix with a few tablespoons of cooking liquid to help the sauce become smoother and the saucy vegetables stick to the pasta.
5. Gently mix in the Mozzarella and basil. Drizzle with the balsamic vinegar. Serve from the baking sheet or pour the pasta into a large bowl.

Per Serving

calories: 147 | fat: 3.0g | protein: 16.0g | carbs: 17.0g | fiber: 5.0g | sodium: 420mg

Garlic Shrimp Fettuccine

Prep time: 10 minutes | Cook time: 15 minutes | Serves 4 to 6

8 ounces (227 g) fettuccine pasta

¼ cup extra-virgin olive oil

3 tablespoons garlic, minced

1 pound (454 g) large shrimp, peeled and deveined

⅓ cup lemon juice

1 tablespoon lemon zest

½ teaspoon salt

½ teaspoon freshly ground black pepper

1. Bring a large pot of salted water to a boil. Add the fettuccine and cook for 8 minutes. Reserve ½ cup of the cooking liquid and drain the pasta.
2. In a large saucepan over medium heat, heat the olive oil. Add the garlic and sauté for 1 minute.
3. Add the shrimp to the saucepan and cook each side for 3 minutes. Remove the shrimp from the pan and set aside.
4. Add the remaining to the saucepan. Stir in the cooking liquid. Add the pasta and toss together to evenly coat the pasta.
5. Transfer the pasta to a serving dish and serve topped with the cooked shrimp.

Per Serving

calories: 615 | fat: 17.0g | protein: 33.0g | carbs: 89.0g | fiber: 4.0g | sodium: 407mg

Spaghetti with Pine Nuts and Cheese

Prep time: 10 minutes | Cook time: 11 minutes | Serves 4 to 6

8 ounces (227 g) spaghetti

4 tablespoons almond butter

1 teaspoon freshly ground black pepper

½ cup pine nuts

1 cup fresh grated Parmesan cheese, divided

1. Bring a large pot of salted water to a boil. Add the pasta and cook for 8 minutes.
2. In a large saucepan over medium heat, combine the butter, black pepper, and pine nuts. Cook for 2 to 3 minutes, or until the pine nuts are lightly toasted.
3. Reserve ½ cup of the pasta water. Drain the pasta and place it into the pan with the pine nuts.
4. Add ¾ cup of the Parmesan cheese and the reserved pasta water to the pasta and toss everything together to evenly coat the pasta.
5. Transfer the pasta to a serving dish and top with the remaining ¼ cup of the Parmesan cheese. Serve immediately.

Per Serving

calories: 542 | fat: 32.0g | protein: 20.0g | carbs: 46.0g | fiber: 2.0g | sodium: 552mg

Creamy Garlic Parmesan Chicken Pasta

Prep time: 5 minutes | Cook time: 15 minutes | Serves 4

3 tablespoons extra-virgin olive oil

2 boneless, skinless chicken breasts, cut into thin strips

1 large onion, thinly sliced

3 tablespoons garlic, minced

1½ teaspoons salt

1 pound (454 g) fettuccine pasta

1 cup heavy whipping cream

¾ cup freshly grated Parmesan cheese, divided

½ teaspoon freshly ground black pepper

1. In a large skillet over medium heat, heat the olive oil. Add the chicken and cook for 3 minutes.
2. Add the onion, garlic and salt to the skillet. Cook for 7 minutes, stirring occasionally.
3. Meanwhile, bring a large pot of salted water to a boil and add the pasta, then cook for 7 minutes.
4. While the pasta is cooking, add the heavy cream, ½ cup of the Parmesan cheese and black pepper to the chicken. Simmer for 3 minutes.
5. Reserve ½ cup of the pasta water. Drain the pasta and add it to the chicken cream sauce.
6. Add the reserved pasta water to the pasta and toss together. Simmer for 2 minutes. Top with the remaining ¼ cup of the Parmesan cheese and serve warm.

Per Serving

calories: 879 | fat: 42.0g | protein: 35.0g | carbs: 90.0g | fiber: 5.0g | sodium: 1336mg

Bulgur Pilaf with Garbanzo

Prep time: 5 minutes | Cook time: 20 minutes | Serves 4 to 6

3 tablespoons extra-virgin olive oil
1 large onion, chopped
1 (1-pound / 454-g) can garbanzo beans, rinsed and drained
2 cups bulgur wheat, rinsed and drained
1½ teaspoons salt
½ teaspoon cinnamon
4 cups water

1. In a large pot over medium heat, heat the olive oil. Add the onion and cook for 5 minutes.
2. Add the garbanzo beans and cook for an additional 5 minutes.
3. Stir in the remaining .
4. Reduce the heat to low. Cover and cook for 10 minutes.
5. When done, fluff the pilaf with a fork. Cover and let sit for another 5 minutes before serving.

Per Serving

calories: 462 | fat: 13.0g | protein: 15.0g | carbs: 76.0g | fiber: 19.0g | sodium: 890mg

Pearl Barley Risotto with Parmesan Cheese

Prep time: 5 minutes | Cook time: 20 minutes | Serves 6

4 cups low-sodium or no-salt-added vegetable broth
1 tablespoon extra-virgin olive oil
1 cup chopped yellow onion
2 cups uncooked pearl barley
½ cup dry white wine
1 cup freshly grated Parmesan cheese, divided
¼ teaspoon kosher or sea salt
¼ teaspoon freshly ground black pepper
Fresh chopped chives and lemon wedges, for serving (optional)

1. Pour the broth into a medium saucepan and bring to a simmer.
2. Heat the olive oil in a large stockpot over medium-high heat. Add the onion and cook for about 4 minutes, stirring occasionally.
3. Add the barley and cook for 2 minutes, stirring, or until the barley is toasted. Pour in the wine and cook for about 1 minute, or until most of the liquid evaporates. Add 1 cup of the warm broth into the pot and cook, stirring, for about 2 minutes, or until most of the liquid is absorbed.
4. Add the remaining broth, 1 cup at a time, cooking until each cup is absorbed (about 2 minutes each time) before adding the next. The last addition of broth will take a bit longer to absorb, about 4 minutes.
5. Remove the pot from the heat, and stir in ½ cup of the cheese, and the salt and pepper.
6. Serve with the remaining ½ cup of the cheese on the side, along with the chives and lemon wedges (if desired).

Per Serving calories: 421 | fat: 11.0g | protein: 15.0g | carbs: 67.0g | fiber: 11.0g | sodium: 641mg

Israeli Couscous with Asparagus

Prep time: 5 minutes | Cook time: 25 minutes | Serves 6

1½ pounds (680 g) asparagus spears, ends trimmed and stalks chopped into 1-inch pieces
1 garlic clove, minced
1 tablespoon extra-virgin olive oil
¼ teaspoon freshly ground black pepper
1¾ cups water
1 (8-ounce / 227-g) box uncooked whole-wheat or regular Israeli couscous (about 1⅓ cups)
¼ teaspoon kosher salt
1 cup garlic-and-herb goat cheese, at room temperature

1. Preheat the oven to 425ºF (220ºC).
2. In a large bowl, stir together the asparagus, garlic, oil, and pepper. Spread the asparagus on a large, rimmed baking sheet and roast for 10 minutes, stirring a few times. Remove the pan from the oven, and spoon the asparagus into a large serving bowl. Set aside.
3. While the asparagus is roasting, bring the water to a boil in a medium saucepan. Add the couscous and season with salt, stirring well.
4. Reduce the heat to medium-low. Cover and cook for 12 minutes, or until the water is absorbed.
5. Pour the hot couscous into the bowl with the asparagus. Add the goat cheese and mix thoroughly until completely melted. Serve immediately.

Per Serving calories: 103 | fat: 2.0g | protein: 6.0g | carbs: 18.0g | fiber: 5.0g | sodium: 343mg

Freekeh Pilaf with Dates and Pistachios

Prep time: 10 minutes | Cook time: 10 minutes | Serves 4 to 6

2 tablespoons extra-virgin olive oil, plus extra for drizzling
1 shallot, minced
1½ teaspoons grated fresh ginger
¼ teaspoon ground coriander
¼ teaspoon ground cumin
Salt and pepper, to taste
1¾ cups water
1½ cups cracked freekeh, rinsed
3 ounces (85 g) pitted dates, chopped
¼ cup shelled pistachios, toasted and coarsely chopped
1½ tablespoons lemon juice
¼ cup chopped fresh mint

1. Set the Instant Pot to Sauté mode and heat the olive oil until shimmering. Add the shallot, ginger, coriander, cumin, salt, and pepper to the pot and cook for about 2 minutes, or until the shallot is softened. Stir in the water and freekeh.
2. Secure the lid. Select the Manual mode and set the cooking time for 4 minutes at High Pressure. Once cooking is complete, do a quick pressure release. Carefully open the lid. Add the dates, pistachios and lemon juice and gently fluff the freekeh with a fork to combine. Season to taste with salt and pepper.
3. Transfer to a serving dish and sprinkle with the mint. Serve drizzled with extra olive oil.

Per Serving calories: 280 | fat: 8.0g | protein: 8.0g | carbs: 46.0g | fiber: 9.0g | sodium: 200mg

Quinoa with Baby Potatoes and Broccoli

Prep time: 5 minutes | Cook time: 10 minutes | Serves 4

2 tablespoons olive oil
1 cup baby potatoes, cut in half
1 cup broccoli florets
2 cups cooked quinoa
Zest of 1 lemon
Sea salt and freshly ground pepper, to taste

1. Heat the olive oil in a large skillet over medium heat until shimmering. Add the potatoes and cook for about 6 to 7 minutes, or until softened and golden brown. Add the broccoli and cook for about 3 minutes, or until tender.
2. Remove from the heat and add the quinoa and lemon zest. Season with salt and pepper to taste, then serve.

Per Serving calories: 205 | fat: 8.6g | protein: 5.1g | carbs: 27.3g | fiber: 3.7g | sodium: 158mg

Black-Eyed Pea and Vegetable Stew

Prep time: 15 minutes | Cook time: 40 minutes | Serves 2

½ cup black-eyed peas, soaked in water overnight
3 cups water, plus more as needed
1 large carrot, peeled and cut into ½-inch pieces (about ¾ cup)
1 large beet, peeled and cut into ½-inch pieces (about ¾ cup)
¼ teaspoon turmeric
¼ teaspoon cayenne pepper
¼ teaspoon ground cumin seeds, toasted
¼ cup finely chopped parsley
¼ teaspoon salt (optional)
½ teaspoon fresh lime juice

1. Pour the black-eyed peas and water into a large pot, then cook over medium heat for 25 minutes. Add the carrot and beet to the pot and cook for 10 minutes more, adding more water as needed.
2. Add the turmeric, cayenne pepper, cumin, and parsley to the pot and cook for another 6 minutes, or until the vegetables are softened.
3. Stir the mixture periodically. Season with salt, if desired.
4. Serve drizzled with the fresh lime juice.

Per Serving
calories: 89 | fat: 0.7g | protein: 4.1g | carbs: 16.6g | fiber: 4.5g | sodium: 367mg

Chickpea Salad with Tomatoes and Basil

Prep time: 5 minutes | Cook time: 45 minutes | Serves 2

1 cup dried chickpeas, rinsed
1 quart water, or enough to cover the chickpeas by 3 to 4 inches
1½ cups halved grape tomatoes
1 cup chopped fresh basil leaves
2 to 3 tablespoons balsamic vinegar
½ teaspoon garlic powder
½ teaspoon salt, or more to taste

1. In your Instant Pot, combine the chickpeas and water.
2. Secure the lid. Select the Manual mode and set the cooking time for 45 minutes at High Pressure.
3. Once cooking is complete, do a natural pressure release for 20 minutes, then release any remaining pressure. Carefully open the lid and drain the chickpeas. Refrigerate to cool (unless you want to serve this warm, which is good, too).
4. While the chickpeas cool, in a large bowl, stir together the basil, tomatoes, vinegar, garlic powder, and salt. Add the beans, stir to combine, and serve.

Per Serving
calories: 395 | fat: 6.0g | protein: 19.8g | carbs: 67.1g | fiber: 19.0g | sodium: 612mg

Mediterranean Lentils

Prep time: 7 minutes | Cook time: 24 minutes | Serves 2

1 tablespoon olive oil
1 small sweet or yellow onion, diced
1 garlic clove, diced
1 teaspoon dried oregano
½ teaspoon ground cumin
½ teaspoon dried parsley
½ teaspoon salt, plus more as needed
¼ teaspoon freshly ground black pepper, plus more as needed
1 tomato, diced
1 cup brown or green lentils
2½ cups vegetable stock
1 bay leaf

1. Set your Instant Pot to Sauté and heat the olive oil until it shimmers. Add the onion and cook for 3 to 4 minutes until soft. Turn off the Instant Pot and add the garlic, oregano, cumin, parsley, salt, and pepper. Cook until fragrant, about 1 minute.
2. Stir in the tomato, lentils, stock, and bay leaf.
3. Lock the lid. Select the Manual mode and set the cooking time for 18 minutes at High Pressure.
4. When the timer beeps, perform a natural pressure release for 10 minutes, then release any remaining pressure. Carefully open the lid. Remove and discard the bay leaf. Taste and season with more salt and pepper, as needed. If there's too much liquid remaining, select Sauté and cook until it evaporates. Serve warm.

Per Serving calories: 426 | fat: 8.1g | protein: 26.2g | carbs: 63.8g | fiber: 31.0g | sodium: 591mg

Mediterranean-Style Beans and Greens

Prep time: 10 minutes | Cook time: 15 minutes | Serves 2

1 (14.5-ounce / 411-g) can diced tomatoes with juice
1 (15-ounce / 425-g) can cannellini beans, drained and rinsed
2 tablespoons chopped green olives, plus 1 or 2 sliced for garnish
¼ cup vegetable broth, plus more as needed
1 teaspoon extra-virgin olive oil
2 cloves garlic, minced
4 cups arugula
¼ cup freshly squeezed lemon juice

1. In a medium saucepan, bring the tomatoes, beans, and chopped olives to a low boil, adding just enough broth to make the saucy (you may need more than ¼ cup if your canned tomatoes don't have a lot of juice). Reduce heat to low and simmer for about 5 minutes.
2. Meanwhile, in a large skillet, heat the olive oil over medium-high heat. When the oil is hot and starts to shimmer, add garlic and sauté just until it starts to turn slightly tan, about 30 seconds. Add the arugula and lemon juice, stirring to coat leaves with the olive oil and juice. Cover, reduce the heat to low, and simmer for 3 to 5 minutes. Serve the beans over the greens and garnish with olive slices.

Per Serving calories: 262 | fat: 5.9g | protein: 13.2g | carbs: 40.4g | fiber: 9.8g | sodium: 897mg

Rich Cauliflower Alfredo

Prep time: 35 minutes | Cook time: 30 minutes | Serves 4

Cauliflower Alfredo Sauce:
1 tablespoon avocado oil
½ yellow onion, diced
2 cups cauliflower florets
2 garlic cloves, minced
1½ teaspoons miso
1 teaspoon Dijon mustard
Pinch of ground nutmeg
½ cup unsweetened almond milk
1½ tbs fresh lemon juice
2 tablespoons nutritional yeast
Sea salt and ground black pepper, to taste

Fettuccine:
1 tablespoon avocado oil
½ yellow onion, diced
1 cup broccoli florets
1 zucchini, halved lengthwise and cut into ¼-inch-thick half-moons
Sea salt and ground black pepper, to taste
½ cup sun-dried tomatoes, drained if packed in oil
8 ounces (227 g) cooked whole-wheat fettuccine
½ cup fresh basil, cut into ribbons

Make the Sauce

1. Heat the avocado oil in a nonstick skillet over medium-high heat until shimmering.
2. Add half of the onion to the skillet and sauté for 5 minutes or until translucent. Add the cauliflower and garlic to the skillet. Reduce the heat to low and cook for 8 minutes or until the cauliflower is tender.
3. Pour them in a food processor, add the remaining for the sauce and pulse to combine well. Set aside.

Make the Fettuccine

4. Heat the avocado oil in a nonstick skillet over medium-high heat. Add the remaining half of onion and sauté for 5 minutes or until translucent.
5. Add the broccoli and zucchini. Sprinkle with salt and ground black pepper, then sauté for 5 minutes or until tender.
6. Add the sun-dried tomatoes, reserved sauce, and fettuccine. Sauté for 3 minutes or until well-coated and heated through. Serve the fettuccine on a large plate and spread with basil before serving.

Per Serving calories: 288 | fat: 15.9g | protein: 10.1g | carbs: 32.5g | fiber: 8.1g | sodium: 185mg

Tomato Sauce and Basil Pesto Fettuccine

Prep time: 15 minutes | Cook time: 15 minutes | Serves 4

4 Roma tomatoes, diced
2 teaspoons no-salt-added tomato paste
1 tablespoon chopped fresh oregano
2 garlic cloves, minced
1 cup low-sodium vegetable soup
½ teaspoon sea salt

1 packed cup fresh basil leaves
¼ cup pine nuts
¼ cup grated Parmesan cheese
2 tablespoons extra-virgin olive oil
1 pound (454 g) cooked whole-grain fettuccine

1. Put the tomatoes, tomato paste, oregano, garlic, vegetable soup, and salt in a skillet. Stir to mix well.
2. Cook over medium heat for 10 minutes or until lightly thickened. Put the remaining , except for the fettuccine, in a food processor and pulse to combine until smooth.
3. Pour the puréed basil mixture into the tomato mixture, then add the fettuccine. Cook for a few minutes or until heated through and the fettuccine is well coated. Serve immediately.

Per Serving calories: 389 | fat: 22.7g | protein: 9.7g | carbs: 40.2g | fiber: 4.8g | sodium: 616mg

Butternut Squash and Zucchini with Penne

Prep time: 15 minutes | Cook time: 30 minutes | Serves 6

1 large zucchini, diced
1 large butternut squash, peeled and diced
1 large yellow onion, chopped
2 tablespoons extra-virgin olive oil
1 teaspoon paprika
½ teaspoon garlic powder

½ teaspoon sea salt
½ teaspoon freshly ground black pepper
1 pound (454 g) whole-grain penne
½ cup dry white wine
2 tablespoons grated Parmesan cheese

1. Preheat the oven to 400°F (205°C). Line a baking sheet with aluminum foil. Combine the zucchini, butternut squash, and onion in a large bowl. Drizzle with olive oil and sprinkle with paprika, garlic powder, salt, and ground black pepper. Toss to coat well.
2. Spread the vegetables in the single layer on the baking sheet, then roast in the preheated oven for 25 minutes or until the vegetables are tender.
3. Meanwhile, bring a pot of water to a boil, then add the penne and cook for 14 minutes or until al dente. Drain the penne through a colander.
4. Transfer ½ cup of roasted vegetables in a food processor, then pour in the dry white wine. Pulse until smooth.
5. Pour the puréed vegetables in a nonstick skillet and cook with penne over medium-high heat for a few minutes to heat through. Transfer the penne with the purée on a large serving plate, then spread the remaining roasted vegetables and Parmesan on top before serving.

Per Serving calories: 340 | fat: 6.2g | protein: 8.0g | carbs: 66.8g | fiber: 9.1g | sodium: 297mg

Small Pasta and Beans Pot

Prep time: 20 minutes | Cook time: 15 minutes | Serves 2 to 4

1 pound (454 g) small whole wheat pasta
1 (14.5-ounce / 411-g) can diced tomatoes, juice reserved
1 (15-ounce / 425-g) can cannellini beans, drained and rinsed
2 tablespoons no-salt-added tomato paste
1 red or yellow bell pepper, chopped
1 yellow onion, chopped

1 tablespoon Italian seasoning mix
3 garlic cloves, minced
¼ teaspoon crushed red pepper flakes, optional
1 tablespoon extra-virgin olive oil
5 cups water
1 bunch kale, stemmed and chopped
½ cup pitted Kalamata olives, chopped
1 cup sliced basil

1. Except for the kale, olives, and basil, combine all the in a pot. Stir to mix well. Bring to a boil over high heat. Stir constantly. Reduce the heat to medium high and add the kale.
2. Cook for 10 minutes or until the pasta is al dente. Stir constantly. Transfer all of them on a large plate and serve with olives and basil on top.

Per Serving calories: 357 | fat: 7.6g | protein: 18.2g | carbs: 64.5g | fiber: 10.1g | sodium: 454mg

Swoodles with Almond Butter Sauce

Prep time: 20 minutes | Cook time: 20 minutes | Serves 4

Sauce:
1 garlic clove
1-inch piece fresh ginger, peeled and sliced
¼ cup chopped yellow onion
¾ cup almond butter
1 tablespoon tamari
1 tablespoon raw honey
1 teaspoon paprika
1 tablespoon fresh lemon juice
⅛ teaspoon ground red pepper
Sea salt and ground black pepper, to taste

¼ cup water
Swoodles:
2 large sweet potatoes, spiralized
2 tablespoons coconut oil, melted
Sea salt and ground black pepper, to taste
For Serving:
½ cup fresh parsley, chopped
½ cup thinly sliced scallions

Make the Sauce
1. Put the garlic, ginger, and onion in a food processor, then pulse to combine well.
2. Add the almond butter, tamari, honey, paprika, lemon juice, ground red pepper, salt, and black pepper to the food processor. Pulse to combine well.
3. Pour in the water during the pulsing until the mixture is thick and smooth.

Make the Swoodles
4. Preheat the oven to 425°F (220°C). Line a baking sheet with parchment paper. Put the spiralized sweet potato in a bowl, then drizzle with olive oil. Toss to coat well. Transfer them on the baking sheet. Sprinkle with salt and pepper.
5. Bake in the preheated oven for 20 minutes or until lightly browned and al dente.
6. Check the doneness during the baking and remove any well- cooked swoodles.
7. Transfer the swoodles on a large plate and spread with sauce, parsley, and scallions. Toss to serve.

Per Serving calories: 441 | fat: 33.6g | protein: 12.0g | carbs: 29.6g | fiber: 7.8g | sodium: 479mg

Broccoli and Carrot Pasta Salad

Prep time: 5 minutes | Cook time: 10 minutes | Serves 2

8 ounces (227 g) whole-wheat pasta
2 cups broccoli florets
1 cup peeled and shredded carrots
¼ cup plain Greek yogurt

Juice of 1 lemon
1 teaspoon red pepper flakes
Sea salt and freshly ground pepper, to taste

1. Bring a large pot of lightly salted water to a boil. Add the pasta to the boiling water and cook until al dente, about 8 to 10 minutes. Drain the pasta and let rest for a few minutes.
2. When cooled, combine the pasta with the veggies, yogurt, lemon juice, and red pepper flakes in a large bowl, and stir thoroughly to combine.
3. Taste and season to taste with salt and pepper. Serve immediately.

Per Serving
calories: 428 | fat: 2.9g | protein: 15.9g | carbs: 84.6g | fiber: 11.7g | sodium: 642mg

Bean and Veggie Pasta

Prep time: 10 minutes | Cook time: 15 minutes | Serves 2

16 ounces (454 g) small whole wheat pasta, such as penne, farfalle, or macaroni
5 cups water
1 (15-ounce / 425-g) can cannellini beans, drained and rinsed
1 (14.5-ounce / 411-g) can diced (with juice) or crushed tomatoes
1 yellow onion, chopped
1 red or yellow bell pepper, chopped

2 tablespoons tomato paste
1 tablespoon olive oil
3 garlic cloves, minced
¼ teaspoon crushed red pepper (optional)
1 bunch kale, stemmed and chopped
1 cup sliced basil
½ cup pitted Kalamata olives, chopped

1. Add the pasta, water, beans, tomatoes (with juice if using diced), onion, bell pepper, tomato paste, oil, garlic, and crushed red pepper (if desired), to a large stockpot. Bring to a boil over high heat, stirring often.
2. Reduce the heat to medium-high, add the kale, and cook, continuing to stir often, until the pasta is al dente, about 10 minutes.
3. Remove from the heat and let sit for 5 minutes. Garnish with the basil and olives and serve.

Per Serving
calories: 565 | fat: 17.7g | protein: 18.0g | carbs: 85.5g | fiber: 16.5g | sodium: 540mg

Lentil and Mushroom Pasta

Prep time: 10 minutes | Cook time: 50 minutes | Serves 2

2 tablespoons olive oil
1 large yellow onion, finely diced
2 portobello mushrooms, trimmed and chopped finely
2 tablespoons tomato paste
3 garlic cloves, chopped
1 teaspoon oregano
2½ cups water

1 cup brown lentils
1 (28-ounce / 794-g) can diced tomatoes with basil (with juice if diced)
1 tablespoon balsamic vinegar
Salt and black pepper, to taste
Chopped basil, for garnish
8 ounces (227 g) pasta of choice, cooked

1. Place a large stockpot over medium heat and add the olive oil. Once the oil is hot, add the onion and mushrooms. Cover and cook until both are soft, about 5 minutes. Add the tomato paste, garlic, and oregano and cook 2 minutes, stirring constantly. Stir in the water and lentils. Bring to a boil, then reduce the heat to medium-low and cook covered for 5 minutes. Add the tomatoes (and juice if using diced) and vinegar. Reduce the heat to low and cook until the lentils are tender, about 30 minutes.
2. Remove from the heat and season with salt and pepper to taste. Garnish with the basil and serve over the cooked pasta.

Per Serving
calories: 463 | fat: 15.9g | protein: 12.5g | carbs: 70.8g | fiber: 16.9g | sodium: 155mg

Roasted Ratatouille Pasta

Prep time: 10 minutes | Cook time: 30 minutes | Serves 2

1 small eggplant (about 8 ounces / 227 g)
1 small zucchini
1 portobello mushroom
1 Roma tomato, halved
½ medium sweet red pepper, seeded
½ teaspoon salt, plus additional for the pasta water
1 teaspoon Italian herb seasoning
1 tablespoon olive oil
2 cups farfalle pasta (about 8 ounces / 227 g)
2 tablespoons minced sun-dried tomatoes in olive oil with herbs
2 tablespoons prepared pesto

1. Slice the ends off the eggplant and zucchini. Cut them lengthwise into ½- inch slices. Place the eggplant, zucchini, mushroom, tomato, and red pepper in a large bowl and sprinkle with ½ teaspoon of salt. Using your hands, toss the vegetables well so that they're covered evenly with the salt. Let them rest for about 10 minutes.
2. While the vegetables are resting, preheat the oven to 400°F (205°C). Line a baking sheet with parchment paper.
3. When the oven is hot, drain off any liquid from the vegetables and pat them dry with a paper towel. Add the Italian herb seasoning and olive oil to the vegetables and toss well to coat both sides.
4. Lay the vegetables out in a single layer on the baking sheet. Roast them for 15 to 20 minutes, flipping them over after about 10 minutes or once they start to brown on the underside. When the vegetables are charred in spots, remove them from the oven.
5. While the vegetables are roasting, fill a large saucepan with water. Add salt and cook the pasta until al dente, about 8 to 10 minutes. Drain the pasta, reserving ½ cup of the pasta water. When cool enough to handle, cut the vegetables into large chunks (about 2 inches) and add them to the hot pasta. Stir in the sun-dried tomatoes and pesto and toss everything well. Serve immediately.

Per Serving calories: 613 | fat: 16.0g | protein: 23.1g | carbs: 108.5g | fiber: 23.0g | sodium: 775mg

Tomato Basil Pasta

Prep time: 3 minutes | Cook time: 2 minutes | Serves 2

2 cups dried campanelle or similar pasta
1¾ cups vegetable stock
½ teaspoon salt, plus more as needed
2 tomatoes, cut into large dices
1 or 2 pinches red pepper flakes
½ teaspoon garlic powder
½ teaspoon dried oregano
10 to 12 fresh sweet basil leaves
Freshly ground black pepper, to taste

1. In your Instant Pot, stir together the pasta, stock, and salt. Scatter the tomatoes on top (do not stir).
2. Secure the lid. Select the Manual mode and set the cooking time for 2 minutes at High Pressure.
3. Once cooking is complete, do a quick pressure release. Carefully open the lid.
4. Stir in the red pepper flakes, oregano, and garlic powder. If there's more than a few tablespoons of liquid in the bottom, select Sauté and cook for 2 to 3 minutes until it evaporates.
5. When ready to serve, chiffonade the basil and stir it in. Taste and season with more salt and pepper, as needed. Serve warm.

Per Serving
calories: 415 | fat: 2.0g | protein: 15.2g | carbs: 84.2g | fiber: 5.0g | sodium: 485mg

Lentil Risotto

Prep time: 10 minutes | Cook time: 20 minutes | Serves 2

½ tablespoon olive oil
½ medium onion, chopped
½ cup dry lentils, soaked overnight
½ celery stalk, chopped
1 sprig parsley, chopped
½ cup Arborio (short-grain Italian) rice
1 garlic clove, lightly mashed
2 cups vegetable stock

1. Press the Sauté button to heat your Instant Pot.
2. Add the oil and onion to the Instant Pot and sauté for 5 minutes.
3. Add the remaining to the Instant Pot, stirring well.
4. Secure the lid. Select the Manual mode and set the cooking time for 15 minutes at High Pressure.
5. Once cooking is complete, do a natural pressure release for 20 minutes, then release any remaining pressure. Carefully open the lid.
6. Stir and serve hot.

Per Serving
calories: 261 | fat: 3.6g | protein: 10.6g | carbs: 47.1g | fiber: 8.4g | sodium: 247mg

Bulgur Pilaf with Kale and Tomatoes

Prep time: 10 minutes | Cook time: 10 minutes | Serves 2

2 tablespoons olive oil,
2 cloves garlic, minced
1 bunch kale, trimmed and cut into bite-sized pieces
Juice of 1 lemon
2 cups cooked bulgur wheat
1 pint cherry tomatoes, halved
Sea salt and freshly ground pepper, to taste

1. Heat the olive oil in a large skillet over medium heat. Add the garlic and sauté for 1 minute.
2. Add the kale leaves and stir to coat. Cook for 5 minutes until leaves are cooked through and thoroughly wilted.
3. Add the lemon juice, bulgur and tomatoes. Season with sea salt and freshly ground pepper to taste, then serve.

Per Serving
calories: 300 | fat: 14.0g | protein: 6.2g | carbs: 37.8g | fiber: 8.7g | sodium: 595mg

Cranberry and Almond Quinoa

Prep time: 5 minutes | Cook time: 10 minutes | Serves 2

2 cups water
1 cup quinoa, rinsed
¼ cup salted sunflower seeds
½ cup slivered almonds
1 cup dried cranberries

1. Combine water and quinoa in the Instant Pot.
2. Secure the lid. Select the Manual mode and set the cooking time for 10 minutes at High Pressure.
3. Once cooking is complete, do a quick pressure release. Carefully open the lid.
4. Add sunflower seeds, almonds, and dried cranberries and gently mix until well combined.
5. Serve hot.

Per Serving
calories: 445 | fat: 14.8g | protein: 15.1g | carbs: 64.1g | fiber: 10.2g | sodium: 113mg

Pork and Spinach Spaghetti

Prep time: 15 minutes | Cook time: 16 minutes | Serves 4

2 tablespoons olive oil
½ cup onion, chopped
1 garlic clove, minced
1 pound (454 g) ground pork
2 cups water
1 (14-ounce / 397-g) can diced tomatoes, drained
½ cup sun-dried tomatoes
1 tablespoon dried oregano
1 teaspoon Italian seasoning
1 fresh jalapeño chile, stemmed, seeded, and minced
1 teaspoon salt
8 ounces (227 g) dried spaghetti, halved
1 cup spinach

1. Warm oil onSauté. Add onion and garlic and cook for 2 minutes until softened. Stir in pork and cook for 5 minutes. Stir in jalapeño, water, sun- dried tomatoes, Italian seasoning, oregano, diced tomatoes, and salt with the chicken; mix spaghetti and press to submerge into the sauce.
2. Seal the lid and cook on High Pressure for 9 minutes. Release the pressure quickly. Stir in spinach, close lid again, and simmer on Keep Warm for 5 minutes until spinach is wilted.

Per Serving

calories: 621 | fat: 32.2g | protein: 29.1g | carbs: 53.9g | fiber: 5.9g | sodium: 738mg

Rigatoni and Zucchini Minestrone

Prep time: 20 minutes | Cook time: 7 minutes | Serves 4

3 tablespoons olive oil
1 onion, diced
1 celery stalk, diced
1 large carrot, peeled and diced
14 ounces (397 g) canned chopped tomatoes
4 ounces (113 g) rigatoni
3 cups water
1 cup chopped zucchini
1 bay leaf
1 teaspoon mixed herbs
¼ teaspoon cayenne pepper
½ teaspoon salt
¼ cup shredded Pecorino Romano cheese
1 garlic clove, minced
⅓ cup olive oil-based pesto

1. Heat oil on Sauté and cook onion, celery, garlic, and carrot for 3 minutes, stirring occasionally until the vegetables are softened. Stir in rigatoni, tomatoes, water, zucchini, bay leaf, herbs, cayenne, and salt. Seal the lid and cook on High for 4 minutes. Do a natural pressure release for 5 minutes. Adjust the taste of the soup with salt and black pepper, and remove the bay leaf. Ladle the soup into serving bowls and drizzle the pesto over. Serve with the garlic toasts.

Per Serving calories: 278 | fat: 23.4g | protein: 6.7g | carbs: 12.2g | fiber: 3.5g | sodium: 793mg

Asparagus and Broccoli Primavera Farfalle

Prep time: 15 minutes | Cook time: 12 minutes | Serves 4

1 bunch asparagus, trimmed, cut into 1-inch pieces
2 cups broccoli florets
3 tablespoons olive oil
3 teaspoons salt
10 ounces (283 g) egg noodles
3 garlic cloves, minced
2½ cups vegetable stock
½ cup heavy cream
1 cup small tomatoes, halved
¼ cup chopped basil
½ cup grated Parmesan cheese

1. Pour 2 cups of water, add the noodles, 2 tablespoons of olive oil, garlic and salt. Place a trivet over the water. Combine asparagus, broccoli, remaining olive oil and salt in a bowl. Place the vegetables on the trivet.Seal the lid and cook on Steam for 12 minutes on High. Do a quick release. Remove the vegetables to a plate. Stir the heavy cream and tomatoes in the pasta. Press Sauté and simmer the cream until desired consistency.
2. Gently mix in the asparagus and broccoli. Garnish with basil and Parmesan, to serve.

Per Serving calories: 544 | fat: 23.8g | protein: 18.5g | carbs: 66.1g | fiber: 6.0g | sodium: 2354mg

Gouda Beef and Spinach Fettuccine

Prep time: 10 minutes | Cook time: 15 minutes | Serves 6

10 ounces (283 g) ground beef
1 pound (454 g) fettuccine pasta
1 cup gouda cheese, shredded
1 cup fresh spinach, torn
1 medium onion, chopped
2 cups tomatoes, diced
1 tablespoon olive oil
1 teaspoon salt
½ teaspoon ground black pepper

1. Heat the olive oil on Sauté mode in the Instant Pot. Stir-fry the beef and onion for 5 minutes. Add the pasta. Pour water enough to cover and season with salt and pepper. Cook on High Pressure for 5 minutes. Do a quick release. Press Sauté and stir in the tomato and spinach; cook for 5 minutes. Top with Gouda to serve.

Per Serving calories: 493 | fat: 17.7g | protein: 20.6g | carbs: 64.3g | fiber: 9.5g | sodium: 561mg

Super Cheesy Tagliatelle

Prep time: 10 minutes | Cook time: 20 minutes | Serves 6

¼ cup goat cheese, chevre
¼ cup grated Pecorino cheese
½ cup grated Parmesan
1 cup heavy cream
½ cup grated Gouda
2 tablespoons olive oil
1 tablespoon Italian Seasoning mix
1 cup vegetable broth
1 pound (454 g) tagliatelle

1. In a bowl, mix goat cheese, pecorino, Parmesan, and heavy cream. Stir in Italian seasoning. Transfer to your instant pot. Stir in the broth and olive oil.
2. Seal the lid and cook on High Pressure for 4 minutes. Do a quick release.
1. Meanwhile, drop the tagliatelle in boiling water and cook for 6 minutes.
2. Remove the instant pot's lid and stir in the tagliatelle. Top with grated gouda and let simmer for about 10 minutes on Sauté mode.

Per Serving

calories: 511 | fat: 22.0g | protein: 14.5g | carbs: 65.7g | fiber: 9.0g | sodium: 548mg

Chickpea Curry

Prep time: 10 minutes | Cook time: 24 minutes | Serves 4

½ cup raw chickpeas
1½ tablespoons cooking oil
½ cup chopped onions
1 bay leaf
½ tablespoon grated garlic
¼ tablespoon grated ginger
¾ cup water
1 cup fresh tomato purée
½ green chili, finely chopped
¼ teaspoon turmeric
½ teaspoon coriander powder
1 teaspoon chili powder
1 cup chopped baby spinach
Salt, to taste
Boiled white rice, for serving

1. Add the oil and onions to the Instant Pot. Sauté for 5 minutes.
2. Stir in ginger, garlic paste, green chili and bay leaf. Cook for 1 minute, then add all the spices.
3. Add the chickpeas, tomato purée and the water to the pot.
4. Cover and secure the lid. Turn its pressure release handle to the sealing position.
5. Cook on the Manual function with High Pressure for 15 mins.
6. After the beep, do a Natural release for 20 minutes.
7. Stir in spinach and cook for 3 minutes on the Sauté setting.
8. Serve hot with boiled white rice.

Per Serving

calories: 176 | fat: 6.8g | protein: 6.7g | carbs: 24.1g | fiber: 5.1g | sodium: 185mg

Rice and Sweet Potato Pilaf

Prep time: 15 minutes | Cook time: 10 minutes | Serves 4 to 6

2 tablespoons extra-virgin olive oil
1 onion, chopped fine
½ teaspoon table salt
2 garlic cloves, minced
1½ teaspoons ground turmeric
1 teaspoon ground coriander
⅛ teaspoon cayenne pepper
2 cups chicken broth
1½ cups long-grain white rice, rinsed
12 ounces (340 g) sweet potato, peeled, quartered lengthwise, and sliced ½ inch thick
½ preserved lemon, pulp and white pith removed, rind rinsed and minced (2 tablespoons)
½ cup shelled pistachios, toasted and chopped
¼ cup fresh cilantro leaves
¼ cup pomegranate seeds

1. Using highest Sauté function, heat oil in Instant Pot until shimmering. Add onion and salt and cook until onion is softened, about 5 minutes.
2. Stir in garlic, turmeric, coriander, and cayenne and cook until fragrant, about 30 seconds. Stir in broth, rice, and sweet potato. Lock lid in place and close pressure release valve. Select Manual function and cook for 4 minutes. Turn off Instant Pot and quick release pressure. Carefully remove lid, allowing steam to escape away from you.
3. Add preserved lemon and gently fluff rice with fork to combine. Lay clean dish towel over pot, replace lid, and let sit for 5 minutes. Season with salt and pepper to taste. Transfer to serving dish and sprinkle with pistachios, cilantro, and pomegranate seeds. Serve.

Per Serving

calories: 698 | fat: 22.8g | protein: 36.8g | carbs: 85.5g | fiber: 5.9g | sodium: 802mg

Cumin Quinoa Pilaf

Prep time: 5 minutes | Cook time: 5 minutes | Serves 2

2 tablespoons extra virgin olive oil
2 cloves garlic, minced
3 cups water
2 cups quinoa, rinsed
2 teaspoons ground cumin
2 teaspoons turmeric
Salt, to taste
1 handful parsley, chopped

1. Press the Sauté button to heat your Instant Pot.
2. Once hot, add the oil and garlic to the pot, stir and cook for 1 minute. Add water, quinoa, cumin, turmeric, and salt, stirring well. Lock the lid. Select the Manual mode and set the cooking time for 1 minute at High Pressure.
3. When the timer beeps, perform a natural pressure release for 10 minutes, then release any remaining pressure. Carefully remove the lid.
4. Fluff the quinoa with a fork. Season with more salt, if needed.
5. Sprinkle the chopped parsley on top and serve.

Per Serving

calories: 384 | fat: 12.3g | protein: 12.8g | carbs: 57.4g | fiber: 6.9g | sodium: 448mg

Pancetta with Garbanzo Beans

Prep time: 10 minutes | Cook time: 38 minutes | Serves 6

3 strips pancetta
1 onion, diced
15 ounces (425 g) canned garbanzo beans
2 cups water
1 cup apple cider
2 garlic cloves, minced
½ cup ketchup
¼ cup sugar
1 teaspoon ground mustard powder
1 teaspoon salt
1 teaspoon black pepper
Fresh parsley, for garnish

1. Cook pancetta for 5 minutes, until crispy, on Sauté mode. Add onion and garlic, and cook for 3 minutes until soft. Mix in garbanzo beans, ketchup, sugar, salt, apple cider, mustard powder, water, and pepper.
2. Seal the lid, press Bean/Chili and cook on High Pressure for 30 minutes. Release pressure naturally for 10 minutes. Serve in bowls garnished with parsley.

Per Serving

calories: 163 | fat: 5.7g | protein: 5.4g | carbs: 22.1g | fiber: 3.7g | sodium: 705mg

Mint Brown Rice

Prep time: 5 minutes | Cook time: 22 minutes | Serves 2

2 cloves garlic, minced
¼ cup chopped fresh mint, plus more for garnish
1 tablespoon chopped dried chives
1 cup short- or long-grain brown rice
1½ cups water or low-sodium vegetable broth
½ to 1 teaspoon sea salt

1. Place the garlic, mint, chives, rice, and water in the Instant Pot. Stir to combine.
2. Secure the lid. Select the Manual mode and set the cooking time for 22 minutes at High Pressure.
3. Once cooking is complete, do a natural pressure release for 10 minutes, then release any remaining pressure. Carefully open the lid.
4. Add salt to taste and serve garnished with more mint.

Per Serving

calories: 514 | fat: 6.6g | protein: 20.7g | carbs: 80.4g | fiber: 3.3g | sodium: 786mg

Spinach and Ricotta Stuffed Pasta Shells

Prep time: 15 minutes | Cook time: 35 minutes | Serves 6

2 cups onion, chopped	1½ cups feta cheese,
1 cup carrot, chopped	crumbled
3 garlic cloves, minced	2 cups spinach, chopped
3½ tablespoons olive oil,	¾ cup grated Pecorino
1 (28-ounce / 794-g)	Romano cheese
canned tomatoes, crushed	2 tablespoons chopped
12 ounces (340 g) conchiglie	fresh chives
pasta	1 tablespoon chopped fresh dill
1 tablespoon olive oil	Salt and ground black
2 cups ricotta cheese,	pepper to taste
crumbled	1 cup shredded Cheddar
	cheese

1. Warm olive oil on Sauté. Add onion, carrot, and garlic, and cook for 5 minutes until tender. Stir in tomatoes and cook for another 10 minutes.
2. Remove to a bowl and set aside.
3. Wipe the pot with a damp cloth, add pasta and cover with enough water. Seal the lid and cook for 5 minutes on High Pressure. Do a quick release and drain the pasta. Lightly Grease olive oil to a baking sheet.
4. In a bowl, combine feta and ricotta cheese.
5. Add spinach, Pecorino Romano cheese, dill, and chives, and stir well. Adjust the seasonings. Using a spoon, fill the shells with the mixture.
6. Spread 4 cups tomato sauce on the baking sheet. Place the stuffed shells over with seam-sides down and sprinkle Cheddar cheese atop. Use aluminum foil to the cover the baking dish.
7. Pour 1 cup of water in the pot of the Pressure cooker and insert the trivet. Lower the baking dish onto the trivet. Seal the lid, and cook for 15 minutes on High Pressure.
8. Do a quick pressure release. Take away the foil. Place the stuffed shells to serving plates and top with tomato sauce before serving.

Per Serving

calories: 730 | fat: 41.5g | protein: 30.0g | carbs: 62.7g | fiber: 10.6g | sodium: 966mg

Chili Halloumi Cheese with Rice

Prep time: 10 minutes | Cook time: 8 minutes | Serves 6

2 cups water	1 teaspoon fresh minced
2 tablespoons brown sugar	garlic
2 tablespoons rice vinegar	20 ounces (567 g) Halloumi
1 tablespoon sweet chili	cheese, cubed
sauce	1 cup rice
1 tablespoon olive oil	¼ cup chopped fresh chives,
	for garnish

1. Heat the oil on Sauté and fry the halloumi for 5 minutes until golden brown. Set aside.
2. To the pot, add water, garlic, olive oil, vinegar, sugar, soy sauce, and chili sauce and mix well until smooth. Stir in rice noodles. Seal the lid and cook on High Pressure for 3 minutes. Release the pressure quickly. Split the rice between bowls. Top with fried halloumi and sprinkle with fresh chives before serving.

Per Serving

calories: 534 | fat: 34.3g | protein: 24.9g | carbs: 30.1g | fiber: 1.0g | sodium: 652mg

Shrimp and Asparagus Risotto

Prep time: 15 minutes | Cook time: 58 minutes | Serves 4

1 tablespoon olive oil	1¼ cups chicken broth
1 pound (454 g) asparagus,	¾ cup milk
trimmed and roughly	1 tablespoon coconut oil
chopped	16 shrimp, cleaned and
1 cup spinach, chopped	deveined
1½ cups mushrooms,	Salt and ground black
chopped	pepper, to taste
1 cup rice, rinsed and	¾ cup Parmesan cheese,
drained	shredded

1. Warm the oil on Sauté. Add spinach, mushrooms and asparagus and Sauté for 10 minutes until cooked through. Press Cancel. Add rice, milk and chicken broth to the pot as you stir. Seal the lid, press Multigrain and cook for 40 minutes on High Pressure. Do a quick release, open the lid and put the rice on a serving plate.
2. Take back the empty pot to the pressure cooker, add coconut oil and press Sauté. Add shrimp and cook each side for 4 minutes until cooked through and turns pink. Set shrimp over rice, add pepper and salt for seasoning. Serve topped with shredded Parmesan cheese.

Per Serving calories: 385 | fat: 14.3g | protein: 16.5g | carbs: 48.4g | fiber: 4.1g | sodium: 771mg

Brown Rice Stuffed Portobello Mushrooms

Prep time: 15 minutes | Cook time: 10 minutes | Serves 4

4 large portobello	1 green bell pepper, seeded
mushrooms, stems and gills	and diced
removed	½ cup feta cheese,
2 tablespoons olive oil	crumbled
½ cup brown rice, cooked	Juice of 1 lemon
1 tomato, seed removed and	½ teaspoon salt
chopped	½ teaspoon ground black
¼ cup black olives, pitted	pepper
and chopped	Minced fresh cilantro, for
	garnish
	1 cup vegetable broth

1. Brush the mushrooms with olive oil.
2. Arrange the mushrooms in a single layer in an oiled baking pan. In a bowl, mix the rice, tomato, olives, bell pepper, feta cheese, lemon juice, salt, and black pepper.
3. Spoon the rice mixture into the mushrooms. Pour in the broth, seal the lid and cook on High Pressure for 10 minutes. Do a quick release. Garnish with fresh cilantro and serve immediately.

Per Serving

calories: 190 | fat: 12.5g | protein: 5.9g | carbs: 15.2g | fiber: 2.6g | sodium: 682mg

Grana Padano Risotto

Prep time: 10 minutes | Cook time: 23 minutes | Serves 6

1 tablespoon olive oil	1 teaspoon salt
1 white onion, chopped	½ teaspoon ground white
2 cups Carnaroli rice, rinsed	pepper
¼ cup dry white wine	2 tablespoons Grana padano
4 cups chicken stock	cheese, grated
	¼ tablespoon Grana padano
	cheese, flakes

1. Warm oil on Sauté. Stir-fry onion for 3 minutes until soft and translucent. Add rice and cook for 5 minutes stirring occasionally.
2. Pour wine into the pot to deglaze, scrape away any browned bits of food from the pan.
3. Stir in stock, pepper, and salt to the pot. Seal the lid, press Rice and cook on High Pressure for 15 minutes. Release the pressure quickly.
4. Sprinkle with grated Parmesan cheese and stir well. Top with flaked cheese for garnish before serving.

Per Serving

calories: 307 | fat: 6.0g | protein: 8.2g | carbs: 53.2g | fiber: 2.1g | sodium: 945mg

Turkey and Bell Pepper Tortiglioni

Prep time: 20 minutes | Cook time: 10 minutes | Serves 6

2 teaspoons chili powder	1 cup salsa
1 teaspoon salt	1 pound (454 g) tortiglioni
1 teaspoon cumin	1 red bell pepper, chopped
1 teaspoon onion powder	diagonally
1 teaspoon garlic powder	1 yellow bell pepper,
½ teaspoon thyme	chopped diagonally
1½ pounds (680 g) turkey	1 green bell pepper, chopped
breast, cut into strips	diagonally
1 tablespoon olive oil	1 cup shredded Gouda
1 red onion, cut into wedges	cheese
4 garlic cloves, minced	½ cup sour cream
3 cups chicken broth	½ cup chopped parsley

1. In a bowl, mix chili powder, cumin, garlic powder, onion powder, salt, and oregano. Reserve 1 teaspoon of seasoning. Coat turkey with the remaining seasoning.
2. Warm oil on Sauté. Add turkey strips and sauté for 4 to 5 minutes until browned. Place the turkey in a bowl. Sauté the onion and garlic for 1 minute in the cooker until soft. Press Cancel. Mix in salsa, broth, and scrape the bottom of any brown bits. Into the broth mixture, stir in tortiglioni pasta and cover with bell peppers and chicken.
3. Seal the lid and cook for 5 minutes on High Pressure. Do a quick Pressure release.
4. Open the lid and sprinkle with shredded gouda cheese and reserved seasoning, and stir well. Divide into plates and top with sour cream. Add parsley for garnishing and serve.

Per Serving calories: 646 | fat: 21.7g | protein: 41.1g | carbs: 72.9g | fiber: 11.1g | sodium: 1331mg

Roasted Butternut Squash and Rice

Prep time: 15 minutes | Cook time: 15 minutes | Serves 4

½ cup water	1 teaspoon freshly ground
2 cups vegetable broth	black pepper
1 small butternut squash,	1 cup feta cheese, cubed
peeled and sliced	1 tablespoon coconut
2 tablespoons olive oil,	aminos
divided	2 teaspoons arrowroot
1 teaspoon salt	starch
	1 cup jasmine rice, cooked

1. Pour the rice and broth in the pot and stir to combine. In a bowl, toss butternut squash with 1 tablespoon of olive oil and season with salt and black pepper.
2. In another bowl, mix the remaining olive oil, water and coconut aminos. Toss feta in the mixture, add the arrowroot starch, and toss again to combine well. Transfer to a greased baking dish.
3. Lay a trivet over the rice and place the baking dish on the trivet. Seal the lid and cook on High for 15 minutes. Do a quick pressure release. Fluff the rice with a fork and serve with squash and feta.

Per Serving

calories: 258 | fat: 14.9g | protein: 7.8g | carbs: 23.2g | fiber: 1.2g | sodium: 1180mg

Pesto Arborio Rice and Veggie Bowls

Prep time: 10 minutes | Cook time: 1 minute | Serves 2

1 cup arborio rice, rinsed and	1 bunch baby carrots, peeled
drained	¼ cabbage, chopped
2 cups vegetable broth	2 eggs
Salt and black pepper to taste	¼ cup pesto sauce
1 potato, peeled, cubed	Lemon wedges, for serving
1 head broccoli, cut into	
small florets	

1. In the pot, mix broth, pepper, rice and salt. Set trivet to the inner pot on top of rice and add a steamer basket to the top of the trivet. Mix carrots, potato, eggs and broccoli in the steamer basket. Add pepper and salt for seasoning.
2. Seal the lid and cook for 1 minute on High Pressure. Quick release the pressure. Take away the trivet and steamer basket from the pot.
3. Set the eggs in a bowl of ice water. Then peel and halve the eggs. Use a fork to fluff rice.
4. Adjust the seasonings. In two bowls, equally divide rice, broccoli, eggs, carrots, sweet potatoes, and a dollop of pesto. Serve alongside a lemon wedge.

Per Serving calories: 858 | fat: 24.4g | protein: 26.4g | carbs: 136.2g | fiber: 14.1g | sodium: 985mg

Rice and Bean Stuffed Zucchini

Prep time: 10 minutes | Cook time: 15 minutes | Serves 4

2 small zucchinis, halved lengthwise
½ cup cooked rice
½ cup canned white beans, drained and rinsed
½ cup chopped tomatoes
½ cup chopped toasted cashew nuts
½ cup grated Parmesan cheese
1 tablespoon olive oil
½ teaspoon salt
½ teaspoon freshly ground black pepper

1. Pour 1 cup of water in the instant pot and insert a trivet. Scoop out the pulp of zucchini and chop roughly.
2. In a bowl, mix the zucchini pulp, rice, tomatoes, cashew nuts, ¼ cup of Parmesan, olive oil, salt, and black pepper. Fill the zucchini boats with the mixture, and arrange the stuffed boats in a single layer on the trivet. Seal the lid and cook for 15 minutes on Steam on High. Do a quick release and serve.

Per Serving calories: 239 | fat: 14.7g | protein: 9.4g | carbs: 19.0g | fiber: 2.6g | sodium: 570mg

Chard and Mushroom Risotto

Prep time: 15 minutes | Cook time: 20 minutes | Serves 4

3 tablespoons olive oil
1 onion, chopped
2 Swiss chard, stemmed and chopped
1 cup risotto rice
⅓ cup white wine
3 cups vegetable stock
½ teaspoon salt
½ cup mushrooms
4 tablespoons pumpkin seeds, toasted
⅓ cup grated Pecorino Romano cheese

1. Heat oil on Sauté, and cook onion and mushrooms for 5 minutes, stirring, until tender. Add the rice and cook for a minute. Stir in wine and cook for 2 to 3 minutes until almost evaporated.
2. Pour in stock and season with salt. Seal the lid and cook on High Pressure for 10 minutes.
3. Do a quick release. Stir in chard until wilted, mix in cheese to melt, and serve scattered with pumpkin seeds.

Per Serving calories: 420 | fat: 17.7g | protein: 11.8g | carbs: 54.9g | fiber: 4.9g | sodium: 927mg

Carrot Risoni

Prep time: 5 minutes | Cook time: 11 minutes | Serves 6

1 cup orzo, rinsed
2 cups water
2 carrots, cut into sticks
1 large onion, chopped
2 tablespoons olive oil
Salt, to taste
Fresh cilantro, chopped, for garnish

1. Heat oil on Sauté. Add onion and carrots and stir-fry for about 10 minutes until tender and crispy. Remove to a plate and set aside. Add water, salt and orzo in the instant pot.
2. Seal the lid and cook on High Pressure for 1 minute. Do a quick release. Fluff the cooked orzo with a fork. Transfer to a serving plate and top with the carrots and onion. Serve scattered with cilantro.

Per Serving
calories: 121 | fat: 4.9g | protein: 1.7g | carbs: 18.1g | fiber: 2.9g | sodium: 17mg

Cheesy Tomato Linguine

Prep time: 15 minutes | Cook time: 11 minutes | Serves 4

2 tablespoons olive oil
1 small onion, diced
2 garlic cloves, minced
1 cup cherry tomatoes, halved
1½ cups vegetable stock
¼ cup julienned basil leaves
1 teaspoon salt
½ teaspoon ground black pepper
¼ teaspoon red chili flakes
1 pound (454 g) Linguine noodles, halved
Fresh basil leaves for garnish
½ cup Parmigiano-Reggiano cheese, grated

1. Warm oil on Sauté. Add onion and Sauté for 2 minutes until soft. Mix garlic and tomatoes and sauté for 4 minutes. To the pot, add vegetable stock, salt, julienned basil, red chili flakes and pepper.
2. Add linguine to the tomato mixture until covered. Seal the lid and cook on High Pressure for 5 minutes.
3. Naturally release the pressure for 5 minutes. Stir the mixture to ensure it is broken down.
4. Divide into plates. Top with basil and Parmigiano-Reggiano cheese and serve.

Per Serving calories: 311 | fat: 11.3g | protein: 10.3g | carbs: 42.1g | fiber: 1.9g | sodium: 1210mg

Beef and Bean Stuffed Pasta Shells

Prep time: 15 minutes | Cook time: 17 minutes | Serves 4

2 tablespoons olive oil
1 pound (454 g) ground beef
1 pound (454 g) pasta shells
2 cups water
15 ounces (425 g) tomato sauce
1 (15-ounce / 425-g) can black beans, drained and rinsed
15 ounces (425 g) canned corn, drained (or 2 cups frozen corn)
10 ounces (283 g) red enchilada sauce
4 ounces (113 g) diced green chiles
1 cup shredded Mozzarella cheese
Salt and ground black pepper to taste
Additional cheese for topping
Finely chopped parsley for garnish

1. Heat oil on Sauté. Add ground beef and cook for 7 minutes until it starts to brown.
2. Mix in pasta, tomato sauce, enchilada sauce, black beans, water, corn, and green chiles and stir to coat well. Add more water if desired.
3. Seal the lid and cook on High Pressure for 10 minutes. Do a quick Pressure release. Into the pasta mixture, mix in Mozzarella cheese until melted; add black pepper and salt. Garnish with parsley to serve.

Per Serving
calories: 1006 | fat: 30.0g | protein: 53.3g | carbs: 138.9g | fiber: 24.4g | sodium: 1139mg

Chicken and Spaghetti Ragù Bolognese

Prep time: 15 minutes | Cook time: 42 minutes | Serves 8

2 tablespoons olive oil	¼ teaspoon crushed red pepper flakes
6 ounces (170 g) bacon, cubed	1½ pounds (680 g) ground chicken
1 onion, minced	½ cup white wine
1 carrot, minced	1 cup milk
1 celery stalk, minced	1 cup chicken broth
2 garlic cloves, crushed	Salt, to taste
¼ cup tomato paste	1 pound (454 g) spaghetti

1. Warm oil on Sauté. Add bacon and fry for 5 minutes until crispy.
2. Add celery, carrot, garlic and onion and cook for 5 minutes until fragrant. Mix in red pepper flakes and tomato paste, and cook for 2 minutes. Break chicken into small pieces and place in the pot.
3. Cook for 10 minutes, as you stir, until browned. Pour in wine and simmer for 2 minutes. Add chicken broth and milk. Seal the lid and cook for 15 minutes on High Pressure. Release the pressure quickly.
4. Add the spaghetti and stir. Seal the lid, and cook on High Pressure for another 5 minutes.
5. Release the pressure quickly. Check the pasta for doneness. Taste, adjust the seasoning and serve hot.

Per Serving calories: 477 | fat: 20.6g | protein: 28.1g | carbs: 48.5g | fiber: 5.3g | sodium: 279mg

Parmesan Squash Linguine

Prep time: 15 minutes | Cook time: 5 minutes | Serves 4

1 cup flour	1 yellow squash, peeled and sliced
2 teaspoons salt	1 pound (454 g) linguine
2 eggs	24 ounces (680 g) canned seasoned tomato sauce
4 cups water	2 tablespoons olive oil
1 cup seasoned breadcrumbs	1 cup shredded Mozzarella cheese
½ cup grated Parmesan cheese, plus more for garnish	Minced fresh basil, for garnish

1. Break the linguine in half. Put it in the pot and add water and half of salt. Seal the lid and cook on High Pressure for 5 minutes. Combine the flour and 1 teaspoon of salt in a bowl. In another bowl, whisk the eggs and 2 tablespoons of water. In a third bowl, mix the breadcrumbs and Mozzarella cheese.
2. Coat each squash slices in the flour. Shake off excess flour, dip in the egg wash, and dredge in the bread crumbs. Set aside. Quickly release the pressure. Remove linguine to a serving bowl and mix in the tomato sauce and sprinkle with fresh basil. Heat oil on Sauté and fry breaded squash until crispy.
3. Serve the squash topped Mozzarella cheese with the linguine on side.

Per Serving

calories: 857 | fat: 17.0g | protein: 33.2g | carbs: 146.7g | fiber: 18.1g | sodium: 1856mg

Red Bean Curry

Prep time: 10 minutes | Cook time: 24 minutes | Serves 4

½ cup raw red beans	½ green chili, finely chopped
1½ tablespoons cooking oil	¼ teaspoon turmeric
½ cup chopped onions	½ teaspoon coriander powder
1 bay leaf	1 teaspoon chili powder
½ tablespoon grated garlic	1 cup chopped baby spinach
¼ tablespoon grated ginger	Salt, to taste
¾ cup water	Boiled white rice or quinoa, for serve
1 cup fresh tomato purée	

1. Add the oil and onions to the Instant Pot. Sauté for 5 minutes.
2. Stir in ginger, garlic paste, green chili and bay leaf. Cook for 1 minute, then add all the spices.
3. Add the red beans, tomato purée and water to the pot.
4. Cover and secure the lid. Turn its pressure release handle to the sealing position.
5. Cook on the Manual function with High Pressure for 15 minutes.
6. After the beep, do a Natural release for 20 minutes.
7. Stir in spinach and cook for 3 minutes on the Sauté setting.
8. Serve hot with boiled white rice or quinoa.

Per Serving

calories: 159 | fat: 5.6g | protein: 6.8g | carbs: 22.5g | fiber: 5.5g | sodium: 182mg

Easy Simple Pesto Pasta (Italian)

Preparation Time: 10 minutes Cooking Time: 8 minutes
Servings: 4 to 6

1-pound (454 g) spaghetti	4 cups fresh basil leaves, stems removed 3 cloves garlic
1 teaspoon salt	1/2 teaspoon freshly ground black pepper 1/2 cup toasted pine nuts
1/4 cup lemon juice	1/2 cup grated Parmesan cheese 1 cup extra-virgin olive oil

1. Bring a large pot of salted water to a boil. Add the spaghetti to the pot and cook for 8 minutes.
2. In a food processor, place the remaining , except for the olive oil, and pulse.
3. While the processor is running, slowly drizzle the olive oil through the top opening. Process until all the olive oil has been added.
4. Reserve ½ cup of the cooking liquid. Drain the pasta and put it into a large bowl. Add the pesto and cooking liquid to the bowl of pasta and toss everything together.
5. Serve immediately.

Nutrition: calories: 1067 fat: 72.0g protein: 23.0g carbs: 91.0g fiber: 6.0g sodium: 817mg

Italian Chicken Pasta (Italian)

Preparation Time: 10 minutes Cooking Time: 9 minutes
Servings: 8

1 lb. chicken breast, skinless, boneless, and cut into chunks 1/2 cup cream cheese	1 cup mozzarella cheese, shredded 1 1/2 tsp Italian seasoning
1 tsp garlic, minced	1cup mushrooms, diced 1/2 onion, diced
2tomatoes, diced 2 cups of water	16 oz whole wheat penne pasta Pepper, Salt

1. Add all except cheeses into the inner pot of instant pot and stir well.
2. Seal pot with lid and cook on high for 9 minutes.
3. Once done, allow to release pressure naturally for 5 minutes then release remaining using quick release. Remove lid.
4. Add cheeses and stir well and serve.

Nutrition: Calories 328 Fat 8.5 g Carbohydrates 42.7 g Sugar 1.4 g Protein 23.7 g Cholesterol 55 mg

Pesto Chicken Pasta (Italian)

Preparation Time: 10 minutes Cooking Time: 10 minutes
Servings: 6

1 lb. chicken breast, skinless, boneless, and diced	1/2 cup parmesan cheese, shredded 1 tsp Italian seasoning
3 tbsp olive oil	
1/4 cup heavy cream	16 oz whole wheat pasta 6 oz basil pesto
3 1/2 cups water Pepper	Salt

1. Season chicken with Italian seasoning, pepper, and salt.
2. Add oil into the inner pot of instant pot and set the pot on sauté mode.
3. Add chicken to the pot and sauté until brown.
4. Add remaining except for parmesan cheese, heavy cream, and pesto and stir well.
5. Seal pot with lid and cook on high for 5 minutes.
6. Once done, release pressure using quick release. Remove lid.
7. Stir in parmesan cheese, heavy cream, and pesto and serve.

Nutrition: Calories 475 Fat 14.7 g Carbohydrates 57 g Sugar 2.8 g Protein 28.7 g Cholesterol 61 mg

Mac & Cheese (Italian)

Preparation Time: 10 minutes Cooking Time: 4 minutes
Servings: 8

1 lb. whole grain pasta	1/2 cup parmesan cheese, grated 4 cups cheddar cheese, shredded 1 cup milk
1/4 tsp garlic powder 1/2 tsp ground mustard 2 tbsp olive oil	4 cups of water Pepper Salt

1. Add pasta, garlic powder, mustard, oil, water, pepper, and salt into the instant pot. Seal pot with lid and cook on high for 4 minutes. Once done, release pressure using quick release. Remove lid. Add remaining and stir well and serve.

Nutrition: Calories 509 Fat 25.7 g Carbohydrates 43.8 g Sugar 3.8 g Protein 27.3g Cholesterol 66 mg

Fresh Sauce Pasta (Italian)

Preparation Time: 15 minutes Cooking Time: 15 minutes
Servings: 4

1/8 teaspoon salt, plus more for cooking the pasta 1-pound penne pasta	1/4 cup olive oil
1 garlic clove, crushed	3 cups chopped scallions, white and green parts 3 tomatoes, diced
2 tablespoons chopped fresh basil	1/8 teaspoon freshly ground black pepper Freshly grated Parmesan cheese, for serving

1. Bring a large pot of salted water to a boil over high heat. Drop in the pasta, stir, and return the water to a boil. Boil the pasta for about 6 minutes or until al dente.
2. A couple minutes before the pasta is completely cooked, in a medium saucepan over medium heat, heat the olive oil.
3. Add the garlic and cook for 30 seconds.
4. Stir in the scallions and tomatoes. Cover the pan and cook for 2 to 3 minutes.
5. Drain the pasta and add it to the vegetables. Stir in the basil and season with the salt and pepper. Top with the Parmesan cheese.

Nutrition: Calories: 477; Total Fat: 16g; Saturated Fat: 2g; Carbohydrates: 72g; Fiber: 3g; Protein: 15g; Sodium: 120mg

Caprese Fusilli

Prep time: 15 minutes | Cook time: 7 minutes | Serves 3

1 tablespoon olive oil	1 cup tomatoes, halved
1 onion, thinly chopped	1 cup water
6 garlic cloves, minced	¼ cup basil leaves
1 teaspoon red pepper flakes	1 teaspoon salt
2½ cups dried fusilli	1 cup Ricotta cheese, crumbled
1 (15-ounce / 425-g) can tomato sauce	2 tablespoons chopped fresh basil

1. Warm oil on Sauté. Add red pepper flakes, garlic and onion and cook for 3 minutes until soft.
2. Mix in fusilli, tomatoes, half of the basil leaves, water, tomato sauce, and salt. Seal the lid, and cook on High Pressure for 4 minutes. Release the pressure quickly.
3. Transfer the pasta to a serving platter and top with the crumbled ricotta and remaining chopped basil.

Per Serving

calories: 589 | fat: 17.7g | protein: 19.5g | carbs: 92.8g | fiber: 13.8g | sodium: 879mg

Three Sauces Lasagna (Italian)

Preparation Time: 30 minutes Cooking Time: 45 minutes
Servings: 8

3 chicken breasts, skinless, boneless, cut into pieces 9 oz whole-grain pasta	1/2 cup olives, sliced
1/2 cup sun-dried tomatoes	1tbsp roasted red peppers, chopped 14 oz can tomato, diced
2cups marinara sauce 1 cup chicken broth Pepper	Salt

1. Add all except whole-grain pasta into the instant pot and stir well.
2. Seal pot with lid and cook on high for 12 minutes.
3. Once done, allow to release pressure naturally. Remove lid.
4. Add pasta and stir well. Seal pot again and select manual and set timer for 5 minutes.
5. Once done, allow to release pressure naturally for 5 minutes then release remaining using quick release. Remove lid.
6. Stir well and serve.

Nutrition: Calories 615 Fat 15.4 g Carbohydrates 71 g Sugar 17.6 g Protein 48 g Cholesterol 100 mg

Spinach Pesto Pasta (Italian)

Prep Time: 10 minutes Cooking Time: 10 minutes Servings: 4

8 oz whole-grain pasta	1/3 cup mozzarella cheese, grated 1/2 cup pesto
5 oz fresh spinach 1 3/4 cup water Pepper Salt	8 oz mushrooms, chopped 1 tbsp olive oil

1. Add oil into the inner pot of instant pot and set the pot on sauté mode.
2. Add mushrooms and sauté for 5 minutes.
3. Add water and pasta and stir well.
4. Seal pot with lid and cook on high for 5 minutes.
5. Once done, release pressure using quick release. Remove lid.
6. Stir in remaining and serve.

Nutrition: Calories 213 Fat 17.3 g Carbohydrates 9.5 g Sugar 4.5 g Protein 7.4g Cholesterol 9 mg

Broccoli Pesto Spaghetti (Italian)

Preparation Time:5 minutes Cooking Time:35 minutes
Servings: 4

8 oz. spaghetti	1-pound broccoli, cut into florets 2 tablespoons olive oil
4 garlic cloves, chopped 4 basil leaves Salt and pepper to taste	2tablespoons blanched almonds 1 lemon, juiced

1. For the pesto, combine the broccoli, oil, garlic, basil, lemon juice and almonds in a blender and pulse until well mixed and smooth.
2. Cook the spaghetti in a large pot of salty water for 8 minutes or until al dente. Drain well.
3. Mix the warm spaghetti with the broccoli pesto and serve right away.

Nutrition: Calories: 284, Fat:10.2g, Protein:10.4g, Carbohydrates:40.2g

Very Vegan Patras Pasta (Italian)

Prep Time: 5 minutes Cooking Time: 10 minutes Servings: 6
4 quarts salted water

10 oz. gluten-free and whole-grain pasta 5 cloves garlic, minced	1 cup hummus Salt and pepper 1/3 cup water
½ cup walnuts 2 tbsp dried cranberries (optional)	½ cup olives

1. Bring the salted water to a boil for cooking the pasta.
2. In the meantime, prepare for the hummus sauce. Combine the garlic, hummus, salt, and pepper with water in a mixing bowl. Add the walnuts, olive, and dried cranberries, if desired. Set aside.
3. Add the pasta in the boiling water. Cook the pasta following the manufacturer's specifications until attaining an al dente texture. Drain the pasta.
4. Transfer the pasta to a large serving bowl and combine with the sauce.

Nutrition: Calories: 329 Protein: 12 g Fat: 13 g Carbs: 43 g

Cheesy Spaghetti with Pine Nuts (Italian)

Prep Time: 10 minutes Cooking Time: 10 minutes Servings: 4

8 oz. spaghetti	4 tbsp. (½ stick) unsalted butter
1 tsp. freshly ground black pepper	½ cup pine nuts
1 cup fresh grated Parmesan cheese, divided	

1. Bring a large pot of salted water to a boil. Add the pasta and cook for 8 minutes.
2. In a large saucepan over medium heat, combine the butter, black pepper, and pine nuts. Cook for 2 to 3 minutes or until the pine nuts are lightly toasted.
3. Reserve ½ cup of the pasta water. Drain the pasta and put it into the pan with the pine nuts.
4. Add ¾ cup of Parmesan cheese and the reserved pasta water to the pasta and toss everything together to coat the pasta evenly.
5. To serve, put the pasta in a serving dish and top with the remaining ¼ cup of Parmesan cheese.

Nutrition: Calories: 238; Protein: 12.3g; Carbs: 3.4g; Fat: 6.3g

Italian Mac & Cheese (Italian)

Prep Time: 10 minutes Cooking Time: 6 minutes Servings: 4

1 lb. whole grain pasta 2 tsp Italian seasoning 1 1/2 tsp garlic powder	4 cups of water 1 cup sour cream
4 oz parmesan cheese, shredded 12 oz ricotta cheese	Pepper Salt 1 1/2 tsp onion powder

1. Add all except ricotta cheese into the inner pot of instant pot and stir well.
2. Seal pot with lid and cook on high for 6 minutes.
3. Once done, allow to release pressure naturally for 5 minutes then release remaining using quick release. Remove lid.
4. Add ricotta cheese and stir well and serve.

Nutrition: Calories 388 Fat 25.8 g Carbohydrates 18.1 g Sugar 4 g Protein 22.8 g Cholesterol 74 mg

Penne Bolognese Pasta (Italian)

Preparation Time: 15 minutes Cooking Time: 20 minutes
Servings: 2

Penne pasta 7 oz. Beef 5 oz.	Parmesan Cheese 1 oz. Celery Stalk 1 oz.
Shallots 26 g	Carrot 1.5 oz.
Garlic 1 clove	Thyme 1 g
Tomatoes in own juice 6 oz.	Oregano 1 g
Parsley 3 g	
Butter 20 g	Dry white wine 50 ml Olive oil 40 ml

1. Pour the penne into boiling salted water and cook for 9 minutes.
2. Roll the beef through a meat grinder.
3. Dice onion, celery, carrots and garlic in a small cube.
4. Fry the chopped vegetables in a heated frying pan in olive oil with minced meat for 4–5 minutes, salt and pepper.
5. Add oregano to the fried minced meat and vegetables, pour 50 ml of wine, add the tomatoes along with the juice and simmer for 10 minutes until the tomatoes are completely softened.
6. Add the boiled penne and butter to the sauce and simmer for 1-2 minutes, stirring continuously.
7. Put in a plate, sprinkle with grated Parmesan and chopped parsley, decorate with a sprig of thyme and serve.

Nutrition: Calories: 435 Protein: 18 g Fat: 14 g Carbs: 33 g

Spaghetti all 'Olio (Italian)

Preparation Time:5 minutes Cooking Time:30 minutes
Servings: 4

8 oz. spaghetti	2tablespoons olive oil 4 garlic cloves, minced 2 red peppers, sliced
1 tablespoon lemon juice	½ cup grated parmesan
Salt and pepper to taste	cheese

1. Heat the oil in a skillet and add the garlic. Cook for 30 seconds then stir in the red peppers and cook for 1 more minute on low heat, making sure only to infuse them, not to burn or fry them.
2. Add the lemon juice and remove off heat.
3. Cook the spaghetti in a large pot of salty water for 8 minutes or as stated on the package, just until they become al dente.
4. Drain the spaghetti well and mix them with the garlic and pepper oil.
5. Serve right away.

Nutrition: Calories:268, Fat:11.9g, Protein:7.1g, Carbohydrates:34.1g

Pasta with Pesto (Italian)

Preparation Time: 10 minutes Cooking Time: 0 minutes
Servings: 4

3 tablespoons extra-virgin olive oil 3 garlic cloves, finely minced	½ cup fresh basil leaves
¼ cup (about 2 ounces) grated Parmesan cheese	¼ cup pine nuts
8 ounces whole-wheat pasta, cooked	according to package instructions and drained

1. In a blender or food processor, combine the olive oil, garlic, basil, cheese, and pine nuts. Pulse for 10 to 20 (1-second) pulses until everything is chopped and blended.
2. Toss with the hot pasta and serve.

Nutrition: Calories: 405; Protein: 13g; Total Carbohydrates: 44g; Sugars:2g; Fiber: 5g;Total Fat: 21g; Saturated Fat: 4g; Cholesterol: 10mg; Sodium: 141mg

Vegan Olive Pasta (Italian)

Preparation Time: 10 minutes Cooking Time: 5 minutes
Servings: 4

4 cups whole grain penne pasta 1/2 cup olives, sliced	1 tbsp capers
1/4 tsp red pepper flakes 3 cups of water	4 cups pasta sauce, homemade 1 tbsp garlic, minced
Pepper Salt	

1. Add all into the inner pot of instant pot and stir well.
2. Seal pot with lid and cook on high for 5 minutes.
3. Once done, release pressure using quick release. Remove lid.
4. Stir and serve.

Nutrition: Calories 441 Fat 10.1 g Carbohydrates 77.3 g Sugar 24.1 g Protein 11.8 g Cholesterol 5 mg

Penne In Tomato and Caper Sauce (Italian)

Preparation Time: 10 minutes Cooking Time: 15 minutes
Servings: 4

2 tablespoons olive oil 2 garlic cloves, minced	1cup sliced cherry tomatoes
2cups Basic Tomato Basil Sauce, or store-bought	1 cup capers, drained and rinsed
4 cups penne pasta	Salt

1. Set a large pot of salted water over high heat to boil.
2. In a medium saucepan over medium heat, heat the olive oil. Add the garlic and cook for 30 seconds. Add the cherry tomatoes and cook for 2 to 3 minutes.
3. Pour in the tomato sauce and bring the mixture to a boil. Stir in the capers and turn off the heat.
4. Once boiling add the pasta to the pot of water and cook for about 7 minutes until al dente.
5. Drain the pasta and stir it into the sauce. Toss gently and cook over medium heat for 1 minute or until warmed through.

Nutrition: Calories: 329; Total Fat: 8g; Saturated Fat: 1g; Carbohydrates: 55g; Fiber: 6g; Protein: 10g; Sodium: 612mg

Swoodles with Almond Butter Sauce (Italian)

Preparation Time: 20 minutes Cooking Time: 20 minutes
Servings: 4

1 garlic clove	1-inch piece fresh ginger, peeled and sliced 1/4 cup chopped yellow onion
3/4 cup almond butter 1 tablespoon tamari	1 tablespoon raw honey 1 teaspoon paprika
1tablespoon fresh lemon juice 1/8 teaspoon ground red pepper	Sea salt and ground black pepper, to taste 1/4 cup water
Swoodles:	2large sweet potatoes, spiralized 2 tablespoons coconut oil, melted
Sea salt and ground black pepper, to taste For Servings:	½ cup fresh parsley, chopped
½ cup thinly sliced scallions	

1. Make the Sauce:
2. Put the garlic, ginger, and onion in a food processor, then pulse to combine well.
3. Add the almond butter, tamari, honey, paprika, lemon juice, ground red pepper, salt, and black pepper to the food processor. Pulse to combine well. Pour in the water during the pulsing until the mixture is thick and smooth.
4. Make the Swoodles:
5. Preheat the oven to 425ºF (220ºC). Line a baking sheet with parchment paper.
6. Put the spiralized sweet potato in a bowl, then drizzle with olive oil. Toss to coat well. Transfer them on the baking sheet. Sprinkle with salt and pepper.
7. Bake in the preheated oven for 20 minutes or until lightly browned and al dente. Check the doneness during the baking and remove any well- cooked swoodles.
8. Transfer the swoodles on a large plate and spread with sauce, parsley, and scallions. Toss to serve.
9. Tips: To make this a complete meal, you can serve it along with cashew slaw.
10. You can use the store-bought swoodles or spiralize the sweet potatoes with spiralizer yourself.

Nutrition: calories: 441 fats: 33.6g protein: 12.0g carbs: 29.6g fiber: 7.8g sodium: 479mg

Small Pasta and Beans Pot (Italian)

Preparation Time: 20 minutes Cooking Time: 15 minutes
Servings: 2 to 4

1 pound (454 g) small whole wheat pasta	1 (14.5-ounce / 411-g) can diced tomatoes, juice reserved
1 (15-ounce / 425-g) can cannellini beans, drained and rinsed 2 tablespoons no-salt-added tomato paste	1 red or yellow bell pepper, chopped 1 yellow onion, chopped
1 tablespoon Italian seasoning mix 3 garlic cloves, minced	¼ teaspoon crushed red pepper flakes, optional 1 tablespoon extra-virgin olive oil
5 cups water	1 bunch kale, stemmed and chopped
½ cup pitted Kalamata olives, chopped 1 cup sliced basil	

1. Except for the kale, olives, and basil, combine all the in a pot. Stir to mix well. Bring to a boil over high heat. Stir constantly.
2. Reduce the heat to medium high and add the kale. Cook for 10 minutes or until the pasta is al dente. Stir constantly.
3. Transfer all of them on a large plate and serve with olives and basil on top.

Tip: You can use the small whole-wheat pasta like penne, farfalle, shell, corkscrew, macaroni, or alphabet pasta.

Nutrition: calories: 357 fats: 7.6g protein: 18.2g carbs: 64.5g fiber: 10.1g sodium: 454mg

Tomato Sauce and Basil Pesto Fettuccine (Italian)

Preparation Time: 15 minutes Cooking Time: 15 minutes
Servings: 4

4 Roma tomatoes, diced	2 teaspoons no-salt-added tomato paste 1 tablespoon chopped fresh oregano
2 garlic cloves, minced	1 cup low-sodium vegetable soup
½ teaspoon sea salt	1packed cup fresh basil leaves
¼ cup pine nuts	¼ cup grated Parmesan cheese
2tablespoons extra-virgin olive oil	1 pound (454 g) cooked whole-grain fettuccine

1. Put the tomatoes, tomato paste, oregano, garlic, vegetable soup, and salt in a skillet. Stir to mix well.
2. Cook over medium heat for 10 minutes or until lightly thickened.
3. Put the remaining , except for the fettuccine, in a food processor and pulse to combine until smooth.
4. Pour the puréed basil mixture into the tomato mixture, then add the fettuccine. Cook for a few minutes or until heated through and the fettuccine is well coated. Serve immediately.

Tip: How to cook the fettuccine: Bring a large pot of water to a boil, then add the fettuccine and cook for 8 minutes or until al dente. Drain the fettuccine in a colander before using.

Nutrition: calories: 389 fats: 22.7g protein: 9.7g carbs: 40.2g fiber: 4.8g sodium: 616mg

Roasted Butternut Squash and Zucchini with Penne (Italian)

Preparation Time: 15 minutes Cooking Time: 30 minutes Servings: 6

1 large zucchini, diced	1large butternut squash, peeled and diced 1 large yellow onion, chopped
2tablespoons extra-virgin olive oil 1 teaspoon paprika 1/2 teaspoon freshly ground black pepper 1-pound (454 g) whole-grain penne	1/2 teaspoon garlic powder 1/2 teaspoon sea salt 2 tablespoons grated Parmesan cheese

1. Preheat the oven to 400°F (205°C). Line a baking sheet with aluminum foil.
2. Combine the zucchini, butternut squash, and onion in a large bowl. Drizzle with olive oil and sprinkle with paprika, garlic powder, salt, and ground black pepper. Toss to coat well.
3. Spread the vegetables in the single layer on the baking sheet, then roast in the preheated oven for 25 minutes or until the vegetables are tender.
4. Meanwhile, bring a pot of water to a boil, then add the penne and cook for 14 minutes or until al dente. Drain the penne through a colander.
5. Transfer ½ cup of roasted vegetables in a food processor, then pour in the dry white wine. Pulse until smooth.
6. Pour the puréed vegetables in a nonstick skillet and cook with penne over medium-high heat for a few minutes to heat through.
7. Transfer the penne with the purée on a large serving plate, then spread the remaining roasted vegetables and Parmesan on top before serving.

Tip: Instead of dry white wine, you can use the same amount of low-sodium chicken broth to replace it.

Nutrition: calories: 340 fats: 6.2g protein: 8.0g carbs: 66.8g fiber: 9.1g sodium: 297mg

Delicious Greek Chicken Pasta (Italian)

Preparation Time: 10 minutes Cooking Time: 10 minutes Servings: 6

2 chicken breasts, skinless, boneless, and cut into chunks	2 cups vegetable stock 1/2 cup olives, sliced
12 oz Greek vinaigrette dressing	Pepper Salt 1 lb. whole grain pasta

1. Add all into the inner pot of instant pot and stir well.
2. Seal pot with lid and cook on high for 10 minutes.
3. Once done, release pressure using quick release. Remove lid.
4. Stir well and serve.

Nutrition: Calories 325 Fat 25.8 g Carbohydrates 10.5 g Sugar 4 g Protein 15.6 g Cholesterol 43 mg

Minestrone Chickpeas and Macaroni Casserole (Italian)

Prep Time: 20 mins Cooking Time: 7 hours 20 mins Servings: 5

1 (15-ounce / 425-g) can chickpeas, drained and rinsed 1 (28-ounce / 794-g) can diced tomatoes, with the juice 1 (6-ounce / 170-g) can no-salt-added tomato paste	3 medium carrots, sliced 3 cloves garlic, minced 2ounces (57 g) Parmesan cheese, grated
1 medium yellow onion, chopped 1 cup low-sodium vegetable soup ½ teaspoon sea salt	½ teaspoon dried rosemary 1 teaspoon dried oregano 2 teaspoons maple syrup ¼ teaspoon ground black pepper
½ pound (227-g) fresh green beans, trimmed and cut into bite-size pieces	1cup macaroni pasta

1. Except for the green beans, pasta, and Parmesan cheese, combine all the in the slow cooker and stir to mix well.
2. Put the slow cooker lid on and cook on low for 7 hours.
3. Fold in the pasta and green beans. Put the lid on and cook on high for 20 minutes or until the vegetable are soft and the pasta is al dente.
4. Pour them in a large serving bowl and spread with Parmesan cheese before serving.

Tip: Instead of chickpeas, you can also use kidney beans, great northern beans, or cannellini beans.

Nutrition: calories: 349 fats: 6.7g protein: 16.5g carbs: 59.9g fiber: 12.9g sodium: 937mg

Easy Walnut and Ricotta Spaghetti (Italian)

Prep Time: 15 minutes Cooking Time: 10 minutes Serving 6

1 pound (454 g) cooked whole-wheat spaghetti 2 tablespoons extra-virgin olive oil	4 cloves garlic, minced
¾ cup walnuts, toasted and finely chopped 2 tablespoons ricotta cheese	¼ cup flat-leaf parsley, chopped
½ cup grated Parmesan cheese	Sea salt and freshly ground pepper, to taste

1. Reserve a cup of spaghetti water while cooking the spaghetti.
2. Heat the olive oil in a nonstick skillet over medium-low heat or until shimmering.
3. Add the garlic and sauté for a minute or until fragrant.
4. Pour the spaghetti water into the skillet and cook for 8 more mins.
5. Turn off the heat and mix in the walnuts and ricotta cheese.
6. Put the cooked spaghetti on a large serving plate, then pour the walnut sauce over. Spread with parsley and Parmesan, then sprinkle with salt and ground pepper. Toss to serve.
7. Tip: How to cook the spaghetti: Bring a large pot of water to a boil, then add the spaghetti and cook for 10 minutes or until al dente. Drain the spaghetti in a colander before using.

Nutrition: calories: 264 fats: 16.8g protein: 8.6g carbs: 22.8g fiber: 4.0g sodium: 336mg

Italian Chicken with Zucchini Noodles (Italian)

Preparation Time: 1 hour and 10 minutes Cooking Time: 6 hours

Servings: 6

½ c. chicken broth	1 tsp. Italian seasoning 4 tsps. tomato paste
1-pound chicken breast 2 tomatoes, chopped	1 ½ c. asparagus
1 c. snap peas halved	4 zucchini noodles, cut into noodle-like strips 1 c. commercial pesto
Pepper and salt to taste	

Parmesan cheese for garnish Basil for garnish

1. Take the chicken broth, Italian seasoning, tomato paste, chicken breasts, tomatoes, asparagus, and peas in the Crockpot. Give a swirl and season with pepper and salt to
2. Close the lid and then cook on low for 6 hours. Let it cool before assembling.
3. Assemble the noodles by placing the chicken mixture on top of the zucchini noodles. Add commercial pesto and garnish with parmesan cheese and basil leaves.

Nutrition: Calories: 429.7 Carbohydrates: 6g Protein: 32g Fat: 26g

Spaghetti Squash with Shrimp Scampi (Italian)

Preparation Time: 30 minutes Cooking Time: 30 minutes

Servings: 4

2 c. chicken broth	1small onion, chopped
2½ tsp. lemon-garlic seasoning 1 tbsp. butter or ghee	3pounds spaghetti squash, cut crosswise and seeds removed
¾ pounds shrimp, shelled and deveined Pepper and salt to taste.	

1. Pour broth in the Crockpot and stir in the lemon garlic seasoning, onion, and butter.
2. Take the spaghetti squash and cook on high for hours.
3. Once cooked, remove the spaghetti squash from the Crockpot and run a fork through the meat to create the strands.
4. Take the squash strands back to the Crockpot and add the shrimps.
5. Season with pepper and salt.
6. Continue cooking on high for 30 minutes or until the shrimps have turned pink.

Nutrition: Calories: 363.3 Carbohydrates: 1g Protein: 33g Fat: 21.2g

Shrimp and Leek Spaghetti (Italian)

Preparation Time: 10 minutes Cooking Time: 20 minutes

Servings: 4

2 cups leek, chopped	8 oz. spaghetti uncooked whole-grain
1/4 cup heavy cream	1 lb. raw medium shrimp peeled deveined
2 teaspoons lemon zest	1tablespoon garlic, chopped
1/2 teaspoon black pepper	2cups baby sweet peas, frozen, thawed
1 1/2 tablespoons olive oil divided	3/4 teaspoon kosher salt divided
2 tablespoons fresh lemon juice	2 tablespoons fresh dill chopped

1. Cook the pasta, drain and reserve ½ cup of the cooking liquid. Cover the cooked pasta and keep warm.
2. In the meantime, pat dries the shrimp with the paper towels, season with pepper, and ¼ teaspoon of salt.
3. Heat ½ of olive oil in a nonstick skillet over high heat, then add shrimp. Cook for about 3-4 minutes as you stir often until the shrimp is cooked through. Transfer the cooked shrimp into a plate and cover it to keep warm.
4. Reduce the heat to medium-high and add leek to the same skillet along with garlic, remaining ½ teaspoon of salt, and the remaining oil. Cook for about 2-3 minutes as you stir often until the leek has become slightly tender.
5. Add the peas to the skillet along with cream, lemon juice, lemon zest and the reserved ½ cup of the cooking liquid. Reduce the heat to medium and simmer for 2-3 minutes until the sauce has slightly thickened. Add in the shrimp and toss well until coated.
6. When through, divide the cooked pasta among the serving bowls and top with the shrimp and sauce evenly. Sprinkle with the chopped fresh dill. Serve immediately and enjoy!

Nutrition: Calories: 446 Fat: 13 g Carbs: 59 g Protein: 28 g

Garlic Shrimp Fettuccine (Italian)

Prep Time: 10 minutes Cooking Time: 15 minutes Servings: 4 to 6

8 ounces (227 g) fettuccine pasta 1/4 cup extra-virgin olive oil	3 tablespoons garlic, minced
1 pound (454 g) large shrimp, peeled and deveined	1 tablespoon lemon zest
1/3 cup lemon juice	1/2 teaspoon salt
1/2 teaspoon freshly ground black pepper	

1. Bring a large pot of salted water to a boil. Add the fettuccine and cook for 8 minutes. Reserve ½ cup of the cooking liquid and drain the pasta.
2. In a large saucepan over medium heat, heat the olive oil. Add the garlic and sauté for 1 minute.
3. Add the shrimp to the saucepan and cook each side for 3 minutes. Remove the shrimp from the pan and set aside.
4. Add the remaining to the saucepan. Stir in the cooking liquid. Add the pasta and toss together to coat the pasta evenly.
5. Transfer the pasta to a serving dish and serve topped with the cooked shrimp.

Nutrition: calories: 615 fats: 17.0g protein: 33.0g carbs: 89.0g fiber: 4.0g sodium: 407mg

Hearty Butternut Spinach, and Cheeses Lasagna(Italian)

Preparation Time: 30 minutes Cooking Time: 3 hours 45 minutes Servings: 4 to 6

2 tablespoons extra-virgin olive oil, divided	1 butternut squash, halved lengthwise and deseeded
½ teaspoon sage	½ teaspoon sea salt
¼ teaspoon ground black pepper	¼ cup grated Parmesan cheese 2 cups ricotta cheese
½ cup unsweetened almond milk	5 layers whole-wheat lasagna noodles (about 12 ounces / 340 g in total) 4 ounces (113 g) fresh spinach leaves, divided

½ cup shredded part skim Mozzarella, for garnish

1. Preheat the oven to 400°F (205°C). Line a baking sheet with parchment paper.
2. Brush 1 tablespoon of olive oil on the cut side of the butternut squash, then place the squash on the baking sheet.
3. Bake in the preheated oven for 45 minutes or until the squash is tender.
4. Allow to cool until you can handle it, then scoop the flesh out and put the flesh in a food processor to purée.
5. Combine the puréed butternut squash flesh with sage, salt, and ground black pepper in a large bowl. Stir to mix well.
6. Combine the cheeses and milk in a separate bowl, then sprinkle with salt and pepper, to taste.
7. Grease the slow cooker with 1 tablespoon of olive oil, then add a layer of lasagna noodles to coat the bottom of the slow cooker.
8. Spread half of the squash mixture on top of the noodles, then top the squash mixture with another layer of lasagna noodles.
9. Spread half of the spinach over the noodles, then top the spinach with half of cheese mixture. Repeat with remaining 3 layers of lasagna noodles, squash mixture, spinach, and cheese mixture.
10. Top the cheese mixture with Mozzarella, then put the lid on and cook on low for 3 hours or until the lasagna noodles are al dente.
11. Serve immediately.

Tip: To make this a complete meal, you can serve it with fresh cucumber soup and green leafy salad.

Nutrition: calories: 657 fats: 37.1g protein: 30.9g carbs: 57.2g fiber: 8.3g sodium: 918mg

Pasta Salad with Tomatoes and Eggplant (Italian)

Prep Time: 10 minutes Cooking Time: 15 minutes Servings: 4

1 tablespoon garlic, minced	8 oz. casarecce, fusilli, or penne pasta, uncooked
8 oz. haricots verts (French green beans), trimmed 1/4 cup dry white wine	1tablespoon olive oil 6 oz. burrata
2cups Japanese eggplant, chopped 1/2 teaspoon kosher salt	2 teaspoons fresh thyme, chopped
4 cups cherry tomatoes, halved, divided 1/2 teaspoon black pepper	2 teaspoons white wine vinegar

1. Cook the pasta according to the package instructions. Next, add in the beans 3 minutes before the cooking time is over. Drain and reserve 1 cup of cooking liquid.
2. In the meantime, heat the oil in a skillet over medium-high heat, add in the eggplant. Cook for 4-5 minutes as you stir occasionally until the eggplant has become tender.
3. Add the garlic to the skillet and cook for 1 minute until fragrant, add half of tomatoes. Continue cooking for an additional 2-3 minutes.
4. Add the wine to the skillet as you stir often until most wine has evaporated, then add in pasta and beans. Toss well to combine. If the mixture is too dry, add in a couple of tablespoons of the reserved pasta cooking liquid at a time.
5. Stir the remaining tomatoes in the skillet, along with salt and vinegar. Divide the pasta mixture among the serving bowls and top with burrata, pepper, and thyme. Serve and enjoy!

Nutrition: Calories: 428 Fat: 14 g Carbs: 56 g Protein: 17 g

Vegetarian Lasagna (Italian)

Preparation Time: 15 minutes Cooking Time: 1 hour Servings: 6

1Sweet Onion, Sliced Thick	2Zucchini, Sliced Lengthwise
1 Eggplant, Sliced Thick	2 Tablespoons Olive Oil
28 Ounces Canned tomatoes, Diced & Sodium Free	1Cup Quartered, Canned & Water Packed Artichokes, Drained 2 Teaspoons Basil, Fresh & Chopped
2 Teaspoons Garlic, Minced	2 Teaspoons Oregano, Fresh & Chopped
12 Lasagna Noodles, Whole Grain & No-Boil	¼ Teaspoon Red Pepper Flakes
¾ Cup Asiago Cheese, Grated	

1. Start by heating your oven to 400, and then get out a baking sheet. Line it with foil before placing it to the side.
2. Get out a large bowl and toss your zucchini, yellow squash, eggplant, onion, and olive oil, making sure it's coated well.
3. Arrange your vegetables on the baking sheet, roasting for twenty minutes. They should be lightly caramelized and tender.
4. Chop your roasted vegetables before placing them in a bowl.
5. Stir in your garlic, basil, oregano, artichoke hearts, tomatoes, and red pepper flakes, spooning a quarter of this mixture in the bottom of a nine by thirteen baking dish. Arrange four lasagna noodles over this sauce, and continue by alternating it. Sprinkle with asiago cheese on top, baking for a half hour.
6. Allow it to cool for fifteen minutes before slicing to serve.

Nutrition: Calories: 386 Protein: 15 g Fat: 11 g Carbs: 59 g

Simple Pesto Pasta (Italian)

Preparation Time: 10 minutes Cooking Time: 10 minutes
Servings: 4

1 lb. spaghetti	4 cups fresh basil leaves, stems removed 3 cloves garlic
1 tsp. salt	1/2 tsp. freshly ground black pepper 1/4 cup lemon juice
1/2 cup pine nuts, toasted	1/2 cup grated Parmesan cheese 1 cup extra-virgin olive oil

1. Bring a large pot of salted water to a boil. Add the spaghetti to the pot and cook for 8 minutes.
2. Put basil, garlic, salt, pepper, lemon juice, pine nuts, and Parmesan cheese in a food processor bowl with chopping blade and purée.
3. While the processor is running, slowly drizzle the olive oil through the top opening. Process until all the olive oil has been added.
4. Reserve ½ cup of the pasta water. Drain the pasta and put it into a bowl. Immediately add the pesto and pasta water to the pasta and toss everything together. Serve warm.

Nutrition: Calories: 113; Protein: 12.3g; Carbs: 3.4g; Fat: 6.3g

Asparagus Pasta (Italian)

Preparation Time: 10 minutes Cooking Time: 25 minutes
Servings: 6

8 Oz. Farfalle Pasta, Uncooked	1½ Cups Asparagus, Fresh, Trimmed & Chopped into 1 Inch Pieces 1 Pint Grape Tomatoes, Halved
2tbsp. Olive Oil	Sea Salt & Black Pepper to Taste
2 Cups Mozzarella, Fresh & Drained 1/3 Cup Basil Leaves, Fresh & Torn 2 tbsp. Balsamic Vinegar	

1. Start by heating the oven to 400°F, and then get out a stockpot. Cook your pasta per package instructions, and reserve ¼ cup of pasta water.
2. Get out a bowl and toss the tomatoes, oil, asparagus, and season with salt and pepper. Spread this mixture on a baking sheet, and bake for fifteen minutes. Stir twice in this time.
3. Remove your vegetables from the oven, and then add the cooked pasta to your baking sheet. Mix with a few tbsp. of pasta water so that your sauce becomes smoother.
4. Mix in your basil and mozzarella, drizzling with balsamic vinegar. Serve warm.

Nutrition: Calories: 307 Protein: 18 g Fat: 14 g Carbs: 33 g

Spaghetti Pesto Cake (Italian)

Preparation Time: 10 minutes Cooking Time: 40 minutes
Serving: 6

12 ounces ricotta	1 cup Basil Pesto, or store-bought 2 tablespoons olive oil
¼ cup freshly grated Parmesan cheese Salt	1-pound spaghetti

1. Preheat the oven to 400°F. Set a large pot of salted water to boil over high heat.
2. In a food processor, combine the ricotta and basil pesto. Purée into a smooth cream and transfer to a large bowl. Set aside.
3. Coat a 10-cup Bundt pan with the olive oil and sprinkle with the Parmesan cheese. Set aside.
4. Once the water is boiling, add the pasta to the pot and cook for about 6 minutes until al dente.
5. Drain the pasta well and add it to the pesto cream. Mix well until all the pasta is saturated with the sauce.
6. Spoon the pasta into the prepared pan, pressing to ensure it is tightly packed. Bake for 30 minutes.
7. Place a flat serving platter on top of the cake pan. Quickly and carefully invert the pasta cake. Gently remove the pan. Cut into slices and serve topped with your favorite sauce, if desired.

Nutrition: Calories: 622; Total Fat: 30g; Saturated Fat: 7g; Carbohydrates: 67g; Fiber: 3g; Protein: 20g; Sodium: 425mg

Artichokes, Olives & Tuna Pasta (Italian)

Preparation Time: 10 minutes Cooking Time: 15 minutes
Servings: 4

¼ cup chopped fresh basil	¼ cup chopped green olives
¼ tsp freshly ground pepper	½ cup white wine
½ tsp salt, divided	110 oz package frozen artichoke hearts, thawed and squeezed dry 2 cups grape tomatoes, halved
2 tsp chopped fresh rosemary	
2 tsp freshly grated lemon zest 2tbsp lemon juice	3 cloves garlic, minced
4 tbsp extra virgin olive oil, divided 6 oz whole wheat penne pasta	8 oz tuna steak, cut into 3 pieces

1. Cook penne pasta according to package instructions. Drain and set aside.
2. Preheat grill to medium high.
3. In bowl, toss and mix ¼ tsp pepper, ¼ tsp salt, 1 tsp rosemary, lemon zest, 1 tbsp oil and tuna pieces.
4. Grill tuna for 3 minutes per side. Allow to cool and flake into bite sized pieces.
5. On medium fire, place a large nonstick saucepan and heat 3 tbsp oil.
6. Sauté remaining rosemary, garlic olives, and artichoke hearts for 4 minutes Add wine and tomatoes, bring to a boil and cook for 3 minutes while stirring once in a while.
7. Add remaining salt, lemon juice, tuna pieces and pasta. Cook until heated through.
8. To serve, garnish with basil and enjoy.

Nutrition: Calories 127.6; Carbohydrates 13 g; Protein 7.2 g; Fat 5.2 g

Roasted Vegetarian Lasagna (Italian)

Prep Time: 25 minutes Cooking Time: 50 minutes Servings: 6

1 eggplant, thickly sliced
1 yellow squash, sliced lengthwise 1 sweet onion, thickly sliced
1 (28-ounce) can sodium-free diced tomatoes 2 teaspoons minced garlic
2 teaspoons chopped fresh basil
12 no-boil whole-grain lasagna noodles

2 zucchinis, sliced lengthwise
2 tablespoons extra-virgin olive oil

1 cup quartered, canned, water-packed artichoke hearts, drained
2 teaspoons chopped fresh oregano Pinch red pepper flakes
¾ cup grated Asiago cheese

1. Preheat the oven to 400°F.
2. Line a baking sheet with aluminum foil and set aside.
3. In a large bowl, toss together the eggplant, zucchini, yellow squash, onion, and olive oil to coat.
4. Arrange the vegetables on the prepared sheet and roast for about 20 minutes, or until tender and lightly caramelized.
5. Chop the roasted vegetables well and transfer them to a large bowl.
6. Stir in the tomatoes, artichoke hearts, garlic, basil, oregano, and red pepper flakes
7. Spoon one-quarter of the vegetable mixture into the bottom of a deep 9- by-13-inch baking dish.
8. Arrange 4 lasagna noodles over the sauce.
9. Repeat, alternating sauce and noodles, ending with sauce.
10. Sprinkle the Asiago cheese evenly over the top. Bake for about 30 minutes until bubbly and hot.
11. Remove from the oven and cool for 15 minutes before serving.
12. Substitution tip: If having a vegetarian meal is not a requirement, lean ground beef (92%) or ground chicken can be added to the roasted vegetable sauce for a more robust meal. Brown the ground meat in a skillet and add it to the finished sauce before assembling the lasagna.

Nutrition: Calories: 386; Total Fat: 11g; Saturated Fat: 3g; Carbohydrates: 59g; Fiber: 12g; Protein: 15g

Pasta with Lemon and Artichokes (Italian)

Preparation Time: 10 minutes Cooking Time: 15 minutes Servings: 4

16 ounces linguine or angel hair pasta 1/4 cup extra-virgin olive oil
2 (15-ounce) jars water-packed artichoke hearts, drained and quartered 2 tablespoons freshly squeezed lemon juice
Freshly ground black pepper

8 garlic cloves, finely minced or pressed

1/4 cup thinly sliced fresh basil 1 teaspoon of sea salt

1. Boil a pot of water on high heat and cook the pasta.
2. While the pasta is cooking, heat the oil in a skillet over medium heat and cook the garlic, stirring often, for 1 to 2 minutes until it just begins to brown. Toss the garlic with the artichokes in a large bowl.
3. When the pasta is cooked, drain it very carefully and add it to the artichoke mixture, then add the lemon juice, basil, salt, and pepper. Gently stir and serve.

Nutrition: Calories: 423 Protein: 15 g Fat: 14 g

Spicy Pasta Puttanesca (Italian)

Prep Time: 10 minutes Cooking Time: 20 minutes Servings: 4

2 teaspoons extra-virgin olive oil

1 (28-ounce) can sodium-free diced tomatoes
2 teaspoons chopped fresh oregano 2 teaspoons chopped fresh basil
½ cup quartered Kalamata olives
1 tablespoon capers, drained and rinsed Juice of

½ sweet onion, finely chopped 2 teaspoons minced garlic
½ cup chopped anchovies

½ teaspoon red pepper flakes
1 lemon
¼ cup sodium-free chicken broth
4 cups cooked whole-grain penne

1. In a large saucepan over medium heat, heat the olive oil.
2. Add the onion and garlic, and sauté for about 3 minutes until softened.
3. Stir in the tomatoes, anchovies, oregano, basil, and red pepper flakes. Bring the sauce to a boil and reduce the heat to low. Simmer for 15 minutes, stirring occasionally.
4. Stir in the olives, chicken broth, capers, and lemon juice.
5. Cook the pasta according to the package directions and serve topped with the sauce.
6. Ingredient tip: Do not mistake sardines for anchovies, although they are both small, silvery fish sold in cans. Anchovies are usually salted in brine and matured to create a distinctive, rich taste.

Nutrition: Calories: 303; Total Fat: 6g; Saturated Fat: 0g; Carbohydrates: 54g; Fiber: 9g; Protein: 9g

Herb-Topped Focaccia (Italian)

Prep Time: 20 minutes Cooking Time: 2 hours Servings: 10

1 tbsp. dried rosemary or 3 tbsp. minced fresh rosemary
1 tbsp. dried thyme or 3 tbsp. minced fresh thyme leaves
1 cup warm water

1 tsp. sugar
1/2 cups flour, divided 1 tsp. salt
1/2 cup extra-virgin olive oil
1 packet active dry yeast 2

1. In a small bowl, combine the rosemary and thyme with the olive oil.
2. In a large bowl, whisk together the sugar, water, and yeast. Let stand for 5 minutes.
3. Add 1 cup of flour, half of the olive oil mixture, and the salt to the mixture in the large bowl. Stir to combine.
4. Add the remaining 1½ cups flour to the large bowl. Using your hands, combine dough until it starts to pull away from the sides of the bowl.
5. Put the dough on a floured board or countertop and knead 10 to 12 times. Place the dough in a well-oiled bowl and cover with plastic wrap. Put it in a warm, dry space for 1 hour.
6. Oil a 9-by-13-inch baking pan. Turn the dough onto the baking pan, and using your hands gently push the dough out to fit the pan.
7. Using your fingers, make dimples into the dough. Evenly pour the remaining half of the olive oil mixture over the dough. Let the dough rise for another 30 minutes.
8. Preheat the oven to 450°F. Place the dough into the oven and let cook for 18 to 20 minutes, until you see it turn a golden brown.

Nutrition: Calories: 53; Protein: 12.3g; Carbs: 3.4g; Fat: 6.3g

Artichoke Chicken Pasta (Italian)

Preparation Time: 20 minutes Cooking Time: 5 minutes
Servings: 4

1cloves garlic, crushed 2 lemons, wedged	2 tbsp. lemon juice
14 oz. artichoke hearts, chopped 1-lb. chicken breast fillet, diced	½ cup feta cheese, crumbled 1 tbsp. olive oil
16 oz. whole-wheat (gluten-free) pasta of your choice 3 tbsp. parsley, chopped	½ cup red onion, chopped 2 tsp. oregano
1 tomato, chopped	Ground black pepper and salt, to taste

1. Pour the water into a deep saucepan and boil it. Add the pasta and some salt; cook it as per package directions. Drain the water and set aside the pasta.
2. Over medium stove flame, heat the oil in a skillet or saucepan (preferably of medium size).
3. Sauté the onions and garlic until softened and translucent, stir in between.
4. Add the chicken and cook until it is no longer pink.
5. Mix in the tomatoes, artichoke hearts, parsley, feta cheese, oregano, lemon juice and the cooked pasta.
6. Combine well and cook for 3-4 minutes, stirring frequently.
7. Season with black pepper and salt. Garnish with lemon wedges and serve warm.

Nutrition: Calories 486 | Fat 10g | Carbs 42g | Fiber 9g | Protein 37g

Spinach Beef Pasta (Italian)

Preparation Time: 30 minutes Cooking Time: 10 minutes
Servings: 4

1 ¼ cups uncooked orzo pasta	¾ cup baby spinach 2 tbsp. olive oil
1 ½ lb. beef tenderloin	¾ cup feta cheese 2 quarts water
1 cup cherry tomatoes, halved	¼ tsp. salt

1. Rub the meat with pepper and cut into small cubes.
2. Over medium stove flame; heat the oil in a deep saucepan (preferably of medium size).
3. Add and stir-fry the meat until it is evenly brown.
4. Add the water and boil the mixture; stir in the orzo and salt.
5. Cook the mixture for 7-8 minutes. Add the spinach and cook until it wilts.
6. Add the tomatoes and cheese; combine and serve warm.

Nutrition: Calories 334 | Fat 13g | Carbs 36g | Fiber 6g | Protein 16g

Asparagus Parmesan Pasta (Italian)

Preparation Time: 25 minutes
Cooking Time: 4 minutes Servings: 2

1tsp. extra-virgin olive oil 1 tsp. lemon juice	¾ cup whole milk
½ bunch asparagus, trimmed and cut into small pieces	½ cup parmesan cheese, grated 2 tbsp. garlic, minced
2tbsp. almond flour	2 tsp. whole grain mustard
4 oz. whole-wheat penne pasta 1 tsp. tarragon, minced	Ground black pepper and salt, to taste

1. Pour the water into a deep saucepan and boil it. Add the pasta and some salt; cook it as per package directions. Drain the water and set aside the pasta.
2. Take another pan, pour 8 cups of water and let it come to boiling. Add the asparagus and boil until it is soft. Drain and set aside.
3. In a mixing bowl, combine the milk, flour, mustard, black pepper and salt. Set aside.
4. Over medium stove flame, heat the oil in a skillet or saucepan (preferably of medium size).
5. Sauté the garlic until softened and fragrant, stirring in between.
6. Add the milk mixture and let it simmer. Add the tarragon, lemon juice and lemon zest; mix to combine.
7. Add the cooked pasta, asparagus, and simmer until the sauce thickens, stirring frequently.
8. Top with parmesan cheese and serve warm.

Nutrition: Calories 402 Fat 31gCarbs 33g Fiber 6gProtein 44g

Chickpea Pasta Salad (Italian)

Preparation Time: 10 minutes Cooking Time: 15 minutes
Servings: 6

2 Tablespoons Olive Oil 16 Ounces Rotelle Pasta	½ Cup Cured Olives, Chopped
2 Tablespoons Oregano, Fresh & Minced 2 Tablespoons Parsley, Fresh & Chopped	¼ Cup Red Wine Vinegar 1 Bunch Green Onions, Chopped
15 Ounces Canned Garbanzo Beans, Drained & Rinsed	½ Cup Parmesan Cheese, Grated Sea Salt & Black Pepper to Taste

1. Bring a pot of water to a boil and cook your pasta al dente per package instructions. Drain it and rinse it using cold water.
2. Get out a skillet and heat up your olive oil over medium heat. Add in your scallions, chickpeas, parsley, oregano and olives. Lower the heat to low, and cook for twenty minutes more. Allow this mixture to cool.
3. Toss your chickpea mixture with your pasta, and then add in your grated cheese, salt, pepper and vinegar. Let it chill for four hours or overnight before serving.

Nutrition: Calories: 424 Protein: 16 g Fat: 10 g Carbs: 69 g

Authentic Pasta e Fagioli (Italian)

Preparation Time: 6 minutes Cooking Time: 15 minutes
Servings: 4

2 tablespoons olive oil	1 teaspoon garlic, pressed
4 small-sized potatoes, peeled and diced 1 parsnip, chopped	1 carrot, chopped
1 celery rib, chopped 1 leek, chopped	1(6-ounce) can tomato paste 4 cups water
2vegetable bouillon cubes	8 ounces cannellini beans, soaked overnight 6 ounces elbow pasta
1/2 teaspoon oregano 1/2 teaspoon basil	1/2 teaspoon fennel seeds Sea salt, to taste
1/4 teaspoon freshly cracked black pepper	2 tablespoons Italian parsley, roughly chopped

1. Press the "Sauté" button to preheat your Instant Pot. Heat the oil and sauté the garlic, potatoes, parsnip, carrot, celery, and leek until they have softened.
2. Now, add in the tomato paste, water, bouillon cubes, cannellini beans, elbow pasta, oregano, basil, fennel seeds, freshly cracked black pepper, and sea salt.
3. Secure the lid. Choose the "Manual" mode and cook for 9 minutes at High pressure. Once cooking is complete, use a quick pressure release; carefully remove the lid.
4. Serve with fresh Italian parsley. Bon appétit!

Nutrition: 486 Calories; 8.3g Fat; 95g Carbs; 12.4g Protein; 11.4g Sugars; 14.8g Fiber

Creamy Garlic-Parmesan Chicken Pasta(Italian)

Preparation Time: 5 minutes Cooking Time: 25 minutes
Servings: 6

2 boneless, skinless chicken breasts 3 tbsp. extra-virgin olive oil	1½ tsp. salt
1 large onion, thinly sliced 3 tbsp. garlic, minced	1 lb. fettuccine pasta
1 cup heavy (whipping) cream	¾ cup freshly grated Parmesan cheese, divided
½ tsp. freshly ground black pepper	

1. Bring a large pot of salted water to a simmer.
2. Cut the chicken into thin strips.
3. In a large skillet over medium heat, cook the olive oil and chicken for 3 minutes.
4. Next add the salt, onion, and garlic to the pan with the chicken. Cook for 7 minutes.
5. Bring the pot of salted water to a boil and add the pasta, then let it cook for 7 minutes.
6. While the pasta is cooking, add the cream, ½ cup of Parmesan cheese, and black pepper to the chicken; simmer for 3 minutes.
7. Reserve ½ cup of the pasta water. Drain the pasta and add it to the chicken cream sauce.
8. Add the reserved pasta water to the pasta and toss together. Let simmer for 2 minutes. Top with the remaining ¼ cup Parmesan cheese and serve warm.

Nutrition: Calories: 153; Protein: 12.3g; Carbs: 3.4g; Fat: 6.3g

Tomato and Almond Pesto (Italian)

Prep Time: 15 minutes Cooking Time: None Servings: 4 cups

¾ Cup slivered almonds	one 28-oz. can dice tomatoes, drained
one 14-oz. can tomato, fire-roasted, drained	¾ cup of extra-virgin olive oil
½ cup grated parmesan cheese salt and pepper to taste	1 cup fresh basil leaves 1 tbsp red wine vinegar

1. Begin by heating a frying pan over a medium to high flame. After heating the pan put the almonds into the pan and let them cook for 4 to 5 minutes.
2. Once the almonds have reached a golden-brown color, place it into a food processor until you reach the consistency of fine powder.
3. Mix into the food processor the basil, red wine vinegar, and the tomatoes. Wait until the mixture becomes smooth and add the olive oil.
4. Continue processing for 35 seconds before adding the salt, pepper, and Parmesan. After a few pulses, the mix is ready to serve.
5. You can refrigerate for a cooler mix.

Nutrition: Calories: 167 Carbohydrates: 18 g Fats: 6 g Proteins: 3 g

Roasted Tomato Sauce with Pasta (Italian)

Preparation Time: 5 minutes Cooking Time: 35 minutes
Servings: 2

large tomatoes, quartered 4 garlic cloves, unpeeled	3 basil sprigs, plus more for garnish
1 teaspoon salt, plus more for the pasta water 1/2 teaspoon freshly ground black pepper	8 ounces whole-wheat pasta 1/4 cup grated Parmesan or Romano cheese 3 tablespoons extra-virgin olive oil

1. Preheat the oven to 450°F.
2. In a small baking dish, put the tomatoes, garlic cloves, and basil sprigs. Add the olive oil, salt, and pepper and toss to coat. Push the basil to the bottom so that it doesn't dry out.
3. Roast for 30 minutes.
4. Meanwhile, bring a large pot of water to boil over high heat. Once boiling, salt the water to your liking, stir, and return to a boil. Add the pasta and cook for 1 to 2 minutes less than the package directions for al dente, as it will continue to cook later with the sauce. Drain, reserving about ½ cup of the cooking water.
5. Remove the tomatoes from the oven. Discard the basil. Squeeze the roasted garlic from their skins and discard the skins.
6. Using a potato masher or large spoon, mash the tomato mixture. Be careful, as it will be hot, and the juices can squirt out at you. Pull out any tomato skins; they should slip right off after being roasted.
7. Transfer the tomato mixture to a large skillet, set over medium-low heat, and add the cooked pasta. Toss, adding the reserved cooking water as needed to achieve the desired consistency.
8. Add the Parmesan. Continue to cook for 2 to 3 minutes, until everything is blended.
9. Garnish with fresh basil.

Nutrition: Calories: 727; Total Fat: 26g; Saturated Fat: 5g; Protein: 22g; Total Carbohydrates: 102g; Fiber: 8g; Sugar: 13g; Cholesterol: 11mg

Spaghetti with Garlic, Olive Oil, And Red Pepper (Italian)

Preparation Time: 5 minutes Cooking Time: 10 minutes
Servings: 2

Salt	8 ounces spaghetti
1/4 cup extra-virgin olive oil	garlic cloves, 3 lightly smashed, and 1 minced 1/2 teaspoon red pepper flakes
1/4 cup grated Parmesan cheese	1 tablespoon chopped fresh flat-leaf parsley

1. Bring a large pot of water to a boil over high heat. Once boiling, salt the water to your liking, stir, and return to a boil. Add the spaghetti and cook according to package directions until al dente. Drain, reserving about ½ cup of the cooking water.
2. In a large skillet, heat the olive oil over low heat. Add the smashed garlic cloves and cook until golden brown. Remove the garlic from the pan and discard.
3. Add the red pepper flakes to the garlic-infused oil and warm for 1 minute before turning off the heat.
4. Once the spaghetti is cooked, add it to the pan.
5. Add the minced garlic and toss the spaghetti in the oil to coat. Add the reserved pasta water, a little at a time, as needed to help everything combine.
6. Sprinkle with Parmesan and parsley.
7. Cooking tip: When making pasta, it is important to salt the water for a flavorful dish generously. I generally use about 2 tablespoons of salt per pound of pasta. Add the salt after the water boils, stir to dissolve, and wait for the water to return to a boil, then add the pasta.

Nutrition: Calories: 722; Total Fat: 32g; Saturated Fat: 6g; Protein: 19g; Total Carbohydrates: 89g; Fiber: 4g; Sugar: 3g; Cholesterol: 11mg

Spaghetti With Anchovy Sauce (Italian)

Preparation Time: 5 minutes Cooking Time: 10 minutes
Servings: 4

Salt	1-pound spaghetti
1/4 cup extra-virgin olive oil	1 can oil-packed anchovy fillets, undrained 3 garlic cloves, minced
1/4 cup chopped fresh flat-leaf parsley 1 teaspoon red pepper flakes	1/4 teaspoon freshly ground black pepper 1 tablespoon bread crumbs

1. Bring a large pot of water to a boil over high heat. Once boiling, salt the water to your liking, stir, and return to a boil. Add the spaghetti and cook according to package directions until al dente. Drain, reserving about ½ cup of the cooking water.
2. Meanwhile, in a large skillet, heat the olive oil over low heat. Add the anchovy fillets with their oil and the garlic. Cook for 7 to 10 minutes, until the pasta, is ready, stirring until the anchovies melt away and form a sauce.
3. Add the spaghetti, parsley, red pepper flakes, black pepper, and a little of the reserved cooking water, as needed, and toss to combine all the .
4. Sprinkle with the bread crumbs.

Nutrition: Calories: 581; Total Fat: 17g; Saturated Fat: 3g; Protein: 19g; Total Carbohydrates: 87g; Fiber: 4g; Sugar: 3g; Cholesterol: 12mg

Alethea's Lemony Asparagus Pasta (Italian)

Preparation Time: 10 minutes Cooking Time: 20 minutes
Servings: 6

1-pound spaghetti, linguini, or angel hair pasta 2 crusty bread slices	½ cup plus 1 tablespoon avocado oil, divided 3 cups chopped asparagus (1½-inch pieces)
½ cup vegan "chicken" broth or vegetable broth, divided 6 tablespoons freshly squeezed lemon juice	8 garlic cloves, minced or pressed
3 tablespoons finely chopped fresh curly parsley 1 tablespoon grated lemon zest	1½ teaspoons sea salt

1. Boil a large pot of water on high heat and cook the pasta until al dente according to the instructions on the package.
2. Meanwhile, in a medium skillet, crumble the bread into coarse crumbs. Put 1 tablespoon of oil on the pan and then stir well to combine over medium heat. Cook for about 5 minutes while stirring it often, until the crumbs are golden brown. Remove from the skillet and set aside.
3. Add the chopped asparagus and ¼ cup of broth in the skillet and cook over medium-high heat until the asparagus becomes bright green and crisp about 5 minutes. Transfer the asparagus to a very large bowl.
4. Add the remaining ½ cup of oil, remaining ¼ cup of broth, lemon juice, garlic, parsley, zest, and salt to the asparagus bowl and stir well.
5. When the noodles are cooked, drain it very well, and then add them to the bowl. Gently toss with the asparagus mixture. Before serving, stir in the toasted bread crumbs. Store leftovers in an airtight container in the refrigerator for up 2 days.

Nutrition: Calories: 256 Protein: 13 g Fat: 23 g Carbs: 68 g

Meaty Baked Penne (Italian)

Preparation Time: 10 minutes Cooking Time: 40 minutes
Servings: 6

1 lb. penne pasta 1 lb. ground beef 1 tsp. salt	1 (25-oz.) jar marinara sauce
1 (1-lb.) bag baby spinach, washed	3 cups shredded mozzarella cheese, divided

1. Bring a large pot of salted water to a boil, add the penne, and cook for 7 minutes. Reserve 2 cups of e pasta water and drain the pasta.
2. Preheat the oven to 350°F.
3. In a large saucepan over medium heat, cook the ground beef and salt. Brown the ground beef for about 5 minutes.
4. Stir in marinara sauce, and 2 cups of pasta water. Let simmer for 5 minutes.
5. Add a handful of spinach at a time into the sauce, and cook for another 3 minutes.
6. To assemble, in a 9-by-13-inch baking dish, add the pasta and pour the pasta sauce over it. Stir in 1½ cups of the mozzarella cheese. Cover the dish with foil and bake for 20 minutes.
7. After 20 minutes, remove the foil, top with the rest of the mozzarella, and bake for another 10 minutes. Serve warm.

Nutrition: Calories: 173; Protein: 12.3g; Carbs: 3.4g; Fat: 6.3g

Spaghetti with Pine Nuts and Cheese (Italian)

Preparation Time: 10 minutes Cooking Time: 11 minutes
Servings: 4 to 6

8 ounces (227 g) spaghetti 4 tablespoons almond butter

1 teaspoon freshly ground black pepper 1/2 cup pine nuts

1 cup fresh grated Parmesan cheese, divided

1. Bring a large pot of salted water to a boil. Add the pasta and cook for 8 minutes.
2. In a large saucepan over medium heat, combine the butter, black pepper, and pine nuts. Cook for 2 to 3 minutes, or until the pine nuts are lightly toasted.
3. Reserve ½ cup of the pasta water. Drain the pasta and place it into the pan with the pine nuts.
4. Add ¾ cup of the Parmesan cheese and the reserved pasta water to the pasta and toss everything together to coat the pasta evenly.
5. Transfer the pasta to a serving dish and top with the remaining ¼ cup of the Parmesan cheese. Serve immediately.

Nutrition: calories: 542 fats: 32.0g protein: 20.0g carbs: 46.0g fiber: 2.0g sodium: 552mg

Creamy Garlic Parmesan Chicken Pasta (Italian)

Preparation Time: 5 minutes Cooking Time: 15 minutes
Servings: 4

3 tablespoons extra-virgin olive oil

2 boneless, skinless chicken breasts, cut into thin strips 1 large onion, thinly sliced

3 tablespoons garlic, minced
1½ teaspoons salt

1-pound (454 g) fettuccine pasta 1 cup heavy whipping cream

3/4 cup freshly grated Parmesan cheese, divided
1/2 teaspoon freshly ground black pepper

1. In a large skillet over medium heat, heat the olive oil. Add the chicken and cook for 3 minutes.
2. Add the onion, garlic and salt to the skillet. Cook for 7 minutes, stirring occasionally.
3. Meanwhile, bring a large pot of salted water to a boil and add the pasta, then cook for 7 minutes.
4. While the pasta is cooking, add the heavy cream, ½ cup of the Parmesan cheese and black pepper to the chicken. Simmer for 3 minutes.
5. Reserve ½ cup of the pasta water. Drain the pasta and add it to the chicken cream sauce.
6. Add the reserved pasta water to the pasta and toss together. Simmer for 2 minutes. Top with the remaining ¼ cup of the Parmesan cheese and serve warm.

Nutrition: calories: 879 fats: 42.0g protein: 35.0g carbs: 90.0g fiber: 5.0g sodium: 1336mg

Arugula Pasta Soup (Italian)

Preparation Time: 15 minutes Cooking Time: 5 minutes
Servings: 6

7 oz. chickpeas, rinsed 4 eggs, lightly beaten 2 tbsp. lemon juice
1 pinch of nutmeg

3 cups arugula, chopped 6 tbsp. parmesan cheese 6 cups chicken broth
1bunch scallions, sliced (greens and whites sliced separately) 1 1/3 cups whole-wheat pasta shells

2 cups water

Ground black pepper, to taste

1. In a cooking pot or deep saucepan, combine the pasta, scallion whites, chickpeas, water, broth and nutmeg.
2. Heat the mixture; cover and bring to a boil.
3. Take off the lid and simmer the mixture for about 4 minutes. Add the arugula and cook until it is wilted.
4. Mix in the eggs and season with black pepper and salt.
5. Mix in the lemon juice and scallion greens. Top with the parmesan cheese; serve warm.

Nutrition: Calories 317 Fat 7g Carbs 32g Fiber 6g Protein 38g

Stuffed Pasta Shells (Italian)

Preparation Time: 15 minutes Cooking Time: 10 minutes
Servings: 4

5 Cups Marinara Sauce 15 Oz. Ricotta Cheese
¾ Cup Parmesan Cheese, Grated 2 tbsp. Parsley, Fresh & Chopped
½ tsp. Thyme

1 ½ Cups Mozzarella Cheese, Grated
¼ Cup Basil Leaves, Fresh & Chopped 8 Oz. Spinach, Fresh & Chopped
Sea Salt & Black Pepper to Taste 1 lb. Ground Beef

1Cup Onions, Chopped 4 Cloves Garlic, Diced

2tbsp. Olive Oil, Divided 12 Oz. Jumbo Pasta Shells

1. Start by cooking your pasta shells by following your package instructions. Once they're cooked, then set them to the side.
2. Press sauté and then add in half of your olive oil. Cook your garlic and onions, which should take about four minutes. Your onions should be tender, and your garlic should be fragrant.
3. Add your ground beef in, seasoning it with thyme, salt, and pepper, cooking for another four minutes.
4. Add in your basil, parsley, spinach and marinara sauce.
5. Cover your pot, and cook for five minutes on low pressure.
6. Use a quick release, and top with cheeses.
7. Press sauté again, making sure that it stays warm until your cheese melts.
8. Take a tbsp. of the mixture, stuffing it into your pasta shells.
9. Top with your remaining sauce before serving warm.

Nutrition: Calories: 710, Protein: 45.2 g, Fat: 23.1 g, Carbs: 70 g

Homemade Pasta Bolognese (Italian)

Preparation Time: 20 minutes Cooking Time: 10 minutes
Servings: 4

Minced meat 17 oz. Pasta 12 oz.	Sweet red onion1 piece Garlic 2 cloves Vegetable oil 1 tbsp.
Tomato pastes 3 tbsp.	Grated Parmesan Cheese 2 oz. Bacon 3 pieces

1. Fry finely chopped onions and garlic in a frying pan in vegetable oil until a characteristic smell.
2. Add minced meat and chopped bacon to the pan. Constantly break the lumps with a spatula and mix so that the minced meat is crumbly.
3. When the mince is ready, add tomato paste, grated Parmesan to the pan, mix, reduce heat and leave to simmer.
4. At this time, boil the pasta. I don't salt water, because for me tomato paste and sauce as a whole turn out to be quite salty.
5. When the pasta is ready, discard it in a colander, arrange it on plates, add meat sauce with tomato paste on top of each serving.

Nutrition: Calories: 1091, Fat: 54.7g, Carbs: 92.8g, Protein: 74g

Mediterranean Pasta with Tomato Sauce and Vegetables (Italian)

Preparation Time: 15 minutes Cooking Time: 25 minutes
Servings: 8

8 oz. linguine or spaghetti, cooked 1 tsp. garlic powder	1 (28 oz.) can whole peeled tomatoes, drained and sliced 1 tbsp. olive oil
1 (8 oz.) can tomato sauce	½ tsp. Italian seasoning 8 oz. mushrooms, sliced
8 oz. yellow squash, sliced 8 oz. zucchini, sliced ½ cup grated Parmesan cheese	½ tsp. sugar

1. In a medium saucepan, mix tomato sauce, tomatoes, sugar, Italian seasoning, and garlic powder. Bring to boil on medium heat. Reduce heat to low. Cover and simmer for 20 minutes.
2. In a large skillet, heat olive oil on medium-high heat.
3. Add squash, mushrooms, and zucchini. Cook, stirring, for 4 minutes or until tender-crisp.
4. Stir vegetables into the tomato sauce.
5. Place pasta in a serving bowl.
6. Spoon vegetable mixture over pasta and toss to coat.
7. Top with grated Parmesan cheese.

Nutrition: Calories: 154 Protein: 6 gFat: 2 gCarbs: 28 g

White Bean Alfredo Pasta (Italian)

Preparation Time: 10 minutes Cooking Time: 15 minutes
Servings: 4

1teaspoon salt, plus more for the pasta water 1-pound fettuccine	2tablespoons extra-virgin olive oil garlic cloves, minced
¼ teaspoon red pepper flakes	(15-ounce) cans cannellini beans, rinsed and drained 2 cups vegetable broth
½ cup almond milk	¼ cup low-fat Pecorino cheese
¼ teaspoon ground nutmeg	Chopped fresh flat-leaf parsley for garnish

1. Bring a large pot of water to boil over high heat. Once boiling, salt the water to your liking, stir, and return to a boil. Add the fettuccine and cook according to package directions until al dente. Drain, reserving about ½ cup of the cooking water.
2. Meanwhile, in a large skillet, heat the olive oil over medium heat. Add the garlic and red pepper flakes and cook for about 1 minute, until fragrant.
3. Add the beans, broth, and almond milk to the pan and bring to a boil. Remove the pan from the heat.
4. Using a slotted spoon, transfer the beans to a food processor or blender and process until smooth.
5. Return the pureed beans to the skillet. Add the Romano, salt, and nutmeg and bring to a simmer.
6. Add the cooked pasta to the bean mixture and stir to coat, adding the reserved cooking water, a little at a time, as needed—Cook for about 2 minutes.
7. Garnish with parsley.
8. Variation tip: Try adding steamed broccoli florets or chopped sun-dried tomatoes for an extra burst of flavor, color, and nutrients.

Nutrition: Calories: 697; Total Fat: 12g; Saturated Fat: 3g; Protein: 30g; Total Carbohydrates: 118g; Fiber: 12g; Sugar: 5g; Cholesterol: 5mg

Pasta with Garlic and Hot Pepper (Italian)

Preparation Time: 25 minutes Cooking Time: 4 minutes
Servings: 4

400g Spaghetti	8 tbsp. Extra virgin olive oil 4 cloves garlic, chopped
1 Chili pepper Coarse salt	

1. Put the water to boil, when it comes to a boil add salt and dip the spaghetti.
2. Meanwhile, in a saucepan heat the oil with the garlic deprived of the inner and chopped germ and the chopped peppers. Be careful: the flame should be sweet and the garlic should not darken.
3. Halfway through cooking, remove the spaghetti and continue cooking in the pan with the oil and garlic, adding the cooking water as if it were a risotto.
4. When cooked, serve the spaghetti.

Nutrition: Calories 201, Fat 4.3g, Protein 5.8g, Carbs 20.1g

Fusilli Arrabbiata (Italian)

Prep Time: 5 minutes Cooking Time: 20 minutes Servings: 4

1tablespoons extra-virgin olive oil 1 small onion, finely chopped Splash dry red wine (optional)	½ serrano pepper, seeded and minced 2 garlic cloves, minced 1/2 teaspoon freshly ground black pepper
1 (28-ounce) can crushed tomatoes 1 (6-ounce) can tomato paste	¾ cup water, 1/4 cup grated Parmesan or Romano cheese
½ to 1 teaspoon red pepper flakes	1 teaspoon dried basil 1 tablespoon dried oregano
1 teaspoon salt, plus more for the pasta water	1-pound fusilli or rotini

1. In a large, deep skillet, heat the olive oil over medium heat. Add the onion and cook for about 3 minutes, until just starting to soften.
2. Add a little red wine (if using) and cook for about 3 minutes, until the alcohol is burned off.
3. Add the serrano pepper and garlic and cook for about 1 minute, until fragrant.
4. Pour in the crushed tomatoes and stir everything together. Add the tomato paste and water and stir until the paste is blended in.
5. Add the red pepper flakes. You may want to do this a little at a time until you get your desired level of heat. You can always add more, but you can't take it out.
6. Season the recipe with oregano, basil, salt, and black pepper.
7. Bring the sauce to a boil, then reduce the heat to a simmer.
8. Bring a large pot of water to a boil over high heat. Once boiling, salt the water to your liking, stir, and return to a boil. Add the fusilli and cook according to package directions until al dente. Drain.
9. Ladle the sauce over the pasta and top with the Parmesan cheese.

Nutrition: Calories: 619; Total Fat: 14g; Saturated Fat: 3g; Protein: 21g; Total Carbohydrates: 104g; Fiber:10g; Sugar: 15g; Cholesterol: 5mg

Triple-Green Pasta with Cheese (Italian)

Prep Time: 5 minutes Cooking Time: 14 to 16 minutes Servings: 4

8 ounces (227 g) uncooked penne	1/4 teaspoon crushed red pepper 2 garlic cloves, minced
2 cups chopped fresh flat-leaf parsley, including stems 5 cups loosely packed baby spinach	1/4 teaspoon ground nutmeg 1/4 teaspoon kosher salt 1 tbsp extra-virgin olive oil
1/4 teaspoon freshly ground black pepper	1/3 cup Castelvetrano olives, pitted and sliced 1/3 cup grated Parmesan cheese

1. In a large stockpot of salted water, cook the pasta for about 8 to 10 minutes. Drain the pasta and reserve ¼ cup of the cooking liquid.
2. Meanwhile, heat the olive oil in a large skillet over medium heat. Add the garlic and red pepper and cook for 30 secs, stirring constantly.
3. Add the parsley and cook for 1 minute, stirring constantly. Add the spinach, nutmeg, salt, and pepper, and cook for 3 minutes, stirring occasionally, or until the spinach is wilted.
4. Add the cooked pasta and the reserved ¼ cup cooking liquid to the skillet. Stir in the olives and cook for about 2 minutes, or until most of the pasta water has been absorbed.
5. Remove from the heat and stir in the cheese before serving.

Nutrition: calories: 262 fats: 4.0g protein: 15.0g carbs: 51.0g fiber: 13.0g sodium: 1180mg

Caprese Pasta with Roasted Asparagus(Italian)

Preparation Time: 5 minutes Cooking Time: 25 minutes Servings: 6

8 ounces (227 g) uncooked small pasta, like orecchiette (little ears) or farfalle (bow ties)	1½ pounds (680 g) fresh asparagus, ends trimmed & stalks chopped into 1-inch pieces
1½ cups grape tomatoes, halved	2 tablespoons extra-virgin olive oil 1/4 teaspoon kosher salt
1/4 teaspoon freshly ground black pepper 2 tablespoons balsamic vinegar	2 cups fresh Mozzarella, drained and cut into bite-size pieces (about 8 ounces / 227 g)
1/3 cup torn fresh basil leaves	

1. Preheat the oven to 400°F (205°C).
2. In a large stockpot of salted water, cook the pasta for about 8 to 10 minutes. Drain and reserve about ¼ cup of the cooking liquid.
3. Meanwhile, in a large bowl, toss together the asparagus, tomatoes, oil, salt and pepper. Spread the mixture onto a large, rimmed baking sheet and bake in the oven for 15 minutes, stirring twice during cooking.
4. Remove the vegetables from the oven and add the cooked pasta to the baking sheet. Mix with a few tablespoons of cooking liquid to help the sauce become smoother and the saucy vegetables stick to the pasta.
5. Gently mix in the Mozzarella and basil. Drizzle with the balsamic vinegar. Serve from the baking sheet or pour the pasta into a large bowl.

Nutrition: calories: 147 fats: 3.0g protein: 16.0g carbs: 17.0g fiber: 5.0g sodium: 420mg

Bean and Veggie Pasta (Italian)

Preparation Time: 10 minutes Cooking Time: 15 minutes Servings: 2

16 ounces (454 g) small whole wheat pasta, such as penne, farfalle, or macaroni	5 cups water
1 (15-ounce / 425-g) can cannellini beans, drained and rinsed	1 (14.5-ounce / 411-g) can diced (with juice) or crushed tomatoes 1 yellow onion, chopped
2 tablespoons tomato paste 1 red or yellow bell pepper, chopped	1 tablespoon olive oil 3 garlic cloves, minced
¼ teaspoon crushed red pepper (optional) 1 bunch kale, stemmed and chopped	1 cup sliced basil ½ cup pitted Kalamata olives, chopped

1. Add the pasta, water, beans, tomatoes (with juice if using diced), onion, bell pepper, tomato paste, oil, garlic, and crushed red pepper (if desired), to a large stockpot or deep skillet with a lid. Bring to a boil over high heat, stirring often.
2. Reduce the heat to medium-high, add the kale, and cook, continuing to stir often, until the pasta is al dente, about 10 mins.
3. Remove from the heat and let sit for 5 minutes. Garnish with the basil and olives and serve.

Nutrition: calories: 565 fats: 17.7g protein: 18.0g carbs: 85.5g fiber: 16.5g sodium: 540mg

Roasted Ratatouille Pasta (Italian)

Preparation Time: 10 minutes Cooking Time: 30 minutes
Servings: 2

1 small eggplant (about 8 ounces / 227 g)	1 small zucchini
1 portobello mushroom 1 Roma tomato, halved	½ medium sweet red pepper, seeded
½ teaspoon salt, plus additional for the pasta water 1 teaspoon Italian herb seasoning	1 tablespoon olive oil
2 cups farfalle pasta (about 8 ounces / 227 g)	2 tablespoons minced sun-dried tomatoes in olive oil with herbs 2 tablespoons prepared pesto

1. Slice the ends off the eggplant and zucchini. Cut them lengthwise into
1. ½-inch slices.
2. Place the eggplant, zucchini, mushroom, tomato, and red pepper in a large bowl and sprinkle with ½ teaspoon of salt. Using your hands, toss the vegetables well so that they're covered evenly with the salt. Let them rest for about 10 minutes.
3. While the vegetables are resting, preheat the oven to 400°F (205°C). Line a baking sheet with parchment paper.
4. When the oven is hot, drain off any liquid from the vegetables and pat them dry with a paper towel. Add the Italian herb seasoning and olive oil to the vegetables and toss well to coat both sides.
5. Lay the vegetables out in a single layer on the baking sheet. Roast them for 15 to 20 minutes, flipping them over after about 10 minutes or once they start to brown on the underside. When the vegetables are charred in spots, remove them from the oven.
6. While the vegetables are roasting, fill a large saucepan with water. Add salt and cook the pasta until al dente, about 8 to 10 minutes. Drain the pasta, reserving ½ cup of the pasta water.
7. When cool enough to handle, cut the vegetables into large chunks (about 2 inches) and add them to the hot pasta.
8. Stir in the sun-dried tomatoes and pesto and toss everything well. Serve immediately.

Nutrition: calories: 613 fats: 16.0g protein: 23.1g carbs: 108.5g fiber: 23.0g sodium: 775mg

Lentil and Mushroom Pasta (Italian)

Preparation Time: 10 minutes Cooking Time: 50 minutes
Servings: 2

2 tablespoons olive oil	1 large yellow onion, finely diced
2 portobello mushrooms, trimmed and chopped finely	3 garlic cloves, chopped 1 teaspoon oregano
2 tablespoons tomato paste 2½ cups water	1 cup brown lentils
1 (28-ounce / 794-g) can diced tomatoes with basil (with juice if diced) 1 tablespoon balsamic vinegar Chopped basil, for garnish	8 ounces (227 g) pasta of choice, cooked Salt and black pepper, to taste

1. Place a large stockpot over medium heat. Add the oil. Once the oil is hot, add the onion and mushrooms. Cover and cook until both are soft, about 5 minutes. Add the tomato paste, garlic, and oregano and cook 2 minutes, stirring constantly.
2. Stir in the water and lentils. Bring to a boil, then reduce the heat to medium-low and cook for 5 minutes, covered.
3. Add the tomatoes (and juice if using diced) and vinegar. Replace the lid, reduce the heat to low and cook until the lentils are tender, about 30 minutes.
4. Remove the sauce from the heat and season with salt and pepper to taste. Garnish with the basil and serve over the cooked pasta.

Nutrition: calories: 463 fats: 15.9g protein: 12.5g carbs: 70.8g fiber: 16.9g sodium: 155mg

Penne Pasta with Tomato Sauce and MitzithraCheese (Italian)

Preparation Time: 15 minutes Cooking Time: 20 minutes
Servings: 5

2 tablespoons olive oil	2 scallion stalks, chopped
2 green garlic stalks, minced 10 ounces penne	1/3 teaspoon ground black pepper, to taste Sea salt, to taste
1/4 teaspoon cayenne pepper 1/4 teaspoon dried marjoram 1/2 teaspoon dried oregano 1/2 teaspoon dried basil	1/2 cup marinara sauce 2 cups vegetable broth
2 overripe tomatoes, pureed	1 cup Mitzithra cheese, grated

1. Press the "Sauté" button to preheat your Instant Pot. Heat the oil until sizzling. Now, sauté the scallions and garlic until just tender and fragrant.
2. Stir in the penne pasta, spices, marinara sauce, broth, and pureed tomatoes; do not stir, but your pasta should be covered with the liquid.
3. Secure the lid. Choose the "Manual" mode and cook for 7 minutes at High pressure. Once cooking is complete, use a natural pressure release for 5 minutes; carefully remove the lid.
4. Fold in the cheese and seal the lid. Let it sit in the residual heat until the cheese melts. Bon appetite

Nutrition: 395 Calories; 15.6g Fat; 51.8g Carbs; 14.9g Protein; 2.5g Sugars; 7.5g Fiber

125

Chapter 6
Vegetable Mains

Stuffed Portobello Mushrooms with Spinach

Prep time: 5 minutes | Cook time: 20 minutes | Serves 4

8 large portobello mushrooms, stems removed	1 medium red bell pepper, diced
3 teaspoons extra-virgin olive oil, divided	4 cups fresh spinach
	¼ cup crumbled feta cheese

1. Preheat the oven to 450°F (235°C).
2. Using a spoon to scoop out the gills of the mushrooms and discard them. Brush the mushrooms with 2 teaspoons of olive oil.
3. Arrange the mushrooms (cap-side down) on a baking sheet. Roast in the preheated oven for 20 minutes.
4. Meantime, in a medium skillet, heat the remaining olive oil over medium heat until it shimmers.
5. Add the bell pepper and spinach and sauté for 8 to 10 minutes, stirring occasionally, or until the spinach is wilted.
6. Remove the mushrooms from the oven to a paper towel-lined plate. Using a spoon to stuff each mushroom with the bell pepper and spinach mixture. Scatter the feta cheese all over.
7. Serve immediately.

Per Serving (2 mushrooms)

calories: 115 | fat: 5.9g | protein: 7.2g | carbs: 11.5g | fiber: 4.0g | sodium: 125mg

Zoodles with Walnut Pesto

Prep time: 10 minutes | Cook time: 10 minutes | Serves 4

4 medium zucchinis, spiralized	¼ teaspoon kosher salt, divided
¼ cup extra-virgin olive oil, divided	2 tablespoons grated Parmesan cheese, divided
1 tbsp minced garlic, divided	1 cup packed fresh basil leaves
½ teaspoon crushed red pepper	¾ cup walnut pieces, divided
¼ teaspoon freshly ground black pepper, divided	

1. In a large bowl, stir together the zoodles, 1 tablespoon of the olive oil, ½ teaspoon of the minced garlic, red pepper, ⅛ teaspoon of the black pepper and ⅛ teaspoon of the salt. Set aside.
2. Heat ½ tablespoon of the oil in a large skillet over medium-high heat. Add half of the zoodles to the skillet and cook for 5 minutes, stirring constantly. Transfer the cooked zoodles into a bowl. Repeat with another ½ tablespoon of the oil and the remaining zoodles. When done, add the cooked zoodles to the bowl.
3. Make the pesto: In a food processor, combine the remaining ½ teaspoon of the minced garlic, ⅛ teaspoon of the black pepper and ⅛ teaspoon of the salt, 1 tablespoon of the Parmesan, basil leaves and ¼ cup of the walnuts. Pulse until smooth and then slowly drizzle the remaining 2 tablespoons of the oil into the pesto. Pulse again until well combined.
4. Add the pesto to the zoodles along with the remaining 1 tablespoon of the Parmesan and the remaining ½ cup of the walnuts. Toss to coat well. Serve immediately.

Per Serving

calories: 166 | fat: 16.0g | protein: 4.0g | carbs: 3.0g | fiber:

2.0g | sodium: 307mg

Chickpea Lettuce Wraps with Celery

Prep time: 10 minutes | Cook time: 0 minutes | Serves 4

1 (15-ounce / 425-g) can low-sodium chickpeas, drained and rinsed	2 tablespoons unsalted tahini
1 celery stalk, thinly sliced	3 tablespoons honey mustard
2 tablespoons finely chopped red onion	1 tablespoon capers, undrained
	12 butter lettuce leaves

1. In a bowl, mash the chickpeas with a potato masher or the back of a fork until mostly smooth.
2. Add the celery, red onion, tahini, honey mustard, and capers to the bowl and stir until well incorporated.
3. For each serving, place three overlapping lettuce leaves on a plate and top with ¼ of the mashed chickpea filling, then roll up. Repeat with the remaining lettuce leaves and chickpea mixture.

Per Serving

calories: 182 | fat: 7.1g | protein: 10.3g | carbs: 19.6g | fiber: 3.0g | sodium: 171mg

Cheesy Sweet Potato Burgers

Prep time: 10 minutes | Cook time: 19 to 20 minutes | Serves 4

1 large sweet potato (about 8 ounces / 227 g)	1 garlic clove
2 tablespoons extra-virgin olive oil, divided	1 cup old-fashioned rolled oats
	1 tablespoon dried oregano
1 cup chopped onion	1 tablespoon balsamic vinegar
1 large egg	¼ teaspoon kosher salt
	½ cup crumbled Gorgonzola cheese

1. Using a fork, pierce the sweet potato all over and microwave on high for 4 to 5 minutes, until softened in the center. Cool slightly before slicing in half.
2. Meanwhile, in a large skillet over medium-high heat, heat 1 tablespoon of the olive oil. Add the onion and sauté for 5 minutes.
3. Spoon the sweet potato flesh out of the skin and put the flesh in a food processor. Add the cooked onion, egg, garlic, oats, oregano, vinegar and salt. Pulse until smooth. Add the cheese and pulse four times to barely combine.
4. Form the mixture into four burgers. Place the burgers on a plate, and press to flatten each to about ¾-inch thick.
5. Wipe out the skillet with a paper towel. Heat the remaining 1 tablespoon of the oil over medium-high heat for about 2 minutes. Add the burgers to the hot oil, then reduce the heat to medium. Cook the burgers for 5 minutes per side.
6. Transfer the burgers to a plate and serve.

Per Serving

calories: 290 | fat: 12.0g | protein: 12.0g | carbs: 43.0g | fiber: 8.0g | sodium: 566mg

Eggplant and Zucchini Gratin

Prep time: 10 minutes | Cook time: 19 minutes | Serves 6

2 large zucchinis, finely chopped	¾ cup unsweetened almond milk
1 large eggplant, finely chopped	1 tablespoon all-purpose flour
¼ teaspoon kosher salt	⅓ cup plus 2 tablespoons grated Parmesan cheese, divided
¼ teaspoon freshly ground black pepper	
3 tablespoons extra-virgin olive oil, divided	1 cup chopped tomato
	1 cup diced fresh Mozzarella
	¼ cup fresh basil leaves

1. Preheat the oven to 425°F (220°C).
2. In a large bowl, toss together the zucchini, eggplant, salt and pepper.
3. In a large skillet over medium-high heat, heat 1 tablespoon of the oil. Add half of the veggie mixture to the skillet. Stir a few times, then cover and cook for about 4 minutes, stirring occasionally. Pour the cooked veggies into a baking dish. Place the skillet back on the heat, add 1 tablespoon of the oil and repeat with the remaining veggies. Add the veggies to the baking dish.
4. Meanwhile, heat the milk in the microwave for 1 minute. Set aside.
5. Place a medium saucepan over medium heat. Add the remaining 1 tablespoon of the oil and flour to the saucepan. Whisk together until well blended.
6. Slowly pour the warm milk into the saucepan, whisking the entire time. Continue to whisk frequently until the mixture thickens a bit. Add ⅓ cup of the Parmesan cheese and whisk until melted. Pour the cheese sauce over the vegetables in the baking dish and mix well.
7. Fold in the tomatoes and Mozzarella cheese. Roast in the oven for 10 minutes, or until the gratin is almost set and not runny.
8. Top with the fresh basil leaves and the remaining 2 tablespoons of the Parmesan cheese before serving.

Per Serving

calories: 122 | fat: 5.0g | protein: 10.0g | carbs: 11.0g | fiber: 4.0g | sodium: 364mg

Veggie-Stuffed Portabello Mushrooms

Prep time: 5 minutes | Cook time: 24 to 25 minutes | Serves 6

3 tablespoons extra-virgin olive oil, divided	¼ teaspoon kosher salt
1 cup diced onion	¼ teaspoon crushed red pepper
2 garlic cloves, minced	6 large portabello mushrooms, stems and gills removed
1 large zucchini, diced	
3 cups chopped mushrooms	
1 cup chopped tomato	Cooking spray
1 teaspoon dried oregano	4 ounces (113 g) fresh Mozzarella cheese, shredded

1. In a large skillet over medium heat, heat 2 tablespoons of the oil. Add the onion and sauté for 4 minutes. Stir in the garlic and sauté for 1 minute.
2. Stir in the zucchini, mushrooms, tomato, oregano, salt and red pepper. Cook for 10 minutes, stirring constantly. Remove from the heat.
3. Meanwhile, heat a grill pan over medium-high heat.
4. Brush the remaining 1 tablespoon of the oil over the portabello mushroom caps. Place the mushrooms, bottom-side down, on the grill pan. Cover with a sheet of aluminum foil sprayed with nonstick cooking spray. Cook for 5 minutes.
5. Flip the mushroom caps over, and spoon about ½ cup of the cooked vegetable mixture into each cap. Top each with about 2½ tablespoons of the Mozzarella.
6. Cover and grill for 4 to 5 minutes, or until the cheese is melted.
7. Using a spatula, transfer the portabello mushrooms to a plate. Let cool for about 5 minutes before serving.

Per Serving

calories: 111 | fat: 4.0g | protein: 11.0g | carbs: 11.0g | fiber: 4.0g | sodium: 314mg

Stir-Fried Eggplant

Prep time: 25 minutes | Cook time: 15 minutes | Serves 2

1 cup water, plus more as needed
½ cup chopped red onion
1 tablespoon finely chopped garlic
1 tablespoon dried Italian herb seasoning
1 teaspoon ground cumin
1 small eggplant (about 8 ounces / 227 g), peeled and cut into ½-inch cubes
1 medium carrot, sliced
2 cups green beans, cut into 1-inch pieces
2 ribs celery, sliced
1 cup corn kernels
2 tablespoons almond butter
2 medium tomatoes, chopped

1. Heat 1 tablespoon of water in a large soup pot over medium-high heat until it sputters.
2. Cook the onion for 2 minutes, adding a little more water as needed.
3. Add the garlic, Italian seasoning, cumin, and eggplant and stir-fry for 2 to 3 minutes, adding a little more water as needed.
4. Add the carrot, green beans, celery, corn kernels, and ½ cup of water and stir well. Reduce the heat to medium, cover, and cook for 8 to 10 minutes, stirring occasionally, or until the vegetables are tender.
5. Meanwhile, in a bowl, stir together the almond butter and ½ cup of water.
6. Remove the vegetables from the heat and stir in the almond butter mixture and chopped tomatoes. Cool for a few minutes before serving.

Per Serving

calories: 176 | fat: 5.5g | protein: 5.8g | carbs: 25.4g | fiber: 8.6g | sodium: 198mg

Honey-Glazed Baby Carrots

Prep time: 5 minutes | Cook time: 6 minutes | Serves 2

⅔ cup water
1½ pounds (680 g) baby carrots
4 tablespoons almond butter
½ cup honey
1 teaspoon dried thyme
1½ teaspoons dried dill Salt, to taste

1. Pour the water into the Instant Pot and add a steamer basket. Place the baby carrots in the basket.
2. Secure the lid. Select the Manual mode and set the cooking time for 4 minutes at High Pressure.
3. Once cooking is complete, do a quick pressure release. Carefully open the lid.
4. Transfer the carrots to a plate and set aside.
5. Pour the water out of the Instant Pot and dry it.
6. Press the Sauté button on the Instant Pot and heat the almond butter.
7. Stir in the honey, thyme, and dill.
8. Return the carrots to the Instant Pot and stir until well coated. Sauté for another 1 minute.
9. Taste and season with salt as needed. Serve warm.

Per Serving

calories: 575 | fat: 23.5g | protein: 2.8g | carbs: 90.6g | fiber: 10.3g | sodium: 547mg

Quick Steamed Broccoli

Prep time: 5 minutes | Cook time: 0 minutes | Serves 2

¼ cup water
3 cups broccoli florets
Salt and ground black pepper, to taste

1. Pour the water into the Instant Pot and insert a steamer basket. Place the broccoli florets in the basket.
2. Secure the lid. Select the Manual mode and set the cooking time for 0 minutes at High Pressure.
3. Once cooking is complete, do a quick pressure release. Carefully open the lid.
4. Transfer the broccoli florets to a bowl with cold water to keep bright green color.
5. Season the broccoli with salt and pepper to taste, then serve.

Per Serving

calories: 16 | fat: 0.2g | protein: 1.9g | carbs: 1.7g | fiber: 1.6g | sodium: 292mg

Garlic-Butter Asparagus with Parmesan

Prep time: 5 minutes | Cook time: 8 minutes | Serves 2

1 cup water
1 pound (454 g) asparagus, trimmed
2 cloves garlic, chopped
3 tablespoons almond butter
Salt and ground black pepper, to taste
3 tablespoons grated Parmesan cheese

1. Pour the water into the Instant Pot and insert a trivet.
2. Put the asparagus on a tin foil add the butter and garlic. Season to taste with salt and pepper.
3. Fold over the foil and seal the asparagus inside so the foil doesn't come open. Arrange the asparagus on the trivet.
4. Secure the lid. Select the Manual mode and set the cooking time for 8 minutes at High Pressure.
5. Once cooking is complete, do a quick pressure release. Carefully open the lid. Unwrap the foil packet and serve sprinkled with the Parmesan cheese.

Per Serving calories: 243 | fat: 15.7g | protein: 12.3g | carbs: 15.3g | fiber: 7.3g | sodium: 435mg

Ratatouille

Prep time: 10 minutes | Cook time: 6 minutes | Serves 4

2 large zucchinis, sliced
2 medium eggplants, sliced
4 medium tomatoes, sliced
2 small red onions, sliced
4 cloves garlic, chopped
2 tablespoons thyme leaves
2 teaspoons sea salt
1 teaspoon black pepper
2 tablespoons balsamic vinegar
4 tablespoons olive oil
2 cups water

1. Line a springform pan with foil and place the chopped garlic in the bottom.
2. Now arrange the vegetable slices, alternately, in circles.
3. Sprinkle the thyme, pepper and salt over the vegetables. Top with oil and vinegar.
4. Pour a cup of water into the instant pot and place the trivet inside. Secure the lid and cook on Manual function for 6 minutes at High Pressure.
5. Release the pressure naturally and remove the lid.
6. Remove the vegetables along with the tin foil.
7. Serve on a platter and enjoy.

Per Serving calories: 240 | fat: 14.3g | protein: 4.7g | carbs: 27.5g | fiber: 10.8g | sodium: 1181mg

Mushroom and Potato Teriyaki

Prep time: 10 minutes | Cook time: 18 minutes | Serves 4

¾ large yellow or white onion, chopped
1½ medium carrots, diced
1½ ribs celery, chopped
1 medium portabella mushroom, diced
¾ tablespoon garlic, chopped
2 cups water
1 pound (454 g) white potatoes, peeled and diced
¼ cup tomato paste
½ tablespoon sesame oil
2 teaspoons sesame seeds
½ tablespoon paprika
1 teaspoon fresh rosemary
¾ cups peas
¼ cup fresh parsley for garnishing, chopped

1. Add the oil, sesame seeds, and all the vegetables in the instant pot and Sauté for 5 minutes.
2. Stir in the remaining and secure the lid.
3. Cook on Manual function for 13 minutes at High Pressure.
4. After the beep, natural release the pressure and remove the lid.
5. Garnish with fresh parsley and serve hot.

Per Serving

calories: 160 | fat: 3.0g | protein: 4.7g | carbs: 30.6g | fiber: 5.5g | sodium: 52mg

Peanut and Coconut Stuffed Eggplants

Prep time: 15 minutes | Cook time: 9 minutes | Serves 4

1 tablespoon coriander seeds
½ teaspoon cumin seeds
½ teaspoon mustard seeds
2 to 3 tablespoons chickpea flour
2 tablespoons chopped peanuts
2 tablespoons coconut shreds
1-inch ginger, chopped
2 cloves garlic, chopped
1 hot green chili, chopped
½ teaspoon ground cardamom
A pinch of cinnamon
⅓ to ½ teaspoon cayenne
½ teaspoon turmeric
½ teaspoon raw sugar
½ to ¾ teaspoon salt
1 teaspoon lemon juice
Water as needed
4 baby eggplants
Fresh Cilantro for garnishing

1. Add the coriander, mustard seeds and cumin in the instant pot.
2. Roast on Sauté function for 2 minutes.
3. Add the chickpea flour, nuts and coconut shred to the pot, and roast for 2 minutes.
4. Blend this mixture in a blender, then transfer to a medium-sized bowl. Roughly blend the ginger, garlic, raw sugar, chili, and all the spices in a blender.
5. Add the water and lemon juice to make a paste. Combine it with the dry flour mixture.
6. Cut the eggplants from one side and stuff with the spice mixture. Add 1 cup of water to the instant pot and place the stuffed eggplants inside.
7. Sprinkle some salt on top and secure the lid.
8. Cook on Manual for 5 minutes at High Pressure, then quick release the steam. Remove the lid and garnish with fresh cilantro, then serve hot.

Per Serving calories: 207 | fat: 4.9g | protein: 7.9g | carbs: 39.6g | fiber: 18.3g | sodium: 315mg

Cauliflower with Sweet Potato

Prep time: 15 minutes | Cook time: 8 minutes | Serves 8

1 small onion
4 tomatoes
4 garlic cloves, chopped
2-inch ginger, chopped
2 teaspoons olive oil
1 teaspoon turmeric
2 teaspoons ground cumin
Salt, to taste
1 teaspoon paprika
2 medium sweet potatoes, cubed small
2 small cauliflowers, diced
2 tablespoons fresh cilantro for topping, chopped

1. Blend the tomatoes, garlic, ginger and onion in a blender.
2. Add the oil and cumin in the instant pot and Sauté for 1 minute.
3. Stir in the blended mixture and the remaining spices.
4. Add the sweet potatoes and cook for 5 minutes on Sauté
5. Add the cauliflower chunks and secure the lid.
6. Cook on Manual for 2 minutes at High Pressure.
7. Once done, Quick release the pressure and remove the lid.
8. Stir and serve with cilantro on top.

Per Serving

calories: 76 | fat: 1.6g | protein: 2.7g | carbs: 14.4g | fiber: 3.4g | sodium: 55mg

Mushroom, Potato, and Green Bean Mix

Prep time: 10 minutes | Cook time: 18 minutes | Serves 3

1 tablespoon olive oil
½ carrot, peeled and minced
½ celery stalk, minced
½ small onion, minced
1 garlic clove, minced
½ teaspoon dried sage, crushed
½ teaspoon dried rosemary, crushed
4 ounces (113 g) fresh Portabella mushrooms, sliced
4 ounces (113 g) fresh white mushrooms, sliced
¼ cup red wine
1 Yukon Gold potato, peeled and diced
¾ cup fresh green beans, trimmed and chopped
1 cup tomatoes, chopped
½ cup tomato paste
½ tablespoon balsamic vinegar
3 cups water
Salt and freshly ground black pepper to taste
2 ounces (57 g) frozen peas
½ lemon juice
2 tablespoons fresh cilantro for garnishing, chopped

1. Put the oil, onion, tomatoes and celery into the instant pot and Sauté for 5 minutes. Stir in the herbs and garlic and cook for 1 minute. Add the mushrooms and sauté for 5 minutes. Stir in the wine and cook for a further 2 minutes
2. Add the diced potatoes and mix. Cover the pot with a lid and let the potatoes cook for 2-3 minutes.
3. Now add the green beans, carrots, tomato paste, peas, salt, pepper, water and vinegar.
4. Secure the lid and cook on Manual function for 8 minutes at High Pressure with the pressure valve in the sealing position. Do a Quick release and open the pot, stir the veggies and then add lemon juice and cilantro, then serve with rice or any other of your choice.

Per Serving calories: 238 | fat: 5.4g | protein: 8.3g | carbs: 42.7g | fiber: 8.5g | sodium: 113mg

Mushroom Tacos

Prep time: 10 minutes | Cook time: 13 minutes | Serves 3

4 large guajillo chilies
2 teaspoons oil
2 bay leaves
2 large onions, sliced
2 garlic cloves
2 chipotle chillies in adobo sauce
2 teaspoons ground cumin
1 teaspoon dried oregano
1 teaspoon smoked hot paprika

½ teaspoon ground cinnamon, Salt, to taste
¾ cup vegetable broth
1 teaspoon apple cider vinegar
3 teaspoons lime juice
¼ teaspoon sugar
8 ounces (227 g) mushrooms chopped
Whole-wheat tacos, for serving

1. Put the oil, onion, garlic, salt and bay leaves into the instant pot and Sauté for 5 minutes.
2. Blend the half of this mixture, in a blender, with all the spices and chillies.
3. Add the mushrooms to the remaining onions and Sauté for 3 minutes. Pour the blended mixture into the pot and secure the lid. Cook on Manual function for 5 minutes at High Pressure. Once done, Quick release the pressure and remove the lid. Stir well and serve with tacos.

Per Serving calories: 138 | fat: 4.1g | protein: 5.7g | carbs: 23.8g | fiber: 4.8g | sodium: 208mg

Lentils and Eggplant Curry

Prep time: 10 minutes | Cook time: 22 minutes | Serves 4

¾ cup lentils, soaked and rinsed
1 teaspoon olive oil
½ onion, chopped
4 garlic cloves, chopped
1 teaspoon ginger, chopped
1 hot green chili, chopped
¼ teaspoon turmeric
½ teaspoon ground cumin

2 tomatoes, chopped
1 cup eggplant, chopped
1 cup sweet potatoes, cubed
¾ teaspoon salt
2 cups water
1 cup baby spinach leaves
Cayenne and lemon/lime to taste
Pepper flakes (garnish)

1. Add the oil, garlic, ginger, chili and salt into the instant pot and Sauté for 3 minutes.
2. Stir in the tomatoes and all the spices. Cook for 5 minutes.
3. Add all the remaining , except the spinach leaves and garnish.
4. Secure the lid and cook on Manual function for 12 minutes at High Pressure.
5. After the beep, release the pressure naturally and remove the lid.
6. Stir in the spinach leaves and let the pot simmer for 2 minutes on Sauté.
7. Garnish with the pepper flakes and serve warm.

Per Serving
calories: 88 | fat: 1.5g | protein: 3.4g | carbs: 17.4g | fiber: 3.3g | sodium: 470mg

Sweet Potato and Tomato Curry

Prep time: 5 minutes | Cook time: 8 minutes | Serves 8

2 large brown onions, finely diced
4 tablespoons olive oil
4 teaspoons salt
4 large garlic cloves, diced
1 red chili, sliced
4 tablespoons cilantro, chopped
4 teaspoons ground cumin

2 teaspoons ground coriander
2 teaspoons paprika
2 pounds (907 g) sweet potato, diced
4 cups chopped, tinned tomatoes
2 cups water
2 cups vegetable stock
Lemon juice and cilantro (garnish)

1. Put the oil and onions into the instant pot and Sauté for 5 minutes.
2. Stir in the remaining and secure the lid.
3. Cook on Manual function for 3 minutes at High Pressure.
4. Once done, Quick release the pressure and remove the lid.
5. Garnish with cilantro and lemon juice.
6. Serve.

Per Serving
calories: 224 | fat: 8.0g | protein: 4.6g | carbs: 35.9g | fiber: 7.5g | sodium: 1385mg

Cabbage Stuffed Acorn Squash

Prep time: 15 minutes | Cook time: 23 minutes | Serves 4

½ tablespoon olive oil
2 medium Acorn squashes
¼ small yellow onion, chopped
1 jalapeño pepper, chopped
½ cup green onions, chopped
½ cup carrots, chopped
¼ cup cabbage, chopped
1 garlic clove, minced

½ (6-ounce / 170-g) can sugar-free tomato sauce
½ tablespoon chili powder
½ tablespoon ground cumin
Salt and freshly ground black pepper to taste
2 cups water
¼ cup Cheddar cheese, shredded

1. Pour the water into the instant pot and place the trivet inside.
2. Slice the squash into 2 halves and remove the seeds.
3. Place over the trivet, skin side down, and sprinkle some salt and pepper over it.
4. Secure the lid and cook on Manual for 15 minutes at High Pressure.
5. Release the pressure naturally and remove the lid. Empty the pot into a bowl.
6. Now add the oil, onion, and garlic in the instant pot and Sauté for 5 minutes.
7. Stir in the remaining vegetables and stir-fry for 3 minutes.
8. Add the remaining and secure the lid.
9. Cook on Manual function for 2 minutes at High Pressure.
10. After the beep, natural release the pressure and remove the lid.
11. Stuff the squashes with the prepared mixture and serve warm.

Per Serving
calories: 163 | fat: 5.1g | protein: 4.8g | carbs: 28.4g | fiber: 4.9g | sodium: 146mg

Potato Curry

Prep time: 10 minutes | Cook time: 30 minutes | Serves 2

2 large potatoes, peeled and diced
1 small onion, peeled and diced
8 ounces (227 g) fresh tomatoes
1 tablespoon olive oil
1 cup water
2 tablespoons garlic cloves, grated
½ tablespoon rosemary
½ tablespoon cayenne pepper
1½ tablespoons thyme
Salt and pepper, to taste

1. Pour a cup of water into the instant pot and place the steamer trivet inside.
2. Place the potatoes and half the garlic over the trivet and sprinkle some salt and pepper on top.
3. Secure the lid and cook on Steam function for 20 minutes.
4. After the beep, natural release the pressure and remove the lid.
5. Put the potatoes to one side and empty the pot.
6. Add the remaining to the cooker and Sauté for 10 minutes.
7. Use an immerse blender to purée the cooked mixture.
8. Stir in the steamed potatoes and serve hot.

Per Serving

calories: 398 | fat: 7.6g | protein: 9.6g | carbs: 76.2g | fiber: 10.9g | sodium: 111mg

Veggie Chili

Prep time: 15 minutes | Cook time: 10 minutes | Serves 3

½ tablespoon olive oil
1 small yellow onion, chopped
4 garlic cloves, minced
¾ (15-ounce / 425-g) can diced tomatoes
1 ounce (28 g) sugar-free tomato paste
½ (4-ounce / 113-g) can green chilies with liquid
1 tablespoon Worcestershire sauce
2 tablespoons red chili powder
½ cup carrots, diced
½ cup scallions, chopped
½ cup green bell pepper, chopped
¼ cup peas
1 tablespoon ground cumin
½ tablespoon dried oregano, crushed
Salt and freshly ground black pepper to taste

1. Add the oil, onion, and garlic into the instant pot and Sauté for 5 minutes.
2. Stir in the remaining vegetables and stir-fry for 3 minutes.
3. Add the remaining and secure the lid.
4. Cook on Manual function for 2 minutes at High Pressure.
5. After the beep, natural release the pressure and remove the lid.
6. Stir well and serve warm.

Per Serving

calories: 106 | fat: 3.9g | protein: 3.4g | carbs: 18.0g | fiber: 6.2g | sodium: 492mg

Radish and Cabbage Congee

Prep time: 5 minutes | Cook time: 20 minutes | Serves 3

1 cup carrots, diced
½ cup radish, diced
6 cups vegetable broth
Salt, to taste
1½ cups short grain rice, rinsed
1 tablespoon grated fresh ginger
4 cups cabbage, shredded
Green onions for garnishing, chopped

1. Add all the , except the cabbage and green onions, into the instant pot.
2. Select the Porridge function and cook on the default time and settings.
3. After the beep, Quick release the pressure and remove the lid Stir in the shredded cabbage and cover with the lid.
4. Serve after 10 minutes with chopped green onions on top.

Per Serving calories: 438 | fat: 0.8g | protein: 8.7g | carbs: 98.4g | fiber: 6.7g | sodium: 1218mg

Creamy Potato Curry

Prep time: 10 minutes | Cook time: 18 minutes | Serves 4

¾ large yellow or white onion, chopped
1½ ribs celery, chopped
¼ cup carrots, diced
¼ cup green onions
½ cup coconut milk
¾ tablespoon garlic, chopped
1½ cups water
¼ cup heavy cream
¼ teaspoon thyme
¼ teaspoon rosemary
½ tablespoon black pepper
¾ cup peas Salt, to taste
2 tablespoons fresh cilantro for garnishing, chopped
1 pound (454 g) white potatoes, peeled and diced

1. Add the oil and all the vegetables in the instant pot and Sauté for 5 minutes.
2. Stir in the remaining and secure the lid.
3. Cook on Manual function for 13 minutes at High Pressure.
4. Once it beeps, natural release the pressure and remove the lid.
5. Garnish with fresh cilantro and serve hot.

Per Serving

calories: 210 | fat: 10.1g | protein: 4.1g | carbs: 27.6g | fiber: 4.7g | sodium: 74mg

Mushroom and Spinach Stuffed Peppers

Prep time: 15 minutes | Cook time: 8 minutes | Serves 7

7 mini sweet peppers
1 cup button mushrooms, minced
5 ounces (142 g) organic baby spinach
½ teaspoon fresh garlic
½ teaspoon coarse sea salt
¼ teaspoon cracked mixed pepper
2 tablespoons water
1 tablespoon olive oil
Organic Mozzarella cheese, diced

1. Put the sweet peppers and water in the instant pot and Sauté for 2 minutes.
2. Remove the peppers and put the olive oil into the pot.
3. Stir in the mushrooms, garlic, spices and spinach.
4. Cook on Sauté until the mixture is dry.
5. Stuff each sweet pepper with the cheese and spinach mixture.
6. Bake the stuffed peppers in an oven for 6 minutes at 400ºF (205ºC).
7. Once done, serve hot.

Per Serving

calories: 81 | fat: 2.4g | protein: 4.1g | carbs: 13.2g | fiber: 2.4g | sodium: 217mg

Black Bean and Corn Tortilla Bowls

Prep time: 10 minutes | Cook time: 8 minutes | Serves 4

1½ cups vegetable broth	2 small potatoes, cubed
½ cup tomatoes, undrained diced	½ cup bell pepper, chopped
1 small onion, diced	½ can black beans, drained and rinsed
2 garlic cloves, finely minced	1 cup frozen corn kernels
1 teaspoon chili powder	½ tablespoon lime juice
1 teaspoon cumin	2 tablespoons cilantro for topping, chopped
½ teaspoon paprika	Whole-wheat tortilla chips
½ teaspoon ground coriander	
Salt and pepper to taste	
½ cup carrots, diced	

1. Add the oil and all the vegetables into the instant pot and Sauté for 3 minutes.
2. Add all the spices, corn, lime juice, and broth, along with the beans, to the pot.
3. Seal the lid and cook on Manual setting at High Pressure for 5 minutes.
4. Once done, natural release the pressure when the timer goes off. Remove the lid.
5. To serve, put the prepared mixture into a bowl.
6. Top with tortilla chips and fresh cilantro. Serve.

Per Serving

calories: 183 | fat: 0.9g | protein: 7.1g | carbs: 39.8g | fiber: 8.3g | sodium: 387mg

Potato, Corn, and Spinach Medley

Prep time: 10 minutes | Cook time: 10 minutes | Serves 6

1 tablespoon olive oil	1 tablespoon fish sauce
3 scallions, chopped	2 tablespoons light soy sauce
½ cup onion, chopped	2 large cloves garlic, diced
2 large white potatoes, peeled and diced	⅓ teaspoon white pepper
1 tablespoon ginger, grated	1 teaspoon salt
3 cups frozen corn kernels	3-4 handfuls baby spinach leaves
1 cup vegetable stock	Juice of ½ lemon

1. Put the oil, ginger, garlic and onions in the instant pot and Sauté for 5 minutes. Add all the remaining except the spinach leaves and lime juice
2. Secure the lid and cook on the Manual setting for 5 minutes at High Pressure. After the beep, Quick release the pressure and remove the lid.
3. Add the spinach and cook for 3 minutes on Sauté
4. Drizzle the lime juice over the dish and serve hot.

Per Serving

calories: 217 | fat: 3.4g | protein: 6.5g | carbs: 44.5g | fiber: 6.3g | sodium: 892mg

Cauliflower and Broccoli Bowls

Prep time: 5 minutes | Cook time: 7 minutes | Serves 3

½ medium onion, diced	½ pound (227 g) broccoli florets
2 teaspoons olive oil	
1 garlic clove, minced	½ cup vegetable broth
½ cup tomato paste	½ teaspoon paprika
½ pound (227 g) frozen cauliflower	¼ teaspoon dried thyme
	2 pinches sea salt

1. Add the oil, onion and garlic into the instant pot and Sauté for 2 minutes.
2. Add the broth, tomato paste, cauliflower, broccoli, and all the spices, to the pot.
3. Secure the lid. Cook on the Manual setting at with pressure for 5 minutes.
4. After the beep, Quick release the pressure and remove the lid.
5. Stir well and serve hot.

Per Serving

calories: 109 | fat: 3.8g | protein: 6.1g | carbs: 16.7g | fiber: 6.1g | sodium: 265mg

Mushroom and Potato Oat Burgers

Prep time: 20 minutes | Cook time: 21 minutes | Serves 5

½ cup minced onion	2 tablespoons chopped cilantro
1 teaspoon grated fresh ginger	1 tablespoon curry powder
½ cup minced mushrooms	1 cup quick oats
½ cup red lentils, rinsed	Brown rice flour, optional
¾ sweet potato, peeled and diced	5 tomato slices
1 cup vegetable stock	Lettuce leaves
2 tablespoons hemp seeds	5 whole-wheat buns
2 tablespoons chopped parsley	

1. Add the oil, ginger, mushrooms and onion into the instant pot and Sauté for 5 minutes.
2. Stir in the lentils, stock, and the sweet potatoes.
3. Secure the lid and cook on the Manual function for 6 minutes at High Pressure.
4. After the beep, natural release the pressure and remove the lid. Meanwhile, heat the oven to 375°F (190°C) and line a baking tray with parchment paper.
5. Mash the prepared lentil mixture with a potato masher.
6. Add the oats and the remaining spices. Put in some brown rice flour if the mixture is not thick enough.
7. Wet your hands and prepare 5 patties, using the mixture, and place them on the baking tray.
8. Bake the patties for 10 minutes in the preheated oven.
9. Slice the buns in half and stack each with a tomato slice, a vegetable patty and lettuce leaves. Serve and enjoy.

Per Serving calories: 266 | fat: 5.3g | protein: 14.5g | carbs: 48.7g | fiber: 9.6g | sodium: 276mg

Potato and Broccoli Medley

Prep time: 10 minutes | Cook time: 20 minutes | Serves 3

½ white onion, diced	1 pound (454 g) baby carrots, cut in half
1½ cloves garlic, finely chopped	¼ cup vegetable broth
1 pound (454 g) potatoes, cut into chunks	½ tbsp Italian seasoning
1 pound (454 g) broccoli florets, diced	½ tbsp Spike original seasoning
	Fresh parsley for garnishing
	1 tablespoon olive oil

1. Put the oil and onion into the instant pot and Sauté for 5 minutes. Stir in the carrots, and garlic and stir-fry for 5 minutes. Add the remaining and secure the lid.
2. Cook on the Manual function for 10 minutes at High Pressure. After the beep, Quick release the pressure and remove the lid. Stir gently and garnish with fresh parsley , then serve.

Per Serving calories: 256 | fat: 5.6g | protein: 9.1g | carbs: 46.1g | fiber: 12.2g | sodium: 274mg

Italian Zucchini Pomodoro

Prep time: 10 minutes | Cook time: 12 minutes | Serves 4

1 tablespoon avocado oil	½ cup water
1 large onion, peeled and diced	1 tbsp Italian seasoning
3 cloves garlic, minced	1 teaspoon sea salt
1 (28-ounce / 794-g) can diced tomatoes, including juice	½ teaspoon ground black pepper
	2 medium zucchini, spiraled

1. Press Sauté button on the Instant Pot. Heat avocado oil. Add onions and stir-fry for 3 to 5 minutes until translucent. Add garlic and cook for an additional minute. Add tomatoes, water, Italian seasoning, salt, and pepper. Add zucchini and toss to combine. Lock lid.
2. Press the Manual button and adjust time to 1 minute. When timer beeps, let pressure release naturally for 5 minutes. Quick release any additional pressure until float valve drops and then unlock lid.
3. Transfer zucchini to four bowls. Press Sauté button, press Adjust button to change the temperature to Less, and simmer sauce in the Instant Pot unlidded for 5 minutes. Ladle over zucchini and serve immediately.

Per Serving calories: 92 | fat: 4.1g | protein: 2.5g | carbs: 13.1g | fiber: 5.1g | sodium: 980mg

Parmesan Stuffed Zucchini Boats

Prep time: 5 minutes | Cook time: 15 minutes | Serves 4

1 cup canned low-sodium chickpeas, drained and rinsed	2 zucchinis
1 cup no-sugar-added spaghetti sauce	¼ cup shredded Parmesan cheese

1. Preheat the oven to 425°F (220°C).
2. In a medium bowl, stir together the chickpeas and spaghetti sauce.
3. Cut the zucchini in half lengthwise and scrape a spoon gently down the length of each half to remove the seeds.
4. Fill each zucchini half with the chickpea sauce and top with one-quarter of the Parmesan cheese.
5. Place the zucchini halves on a baking sheet and roast in the oven for 15 minutes.
6. Transfer to a plate. Let rest for 5 minutes before serving.

Per Serving

calories: 139 | fat: 4.0g | protein: 8.0g | carbs: 20.0g | fiber: 5.0g | sodium: 344mg

Mushroom Swoodles

Prep time: 5 minutes | Cook time: 3 minutes | Serves 4

2 tablespoons coconut aminos	3 cloves garlic, minced
1 tablespoon white vinegar	1 large sweet potato, peeled and spiraled
2 teaspoons olive oil	1 pound (454 g) shiitake mushrooms, sliced
1 teaspoon sesame oil	
1 tablespoon honey	1 cup vegetable broth
¼ teaspoon red pepper flakes	¼ cup chopped fresh parsley

1. In a large bowl, whisk together coconut aminos, vinegar, olive oil, sesame oil, honey, red pepper flakes, and garlic.
2. Toss sweet potato and shiitake mushrooms in sauce. Refrigerate covered for 30 minutes.
3. Pour vegetable broth into Instant Pot. Add trivet. Lower steamer basket onto trivet and add the sweet potato mixture to the basket. Lock lid.
4. Press the Manual button and adjust time to 3 minutes. When timer beeps, let pressure release naturally for 5 minutes. Quick release any additional pressure until float valve drops and then unlock lid.
5. Remove basket from the Instant Pot and distribute sweet potatoes and mushrooms evenly among four bowls; pour liquid from the Instant Pot over bowls and garnish with chopped parsley.

Per Serving calories: 127 | fat: 4.0g | protein: 4.2g | carbs: 20.9g | fiber: 4.1g | sodium: 671mg

Rice, Corn, and Bean Stuffed Peppers

Prep time: 15 minutes | Cook time: 15 minutes | Serves 4

4 large bell peppers	¼ cup canned cannellini beans, rinsed and drained
2 cups cooked white rice	¼ cup canned black beans, rinsed and drained
1 medium onion, peeled and diced	
3 small Roma tomatoes, diced	1 teaspoon sea salt
	1 teaspoon garlic powder
¼ cup marinara sauce	½ cup vegetable broth
1 cup corn kernels (cut from the cob is preferred)	2 tablespoons grated Parmesan cheese
¼ cup sliced black olives	

1. Cut off the bell pepper tops as close to the tops as possible. Hollow out and discard seeds. Poke a few small holes in the bottom of the peppers to allow drippings to drain.
2. In a medium bowl, combine remaining except for broth and Parmesan cheese. Stuff equal amounts of mixture into each of the bell peppers.
3. Place trivet into the Instant Pot and pour in the broth. Set the peppers upright on the trivet. Lock lid.
4. Press the Manual button and adjust time to 15 minutes. When timer beeps, let pressure release naturally until float valve drops and then unlock lid.
5. Serve immediately and garnish with Parmesan cheese.

Per Serving calories: 265 | fat: 3.0g | protein: 8.1g | carbs: 53.1g | fiber: 8.0g | sodium: 834mg

Carrot and Turnip Purée

Prep time: 10 minutes | Cook time: 10 minutes | Serves 6

2 tablespoons olive oil, divided	2 cups vegetable broth
3 large turnips, peeled and quartered	1 teaspoon salt
4 large carrots, peeled and cut into 2-inch pieces	½ teaspoon ground nutmeg
	2 tablespoons sour cream

1. Press the Sauté button on Instant Pot. Heat 1 tablespoon olive oil. Toss turnips and carrots in oil for 1 minute. Add broth. Lock lid. Press the Manual button and adjust time to 8 minutes. When timer beeps, quick release pressure until float valve drops and then unlock lid.
2. Drain vegetables and reserve liquid; set liquid aside. Add 2 tablespoons of reserved liquid plus remaining to vegetables in the Instant Pot.
3. Use an immersion blender to blend until desired smoothness. If too thick, add more liquid 1 tablespoon at a time. Serve warm.

Per Serving calories: 95 | fat: 5.2g | protein: 1.4g | carbs: 11.8g | fiber: 3.0g | sodium: 669mg

Brussels Sprouts Linguine

Prep time: 5 minutes | Cook time: 25 minutes | Serves 4

8 ounces (227 g) whole-wheat linguine	8 ounces (227 g) Brussels sprouts, chopped
⅓ cup plus 2 tablespoons extra-virgin olive oil, divided	½ cup chicken stock
1 medium sweet onion, diced	⅓ cup dry white wine
2 to 3 garlic cloves, smashed	½ cup shredded Parmesan cheese
	1 lemon, quartered

1. Bring a large pot of water to a boil and cook the pasta for about 5 minutes, or until al dente. Drain the pasta and reserve 1 cup of the pasta water. Mix the cooked pasta with 2 tablespoons of the olive oil. Set aside.
2. In a large skillet, heat the remaining ⅓ cup of the olive oil over medium heat. Add the onion to the skillet and sauté for about 4 minutes, or until tender. Add the smashed garlic cloves and sauté for 1 minute, or until fragrant.
3. Stir in the Brussels sprouts and cook covered for 10 minutes. Pour in the chicken stock to prevent burning. Once the Brussels sprouts have wilted and are fork-tender, add white wine and cook for about 5 minutes, or until reduced.
4. Add the pasta to the skillet and add the pasta water as needed.
5. Top with the Parmesan cheese and squeeze the lemon over the dish right before eating.

Per Serving

calories: 502 | fat: 31.0g | protein: 15.0g | carbs: 50.0g | fiber: 9.0g | sodium: 246mg

Beet and Watercress Salad

Prep time: 15 minutes | Cook time: 8 minutes | Serves 4

2 pounds (907 g) beets, scrubbed, trimmed and cut into ¾-inch pieces	1 tablespoon extra-virgin olive oil, divided, plus more for drizzling
½ cup water	1 tablespoon white wine vinegar, divided
1 teaspoon caraway seeds	Black pepper, to taste
½ teaspoon table salt, plus more for seasoning	1 teaspoon grated orange zest
1 cup plain Greek yogurt	2 tablespoons orange juice
1 small garlic clove, minced	¼ cup coarsely chopped fresh dill
5 ounces (142 g) watercress, torn into bite-size pieces	¼ cup hazelnuts, toasted, skinned and chopped
	Coarse sea salt, to taste

1. Combine the beets, water, caraway seeds and table salt in the Instant Pot. Set the lid in place. Select the Manual mode and set the cooking time for 8 minutes on High Pressure. When the timer goes off, do a quick pressure release.
2. Carefully open the lid. Using a slotted spoon, transfer the beets to a plate. Set aside to cool slightly.
3. In a small bowl, combine the yogurt, garlic and 3 tablespoons of the beet cooking liquid. In a large bowl, toss the watercress with 2 teaspoons of the oil and 1 teaspoon of the vinegar. Season with table salt and pepper.
4. Spread the yogurt mixture over a serving dish. Arrange the watercress on top of the yogurt mixture, leaving 1-inch border of the yogurt mixture. Add the beets to now-empty large bowl and toss with the orange zest and juice, the remaining 2 teaspoons of the vinegar and the remaining 1 teaspoon of the oil. Season with table salt and pepper.
5. Arrange the beets on top of the watercress mixture. Drizzle with the olive oil and sprinkle with the dill, hazelnuts and sea salt. Serve immediately.

Per Serving calories: 240 | fat: 15.0g | protein: 9.0g | carbs: 19.0g | fiber: 5.0g | sodium: 440mg

Garlicky Broccoli Rabe

Prep time: 10 minutes | Cook time: 5 to 6 minutes | Serves 4

14 ounces (397 g) broccoli rabe, trimmed and cut into 1-inch pieces	Black pepper, to taste
2 teaspoons salt, plus more for seasoning	2 tablespoons extra-virgin olive oil
	3 garlic cloves, minced
	¼ teaspoon red pepper flakes

1. Bring 3 quarts water to a boil in a large saucepan. Add the broccoli rabe and 2 teaspoons of the salt to the boiling water and cook for 2 to 3 minutes, or until wilted and tender. Drain the broccoli rabe. Transfer to ice water and let sit until chilled. Drain again and pat dry.
2. In a skillet over medium heat, heat the oil and add the garlic and red pepper flakes. Sauté for about 2 minutes, or until the garlic begins to sizzle. Increase the heat to medium-high. Stir in the broccoli rabe and cook for about 1 minute, or until heated through, stirring constantly. Season with salt and pepper. Serve immediately.

Per Serving calories: 87 | fat: 7.3g | protein: 3.4g | carbs: 4.0g | fiber: 2.9g | sodium: 1196mg

Sautéed Cabbage with Parsley

Prep time: 10 minutes | Cook time: 12 to 14 minutes | Serves 4 to 6

1 small head green cabbage (about 1¼ pounds / 567 g), cored and sliced thin
2 tablespoons extra-virgin olive oil, divided
1 onion, halved and sliced thin
¾ teaspoon salt, divided
¼ teaspoon black pepper
¼ cup chopped fresh parsley
1½ teaspoons lemon juice

1. Place the cabbage in a large bowl with cold water. Let sit for 3 minutes. Drain well. Heat 1 tablespoon of the oil in a skillet over medium-high heat until shimmering. Add the onion and ¼ teaspoon of the salt and cook for 5 to 7 minutes, or until softened and lightly browned. Transfer to a bowl. Heat the remaining 1 tablespoon of the oil in now-empty skillet over medium-high heat until shimmering. Add the cabbage and sprinkle with the remaining ½ teaspoon of the salt and black pepper. Cover and cook for about 3 minutes, without stirring, or until cabbage is wilted and lightly browned on bottom.
2. Stir and continue to cook for about 4 minutes, uncovered, or until the cabbage is crisp-tender and lightly browned in places, stirring once halfway through cooking. Off heat, stir in the cooked onion, parsley and lemon juice.
3. Transfer to a plate and serve.

Per Serving calories: 117 | fat: 7.0g | protein: 2.7g | carbs: 13.4g | fiber: 5.1g | sodium: 472mg

Braised Cauliflower with White Wine

Prep time: 10 minutes | Cook time: 12 to 16 minutes | Serves 4 to 6

3 tablespoons plus 1 teaspoon extra-virgin olive oil, divided
3 garlic cloves, minced
⅛ teaspoon red pepper flakes
1 head cauliflower (2 pounds / 907 g), cored and cut into 1½-inch florets
¼ teaspoon salt, plus more for seasoning
Black pepper, to taste
⅓ cup vegetable broth
⅓ cup dry white wine
2 tablespoons minced fresh parsley

1. Combine 1 teaspoon of the oil, garlic and pepper flakes in small bowl.
2. Heat the remaining 3 tablespoons of the oil in a skillet over medium-high heat until shimmering. Add the cauliflower and ¼ teaspoon of the salt and cook for 7 to 9 minutes, stirring occasionally, or until florets are golden brown.
3. Push the cauliflower to sides of the skillet. Add the garlic mixture to the center of the skillet. Cook for about 30 seconds, or until fragrant. Stir the garlic mixture into the cauliflower.
4. Pour in the broth and wine and bring to simmer. Reduce the heat to medium-low. Cover and cook for 4 to 6 minutes, or until the cauliflower is crisp-tender. Off heat, stir in the parsley and season with salt and pepper.
5. Serve immediately.

Per Serving
calories: 143 | fat: 11.7g | protein: 3.1g | carbs: 8.7g | fiber: 3.1g | sodium: 263mg

Cauliflower Steaks with Arugula

Prep time: 5 minutes | Cook time: 20 minutes | Serves 4

Cauliflower:
1 head cauliflower
Cooking spray
½ teaspoon garlic powder
4 cups arugula
Dressing:
1½ tablespoons extra-virgin olive oil
1½ tablespoons honey mustard
1 teaspoon freshly squeezed lemon juice

1. Preheat the oven to 425ºF (220ºC).
2. Remove the leaves from the cauliflower head, and cut it in half lengthwise. Cut 1½-inch-thick steaks from each half.
3. Spritz both sides of each steak with cooking spray and season both sides with the garlic powder.
4. Place the cauliflower steaks on a baking sheet, cover with foil, and roast in the oven for 10 minutes.
5. Remove the baking sheet from the oven and gently pull back the foil to avoid the steam. Flip the steaks, then roast uncovered for 10 minutes more.
6. Meanwhile, make the dressing: Whisk together the olive oil, honey mustard and lemon juice in a small bowl.
7. When the cauliflower steaks are done, divide into four equal portions. Top each portion with one-quarter of the arugula and dressing. Serve immediately.

Per Serving
calories: 115 | fat: 6.0g | protein: 5.0g | carbs: 14.0g | fiber: 4.0g | sodium: 97mg

Baby Kale and Cabbage Salad

Prep time: 10 minutes | Cook time: 0 minutes | Serves 6

2 bunches baby kale, thinly sliced
½ head green savoy cabbage, cored and thinly sliced
1 medium red bell pepper, thinly sliced
1 garlic clove, thinly sliced
Dressing:
Juice of 1 lemon
¼ cup apple cider vinegar
1 teaspoon ground cumin
¼ teaspoon smoked paprika
1 cup toasted peanuts

1. In a large mixing bowl, toss together the kale and cabbage.
2. Make the dressing: Whisk together the lemon juice, vinegar, cumin and paprika in a small bowl.
3. Pour the dressing over the greens and gently massage with your hands. Add the pepper, garlic and peanuts to the mixing bowl. Toss to combine. Serve immediately.

Per Serving calories: 199 | fat: 12.0g | protein: 10.0g | carbs: 17.0g | fiber: 5.0g | sodium: 46mg

Grilled Romaine Lettuce

Prep time: 5 minutes | Cook time: 3 to 5 minutes | Serves 4

Romaine:
2 heads romaine lettuce, halved lengthwise
2 tablespoons extra-virgin olive oil
Dressing:
½ cup unsweetened almond milk
1 tablespoon extra-virgin olive oil
¼ bunch fresh chives, thinly chopped
1 garlic clove, pressed
1 pinch red pepper flakes

1. Heat a grill pan over medium heat.
2. Brush each lettuce half with the olive oil. Place the lettuce halves, flat-side down, on the grill. Grill for 3 to 5 minutes, or until the lettuce slightly wilts and develops light grill marks. Meanwhile, whisk together all the for the dressing in a small bowl. Drizzle 2 tablespoons of the dressing over each romaine half and serve.

Per Serving calories: 126 | fat: 11.0g | protein: 2.0g | carbs: 7.0g | fiber: 1.0g | sodium: 41mg

Mini Crustless Spinach Quiches

Prep time: 10 minutes | Cook time: 20 minutes | Serves 6

2 tablespoons extra-virgin olive oil
1 onion, finely chopped
2 cups baby spinach
2 garlic cloves, minced
8 large eggs, beaten
¼ cup unsweetened almond milk
½ teaspoon sea salt
¼ teaspoon freshly ground black pepper
1 cup shredded Swiss cheese
Cooking spray

1. Preheat the oven to 375ºF (190ºC). Spritz a 6-cup muffin tin with cooking spray. Set aside.
2. In a large skillet over medium-high heat, heat the olive oil until shimmering. Add the onion and cook for about 4 minutes, or until soft. Add the spinach and cook for about 1 minute, stirring constantly, or until the spinach softens. Add the garlic and sauté for 30 seconds. Remove from the heat and let cool.
3. In a medium bowl, whisk together the eggs, milk, salt and pepper. Stir the cooled vegetables and the cheese into the egg mixture. Spoon the mixture into the prepared muffin tins. Bake for about 15 minutes, or until the eggs are set.
4. Let rest for 5 minutes before serving.

Per Serving calories: 218 | fat: 17.0g | protein: 14.0g | carbs: 4.0g | fiber: 1.0g | sodium: 237mg

Potato Tortilla with Leeks and Mushrooms

Prep time: 30 minutes | Cook time: 50 minutes | Serves 2

1 tablespoon olive oil
1 cup thinly sliced leeks
4 ounces (113 g) baby bella (cremini) mushrooms, stemmed and sliced
1 small potato, peeled and sliced ¼-inch thick
½ cup unsweetened almond milk
5 large eggs, beaten
1 teaspoon Dijon mustard
½ teaspoon salt
½ teaspoon dried thyme
Pinch freshly ground black pepper
3 ounces (85 g) Gruyère cheese, shredded

1. Preheat the oven to 350ºF (180ºC).
2. In a large sauté pan over medium-high heat, heat the olive oil. Add the leeks, mushrooms, and potato and sauté for about 10 minutes, or until the potato starts to brown.
3. Reduce the heat to medium-low, cover, and cook for an additional 10 minutes, or until the potato begins to soften. Add 1 to 2 tablespoons of water to prevent sticking to the bottom of the pan, if needed.
4. Meanwhile, whisk together the milk, beaten eggs, mustard, salt, thyme, black pepper, and cheese in a medium bowl until combined. When the potatoes are fork-tender, turn off the heat. Transfer the cooked vegetables to an oiled nonstick ovenproof pan and arrange them in a nice layer along the bottom and slightly up the sides of the pan. Pour the milk mixture evenly over the vegetables.
5. Bake in the preheated oven for 25 to 30 minutes, or until the eggs are completely set and the top is golden and puffed. Remove from the oven and cool for 5 minutes before cutting and serving.

Per Serving calories: 541 | fat: 33.1g | protein: 32.8g | carbs: 31.0g | fiber: 4.0g | sodium: 912mg

Mushrooms Ragu with Cheesy Polenta

Prep time: 20 minutes | Cook time: 30 minutes | Serves 2

½ ounce (14 g) dried porcini mushrooms
1 pound (454 g) baby bella (cremini) mushrooms, quartered
2 tablespoons olive oil
1 garlic clove, minced
1 large shallot, minced
1 tablespoon flour
2 teaspoons tomato paste
½ cup red wine
1 cup mushroom stock (or reserved liquid from soaking the porcini mushrooms, if using)
1 fresh rosemary sprig
½ teaspoon dried thyme
1½ cups water
½ teaspoon salt, plus more as needed
⅓ cup instant polenta
2 tablespoons grated Parmesan cheese

1. Soak the dried porcini mushrooms in 1 cup of hot water for about 15 minutes to soften them. When ready, scoop them out of the water, reserving the soaking liquid. Mince the porcini mushrooms. Heat the olive oil in a large sauté pan over medium-high heat. Add the mushrooms, garlic, and shallot and sauté for 10 minutes, or until the vegetables are beginning to caramelize.
2. Stir in the flour and tomato paste and cook for an additional 30 seconds. Add the red wine, mushroom stock, rosemary, and thyme. Bring the mixture to a boil, stirring constantly, or until it has thickened.
3. Reduce the heat and allow to simmer for 10 minutes.
4. Meanwhile, bring the water to a boil in a saucepan and sprinkle with the salt.
5. Add the instant polenta and stir quickly while it thickens. Scatter with the grated Parmesan cheese. Taste and season with more salt as needed. Serve warm.

Per Serving calories: 450 | fat: 16.0g | protein: 14.1g | carbs: 57.8g | fiber: 5.0g | sodium: 165mg

Veggie Rice Bowls with Pesto Sauce

Prep time: 15 minutes | Cook time: 1 minute | Serves 2

2 cups water
1 cup arborio rice, rinsed
Salt and ground black pepper, to taste
2 eggs
1 cup broccoli florets
½ pound (227 g) Brussels sprouts
1 carrot, peeled and chopped
1 small beet, peeled and cubed
¼ cup pesto sauce
Lemon wedges, for serving

1. Combine the water, rice, salt, and pepper in the Instant Pot. Insert a trivet over rice and place a steamer basket on top. Add the eggs, broccoli, Brussels sprouts, carrots, beet cubes, salt, and pepper to the steamer basket.
2. Lock the lid. Select the Manual mode and set the cooking time for 1 minute at High Pressure.
3. When the timer beeps, perform a natural pressure release for 10 minutes, then release any remaining pressure. Carefully open the lid. Remove the steamer basket and trivet from the pot and transfer the eggs to a bowl of ice water. Peel and halve the eggs. Use a fork to fluff the rice.
4. Divide the rice, broccoli, Brussels sprouts, carrot, beet cubes, and eggs into two bowls. Top with a dollop of pesto sauce and serve with the lemon wedges.

Per Serving calories: 590 | fat: 34.1g | protein: 21.9g | carbs: 50.0g | fiber: 19.6g | sodium: 670mg

Roasted Cauliflower and Carrots

Prep time: 10 minutes | Cook time: 30 minutes | Serves 2

4 cups cauliflower florets (about ½ small head)	2 teaspoons za'atar spice mix, divided
2 medium carrots, peeled, halved, and then sliced into quarters lengthwise	1 (15-ounce / 425-g) can chickpeas, drained, rinsed, and patted dry
2 tablespoons olive oil, divided	¾ cup plain Greek yogurt
½ teaspoon salt, divided	1 teaspoon harissa spice paste, plus additional as needed
½ teaspoon garlic powder, divided	

1. Preheat the oven to 400ºF (205ºC). Line a sheet pan with foil or parchment paper.
2. Put the cauliflower and carrots in a large bowl. Drizzle with 1 tablespoon of olive oil and sprinkle with ¼ teaspoon of salt, ¼ teaspoon of garlic powder, and 1 teaspoon of za'atar. Toss to combine well.
3. Spread the vegetables onto one half of the prepared sheet pan in a single layer.
4. Put the chickpeas in the same bowl and season with the remaining 1 tablespoon of olive oil, ¼ teaspoon of salt, ¼ teaspoon of garlic powder, and the remaining 1 teaspoon of za'atar. Toss to combine well.
5. Spread the chickpeas onto the other half of the sheet pan.
6. Roast in the preheated oven for 30 minutes, or until the vegetables are crisp-tender. Flip the vegetables halfway through and give the chickpeas a stir so they cook evenly.
7. Meanwhile, whisk the yogurt and harissa together in a small bowl. Taste and add additional harissa as needed.
8. Serve the vegetables and chickpeas with the yogurt mixture on the side.

Per Serving calories: 468 | fat: 23.0g | protein: 18.1g | carbs: 54.1g | fiber: 13.8g | sodium: 631mg

Butternut Noodles with Mushrooms

Prep time: 10 minutes | Cook time: 12 minutes | Serves 4

¼ cup extra-virgin olive oil	3 garlic cloves, minced
1 pound (454 g) cremini mushrooms, sliced	½ cup dry white wine
½ red onion, finely chopped	Pinch of red pepper flakes
1 teaspoon dried thyme	4 cups butternut noodles
½ teaspoon sea salt	4 ounces (113 g) grated Parmesan cheese

1. In a large skillet over medium-high heat, heat the olive oil until shimmering. Add the mushrooms, onion, thyme, and salt to the skillet. Cook for about 6 minutes, stirring occasionally, or until the mushrooms start to brown. Add the garlic and sauté for 30 seconds. Stir in the white wine and red pepper flakes. Fold in the noodles. Cook for about 5 minutes, stirring occasionally, or until the noodles are tender. Serve topped with the grated Parmesan.

Per Serving calories: 244 | fat: 14.0g | protein: 4.0g | carbs: 22.0g | fiber: 4.0g | sodium: 159mg

Zoodles with Beet Pesto

Prep time: 10 minutes | Cook time: 50 minutes | Serves 2

1 medium red beet, peeled, chopped	2 tablespoons plus 2 teaspoons extra-virgin olive oil, divided
½ cup walnut pieces	¼ teaspoon salt
½ cup crumbled goat cheese	4 small zucchinis, spiralized
3 garlic cloves	
2 tablespoons freshly squeezed lemon juice	

1. Preheat the oven to 375ºF (190ºC).
2. Wrap the chopped beet in a piece of aluminum foil and seal well.
3. Roast in the preheated oven for 30 to 40 minutes until tender.
4. Meanwhile, heat a skillet over medium-high heat until hot. Add the walnuts and toast for 5 to 7 minutes, or until fragrant and lightly browned.
5. Remove the cooked beets from the oven and place in a food processor. Add the toasted walnuts, goat cheese, garlic, lemon juice, 2 tablespoons of olive oil, and salt. Pulse until smoothly blended. Set aside.
6. Heat the remaining 2 teaspoons of olive oil in a large skillet over medium heat. Add the zucchini and toss to coat in the oil. Cook for 2 to 3 minutes, stirring gently, or until the zucchini is softened. Transfer the zucchini to a serving plate and toss with the beet pesto, then serve.

Per Serving
calories: 423 | fat: 38.8g | protein: 8.0g | carbs: 17.1g | fiber: 6.0g | sodium: 338mg

Fried Eggplant Rolls

Prep time: 20 minutes | Cook time: 10 minutes | Serves 4 to 6

1 large eggplants, trimmed and cut lengthwise into ¼-inch-thick slices	4 ounces (113 g) goat cheese, shredded
1 teaspoon salt	¼ cup finely chopped fresh basil
1 cup ricotta cheese	½ teaspoon freshly ground black pepper
	Olive oil spray

1. Add the eggplant slices to a colander and season with salt. Set aside for 15 to 20 minutes.
2. Mix together the ricotta and goat cheese, basil, and black pepper in a large bowl and stir to combine. Set aside.
3. Dry the eggplant slices with paper towels and lightly mist them with olive oil spray.
4. Heat a large skillet over medium heat and lightly spray it with olive oil spray.
5. Arrange the eggplant slices in the skillet and fry each side for 3 minutes until golden brown.
6. Remove from the heat to a paper towel-lined plate and rest for 5 minutes.
7. Make the eggplant rolls: Lay the eggplant slices on a flat work surface and top each slice with a tablespoon of the prepared cheese mixture. Roll them up and serve immediately.

Per Serving
calories: 254 | fat: 14.9g | protein: 15.3g | carbs: 18.6g | fiber: 7.1g | sodium: 745mg

Roasted Veggies and Brown Rice Bowl

Prep time: 15 minutes | Cook time: 20 minutes | Serves 4

2 cups cauliflower florets
2 cups broccoli florets
1 (15-ounce / 425-g) can chickpeas, drained and rinsed
1 cup carrot slices (about 1 inch thick)
2 to 3 tablespoons extra-virgin olive oil, divided
Salt and freshly ground black pepper, to taste
Nonstick cooking spray

2 cups cooked brown rice
2 to 3 tablespoons sesame seeds, for garnish

Dressing:
3 to 4 tablespoons tahini
2 tablespoons honey
1 lemon, juiced
1 garlic clove, minced
Salt and freshly ground black pepper, to taste

1. Preheat the oven to 400°F (205°C). Spritz two baking sheets with nonstick cooking spray.
2. Spread the cauliflower and broccoli on the first baking sheet and the second with the chickpeas and carrot slices.
3. Drizzle each sheet with half of the olive oil and sprinkle with salt and pepper. Toss to coat well.
4. Roast the chickpeas and carrot slices in the preheated oven for 10 minutes, leaving the carrots tender but crisp, and the cauliflower and broccoli for 20 minutes until fork-tender. Stir them once halfway through the cooking time.
5. Meanwhile, make the dressing: Whisk together the tahini, honey, lemon juice, garlic, salt, and pepper in a small bowl.
6. Divide the cooked brown rice among four bowls. Top each bowl evenly with roasted vegetables and dressing. Sprinkle the sesame seeds on top for garnish before serving.

Per Serving

calories: 453 | fat: 17.8g | protein: 12.1g | carbs: 61.8g | fiber: 11.2g | sodium: 60mg

Zucchini and Artichokes Bowl with Farro

Prep time: 15 minutes | Cook time: 10 minutes | Serves 4 to 6

⅓ cup extra-virgin olive oil
⅓ cup chopped red onions
½ cup chopped red bell pepper
2 garlic cloves, minced
1 cup zucchini, cut into ½-inch-thick slices
½ cup coarsely chopped artichokes
½ cup canned chickpeas, drained and rinsed
3 cups cooked farro

Salt and freshly ground black pepper, to taste
½ cup crumbled feta cheese, for serving (optional)
¼ cup sliced olives, for serving (optional)
2 tablespoons fresh basil, chiffonade, for serving (optional)
3 tablespoons balsamic vinegar, for serving (optional)

1. Heat the olive oil in a large skillet over medium heat until it shimmers. Add the onions, bell pepper, and garlic and sauté for 5 minutes, stirring occasionally, until softened.
2. Stir in the zucchini slices, artichokes, and chickpeas and sauté for about 5 minutes until slightly tender.
3. Add the cooked farro and toss to combine until heated through. Sprinkle the salt and pepper to season.
4. Divide the mixture into bowls. Top each bowl evenly with feta cheese, olive slices, and basil and sprinkle with the balsamic vinegar, if desired.

Per Serving calories: 366 | fat: 19.9g | protein: 9.3g | carbs: 50.7g | fiber: 9.0g | sodium: 86mg

Cauliflower Hash with Carrots

Prep time: 10 minutes | Cook time: 10 minutes | Serves 4

3 tablespoons extra-virgin olive oil
1 large onion, chopped
1 tablespoon minced garlic

2 cups diced carrots
4 cups cauliflower florets
½ teaspoon ground cumin
1 teaspoon salt

1. In a large skillet, heat the olive oil over medium heat.
2. Add the onion and garlic and sauté for 1 minute. Stir in the carrots and stir-fry for 3 minutes.
3. Add the cauliflower florets, cumin, and salt and toss to combine.
4. Cover and cook for 3 minutes until lightly browned. Stir well and cook, uncovered, for 3 to 4 minutes, until softened.
5. Remove from the heat and serve warm.

Per Serving

calories: 158 | fat: 10.8g | protein: 3.1g | carbs: 14.9g | fiber: 5.1g | sodium: 656mg

Zucchini Fritters

Prep time: 15 minutes | Cook time: 5 minutes | Makes 14 fritters

4 cups grated zucchini
Salt, to taste
2 large eggs, lightly beaten
⅓ cup sliced scallions (green and white parts)

⅔ all-purpose flour
⅛ teaspoon black pepper
2 tablespoons olive oil

1. Put the grated zucchini in a colander and lightly season with salt. Set aside to rest for 10 minutes. Squeeze out as much liquid from the grated zucchini as possible.
2. Pour the grated zucchini into a bowl. Fold in the beaten eggs, scallions, flour, salt, and pepper and stir until everything is well combined.
3. Heat the olive oil in a large skillet over medium heat until hot.
4. Drop 3 tablespoons mounds of the zucchini mixture onto the hot skillet to make each fritter, pressing them lightly into rounds and spacing them about 2 inches apart.
5. Cook for 2 to 3 minutes. Flip the zucchini fritters and cook for 2 minutes more, or until they are golden brown and cooked through.
6. Remove from the heat to a plate lined with paper towels. Repeat with the remaining zucchini mixture. Serve hot.

Per Serving (2 fritters)

calories: 113 | fat: 6.1g | protein: 4.0g | carbs: 12.2g | fiber: 1.0g | sodium: 25mg

Sautéed Spinach and Leeks

Prep time: 5 minutes | Cook time: 8 minutes | Serves 2

3 tablespoons olive oil
2 garlic cloves, crushed
2 leeks, chopped
2 red onions, chopped

9 ounces (255 g) fresh spinach
1 teaspoon kosher salt
½ cup crumbled goat cheese

1. Coat the bottom of the Instant Pot with the olive oil.
2. Add the garlic, leek, and onions and stir-fry for about 5 minutes, on Sauté mode.
3. Stir in the spinach. Sprinkle with the salt and sauté for an additional 3 minutes, stirring constantly.
4. Transfer to a plate and scatter with the goat cheese before serving.

Per Serving

calories: 447 | fat: 31.2g | protein: 14.6g | carbs: 28.7g | fiber: 6.3g | sodium: 937mg

Moroccan Tagine with Vegetables

Prep time: 20 minutes | Cook time: 40 minutes | Serves 2

2 tablespoons olive oil	2 small red potatoes, cut into
½ onion, diced	1-inch pieces
1 garlic clove, minced	1 cup water
2 cups cauliflower florets	1 teaspoon pure maple syrup
1 medium carrot, cut into 1-inch pieces	½ teaspoon cinnamon
1 cup diced eggplant	½ teaspoon turmeric
1 (28-ounce / 794-g) can whole tomatoes with their juices	1 teaspoon cumin
	½ teaspoon salt
1 (15-ounce / 425-g) can chickpeas, drained and rinsed	1 to 2 teaspoons harissa paste

1. In a Dutch oven, heat the olive oil over medium-high heat. Sauté the onion for 5 minutes, stirring occasionally, or until the onion is translucent.
2. Stir in the garlic, cauliflower florets, carrot, eggplant, tomatoes, and potatoes. Using a wooden spoon or spatula to break up the tomatoes into smaller pieces.
3. Add the chickpeas, water, maple syrup, cinnamon, turmeric, cumin, and salt and stir to incorporate. Bring the mixture to a boil.
4. Once it starts to boil, reduce the heat to medium-low. Stir in the harissa paste, cover, allow to simmer for about 40 minutes, or until the vegetables are softened. Taste and adjust seasoning as needed.
5. Let the mixture cool for 5 minutes before serving.

Per Serving

calories: 293 | fat: 9.9g | protein: 11.2g | carbs: 45.5g | fiber: 12.1g | sodium: 337mg

Vegan Lentil Bolognese

Prep time: 15 minutes | Cook time: 50 minutes | Serves 2

1 medium celery stalk	1 cup red wine
1 large carrot	½ teaspoon salt, plus more as needed
½ large onion	
1 garlic clove	½ teaspoon pure maple syrup
2 tablespoons olive oil	
1 (28-ounce / 794-g) can crushed tomatoes	1 cup cooked lentils (prepared from ½ cup dry)

1. Add the celery, carrot, onion, and garlic to a food processor and process until everything is finely chopped.
2. In a Dutch oven, heat the olive oil over medium-high heat. Add the chopped mixture and sauté for about 10 minutes, stirring occasionally, or until the vegetables are lightly browned.
3. Stir in the tomatoes, wine, salt, and maple syrup and bring to a boil.
4. Once the sauce starts to boil, cover, and reduce the heat to medium-low. Simmer for 30 minutes, stirring occasionally, or until the vegetables are softened.
5. Stir in the cooked lentils and cook for an additional 5 minutes until warmed through.
6. Taste and add additional salt, if needed. Serve warm.

Per Serving

calories: 367 | fat: 15.0g | protein: 13.7g | carbs: 44.5g | fiber: 17.6g | sodium: 1108mg

Grilled Vegetable Skewers

Prep time: 15 minutes | Cook time: 10 minutes | Serves 4

4 medium red onions, peeled and sliced into 6 wedges	2 orange bell peppers, cut into 2-inch squares
4 medium zucchinis, cut into 1-inch-thick slices	2 yellow bell peppers, cut into 2-inch squares
2 beefsteak tomatoes, cut into quarters	2 tablespoons plus 1 teaspoon olive oil, divided
4 red bell peppers, cut into 2-inch squares	Special Equipment:
	4 wooden skewers, soaked in water for at least 30 minutes

1. Preheat the grill to medium-high heat.
2. Skewer the vegetables by alternating between red onion, zucchini, tomatoes, and the different colored bell peppers. Brush them with 2 tablespoons of olive oil.
3. Oil the grill grates with 1 teaspoon of olive oil and grill the vegetable skewers for 5 minutes. Flip the skewers and grill for 5 minutes more, or until they are cooked to your liking.
4. Let the skewers cool for 5 minutes before serving.

Per Serving

calories: 115 | fat: 3.0g | protein: 3.5g | carbs: 18.7g | fiber: 4.7g | sodium: 12mg

Stuffed Portobello Mushroom with Tomatoes

Prep time: 10 minutes | Cook time: 15 minutes | Serves 4

4 large portobello mushroom caps	4 sun-dried tomatoes
3 tablespoons extra-virgin olive oil	1 cup shredded mozzarella cheese, divided
Salt and freshly ground black pepper, to taste	½ to ¾ cup low-sodium tomato sauce

1. Preheat the broiler to High.
2. Arrange the mushroom caps on a baking sheet and drizzle with olive oil.
1. Sprinkle with salt and pepper.
2. Broil for 10 minutes, flipping the mushroom caps halfway through, until browned on the top.
3. Remove from the broil. Spoon 1 tomato, 2 tablespoons of cheese, and 2 to 3 tablespoons of sauce onto each mushroom cap.
4. Return the mushroom caps to the broiler and continue broiling for 2 to 3 minutes.
5. Cool for 5 minutes before serving.

Per Serving

calories: 217 | fat: 15.8g | protein: 11.2g | carbs: 11.7g | fiber: 2.0g | sodium: 243mg

Zoodles

Prep time: 10 minutes | Cook time: 5 minutes | Serves 2

2 tablespoons avocado oil	¼ teaspoon salt
2 medium zucchini, spiralized	Freshly ground black pepper

1. Heat the avocado oil in a large skillet over medium heat until it shimmers.
2. Add the zucchini noodles, salt, and black pepper to the skillet and toss to coat. Cook for 1 to 2 minutes, stirring constantly, until tender.
3. Serve warm.

Per Serving

calories: 128 | fat: 14.0g | protein: 0.3g | carbs: 0.3g | fiber: 0.1g | sodium: 291mg

Wilted Dandelion Greens with Sweet Onion

Prep time: 15 minutes | Cook time: 15 minutes | Serves 4

1 tablespoon extra-virgin olive oil
1 Vidalia onion, thinly sliced
½ cup low-sodium vegetable broth
2 bunches dandelion greens, roughly chopped
Freshly ground black pepper, to taste
2 garlic cloves, minced

1. Heat the olive oil in a large skillet over low heat.
2. Add the garlic and onion and cook for 2 to 3 minutes, stirring occasionally, or until the onion is translucent.
3. Fold in the vegetable broth and dandelion greens and cook for 5 to 7 minutes until wilted, stirring frequently.
4. Sprinkle with the black pepper and serve on a plate while warm.

Per Serving

calories: 81 | fat: 3.9g | protein: 3.2g | carbs: 10.8g | fiber: 4.0g | sodium: 72mg

Garlicky Zucchini Cubes with Mint

Prep time: 5 minutes | Cook time: 10 minutes | Serves 4

3 large green zucchini, cut into ½-inch cubes
3 tablespoons extra-virgin olive oil
1 large onion, chopped
3 cloves garlic, minced
1 teaspoon salt
1 teaspoon dried mint

1. Heat the olive oil in a large skillet over medium heat.
2. Add the onion and garlic and sauté for 3 minutes, stirring constantly, or until softened.
3. Stir in the zucchini cubes and salt and cook for 5 minutes, or until the zucchini is browned and tender.
4. Add the mint to the skillet and toss to combine, then continue cooking for 2 minutes. Serve warm.

Per Serving calories: 146 | fat: 10.6g | protein: 4.2g | carbs: 11.8g | fiber: 3.0g | sodium: 606mg

Vegetable and Tofu Scramble

Prep time: 5 minutes | Cook time: 10 minutes | Serves 2

2 tablespoons extra-virgin olive oil
½ red onion, finely chopped
1 cup chopped kale
8 ounces (227 g) mushrooms, sliced
8 ounces (227 g) tofu, cut into pieces
2 garlic cloves, minced
Pinch red pepper flakes
½ teaspoon sea salt
⅛ teaspoon freshly ground black pepper

1. Heat the olive oil in a medium nonstick skillet over medium-high heat until shimmering.
2. Add the onion, kale, and mushrooms to the skillet and cook for about 5 minutes, stirring occasionally, or until the vegetables start to brown.
3. Add the tofu and stir-fry for 3 to 4 minutes until softened.
4. Stir in the garlic, red pepper flakes, salt, and black pepper and cook for 30 seconds.
5. Let the mixture cool for 5 minutes before serving.

Per Serving

calories: 233 | fat: 15.9g | protein: 13.4g | carbs: 11.9g | fiber: 2.0g | sodium: 672mg

Lentil and Tomato Collard Wraps

Prep time: 15 minutes | Cook time: 0 minutes | Serves 4

2 cups cooked lentils
5 Roma tomatoes, diced
½ cup crumbled feta cheese
10 large fresh basil leaves, thinly sliced
¼ cup extra-virgin olive oil
1 tablespoon balsamic vinegar
2 garlic cloves, minced
½ teaspoon raw honey
½ teaspoon salt
¼ teaspoon freshly ground black pepper
4 large collard leaves, stems removed

1. Combine the lentils, tomatoes, cheese, basil leaves, olive oil, vinegar, garlic, honey, salt, and black pepper in a large bowl and stir until well blended.
2. Lay the collard leaves on a flat work surface. Spoon the equal-sized amounts of the lentil mixture onto the edges of the leaves. Roll them up and slice in half to serve.

Per Serving

calories: 318 | fat: 17.6g | protein: 13.2g | carbs: 27.5g | fiber: 9.9g | sodium: 475mg

Stir-Fry Baby Bok Choy

Prep time: 12 minutes | Cook time: 10 to 13 minutes | Serves 6

2 tablespoons coconut oil
1 large onion, finely diced
2 teaspoons ground cumin
1-inch piece fresh ginger, grated
1 teaspoon ground turmeric
½ teaspoon salt
12 baby bok choy heads, ends trimmed and sliced lengthwise
Water, as needed
3 cups cooked brown rice

1. Heat the coconut oil in a large pan over medium heat.
2. Sauté the onion for 5 minutes, stirring occasionally, or until the onion is translucent. Fold in the cumin, ginger, turmeric, and salt and stir to coat well.
3. Add the bok choy and cook for 5 to 8 minutes, stirring occasionally, or until the bok choy is tender but crisp. You can add 1 tablespoon of water at a time, if the skillet gets dry until you finish sautéing. Transfer the bok choy to a plate and serve over the cooked brown rice.

Per Serving calories: 443 | fat: 8.8g | protein: 30.3g | carbs: 75.7g | fiber: 19.0g | sodium: 1289mg

Celery and Mustard Greens

Prep time: 10 minutes | Cook time: 15 minutes | Serves 4

½ cup low-sodium vegetable broth
1 celery stalk, roughly chopped
½ sweet onion, chopped
½ large red bell pepper, thinly sliced
2 garlic cloves, minced
1 bunch mustard greens, roughly chopped

1. Pour the vegetable broth into a large cast iron pan and bring it to a simmer over medium heat.
2. Stir in the celery, onion, bell pepper, and garlic. Cook uncovered for about 3 to 5 minutes, or until the onion is softened.
3. Add the mustard greens to the pan and stir well. Cover, reduce the heat to low, and cook for an additional 10 minutes, or until the liquid is evaporated and the greens are wilted. Remove from the heat and serve warm.

Per Serving (1 cup) calories: 39 | fat: 0g | protein: 3.1g | carbs: 6.8g | fiber: 3.0g | sodium: 120mg

Sweet Pepper Stew

Prep time: 20 minutes | Cook time: 50 minutes | Serves 2

2 tablespoons olive oil	1 teaspoon oregano
2 sweet peppers, diced (about 2 cups)	1 cup low-sodium tomato juice
½ large onion, minced	1 cup low-sodium vegetable stock
1 garlic clove, minced	¼ cup brown rice
1 tablespoon gluten-free Worcestershire sauce	¼ cup brown lentils
	Salt, to taste

1. In a Dutch oven, heat the olive oil over medium-high heat.
2. Sauté the sweet peppers and onion for 10 minutes, stirring occasionally, or until the onion begins to turn golden and the peppers are wilted.
3. Stir in the garlic, Worcestershire sauce, and oregano and cook for 30 seconds more. Add the tomato juice, vegetable stock, rice, and lentils to the Dutch oven and stir to mix well. Bring the mixture to a boil and then reduce the heat to medium-low. Let it simmer covered for about 45 minutes, or until the rice is cooked through and the lentils are tender. Sprinkle with salt and serve warm.

Per Serving
calories: 378 | fat: 15.6g | protein: 11.4g | carbs: 52.8g | fiber: 7.0g | sodium: 391mg

Roasted Vegetables

Prep time: 20 minutes | Cook time: 35 minutes | Serves 2

6 teaspoons extra-virgin olive oil, divided	2 cups fresh cauliflower florets
12 to 15 Brussels sprouts, halved	1 medium zucchini, cut into 1-inch rounds
1 medium sweet potato, peeled and cut into 2-inch cubes	1 red bell pepper, cut into 1-inch slices
	Salt, to taste

1. Preheat the oven to 425°F (220°C).
2. Add 2 teaspoons of olive oil, Brussels sprouts, sweet potato, and salt to a large bowl and toss until they are completely coated.
3. Transfer them to a large roasting pan and roast for 10 minutes, or until the Brussels sprouts are lightly browned.
4. Meantime, combine the cauliflower florets with 2 teaspoons of olive oil and salt in a separate bowl.
5. Remove from the oven. Add the cauliflower florets to the roasting pan and roast for 10 minutes more.
6. Meanwhile, toss the zucchini and bell pepper with the remaining olive oil in a medium bowl until well coated. Season with salt.
7. Remove the roasting pan from the oven and stir in the zucchini and bell pepper. Continue roasting for 15 minutes, or until the vegetables are fork- tender.
8. Divide the roasted vegetables between two plates and serve warm. **Per Serving** calories: 333 | fat: 16.8g | protein: 12.2g | carbs: 37.6g | fiber: 11.0g | sodium: 329mg

Ratatouille

Prep time: 10 minutes | Cook time: 30 minutes | Serves 4

4 tablespoons extra-virgin olive oil, divided	1 (15-ounce / 425-g) can no-salt-added diced tomatoes
1 cup diced zucchini	½ teaspoon garlic powder
2 cups diced eggplant	1 teaspoon ground thyme
1 cup diced onion	Salt and freshly ground black pepper, to taste
1 cup chopped green bell pepper	

1. Heat 2 tablespoons of olive oil in a large saucepan over medium heat until it shimmers.
2. Add the zucchini and eggplant and sauté for 10 minutes, stirring occasionally. If necessary, add the remaining olive oil. Stir in the onion and bell pepper and sauté for 5 minutes until softened.
3. Add the diced tomatoes with their juice, garlic powder, and thyme and stir to combine. Continue cooking for 15 minutes until the vegetables are cooked through, stirring occasionally. Sprinkle with salt and black pepper.
4. Remove from the heat and serve on a plate.

Per Serving calories: 189 | fat: 13.7g | protein: 3.1g | carbs: 14.8g | fiber: 4.0g | sodium: 27mg

Sauté ed Green Beans with Tomatoes

Prep time: 10 minutes | Cook time: 20 minutes | Serves 4

¼ cup extra-virgin olive oil	1½ teaspoons salt, divided
1 large onion, chopped	1 (15-ounce / 425-g) can diced tomatoes
4 cloves garlic, finely chopped	½ teaspoon freshly ground black pepper
1 pound (454 g) green beans, fresh or frozen, cut into 2-inch pieces	

1. Heat the olive oil in a large skillet over medium heat.
2. Add the onion and garlic and sauté for 1 minute until fragrant.
3. Stir in the green beans and sauté for 3 minutes. Sprinkle with ½ teaspoon of salt.
4. Add the tomatoes, remaining salt, and pepper and stir to mix well. Cook for an additional 12 minutes, stirring occasionally, or until the green beans are crisp and tender.
5. Remove from the heat and serve warm.

Per Serving calories: 219 | fat: 13.9g | protein: 4.0g | carbs: 17.7g | fiber: 6.2g | sodium: 843mg

Vegetable and Red Lentil Stew

Prep time: 10 minutes | Cook time: 35 minutes | Serves 6

1 tablespoon extra-virgin olive oil	4 celery stalks, finely diced
2 onions, peeled and finely diced	3 cups red lentils
6½ cups water	1 teaspoon dried oregano
2 zucchini, finely diced	1 teaspoon salt, plus more as needed

1. Heat the olive oil in a large pot over medium heat.
2. Add the onions and sauté for about 5 minutes, stirring constantly, or until the onions are softened.
3. Stir in the water, zucchini, celery, lentils, oregano, and salt and bring the mixture to a boil.
4. Reduce the heat to low and let simmer covered for 30 minutes, stirring occasionally, or until the lentils are tender.
5. Taste and adjust the seasoning as needed.

Per Serving calories: 387 | fat: 4.4g | protein: 24.0g | carbs: 63.7g | fiber: 11.7g | sodium: 418mg

Baked Tomatoes and Chickpeas

Prep time: 15 minutes | Cook time: 40 to 45 minutes | Serves 4

1 tablespoon extra-virgin olive oil	2 (15-ounce / 425-g) cans chickpeas, drained and rinsed
½ medium onion, chopped	
3 garlic cloves, chopped	4 cups halved cherry tomatoes
¼ teaspoon ground cumin	
2 teaspoons smoked paprika	½ cup plain Greek yogurt, for serving
	1 cup crumbled feta cheese, for serving

1. Preheat the oven to 425°F (220°C).
2. Heat the olive oil in an ovenproof skillet over medium heat.
3. Add the onion and garlic and sauté for about 5 minutes, stirring occasionally, or until tender and fragrant.
4. Add the paprika and cumin and cook for 2 minutes. Stir in the chickpeas and tomatoes and allow to simmer for 5 to 10 minutes.
5. Transfer the skillet to the preheated oven and roast for 25 to 30 minutes, or until the mixture bubbles and thickens.
6. Remove from the oven and serve topped with yogurt and crumbled feta cheese.

Per Serving calories: 411 | fat: 14.9g | protein: 20.2g | carbs: 50.7g | fiber: 13.3g | sodium: 443mg

Sweet Potato Chickpea Buddha Bowl

Prep time: 10 minutes | Cook time: 10 to 15 minutes | Serves 2

Sauce:	Bowl:
1 tablespoon tahini	1 small sweet potato, peeled and finely diced
2 tablespoons plain Greek yogurt	
2 tablespoons hemp seeds	1 teaspoon extra-virgin olive oil
1 garlic clove, minced Pinch salt	1 cup from 1 (15-ounce / 425-g) can low-sodium chickpeas, drained and rinsed
Freshly ground black pepper, to taste	
	2 cups baby kale

Make the Sauce
1. Whisk together the tahini and yogurt in a small bowl.
2. Stir in the hemp seeds and minced garlic. Season with salt pepper. Add 2 to 3 tablespoons water to create a creamy yet pourable consistency and set aside.

Make the Bowl
3. Preheat the oven to 425°F (220°C). Line a baking sheet with parchment paper.
4. Place the sweet potato on the prepared baking sheet and drizzle with the olive oil. Toss well
5. Roast in the preheated oven for 10 to 15 minutes, stirring once during cooking, or until fork-tender and browned.
6. In each of 2 bowls, place ½ cup of chickpeas, 1 cup of baby kale, and half of the cooked sweet potato. Serve drizzled with half of the prepared sauce.

Per Serving

calories: 323 | fat: 14.1g | protein: 17.0g | carbs: 36.0 g | fiber: 7.9g | sodium: 304mg

Zucchini Patties

Prep time: 15 minutes | Cook time: 5 minutes | Serves 2

2 medium zucchinis, shredded	1 tbsp chopped fresh mint
1 teaspoon salt, divided	1 scallion, chopped
2 eggs	2 tablespoons extra-virgin olive oil
2 tablespoons chickpea flour	

1. Put the shredded zucchini in a fine-mesh strainer and season with ½ teaspoon of salt. Set aside.
2. Beat together the eggs, chickpea flour, mint, scallion, and remaining ½ teaspoon of salt in a medium bowl.
3. Squeeze the zucchini to drain as much liquid as possible. Add the zucchini to the egg mixture and stir until well incorporated.
4. Heat the olive oil in a large skillet over medium-high heat.
5. Drop the zucchini mixture by spoonfuls into the skillet. Gently flatten the zucchini with the back of a spatula.
6. Cook for 2 to 3 minutes or until golden brown. Flip and cook for an additional 2 minutes.
7. Remove from the heat and serve on a plate.

Per Serving

calories: 264 | fat: 20.0g | protein: 9.8g | carbs: 16.1g | fiber: 4.0g | sodium: 1780mg

Cauliflower Rice Risotto with Mushrooms

Prep time: 5 minutes | Cook time: 10 minutes | Serves 4

1 teaspoon extra-virgin olive oil	½ cup plain Greek yogurt
½ cup chopped portobello mushrooms	¼ cup low-sodium vegetable broth
4 cups cauliflower rice	1 cup shredded Parmesan cheese

1. In a medium skillet, heat the olive oil over medium-low heat until shimmering.
2. Add the mushrooms and stir-fry for 3 minutes.
3. Stir in the cauliflower rice, yogurt, and vegetable broth. Cover and bring to a boil over high heat for 5 minutes, stirring occasionally.
4. Add the Parmesan cheese and stir to combine. Continue cooking for an additional 3 minutes until the cheese is melted.
5. Divide the mixture into four bowls and serve warm.

Per Serving calories: 167 | fat: 10.7g | protein: 12.1g | carbs: 8.1g | fiber: 3.0g | sodium: 326mg

Creamy Cauliflower Chickpea Curry

Prep time: 5 minutes | Cook time: 15 minutes | Serves 4

3 cups fresh or frozen cauliflower florets	1 tablespoon curry powder
2 cups unsweetened almond milk	¼ teaspoon garlic powder
	¼ teaspoon ground ginger
1 (15-ounce / 425-g) can low-sodium chickpeas, drained and rinsed	⅛ teaspoon onion powder
	¼ teaspoon salt
	1 (15-ounce / 425-g) can coconut milk

1. Add the cauliflower florets, almond milk, chickpeas, coconut milk, curry powder, garlic powder, ginger, and onion powder to a large stockpot and stir to combine.
2. Cover and cook over medium-high heat for 10 minutes, stirring occasionally.
3. Reduce the heat to low and continue cooking uncovered for 5 minutes, or until the cauliflower is tender.
4. Sprinkle with the salt and stir well. Serve warm.

Per Serving

calories: 409 | fat: 29.6g | protein: 10.0g | carbs: 29.8g | fiber: 9.1g | sodium: 117mg

Zucchini Crisp

Prep time: 10 minutes | Cook time: 20 minutes | Serves 2

4 zucchinis, sliced into ½-inch rounds
½ cup unsweetened almond milk
1 teaspoon fresh lemon juice
1 teaspoon arrowroot powder
½ teaspoon salt, divided

½ cup whole wheat bread crumbs
¼ cup nutritional yeast
¼ cup hemp seeds
½ teaspoon garlic powder
¼ teaspoon crushed red pepper
¼ teaspoon black pepper

1. Preheat the oven to 375ºF (190ºC). Line two baking sheets with parchment paper and set aside.
2. Put the zucchini in a medium bowl with the almond milk, lemon juice, arrowroot powder, and ¼ teaspoon of salt. Stir to mix well.
3. In a large bowl with a lid, thoroughly combine the bread crumbs, nutritional yeast, hemp seeds, garlic powder, crushed red pepper and black pepper. Add the zucchini in batches and shake until the slices are evenly coated.
4. Arrange the zucchini on the prepared baking sheets in a single layer.
5. Bake in the preheated oven for about 20 minutes, or until the zucchini slices are golden brown.
6. Season with the remaining ¼ teaspoon of salt before serving.

Per Serving
calories: 255 | fat: 11.3g | protein: 8.6g | carbs: 31.9g | fiber: 3.8g | sodium: 826mg

Creamy Sweet Potatoes and Collards

Prep time: 20 minutes | Cook time: 35 minutes | Serves 2

1 tablespoon avocado oil
3 garlic cloves, chopped
1 yellow onion, diced
½ teaspoon crushed red pepper flakes
1 large sweet potato, peeled and diced
2 bunches collard greens (about 2 pounds/907 g), stemmed, leaves chopped int

1-inch squares
1 (14.5-ounce / 411-g) can diced tomatoes with juice
1 (15-ounce / 425-g) can red kidney beans or chickpeas, drained and rinsed
1½ cups water
½ cup unsweetened coconut milk
Salt and black pepper, to taste

1. In a large, deep skillet over medium heat, melt the avocado oil.
2. Add the garlic, onion, and red pepper flakes and cook for 3 minutes. Stir in the sweet potato and collards.
3. Add the tomatoes with their juice, beans, water, and coconut milk and mix well. Bring the mixture just to a boil.
4. Reduce the heat to medium-low, cover, and simmer for about 30 minutes, or until softened.
5. Season to taste with salt and pepper and serve.

Per Serving calories: 445 | fat: 9.6g | protein: 18.1g | carbs: 73.1g | fiber: 22.1g | sodium: 703mg

Paprika Cauliflower Steaks with Walnut Sauce

Prep time: 5 minutes | Cook time: 30 minutes | Serves 2

Walnut Sauce:
½ cup raw walnut halves
2 tablespoons virgin olive oil, divided
1 clove garlic, chopped
1 small yellow onion, chopped
½ cup unsweetened almond milk

Salt and pepper, to taste
2 tablespoons fresh lemon juice
Paprika Cauliflower:
1 medium head cauliflower
1 teaspoon sweet paprika
1 teaspoon minced fresh thyme leaves (about 2 sprigs)

1. Preheat the oven to 350ºF (180ºC).
2. Make the walnut sauce: Toast the walnuts in a large, ovenproof skillet over medium heat until fragrant and slightly darkened, about 5 minutes. Transfer the walnuts to a blender. Heat 1 tablespoon of olive oil in the skillet. Add the garlic and onion and sauté for about 2 minutes, or until slightly softened. Transfer the garlic and onion into the blender, along with the almond milk, lemon juice, salt, and pepper. Blend the until smooth and creamy. Keep the sauce warm while you prepare the cauliflower.
3. Make the paprika cauliflower: Cut two 1-inch-thick "steaks" from the center of the cauliflower. Lightly moisten the steaks with water and season both sides with paprika, thyme, salt, and pepper. Heat the remaining 1 tablespoon of olive oil in the skillet over medium- high heat. Add the cauliflower steaks and sear for about 3 minutes until evenly browned. Flip the cauliflower steaks and transfer the skillet to the oven. Roast in the preheated oven for about 20 minutes until crisp-tender. Serve the cauliflower steaks warm with the walnut sauce on the side.

Per Serving calories: 367 | fat: 27.9g | protein: 7.0g | carbs: 22.7g | fiber: 5.8g | sodium: 173mg

Potato and Kale Bowls

Prep time: 10 minutes | Cook time: 10 minutes | Serves 4

1 tablespoon olive oil
1 small onion, peeled and diced
1 stalk celery, diced
2 cloves garlic, minced
4 medium potatoes, peeled and diced
2 bunches kale, washed, deveined, and chopped

1½ cups vegetable broth
2 teaspoons salt
½ teaspoon ground black pepper
¼ teaspoon caraway seeds
1 tablespoon apple cider vinegar
4 tablespoons sour cream

1. Press the Sauté button on Instant Pot. Heat oil. Add onion and celery and stir-fry for 3 to 5 minutes until onions are translucent. Add garlic and cook for an additional minute. Add potatoes in an even layer. Add chopped kale in an even layer. Add broth. Lock lid.
2. Press the Manual button and adjust time to 5 minutes. Let the pressure release naturally for 10 minutes. Quick release any additional pressure until float valve drops and then unlock lid; then drain broth. Stir in salt, pepper, caraway seeds, and vinegar; slightly mash the potatoes in the Instant Pot. Garnish each serving with 1 tablespoon sour cream.

Per Serving calories: 259 | fat: 5.5g | protein: 7.9g | carbs: 47.6g | fiber: 7.6g | sodium: 1422mg

Eggplant and Millet Pilaf

Prep time: 5 minutes | Cook time: 17 minutes | Serves 4

1 tablespoon olive oil	2 cups vegetable broth
¼ cup peeled and diced onion	1 teaspoon sea salt
1 cup peeled and diced eggplant	¼ teaspoon ground black pepper
1 small Roma tomato, seeded and diced	⅛ teaspoon saffron
1 cup millet	⅛ teaspoon cayenne pepper
	1 tablespoon chopped fresh chives

1. Press Sauté button on Instant Pot. Add the olive oil. Add onion and cook for 3 to 5 minutes until translucent. Toss in eggplant and stir-fry for 2 more minutes. Add diced tomato.
2. Add millet to Instant Pot in an even layer. Gently pour in broth. Lock lid.
3. Press the Rice button (the Instant Pot will determine the time, about 10 minutes pressurized cooking time). When timer beeps, let pressure release naturally for 5 minutes. Quick release any additional pressure until float valve drops and then unlock lid.
4. Transfer pot to a serving bowl. Season with salt, pepper, saffron, and cayenne pepper. Garnish with chives.

Per Serving

calories: 238 | fat: 5.6g | protein: 6.0g | carbs: 40.8g | fiber: 5.3g | sodium: 861mg

Sautéed Cabbage (Spanish)

Preparation time: 10 minutes
Cooking time: 12 to 14 minutes
Serving: 4 to 6

1small head green cabbage (about 1¼ pounds / 567 g), cored and sliced thin	2tablespoons extra-virgin olive oil, divided 1 onion, halved and sliced thin
3/4 teaspoon salt, divided	¼ teaspoon black pepper
¼ cup chopped fresh parsley 1½ teaspoons lemon juice	

1. Place the cabbage in a large bowl with cold water. Let sit for 3 minutes. Drain well.
2. Heat 1 tablespoon of the oil in a skillet over medium-high heat until shimmering. Add the onion and ¼ teaspoon of the salt and cook for 5 to 7 minutes, or until softened and lightly browned. Transfer to a bowl.
3. Heat the remaining 1 tablespoon of the oil in now-empty skillet over medium-high heat until shimmering. Add the cabbage and sprinkle with the remaining ½ teaspoon of the salt and black pepper. Cover and cook for about 3 minutes, without stirring, or until cabbage is wilted and lightly browned on bottom.
4. Stir and continue to cook for about 4 minutes, uncovered, or until the cabbage is crisp-tender and lightly browned in places, stirring once halfway through cooking. Off heat, stir in the cooked onion, parsley and lemon juice.
5. Transfer to a plate and serve.

Nutrition: calories: 117 fat: 7g protein: 3g carbs: 13g fiber: 5g sodium: 472mg

Ratatouille (Italian)

Preparation time: 15 minutes
Cooking time: 40 minutes Serving: 6

2 russet potatoes, cubed	½ cup Roma tomatoes, cubed 1 eggplant, cubed
1 zucchini, cubed	1 red onion, chopped
1 red bell pepper, chopped	1 teaspoon dried mint
2 garlic cloves, minced	
1 teaspoon dried parsley 1 teaspoon dried oregano	½ teaspoon salt
½ teaspoon black pepper	¼ teaspoon red pepper flakes 1/3 cup olive oil
1 (8-ounce / 227-g) can tomato paste	¼ cup vegetable broth
¼ cup water	

1. Preheat the air fryer to 320ºF (160ºC).
2. In a large bowl, combine the potatoes, tomatoes, eggplant, zucchini, onion, bell pepper, garlic, mint, parsley, oregano, salt, black pepper, and red pepper flakes.
3. In a small bowl, mix together the olive oil, tomato paste, broth, and water.
4. Pour the oil-and-tomato-paste mixture over the vegetables and toss until everything is coated.
5. Pour the coated vegetables into the air fryer basket in an even layer and roast for 20 minutes. After 20 minutes, stir well and spread out again. Roast for an additional 10 minutes, then repeat the process and cook for another 10 minutes.

Nutrition: calories: 280 fat: 13g protein: 6g carbs: 40g fiber: 7g sodium: 264mg

Celeriac Mix with Cauliflower (Italian)

Preparation Time: 10 minutes Cooking Time: 12 minutes
Servings: 6

1 head cauliflower 1 small celery root	¼ cup butter
1 tablespoon. chopped rosemary	1 tablespoon. chopped thyme
	1 cup cream cheese

1. Skin the celery root and cut it into small pieces.
2. Cut the cauliflower into similar sized pieces and combine.
3. Toast the herbs in the butter in a large pan, until they become fragrant.
4. Add the cauliflower and celery root and stir to combine.
5. Season and cook at medium-high until moisture in the vegetables releases itself, then cover and cook on low for 10-12 minutes.
6. Once the vegetables are soft, remove them from the heat and place them in the blender.
7. Make it smooth, then put the cream cheese and puree again.
8. Season and serve.

Nutrition: 225 Calories 20g Fat 5g Protein

Veggie-Stuffed Mushrooms (Italian)

Preparation time: 5 minutes Cooking time: 24 to 25 minutes
Serving: 6

3 tablespoons extra-virgin olive oil, divided 1 cup diced onion	2garlic cloves, minced 1 large zucchini, diced
3cups chopped mushrooms 1 cup chopped tomato	1 teaspoon dried oregano
¼ teaspoon kosher salt	¼ teaspoon crushed red pepper
6 large portobello mushrooms, stems and gills removed Cooking spray	4 ounces (113 g) fresh Mozzarella cheese, shredded

1. In a large skillet over medium heat, heat 2 tablespoons of the oil. Add the onion and sauté for 4 minutes. Stir in the garlic and sauté for 1 minute.
2. Stir in the zucchini, mushrooms, tomato, oregano, salt and red pepper. Cook for 10 minutes, stirring constantly. Remove from the heat.
3. Meanwhile, heat a grill pan over medium-high heat.
4. Brush the remaining 1 tablespoon of the oil over the portobello mushroom caps. Place the mushrooms, bottom-side down, on the grill pan. Cover with a sheet of aluminum foil sprayed with nonstick cooking spray. Cook for 5 minutes.
5. Flip the mushroom caps over, and spoon about ½ cup of the cooked vegetable mixture into each cap. Top each with about 2½ tablespoons of the Mozzarella.
6. Cover and grill for 4 to 5 minutes, or until the cheese is melted.
7. Using a spatula, transfer the portobello mushrooms to a plate. Let cool for about 5 minutes before serving.

Nutrition: calories: 111 fat: 4g protein: 11g carbs: 11g fiber: 4g sodium: 314mg

Roasted Root Veggies (Spanish)

Preparation time: 20 minutes Cooking time: 1 hour 30 minutes
Servings: 6

2 tablespoon olive oil	1 head garlic, cloves separated and peeled
1 large turnip, peeled and cut into ½-inch pieces 1 medium sized red onion, cut into ½-inch pieces	1 ½ lbs. beets, trimmed but not peeled, scrubbed and cut into ½-inch pieces
1 ½ lbs. Yukon gold potatoes, unpeeled, cut into ½-inch pieces 2 ½ lbs. pieces	butternut squash, peeled, seeded, cut into ½-inch pieces

1. Grease 2 rimmed and large baking sheets. Preheat oven to 425oF.
2. In a large bowl, mix all thoroughly.
3. Into the two baking sheets, evenly divide the root vegetables, spread in one layer.
4. Season generously with pepper and salt.
5. Pop into the oven and roast for 1 hour and 15 minute or until golden brown and tender.
6. Remove from oven and let it cool for at least 15 minutes before serving.

Nutrition: Calories: 298; Carbs: 61.1g; Protein: 7.4g; Fat: 5.0g

Delicious Feta with Fresh Spinach (Greek)

Preparation Time: 10 minutes Cooking Time: 0 minutes
Servings: 6

6 cups fresh baby spinach, chopped	¼ cup scallions, white and green parts, chopped
1(16-ounce)packageorzo pasta,cookedaccordingto package directions, rinsed, drained, and cooled	3/4 cup crumbled feta cheese 1/4 cup halved Kalamata olives 1/2 cup red wine vinegar
1/4 cup extra-virgin olive oil	1½ teaspoons freshly squeezed lemon juice Sea salt
Freshly ground black pepper	

1. In a large bowl, combine the spinach, scallions, and cooled orzo.
2. Sprinkle with the feta and olives.
3. In a small bowl, whisk the vinegar, olive oil, and lemon juice. Season with sea salt and pepper.
4. Add the dressing to the salad and gently toss to combine. Refrigerate until serving.

Nutrition: 255 Calories 8g Protein 8g Fat

Cheddar Fondue with Tomato Sauce (Italian)

Preparation Time: 10 minutes Cooking Time: 30 minutes
Servings: 4

1 garlic clove, halved	6 medium tomatoes, seeded and diced 2/3 cup dry white wine
6 tablespoons. Butter, cubed 1-½ teaspoons. Dried basil Dash cayenne pepper Cubed French bread and cooked shrimp	2 cups shredded cheddar cheese 1 tablespoon. All-purpose flour

1. Rub the bottom and sides of a fondue pot with a garlic clove.
2. Set aside and discard the garlic.
1. 3.Combinewine,butter,basil,cayenne,andtomatoesinalarge saucepan.
3. On a medium-low heat, bring the mixture to a simmer, then decrease the heat to low.
4. Mix cheese with flour.
5. Add to tomato mixture gradually while stirring after each addition until cheese is melted.
6. Pour into the preparation fondue pot and keep warm.
7. Enjoy with shrimp and bread cubes.

Nutrition: 118 Calories 10g Fat 4g Protein

Quick Spinach Focaccia (Italian)

Preparation Time: 10 minutes Cooking Time: 25 minutes
Servings: 12

10 eggs	2 cups spinach, chopped
¼ tsp garlic powder	¼ tsp onion powder
½ tsp dried basil	1 ½ cups parmesan cheese, grated Salt

1. Preheat the oven to 400 F. Grease muffin tin and set aside.
2. In a large bowl, whisk eggs with basil, garlic powder, onion powder, and salt.
3. Add cheese and spinach and stir well.
4. Pour egg mixture into the prepared muffin tin and bake 15 minutes.
5. Serve and enjoy.

Nutrition: 110 Calories 7g Fat 9g Protein

Triumph of Cucumbers and Avocados (Spanish)

Preparation Time: 10 minutes Cooking Time: 15 minutes
Servings: 4

12 oz cherry tomatoes, cut in half 5 small cucumbers, chopped	3 small avocados, chopped
½ tsp ground black pepper 2 tbsp olive oil	2 tbsp fresh lemon juice
¼ cup fresh cilantro, chopped	1 tsp sea salt

1. Add cherry tomatoes, cucumbers, avocados, and cilantro into the large mixing bowl and mix well.
2. Mix olive oil, lemon juice, black pepper, and salt and pour over salad.
3. Toss well and serve immediately.

Nutrition: 442 Calories 37g Fat 6.2g Protein

Roasted Vegetables and Zucchini Pasta (Italian)

Preparation time: 10 minutes
Cooking time: 7 minutes Servings: 2

¼ cup raw pine nuts	4 cups leftover vegetables 2 garlic cloves, minced
1 tablespoon extra-virgin olive oil	4 medium zucchinis, cut into long strips resembling noodles

1. Heat oil in a large skillet over medium heat and sauté the garlic for 2 minutes.
2. Add the leftover vegetables and place the zucchini noodles on top. Let it cook for five minutes. Garnish with pine nuts.

Nutrition: Calories: 288; Carbs: 23.6g; Protein: 8.2g; Fat: 19.2g

Mediterranean Baked Chickpeas (Spanish)

Preparation time: 15 minutes Cooking time: 15 minutes
Servings: 6

1 tablespoon extra-virgin olive oil	½ medium onion, chopped
2 teaspoons smoked paprika	3 garlic cloves, chopped
4 cups halved cherry tomatoes	¼ teaspoon ground cumin
	2 (15-ounce) cans chickpeas, drained and rinsed

½ cup plain, unsweetened, full-fat Greek yogurt, for serving 1 cup crumbled feta, for serving

1. Preheat the oven to 425°F.
2. In an oven-safe sauté pan or skillet, heat the oil over medium heat and sauté the onion and garlic. Cook for about 5 minutes, until softened and fragrant. Stir in the paprika and cumin and cook for 2 minutes. Stir in the tomatoes and chickpeas.
3. Bring to a simmer for 5 to 10 minutes before placing in the oven.
4. Roast in oven for 25 to 30 minutes, until bubbling and thickened. To serve, top with Greek yogurt and feta.

Nutrition: Calories: 330; Carbs: 75.4g; Protein: 9.0g; Fat: 18.5g

Falafel Bites (Italian)

Preparation time: 10 minutes Cooking time: 15 minutes
Servings: 4

1 2/3 cups falafel mix 1¼ cups water	Extra-virgin olive oil spray
1 tablespoon Pickled Onions (optional) 1 tablespoon Pickled Turnips (optional)	2 tablespoons Tzatziki Sauce (optional)

1. In a large bowl, carefully stir the falafel mix into the water. Mix well. Let stand 15 minutes to absorb the water. Form mixes into 1-inch balls and arrange on a baking sheet.
2. Preheat the broiler to high.
3. Take the balls and flatten slightly with your thumb (so they won't roll around on the baking sheet). Spray with olive oil, and then broil for 2 to 3 minutes on each side, until crispy and brown.
4. To fry the falafel, fill a pot with ½ inch of cooking oil and heat over medium-high heat to 375°F. Fry the balls for about 3 minutes, until brown and crisp. Drain on paper towels and serve with pickled onions, pickled turnips, and tzatziki sauce (if using).

Nutrition: Calories: 530; Carbs: 95.4g; Protein: 8.0g; Fat: 18.5g

Quick Vegetable Kebabs (Spanish)

Preparation time: 15 minutes Cooking time: 20 minutes
Servings: 6

4 medium red onions, peeled and sliced into 6 wedges 4 medium zucchinis, cut into 1-inch-thick slices	4 bell peppers, cut into 2-inch squares
2 yellow bell peppers, cut into 2-inch squares 2 orange bell peppers, cut into 2-inch squares 2 beefsteak tomatoes, cut into quarters	3 tablespoons Herbed Oil

1. Preheat the oven or grill to medium-high or 350°F.
2. Thread 1-piece red onion, zucchini, different colored bell peppers, and tomatoes onto a skewer. Repeat until the skewer is full of vegetables, up to 2 inches away from the skewer end, and continue until all skewers are complete.
3. Put the skewers on a baking sheet and cook in the oven for 10 minutes or grill for 5 minutes on each side. The vegetables will be done with they reach your desired crunch or softness.
4. Remove the skewers from heat and drizzle with Herbed Oil.

Nutrition: Calories: 235; Carbs: 30.4g; Protein: 8.0g; Fat: 14.5g

Sautéed Collard Greens (Spanish)

Preparation time: 10 minutes Cooking time: 0 minute
Servings: 4

1-pound fresh collard greens, cut into 2-inch pieces 1 pinch red pepper flakes	3 cups chicken broth 1 teaspoon pepper
1 teaspoon salt	2 cloves garlic, minced 1 large onion, chopped 3 slices bacon
1 tablespoon olive oil	

1. Using a large skillet, heat oil on medium-high heat. Sauté bacon until crisp. Remove it from the pan and crumble it once cooled. Set it aside.
2. Using the same pan, sauté onion and cook until tender. Add garlic until fragrant. Add the collard greens and cook until they start to wilt.
3. Pour in the chicken broth and season with pepper, salt and red pepper flakes. Reduce the heat to low and simmer for 45 minutes.

Nutrition: Calories: 20; Carbs: 3.0g; Protein: 1.0g; Fat: 1.0g

Tortellini in Red Pepper Sauce (Italian)

Prep time: 15 minutes Cooking time: 10 minutes Servings: 4

1 (16-ounce) container fresh cheese tortellini (usually green and white pasta)	1 (16-ounce) jar roasted red peppers, drained 1 teaspoon garlic powder
¼ cup tahini	1 tablespoon red pepper oil (optional)

Description

1. Bring a large pot of water to a boil and cook the tortellini according to package directions.
2. In a blender, combine the red peppers with the garlic powder and process until smooth. Once blended, add the tahini until the sauce is thickened. If the sauce gets too thick, add up to 1 tablespoon red pepper oil (if using).
3. Once tortellini are cooked, drain and leave pasta in colander. Add the sauce to the bottom of the empty pot and heat for 2 minutes. Then, add the tortellini back into the pot and cook for 2 more minutes. Serve and enjoy!

Nutrition: Calories: 530; Carbs: 95.4g; Protein: 8.0g; Fat: 18.5g

Vegetable Hummus Wraps (Greek)

Prep time: 15 minutes Cooking time: 10 minutes Serving: 6

1 large eggplant	1 large onion
½ cup extra-virgin olive oil	6 lavash wraps or large pita bread 1 cup hummus
1 teaspoon salt	

1. Preheat a grill, large grill pan, or lightly oiled large skillet on medium heat.
2. Slice the eggplant and onion into circles. Brush the vegetables with olive oil and sprinkle with salt.
3. Cook the vegetables on both sides, about 3 to 4 minutes each side.
4. To make the wrap, lay the lavash or pita flat. Spread about 2 tablespoons of hummus on the wrap.
5. Evenly divide the vegetables among the wraps, layering them along one side of the wrap. Gently fold over the side of the wrap with the vegetables, tucking them in and making a tight wrap.
6. Lay the wrap seam side-down and cut in half or thirds.
7. You can also wrap each sandwich with plastic wrap to help it hold its shape and eat it later.

Nutrition: calories: 362 | fat: 26g | protein: 15g | carbs: 28g | fiber: 11g | sodium: 1069mg

Zucchini Garlic Fries (Italian)

Preparation time: 15 minutes Cooking time: 20 minutes
Servings: 6

¼ teaspoon garlic powder	½ cup almond flour
2 large egg whites, beaten	3 medium zucchinis, sliced into fry sticks Salt and pepper to taste

1. Preheat oven to 400oF.
2. Mix all in a bowl until the zucchini fries are well coated.
3. Place fries on cookie sheet and spread evenly.
4. Put in oven and cook for 20 minutes.
5. Halfway through cooking time, stir fries.

Nutrition: Calories: 11; Carbs: 1.1g; Protein: 1.5g; Fat: 0.1g

147

Beet and Watercress Salad (Greek)

Preparation time: 15 minutes Cooking time: 8 minutes
Serving: 4

1pounds (907 g) beets, scrubbed, trimmed and cut into ¾-inch pieces	½ cup water
1 teaspoon caraway seeds	½ teaspoon table salt, plus more for seasoning 1 cup plain Greek yogurt
1 small garlic clove, minced	5 ounces (142 g) watercress, torn into bite-size pieces
1 tablespoon extra-virgin olive oil, divided, plus more for drizzling 1 tablespoon white wine vinegar, divided	Black pepper, to taste
1 teaspoon grated orange zest 2 tablespoons orange juice	¼ cup coarsely chopped fresh dill
¼ cup hazelnuts, toasted, skinned and chopped	Coarse sea salt, to taste

1. Combine the beets, water, caraway seeds and table salt in the Instant Pot. Set the lid in place. Select the Manual mode and set the cooking time for 8 minutes on High Pressure. When the timer goes off, do a quick pressure release.
2. Carefully open the lid. Using a slotted spoon, transfer the beets to a plate. Set aside to cool slightly.
3. In a small bowl, combine the yogurt, garlic and 3 tablespoons of the beet cooking liquid. In a large bowl, toss the watercress with 2 teaspoons of the oil and 1 teaspoon of the vinegar. Season with table salt and pepper.
4. Spread the yogurt mixture over a serving dish. Arrange the watercress on top of the yogurt mixture, leaving 1-inch border of the yogurt mixture.
5. Add the beets to now-empty large bowl and toss with the orange zest and juice, the remaining 2 teaspoons of the vinegar and the remaining 1 teaspoon of the oil. Season with table salt and pepper.
6. Arrange the beets on top of the watercress mixture. Drizzle with the olive oil and sprinkle with the dill, hazelnuts and sea salt.
7. Serve immediately.

Nutrition: calories: 240 | fat: 15g | protein: 9g | carbs: 19g | fiber: 5g | sodium: 440mg

Easy Roasted Radishes (Greek)

Preparation time: 5 minutes Cooking time: 18 minutes
Serving: 4

1-pound (454 g) radishes, ends trimmed	½ teaspoon sea salt if needed 2 tbsp olive oil

1. Preheat the air fryer to 360°F (182°C).
2. In a large bowl, combine the radishes with olive oil and sea salt.
3. Pour the radishes into the air fryer and cook for 10 minutes. Stir or turn the radishes over and cook for 8 minutes more, then serve.

Nutrition: calories: 78 | fat: 9g | protein: 1g | carbs: 4g | fiber: 2g | sodium: 335mg

Walnut Pesto Zoodles (Italian)

Preparation Time: 15 minutes Cooking Time: 10 minutes
Servings: 4

4 medium zucchini (makes about 8 cups of zoodles)	¼ cup extra-virgin olive oil, divided
2 garlic cloves, minced (about 1 teaspoon), divided	½ teaspoon crushed red pepper
¼ teaspoon freshly ground black pepper, divided	¼ teaspoon kosher or sea salt, divided
2 tablespoons grated Parmesan cheese, divided 1 cup packed fresh basil leaves	¾ cup walnut pieces, divided

1. Make the zucchini noodles (zoodles) using a spiralizer or your vegetable peeler to make ribbons (run the peeler down the zucchini to make long strips). In a large bowl, gently mix to combine the zoodles with 1 tablespoon of oil, 1 minced garlic clove, all the crushed red pepper, 1/8 teaspoon of black pepper, and 1/8 teaspoon of salt. Set aside.
2. In a large skillet over medium-high heat, heat ½ tablespoon of oil. Add half of the zoodles to the pan and cook for 5 minutes, stirring every minute or so. Pour the cooked zoodles into a large serving bowl, and repeat with another ½ tablespoon of oil and the remaining zoodles. Add those zoodles to the serving bowl when they are done cooking.
3. While the zoodles are cooking, make the pesto. If you're using a food processor, add the remaining minced garlic clove, 1/8 teaspoon of black pepper, and 1/8 teaspoon of salt, 1 tablespoon of Parmesan, all the basil leaves, and ¼ cup of walnuts. Turn on the processor, and slowly drizzle the remaining 2 tablespoons of oil into the opening until the pesto is completely blended. If you're using a high-powered blender, add the 2 tablespoons of oil first and then the rest of the pesto . Pulse until the pesto is completely blended.
4. Add the pesto to the zoodles along with the remaining 1 tablespoon of Parmesan and the remaining ½ cup of walnuts. Mix together well and serve.

Nutrition: Calories: 301 Total Fat: 28g Saturated Fat: 4g Cholesterol: 3mg Sodium: 170mg Total Carbohydrates: 11g Fiber: 4g Protein: 7g

Instant Pot Millet Pilaf (Italian)

Prep Time: 20 minutes Cooking Time: 11 minutes Servings: 4-5

1 cup millet	Cup apricot and shelled pistachios (roughly chopped)
1 lemon juice and zest	
tbsp olive oil	Cup parsley (fresh)

1. Pour one and three-quarter cup of water in your instant pot. Place the millet and lid the instant pot.
2. Adjust time for 10 minutes on high pressure. When the time has elapsed, release pressure naturally.
3. Remove the lid and add all other. Stir while adjusting the seasonings. Serve and enjoy

Nutrition: 308 Calories 11g Fat 6g Fiber

Cauliflower Steaks with Eggplant Relish (Spanish)

Prep Time: 5 minutes Cooking Time: 25 minutes Servings: 4

2 small heads cauliflower (about 3 pounds)	¼ teaspoon kosher or sea salt¼ teaspoon smoked paprika extra-virgin olive oil, divided

1. 1 recipe Eggplant Relish Spread or 1 container store-bought baba ghanoush
2. Place a large, rimmed baking sheet in the oven. Preheat the oven to 400°F with the pan inside.
3. Stand one head of cauliflower on a cutting board, stem-end down. With a long chef's knife, slice down through the very center of the head, including the stem. Starting at the cut edge, measure about 1 inch and cut one thick slice from each cauliflower half, including as much of the stem as possible, to make two cauliflower "steaks." Reserve the remaining cauliflower for another use. Repeat with the second cauliflower head.
4. Dry each steak well with a clean towel. Sprinkle the salt and smoked paprika evenly over both sides of each cauliflower steak.
5. In a large skillet over medium-high heat, heat 2 tablespoons of oil. When the oil is very hot, add two cauliflower steaks to the pan and cook for about 3 minutes, until golden and crispy. Flip and cook for 2 more minutes. Transfer the steaks to a plate. Use a pair of tongs to hold a paper towel and wipe out the pan to remove most of the hot oil (which will contain a few burnt bits of cauliflower). Repeat the cooking process with the remaining 2 tablespoons of oil and the remaining two steaks.
6. Using oven mitts, carefully remove the baking sheet from the oven and place the cauliflower on the baking sheet. Roast in the oven for 12 to 15 minutes, until the cauliflower steaks are just fork tender; they will still be somewhat firm. Serve the steaks with the Eggplant Relish Spread, baba ghanoush, or the homemade ketchup from our Italian Baked Beans recipe.

Nutrition: Calories: 282 Total Fat: 22g Saturated Fat: 3g Cholesterol: 7mg Sodium: 380mg Total Carbohydrates: 20g Fiber: 9g Protein: 8g

Summer Veggies in Instant Pot (Spanish)

Prep time: 10 minutes Cooking time: 7 minutes Servings: 6

2 cups okra, sliced	1 cup grape tomatoes
1cup mushroom, sliced 1 ½ cups onion, sliced	2cups bell pepper, sliced 2 ½ cups zucchini, sliced
2 tablespoons basil, chopped 1 tablespoon thyme, chopped	½ cups balsamic vinegar ½ cups olive oil Salt and pepper

1. Place all in the Instant Pot.
2. Stir the contents and close the lid.
3. Close the lid and press the Manual button.
4. Adjust the cooking time to 7 minutes.
5. Do quick pressure release.
6. Once cooled, evenly divide into serving size, keep in your preferred container, and refrigerate until ready to eat.

Nutrition: Calories per serving: 233; Carbs: 7g; Protein: 3g; Fat: 18g

Mediterranean Lentil Sloppy Joes (Italian)

Preparation Time: 5 minutes Cooking Time: 15 minutes Servings: 4

1 tablespoon extra-virgin olive oil	1 cup chopped onion (about ½ medium onion)
1 cup chopped bell pepper, any color (about 1 medium bell pepper) 2 garlic cloves, minced (about 1 teaspoon)	1 (15-ounce) can lentils, drained and rinsed
1(14.5-ounce)canlow-sodiumorno-salt-addeddiced tomatoes, undrained	1 teaspoon ground cumin 1 teaspoon dried thyme
¼ teaspoon kosher or sea salt	4 whole-wheat pita breads, split open
1½ cups chopped seedless cucumber (1 medium cucumber) 1 cup chopped romaine lettuce	

1. In a medium saucepan over medium-high heat, heat the oil. Add the onion and bell pepper and cook for 4 minutes, stirring frequently. Add the garlic and cook for 1 minute, stirring frequently. Add the lentils, tomatoes (with their liquid), cumin, thyme, and salt. Turn the heat to medium and cook, stirring occasionally, for 10 minutes, or until most of the liquid has evaporated.
2. Stuff the lentil mixture inside each pita. Lay the cucumbers and lettuce on top of the lentil mixture and serve.

Nutrition: Calories: 334 Total Fat: 5g Saturated Fat: 1g Cholesterol: 0mg Sodium: 610mg Total Carbohydrates: 58g Fiber: 10g Protein: 16g

Stir Fried Bok Choy (Spanish)

Preparation time: 5 minutes Cooking time: 13 minutes Servings: 4

3 tablespoons coconut oil 4 cloves of garlic, minced 1 onion, chopped	2 heads bok choy, rinsed and chopped 2 teaspoons coconut aminos
Salt and pepper to taste 2 tablespoons sesame oil	2 tablespoons sesame seeds, toasted

1. Heat the oil in a pot for 2 minutes.
2. Sauté the garlic and onions until fragrant, around 3 minutes.
3. Stir in the bok choy, coconut aminos, salt and pepper.
4. Cover pan and cook for 5 minutes.
5. Stir and continue cooking for another 3 minutes.
6. Drizzle with sesame oil and sesame seeds on top before serving.

Nutrition: Calories: 358; Carbs: 5.2g; Protein: 21.5g; Fat: 28.4g

Zucchini Pasta with Mango-Kiwi Sauce (Italian)

Preparation time: 5 minutes Cooking time: 20 minutes
Servings: 2

1 teaspoon dried herbs – optional	½ Cup Raw Kale leaves, shredded 2 small dried figs
3 medjool dates	4 medium kiwis
2 big mangos, seed discarded 2 cup zucchini, spiralized	¼ cup roasted cashew

1. On a salad bowl, place kale then topped with zucchini noodles and sprinkle with dried herbs. Set aside.
2. In a food processor, grind to a powder the cashews. Add figs, dates, kiwis and mangoes then puree to a smooth consistency.
3. Pour over zucchini pasta, serve and enjoy.

Nutrition: Calories: 530; Carbs: 95.4g; Protein: 8.0g; Fat: 18.5g

Quinoa with Almonds and Cranberries (Greek)

Preparation time: 10 minutes Cooking time: 15 minutes
Servings: 4

2 cups cooked quinoa	1/3 teaspoon cranberries or currants
¼ cup sliced almonds 2 garlic cloves, minced 1¼ teaspoons salt	½ teaspoon ground cumin
½ teaspoon turmeric	¼ teaspoon ground cinnamon
¼ teaspoon freshly ground black pepper	

1. In a large bowl, toss the quinoa, cranberries, almonds, garlic, salt, cumin, turmeric, cinnamon, and pepper and stir to combine. Enjoy alone or with roasted cauliflower.

Nutrition: Calories: 430; Carbs: 65.4g; Protein: 8.0g; Fat: 15.5g

Freekeh, Chickpea, and Herb Salad (Spanish)

Preparation time: 15 minutes Cooking time: 10 minutes
Servings: 6

1 (15-ounce) can chickpeas, rinsed and drained 1 cup cooked freekeh	1 cup thinly sliced celery
1 bunch scallions, both white & green parts, finely chopped	½ cup chopped fresh flat-leaf parsley
¼ cup chopped fresh mint	3 tablespoons chopped celery leaves
½ teaspoon kosher salt	1/3 cup extra-virgin olive oil
¼ cup freshly squeezed lemon juice	¼ teaspoon cumin seeds 1 teaspoon garlic powder

1. In a large bowl, combine the chickpeas, freekeh, celery, scallions, parsley, mint, celery leaves, and salt and toss lightly.
2. In a small bowl, whisk together the olive oil, lemon juice, cumin seeds, and garlic powder. Once combined, add to freekeh salad.

Nutrition: Calories: 230; Carbs: 25.4g; Protein: 8.0g; Fat: 18.5g

Sumptuous Tomato Soup (Spanish)

Preparation time: 10 minutes Cooking time: 30 minutes
Servings: 2

Pepper and salt to taste	2 tablespoon tomato paste 1 ½ cups vegetable broth
1 tablespoon chopped parsley 1 tablespoon olive oil	5 garlic cloves
½ medium yellow onion 4 large ripe tomatoes	

1. Preheat oven to 350oF.
2. Chop onion and tomatoes into thin wedges. Place on a rimmed baking sheet. Season with parsley, pepper, salt, and olive oil. Toss to combine well. Hide the garlic cloves inside tomatoes to keep it from burning.
3. Pop in the oven and bake for 30 minutes.
4. On medium pot, bring vegetable stock to a simmer. Add tomato paste.
5. Pour baked tomato mixture into pot. Continue simmering for another 10 minutes.
6. With an immersion blender, puree soup.
7. Adjust salt and pepper to taste before serving.

Nutrition: Calories: 179; Carbs: 26.7g; Protein: 5.2g; Fat: 7.7g

Superfast Cajun Asparagus (Spanish)

Preparation time: 10 minutes Cooking time: 8 minutes
Servings: 2

1 teaspoon Cajun seasoning	1 teaspoon Olive oil
1-pound asparagus	

1. Snap the asparagus and make sure that you use the tender part of the vegetable.
2. Place a large skillet on stovetop and heat on high for a minute.
3. Then grease skillet with cooking spray and spread asparagus in one layer.
4. Cover skillet and continue cooking on high for 5 to eight minutes.
5. Halfway through cooking time, stir skillet and then cover and continue to cook.
6. Once done cooking, transfer to plates, serve, and enjoy!

Nutrition: Calories: 81; Carbs: 0g; Protein: 0g; Fat: 9g

Nutritious Vegan Cabbage (Spanish)

Preparation Time: 35 minutes Cooking Time: 15 minutes
Servings: 6

3 cups green cabbage 1 can tomatoes	onion Cups vegetable broth 3 stalks celery
carrots 2 tbsp. vinegar	sage

1. Mix 1 tbsp. of lemon juice. 2 garlic cloves and the rest of in the instant pot and. Lid and set time for fifteen minutes on high pressure.
2. Release pressure naturally then remove the lid. Remove the soup from the instant pot.
3. Serve and enjoy.

Nutrition: 67 Calories 0.4g Fat 3.8g Fiber

Vegetable Soup Moroccan Style (Greek)

Prep time: 10 minutes Cooking time: 10 minutes Servings: 6

½ teaspoon pepper 1 teaspoon salt

2 oz whole wheat orzo

1large zucchini, peeled and cut into ¼-insh cubes 8 sprigs fresh cilantro, plus more leaves for garnish 12 sprigs flat leaf parsley, plus more for garnish

A pinch of saffron threads

2stalks celery leaves included, sliced thinly 2 carrots, diced

2 small turnips, peeled and diced 1 14-oz can dice tomatoes

6 cups water

1 lb. lamb stew meat, trimmed and cut into ½-inch cubes 2 teaspoon ground turmeric

1medium onion, diced finely

2tablespoon extra-virgin olive oil

1. On medium high fire, place a large Dutch oven and heat oil.
2. Add turmeric and onion, stir fry for two minutes.
3. Add meat and sauté for 5 minutes.
4. Add saffron, celery, carrots, turnips, tomatoes and juice, and water.
5. With a kitchen string, tie cilantro and parsley sprigs together and into pot.
6. Cover and bring to a boil. Once boiling reduce fire to a simmer and continue to cook for 45 to 50 minutes or until meat is tender.
7. Once meat is tender, stir in zucchini. Cover and cook for 8 mins.
8. Add orzo; cook for 10 minutes or until soft.
9. Remove and discard cilantro and parsley sprigs.
10. 1 Season with pepper and salt.
11. 1 Transfer to a serving bowl and garnish with cilantro and parsley leaves before serving.

Nutrition: Calories: 268; Carbs: 12.9g; Protein: 28.1g; Fat: 11.7g

Colorful Vegetable Medley (Spanish)

Prep Time: 10 minutes Cooking Time: 3 minutes Servings: 4

1 small head broccoli, broken into florets 16 asparagus, trimmed

1small head cauliflower, broken into florets 5 ounces green beans

2carrots, peeled and cut on the bias 1 cup of water

Salt to taste

1. Add water and set trivet on top of the water
2. Place steamer basket on top
3. Spread green beans, cauliflower, asparagus, carrots, broccoli in a steamer basket
4. Close the lid
5. Steam for 3 minutes on High
6. Release the pressure quickly
7. Season with salt
8. Serve and enjoy!

Nutrition Calories: 223 Fat: 21g Carbohydrates: 8g Protein: 3g

Veggie Ramen Miso Soup (Italian)

Preparation time: 5 minutes Cooking time: 20 minutes Servings: 1

2 teaspoons thinly sliced green onion A pinch of salt

½ teaspoon shoyu

2 tablespoon mellow white miso

1cup zucchini, cut into angel hair spirals

½ cup thinly sliced cremini mushrooms

½ medium carrot, cut into angel hair spirals 1/2 cup baby spinach leaves – optional

2¼ cups water

½ box of medium firm tofu, cut into ¼-inch cubes 1 hardboiled egg

1. In a small bowl, mix ¼ cup of water and miso. Set aside.
2. In a small saucepan on medium high fire, bring to a boil 2 cups water, mushrooms, tofu and carrots. Add salt, shoyu and miso mixture. Allow to boil for 5 minutes. Remove from fire and add green onion, zucchini and baby spinach leaves if using.
3. Let soup stand for 5 minutes before transferring to individual bowls. Garnish with ½ of hardboiled egg per bowl, serve and enjoy.

Nutrition: Calories: 335; Carbs: 19.0g; Protein: 30.6g; Fat: 17.6g

Yummy Cauliflower Fritters (Greek)

Preparation time: 10 minutes Cooking time: 15 minutes Servings: 6

1 large cauliflower head, cut into florets 2 eggs, beaten

½ teaspoon turmeric

½ teaspoon salt

¼ teaspoon black pepper 6 tablespoons coconut oil

1. Place the cauliflower florets in a pot with water.
2. Bring to a boil and drain once cooked.
3. Place the cauliflower, eggs, turmeric, salt, and pepper into the food processor.
4. Pulse until the mixture becomes coarse.
5. Transfer into a bowl. Using your hands, form six small flattened balls and place in the fridge for at least 1 hour until the mixture hardens.
6. Heat the oil in a skillet and fry the cauliflower patties for 3 minutes on each side
7. Place in individual containers.
8. Put a label and store in the fridge.
9. Allow to thaw at room temperature before heating in the microwave oven.

Nutrition: Calories per serving: 157; Carbs: 2.8g; Protein: 3.9g; Fat: 15.3g; Fiber: 0.9g

Vegetable Stew (Spanish)

Preparation Time: 10 minutes
Cooking Time: 45 minutes Servings: 4

1-pound potatoes, peeled and cut into bite-sized pieces 2 tablespoons coconut oil, unsalted	3 tablespoons olive oil 2 cups vegetable broth
2 carrots, peeled and chopped 3 celery stalks, chopped	2 onions, peeled and chopped
1 zucchini, cut into ½ inch thick slices 1 tablespoon paprika	1 tablespoon salt
1 teaspoon black pepper	A handful of fresh celery leaves

1. Warm oil on Sauté mode
2. Stir-fry onions for 3-4 minutes
3. Add celery, zucchini, carrots, and ¼ cup broth
4. Cook for 10 minutes more and keep stirring continuously
5. Stir in potatoes, cayenne pepper, bay leaves, remaining broth, celery leaves, salt and pepper
6. Close the lid
7. Cook at Meat/Stew for 30 minutes on High
8. Quick-release the pressure
9. Serve and enjoy!

Nutrition: Calories: 331 Fat: 14g Carbohydrates: 44g Protein: 17g

Asparagus with Feta (Greek)

Preparation Time: 10 minutes Cooking Time: 5 minutes
Servings: 4

1 cup feta cheese, cubed	1-pound asparagus spears end trimmed 1 tablespoon olive oil
1 cup of water 1 lemon	Salt and freshly ground black pepper, to taste

1. Add water into a pot and set trivet over the water
2. Place steamer basket on the trivet
3. Place the asparagus into the steamer basket
4. Close the lid
5. Cook for 1 minute on high pressure
6. Release the pressure quickly
7. Take a bowl and add olive oil into it
8. Toss in asparagus until well-coated
9. Season with pepper and salt
10. Serve with feta cheese and lemon
11. Enjoy!

Nutrition: Calories: 170 Fat: 18g Carbohydrates: 2g Protein: 3g

Rosemary Sweet Potato Medallions (Spanish)

Preparation Time: 10 minutes
Cooking Time: 18 minutes Servings: 4

4 sweet potatoes	2 tablespoons coconut oil 1 cup of water
1 tablespoon rosemary	1 teaspoon garlic powder Salt, to taste

1. Add water and place steamer rack over the water
2. Using a fork, prick sweet potatoes all over
3. Then set on a steamer rack
4. Close the lid and cook for 12 minutes on High pressure
5. Release the pressure quickly
6. Cut the sweet potatoes into ½ inch
7. Melt the coconut oil on Sauté mode
8. Add in the medallions
9. Cook each side for 2 to 3 minutes until browned
10. Season with salt and garlic powder
11. Add rosemary on top
12. Serve and enjoy!

Nutrition: Calories: 291 Fat: 10g Carbohydrates: 30g Protein: 5g

Garlic Eggplant Slices (Spanish)

Preparation time: 5 minutes Cooking time: 25 minutes
Serving: 4

1 egg	1 tablespoon water
½ cup whole wheat bread crumbs 1 teaspoon garlic powder	½ teaspoon dried oregano
½ teaspoon salt	½ teaspoon paprika
1 medium eggplant, sliced into ¼-inch-thick rounds 1 tablespoon olive oil	

1. Preheat the air fryer to 360°F (182°C).
2. In a medium shallow bowl, beat together the egg and water until frothy.
3. In a separate medium shallow bowl, mix together bread crumbs, garlic powder, oregano, salt, and paprika.
4. Dip each eggplant slice into the egg mixture, then into the bread crumb mixture, coating the outside with crumbs. Place the slices in a single layer in the bottom of the air fryer basket.
5. Drizzle the tops of the eggplant slices with the olive oil, then fry for 15 minutes. Turn each slice and cook for an additional 10 minutes.

Nutrition: calories: 137 | fat: 5g | protein: 5g | carbs: 19g | fiber: 5g | sodium: 409mg

Delicious Tomato Broth (Spanish)

Preparation Time: 10 minutes Cooking Time: 15 minutes
Servings: 2

14 oz can fire-roasted tomatoes	½ tsp dried basil
½ cup heavy cream	½ cup parmesan cheese, grated 1 cup cheddar cheese, grated
1 ½ cups vegetable stock	¼ cup zucchini, grated
½ tsp dried oregano Pepper	Salt

1. Add tomatoes, stock, zucchini, oregano, basil, pepper, and salt into the instant pot and stir well.
2. Seal pot and cook on high pressure for 5 minutes.
3. Release pressure using quick release. Remove lid.
4. Set pot on sauté mode. Add heavy cream, parmesan cheese, and cheddar cheese and stir well and cook until cheese is melted.
5. Serve and enjoy.

Nutrition: 460 Calories 35g Fat 24g Protein

Crispy Artichokes (Spanish)

Preparation time: 10 minutes Cooking time: 15 minutes
Serving: 2

1 large sweet potato (about 8 ounces / 227 g) 2 tablespoons extra-virgin olive oil, divided 1 cup chopped onion	1 large egg
1 garlic clove	1 cup old-fashioned rolled oats 1 tablespoon dried oregano
1 tablespoon balsamic vinegar	¼ teaspoon kosher salt
½ cup crumbled Gorgonzola cheese	

1. Using a fork, pierce the sweet potato all over and microwave on high for 4 to 5 minutes, until softened in the center. Cool slightly before slicing in half.
2. Meanwhile, in a large skillet over medium-high heat, heat 1 tablespoon of the olive oil. Add the onion and sauté for 5 minutes.
3. Spoon the sweet potato flesh out of the skin and put the flesh in a food processor. Add the cooked onion, egg, garlic, oats, oregano, vinegar and salt. Pulse until smooth. Add the cheese and pulse four times to barely combine.
4. Form the mixture into four burgers. Place the burgers on a plate, and press to flatten each to about ¾-inch thick.
5. Wipe out the skillet with a paper towel. Heat the remaining 1 tablespoon of the oil over medium-high heat for about 2 minutes. Add the burgers to the hot oil, then reduce the heat to medium. Cook the burgers for 5 minutes per side.
6. Transfer the burgers to a plate and serve.

Nutrition: calories: 290 | fat: 12g | protein: 12g | carbs: 43g | fiber: 8g | sodium: 566mg

Rosemary Roasted Red Potatoes (Greek)

Preparation time: 5 minutes Cooking time: 20 minutes
Serving: 6

1 pound (454 g) red potatoes, quartered	¼ cup olive oil
½ teaspoon kosher salt	¼ teaspoon black pepper 1 garlic clove, minced
4 rosemary sprigs	

1. Preheat the air fryer to 360ºF (182ºC).
2. In a large bowl, toss the potatoes with the olive oil, salt, pepper, and garlic until well coated.
3. Pour the potatoes into the air fryer basket and top with the sprigs of rosemary.
4. Roast for 10 minutes, then stir or toss the potatoes and roast for 10 minutes more.
5. Remove the rosemary sprigs and serve the potatoes. Season with additional salt and pepper, if needed.

Nutrition: calories: 133 | fat: 9g | protein: 1g | carbs: 12g | fiber: 1g | sodium: 199mg

Kate's Warm Mediterranean Farro Bowl (Italian)

Preparation time: 15 minutes Cooking time: 10 minutes
Servings: 4

1/3 cup extra-virgin olive oil	½ cup chopped red bell pepper 1/3 cup chopped red onions
2 garlic cloves, minced	1cup zucchini, cut in ½-inch slices
½ cup canned chickpeas, drained and rinsed	½ cup coarsely chopped artichokes 3 cups cooked farro
Salt	Freshly ground black pepper
¼ cup sliced olives, for serving (optional) 2tablespoons fresh basil, chiffonade, for serving (optional) 3 tablespoons balsamic reduction, for serving (optional)	½ cup crumbled feta cheese, for serving (optional)

1. In a large sauté pan or skillet, heat the oil over medium heat and sauté the pepper, onions, and garlic for about 5 minutes, until tender.
2. Add the zucchini, chickpeas, and artichokes, then stir and continue to sauté vegetables, approximately 5 more minutes, until just soft.
3. Stir in the cooked farro, tossing to combine and cooking enough to heat through. Season with salt and pepper and remove from the heat.
4. Transfer the contents of the pan into the serving vessels or bowls.
5. Top with olives, feta, and basil (if using). Drizzle with balsamic reduction (if using) to finish.

Nutrition: Calories: 530; Carbs: 95.4g; Protein: 8.0g; Fat: 13.5g

Savoy Cabbage with Coconut Cream Sauce (Spanish)

Prep time: 5 minutes Cooking time: 20 minutes Servings: 4

1tablespoons olive oil 1 onion, chopped	2cloves of garlic, minced
1 head savoy cabbage, chopped finely 2 cups bone broth	1cup coconut milk, freshly squeezed 1 bay leaf
Salt and pepper to taste	2tablespoons chopped parsley

1. Heat oil in a pot for 2 minutes.
2. Stir in the onions, bay leaf, and garlic until fragrant, around 3 minutes.
3. Add the rest of the , except for the parsley and mix well.
4. Cover pot, bring to a boil, and let it simmer for 5 minutes or until cabbage is tender to taste.
5. Stir in parsley and serve.

Nutrition: Calories: 195; Carbs: 12.3g; Protein: 2.7g; Fat: 19.7g

Slow Cooked Buttery Mushrooms (Spanish)

Prep time: 10 minutes Cooking time: 10 minutes Servings: 2

2 tablespoons butter	2tablespoons olive oil
3cloves of garlic, minced	16 ounces fresh brown mushrooms, sliced 7 ounces fresh shiitake mushrooms, sliced A dash of thyme
Salt and pepper to taste	

1. Heat the butter and oil in a pot.
2. Sauté the garlic until fragrant, around 1 minute.
3. Stir in the rest of the and cook until soft, around 9 minutes.

Nutrition: Calories: 192; Carbs: 12.7g; Protein: 3.8g; Fat: 15.5g

Steamed Zucchini-Paprika (Italian)

Preparation time: 15 minutes Cooking time: 30 minutes Servings: 2

4 tablespoons olive oil	3 cloves of garlic, minced 1 onion, chopped
3 medium-sized zucchinis, sliced thinly A dash of paprika	Salt and pepper to taste

1. Place all in the Instant Pot.
2. Give a good stir to combine all .
3. Close the lid and make sure that the steam release valve is set to "Venting."
4. Press the "Slow Cook" button and adjust the cooking time to 4 hours.
5. Halfway through the cooking time, open the lid and give a good stir to brown the other side.

Nutrition: Calories: 93; Carbs: 3.1g; Protein: 0.6g; Fat: 10.2g

Steamed Squash Chowder (Spanish)

Preparation time: 20 minutes Cooking time: 40 minutes Servings: 4

3 cups chicken broth 2 tablespoon ghee	1teaspoon chili powder
½ teaspoon cumin 1 ½ teaspoon salt	2teaspoon cinnamons 3 tablespoon olive oil 2 carrots, chopped
1 small yellow onion, chopped 1 green apple, sliced and cored	1 large butternut squash, peeled, seeded, and chopped to ½-inch cubes

1. In a large pot on medium high fire, melt ghee.
2. Once ghee is hot, sauté onions for 5 minutes or until soft and translucent.
3. Add olive oil, chili powder, cumin, salt, and cinnamon. Sauté for half a minute.
4. Add chopped squash and apples.
5. Sauté for 10 minutes while stirring once in a while.
6. Add broth, cover and cook on medium fire for twenty minutes or until apples and squash are tender.
7. With an immersion blender, puree chowder. Adjust consistency by adding more water.
8. Add more salt or pepper depending on desire.
9. Serve and enjoy.

Nutrition: Calories: 228; Carbs: 17.9g; Protein: 2.2g; Fat: 18.0g

Stir Fried Brussels Sprouts and Carrots(Spanish)

Preparation time: 10 minutes Cooking time: 15 minutes Servings: 6

1 tablespoon cider vinegar 1/3 cup water	1 lb. Brussels sprouts, halved lengthwise
1lb. carrots cut diagonally into ½-inch thick lengths 3 tablespoon unsalted butter, divided	2tablespoon chopped shallot
½ teaspoon pepper	¾ teaspoon salt

1. On medium high fire, place a nonstick medium fry pan and heat 2 tablespoon butter.
2. Add shallots and cook until softened, around one to two minutes while occasionally stirring.
3. Add pepper salt, Brussels sprouts and carrots. Stir fry until vegetables starts to brown on the edges, around 3 to 4 minutes.
4. Add water, cook and cover.
5. After 5 to 8 minutes, or when veggies are already soft, add remaining butter.
6. If needed season with more pepper and salt to taste.
7. Turn off fire, transfer to a platter, serve and enjoy.

Nutrition: Calories: 98; Carbs: 13.9g; Protein: 3.5g; Fat: 4.2g

Stir Fried Eggplant (Spanish)

Preparation time: 10 minutes Cooking time: 30 minutes
Servings: 2

1teaspoon cornstarch + 2 tablespoon water, mixed 1 teaspoon brown sugar	2tablespoon oyster sauce 1 tablespoon fish sauce
2 tablespoon soy sauce	½ cup fresh basil 2 tablespoon oils
¼ cup water	2 cups Chinese eggplant, spiral 1 red chili
6 cloves garlic, minced	½ purple onion, sliced thinly
13-oz package medium firm tofu, cut into slivers	

1. Prepare sauce by mixing cornstarch and water in a small bowl. In another bowl mix brown sugar, oyster sauce and fish sauce and set aside.
2. On medium high fire, place a large nonstick saucepan and heat 2 tablespoon oil. Sauté chili, garlic and onion for 4 minutes. Add tofu, stir fry for 4 minutes.
3. Add eggplant noodles and stir fry for 10 minutes. If pan dries up, add water in small amounts to moisten pan and cook noodles.
4. Pour in sauce and mix well. Once simmering, slowly add cornstarch mixer while continuing to mix vigorously. Once sauce thickens add fresh basil and cook for a minute.
5. Remove from fire, transfer to a serving plate and enjoy.

Nutrition: Calories: 369; Carbs: 28.4g; Protein: 11.4g; Fat: 25.3g

Grilled Eggplant Rolls (Spanish)

Preparation Time: 30 minutes Cooking Time: 10 minutes
Servings: 5

1large eggplants	4 ounces goat cheese 1 cup ricotta
¼ cup fresh basil, finely chopped	

1. Slice the tops of the eggplants off and cut the eggplants lengthwise into
1. ¼-inch-thick slices. Sprinkle the slices with the salt and place the eggplant in a colander for 15 to 20 minutes.
2. In a large bowl, combine the goat cheese, ricotta, basil, and pepper.
3. Preheat a grill, grill pan, or lightly oiled skillet on medium heat. Pat the eggplant slices dry using paper towel and lightly spray with olive oil spray. Place the eggplant on the grill, grill pan or skillet and cook for 3 minutes on each side.
4. Take out the eggplant from the heat and let cool for 5 minutes.
5. To roll, lay one eggplant slice flat, place a tablespoon of the cheese mixture at the base of the slice, and roll up. Serve immediately or chill until serving.

Nutrition: 255 Calories 15g Protein 19g Carbohydrates

Sweet Chickpea and Mushroom Stew (Spanish)

Preparation Time: 10 minutes Cooking Time: 8 minutes
Servings: 4

½ tablespoon button mushrooms, chopped 1 cup chickpeas, cooked	2 carrots, chopped
2 garlic cloves, crushed 4 cherry tomatoes	1onion, peeled and chopped
A handful of string beans, trimmed 1 apple, cut into 1-inch cubes	½ cup raisins
A handful of fresh mint 1 teaspoon ginger, grated	½ cup orange juice, squeezed
½ teaspoon salt	

1. Place all in your instant pot
2. Pour water to cover
3. Cook on High pressure for 8 minutes
4. Quick-release the pressure over 10 minutes
5. Serve and enjoy!

Nutrition: Calories: 222 Fat: 7g Carbohydrates: 35g Protein: 8g

Instant Pot Horta and Potatoes (Spanish)

Preparation Time: 12 minutes Cooking Time: 17 minutes
Servings: 4

1heads of washed and chopped greens (spinach, Dandelion, kale, mustard green, Swiss chard)	6 potatoes (washed and cut in pieces) 1 cup virgin olive oil
1 lemon juice (reserve slices for serving)	10 garlic cloves (chopped)

1. Position all the in the instant pot and lid setting the vent to sealing.
2. Set time for fifteen minutes. When time is done release pressure.
3. Let the potatoes rest for some time. Serve and enjoy with lemon slices.

Nutrition: 499 Calories 18g Protein 41g Carbohydrates

Instant Pot Jackfruit Curry (Spanish)

Preparation Time: 1 hour Cooking Time: 16 minutes Servings: 2

1 tbsp. oil	Cumin seeds, Mustard seeds 2 tomatoes (purred)
20 oz. can green jackfruit (drained and rinsed)	1 tbsp. coriander powder, turmeric.

1. Turn the instant pot to sauté mode. Add cumin seeds, mustard, ten nigella seeds and allow them to sizzle.
2. Add 2 red chilies and 2 bay leaves and allow cooking for a few seconds.
3. Add chopped 1 onion, 5 garlic cloves, ginger and salt, and pepper to taste. Stir cook for five minutes.
4. Add other and a cup of water then lid the instant pot. Set time for seven minutes on high pressure.
5. When the time has elapsed release pressure naturally, shred the jackfruit and serve.

Nutrition: 369 Calories 3g Fat 6g Fiber

Mozzarella Eggplants (Italian)

Preparation Time: 20 minutes Cooking Time: 40 minutes
Servings: 4

1large eggplants	2tomatoes
3Mozzarella balls	1 tablespoon olive oil 1 teaspoon salt

1. Trim the eggplants and make the cross cuts to get the Hasselback eggplants.
2. Sprinkle the vegetables with salt.
3. After this, slice the tomatoes and Mozzarella balls.
4. Fill the eggplant cuts with Mozzarella and tomatoes and sprinkle with olive oil.
5. Then wrap every eggplant in foil.
6. Bake the vegetables for 40 minutes at 375F.
7. Discard the foil from the eggplants and cut them on 4 servings (1/2 part of eggplant = 1 serving).

Nutrition: calories 195, fat 11.2, fiber 10.8, carbs 19.7, protein 8.5

Greek Style Beans (Greek)

Preparation Time: 10 minutes Cooking Time: 10 hours and 40 minutes Servings: 8

3 cups white beans 1/4 cup olive oil	1 onion, diced
1 clove garlic, peeled	28 oz. canned crushed tomatoes

1. Pour 8 cups of water into the Instant Pot. Add the white beans.
2. Season with a pinch of salt.
3. Let the beans soak for up to 10 hours.
4. Seal the pot. Set it to manual. Choose bean/chili function.
5. Adjust time to 15 minutes at high pressure. Release the pressure naturally.
6. Transfer the white beans into a bowl and set aside.
7. Take 1 cup of the cooking liquid and set aside.
8. Drain the remaining liquid.
9. Press the sauté setting. Heat the olive oil.
10. Cook the onion, garlic and tomatoes for 5 minutes.
11. Add the reserved cooking liquid and the tomatoes.
12. Put the beans back. Stir well. Secure the pot.
13. Choose bean/chili function for 5 minutes at high pressure.
14. Release the pressure naturally.
15. Season with salt and pepper.

Nutrition: Calories 352; Total Fat 7g; Saturated Fat 1.1g; Cholesterol 0mg; Sodium 203mg; Total Carbohydrate 55g; Dietary Fiber 15g; Total Sugars 7.7g; Protein 20.3g; Potassium 1381mg

Simple Baked Okra (Spanish)

Preparation Time: 20 minutes Cooking Time: 10 minutes
Servings: 2

8 oz okra, chopped	½ teaspoon ground black pepper
½ teaspoon salt	1 tablespoon olive oil

1. Line the baking tray with foil.
2. Place the okra in the tray in one layer.
3. Sprinkle the vegetables with ground black pepper and salt Mix up well.
4. Then drizzle the okra with olive oil.
5. Roast the vegetables in the preheated to the 375F oven for 10 minutes.
6. Stir the okra with the help of spatula every 3 minutes.

Nutrition: calories 107, fat 7.2, fiber 3.8, carbs 8.8, protein 2.3

Greek Stuffed Collard Greens (Greek)

Preparation Time: 10 minutes Cooking Time: 20 minutes
Servings: 4

1 (28-ounce) can low-sodium or no-salt-added crushed tomatoes	8 collard green leaves (about 1/3 pound), tough tips of stems cut off
1recipe Mediterranean Lentils and Rice or 2 (10-ounce) bags frozen grain medley (about 4 cups), cooked	2tablespoons grated Parmesan cheese

1. Preheat the oven to 400°F. Pour the tomatoes into a baking pan and set aside.
2. Fill a large stockpot about three-quarters of the way with water and bring to a boil. Add the collard greens and cook for 2 minutes. Drain in a colander. Put the greens on a clean towel or paper towels and blot dry.
3. To assemble the stuffed collards, lay one leaf flat on the counter vertically. Add about ½ cup of the lentils and rice mixture to the middle of the leaf, and spread it evenly along the middle of the leaf. Fold one long side of the leaf over the rice filling, then fold over the other long side so it is slightly overlapping. Take the bottom end, where the stem was, and gently but firmly roll up until you have a slightly square package. Carefully transfer the stuffed leaf to the baking pan, and place it seam-side down in the crushed tomatoes. Repeat with the remaining leaves.
4. Sprinkle the leaves with the grated cheese, and cover the pan with aluminum foil. Bake for 20 minutes, or until the collards are tender- firm, and serve. (If you prefer softer greens, bake for an additional 10 minutes.)

Nutrition: Calories: 205 Total Fat: 8g Saturated Fat: 2g Cholesterol: 3mg Sodium: 524mg Total Carbohydrates: 34g Fiber: 8g Protein: 6g

Chickpea & Lentil Salad (Greek)

Preparation Time: 10 minutes
Cooking Time: 3 Hours And 50 minutes Servings: 4

1 1/2 cups dried chickpeas, rinsed and drained 1 cup green lentils	1 teaspoon herbs de Provence 2 cups vegetable broth
12 oz. cherry tomatoes, sliced in half	

1. Combine the chickpeas, 2 cups water and 1 tablespoon olive oil in the Instant Pot.
2. Mix well.
3. Choose manual mode.
4. Cook at high pressure for 38 minutes.
5. Drain the chickpeas and set aside.
6. Add the lentils, vegetable broth and seasoning.
7. Press slow cook.
8. Adjust time to 3 hours.
9. Toss the lentils, tomatoes and chickpeas in a salad bowl.

Nutrition: Calories 508; Total Fat 8.4g; Saturated Fat 1.1g; Cholesterol 0mg; Sodium 432mg; Total Carbohydrate 78.3g; Dietary Fiber 30g; Total Sugars 11.8g; Protein 31.9g; Potassium 1419mg

Leek and Garlic Cannellini Beans (Greek)

Preparation Time: 15 minutes
Cooking Time: 22 minutes Servings: 4

1-pound cannellini beans, soaked overnight 1 onion, peeled and chopped	2 large leeks, finely chopped 3 garlic cloves, whole
1 teaspoon pepper	1 teaspoon salt
4 tablespoons vegetables oil, for toppings 2 tablespoons flour, for toppings	1 tablespoon cayenne pepper, for toppings

1. Add all except the topping's into your instant pot
2. Press Manual/Pressure Cook
3. Cook for 20 minutes on High
4. Take a skillet and heat 4 tablespoons oil
5. Then add cayenne pepper and flour
6. Stir-fry for 2 minutes and keep them aside
7. Once done, quick release the pressure
8. Pour in the cayenne mixture and give it a good stir
9. Let it sit for 15 minutes before you serve
10. Serve and enjoy!

Nutrition: Calories: 148 Fat: 5g Carbohydrates: 20g Protein: 7g

Butter Potatoes (Spanish)

Preparation Time: 10 minutes Cooking Time: 30 minutes
Servings: 6

1.5-pound finger potatoes	1tablespoon dried rosemary 3 tablespoons butter, softened 1 teaspoon salt

1. Wash the finger potatoes well.
2. With the help of the big knife crush every potato.
3. Place the crushed potatoes in the tray and sprinkle with salt and dried rosemary. Mix up well.
4. Bake the finger potatoes for 30 minutes at 375F. The cooked potatoes will be soft and have a light crust.

Nutrition: calories 158, fat 6, fiber 2.7, carbs 24.3, protein 2.9

Chapter 7
<u>Poultry and Meats</u>

<u>Herbed-Mustard-Coated Pork Tenderloin</u>

Prep time: 10 minutes | Cook time: 15 minutes | Serves 4

3 tablespoons fresh rosemary leaves
¼ cup Dijon mustard
½ cup fresh parsley leaves
6 garlic cloves
½ teaspoon sea salt
¼ teaspoon freshly ground black pepper
1 tablespoon extra-virgin olive oil
1 (1½-pound / 680-g) pork tenderloin

1. Preheat the oven to 400°F (205°C).
2. Put all the , except for the pork tenderloin, in a food processor. Pulse until it has a thick consistency.
3. Put the pork tenderloin on a baking sheet, then rub with the mixture to coat well.
4. Put the sheet in the preheated oven and bake for 15 minutes or until the internal temperature of the pork reaches at least 165°F (74°C). Flip the tenderloin halfway through the cooking time.
5. Transfer the cooked pork tenderloin to a large plate and allow to cool for 5 minutes before serving.

Per Serving calories: 363 | fat: 18.1g | protein: 2.2g | carbs: 4.9g | fiber: 2.0g | sodium: 514mg

<u>Macadamia Pork</u>

Prep time: 10 minutes | Cook time: 10 minutes | Serves 4

1 (1-pound / 454-g) pork tenderloin, cut into ½-inch slices and pounded thin
1 teaspoon sea salt, divided
¼ teaspoon freshly ground black pepper, divided
½ cup macadamia nuts
1 cup unsweetened coconut milk
1 tablespoon extra-virgin olive oil

1. Preheat the oven to 400°F (205°C).
2. On a clean work surface, rub the pork with ½ teaspoon of the salt and ⅛ teaspoon of the ground black pepper. Set aside. Ground the macadamia nuts in a food processor, then combine with remaining salt and black pepper in a bowl. Stir to mix well and set aside.
3. Combine the coconut milk and olive oil in a separate bowl. Stir to mix well.
4. Dredge the pork chops into the bowl of coconut milk mixture, then dunk into the bowl of macadamia nut mixture to coat well. Shake the excess off.
5. Put the well-coated pork chops on a baking sheet, then bake for 10 minutes or until the internal temperature of the pork reaches at least 165°F (74°C).
6. Transfer the pork chops to a serving plate and serve immediately.

Per Serving calories: 436 | fat: 32.8g | protein: 33.1g | carbs: 5.9g | fiber: 3.0g | sodium: 310mg

<u>Grilled Chicken and Zucchini Kebabs</u>

Prep time: 10 minutes | Cook time: 20 minutes | Serves 4

¼ cup extra-virgin olive oil
2 tablespoons balsamic vinegar
1 teaspoon dried oregano, crushed between your fingers
1 pound (454 g) boneless, skinless chicken breasts, cut into 1½-inch pieces
2 medium zucchinis, cut into 1-inch pieces
½ cup Kalamata olives, pitted and halved
2 tablespoons olive brine
¼ cup torn fresh basil leaves
Nonstick cooking spray

Special Equipment:
14 to 15 (12-inch) wooden skewers, soaked for at least 30 minutes

1. Spray the grill grates with nonstick cooking spray. Preheat the grill to medium-high heat.
2. In a small bowl, whisk together the olive oil, vinegar, and oregano. Divide the marinade between two large plastic zip-top bags.
3. Add the chicken to one bag and the zucchini to another. Seal and massage the marinade into both the chicken and zucchini.
4. Thread the chicken onto 6 wooden skewers. Thread the zucchini onto 8 or 9 wooden skewers.
5. Cook the kebabs in batches on the grill for 5 minutes, flip, and grill for 5 minutes more, or until any chicken juices run clear.
6. Remove the chicken and zucchini from the skewers to a large serving bowl. Toss with the olives, olive brine, and basil and serve.

Per Serving
calories: 283 | fat: 15.0g | protein: 11.0g | carbs: 26.0g | fiber: 3.0g | sodium: 575mg

<u>Almond-Crusted Chicken Tenders with Honey</u>

Prep time: 10 minutes | Cook time: 20 minutes | Serves 4

1 tablespoon honey
1 tablespoon whole-grain or Dijon mustard
¼ tbsp freshly ground black pepper
¼ teaspoon kosher or sea salt
1 pound (454 g) boneless, skinless chicken breast tenders or tenderloins
1 cup almonds, roughly chopped
Nonstick cooking spray

1. Preheat the oven to 425°F (220°C). Line a large, rimmed baking sheet with parchment paper. Place a wire cooling rack on the parchment-lined baking sheet, and spray the rack well with nonstick cooking spray.
2. In a large bowl, combine the honey, mustard, pepper, and salt. Add the chicken and toss gently to coat. Set aside.
3. Dump the almonds onto a large sheet of parchment paper and spread them out. Press the coated chicken tenders into the nuts until evenly coated on all sides. Place the chicken on the prepared wire rack.
4. Bake in the preheated oven for 15 to 20 minutes, or until the internal temperature of the chicken measures 165°F (74°C) on a meat thermometer and any juices run clear.
5. Cool for 5 minutes before serving.

Per Serving calories: 222 | fat: 7.0g | protein: 11.0g | carbs: 29.0g | fiber: 2.0g | sodium: 448mg

Parsley-Dijon Chicken and Potatoes

Prep time: 5 minutes | Cook time: 22 minutes | Serves 6

1 tablespoon extra-virgin olive oil	1 cup low-sodium or no-salt-added chicken broth
1½ pounds (680 g) boneless, skinless chicken thighs, cut into 1-inch cubes, patted dry	1 tablespoon Dijon mustard
1½ pounds (680 g) Yukon Gold potatoes, unpeeled, cut into ½-inch cubes	¼ teaspoon freshly ground black pepper
2 garlic cloves, minced	¼ teaspoon kosher or sea salt
¼ cup dry white wine	1 cup chopped fresh flat-leaf (Italian) parsley, including stems
	1 tablespoon freshly squeezed lemon juice

1. In a large skillet over medium-high heat, heat the oil. Add the chicken and cook for 5 minutes, stirring only after the chicken has browned on one side. Remove the chicken and reserve on a plate.
2. Add the potatoes to the skillet and cook for 5 minutes, stirring only after the potatoes have become golden and crispy on one side. Push the potatoes to the side of the skillet, add the garlic, and cook, stirring constantly, for 1 minute. Add the wine and cook for 1 minute, until nearly evaporated. Add the chicken broth, mustard, salt, pepper, and reserved chicken. Turn the heat to high and bring to a boil. Once boiling, cover, reduce the heat to medium-low, and cook for 10 to 12 minutes, until the potatoes are tender and the internal temperature of the chicken measures 165°F (74°C) on a meat thermometer and any juices run clear. During the last minute of cooking, stir in the parsley. Remove from the heat, stir in the lemon juice, and serve.

Per Serving calories: 324 | fat: 9.0g | protein: 16.0g | carbs: 45.0g | fiber: 5.0g | sodium: 560mg

Chicken Bruschetta Burgers

Prep time: 10 minutes | Cook time: 16 minutes | Serves 2

1 tablespoon olive oil	8 ounces (227 g) ground chicken breast
2 garlic cloves, minced	
3 tablespoons finely minced onion	¼ teaspoon salt
1 teaspoon dried basil	3 pieces small Mozzarella balls, minced
3 tablespoons minced sun-dried tomatoes packed in olive oil	

1. Heat the olive oil in a nonstick skillet over medium-high heat. Add the garlic and onion and sauté for 5 minutes until tender. Stir in the basil. Remove from the skillet to a medium bowl. Add the tomatoes, ground chicken, and salt and stir until incorporated. Mix in the Mozzarella balls.
2. Divide the chicken mixture in half and form into two burgers, each about ¾-inch thick.
3. Heat the same skillet over medium-high heat and add the burgers. Cook each side for 5 to 6 minutes, or until they reach an internal temperature of 165°F (74°C).
4. Serve warm.

Per Serving calories: 300 | fat: 17.0g | protein: 32.2g | carbs: 6.0g | fiber: 1.1g | sodium: 724mg

Grilled Pork Chops

Prep time: 20 minutes | Cook time: 10 minutes | Serves 4

¼ cup extra-virgin olive oil	1 teaspoon salt
2 tablespoons fresh thyme leaves	4 pork loin chops, ½-inch-thick
1 teaspoon smoked paprika	

1. In a small bowl, mix together the olive oil, thyme, paprika, and salt. Put the pork chops in a plastic zip-top bag or a bowl and coat them with the spice mix. Let them marinate for 15 minutes.
2. Preheat the grill to high heat. Cook the pork chops for 4 minutes on each side until cooked through. Serve warm.

Per Serving calories: 282 | fat: 23.0g | protein: 21.0g | carbs: 1.0g | fiber: 0g | sodium: 832mg

Potato Lamb and Olive Stew

Prep time: 20 minutes | Cook time: 3 hours 42 minutes | Serves 10

4 tablespoons almond flour	Coarse sea salt and black pepper, to taste
¾ cup low-sodium chicken stock	3½ pounds (1.6 kg) lamb shanks, fat trimmed and cut crosswise into 1½-inch pieces
1¼ pounds (567 g) small potatoes, halved	
3 cloves garlic, minced	2 tablespoons extra-virgin olive oil
4 large shallots, cut into ½-inch wedges	
3 sprigs fresh rosemary	½ cup dry white wine
1 tablespoon lemon zest	1 cup pitted green olives, halved
	2 tablespoons lemon juice

1. Combine 1 tablespoon of almond flour with chicken stock in a bowl. Stir to mix well. Put the flour mixture, potatoes, garlic, shallots, rosemary, and lemon zest in the slow cooker. Sprinkle with salt and black pepper. Stir to mix well. Set aside.
2. Combine the remaining almond flour with salt and black pepper in a large bowl, then dunk the lamb shanks in the flour and toss to coat.
3. Heat the olive oil in a nonstick skillet over medium-high heat until shimmering.
4. Add the well-coated lamb and cook for 10 minutes or until golden brown. Flip the lamb pieces halfway through the cooking time. Transfer the cooked lamb to the slow cooker.
5. Pour the wine in the same skillet, then cook for 2 minutes or until it reduces in half. Pour the wine in the slow cooker.
6. Put the slow cooker lid on and cook on high for 3 hours and 30 minutes or until the lamb is very tender.
7. In the last 20 minutes of the cooking, open the lid and fold in the olive halves to cook.
8. Pour the stew on a large plate, let them sit for 5 minutes, then skim any fat remains over the face of the liquid.
9. Drizzle with lemon juice and sprinkle with salt and pepper. Serve warm.

Per Serving

calories: 309 | fat: 10.3g | protein: 36.9g | carbs: 16.1g | fiber: 2.2g | sodium: 239mg

Slow Cook Lamb Shanks with Cannellini Beans Stew

Prep time: 20 minutes | Cook time: 10 hours 15 minutes | Serves 12

1 (19-ounce / 539-g) can cannellini beans, rinsed and drained
1 large yellow onion, chopped
2 medium-sized carrots, diced
1 large stalk celery, chopped
2 cloves garlic, thinly sliced
4 (1½-pound / 680-g) lamb shanks, fat trimmed
2 teaspoons tarragon
½ teaspoon sea salt
¼ teaspoon ground black pepper
1 (28-ounce / 794-g) can diced tomatoes, with the juice

1. Combine the beans, onion, carrots, celery, and garlic in the slow cooker. Stir to mix well.
2. Add the lamb shanks and sprinkle with tarragon, salt, and ground black pepper.
3. Pour in the tomatoes with juice, then cover the lid and cook on high for an hour.
4. Reduce the heat to low and cook for 9 hours or until the lamb is super tender.
5. Transfer the lamb on a plate, then pour the bean mixture in a colander over a separate bowl to reserve the liquid.
6. Let the liquid sit for 5 minutes until set, then skim the fat from the surface of the liquid. Pour the bean mixture back to the liquid.
7. Remove the bones from the lamb heat and discard the bones. Put the lamb meat and bean mixture back to the slow cooker. Cover and cook to reheat for 15 minutes or until heated through.
8. Pour them on a large serving plate and serve immediately.

Per Serving
calories: 317 | fat: 9.7g | protein: 52.1g | carbs: 7.0g | fiber: 2.1g | sodium: 375mg

Beef Kebabs with Onion and Pepper

Prep time: 15 minutes | Cook time: 10 minutes | Serves 6

2 pounds (907 g) beef fillet
1½ teaspoons salt
1 teaspoon freshly ground black pepper
½ teaspoon ground nutmeg
½ teaspoon ground allspice
⅓ cup extra-virgin olive oil
1 large onion, cut into 8 quarters
1 large red bell pepper, cut into 1-inch cubes

1. Preheat the grill to high heat.
2. Cut the beef into 1-inch cubes and put them in a large bowl.
3. In a small bowl, mix together the salt, black pepper, allspice, and nutmeg.
4. Pour the olive oil over the beef and toss to coat. Evenly sprinkle the seasoning over the beef and toss to coat all pieces.
5. Skewer the beef, alternating every 1 or 2 pieces with a piece of onion or bell pepper.
6. To cook, place the skewers on the preheated grill, and flip every 2 to 3 minutes until all sides have cooked to desired doneness, 6 minutes for medium-rare, 8 minutes for well done. Serve hot.

Per Serving calories: 485 | fat: 36.0g | protein: 35.0g | carbs: 4.0g | fiber: 1.0g | sodium: 1453mg

Greek-Style Lamb Burgers

Prep time: 10 minutes | Cook time: 10 minutes | Serves 4

1 pound (454 g) ground lamb
½ teaspoon salt
½ teaspoon freshly ground black pepper
4 tablespoons crumbled feta cheese
Buns, toppings, and tzatziki, for serving (optional)

1. Preheat the grill to high heat. In a large bowl, using your hands, combine the lamb with the salt and pepper.
2. Divide the meat into 4 portions. Divide each portion in half to make a top and a bottom. Flatten each half into a 3-inch circle. Make a dent in the center of one of the halves and place 1 tablespoon of the feta cheese in the center. Place the second half of the patty on top of the feta cheese and press down to close the 2 halves together, making it resemble a round burger. Grill each side for 3 minutes, for medium-well. Serve on a bun with your favorite toppings and tzatziki sauce, if desired.

Per Serving calories: 345 | fat: 29.0g | protein: 20.0g | carbs: 1.0g | fiber: 0g | sodium: 462mg

Chicken Cacciatore

Prep time: 15 minutes | Cook time: 1 hour and 30 minutes | Serves 2

1½ pounds (680 g) bone-in chicken thighs, skin removed and patted dry
Salt, to taste
2 tablespoons olive oil
½ large onion, thinly sliced
4 ounces (113 g) baby bella mushrooms, sliced
1 red sweet pepper, cut into 1-inch pieces
1 (15-ounce / 425-g) can crushed fire-roasted tomatoes
1 fresh rosemary sprig
½ cup dry red wine
1 teaspoon Italian herb seasoning
½ teaspoon garlic powder
3 tablespoons flour

1. Season the chicken thighs with a generous pinch of salt.
2. Heat the olive oil in a Dutch oven over medium-high heat. Add the chicken and brown for 5 minutes per side.
3. Add the onion, mushrooms, and sweet pepper to the Dutch oven and sauté for another 5 minutes.
4. Add the tomatoes, rosemary, wine, Italian seasoning, garlic powder, and salt, stirring well.
5. Bring the mixture to a boil, then reduce the heat to low. Allow to simmer slowly for at least 1 hour, stirring occasionally, or until the chicken is tender and easily pulls away from the bone.
6. Measure out 1 cup of the sauce from the pot and put it into a bowl. Add the flour and whisk well to make a slurry.
7. Increase the heat to medium-high and slowly whisk the slurry into the pot. Stir until it comes to a boil and cook until the sauce is thickened.
8. Remove the chicken from the bones and shred it, and add it back to the sauce before serving, if desired.

Per Serving calories: 520 | fat: 23.1g | protein: 31.8g | carbs: 37.0g | fiber: 6.0g | sodium: 484mg

Chicken Gyros with Tzatziki Sauce

Prep time: 15 minutes | Cook time: 10 minutes | Serves 2

2 tbsp freshly squeezed lemon juice	1 small zucchini, cut into ½-inch strips lengthwise
2 tbsp olive oil, divided, plus more for oiling the grill	½ red pepper, seeded and cut in half lengthwise
1 tbsp minced fresh oregano	½ English cucumber, peeled and minced
½ teaspoon garlic powder	¾ cup plain Greek yogurt
Salt, to taste	1 tbsp minced fresh dill
8 ounces (227 g) chicken tenders	2 (8-inch) pita breads
1 small eggplant, cut into 1-inch strips lengthwise	

1. Combine the lemon juice, 1 tablespoon of olive oil, oregano, garlic powder, and salt in a medium bowl. Add the chicken and let marinate for 30 minutes.
2. Place the eggplant, zucchini, and red pepper in a large mixing bowl and sprinkle with salt and the remaining 1 tablespoon of olive oil. Toss well to coat. Let the vegetables rest while the chicken is marinating.
3. Make the tzatziki sauce: Combine the cucumber, yogurt, salt, and dill in a medium bowl. Stir well to incorporate and set aside in the refrigerator.
4. When ready, preheat the grill to medium-high heat and oil the grill grates.
5. Drain any liquid from the vegetables and put them on the grill.
6. Remove the chicken tenders from the marinade and put them on the grill.
7. Grill the chicken and vegetables for 3 minutes per side, or until the chicken is no longer pink inside.
8. Remove the chicken and vegetables from the grill and set aside. On the grill, heat the pitas for about 30 seconds, flipping them frequently.
9. Divide the chicken tenders and vegetables between the pitas and top each with ¼ cup of the prepared sauce. Roll the pitas up like a cone and serve.

Per Serving

calories: 586 | fat: 21.9g | protein: 39.0g | carbs: 62.0g | fiber: 11.8g | sodium: 955mg

Spiced Roast Chicken

Prep time: 10 minutes | Cook time: 35 minutes | Serves 6

1 teaspoon garlic powder	½ teaspoon salt
1 teaspoon ground paprika	¼ tbsp. ground cayenne pepper
½ teaspoon ground cumin	6 chicken legs
½ tbsp. ground coriander	1 teaspoon extra-virgin olive oil

1. Preheat the oven to 400°F (205°C).
2. Combine the garlic powder, paprika, cumin, coriander, salt, and cayenne pepper in a small bowl.
3. On a clean work surface, rub the spices all over the chicken legs until completely coated.
4. Heat the olive oil in an ovenproof skillet over medium heat.
5. Add the chicken thighs and sear each side for 8 to 10 minutes, or until the skin is crispy and browned.
6. Transfer the skillet to the preheated oven and continue cooking for 10 to 15 minutes, or until the juices run clear and it registers an internal temperature of 165°F (74°C).
7. Remove from the heat and serve on plates.

Per Serving

calories: 275 | fat: 15.6g | protein: 30.3g | carbs: 0.9g | fiber: 0g | sodium: 255mg

Crispy Pesto Chicken

Prep time: 15 minutes | Cook time: 50 minutes | Serves 2

12 ounces (340 g) small red potatoes (3 or 4 potatoes), scrubbed and diced into 1-inch pieces	½ teaspoon garlic powder
	¼ teaspoon salt
1 tablespoon olive oil	1 (8-ounce / 227-g) boneless, skinless chicken breast
	3 tablespoons prepared pesto

1. Preheat the oven to 425°F (220°C). Line a baking sheet with parchment paper.
2. Combine the potatoes, olive oil, garlic powder, and salt in a medium bowl. Toss well to coat.
3. Arrange the potatoes on the parchment paper and roast for 10 minutes. Flip the potatoes and roast for an additional 10 mins.
4. Meanwhile, put the chicken in the same bowl and toss with the pesto, coating the chicken evenly.
5. Check the potatoes to make sure they are golden brown on the top and bottom. Toss them again and add the chicken breast to the pan.
6. Turn the heat down to 350°F (180°C) and roast the chicken and potatoes for 30 minutes. Check to make sure the chicken reaches an internal temperature of 165°F (74°C) and the potatoes are fork-tender.
7. Let cool for 5 minutes before serving.

Per Serving

calories: 378 | fat: 16.0g | protein: 29.8g | carbs: 30.1g | fiber: 4.0g | sodium: 425mg

Greek Beef Kebabs

Prep time: 15 minutes | Cook time: 20 minutes | Serves 2

6 ounces (170 g) beef sirloin tip, trimmed of fat and cut into 2-inch pieces	¼ cup freshly squeezed lemon juice
	2 tbsp balsamic vinegar
3 cups of any mixture of vegetables: mushrooms, summer squash, zucchini, onions, red peppers, cherry tomatoes	2 teaspoons dried oregano
	1 teaspoon garlic powder
	1 teaspoon salt
	1 tbsp minced fresh rosemary
½ cup olive oil	Cooking spray

1. Put the beef in a plastic freezer bag.
2. Slice the vegetables into similar-size pieces and put them in a second freezer bag.
3. Make the marinade: Mix the olive oil, lemon juice, balsamic vinegar, oregano, garlic powder, salt, and rosemary in a measuring cup. Whisk well to combine. Pour half of the marinade over the beef, and the other half over the vegetables.
4. Put the beef and vegetables in the refrigerator to marinate for 4 hours.
5. When ready, preheat the grill to medium-high heat and spray the grill grates with cooking spray.
6. Thread the meat onto skewers and the vegetables onto separate skewers.
7. Grill the meat for 3 minutes per side. They should only take 10 to 12 minutes to cook, depending on the thickness of the meat.
8. Grill the vegetables for about 3 minutes per side, or until they have grill marks and are softened. Serve hot.

Per Serving calories: 284 | fat: 18.2g | protein: 21.0g | carbs: 9.0g | fiber: 3.9g | sodium: 122mg

Beef Stew with Beans and Zucchini

Prep time: 20 minutes | Cook time: 6 to 8 hours | Serves 2

1 (15-ounce / 425-g) can diced or crushed tomatoes with basil	Pinch freshly ground black pepper
¼ teaspoon salt	¾ cup dry red wine
1 teaspoon beef base	¼ cup minced brined olives
2 tbsp olive oil, divided	1 fresh rosemary sprig
8 ounces (227 g) baby bella (cremini) mushrooms, quartered	1 (15-ounce / 425-g) can white cannellini beans, drained and rinsed
2 garlic cloves, minced	1 medium zucchini, cut in half lengthwise and then cut into 1-inch pieces.
½ large onion, diced	
1 pound (454 g) cubed beef stew meat	3 tablespoons flour

1. Place the tomatoes into a slow cooker and set it to low heat. Add the beef base and stir to incorporate.
2. Heat 1 tablespoon of olive oil in a large sauté pan over medium heat. Add the mushrooms and onion and sauté for 10 minutes, stirring occasionally, or until they're golden. Add the garlic and cook for 30 seconds more. Transfer the vegetables to the slow cooker.
3. In a plastic food storage bag, combine the stew meat with the flour, salt, and pepper. Seal the bag and shake well to combine. Heat the remaining 1 tablespoon of olive oil in the sauté pan over high heat.
4. Add the floured meat and sear to get a crust on the outside edges. Deglaze the pan by adding about half of the red wine and scraping up any browned bits on the bottom. Stir so the wine thickens a bit and transfer to the slow cooker along with any remaining wine.
5. Stir the stew to incorporate the. Stir in the olives and rosemary, cover, and cook for 6 to 8 hours on Low. About 30 minutes before the stew is finished, add the beans and zucchini to let them warm through. Serve warm.

Per Serving calories: 389 | fat: 15.1g | protein: 30.8g | carbs: 25.0g | fiber: 8.0g | sodium: 582mg

Grilled Lemon Chicken

Prep time: 10 minutes | Cook time: 12 to 14 minutes | Serves 2

1 (4-ounce / 113-g) boneless, skinless chicken breasts	1 teaspoon dried basil
	1 teaspoon paprika
	½ teaspoon dried thyme
Marinade:	¼ teaspoon salt
4 tablespoons freshly squeezed lemon juice	¼ teaspoon garlic powder
	2 tablespoons olive oil, plus more for greasing the grill grates

1. Make the marinade: Whisk together the lemon juice, olive oil, basil, paprika, thyme, salt, and garlic powder in a large bowl until well combined.
2. Add the chicken breasts to the bowl and let marinate for at least 30 minutes.
3. When ready to cook, preheat the grill to medium-high heat. Lightly grease the grill grates with the olive oil.
4. Discard the marinade and arrange the chicken breasts on the grill grates.
5. Grill for 12 to 14 minutes, flipping the chicken halfway through, or until a meat thermometer inserted in the center of the chicken reaches 165°F (74°C).
6. Let the chicken cool for 5 minutes and serve warm.

Per Serving
calories: 251 | fat: 15.5g | protein: 27.3g | carbs: 1.9g | fiber: 1.0g | sodium: 371mg

Gyro Burgers with Tahini Sauce

Prep time: 15 minutes | Cook time: 10 minutes | Serves 4

2 tablespoons extra-virgin olive oil	1 medium green bell pepper, halved and seeded
1 tablespoon dried oregano	2 tablespoons tahini or peanut butter
1¼ teaspoons garlic powder, divided	1 tablespoon hot water (optional)
1 teaspoon ground cumin	½ cup plain Greek yogurt
½ teaspoon freshly ground black pepper	1 tablespoon freshly squeezed lemon juice
¼ teaspoon kosher or sea salt	1 cup thinly sliced red onion
1 pound (454 g) beef flank steak, top round steak, or lamb leg steak, center cut, about 1 inch thick	4 (6-inch) whole-wheat pita breads, warmed
	Nonstick cooking spray

1. Set an oven rack about 4 inches below the broiler element. Preheat the oven broiler to high. Line a large, rimmed baking sheet with aluminum foil. Place a wire cooling rack on the foil, and spray the rack with nonstick cooking spray. Set aside.
2. In a small bowl, whisk together the olive oil, oregano, 1 teaspoon of garlic powder, cumin, pepper, and salt. Rub the oil mixture on all sides of the steak, reserving 1 teaspoon of the mixture. Place the steak on the prepared rack. Rub the remaining oil mixture on the bell pepper, and place on the rack, cut-side down. Press the pepper with the heel of your hand to flatten.
3. Broil for 5 minutes. Flip the steak and the pepper pieces, and broil for 2 to 5 minutes more, until the pepper is charred and the internal temperature of the meat measures 145°F (63°C) on a meat thermometer. Put the pepper and steak on a cutting board to rest for 5 minutes.
4. Meanwhile, in a small bowl, whisk the tahini until smooth (adding 1 tablespoon of hot water if your tahini is sticky). Add the remaining ¼ teaspoon of garlic powder and the yogurt and lemon juice, and whisk thoroughly.
5. Slice the steak crosswise into ¼-inch-thick strips. Slice the bell pepper into strips. Divide the steak, bell pepper, and onion among the warm pita breads. Drizzle with tahini sauce and serve.

Per Serving
calories: 348 | fat: 15.0g | protein: 33.0g | carbs: 20.0g | fiber: 3.0g | sodium: 530mg

Beef, Tomato, and Lentils Stew

Prep time: 10 minutes | Cook time: 10 minutes | Serves 4

1 tablespoon extra-virgin olive oil	1 (14-ounce / 397-g) can lentils, drained
1 onion, chopped	½ teaspoon sea salt
1 (14-ounce / 397-g) can chopped tomatoes with garlic and basil, drained	⅛ tbsp. freshly ground black pepper
	1 pound (454 g) extra-lean ground beef

1. Heat the olive oil in a pot over medium-high heat until shimmering.
2. Add the beef and onion to the pot and sauté for 5 minutes or until the beef is lightly browned.
3. Add the remaining. Bring to a boil. Reduce the heat to medium and cook for 4 more minutes or until the lentils are tender. Keep stirring during the cooking.
4. Pour them in a large serving bowl and serve immediately.

Per Serving calories: 460 | fat: 14.8g | protein: 44.2g | carbs: 36.9g | fiber: 17.0g | sodium: 320mg

Quick Chicken Salad Wraps

Prep time: 15 minutes | Cook time: 0 minutes | Serves 2

Tzatziki Sauce:
½ cup plain Greek yogurt
1 tablespoon freshly squeezed lemon juice
Pinch garlic powder
1 teaspoon dried dill
Salt and freshly ground black pepper, to taste

Salad Wraps:
2 (8-inch) whole-grain pita bread
1 cup shredded chicken meat
2 cups mixed greens
2 roasted red bell peppers, thinly sliced
½ English cucumber, peeled if desired and thinly sliced
¼ cup pitted black olives
1 scallion, chopped

1. Make the tzatziki sauce: In a bowl, whisk together the yogurt, lemon juice, garlic powder, dill, salt, and pepper until creamy and smooth.
2. Make the salad wraps: Place the pita bread on a clean work surface and spoon ¼ cup of the tzatziki sauce onto each piece of pita bread, spreading it all over. Top with the shredded chicken, mixed greens, red pepper slices, cucumber slices, black olives, finished by chopped scallion.
3. Roll the salad wraps and enjoy.

Per Serving
calories: 428 | fat: 10.6g | protein: 31.1g | carbs: 50.9g | fiber: 6.0g | sodium: 675mg

Roasted Chicken Thighs With Basmati Rice

Prep time: 15 minutes | Cook time: 50 to 55 minutes | Serves 2

Chicken:
½ teaspoon cumin
½ teaspoon cinnamon
½ teaspoon paprika
¼ teaspoon ginger powder
¼ teaspoon garlic powder
¼ teaspoon coriander
¼ teaspoon salt
⅛ teaspoon cayenne pepper

10 ounces (284 g) boneless, skinless chicken thighs (about 4 pieces)
Rice:
1 tablespoon olive oil
½ small onion, minced
½ cup basmati rice 2 pinches saffron
1 cup low-sodium chicken stock
¼ teaspoon salt

Make the Chicken
1. Preheat the oven to 350°F (180°C).
2. Combine the cumin, cinnamon, paprika, ginger powder, garlic powder, coriander, salt, and cayenne pepper in a small bowl. Using your hands to rub the spice mixture all over the chicken thighs.
3. Transfer the chicken thighs to a baking dish. Roast in the preheated oven for 35 to 40 minutes, or until the internal temperature reaches 165°F (74°C) on a meat thermometer.

Make the Rice
4. Meanwhile, heat the olive oil in a skillet over medium-high heat. Sauté the onion for 5 minutes until fragrant, stirring occasionally.
5. Stir in the basmati rice, saffron, chicken stock, and salt. Reduce the heat to low, cover, and bring to a simmer for 15 minutes, until light and fluffy.
6. Remove the chicken from the oven to a plate and serve with the rice.

Per Serving calories: 400 | fat: 9.6g | protein: 37.2g | carbs: 40.7g | fiber: 2.1g | sodium: 714mg

Panko Grilled Chicken Patties

Prep time: 10 minutes | Cook time: 8 to 10 minutes | Serves 4

1 pound (454 g) ground chicken
3 tbsp crumbled feta cheese
3 tablespoons finely chopped red pepper
¼ cup finely chopped red onion
3 tbsp panko bread crumbs
1 garlic clove, minced
1 tbsp chopped fresh oregano
¼ teaspoon salt
⅛ teaspoon freshly ground black pepper
Cooking spray

1. Mix together the ground chicken, feta cheese, red pepper, red onion, bread crumbs, garlic, oregano, salt, and black pepper in a large bowl, and stir to incorporate.
2. Divide the chicken mixture into 8 equal portions and form each portion into a patty with your hands.
3. Preheat a grill to medium-high heat and oil the grill grates with cooking spray.
4. Arrange the patties on the grill grates and grill each side for 4 to 5 minutes, or until the patties are cooked through.
5. Rest for 5 minutes before serving.

Per Serving calories: 241 | fat: 13.5g | protein: 23.2g | carbs: 6.7g | fiber: 1.1g | sodium: 321mg

Sautéed Ground Turkey with Brown Rice

Prep time: 20 minutes | Cook time: 45 minutes | Serves 2

1 tablespoon olive oil
½ medium onion, minced
2 garlic cloves, minced
8 ounces (227 g) ground turkey breast
½ cup chopped roasted red peppers, (about 2 jarred peppers)
¼ cup sun-dried tomatoes, minced
1¼ cups low-sodium chicken stock
½ cup brown rice
1 tbsp dried oregano Salt, to taste
2 cups lightly packed baby spinach

1. In a skillet, heat the olive oil over medium heat. Sauté the onion for 5 minutes, stirring occasionally.
2. Stir in the garlic and sauté for 30 seconds more until fragrant.
3. Add the turkey breast and cook for about 7 minutes, breaking apart with a wooden spoon, until the turkey is no longer pink.
4. Stir in the roasted red peppers, tomatoes, chicken stock, brown rice, and oregano and bring to a boil.
5. When the mixture starts to boil, cover, and reduce the heat to medium-low. Bring to a simmer until the rice is tender, stirring occasionally, about 30 minutes. Sprinkle with the salt.
6. Add the baby spinach and keep stirring until wilted.
7. Remove from the heat and serve warm.

Per Serving
calories: 445 | fat: 16.8g | protein: 30.2g | carbs: 48.9g | fiber: 5.1g | sodium: 662mg

Tender & Juicy Lamb Roast (Greek)

Prep Time: 10 minutes Cooking Time: 8 hours Servings: 8

4 lbs. lamb roast, boneless
4 garlic cloves, cut into slivers
½ teaspoon marjoram
¼ teaspoon pepper
½ teaspoon thyme
1 teaspoon oregano
2 teaspoon salts

1. Using a sharp knife make small cuts all over meat then insert garlic slivers into the cuts.
2. In a small bowl, mix together marjoram, thyme, oregano, pepper, and salt and rub all over lamb roast.
3. Place lamb roast into the slow cooker.
4. Cover and cook on low for 8 hours. Serve and enjoy.

Nutrition: Calories 605 Fat 48 g Carbohydrates 0.7 g Sugar 1 g Protein 36 g Cholesterol 160 mg

Yogurt Chicken Breasts

Prep time: 10 minutes | Cook time: 10 minutes | Serves 4

1 pound (454 g) boneless, skinless chicken breasts, cut into 2-inch strips	Pinch saffron (3 or 4 threads)
1 tablespoon extra-virgin olive oil	3 garlic cloves, minced
	½ onion, chopped
Yogurt Sauce:	2 tablespoons chopped fresh cilantro
½ cup plain Greek yogurt	Juice of ½ lemon
2 tablespoons water	½ teaspoon salt

1. Make the yogurt sauce: Place the yogurt, water, saffron, garlic, onion, cilantro, lemon juice, and salt in a blender, and pulse until completely mixed.
2. Transfer the yogurt sauce to a large bowl, along with the chicken strips. Toss to coat well.
3. Cover with plastic wrap and marinate in the refrigerator for at least 1 hour, or up to overnight.
4. When ready to cook, heat the olive oil in a large skillet over medium heat.
5. Add the chicken strips to the skillet, discarding any excess marinade. Cook each side for 5 minutes, or until cooked through.
6. Let the chicken cool for 5 minutes before serving.

Per Serving

calories: 154 | fat: 4.8g | protein: 26.3g | carbs: 2.9g | fiber: 0g | sodium: 500mg

Coconut Chicken Tenders

Prep time: 10 minutes | Cook time: 15 to 20 minutes | Serves 6

4 chicken breasts, each cut lengthwise into 3 strips	½ cup coconut flour
	2 eggs
½ teaspoon salt	2 tablespoons unsweetened plain almond milk
¼ teaspoon freshly ground black pepper	1 cup unsweetened coconut flakes

1. Preheat the oven to 400°F (205°C). Line a baking sheet with parchment paper.
2. On a clean work surface, season the chicken with salt and pepper.
3. In a small bowl, add the coconut flour. In a separate bowl, whisk the eggs with almond milk until smooth. Place the coconut flakes on a plate.
4. One at a time, roll the chicken strips in the coconut flour, then dredge them in the egg mixture, shaking off any excess, and finally in the coconut flakes to coat.
5. Arrange the coated chicken pieces on the baking sheet. Bake in the preheated oven for 15 to 20 minutes, flipping the chicken halfway through, or until the chicken is golden brown and cooked through.
6. Remove from the oven and serve on plates.

Per Serving

calories: 215 | fat: 12.6g | protein: 20.2g | carbs: 8.9g | fiber: 6.1g | sodium: 345mg

Baked Teriyaki Turkey Meatballs

Prep time: 20 minutes | Cook time: 20 minutes | Serves 6

1 pound (454 g) lean ground turkey	2 tablespoons reduced-sodium tamari or gluten-free soy sauce
1 egg, whisked	
¼ cup finely chopped scallions, both white and green parts	1 teaspoon grated fresh ginger
	1 tablespoon honey
2 garlic cloves, minced	2 teaspoons mirin
	1 teaspoon olive oil

1. Preheat the oven to 400°F (205°C). Line a baking sheet with parchment paper and set aside.
2. Mix together the ground turkey, whisked egg, scallions, garlic, tamari, ginger, honey, mirin, and olive oil in a large bowl, and stir until well blended.
3. Using a tablespoon to scoop out rounded heaps of the turkey mixture, and then roll them into balls with your hands. Transfer the balls to the prepared baking sheet.
4. Bake in the preheated oven for 20 minutes, flipping the balls with a spatula halfway through, or until the meatballs are browned and cooked through.
5. Serve warm.

Per Serving

calories: 158 | fat: 8.6g | protein: 16.2g | carbs: 4.0g | fiber: 0.2g | sodium: 269mg

Lamb Tagine with Couscous and Almonds

Prep time: 15 minutes | Cook time: 7 hours 7 minutes | Serves 6

2 tablespoons almond flour	¼ teaspoon crushed saffron threads
Juice and zest of 1 navel orange	
	1 teaspoon ground cumin
2 tablespoons extra-virgin olive oil	¼ teaspoon ground red pepper flakes
2 pounds (907 g) boneless lamb leg, fat trimmed and cut into 1½-inch cubes	½ teaspoon sea salt
	2 tablespoons raw honey
½ cup low-sodium chicken stock	1 cup pitted dates
	3 cups cooked couscous, for serving
2 large white onions, chopped	
1 teaspoon pumpkin pie spice	2 tablespoons toasted slivered almonds, for serving

1. Combine the almond flour with orange juice in a large bowl. Stir until smooth, then mix in the orange zest. Set aside.
2. Heat the olive oil in a nonstick skillet over medium-high heat until shimmering.
3. Add the lamb cubes and sauté for 7 minutes or until lightly browned.
4. Pour in the flour mixture and chicken stock, then add the onions, pumpkin pie spice, saffron, cumin, ground red pepper flakes, and salt. Stir to mix well.
5. Pour them in the slow cooker. Cover and cook on low for 6 hours or until the internal temperature of the lamb reaches at least 145°F (63°C).
6. When the cooking is complete, mix in the honey and dates, then cook for another an hour.
7. Put the couscous in a tagine bowl or a large bowl, then top with lamb mixture. Scatter with slivered almonds and serve immediately.

Per Serving

calories: 447 | fat: 10.2g | protein: 36.3g | carbs: 53.5g | fiber: 4.9g | sodium: 329mg

Chermoula Roasted Pork Tenderloin

Prep time: 15 minutes | Cook time: 20 minutes | Serves 2

½ cup fresh cilantro	2 teaspoons cumin
½ cup fresh parsley	1 teaspoon smoked paprika
6 small garlic cloves	½ teaspoon salt, divided
3 tablespoons olive oil, divided	Pinch freshly ground black pepper
3 tablespoons freshly squeezed lemon juice	1 (8-ounce / 227-g) pork tenderloin

1. Preheat the oven to 425°F (220°C).
2. In a food processor, combine the cilantro, parsley, garlic, 2 tablespoons of olive oil, lemon juice, cumin, paprika, and ¼ teaspoon of salt. Pulse 15 to 20 times, or until the mixture is fairly smooth. Scrape the sides down as needed to incorporate all the . Transfer the sauce to a small bowl and set aside.
3. Season the pork tenderloin on all sides with the remaining ¼ teaspoon of salt and a generous pinch of black pepper.
4. Heat the remaining 1 tablespoon of olive oil in a sauté pan.
5. Sear the pork for 3 minutes, turning often, until golden brown on all sides.
6. Transfer the pork to a baking dish and roast in the preheated oven for 15 minutes, or until the internal temperature registers 145°F (63°C).
7. Cool for 5 minutes before serving.

Per Serving

calories: 169 | fat: 13.1g | protein: 11.0g | carbs: 2.9g | fiber: 1.0g | sodium: 332mg

Lamb Kofta (Spiced Meatballs)

Prep time: 15 minutes | Cook time: 30 minutes | Serves 2

¼ cup walnuts	¼ teaspoon cumin
1 garlic clove	¼ teaspoon allspice
½ small onion	¼ teaspoon salt
1 roasted piquillo pepper	Pinch cayenne pepper
2 tablespoons fresh mint	8 ounces (227 g) lean ground lamb
2 tablespoons fresh parsley	

1. Preheat the oven to 350°F (180°C). Line a baking sheet with aluminum foil.
2. In a food processor, combine the walnuts, garlic, onion, roasted pepper, mint, parsley, cumin, allspice, salt, and cayenne pepper. Pulse about 10 times to combine everything.
3. Transfer the spice mixture to a large bowl and add the ground lamb. With your hands or a spatula, mix the spices into the lamb.
4. Roll the lamb into 1½-inch balls (about the size of golf balls).
5. Arrange the meatballs on the prepared baking sheet and bake for 30 minutes, or until cooked to an internal temperature of 165°F (74°C).
6. Serve warm.

Per Serving

calories: 409 | fat: 22.9g | protein: 22.0g | carbs: 7.1g | fiber: 3.0g | sodium: 428mg

Beef, Artichoke & Mushroom Stew (Italian)

Preparation Time: 20 minutes Cooking Time: 2 hours and 15 minutes Servings: 6

For Beef Marinade:1 onion, chopped	1 garlic clove, crushed
2tablespoons fresh thyme, hopped	½ cup dry red wine2 tablespoons tomato puree
2 tablespoons olive oil	1teaspoon cayenne pepper
Pinch of salt and ground black pepper	1½ pounds beef stew meat, cut into large chunks For Stew:2tablespoons olive oil
2 tablespoons all-purpose flour½ cup water	½ cup dry red wine12 ounces jar artichoke hearts, drained and cut into small chunks
4 ounces button mushrooms, sliced	
Salt and ground black pepper, as required	

1. For marinade: in a large bowl, add all the except the beef and mix well.
2. Add the beef and coat with the marinade generously.
3. Refrigerate to marinate overnight.
4. Remove the beef from bowl, reserving the marinade.
5. In a large pan, heat the oil and sear the beef in 2 batches for about 5 minutes or until browned.
6. With a slotted spoon, transfer the beef into a bowl.
7. In the same pan, add the reserved marinade, flour, water and wine and stir to combine.
8. Stir in the cooked beef and bring to a boil.
9. Reduce the heat to low and simmer, covered for about 2 hours, stirring occasionally.
10. Stir in the artichoke hearts and mushrooms and simmer for about 30 minutes.
11. Stir in the salt and black pepper and bring to a boil over high heat.
12. Remove from the eat ad serve hot.

Nutrition: Calories 367 Total Fat 16.6 g Saturated Fat 4 g Cholesterol 101mg Total Carbs 9.6 g Sugar 2.2 g Fiber 3.1 g Sodium 292 mg Potassium 624 mg Protein 36.7 g

Ground Beef, Tomato, and Kidney Bean Chili

Prep time: 10 minutes | Cook time: 15 minutes | Serves 4

1 tbsp extra-virgin olive oil	2 (28-ounce / 794-g) cans chopped tomatoes, juice reserved
1 pound (454 g) extra-lean ground beef	Chili Spice:
1 onion, chopped	1 teaspoon garlic powder
2 (14-ounce / 397-g) cans kidney beans	1 tablespoon chili powder
	½ teaspoon sea salt

1. Heat the olive oil in a pot over medium-high heat until shimmering.
2. Add the beef and onion to the pot and sauté for 5 minutes or until the beef is lightly browned and the onion is translucent.
3. Add the remaining. Bring to a boil. Reduce the heat to medium and cook for 10 more minutes. Keep stirring during the cooking.
4. Pour them in a large serving bowl and serve immediately.

Per Serving

calories: 891 | fat: 20.1g | protein: 116.3g | carbs: 62.9g | fiber: 17.0g | sodium: 561mg

Slow Cooker Mediterranean Beef Stew (Greek)

Prep Time: 10 minutes Cooking Time: 10 hours Servings: 10

Beef meat (for stew) 3 pounds Beef broth 2 cups	Baby mushrooms 16 ounces Garlic, minced 10 cloves Chopped onion 1 large
Dried rosemary 2 tablespoons Tomato sauce 15 ounces Balsamic vinegar ½ cup	Diced tomatoes in a can 14½ ounces Jar capers, drained 2 ounces Drained black olives 6 ounces
Salt ½ tbsp. Pepper ½ tbsp	

1. Put all the except the for garnishing in a 6-quart slow cooker and combine.
2. Cover the cooker and slow cook for 10 hours.
3. Add pepper and salt as required.
4. Garnish with parmesan and chopped parsley while serving.

Nutrition: Calories: 273 Carbohydrate: 16g Protein: 33g Sugars: 6gFat: 9g Sodium: 931mg

Slow Cooker Meatloaf Recipe (Spanish)

Prep Time: 10 mins Cooking Time: 6 hours and 10 mins Servings: 8

Ground bison - 2 pounds Grated zucchini - 1	Eggs – 2 large
Olive oil cooking spray – as required Zucchini, shredded - 1	Parsley, fresh, finely chopped - ½ cup Parmesan cheese, shredded - ½ cup Balsamic vinegar - 3 tablespoons Garlic, grated - 4 cloves
Onion minced, dry - 2 tablespoons Dried oregano - 1 tablespoon Ground black pepper - ½ teaspoon Kosher salt - ½ teaspoon Shredded Mozzarella cheese - ¼ cup Ketchup without sugar - ¼ cup Freshly chopped parsley - ¼ cup	For the topping:

1. Stripe line the inside of a six-quart slow cooker with aluminum foil.
2. Spray non-stick cooking oil over it.
3. In a large bowl combine ground bison or extra-lean ground sirloin, zucchini, eggs, parsley, balsamic vinegar, garlic, dried oregano, sea or kosher salt, minced dry onion, and ground black pepper.
4. Transfer this mixture into the slow cooker and form an oblong shaped loaf.
5. Cover the cooker, set on a low heat and cook for 6 hours.
6. After cooking, open the cooker and spread ketchup all over the meatloaf.
7. Now, place the cheese above the ketchup as a new layer and close the slow cooker.
8. Let the meatloaf sit on these two layers for about 10 minutes or until the cheese starts to melt.
9. Garnish with fresh parsley, and shredded Mozzarella cheese.

Nutrition: Calories: 320 Carbohydrate: 4g Protein: 26g Sugars: 2g Fat: 20g Dietary Fiber: 1g Cholesterol: 131mg Sodium: 403mg Potassium: 507mg

Beef & Tapioca Stew (Greek)

Preparation Time: 20 minutes Cooking Time: 1 hour and 45 minutes Servings: 8

1tablespoon olive oil	2 pounds boneless beef chuck roast, cut into ¾-inch cubes
1 (14½-ounce) can diced tomatoes with juice 3cups sweet potato, peeled and cubed 2 medium onions, cut into thin wedges 2 cups prunes, pitted 2 tbsp ground cinnamon	¼ cup quick-cooking tapioca 1 tablespoon honey ¼ teaspoon garlic powder Ground black pepper, as required¼ cup red wine vinegar 2 cups beef broth

1. In a Dutch oven, heat 1 tablespoon of oil over medium-high heat and sear the beef cubes in 2 batches for bout 4-5 minutes or until browned.
2. Drain off the grease from the pan.
3. Stir in the tomatoes, tapioca, honey, cinnamon, garlic powder, black pepper, vinegar and broth and bring to a boil.
4. Reduce the heat to low and simmer, covered for about 1 hour, stirring occasionally.
5. Stir in the onions and sweet potato and simmer, covered for about 20-30 minutes.
6. Stir in the prunes and cook for about 3-5 minutes.
7. Serve hot.

Nutrition: Calories 675 Total Fat34. 1 g Saturated Fat 13 g Cholesterol 117 mg Total Carbs 59.6 g Sugar 26 g Fiber 7.1 g Sodium 295 mg Potassium 1150 mg Protein 34.1 g

Pork Ribs with Barbecue Sauce (Spanish)

Preparation time: 5 minutes Cooking time: 15 minutes Servings: 6

3 pounds of pork ribs in portions 1 cup of water	1 cup of ketchup
½ cup of water	½ cup vinegar
¼ cup chopped onion	¼ cup sugar
1 teaspoon salt	1 teaspoon chili powder 1 teaspoon celery seeds

1. Put the ribs and water in the pot. Close and secure the lid. Place the pressure regulator on the vent tube and cook 5 minutes once the pressure regulator begins to rock slowly. Cool the pot quickly. Drain the liquid.
2. Mix the remaining and pour them over the ribs in the pot. Stir to cover the ribs.
3. Close and secure the lid. Place the pressure regulator on the vent tube and cook 10 minutes once the pressure regulator begins to rock slowly.
4. Let the pressure decrease on its own. Remove the ribs. Boil the sauce, without the lid, until the desired consistency is achieved.

Nutrition: Calories: 427, Carbohydrates: 0g, Fat: 27g, Protein: 47g, Sugar: 0g, Cholesterol: 107mg

Lemon Beef (Spanish)

Preparation Time: 10 minutes Cooking Time: 6 hours
Servings: 4

1 lb. beef chuck roast 1 fresh lime juice	1 garlic clove, crushed
1 teaspoon chili powder 1/2 teaspoon salt	2 cups lemon-lime soda

1. Place beef chuck roast into the slow cooker.
2. Season roast with garlic, chili powder, and salt.
3. Pour lemon-lime soda over the roast.
4. Cover slow cooker with lid and cook on low for 6 hours. Shred the meat using fork.
5. Add lime juice over shredded roast and serve.

Nutrition: Calories 355 Fat 16.8 g Carbohydrates 14 g Sugar 11.3 g Protein 35.5 g Cholesterol 120 mg

Easy Pork Kabobs (Greek)

Preparation Time: 10 minutes
Cooking Time: 4 hours 20 minutes
Servings: 6

1 lbs. pork tenderloin, cut into 1-inch cubes	1 onion, chopped
½ cup olive oil	2 tablespoon fresh parsley, chopped
½ cup red wine vinegar Pepper Salt	2 garlic cloves, chopped

1. In a large zip-lock bag, mix together red wine vinegar, parsley, garlic, onion, and oil.
2. Add meat to bag and marinate in the refrigerator for overnight.
3. Remove marinated pork from refrigerator and thread onto soaked wooden skewers. Season with pepper and salt.
4. Preheat the grill over high heat.
5. Grill pork for 3-4 minutes on each side.
6. Serve and enjoy.

Nutrition: Calories 375 Fat 22 g Carbohydrates 2.5 g Sugar 1 g Protein 40 g Cholesterol 110 mg

Herb Pork Roast (Spanish)

Preparation Time: 10 minutes
Cooking Time: 14 hours Servings: 10

4lbs. pork roastboneless or bone-in 1 tablespoon dry herb mix	4 garlic clovescut into slivers 1 tablespoon salt

1. Using a sharp knife make small cuts all over meat then insert garlic slivers into the cuts.
2. In a small bowl, mix together Italian herb mix and salt and rub all over pork roast.
3. Place pork roast in the crock pot.
4. Cover and cook on low for 14 hours.
5. Remove meat from crock pot and shred using a fork.
6. Serve and enjoy.

Nutrition: Calories 327 Fat 8 g Carbohydrates 0.5 g Sugar 0 g Protein 59 g Cholesterol 166 mg

Roasted Pork Meat (Spanish)

Preparation time: 5 minutes Cooking time: 55 minutes
Servings: 6

3 pounds of roast pork Salt and pepper 1 sliced onion	1 tablespoon vegetable oil 2 cups of water

1. Pour vegetable oil into the pot. Brown the pork on both sides in medium pressure over medium heat and then remove from the pot.
2. Pour the water into the pot. Put the pork on the rack of the pot. Season with salt, pepper and sliced onions.
3. Close and secure the lid. Place the pressure regulator on the vent tube and cook 55 minutes once the pressure regulator begins to rock slowly. Let the pressure decrease on its own.

Nutrition: Calories: 483, Carbohydrates: 0g, Fat: 27g, Protein: 53g, Cholesterol: 171mg,

Apricot Pork Meat (Spanish)

Preparation time: 5 minutes Cooking time: 60 minutes
Servings: 8

3 pounds boneless rolled pork	½ cup ketchup
½ cup teriyaki sauce	1/3 Cup of canned apricots
¼ cup cider vinegar	¼ cup dark brown sugar, packaged 1 teaspoon of paprika
1 teaspoon dried mustard ¼ teaspoon black pepper 1 large onion sliced	2 cups of water

1. Put the creed meat in a large plastic bag or glass dish. Combine ketchup, teriyaki sauce, canned food, vinegar, brown sugar, paprika, mustard and pepper. Mix together and pour over pork. Refrigerate overnight.
2. Remove the pork from the marinade and keep the marinade. Brown pork on both sides in the pressure cooker over medium heat. Remove pork from the pot.
3. Put the cooking rack, half of the sliced onion and the water inside the pot. Put the pork on the rack of the pot and distribute the remaining onion evenly over the meat. Close and secure the lid.
4. Place the pressure regulator on the vent tube and cook 60 minutes once the pressure regulator begins to rock slowly.
5. Let the pressure decrease on its own. Put in a saucepan the marinade that it kept and boil until it thickens, stirring occasionally.
6. Remove the meat and onions from the pressure cooker. Add onions to the thickened marinade and serve with sliced pork. Onions can be stepped on before adding to the sauce and served with rice, if desired.

Nutrition: Calories: 332, Carbohydrates: 0g, Fat: 13g, Protein: 47g, Sugar: 0g, Cholesterol: 77mg

Pork Loin with Pineapple Glaze (Spanish)

Preparation time: 10 minutes Cooking time: 35 minutes
Servings: 8

Mix to macerate:	½ cup kosher salt
½ cup light brown sugar, compact	1 tablespoon black peppercorns
1 tablespoon coriander seeds 4 bay leaves	1pork loin (clean and fat free (approx. 3½ pounds, 1¾ kg) 5 garlic cloves finely chopped
2tablespoons olive oil	1 pound (½ kg) peeled pearl onion
2 teaspoons chopped fresh rosemary 2 teaspoons chopped fresh thyme½ teaspoon freshly ground black pepper	½ cup dry white wine1½ cups of pineapple juice

1. To macerate the pork, mix the kosher salt, brown sugar, peppercorns, coriander seeds and bay leaves with 2 cups of warm water, in a bowl, until the salt dissolves. Pour 6 cups of cold water. Add the pork (it must be completely submerged in the liquid), cover and refrigerate overnight.
2. Mix the garlic, 2 tablespoons of olive oil, rosemary, and thyme and ground black pepper in the 1-Quart Mixing Bowl. Remove the pork from the mixture where you mashed it and dry it with paper towels (discard the liquid). Cover it completely with the herbal mixture.
3. Preheat the pot at medium-high temperature for about 3 minutes. The temperature is correct when, when spraying a few drops of water, they bounce off the surface without evaporating. Place the pork, reduce the temperature to medium and seal for about 4 minutes, or until golden brown. Turn it carefully and seal for another 4 minutes, or until it is golden.
1. Reduce the temperature to low, cover with the closed valve, and cook for about 20 minutes, or until the pork is fully cooked. Transfer it to a tray and set aside.
2. Pour the wine into the same pot and let it boil at high temperature for 1 minute, or until it almost evaporates. Stir constantly with the Balloon Whisk, to peel off the pork pieces attached to the base.
3. Add the pineapple juice and onion. Continue cooking at medium-high temperature for about 3 minutes. Reduce the temperature to medium, put the pork back in the pot and bathe it with the sauce. Let it cook uncovered for 3 more minutes. Turn off the stove.
4. Carefully remove the pork from the pot and slice it. Top with onions and sauce, and serve immediately with your favorite rice and vegetables.

Nutrition: Calories: 258.6, Carbohydrates: 22.9g, Fat: 6.2g, Protein: 28.4g, Sugar: 19.4g, Cholesterol: 80.6mg

Mexican Lasagna (Italian)

Preparation time: 10 minutes Cooking time: 21 minutes
Servings: 6

1 pound (1/2 kilo) ground beef 2 cups green sauce	½ cup sour cream
1 teaspoon garlic, finely chopped	½ cup onion, finely chopped
1 package of taco seasoning —4 ounces / 113 grams— (taco seasoning) 15 corn tortillas	½ cup green onion, finely chopped
¾ cup red and green peppers, diced 1½ cups shredded Mexican cheese	½ cup Kalamata olives (Kalamata olives), boneless and sliced
1½ cups black beans, previously cooked	½ cup jalapeno pepper with seeds, sliced

1. In a bowl, combine the green sauce with ½ cup of sour cream; reservation.
2. Preheat the skillet at medium-high temperature for 3 minutes or until, after spraying a few drops of water, they roll over the surface without evaporating. Add the meat and cook for 4 minutes, while stirring constantly.
3. Add the garlic, onion and taco seasoning; Stir and cook for 1 more minute. Turn off the stove, remove the pan and place the meat in another container; reservation.
4. In the same pan, carefully distribute a third of the green sauce mixture; cover with 5 tortillas, half of the meat, peppers and ½ cup of grated cheese.
5. Then place 5 more tortillas, the rest of the meat, black beans, jalapeños, a second portion of cheese and a second portion of the mixed green sauce.
6. Cover with the remaining 5 tortillas; Scatter the rest of the sauce mixture, cheese, olives and chives.
7. Cover with the valve open and cook at low temperature for 16 minutes. Turn off the stove, let the lasagna stand for 3 minutes, slice it and serve.

Nutrition: Calories: 545.7, Carbohydrates: 60.5g,Fat: 20.2g, Protein: 34.9g, Sugar: 1g, Cholesterol: 77.4mg

Greek Beef Roast (Greek)

Preparation Time: 10 minutes Cooking Time: 8 hours
Servings: 6

1 lbs. lean top round beef roast	1 tablespoon Italian seasoning 6 garlic cloves, minced
1 onion, sliced	½ cup red wine
2 cups beef broth	1 teaspoon red pepper flakes Pepper Salt

1. Season meat with pepper and salt and place into the crock pot.
2. Pour remaining over meat.
3. Cover and cook on low for 8 hours.
4. Shred the meat using fork.
5. Serve and enjoy.

Nutrition: Calories 231 Fat 6 g Carbohydrates 4 g Sugar 1.4 g Protein 35 g Cholesterol 75 mg

Tomato Pork Chops (Spanish)

Prep Time: 10 minutes Cooking Time: 6 hours Servings: 4

4 pork chops, bone-in1 tablespoon garlic, minced	½ small onion, chopped 6 oz can tomato paste1 bell pepper, chopped
¼ teaspoon red pepper flakes1 teaspoon Worcestershire sauce	1tablespoon dried Italian seasoning oz can tomato, diced2teaspoon olive oil
¼ teaspoon pepper1 teaspoon kosher salt	

1. Heat oil in a pan over medium-high heat.
2. Season pork chops with pepper and salt.
3. Sear pork chops in pan until brown from both the sides.
4. Transfer pork chops into the crock pot.
5. Add remaining over pork chops.
6. Cover and cook on low for 6 hours. Serve and enjoy.

Nutrition: Calories 325 Fat 23.4 g Carbohydrates 10 g Sugar 6 g Protein 20 g Cholesterol 70 mg

Greek Pork Chops (Greek)

Prep Time: 10 minutes Cooking Time: 6 minutes Servings: 8

8 pork chops, boneless4 teaspoon dried oregano	2 tablespoon Worcestershire sauce 3 tablespoon fresh lemon juice¼ cup olive oil
Salt	1teaspoon ground mustard 2 teaspoon garlic powder2 teaspoon onion powder Pepper

1. 1.1.Whisktogetheroil,garlicpowder,onionpowder,oregano, Worcestershire sauce, lemon juice, mustard, pepper, and salt.
2. Place pork chops in a baking dish then pour marinade over pork chops and coat well. Place in refrigerator overnight.
3. Preheat the grill.
4. Place pork chops on hot grill and cook for 3-4 mins on each side.
5. Serve and enjoy.

Nutrition: Calories 324 Fat 26.5 g Carbohydrates 2.5 g Sugar 1.3 g Protein 18 g Cholesterol 69 mg

Pork Cacciatore (Italian)

Prep Time: 10 minutes Cooking Time: 6 hours Servings: 6

1 ½ lbs. pork chops	1 teaspoon dried oregano 1 cup beef broth
3 tablespoon tomato paste 14 oz can tomato, diced 1 garlic clove, minced 2 tablespoon olive oil	2 cups mushrooms, sliced 1 small onion, diced ¼ teaspoon pepper
½ teaspoon salt	

1. Heat oil in a pan over medium-high heat.
2. Add pork chops in pan and cook until brown on both the sides.
3. Transfer pork chops into the crock pot.
4. Pour remaining over the pork chops.
5. Cover and cook on low for 6 hours. Serve and enjoy.

Nutrition: Calories 440 Fat 33 g Carbohydrates 6 g Sugar 3 g Protein 28 g Cholesterol 97 mg

Pork with Tomato & Olives (Greek)

Preparation Time: 10 minutes Cooking Time: 30 minutes Servings: 6

6 pork chops, boneless and cut into thick slices 1/8 teaspoon ground cinnamon 1/4 cup beef broth	1/2 cup olives, pitted and sliced 8 oz can tomato, crushed 2 garlic cloves, chopped 1 large onion, sliced
1 tablespoon olive oil	

1. Heat olive oil in a pan over medium-high heat.
2. Place pork chops in a pan and cook until lightly brown and set aside.
3. Cook garlic and onion in the same pan over medium heat, until onion is softened.
4. Add broth and bring to boil over high heat.
5. Return pork to pan and stir in crushed tomatoes and remaining .
6. Cover and simmer for 20 minutes.
7. Serve and enjoy.

Nutrition: Calories 321 Fat 23 g Carbohydrates 7 g Sugar 1 g Protein 19 g Cholesterol 70 mg

Basil Cheese Pork Roast (Italian)

Preparation Time: 10 minutes Cooking Time: 6 hours Servings: 8

1 lbs. lean pork roast, boneless	1 teaspoon garlic powder
1 tablespoon parsley	1 teaspoon dried oregano 1 teaspoon dried basil Pepper
½ cup cheddar cheese, grated	Salt
30 oz can tomato, diced	

1. Add the meat into the crock pot.
2. Mix together tomatoes, oregano, basil, garlic powder, parsley, cheese, pepper, and salt and pour over meat.
3. Cover and cook on low for 6 hours.
4. Serve and enjoy.

Nutrition: Calories 260 Fat 9 g Carbohydrates 5.5 g Sugar 3.5 g Protein 35 g Cholesterol 97 mg

Feta Lamb Patties (Greek)

Preparation Time: 10 minutes Cooking Time: 12 minutes Servings: 4

1 lb. ground lamb	1/2 teaspoon garlic powder 1/2 cup feta cheese, crumbled 1/4 cup mint leaves, chopped
1/4 cup roasted red pepper, chopped 1/4 cup onion, chopped	Pepper Salt

1. Add all into the bowl and mix until well combined.
2. Spray pan with cooking spray and heat over medium-high heat.
3. Make small patties from meat mixture and place on hot pan and cook for 6-7 minutes on each side. Serve and enjoy.

Nutrition: Calories 270 Fat 12 g Carbohydrates 2.9 g Sugar 1.7 g Protein 34.9 g Cholesterol 119 mg

Tender Lamb Chops (Greek)

Preparation Time: 10 minutes Cooking Time: 6 hours
Servings: 8

8 lamb chops	½ teaspoon dried thyme 1 onion, sliced
1 teaspoon dried oregano	2 garlic cloves, minced Pepper and salt

1. Add sliced onion into the slow cooker.
2. Combine together thyme, oregano, pepper, and salt. Rub over lamb chops.
3. Place lamb chops in slow cooker and top with garlic.
4. Pour ¼ cup water around the lamb chops.
5. Cover and cook on low for 6 hours.
6. Serve and enjoy.

Nutrition: Calories 40 Fat 1.9 g Carbohydrates 2.3 g Sugar 0.6 g Protein 3.4 g Cholesterol 0 mg

Sun-dried Tomato Chuck Roast (Italian)

Preparation Time: 10 minutes Cooking Time: 10 hours
Servings: 6

1 lbs. beef chuck roast	1 teaspoon dried Italian seasoning, crushed
½ cup beef broth	2 tablespoon balsamic vinegar
¼ cup sun-dried tomatoes, chopped 25 garlic cloves, peeled	¼ cup olives, sliced

1. Place meat into the crock pot.
2. Pour remaining over meat.
3. Cover and cook on low for 10 hours.
4. Shred the meat using fork.
5. Serve and enjoy.

Nutrition: Calories 582 Fat 43 g Carbohydrates 5 g Sugar 0.5 g Protein 40g Cholesterol 156 mg

Lemon Lamb Leg (Greek)

Preparation Time: 10 minutesCooking Time: 8 hours Servings: 12

4 lbs. lamb leg, boneless and slice of fat 1 tablespoon rosemary, crushed1/4 cup water	1/4 cup lemon juice1 teaspoon black pepper 1/4 teaspoon salt

1. Place lamb into the crock pot.
2. Add remaining into the crock pot over the lamb.
3. Cover and cook on low for 8 hours.
4. Remove lamb from crock pot and sliced.
5. Serve and enjoy.

Nutrition: Calories 275 Fat 10.2 g Carbohydrates 0.4 g Sugar 0.1 g Protein 42 g Cholesterol 132 mg

Lamb Meatballs (Greek)

Preparation Time: 10 minutes Cooking Time: 20 minutes
Servings: 4

1lb. ground lamb	2teaspoon fresh oregano, chopped
2 tablespoon fresh parsley, chopped	1 tablespoon garlic, minced
1 egg, lightly beaten	3 tablespoon olive oil
¼ teaspoon red pepper flakes	1 teaspoon ground cumin
¼ teaspoon pepper1 teaspoon kosher salt	

1. Preheat the oven to 425 F.
2. Line baking tray with parchment paper.
3. Add all except oil into the mixing bowl and mix until well combined.
4. Make small balls from meat mixture and place on baking tray.
5. Drizzle oil over meatballs and bake for 20 minutes.
6. Serve and enjoy.

Nutrition: Calories 325 Fat 20 g Carbohydrates 2 g Sugar 0.2 g Protein 33 g Cholesterol 143 mg

Herb Ground Beef (Spanish)

Preparation Time: 10 minutes Cooking Time: 15 minutes
Servings: 4

1 lb. ground beef	½ teaspoon dried parsley
½ teaspoon dried basil	½ teaspoon dried oregano 1 teaspoon garlic, minced 1 tablespoon olive oil
1 teaspoon pepper	½ teaspoon dried thyme
¼ teaspoon nutmeg	½ teaspoon dried rosemary 1 teaspoon salt

1.Heat oil in a pan over medium heat.
2.Add ground meat to the pan and fry until cooked.
3.Add remaining and stir well.
4.Serve and enjoy.

Nutrition: Calories 215 Fat 7.2 g Carbohydrates 1 g Sugar 0.2 g Protein 34 g Cholesterol 101 mg

Easy Beef Kofta (Spanish)

Preparation Time: 10 minutes Cooking Time: 10 minutes
Servings: 8

1lbs. ground beef	4 garlic cloves, minced
1 onion, minced	2 teaspoon cumin
1 cup fresh parsley, chopped	¼ teaspoon pepper
1 teaspoon salt	

1. Add all into the mixing bowl and mix until combined.
2. Roll meat mixture into the kabab shapes and cook in a hot pan for 4-6 minutes on each side or until cooked.
3. Serve and enjoy.

Nutrition: Calories 223 Fat 7.3 g Carbohydrates 2.5 g Sugar 0.7 g Protein 35 g Cholesterol 101 mg

Smoky Pork & Cabbage (Italian)

Preparation Time: 10 minutes Cooking Time: 8 hours
Servings: 6

3 lbs. pork roast	1/2 cabbage head, chopped
	1 cup water
1/3 cup liquid smoke	1 tablespoon kosher salt

1. Rub pork with kosher salt and place into the crock pot.
2. Pour liquid smoke over the pork. Add water.
3. Cover and cook on low for 7 hours.
4. Remove pork from crock pot and add cabbage in the bottom of crock pot.
5. Place pork on top of the cabbage.
6. Cover again and cook for 1 hour more.
7. Shred pork with a fork and serve.

Nutrition: Calories 484 Fat 21.5 g Carbohydrates 4 g Sugar 1.9 g Protein 66 g Cholesterol 195 mg

Pork in Red Chili Sauce (Spanish)

Preparation time: 10 minutes Cooking time: 24 minutes
Servings: 4-6

2 pounds (1 kg) pork loin, cut into medium cubes	4 cups zucchini sliced in half moon
1 cup half-moon sliced carrot	1tablespoon finely chopped garlic Salt and black pepper to taste
Red Chile sauce:	2 medium Roma tomatoes
3 tree peppers, peeled and deveined	2 guajillo peppers, peeled and deveined
1 wide chili, peeled and deveined	1 cup chicken broth

1. In the pot, cook all the sauce at medium-high temperature for 6 minutes (uncovered). Remove from the stove and let cool for 5 minutes.
2. In the blender, carefully add all the from the pot; Cover and blend at maximum speed for 1 minute. Reservation.
3. Preheat the 10½-inch skillet at medium-high temperature for about 3 minutes or until, after spraying a few drops of water, they roll over the surface without evaporating.
4. Add the meat, previously seasoned with salt and black pepper. Cook for about 4 minutes with the lid ajar; stir occasionally. Add zucchini, carrot and garlic. Cook at the same temperature for 2 minutes with the lid ajar; stir sporadically.
5. Add the chili sauce to the pan. Cover with the valve open, and cook until it whistles (in about 1 minute and a half). Reduce the temperature to low and, when the valve stops whistling, close it and cook for another 10 minutes. Turn off the stove and let stand for a couple of minutes.
6. Serve with Mexican rice or your favorite beans.

Nutrition: Calories: 465.7, Carbohydrates: 60.5g, Fat: 20.2g, Protein: 34.9g, Sugar: 1g, Cholesterol: 67.4mg

Archehera Ranchera (Spanish)

Preparation time: 10 minutes Cooking time: 14 minutes
Servings: 8

3 pounds (1½ kg) flank steak, cut into strips	8 ounces (227 g) Spanish chorizo, cut into strips
¾ cup purple onion, cut into julienne	1 tablespoon finely chopped garlic1pound (1/2 kg) of nopales cooked and cut into strips (jar or tender)
1½ cups of green pepper, cut into julienne	1½ cups yellow pepper, cut into julienne
1½ cups of red pepper, cut into julienne	¼ cup chopped cilantro
	Sauce for meat:
¾ cup soy sauce½ cup dark beer	2tablespoons of liquid smoke

1. Preheat the 14-inch Paella pan at medium-high temperature for about 3 minutes or until, after spraying a few drops of water, they roll over the surface without evaporating. Add the chorizo and cook for 2 minutes; stir constantly.
2. Add the onion and garlic; Skip for 1 minute. Place the meat and nopales and cook for 1 minute.
3. Add the peppers, cilantro and the three of the sauce. Cover with valve open and cook until the valve whistles (2 minutes). Reduce the temperature to low, close the valve and cook for 8 more minutes.
4. Serve the meat with beans, guacamole and corn tortillas.

Nutrition: Calories: 131, Carbohydrates: 6g, Fat: 1g, Protein: 1g, Sugar: 3g, Cholesterol: 0mg

Lemon Pepper Pork Tenderloin (Spanish)

Preparation Time: 10 minutes
Cooking Time: 25 minutes Servings: 4

1 lb. pork tenderloin	3/4 teaspoon lemon pepper
2 teaspoon dried oregano	1 tablespoon olive oil
3 tablespoon feta cheese, crumbled	3 tablespoon olive tapenades

1. Add pork, oil, lemon pepper, and oregano in a zip-lock bag and rub well and place in a refrigerator for 2 hours.
2. Remove pork from zip-lock bag. Using sharp knife make lengthwise cut through the center of the tenderloin.
3. Spread olive tapenade on half tenderloin and sprinkle with feta cheese.
4. Fold another half of meat over to the original shape of tenderloin.
5. Tie close pork tenderloin with twine at 2-inch intervals.
6. Grill pork tenderloin for 20 minutes.
7. Cut into slices and serve.

Nutrition: Calories 215 Fat 9.1 g Carbohydrates 1 g Sugar 0.5 g Protein 30.8 g Cholesterol 89 mg

Jalapeno Lamb Patties (Spanish)

Prep Time: 10 minutes Cooking Time: 8 minutes Servings: 4

1 lb. ground lamb	1 jalapeno pepper, minced
5 basil leaves, minced	10 mint leaves, minced
1 tablespoon garlic, minced	1 teaspoon dried oregano
¼ cup fresh parsley, chopped	1 cup feta cheese, crumbled
¼ teaspoon pepper	½ teaspoon kosher salt

1. Add all into the mixing bowl and mix until well combined.
2. Preheat the grill to 450 F.
3. Spray grill with cooking spray.
4. Make four equal shape patties from meat mixture and place on hot grill and cook for 3 minutes. Turn patties to another side and cook for 4 minutes. Serve and enjoy.

Nutrition: Calories 317 Fat 16 g Carbohydrates 3 g Sugar 1.7 g Protein 37.5 g Cholesterol 135 mg

Basil Parmesan Pork Roast (Spanish)

Prep Time: 10 minutes Cooking Time: 6 hours Servings: 8

2 lbs. lean pork roast, boneless	1 tablespoon parsley
½ cup parmesan cheese, grated	28 oz can tomato, diced
1 teaspoon dried oregano	1 teaspoon dried basil
Salt	1 tbsp garlic powder Pepper

1. Add the meat into the crock pot.
2. Mix together tomatoes, oregano, basil, garlic powder, parsley, cheese, pepper, and salt and pour over meat.
3. Cover and cook on low for 6 hours. Serve and enjoy.

Nutrition: Calories 294 Fat 11.6 g Carbohydrates 5 g Sugar 3 g Protein 38 g Cholesterol 105 mg

.Turkey Sausage, Fresh Herbs & Feta (Spanish)

Prep Time: 25 minutes Cooking Time: 15 minutes Servings: 6

1 onion, sliced thinly	1 smoked turkey sausage, sliced into rounds
4 tablespoons fresh herbs, chopped (parsley, basil)	1 cup white rice
	4 oz. feta cheese, crumbled

1. Add 1 tablespoon olive oil in the Instant Pot.
2. Cook the onion and sausage for 5 minutes.
3. Season with a little salt and pepper.
4. Add the rice and stir.
5. Add 2 cups chicken stock.
6. Stir well.
7. Seal the pot.
8. Set it to manual.
9. Cook at high pressure for 15 minutes.
10. Release the pressure quickly.
11. Add the herbs and top with the feta cheese.
12. Serving Suggestion: Serve with salad.

Nutrition: Calories 179 Total Fat 4.9g Saturated Fat 3.1g Cholesterol 19mg Sodium 230mg Total Carbohydrate 27.6g Dietary Fiber 1.1g Total Sugars 1.6g Protein 5.6g Potassium 108mg

.Turkey Lasagna (Italian)

Preparation Time: 20 minutes Cooking Time: 10 minutes Servings: 4

4 tortillas	1 1/4 cup salsa
1/2 can refried beans	1 1/2 cups cooked turkey
1 1/4 cup cheddar cheese, shredded	

1. Spray a small pan with oil.
2. Spread the refried beans on each tortilla.
3. Place the first tortilla inside the pan.
4. Add layers of the turkey, salsa and cheese.
5. Place another tortilla and repeat the layers.
6. Pour 1 cup of water inside the Instant Pot.
7. Place the layers on top of a steamer basket.
8. Place the basket inside the Instant Pot.
9. Choose manual setting.
10. Cook at high pressure for 10 minutes.
11. Serving Suggestion: Top with chopped parsley.

Nutrition: Calories 335 Total Fat 15.5g Saturated Fat 8.6g Cholesterol 79mg Sodium 849mg Total Carbohydrate 21.1g Dietary Fiber 4.5g Total Sugars 3g Protein 28.5g Potassium 561mg

Greek Chicken Salad (Greek)

Preparation Time: 10 minutes Cooking Time: 5 minutes Servings: 1

1 cup cooked chicken, shredded 2 teaspoon fresh basil, chopped 1/4 cup cucumber, diced	1 teaspoon vinegar
1 tablespoon sour cream	Salt
Pepper	

1. Add all into the medium bowl and mix well to combine.
2. Season with pepper and salt. Place in refrigerator for 10 minutes.
3. Serve and enjoy.

Nutrition: Calories 243 Fat 6.8 g Carbohydrates 1.6 g Sugar 0.5 g Protein 41.2g Cholesterol 113 mg

Seasoned Pork Chops (Spanish)

Preparation Time: 10 minutes Cooking Time: 4 hours Servings: 4

4 pork chops	2 garlic cloves, minced 1 cup chicken broth
1 tablespoon poultry seasoning 1/4 cup olive oil	Pepper and salt

1. In a bowl, whisk together olive oil, poultry seasoning, garlic, broth, pepper, and salt.
2. Pour olive oil mixture into the slow cooker then place pork chops to the crock pot.
3. Cover and cook on high for 4 hours.
4. Serve and enjoy.

Nutrition: Calories 386 Fat 32.9 g Carbohydrates 3 g Sugar 1 g Protein 20 g Cholesterol 70 mg

Beef Stroganoff (Spanish)

Prep Time: 10 minutes Cooking Time: 8 hours Servings: 2

1/2 lb. beef stew meat10 oz mushroom soup	homemade 1 medium onion chopped
1/2 cup sour cream oz mushrooms	sliced Pepper and salt

Add all except sour cream into the crock pot and mix well.

1. Cover and cook on low for 8 hours.
2. Add sour cream and stir well.
3. Serve and enjoy.

Nutrition: Calories 470 Fat 25 g Carbohydrates 8.6 g Sugar 3 g Protein 49 g Cholesterol 108 mg

.Greek Turkey Burgers (Greek)

Preparation Time: 10 minutes Cooking Time: 15 minutes Servings: 4

1/3 cup feta cheese, crumbled 1 teaspoon dill	1 egg white
7 ounces roasted red bell peppers, sliced	½ cup breadcrumbs 4 whole-wheat buns
¾ cup mint, chopped 1 cup red onion, sliced 1 pound ground turkey	2 tablespoons lemon juice Canola oil as needed
4 Iceberg salad leaves	

1. In a mixing bowl, beat the egg whites. Add the mint, breadcrumbs, onions, feta cheese, lemon juice, dill and turkey; combine well.
2. Form 4 patties from the mixture.
3. Over medium stove flame, heat the oil in a skillet or saucepan (preferably of medium size).
4. Add the patties and cook them until evenly brown on both sides.
5. Serve the patties in the buns topping them with roasted peppers and iceberg leaves.

Nutrition: Calories 362 Fat 13gCarbohydrates 38gFiber 4gProtein 33g

.Mediterranean Chicken (Greek)

Prep Time: 10 minutes Cooking Time: 10 minutes Servings: 6

2 lb. chicken breast fillet, sliced into strips	Wine mixture (1/4 cup white wine mixed with 3 tablespoons red wine)
1 1/2 tbsp dried oregano 6 garlic cloves, chopped	2 tablespoons light brown sugar

1.Pour in the wine mixture to the Instant Pot.
2.Stir in the rest
3.Toss the chicken to coat evenly.
4.Seal the pot.
5.Set it to high pressure.
6.Cook for 10 minutes.
7.Release the pressure naturally.

Nutrition: Calories 304 Total Fat 11.3g Saturated Fat 3.1g Cholesterol 135mg Sodium 131mg Total Carbohydrate 4.2g Dietary Fiber 0.2g Total Sugars 3g Protein 44g Potassium 390mg

.Mediterranean Chicken Wings (Greek)

Prep Time: 1 hour Cooking Time: 20 minutes Servings: 4

8 chicken wings	1tablespoon garlic puree
2 tbsp mixed dried herbs (tarragon, oregano and basil)	1 tablespoon chicken seasoning

1. In a bowl, mix the garlic puree, herbs and seasoning.
2. Marinate the chicken in this mixture for 1 hour.
3. Add 1 tablespoon of coconut oil into the Instant Pot.
4. Set it to sauté.
5. Cook the chicken until brown on both sides.
6. Remove and set aside.
7. Add 1 cup of water to the pot.
8. Place steamer basket inside.
9. Put the chicken on top of the basket.
10. Seal the pot.
11. Set it to manual and cook at high pressure for 10 minutes.
12. Release the pressure naturally.

Nutrition: Calories 280 Total Fat 11.2g Saturated Fat 3g Cholesterol 130mg Sodium 135mg Total Sugars 0g Protein 42.2g Potassium 355mg

.Chicken Meatballs with Carrot (Spanish)

Preparation time: 10 minutes Cooking time: 10 minutes Servings: 8

1/3 cup carrot, grated 1 onion, diced	2 cups ground chicken 1 tablespoon semolina
1 egg, beaten	½ teaspoon salt
1 teaspoon dried oregano 1 teaspoon dried cilantro	1 tablespoon coconut oil 1 teaspoon chili flakes

1. In the mixing bowl combine together grated carrot, diced onion, ground chicken, semolina, egg, salt, dried oregano, cilantro, and chili flakes.
2. With the help of scooper make the meatballs.
3. Heat up the coconut oil in the skillet.
4. When it starts to shimmer, put meatballs in it.
5. Cook the meatballs for 5 minutes from each side over the medium-low heat.

Nutrition: Calories 107, Fat 4.2 g, Fiber 0.8 g, Carbs 2.4 g, Protein 11.2 g

.Turkey Skewers (Italian)

Prep Time: 15 minutes Cooking time: 30 minutes Servings: 6

1½ pounds turkey breast, cubed 3 Spanish peppers, sliced	2zucchinis, cut into thick slices 1 onion, cut into wedges
2 tbsps. olive oil, room temperature	1 tbsp. dry ranch seasoning

1. Alternately thread the turkey pieces, and vegetables onto the bamboo skewers. Sprinkle the skewers with dry ranch dressing, and olive oil.
2. Grill your skewers for about 10 minutes, turning them periodically to ensure even cooking.
3. Wrap skewers in aluminum foil and keeps warm. Serve along with a side of vegetables.

Nutrition: Calories: 280 Carbs: 6.7g Fat: 13.8g Protein: 25.8g Fiber: 1.2g

.Light Caesar (Italian)

Preparation time: 10 minutes Cooking time: 10 minutes
Servings: 4

4 oz chicken fillet, chopped	¼ cup black olives, chopped 2 cups lettuce, chopped
1 tablespoon mayo sauce 1 teaspoon lemon juice	½ oz Parmesan cheese, shaved 1 teaspoon olive oil
½ teaspoon ground black pepper	½ teaspoon coconut oil

1. Sprinkle the chicken fillet with ground black pepper.
2. Heat up coconut oil and add chopped chicken fillet.
3. Roast it got 10 minutes or until it is cooked. Stir it from time to time.
4. Meanwhile, mix up together black olives, lettuce, Parmesan in the bowl.
5. Make mayo dressing: whisk together mayo sauce, olive oil, and lemon juice.
6. Add the cooked chicken in the salad and shake well.
7. Pour the mayo sauce dressing over the salad.

Nutrition: Calories 134, Fat 13.3 g, Fiber 0, Carbs 2 g, Protein 9.4 g

.Chicken Parm (Italian)

Preparation time: 10 minutes Cooking time: 30 minutes
Servings: 4

4 chicken steaks (4 oz each steak)	½ cup crushed tomatoes
¼ cup fresh cilantro 1 garlic clove, diced	½ cup of water 1 onion, diced
1 teaspoon olive oil	3 oz Parmesan, grated
3 tablespoon Panko breadcrumbs 2 eggs, beaten	1 teaspoon ground black pepper

1. Pour olive oil in the saucepan.
2. Add garlic and onion. Roast the vegetables for 3 minutes.
3. Then add fresh cilantro, crushed tomatoes, and water.
4. Simmer the mixture for 5 minutes.
5. Meanwhile, mix up together ground black pepper and eggs.
6. Dip the chicken steaks in the egg mixture.
7. Then coat them in Panko breadcrumbs and again in the egg mixture.
8. Coat the chicken steaks in grated Parmesan.
9. Place the prepared chicken steaks in the crushed tomato mixture.
10. Close the lid and cook chicken Parm for 20 minutes. Flip the chicken steaks after 10 minutes of cooking.
11. Serve the chicken Parm with crushed tomatoes sauce.

Nutrition: Calories 354, Fat 21.3 g, Fiber 2.1, Carbs 12 g, Protein 32.4 g

.Chicken Bolognese (Greek)

Preparation time: 7 minutes Cooking time: 25 minutes
Servings: 4

2 tbsp fresh parsley, chopped 1 tbsp chili pepper	1 teaspoon paprika
½ teaspoon dried oregano	¼ teaspoon garlic, minced
½ teaspoon dried thyme	1cup ground chicken 2 oz
1/3 cup crushed tomatoes	Parmesan, grated 1 tablespoon olive oil

1. Heat up olive oil in the skillet.
2. Add ground chicken and sprinkle it with chili pepper, paprika, dried oregano, dried thyme, and parsley. Mix up well.
3. Cook the chicken for 5 minutes and add crushed tomatoes. Mix up well.
4. Close the lid and simmer the chicken mixture for 10 minutes over the low heat.
5. Then add grated Parmesan and mix up.
6. Cook chicken Bolognese for 5 minutes more over the medium heat.

Nutrition: Calories 154, Fat 9.3 g, Fiber 1.1, Carbs 3 g, Protein 15.4 g

.Cashew Broccoli Chicken (Greek)

Preparation Time: 25 minutes Cooking Time: 30 minutes
Servings: 5

½ cup carrots, chopped 1/3 cup unsalted cashews 3 green onions, chopped 1 cup sugar snap peas	1 red bell pepper, chopped 2 cups broccoli florets
1 pound chicken breasts, cubed 1 tablespoon olive oil	3 cloves garlic, crushed Sauce:
1 teaspoon sesame oil 2 tablespoons honey	3 tablespoons peanut butter
1 tablespoon crushed ginger	3 tablespoons water
4 tablespoons soy sauce	

1. In a mixing bowl, add the sauce and mix them together.
2. Over medium stove flame, heat the oil in a skillet or saucepan (preferably of medium size).
3. Add the chicken and cook it until evenly brown; season with garlic, salt, and black pepper.
4. Add the broccoli, snap peas, bell pepper, and carrots and fry for 5-6 minutes, stirring often.
5. Add the sauce and combine well. Add in the cashews, mix and serve warm.

Nutrition: Calories 235 Fat 9g Carbohydrates 21g Fiber 4g Protein 26g

.Tahini Chicken Rice Bowls with Apricots (Italian)

Preparation Time: 15 minutes Cooking time: 15 minutes
Servings: 4

1cup uncooked instant brown rice	¼ cup tahini or peanut butter (tahini for nut-free)
¼ cup 2% plain Greek yogurt	2tbsps. chopped scallions, green, and white parts 1 tbsp. freshly squeezed lemon juice
1 tbsp. water	1tsp ground cumin
3/4 tsp ground cinnamon	¼ tsp kosher or sea salt
2cups chopped cooked chicken breast	½ cup chopped dried apricots
2 cups peeled, and chopped seedless cucumber 4 tsps. sesame seeds	Fresh mint leaves, for serving

1. In a pot, pour plenty of water, and bring to a boil. When it boils, pour in a handful of salt, and add the rice, and cook for 35-40 minutes (the time indicated on the package).
2. Meanwhile, in a medium bowl, stir together the tahini, yogurt, scallions, lemon juice, water, cumin, cinnamon, and salt. Transfer half of the tahini mixture to another medium bowl.
3. Add the chicken to the first bowl, and stir well to season.
4. When the rice is ready, drain it, and add it to the second bowl of tahini.
5. Have 4 bowls. In each bowl place the chicken in ¼ space. In another ¼ arrange the rice mixture next to the chicken. In the last half of the bowl add the dried apricots, and cucumbers. Sprinkle with the sesame seeds, and top with the mint leaves. Serve, and enjoy.

Nutrition: Calories: 335 Carbs: 30g Fat: 10g Protein: 31g Fiber: 3g

.Turkey And Asparagus Mix (Greek)

Preparation Time: 10 minutes Cooking time: 30 minutes
Servings: 4

1 bunch asparagus, trimmed and halved	1big turkey breast, skinless, boneless, and cut into strips 1 tsp basil, dried
2tbsps. olive oil	A pinch of salt, and black pepper
½ cup tomato sauce	1 tbsp. chives, chopped

1. In a skillet, pour a drizzle of oil, and heat over medium-high heat. Add the turkey, and brown for 3 minutes per side.
2. Add the asparagus, and the rest of the (except the chives), and bring to a boil. When it boils, decrease the heat, and cook over medium-low heat for 25 minutes.
3. Add the chives, divide the mixture among plates, and serve.

Nutrition: Calories: 337 Carbs: 21.4g Fat: 21.2g Protein: 17.6g Fiber: 10.2g

.Artichoke Basil Chicken (Greek)

Preparation Time: 10 minutes Cooking Time: 15 minutes
Servings: 4

1 1/2 lbs. chicken thighs	1 1/2 cup marinated
1/2 teaspoon dried oregano	artichokes 2 cups cherry tomatoes
8 fresh basil leaves	3 tablespoon balsamic vinegar 1/4 teaspoon dried thyme
1/4 teaspoon pepper 1/2 teaspoon salt	

1. Spray a large pan with cooking spray and heat over medium-high heat.
2. Add chicken in a hot pan and cook for 3 minutes on each side.
3. Add tomatoes, marinated artichokes, vinegar, and seasoning and stir well.
4. Turn heat to medium. Cover and simmer for 10 minutes.
5. Turn heat to high and cook until all liquid reduced.
6. Turn chicken and cook until chicken is lightly browned or until cooked through.
7. Garnish with basil and serve.

Nutrition: Calories 400 Fat 18 g Carbohydrates 6 g Sugar 3 g Protein 50 g
Cholesterol 150 mg

.Chicken Burgers (Greek)

Preparation time: 15 minutes Cooking time: 15 minutes
Servings: 4

8 oz ground chicken	1 cup fresh spinach, blended 1 teaspoon minced onion
½ teaspoon salt	1 red bell pepper, grinded 1 egg, beaten
1 teaspoon ground black pepper	4 tablespoons Panko breadcrumbs

1. In the mixing bowl mix up together ground chicken, blended spinach, minced garlic, salt, grinded bell pepper, egg, and ground black pepper.
2. When the chicken mixture is smooth, make 4 burgers from it and coat them in Panko breadcrumbs.
3. Place the burgers in the non-sticky baking dish or line the baking tray with baking paper.
4. Bake the burgers for 15 minutes at 365F.
5. Flip the chicken burgers on another side after 7 minutes of cooking.

Nutrition: Calories 177, Fat 5.2 g, Fiber 1.8 g, Carbs 10.4 g, Protein 13.2 g

.Turkey Verde with Brown Rice (Spanish)

Prep Time: 10 minutes Cooking Time: 24 minutes Servings: 5

2/3 cup chicken broth 1	1 1/2 lb. turkey tenderloins
1/4 cup brown rice	1 onion, sliced
1/2 cup salsa Verde	

1. Add the chicken broth and rice to the Instant Pot.
2. Top with the turkey, onion and salsa.
3. Cover the pot.
4. Set it to manual.
5. Cook at high pressure for 18 minutes.
6. Release the pressure naturally.
7. Wait for 8 minutes before opening the pot.
8. Serving Suggestion: Garnish with fresh cilantro.

Nutrition: Calories 336 Total Fat 3.3g Saturated Fat 0.3g Cholesterol 54mg Sodium 321mg Total Carbohydrate 39.4g Dietary Fiber 2.2g Total Sugars 1.4g Protein 38.5g Potassium 187mg

.Duck Patties (Italian)

Preparation time: 15 minutes Cooking time: 10 minutes Servings: 8

1-pound duck breast, skinless, boneless 1 teaspoon semolina	½ teaspoon cayenne pepper 2 eggs, beaten
1 teaspoon salt	1 tablespoon fresh cilantro, chopped 1 tablespoon olive oil

1. Chop the duck breast on the tiny pieces (grind it) and combine together with semolina, cayenne pepper, salt, and cilantro. Mix up well.
2. Then add eggs and stir gently.
3. Pour olive oil in the skillet and heat it up.
4. Place the duck mixture in the oil with the help of the spoon to make the shape of small patties.
5. Roast the patties for 3 minutes from each side over the medium heat.
6. Then close the lid and cook patties for 4 minutes more over the low heat.

Nutrition: Calories 106, Fat 5.2 g, Fiber 0.8 g, Carbs 0.4 g, Protein 13.2 g

.Creamy Chicken Pate (Spanish)

Prep time: 2 hours Cooking time: 20 minutes Servings: 6

8 oz chicken liver	3 tablespoon butters
1 white onion, chopped 1 bay leaf	1 teaspoon salt
½ tbsp. ground black pepper	½ cup of water

1. Place the chicken liver in the saucepan.
2. Add onion, bay leaf, salt, ground black pepper, and water.
3. Mix up the mixture and close the lid.
4. Cook the liver mixture for 20 minutes over the medium heat.
5. Then transfer it in the blender and blend until smooth.
6. Add butter and mix up until it is melted.
7. Pour the pate mixture in the pate ramekin and refrigerate for 2 hours.

Nutrition: Calories 122, Fat 8.2 g, Fiber 0.8 g, Carbs 2.4 g, Protein 9.2 g

.Curry Chicken Drumsticks (Spanish)

Preparation time: 10 minutes Cooking time: 30 minutes Servings: 4

4 chicken drumsticks	1 apple, grated
1 tablespoon curry paste 4 tablespoons milk	1 teaspoon coconut oil 1 teaspoon chili flakes
½ teaspoon minced ginger	

1. Mix up together grated apple, curry paste, milk, chili flakes, and minced garlic.
2. Put coconut oil in the skillet and melt it.
3. Add apple mixture and stir well.
4. Then add chicken drumsticks and mix up well.
5. Roast the chicken for 2 minutes from each side.
6. Then preheat oven to 360F.
7. Place the skillet with chicken drumsticks in the oven and bake for 25 minutes.

Nutrition: Calories 152, Fat 7.2 g, Fiber 1.8 g, Carbs 9.4 g, Protein 13.2 g

.Turkey Meatballs (Spanish)

Prep Time: 10 minutes Cooking time: 25 minutes Servings: 2

¼ diced yellow onion	14 oz. diced artichoke hearts 1 lb. ground turkey
1 tsp dried parsley 1 tsp oil	4 tbsp chopped basil Pepper, and salt, to taste

1. Preheat the oven to 350°F, and grease a baking sheet.
2. In a saucepan, drizzle olive oil, and heat over medium heat. Add the artichoke hearts, and diced onions, and sauté for 5 minutes. Allow cooling.
3. In a large bowl, add parsley, basil, ground turkey, salt, and pepper, and mix well with a fork. Add artichokes, & mix well.
4. Using your hands, form patties, and place them on the prepared baking sheet.
5. Bake in the oven for about 15-20 minutes. Serve accompanied by a side of vegetables.

Nutrition: Calories: 283 Carbs: 30g Fat: 12g Protein: 12g

.Turkey With Artichokes and Asparagus (Greek)

Prep Time: 5 minutes Cooking time: 30 minutes Servings: 4

2 turkey breasts, boneless, skinless, and halved 3 tbsp. olive oil	1 ½ pounds asparagus, trimmed and halved 1 cup chicken stock
A pinch of salt, and black pepper	1 cup canned artichoke hearts, drained
¼ cup kalamata olives, pitted and sliced 1 shallot, chopped	3 garlic cloves, minced 3 tbsp. dill, chopped

1. Pour a drizzle of oil into a skillet, and heat over medium-high heat. Add the turkey, and garlic, and brown for 4 minutes on each side.
2. Add the asparagus, broth, and the rest of the (except the dill), bring to a boil and cook over medium heat for 20 mins.
3. Add the dill, divide the mixture among plates, and serve.

Nutrition: Calories: 291 Carbs: 22.8g Fat: 16g Protein: 34.5g Fiber: 10.3g

.Turkey With Cranberry Sauce (Greek)

Preparation Time: 10 minutes Cooking time: 50 minutes
Servings: 4

1 cup chicken stock 2 tbsp. avocado oil	½ cup cranberry sauce
1 big turkey breast, skinless, boneless, and sliced 1 yellow onion, roughly chopped	Salt, and black pepper to the taste

1. Preheat the oven to 350°F.
2. Pour a drizzle of avocado oil into the oven-safe skillet, and heat over medium-high heat. Add the onion, and sauté for 5 minutes. Add the turkey, and sauté for 3 minutes on each side. Add the rest of the , and sauté.
3. Transfer the skillet to the oven, and bake for about 40 minutes. Distribute onto serving plates, and serve.

Nutrition: Calories: 382 Carbs: 26.6g Fat: 12.6g Protein: 17.6g Fiber: 9.6g

.Spanish Chicken and Rice (Spanish)

Preparation Time: 15 minutes Cooking time: 30 minutes
Servings: 2

1 tsps. smoked paprika 2 tsps. ground cumin 1½ tsps. garlic salt	¾ tsp chili powder
¼ tsp dried oregano 1 lemon, squeezed	2 boneless, skinless chicken breasts
3 tbsps. extra-virgin olive oil, divided 2 large shallots, diced	1 cup uncooked white rice 2 cups vegetable stock
1 cup broccoli florets 1/3 cup chopped parsley	

1. In a small bowl, whisk together the paprika, cumin, garlic salt, chili powder, and oregano. Divide in half, and set aside.
2. In a medium bowl, add the chicken, and brush with 2 tbsps. of the olive oil. Rub the chicken with half of the seasoning mixture, and set aside.
3. In a saucepan, heat the remaining 1 tbsp. olive oil, and brown the chicken for 3 minutes on each side, remove and set aside.
4. Add the shallots to the casserole, and sauté for 5 minutes. Add the rice, and toast it for a couple of minutes. Add the vegetable broth, lemon juice, and remaining seasoning mix, and stir. Return the chicken to the pan on top of the rice. Cover, and cook for 15 minutes.
5. When the time is up, add the broccoli florets, cover, and cook another 5 minutes, until the liquid is absorbed, the rice is tender, and the chicken is cooked. Plate, sprinkle with chopped parsley and serve immediately.

Nutrition: Calories: 750 Carbs: 101g Fat: 25g Protein: 36g Fiber: 7g

.Spicy Chicken Breasts (Greek)

Preparation Time: 15 minutes Cooking time: 30 minutes
Servings: 6

1 ½ pounds chicken breasts	1 bell pepper, deveined, and chopped 1 leek, chopped
1 tomato, pureed	2 tbsps. coriander
2 garlic cloves, minced 1 tsp cayenne pepper	1 tsp dry thyme
¼ cup coconut amino Sea salt	Ground black pepper

1. Rub each chicken breast with garlic, cayenne pepper, thyme, salt, and black pepper.
2. In a saucepan, drizzle oil, and heat over medium-high heat. Add chicken, and brown for 3 minutes per side.
3. Add the tomato puree, and coconut amino, and bring to a boil. Add the pepper, leek, and cilantro, and reduce the heat to low. Cook partially covered for about 20 minutes, then serve.

Nutrition: Calories: 239 | Carbs: 5.5g | Fat: 6g | Protein: 34.3g | Fiber: 1g

.Pomegranate Chicken Thighs (Greek)

Preparation time: 10 minutes Cooking time: 10 minutes
Servings: 2

1 tablespoon pomegranate molasses	8 oz chicken thighs (4 oz each chicken thigh)
½ teaspoon paprika	1 teaspoon cornstarch
½ teaspoon chili flakes	½ teaspoon ground black pepper 1 teaspoon olive oil
½ teaspoon lime juice	

1. In the shallow bowl mix up together ground black pepper, chili flakes, paprika, and cornstarch.
2. Rub the chicken thighs with spice mixture.
3. Heat up olive oil in the skillet.
4. Add chicken thighs and roast them for 4 minutes from each side over the medium heat.
5. When the chicken thighs are light brown, sprinkle them with pomegranate molasses and roast for 1 minute from each side.

Nutrition: Calories 374, Fat 21.3 g, Fiber 0.1, Carbs 9 g, Protein 30.4 g

.Butter Chicken (Greek)

Prep time: 15 minutes Cooking time: 30 minutes Servings: 5

chicken fillet 1/3 cup butter, softened	½ teaspoon thyme 1 teaspoon salt
½ lemon	1 tablespoon rosemary

1. Churn together thyme, salt, and rosemary.
2. Chop the chicken fillet roughly and mix up with churned butter mixture.
3. Place the prepared chicken in the baking dish.
4. Squeeze the lemon over the chicken.
5. Chop the squeezed lemon and add in the baking dish.
6. Cover the chicken with foil and bake it for 20 minutes at 365F.
7. Then discard the foil and bake the chicken for 10 minutes more.

Nutrition: Calories 254, Fat 19.3 g, Fiber 1.1, Carbs 1 g, Protein 36.4 g

.Chicken Fajitas (Italian)

Preparation time: 15 minutes Cooking time: 15 minutes
Servings: 2

1 bell pepper	½ red onion, peeled 5 oz chicken fillets 1 garlic clove, sliced
1 tablespoon olive oil	1 teaspoon balsamic vinegar 1 teaspoon chili pepper
½ teaspoon salt	1 teaspoon lemon juice 2 flour tortillas

1. Cut the bell pepper and chicken fillet on the wedges.
2. Then slice the onion.
3. Pour olive oil in the skillet and heat it up.
4. Add chicken wedges and sprinkle them with chili pepper and salt.
5. Roast the chicken for 4 minutes. Stir it from time to time.
6. After this, add lemon juice and balsamic vinegar. Mix up well.
7. Add bell pepper, onion, and garlic clove.
8. Roast fajitas for 10 minutes over the medium-high heat. Stir it from time to time.
9. Put the cooked fajitas on the tortillas and transfer in the serving plates.

Nutrition: Calories 346, Fat 14.2 g, Fiber 2.8 g, Carbs 23.4 g, Protein 25.2 g

.BBQ Pulled Chicken (Greek)

Preparation time: 10 minutes Cooking time: 45 minutes
Servings: 6

1.5-pound chicken breast, skinless, boneless 2 tablespoons BBQ sauce	1 tablespoon butter
1 teaspoon Dijon mustard 1 tablespoon olive oil	1 teaspoon cream cheese 1 teaspoon salt
1teaspoon cayenne pepper	

1. Sprinkle the chicken breast with cayenne pepper, salt, and olive oil.
2. Place it in the baking tray and bake for 35 minutes at 365F. Flip it from time to time to avoid burning.
3. When the chicken breast is cooked, transfer it on the chopping board and shred with the help of the fork.
4. Put the shredded chicken in the saucepan.
5. Add butter, cream cheese, mustard, and BBQ sauce. Mix up gently and heat it up until boiling.
6. Remove the cooked meal from the heat and stir well.

Nutrition: Calories 154, Fat 7.3 g, Fiber 1.1, Carbs 2 g, Protein 24.4 g

.Flavorful Lemon Chicken Tacos (Italian)

Prep Time: 10 minutes Cooking Time: 4 hours Servings: 8

1lbs. chicken breasts, boneless oz salsa	1 tablespoon taco seasoning, homemade 2 fresh lime juice
1/4 cup fresh parsley, chopped 1/4 teaspoon red chili powder Pepper	Salt

1. Place chicken into the crockpot.
2. Pour over the chicken.
3. Cover and cook on high for 4 hours.
4. Shred the chicken using a fork and serve.

Nutrition: Calories 235Fat 8 g Carbohydrates 5 g Sugar 2 g Protein 30 g Cholesterol 100 mg

Chicken Stroganoff (Italian)

Prep time: 10 minutes Cooking time: 20 minutes Servings: 4

1 cup cremini mushrooms, sliced 1 onion, sliced	1 tablespoon olive oil
½ teaspoon thyme	1 teaspoon salt
10 oz chicken fillet, chopped	1 cup Plain yogurt

1. Heat up olive oil in the saucepan.
2. Add mushrooms and onion.
3. Sprinkle the vegetables with thyme and salt. Mix up well and cook them for 5 minutes.
4. After this, add chopped chicken fillet and mix up well.
5. Cook the for 5 minutes more.
6. Then add plain yogurt, mix up well, and close the lid.
7. Cook chicken stroganoff for 10 minutes over the low heat.

Nutrition: Calories 224, Fat 9.2 g, Fiber 0.8 g, Carbs 7.4 g, Protein 24.2 g

.Parmesan Chicken Gratin (Greek)

Preparation time: 10 minutes Cooking time: 30 minutes
Servings: 4

1chicken thighs, skinless, boneless 1 teaspoon paprika	1 tablespoon lemon juice
½ teaspoon chili flakes	¼ teaspoon garlic powder 3 oz Parmesan, grated 1/3 cup milk
1onion, sliced	2oz pineapple, sliced

1. Chop the chicken thighs roughly and sprinkle them with paprika, lemon juice, chili flakes, garlic powder, and mix up well.
2. Arrange the chopped chicken thighs in the baking dish in one layer.
3. Then place sliced onion over the chicken.
4. Add the layer of sliced pineapple.
5. Mix up together milk and Parmesan and pour the liquid over the pineapple,
6. Cover the surface of the baking dish with foil and bake gratin for 30 minutes at 355F.

Nutrition: Calories 100, Fat 5.2, Fiber 1, Carbs 6.7, Protein 8.1

.Santa le Skillet Chicken (Italian)

Prep time: 10 minutes Cooking time: 20 minutes Servings: 4

12 oz chicken breast, skinless, boneless, chopped	1tablespoon nut oil
1 tablespoon taco seasoning	
½ teaspoon cayenne pepper	½ teaspoon salt
½ teaspoon garlic, chopped	½ red onion, sliced
1/3 cup black beans, canned, rinsed	½ cup Mozzarella, shredded

1. Rub the chopped chicken breast with taco seasoning, salt, and cayenne pepper.
2. Place the chicken in the skillet, add nut oil and roast it for 10 minutes over the medium heat. Mix up the chicken pieces from time to time to avoid burning.
3. After this, transfer the chicken in the plate.
4. Add sliced onion and garlic in the skillet. Roast the vegetables for 5 minutes. Stir them constantly. Then add black beans and stir well. Cook the for 2 minutes more.
5. Add the chopped chicken and mix up well. Top the meal with Mozzarella cheese.
6. Close the lid and cook the meal for 3 minutes.

Nutrition: Calories 184, Fat 6.3 g, Fiber 2.1, Carbs 13 g, Protein 22.4 g

.Grilled Greek Chicken (Greek)

Prep Time: 10 minutes Cooking Time: 12 minutes Servings: 4

1 1/2 lbs. chicken breasts, skinless and boneless 1 tablespoon garlic, minced	1/4 teaspoon cayenne pepper 1 teaspoon fresh thyme
1/2 teaspoon oregano	1 tablespoon red wine vinegar 3 tablespoon olive oil
3 tablespoon fresh lemon juice 1/2 teaspoon pepper	1/2 teaspoon salt

1. Add chicken into the zip-lock bag. Pour remaining over chicken. Seal bag and shake well.
2. Place marinated chicken into the refrigerator overnight.
3. Heat grill over medium-high heat.
4. Place marinated chicken on hot grill and cook for 4-6 minutes on each side. Serve and enjoy.

Nutrition: Calories 420 Fat 23 g Carbohydrates 1 g Sugar 0.3 g Protein 50 g Cholesterol 150 mg

.Guacamole Chicken Salad (Italian)

Prep Time: 10 minutes Cooking Time: 10 minutes Servings: 3

2 chicken breasts, cooked and cubed 1 cup cilantro, chopped	1tablespoon fresh lime juice 2 avocados, peeled and pitted
2Serrano chili peppers, chopped 1/2 cup celery, chopped	1/2 cup onion, chopped 1 teaspoon kosher salt

1. Add avocados and lime juice into the bowl and mash using a fork.
2. Add remaining into the bowl and stir to combine.
3. Serve and enjoy.

Nutrition: Calories 477 Fat 33.4 g Carbohydrates 15.9 g Sugar 2 g Protein 31.2g Cholesterol 87 mg

.Chicken Enchiladas (Greek)

Preparation time: 20 minutes Cooking time: 15 minutes Servings: 5

5 corn tortillas	10 oz chicken breast, boiled, shredded 1 teaspoon chipotle pepper
3 tablespoons green salsa	½ teaspoon minced garlic
½ cup cream	¼ cup chicken stock
1 cup Mozzarella, shredded	
1 teaspoon butter, softened	

1. Mix up together shredded chicken breast, chipotle pepper, green salsa, and minced garlic.
2. Then put the shredded chicken mixture in the center of every corn tortilla and roll them.
3. Spread the baking dish with softened butter from inside and arrange the rolled corn tortillas.
4. Then pour chicken stock and cream over the tortillas.
5. Top them with shredded Mozzarella.
6. Bake the enchiladas for 15 minutes at 365F.

Nutrition: Calories 152, Fat 5.2 g, Fiber 1.8 g, Carbs 12.4 g, Protein 15.2 g

.Ranch Chicken Salad (Spanish)

Preparation Time: 10 minutes Cooking Time: 5 minutes Servings: 4

1cups cooked chicken, shredded 1/2 cup green onion, chopped 3/4 cup carrots, chopped	1 1/2 cups celery, chopped 1/2 cup mayonnaise
1/4 sweet onion, diced Salt	1 tablespoon ranch seasoning 4 tablespoon hot sauce Pepper

1. In a small bowl, mix together hot sauce, ranch seasoning, and mayonnaise. Add remaining into the large bowl and mix well. Pour hot sauce mixture over salad and mix well. Serve and enjoy.

Nutrition: Calories 275 Fat 13 g Carbohydrates 12 g Sugar 4 g Protein 20 g Cholesterol 65 mg

.Harissa Chicken (Italian)

Preparation Time: 10 minutes Cooking Time: 4 hours Servings: 4

1 lb. chicken breasts, skinless and boneless 1 cup harissa sauce	1/4 teaspoon garlic powder 1/2 teaspoon ground cumin 1/4 teaspoon onion powder 1/2 teaspoon kosher salt

1. Season chicken with garlic powder, onion powder, cumin, and salt.
2. Place chicken into the crockpot. Pour harissa sauce over chicken.
3. Cover and cook on low for 4 hours.
4. Shred the chicken using a fork.
5. Serve and enjoy.

Nutrition: Calories 230 Fat 10 g Carbohydrates 2 g Sugar 0.2 g Protein 33 g Cholesterol 100 mg

.Almond Cranberry Chicken Salad (Spanish)

Preparation Time: 10 minutes
Cooking Time: 5 minutes Servings: 4

1 lb. cooked chicken, shredded 1/4 teaspoon garlic powder	1 celery stalk, chopped 1/4 cup almonds, sliced 1/4 cup cranberries, dried 1/4 cup mayonnaise
1/4 cup sour cream	1/4 teaspoon onion powder 1/4 teaspoon pepper
1/2 teaspoon salt	

1. Add all into the mixing bowl and mix well.
2. Place in refrigerator for 1-2 hours.
3. Serve and enjoy.

Nutrition: Calories 175 Fat 12 g Carbohydrates 6 g Sugar 2 g Protein 8 g Cholesterol 30 mg

.Simple Baked Chicken Breasts (Greek)

Preparation Time: 10 minutes
Cooking Time: 45 minutes Servings: 6

6 chicken breasts, skinless & boneless 1/2 cup olive oil	1/4 cup soy sauce
1tablespoon oregano	2tablespoon fresh lemon juice 1 teaspoon garlic salt

1. Add all into the large zip-lock bag. Seal bag and shake well and place in the fridge for 3-4 hours.
2. Preheat the oven to 350 F.
3. Place marinated chicken into a baking dish and bake for 45 minutes.
4. Serve and enjoy.

Nutrition: Calories 435 Fat 27 g Carbohydrates 2 g Sugar 1 g Protein 43 g Cholesterol 131 mg

.Shredded Turkey Breast (Greek)

Preparation Time: 10 minutes
Cooking Time: 8 hours Servings: 10

4 lbs. turkey breast, skinless, boneless, and halves 1 1/2 tablespoon taco seasoning, homemade	12 oz chicken stock 1/2 cup butter, cubed Pepper
Salt	

1. Place turkey breast into the crockpot.
2. Pour remaining over turkey breast.
3. Cover and cook on low for 8 hours.
4. Shred turkey breast with a fork.
5. Serve and enjoy.

Nutrition: Calories 327 Fat 15.4 g Carbohydrates 11.8 g Sugar 6.5 g Protein 34.3g Cholesterol 111 mg

.Urban Chicken Alfredo (Spanish)

Prep time: 10 minutes Cooking time: 20 minutes Servings: 2

1 onion, chopped	1 sweet red pepper, roasted, chopped 1 cup spinach, chopped
½ cup cream	1 teaspoon cream cheese 1 tablespoon olive oil
½ teaspoon ground black pepper	8 oz chicken breast, skinless, boneless, sliced

1. Mix up together sliced chicken breast with ground black pepper and put in the saucepan.
2. Add olive oil and mix up.
3. Roast the chicken for 5 minutes over the medium-high heat. Stir it from time to time.
4. After this, add chopped sweet pepper, onion, and cream cheese.
5. Mix up well and bring to boil.
6. Add spinach and cream. Mix up well.
7. Close the lid and cook chicken Alfredo for 10 minutes more over the medium heat.

Nutrition: Calories 279, Fat 14 g, Fiber 2.5 g, Protein 26.4 g

.Spicy Chicken with Couscous (Greek)

Prep Time: 15 minutes Cooking time: 40 minutes Servings: 4

16oz lean chicken breasts	1½ tsps. smoked paprika, chili powder, or ras el hanout 1/3 cup sliced preserved lemon, chopped
2 tbsps. olive oil	1tsp dried oregano or ¼ cup chopped fresh herbs (parsley, oregano, or coriander) plus extra fresh coriander, to garnish
2red onions, sliced	14oz pack Birds Eye Steam Fresh Plus Pearl Couscous with Chickpeas 4 small whole meal pita pieces of bread

14oz can no-added-salt chickpeas, rinsed, and drained
6 tbsps. yogurt, to serve

1. Flatten the chicken with a meat tenderizer. Place inside a Ziplock bag along with the ground spices, lemon, oil, herbs, and onions. Shake to evenly coat the , and let sit in the refrigerator for a few hours.
2. Preheat the oven to 375°F.
3. Transfer the marinated chicken to an ovenproof dish, and bake for about 35 minutes, turning halfway through cooking. Pour the couscous into a large bowl. Add a little turmeric powder, and mix well. Pour in hot water, and let stand covered for about 5 minutes. After that, shell it with a fork, add the chickpeas, and mix.
4. Meanwhile, heat or toast the pita bread.
5. Divide the couscous among 4 plates. Slice the chicken, and add it to the couscous. Garnish with a spoonful of yogurt and some cilantro. Serve, and enjoy!

Nutrition: Calories: 564 | Carbs: 60g | Fat: 14g | Protein: 41g | Fiber: 12g

.Chickben & Rice (Greek)

Preparation Time: 20 minute Cooking Time: 30 minutes
Servings: 8

1 whole chicken, sliced into smaller pieces. 2 tablespoons dry Greek seasoning	11/2 cups long grain white rice 1 cup chopped parsley

1. Coat the chicken with the seasoning mix.
2. Add 2 cups of water to the Instant Pot.
3. Add the chicken inside.
4. Seal the pot.
5. Choose manual mode.
6. Cook at high pressure for 30 minutes.
7. Release the pressure naturally.
8. Lift the chicken and place on a baking sheet.
9. Bake in the oven for 5 minutes or until skin is crispy.
10. While waiting, strain the broth from the Instant Pot to remove the chicken residue.
11. Add the rice.
12. Seal the pot.
13. Set it to rice function.
14. Fluff the rice and serve with the chicken.

Nutrition: Calories 412 Total Fat 11.2g Saturated Fat 3.1g Cholesterol 130mg Sodium 249mg Total Carbohydrate 29.3g Dietary Fiber 0.7g Total Sugars 0.1g Protein 45.1g Potassium 450mg

.Arugula Fig Chicken (Greek)

Preparation time: 15 minutes Cooking time: 30 minutes
Servings: 4

1teaspoons cornstarch 2 clove garlic, crushed	¾ cup Mission figs, chopped
¼ cup black or green olives, chopped 1 bag baby arugula	½ cup chicken broth
8 skinless chicken thighs 2 teaspoons olive oil	2 teaspoons brown sugar
½ cup red wine vinegar	Ground black pepper and salt, to taste

1. Over medium stove flame, heat the oil in a skillet or saucepan (preferably of medium size).
2. Add the chicken, sprinkle with some salt and cook until evenly brown. Set it aside.
3. Add and sauté the garlic.
4. In a mixing bowl, combine the vinegar, broth, cornstarch and sugar. Add the mixture into the pan and simmer until the sauce thickens.
5. Add the figs and olives; simmer for a few minutes. Serve warm with chopped arugula on top.

Nutrition: Calories 364 Fat 14g Carbohydrates 29g Fiber 5 g Protein 31g

.Pesto Veggie Chicken (Spanish)

Preparation Time: 10 minutes
Cooking Time: 7 hours Servings: 3

2 chicken breasts, skinless and boneless 1 1/2 cups grape tomatoes, halved	2 tablespoon pesto
2 cups zucchini, chopped Salt	2 cups green beans, chopped Pepper

1. Place chicken into the crockpot.
2. Pour remaining over the chicken.
3. Cover and cook on low for 7 hours.
4. Serve and enjoy.

Nutrition: Calories 281 Fat 12 g Carbohydrates 11.9 g Sugar 5.4 g Protein 32.2g Cholesterol 89 mg

.Italian Chicken (Italian)

Preparation Time: 30 minutes Cooking Time: 10 minutes
Servings: 6

1 carrot, chopped 1/2 lb. mushrooms 8 chicken thighs	1 cup tomato sauce
3 cloves garlic, crushed	

1. Season the chicken with salt and pepper.
2. Cover and marinate for 30 minutes.
3. Press the sauté setting in the Instant Pot.
4. Add 1 tablespoon of ghee.
5. Cook the carrots and mushrooms until soft.
6. Add the tomato sauce and garlic.
7. Add the chicken, tomatoes and olives.
8. Cook and mix well.
9. Seal the pot.
10. Set it to manual.
11. Cook at high pressure for 10 minutes.
12. Release the pressure naturally.

Nutrition: Calories 425 Total Fat 16.9g Saturated Fat 5.3g Cholesterol 179mg Sodium 395mg Total Carbohydrate 7.5g Dietary Fiber 2.1g Total Sugars 4.5g Protein 58.9g Potassium 929mg

.Lemon Garlic Chicken (Greek)

Prep Time: 1 hour Cooking Time: 20 minutes Servings: 6

6 chicken breast fillets 3 tablespoons olive oil	1 tablespoon lemon juice 2 teaspoon dried parsley
3 cloves garlic, crushed and minced	

1. Marinate the chicken breast fillets in a mixture of olive oil, lemon juice, garlic, parsley, and a pinch of salt and pepper.
2. Let sit for 1 hour covered in the refrigerator.
3. Press the sauté setting in the Instant Pot.
4. Pour in the vegetable oil.
5. Cook the chicken for 5 minutes per side or until fully cooked.

Nutrition: Calories 341 Total Fat 17.9g Saturated Fat 4g Cholesterol 130mg Sodium 127mg Total Carbohydrate 0.7g Dietary Fiber 0.1g Total Sugars 0.1g Protein 42.4g Potassium 368mg

.Chicken with Salsa & Cilantro (Spanish)

Prep Time: 20 minutes Cooking Time: 20 minutes Servings: 6

1 ½ lb. chicken breast fillets	1teaspoon garlic, minced 1
2 cups salsa Verde	teaspoon cumin
2tbsp fresh cilantro, chopped	

1. Put the chicken breast fillets inside the Instant Pot.
2. Pour the salsa, garlic and cumin on top.
3. Seal the pot.
4. Set it to poultry.
5. Release the pressure quickly.
6. Remove the chicken and shred.
7. Put it back to the pot.
8. Stir in the cilantro.

Nutrition: Calories 238 Total Fat 8.7g Saturated Fat 2.3g Cholesterol 101mg Sodium 558mg Total Carbohydrate 3.8g Dietary Fiber 0.4g Total Sugars 1.2g Protein 34g Potassium 285mg

.Chicken Zucchini Boats (Greek)

Prep time: 15 minutes Cooking time: 30 minutes Servings: 2

1 zucchini	½ cup ground chicken
½ teaspoon chipotle pepper	½ teaspoon tomato sauce
1 oz Swiss cheese, shredded	½ teaspoon salt
4 tablespoons water	

1. Trim the zucchini and cut it on 2 halves.
2. Remove the zucchini pulp.
3. In the mixing bowl mix up together ground chicken, chipotle pepper, tomato sauce, and salt.
4. Fill the zucchini with chicken mixture and top with Swiss cheese.
5. Place the zucchini boats in the tray. Add water.
6. Bake the boats for 30 minutes at 355F.

Nutrition: Calories 134, Fat 6.3 g, Fiber 1.1, Protein 13.4 g

.Jerk Chicken (Greek)

Preparation time: 10 minutes Cooking time: 30 minutes Servings: 2

2 chicken thighs, skinless, boneless 1 teaspoon fresh ginger, chopped	1 garlic clove, chopped
½ spring onion, chopped 1 teaspoon liquid honey	1 teaspoon fresh parsley, chopped
1 teaspoon fresh coriander, chopped	¼ teaspoon chili flakes
¼ tbsp ground black pepper	2 teaspoons lemon juice

1. Mix up together fresh ginger, garlic, onion, liquid honey, parsley, coriander, chili flakes, and ground black pepper.
2. Rub the chicken thighs with honey mixture generously.
3. Preheat the grill to 385F.
4. Place the chicken thighs in the grill and cook for 30 minutes. Flip the chicken thighs on another side after 15 minutes of cooking. The cooked jerk chicken should have a brown crust.
5. Sprinkle the cooked chicken with lemon juice.

Nutrition: Calories 139, Fat 7.3 g, Fiber 0.1, Carbs 4 g, Protein 19.4 g

.Mediterranean White Wine Chicken (Greek)

Prep Time: 35 minutes Cooking Time: 15 minutes Servings: 4

1cloves garlic, minced	½ cup diced onion
3cups tomatoes, chopped 2 teaspoons olive oil	4skinless, boneless chicken breast halves
½ cup + 2 tablespoons white wine	¼ cup chopped parsley
2 teaspoons chopped thyme	1 tablespoon chopped basil
	Ground black pepper and salt to taste

1. Over medium stove flame, heat the oil and 2 tablespoons white wine in a skillet or saucepan (preferably of medium size).
2. Add the chicken and fry until evenly brown. Set it aside.
3. Add the garlic and sauté for 30 seconds. Add the onion and sauté for 2-3 minutes.
4. Mix in the tomatoes and bring the mixture to a simmer.
5. Reduce the heat and mix in ½ cup white wine; simmer the mix for 10 minutes and add the basil and thyme. Cook for another 5 minutes.
6. Add the chicken; combine and cook over low heat for 7-10 minutes. Add the parsley on top. Season with black pepper and salt. Serve warm.

Nutrition: Cals 293 Fat 8g Carbohydrates 14g Fiber 3g Protein 36g

.Delicious Italian Chicken (Italian)

Prep Time: 10 minutes Cooking Time: 4 hours Servings: 4

4 chicken breasts, skinless and boneless	1 onion, chopped
1tablespoon garlic, minced	2tablespoon fresh lemon juice 2 teaspoon Italian seasoning
1 tablespoon olive oil 2 tablespoon capers	1 cup roasted red peppers, chopped 1 cup olives
Pepper Salt	

1. Season chicken with pepper and salt.
2. Heat oil in a pan over medium heat. Place chicken in the pan and cook until browned from both sides.
3. Transfer chicken into the crockpot.
4. Add remaining over chicken.
5. Cover and cook on low for 4 hours.
6. Serve and enjoy.

Nutrition: Calories 355 Fat 15 g Carbohydrates 9 g Sugar 3 g Protein 43 g Cholesterol 132 mg

.Delicious Chicken Tenders (Greek)

Prep Time: 10 minutes Cooking Time: 15 minutes Servings: 4

11/2 lbs. chicken tenders	2tablespoon BBQ sauce, homemade & sugar-free
1 tablespoon olive oil	
1tbsp poultry seasoning Pepper	Salt

1. Add all except oil in a zip-lock bag. Seal bag and place in the fridge for 2 hours.
2. Heat oil in a pan over medium heat.
3. Place marinated chicken tenders on the hot pan and cook until lightly browned and cooked. Serve and enjoy.

Nutrition: Calories 366 Fat 15 g Carbohydrates 3 g Sugar 2 g Protein 50 g Cholesterol 150 mg

.Flavors Chicken Shawarma (Italian)

Prep Time: 10 minutes Cooking Time: 12 minutes Servings: 4

8 chicken thighs, skinless 1 tablespoon cumin	2 garlic cloves, minced 3 tablespoon olive oil
2 tablespoon lemon juice	1/2 teaspoon cayenne pepper 2 teaspoons paprika
1 tbsp ground cardamom 1 tablespoon coriander	1/4 teaspoon pepper 2 teaspoon salts

1. Add chicken into the zip-lock bag. Pour remaining over chicken. Seal bag and shake well.
2. Place marinated chicken into the refrigerator overnight.
3. Heat grill over medium-high heat.
4. Place marinated chicken on hot grill and cook for 6 minutes on each side. Serve and enjoy.

Nutrition: Calories 665 Fat 33 g Carbohydrates 3 g Sugar 0.5 g Protein 85 g Cholesterol 260 mg

.Moroccan Chicken (Greek)

Prep Time: 20 minutes Cooking time: 45 minutes Servings: 6

1 ½ tbsp all-natural Ras El Hanout 1 ½ tsp ground cinnamon	1 tsp sweet paprika 1 tsp ground ginger
½ to 1 tsp black pepper	3 ½ lb. whole chicken cut into bone-in pieces Kosher salt
extra virgin olive oil	1 medium yellow onion, chopped 4 garlic cloves, peeled, and minced 1 oz chopped fresh cilantro
1 lemon, thinly sliced	¾ cup pitted green olives
¼ cup raisins	¼ cup chopped dry apricots 3 tbsp tomato paste
Toasted slivered almonds, optional	1 ½ cup low-sodium chicken broth

1. In a small bowl, combine Ras El Hanout, and the remaining spices to make the rub.
2. Pat the chicken pieces dry, and season lightly with kosher salt on both sides. Rub the chicken with the spice rub. Let marinate in the refrigerator for 2 hours or overnight.
3. In a deep ceramic skillet, heat 2 tbsps. extra virgin olive oil over medium-high heat. Add the chicken (skin side down, if you kept the skin on), and brown for 5 minutes. Turn, and brown on the other side for about 3 more minutes.
4. Lower the heat to medium-low, and add the onions, garlic, and cilantro. Cover, and cook for 3 minutes, then add lemon slices, olives, raisins, and dried apricots.
5. In a small bowl, mix tomato paste, and chicken broth, and pour mixture
6. over chicken. Bring to a boil for 5 minutes, then, lower the heat, cover, and cook over medium-low heat for about 40 mins.
7. Garnish with fresher cilantro, and toasted almonds, and serve accompanied by couscous.

Nutrition: Calories: 374 Carbs: 16.3g Fat: 21.5g Protein: 31.1g

.Moroccan Chicken Thighs and Vegetable Tagine(Greek)

Preparation Time: 15 minutes Cooking time: 50 minutes Servings: 6

½ cup extra-virgin olive oil, divided	1½ pounds boneless skinless chicken thighs, cut into 1-inch chunks 1½ tsps. salt, divided
½ tsp freshly ground black pepper 1 small red onion, chopped	1 red bell pepper, cut into 1-inch squares
2 medium tomatoes, chopped or 1½ cups diced canned tomatoes 1 cup water	2 medium zucchinis, sliced into ¼-inch-thick half moons
1 cup pitted halved olives (Kalamata or Spanish green work nicely)	¼ cup chopped fresh cilantro or flat-leaf Italian parsley Riced cauliflower or sautéed spinach, for serving

1. In a large rimmed skillet, heat ¼ cup olive oil over medium-high heat.
2. Season chicken with 1 tsp salt, and pepper, and cook 4 minutes per side. Add the onions, and peppers, and sauté for 8 minutes, until wilted. Add the chopped tomatoes, and water, and bring to a boil. When it boils, reduce the heat to low, cover, and simmer for about 40 minutes.
3. Add the remaining ¼ cup olive oil, zucchini, olives, and cilantro, and mix well. Continue to cook over low heat, uncovered, for about 10 minutes, until the zucchini is tender.
4. Serve the chicken warm over the embroidered cauliflower or a bed of sautéed spinach.

Nutrition: Calories: 358 Carbs: 8g Fat: 24g Protein: 25g Fiber: 3g

.Roasted Pepper Chicken (Greek)

Preparation Time: 10 minutes Cooking Time: 4 hours Servings: 4

4 chicken breasts, skinless and boneless	1 cup roasted red peppers, chopped 1 tablespoon garlic, minced
2 tablespoon capers	2 tablespoon lemon juice 3/4 cup olives, sliced
1 medium onion, chopped Salt	3 teaspoon Italian seasoning Pepper

1. Season chicken with pepper and salt.
2. Cook chicken in a pan until lightly browned.
3. Transfer chicken into the crockpot.
4. Add remaining over chicken.
5. Cover and cook on low for 4 hours.
6. Serve and enjoy.

Nutrition: Calories 355 Fat 15 g Carbohydrates 9 g Sugar 3 g Protein 43 g Cholesterol 130 mg

.Oregano Turkey and Peppers (Spanish)

Prep Time: 10 minutes Cooking time: 1 hour Servings: 4

1red bell peppers, cut into strips	2 green bell peppers, cut into strips 1 red onion, chopped
4 garlic cloves, minced	½ cup black olives, pitted and sliced 2 cups chicken stock
1big turkey breast, skinless, boneless, and cut into strips 1 tbsp. oregano, chopped	½ cup cilantro, chopped

1. Preheat the oven to 400 degrees F.
2. Arrange the peppers, turkey, and the rest of the on a baking sheet. Roast in the oven for 1 hour.
3. Divide among plates, serve, and enjoy.

Nutrition: Calories: 229 Carbs: 17.8g Fat: 8.9g Protein: 33.6g Fiber: 8.2g

.Mediterranean Feta Chicken (Spanish)

Preparation Time: 20 minutes Cooking Time: 15 minutes Servings: 4

1tablespoons olive oil	1cup crumbled feta cheese
2(6-ounce) boneless and skinless chicken breast halves 1 teaspoon Greek seasoning	1/3 cup chopped sun-dried tomatoes

1. Preheat your oven to 375 F-190 C. Line a baking pan with parchment paper. Grease it with some avocado oil. (You can also use cooking spray)
2. Mix the feta cheese and tomatoes in a mixing bowl.
3. Coat the chicken with olive oil and season with the seasoning. Add the cheese mixture and roll up chicken breasts. Secure with a toothpick, pinning them.
4. Place the chicken into the pan; bake for 25-30 minutes. Remove the toothpicks and serve warm.

Nutrition: Calories 204 Fat 14g Carbohydrates 9g Fiber 1g Protein 9g

.Roasted Tomato Chicken Curry (Greek)

Preparation Time: 10 minutes Cooking Time: 33 minutes Servings: 4

1 1/2 lbs. chicken thighs, skinless and boneless 14 oz can roast tomatoes, diced 14 oz coconut milk 1 teaspoon salt	1 teaspoon ground ginger 1 tablespoon curry powder 1 tablespoon olive oil

1. Add all into the instant pot and stir well.
2. Cover and cook on high pressure for 22 minutes.
3. Once done, release pressure using quick release. Open the lid.
4. Remove chicken from pot.
5. Set pot on sauté mode and cook for 10 minutes.
6. Cut chicken into small pieces and return into the pot.
7. Stir well and serve.

Nutrition: Calories 612 Fat 40 g Carbohydrates 11.6 g Sugar 5.8 g Protein 52.5 g Cholesterol 151 mg

.Crisp Chicken Carnitas (Spanish)

Preparation Time: 10 minutes Cooking Time: 4 hours Servings: 8

1lbs. chicken breasts, skinless and boneless 1/4 cup fresh parsley, chopped 2tablespoon fresh lime juice 1 tablespoon chili powder 1/2 teaspoon salt	1tablespoon garlic, minced 2 teaspoon cumin powder

1. Add chicken into the crockpot.
2. Pour remaining ingredients over the chicken.
3. Cover and cook on high for 4 hours.
4. Shred the chicken using a fork.
5. Transfer shredded chicken on a baking tray and broil for 5 minutes.
6. Serve and enjoy.

Nutrition: Calories 225 Fat 8.7 g Carbohydrates 2.1 g Sugar 0.3 g Protein 33.2g Cholesterol 101 mg

.Cilantro Lime Chicken Salad (Spanish)

Preparation Time: 10 minutes
Cooking Time: 5 minutes Servings: 2

11/2 cups cooked chicken, shredded 2 tablespoon fresh lime juice 1 teaspoon chili powder Pepper	2tablespoon fresh cilantro, chopped 2 tablespoon green onion, sliced Salt

1. Add all ingredients into the medium bowl and mix well. Season with pepper and salt.

Nutrition: Calories 113 Fat 2 g Carbohydrates 1 g Sugar 0.5 g Protein 20 g Cholesterol 55 mg

.Meatballs (Greek)

Preparation Time: 10 minutes Cooking Time: 18 minutes Servings: 6

1lb. ground chicken	2tablespoon chives, chopped 1/4 cup almond flour
1 1/2 cups zucchini, grated & squeeze out all liquid 1 teaspoon Italian seasoning	1 egg, lightly beaten 1/2 teaspoon salt

1. Preheat the oven to 350 F.
2. Line baking tray with parchment paper and set aside.
3. Add all ingredients into the mixing bowl and mix until well combined.
4. Make small balls from mixture and place on parchment lined baking tray.
5. Bake for 18 minutes.
6. Serve and enjoy.

Nutrition: Calories 189 Fat 8.8 g Carbohydrates 2.1 g Sugar 0.6 g Protein 24.2g Cholesterol 95 mg

.Tasty Chicken Kabobs (Greek)

Preparation Time: 10 minutes Cooking Time: 10 minutes
Servings: 4

1 1/2 lbs. chicken breast, boneless & cut into 1-inch pieces 1 teaspoon dried oregano	1tablespoon fresh lime juice 1 tablespoon olive oil 1/2 teaspoon pepper 1/2 teaspoon sea salt

1. Add chicken into the mixing bowl. Pour remaining ingredients over chicken and coat well and place it in the refrigerator overnight.
2. Heat grill over medium heat.
3. Thread marinated chicken onto the skewers.
4. Place chicken skewers onto the hot grill and cook for 8-10 minutes.
5. Serve and enjoy.

Nutrition: Calories 228 Fat 7.8 g Carbohydrates 1.3 g Sugar 0.2 g Protein 36.2g Cholesterol 109 mg

.Cheesy Salsa Chicken (Italian)

Preparation Time: 10 minutes Cooking Time: 6 hours
Servings: 6

1lbs. chicken breasts, cut into cubes 2 cups cheddar cheese, shredded Pepper Salt	2 tablespoon taco seasoning 2 cups salsa

1. Add all ingredients except cheese into the crock pot.
2. Cover and cook on low for 5 hours 30 minutes.
3. Add cheese and stir well and cook for 30 minutes more.
4. Stir and serve.

Nutrition: Calories 463 Fat 23.8 g Carbohydrates 5.9 g Sugar 2.9 g Protein 54.5 g Cholesterol 174 mg

.Grilled Pesto Chicken (Italian)

Preparation Time: 10 minutes
Cooking Time: 10 minutes Servings: 6

1 1/2 lbs. chicken breasts, skinless, boneless, and slice 1/4 cup pesto Salt	1/2 cup mozzarella cheese, shredded Pepper

1. Place chicken into the large bowl.
2. Add pesto, pepper, and salt over chicken and coat well. Cover and place in the fridge for 2 hours.
3. Heat grill over medium-high heat.
4. Place marinated chicken on hot grill and cook until completely done.
5. Sprinkle cheese over chicken.
6. Serve and enjoy.

Nutrition: Calories 300 Fat 14 g Carbohydrates 1 g Sugar 0.5 g Protein 40 g Cholesterol 120 mg

.European Posole (Greek)

Preparation time: 10 minutes Cooking time: 25 minutes
Servings: 2

1 ½ cup water	6 oz chicken fillet
1 chili pepper, chopped 1 onion, diced	1 teaspoon butter
½ teaspoon salt	½ teaspoon paprika
1 tablespoon fresh dill, chopped	

1. Pour water in the saucepan.
2. Add chicken fillet and salt. Boil it for 15 minutes over the medium heat.
3. Then remove the chicken fillet from water and shred it with the help of the fork.
4. Return it back in the hot water.
5. Melt butter in the skillet and add diced onion. Roast it until light brown and transfer in the shredded chicken.
6. Add paprika, dill, chili pepper, and mix up.
7. Close the lid and simmer Posole for 5 minutes.

Nutrition: Calories 207, Fat 8.3 g, Fiber 1.1, Carbs 6 g, Protein 25.4g

.Mango Chicken Salad (Greek)

Preparation time: 10 minutes Cooking time: 12 minutes
Servings: 3

1 cup lettuce, chopped 1 cup arugula, chopped	1 mango, peeled, chopped
8 oz chicken breast, skinless, boneless 1 tablespoon lime juice	1 teaspoon sesame oil
½ teaspoon salt	½ teaspoon ground black pepper 1 teaspoon butter

1. Sprinkle the chicken breast with salt and ground black pepper.
2. Melt butter in the skillet and add chicken breast.
3. Roast it for 10 minutes over the medium heat. Flip it on another side from time to time.
4. Meanwhile, combine together lettuce, arugula, mango, and sesame oil in the salad bowl.
5. Add lime juice.
6. Chop the cooked chicken breast roughly and chill it to the room temperature.
7. Add it in the mango salad and mix up.

Nutrition: Calories 183, Fat 5.2 g, Fiber 2.8 g, Carbs 17.4 g, Protein 17.2 g

.Turkey with Basil & Tomatoes (Greek)

Preparation Time: 10 minutes Cooking Time: 10 minutes
Servings: 4

4 turkey breast fillets 1
tablespoon olive oil
1 1/2 cups cherry tomatoes,
sliced in half 1/4 cup olive
tapenade

1/4 cup fresh basil,
chopped

1. Season the turkey fillets with salt.
2. Add the olive oil to the Instant Pot.
3. Set it to sauté.
4. Cook the turkey until brown on both sides.
5. Stir in the basil, tomatoes and olive tapenade.
6. Cook for 3 minutes, stirring frequently.
7. Serving Suggestion: Serve with green salad.

Nutrition: Calories 188 Total Fat 5.1g Saturated Fat 1g Cholesterol 0mg Sodium 3mg Total Carbohydrate 2.8g Dietary Fiber 1.6g Total Sugars 1.9g Protein 33.2g Potassium 164mg

.Easy & Tasty Salsa Chicken (Italian)

Preparation Time: 10 minutes Cooking Time: 2 hours
Servings: 6

1 1/2 lbs. chicken tenders,
skinless 1/4 teaspoon garlic
powder
15 oz salsa

Salt

1/8 teaspoon ground cumin
1/8 teaspoon oregano

1/4 teaspoon onion powder
1/4 teaspoon chili powder
Pepper

1. Place chicken tenders into the crockpot.
2. Pour remaining ingredients over chicken.
3. Cover and cook on high for 2 hours.
4. Shred the chicken using a fork and serve.

Nutrition: Calories 235 Fat 8 g Carbohydrates 5 g Sugar 2 g Protein 35 g Cholesterol 100 mg

.Tender Turkey Breast (Greek)

Preparation Time: 10 minutes Cooking Time: 4 hours
Servings: 8

4 lbs. turkey breast, bone-in
1/2 cup chicken stock

Salt

6 garlic cloves, peeled 3
fresh rosemary sprigs
Pepper

1. Place turkey breast into the crockpot. Season with pepper and salt.
2. Add stock, garlic, and rosemary on top.
3. Cover and cook on low for 4 hours.
4. Serve and enjoy.

Nutrition: Calories 235 Fat 3.5 g Carbohydrates 10 g Sugar 8 g Protein 39 g Cholesterol 100 mg

.Roasted Chicken with Red Peppers and LemonGarlic Hummus (Greek)

Preparation Time: 10 minutes Cooking time: 10 minutes
Servings: 6

1¼ pounds boneless,
skinless chicken thighs, cut
into 1-inch pieces

½ tsp dried thyme

¼ tsp kosher or sea salt

Lemony Garlic Hummus,
or a 10-ounce container
prepared hummus
3 (6-inch) whole-wheat pita
bread, cut into eighths

½ sweet or red onion, cut
into 1-inch chunks (about 1
cup) 2 tbsps. extra-virgin
olive oil

¼ tsp freshly ground black
pepper

1 (12-ounce) jar roasted red
peppers, drained, and
chopped

½ medium lemon

1. Line a large baking sheet with aluminum foil, and set it aside.
2. Place the baking sheet 4 inches under the grill, and preheat to maximum temperature.
3. In a large bowl, mix the chicken, onion, oil, thyme, pepper, and salt. Spread the mixture on the hot baking sheet.
4. Place the chicken under the broiler, and cook for 10 minutes, stirring halfway through cooking. Cook until the chicken, and onion begins to char on the tips.
5. Spread the hummus on a large serving platter, and pour the chicken mixture over it. Sprinkle with the juice of half a squeezed lemon, and serve accompanied by pita pieces.

Nutrition: Calories: 324 Carbs: 29g Fat: 11g Protein: 29g Fiber: 6g

Roasted Garlic Chicken Thigh (Greek)

.Preparation Time: 10 minutes Cooking time: 55 minutes
Servings: 2

8 chicken thighs

6 cloves garlic, peeled and
crushed

2cups cherry tomatoes,
halved 1/3 cup capers,
sliced

Salt, and pepper as needed 1
tbsp. extra-virgin olive oil
1jar (10 ounces) roasted red
peppers, drained, and
chopped 1 ½ pounds
potatoes, diced
1 tsp dried Italian seasoning
1 tbsp. fresh basil

1. Preheat the oven to 400°F.
2. Season the chicken with kosher salt, and black pepper.
3. In an oven-safe skillet, pour in the olive oil, and heat over medium-high heat. Brown the chicken on both sides.
1. 4.Addthegarlic,peppers,tomatoes,potatoes,capers,and Italian seasoning, and mix well.
4. Transfer the skillet to the oven, and bake for about 45 minutes. Serve, and enjoy!

Nutrition: Calories: 500 Carbs: 37g Fat: 23g Protein: 35g

.Slow-Cooked Turkey and Brown Rice (Spanish)

Preparation Time: 15 minutes Cooking time: 3 hours 10 minutes Servings: 6

1tbsp. extra-virgin olive oil	2tbsps. chopped fresh sage, divided 2 tbsps. chopped fresh thyme, divided 1 tsp sea salt
1½ pounds ground turkey	
½ tsp ground black pepper	1 (14-ounce / 397-g) can stewed tomatoes, with the juice
2 cups brown rice	
¼ cup pitted and sliced Kalamata olives 3 medium zucchinis, sliced thinly	¼ cup chopped fresh flat-leaf parsley 1 medium yellow onion, chopped
1 tbsp. plus 1 tsp balsamic vinegar 2 cups low-sodium chicken stock 2 garlic cloves, minced	½ cup grated Parmesan cheese, for serving

1. Heat olive oil in a nonstick skillet over medium-high heat. Add ground turkey, and sprinkle with 1 tbsp. sage, 1 tbsp. thyme, salt, and ground black pepper.
2. Brown the turkey 5 minutes per side. Pour into a slow cooker. Add remaining ingredients (except parmesan cheese), and mix well.
3. Place lid on, and cook for 3 hours or until rice, and vegetables are tender. Pour into a large serving dish, sprinkle with grated Parmesan cheese, and serve.

Nutrition: Calories: 449 Carbs: 56.5g Fat: 16.4g Protein: 32.4g

.Tasty Chicken Bites (Spanish)

Preparation Time: 10 minutes Cooking Time: 10 minutes Servings: 2

1 lb. chicken breasts, boneless and cut into cubes	1tablespoon fresh oregano, chopped 2 tablespoon olive oil
2 tablespoon fresh lemon juice	
1/8 teaspoon cayenne pepper Pepper	Salt

1. Place chicken in a bowl.
2. Add reaming ingredients over chicken and toss well. Place in the fridge for 1 hour.
3. Heat grill over medium heat.
4. Spray grill with cooking spray.
5. Thread marinated chicken onto the skewers.
6. Place skewers on hot grill and cooks until chicken is cooked.
7. Serve and enjoy.

Nutrition: Calories 560 Fat 31 g Carbohydrates 2 g Sugar 0.5 g Protein 65 g Cholesterol 200 mg

.Mediterranean Chicken and Potatoes (Greek)

Prep Time: 20 minutes Cooking time: 45 minutes Servings: 6

3lb. chicken pieces, bone-in, and skin on Salt	4gold potatoes, scrubbed clean, cut into thin wedges 1 medium yellow onion, halved then sliced
1 tsp black pepper 1 lemon, sliced	1 cup chicken broth
6 to 12 pitted kalamata olives, optional Fresh parsley, for garnish	¼ cup extra virgin olive oil
¼ cup lemon juice	12 fresh garlic cloves, minced
1 ½ tbsp dried rosemary (or dried oregano)	½ tsp ground nutmeg

1. Preheat the oven to 350°F.
2. Meanwhile, dry the chicken, and season generously with salt.
3. Arrange potato wedges and onions in the bottom of a baking dish or skillet. Season with salt, and 1 tbsp. black pepper, then adds the chicken pieces to the pan.
4. In a small bowl, whisk together ¼ cup extra virgin olive oil with the lemon juice, minced garlic, rosemary, and nutmeg. Pour the sauce evenly over the chicken, and potatoes, and arrange the lemon slices on top.
5. Pour the chicken broth over the side of the baking dish or pan (do not pour the broth over the chicken).
6. Bake in heated the oven uncovered for 45 minutes-1 hours until chicken and potatoes are tender. Remove from the oven, add kalamata olives, garnish with some fresh parsley, and serve

Note: If desired, you can serve the chicken, and potatoes accompanied by Tzatziki sauce, and pita bread.

Nutrition: Calories: 473 Carbs: 28g Fat: 15.8g Protein: 54.4g Fiber: 3.5g

.Baked Lemon Chicken (Italian)

Preparation Time: 10 minutes Cooking Time: 15 minutes Servings: 1

1 chicken breast, boneless	1/2 tablespoon Italian seasoning 1 fresh lemon juice
1fresh lemon, sliced Pepper	Salt

1. Preheat the oven to 350 F.
2. Spray baking dish with cooking spray.
3. Season chicken with Italian seasoning, pepper and salt.
4. Place chicken into the baking dish.
5. Pour lemon juice over chicken and arrange lemon slices on top of chicken.
6. Bake for 15 minutes.
7. Serve and enjoy.

Nutrition: Calories 139 Fat 4.7 g Carbohydrates 1.6 g Sugar 0.9 g Protein
21.4 g Cholesterol 69 mg

.Tender Chicken Quesadilla (Spanish)

Preparation time: 10 minutes Cooking time: 20 minutes
Servings: 4

bread tortillas	1 teaspoon butter
2 teaspoons olive oil	1 teaspoon Taco seasoning
6 oz chicken breast, skinless, boneless, sliced	1 bell pepper, cut on the wedges
1/3 cup Cheddar cheese, shredded	

1. Pour 1 teaspoon of olive oil in the skillet and add chicken.
2. Sprinkle the meat with Taco seasoning and mix up well.
3. Roast chicken for 10 minutes over the medium heat. Stir it from time to time.
4. Then transfer the cooked chicken in the plate.
5. Add remaining olive oil in the skillet.
6. Then add bell pepper and roast it for 5 minutes. Stir it all the time.
7. Mix up together bell pepper with chicken.
8. Toss butter in the skillet and melt it.
9. Put 1 tortilla in the skillet.
10. Put Cheddar cheese on the tortilla and flatten it.
11. Then add chicken-pepper mixture and cover it with the second tortilla.
12. Roast the quesadilla for 2 minutes from each side.
13. Cut the cooked meal on the halves and transfer in the serving plates.

Nutrition: Calories 167, Fat 8.2 g, Fiber 0.8 g, Carbs 16.4 g, Protein 24.2 g

.Crack Chicken (Greek)

Preparation time: 10 minutes Cooking time: 30 minutes
Servings: 4

4 chicken thighs, skinless, boneless 1 teaspoon ground black pepper	½ teaspoon salt
1 teaspoon paprika	¼ cup Cheddar cheese, shredded 1 tablespoon cream cheese
½ teaspoon garlic powder	1 teaspoon fresh dill, chopped 1 tablespoon butter
1 teaspoon olive oil	½ teaspoon ground nutmeg

1. Grease the baking dish with butter.
2. Then heat up olive oil in the skillet.
3. Meanwhile, rub the chicken thighs with ground nutmeg, garlic powder, paprika, and salt. Add ground black pepper.
4. Roast the chicken thighs in the hot oil over the high heat for 2 minutes from each side.
5. Then transfer the chicken thighs in the prepared baking dish.
6. Mix up together Cheddar cheese, cream cheese, and dill.
7. Top every chicken thigh with cheese mixture and bake for 25 minutes at 365F.

Nutrition: Calories 79, Fat 7.3 g, Fiber 0.1, Carbs 1 g, Protein 2.4 g

.Chicken Bacon Salad (Italian)

Prep Time: 10 minutes Cooking Time: 5 minutes Servings: 3

1 cups cooked chicken, shredded 1 cup cheddar cheese, shredded 1 cup celery, chopped	1/2 cup sour cream
/4 cup mayonnaise	1/2 cup bacon, crumbles 3 green onions, sliced 1/4 cup onion, chopped Pepper
Salt	

1. Add all ingredients into the large bowl and mix until well combined.
2. Serve and enjoy.

Nutrition: Calories 482 Fat 31.3 g Carbohydrates 9.9 g Sugar 2.7 g Protein 39.6 g Cholesterol 137 mg

.Mayo Chicken Salad (Italian)

Prep Time: 10 minutes Cooking Time: 5 minutes Servings: 6

1 lbs. cooked chicken, shredded 3 celery stalks, chopped	1 cup mayonnaise
1/4 teaspoon garlic powder	1/4 teaspoon salt
1/4 teaspoon onion powder	
1/4 teaspoon pepper	

1. Add all ingredients into the large mixing bowl and stir to combine.
2. Serve and enjoy.

Nutrition: Calories 445 Fat 24 g Carbohydrates 9 g Sugar 2 g Protein 45 g Cholesterol 144 mg

.Green Salsa Chicken (Italian)

Prep Time: 10 minutes Cooking Time: 3 hours Servings: 6

1 lb. chicken breasts, skinless and boneless	15 oz green salsa Pepper
Salt	

1. Add all ingredients into the crock pot.
2. Cover and cook on high for 3 hours.
3. Shred the chicken using fork.
4. Serve and enjoy.

Nutrition: Calories 166 Fat 6 g Carbohydrates 3 g Sugar 1.4 g Protein 22 g Cholesterol 67 mg

.Chicken Chili (Greek)

Prep Time: 10 minutes Cooking Time: 6 hours Servings: 4

1 lb. chicken breasts, skinless and boneless	14 oz can tomato, diced 2 cups of water
1 jalapeno pepper, chopped	1/2 teaspoon paprika 1/2
1 poblano pepper, chopped	teaspoon dried sage 1/2
12 oz can green chilies	teaspoon cumin
1 teaspoon dried oregano	1 teaspoon sea salt
1/2 cup dried chives	

1. Add all ingredients into the crockpot and stir well.
2. Cover and cook on low for 6 hours.
3. Shred the chicken using a fork.
4. Stir well and serve.

Nutrition: Calories 265 Fat 8.9 g Carbohydrates 11.1 g Sugar 4.2 g Protein 34.9 g Cholesterol 101 mg

.Chicken with Spanish Rice (Spanish)

Preparation Time: 15 minutes Cooking Time: 25 minutes Servings: 12

6 chicken breast fillets, sliced into cubes 4 cloves garlic, minced 28 oz. canned diced tomatoes with green chili	1 onion, chopped 4 cups brown rice

1. Season the chicken with salt and pepper.
2. Pour 1 tablespoon into the Instant Pot.
3. Set it to sauté.
4. Brown the chicken and set aside.
5. Add the garlic, onion and rice.
6. Cook for 2 minutes.
7. Add the canned tomatoes with green chili and 4 ½ cups of water.
8. Seal the pot.
9. Set it to manual.
10. Cook at high pressure for 24 minutes.
11. Release the pressure naturally.
12. Fluff the rice and top with the chicken.
13. Serving Suggestion: Garnish with chopped fresh parsley.

Nutrition: Calories 383 Total Fat 7.2g Saturated Fat 1.8g Cholesterol 65mg Sodium 331mg Total Carbohydrate 51.8g Dietary Fiber 2.4g Total Sugars 0.4g Protein 26.5g Potassium 435mg

Turkey Meatloaf (Greek)

Preparation Time: 15 minutes Cooking Time: 35 minutes Servings: 6

1/2 cup bread crumbs 1/4 cup onion, chopped 1 lb. lean ground turkey	1/4 cup sun dried tomatoes, diced 1/2 cup feta cheese, crumbled

1. Mix all the ingredients in a bowl.
2. Form a loaf and cover with foil.
3. Pour 1 cup of water into the Instant Pot.
4. Add the steamer basket inside.
5. Place the wrapped turkey mixture on top of basket.
6. Cover the pot.
7. Set it to manual.
8. Cook at high pressure for 35 minutes.
9. Release the pressure quickly.
10. Serving Suggestion: Let cool before slicing and serving.

Tip: You can also add a tablespoon of almond milk to the mixture. **Nutrition:** Calories 226 Total Fat 11g Saturated Fat 4.5g Cholesterol 78mg Sodium 330mg Total Carbohydrate 10.2g Dietary Fiber 0.9g Total Sugars 1.5g Protein 21.7g Potassium 424mg

.Chicken Sauté (Spanish)

Prep time: 10 minutes Cooking time: 25 minutes Servings: 2

4 oz chicken fillet 4 tomatoes, peeled 1 cup of water 1 tbsp salt ½ teaspoon saffron	1 bell pepper, chopped 1 teaspoon olive oil 1 chili pepper, chopped

1. Pour water in the pan and bring it to boil.
2. Meanwhile, chop the chicken fillet.
3. Add the chicken fillet in the boiling water and cook it for 10 minutes or until the chicken is tender.
4. After this, put the chopped bell pepper and chili pepper in the skillet.
5. Add olive oil and roast the vegetables for 3 minutes.
6. Add chopped tomatoes and mix up well.
7. Cook the vegetables for 2 minutes more.
8. Then add salt and a ¾ cup of water from chicken.
9. Add chopped chicken fillet and mix up.
10. Cook the sauté for 10 minutes over the medium heat.

Nutrition: Calories 192, Fat 7.2 g, Fiber 3.8 g, Carbs 14.4 g, Protein 19.2 g

.Grilled Marinated Chicken (Greek)

Prep time: 35 minutes Cooking time: 20 minutes Servings: 6

1-pound chicken breast, skinless, boneless 2 tablespoons lemon juice ½ teaspoon ground nutmeg 1 teaspoon onion powder 2 tablespoons olive oil 1 tbsp apple cider vinegar	1 teaspoon sage ½ teaspoon dried oregano 1 tbsp paprika 1 teaspoon chili flakes 1 teaspoon salt

1. Make the marinade: whisk together apple cider vinegar, salt, chili flakes, olive oil, onion powder, paprika, dried oregano, ground nutmeg, sage, and lemon juice.
2. Then rub the chicken with marinade carefully and leave for 25 minutes to marinate.
3. Meanwhile, preheat grill to 385F.
4. Place the marinated chicken breast in the grill and cook it for 10 minutes from each side.
5. Cut the cooked chicken on the servings.

Nutrition: Calories 218 Fat 8.2 g, Fiber 0.8 g, Carbs 0.4 g, Protein 32.2 g

.Turkey With Green Sauce (Greek)

Prep Time: 5 minutes Cooking time: 50 minutes Servings: 4

1 big turkey breast, skinless, boneless, and cubed 1 ½ cups Salsa Verde 1 ½ cups feta cheese, crumbled	Salt, and black pepper to the taste 1 tbsp. olive oil ¼ cup cilantro, chopped

1. Preheat the oven to 400°F.
2. Grease a baking dish with olive oil, add the turkey with the gravy, salt, and pepper, and bake for 50 minutes.
3. Remove from the oven, add the cheese, and cilantro, and toss gently. Divide among plates, and serve.

Nutrition: Calories: 332 Carbs: 22.1g Fat: 15.4g Protein: 34.5g Fiber: 10g

.Turkey With Herbs and Almonds (Greek)

Preparation Time: 10 minutes Cooking time: 40 minutes
Servings: 4

1 big turkey breast, skinless, boneless, and cubed 1 tbsp. olive oil

½ cup chicken stock 1 tbsp. basil, chopped

1 tbsp. rosemary, chopped 1 tbsp. oregano, chopped 1 tbsp. parsley, chopped ½ cup almonds, toasted, and chopped 3 cups tomatoes, chopped

3 garlic cloves, minced

1. Heat a skillet with the oil over medium-high heat. Add the turkey, and garlic, and brown for 3 minutes per side. Add the broth, and the rest of the ingredients, and bring to a boil over medium heat. Cook for 35 minutes covered.
2. Divide the mixture among plates, and serve.

Nutrition: Calories: 297 Carbs: 19.4g Fat: 11.2g Protein: 23.6g Fiber: 9.2g

.Turkey With Lemon and Pine Nuts (Greek)

Preparation Time: 10 minutes Cooking time: 30 minutes
Servings: 4

2 turkey breasts, boneless, skinless, and halved A pinch of salt, and black pepper

2 tbsps. avocado oil Juice of 2 lemons

1tbsp. rosemary, chopped 3 garlic cloves, minced

¼ cup pine nuts, chopped 1 cup chicken stock

1. Heat an oiled skillet over medium-high heat. Add the garlic, and turkey, and brown for 4 minutes on each side.
2. Add the rest of the ingredients, and bring to a boil. When it boils, lower the heat to medium, and cook for 20 minutes.
3. Divide the mixture among plates, and serve with a side salad.

Nutrition: Calories: 293 Carbs: 17.8g Fat: 12.4g Protein: 24.5g Fiber: 9.3g

Chapter 8
Fish and Seafood

Cioppino (Seafood Tomato Stew)

Prep time: 10 minutes | Cook time: 20 minutes | Serves 2

2 tablespoons olive oil	1 (6.5-ounce / 184-g) can
½ small onion, diced	minced clams with their
½ green pepper, diced	juice
2 teaspoons dried basil	8 ounces (227 g) peeled,
2 teaspoons dried oregano	deveined raw shrimp
½ cup dry white wine	4 ounces (113 g) any white
1 (14.5-ounce / 411-g) can	fish (a thick piece works
diced tomatoes with basil	best)
1 (8-ounce / 227-g) can no-	3 tablespoons fresh parsley
salt-added tomato sauce	Salt and freshly ground
	black pepper, to taste

1. In a Dutch oven, heat the olive oil over medium heat.
2. Sauté the onion and green pepper for 5 minutes, or until tender. Stir in the basil, oregano, wine, diced tomatoes, and tomato sauce and bring to a boil.
3. Once boiling, reduce the heat to low and bring to a simmer for 5 minutes.
4. Add the clams, shrimp, and fish and cook for about 10 minutes, or until the shrimp are pink and cooked through.
5. Scatter with the parsley and add the salt and black pepper to taste. Remove from the heat and serve warm.

Per Serving calories: 221 | fat: 7.7g | protein: 23.1g | carbs: 10.9g | fiber: 4.2g | sodium: 720mg

Lemon Grilled Shrimp

Prep time: 20 minutes | Cook time: 4 to 6 minutes | Serves 4

2 tablespoons garlic, minced	1 teaspoon salt
3 tablespoons fresh Italian	2 pounds (907 g) jumbo
parsley, finely chopped	shrimp (21 to 25), peeled and
¼ cup extra-virgin olive oil	deveined
½ cup lemon juice	Special Equipment:
	4 wooden skewers, soaked in
	water for at least 30 minutes

1. Whisk together the garlic, parsley, olive oil, lemon juice, and salt in a large bowl.
2. Add the shrimp to the bowl and toss well, making sure the shrimp are coated in the marinade. Set aside to sit for 15 minutes.
3. When ready, skewer the shrimps by piercing through the center. You can place about 5 to 6 shrimps on each skewer.
4. Preheat the grill to high heat.
5. Grill the shrimp for 4 to 6 minutes, flipping the shrimp halfway through, or until the shrimp are pink on the outside and opaque in the center. Serve hot.

Per Serving
calories: 401 | fat: 17.8g | protein: 56.9g | carbs: 3.9g | fiber: 0g | sodium: 1223mg

Garlic Shrimp with Mushrooms

Prep time: 10 minutes | Cook time: 15 minutes | Serves 4

1 pound (454 g) fresh	4 ounces (113 g) sliced
shrimp, peeled, deveined,	mushrooms (shiitake, baby
and patted dry	bella, or button)
1 teaspoon salt	½ teaspoon red pepper
1 cup extra-virgin olive oil	flakes
8 large garlic cloves, thinly	¼ cup chopped fresh flat-
sliced	leaf Italian parsley

1. In a bowl, season the shrimp with salt. Set aside.
2. Heat the olive oil in a large skillet over medium-low heat.
3. Add the garlic and cook for 3 to 4 minutes until fragrant, stirring occasionally.
4. Sauté the mushrooms for 5 minutes, or until they start to exude their juices. Stir in the shrimp and sprinkle with red pepper flakes and sauté for 3 to 4 minutes more, or until the shrimp start to turn pink.
5. Remove the skillet from the heat and add the parsley. Stir to combine and serve warm.

Per Serving

calories: 619 | fat: 55.5g | protein: 24.1g | carbs: 3.7g | fiber: 0g | sodium: 735mg

Lemony Shrimp with Orzo Salad

Prep time: 10 minutes | Cook time: 22 minutes | Serves 4

1 cup orzo	3 lemons, juiced
1 hothouse cucumber,	Salt and freshly ground black
deseeded and chopped	pepper, to taste
½ cup finely diced red onion	¾ cup crumbled feta cheese
2 tablespoons extra-virgin	2 tablespoons dried dill
olive oil	1 cup chopped fresh flat-leaf
2 pounds (907 g) shrimp,	parsley
peeled and deveined	

1. Bring a large pot of water to a boil. Add the orzo and cook covered for 15 to 18 minutes, or until the orzo is tender. Transfer to a colander to drain and set aside to cool.
2. Mix the cucumber and red onion in a bowl. Set aside.
3. Heat the olive oil in a medium skillet over medium heat until it shimmers.
4. Reduce the heat, add the shrimp, and cook each side for 2 minutes until cooked through.
5. Add the cooked shrimp to the bowl of cucumber and red onion. Mix in the cooked orzo and lemon juice and toss to combine. Sprinkle with salt and pepper. Scatter the top with the feta cheese and dill. Garnish with the parsley and serve immediately.

Per Serving

calories: 565 | fat: 17.8g | protein: 63.3g | carbs: 43.9g | fiber: 4.1g | sodium: 2225mg

Avocado Shrimp Ceviche

Prep time: 15 minutes | Cook time: 0 minutes | Serves 4

1 pound (454 g) fresh shrimp, peeled, deveined, and cut in half lengthwise
1 small red or yellow bell pepper, cut into ½-inch chunks
½ small red onion, cut into thin slivers
½ English cucumber, peeled and cut into ½-inch chunks
¼ cup chopped fresh cilantro
½ cup extra-virgin olive oil
⅓ cup freshly squeezed lime juice
2 tablespoons freshly squeezed clementine juice
2 tablespoons freshly squeezed lemon juice
1 teaspoon salt
½ teaspoon freshly ground black pepper
2 ripe avocados, peeled, pitted, and cut into ½-inch chunks

1. Place the shrimp, bell pepper, red onion, cucumber, and cilantro in a large bowl and toss to combine.
2. In a separate bowl, stir together the olive oil, lime, clementine, and lemon juice, salt, and black pepper until smooth. Pour the mixture into the bowl of shrimp and vegetable mixture and toss until they are completely coated.
3. Cover the bowl with plastic wrap and transfer to the refrigerator to marinate for at least 2 hours, or up to 8 hours.
4. When ready, stir in the avocado chunks and toss to incorporate. Serve immediately.

Per Serving

calories: 496 | fat: 39.5g | protein: 25.3g | carbs: 13.8g | fiber: 6.0g | sodium: 755mg

Spicy Grilled Shrimp with Lemon Wedges

Prep time: 15 minutes | Cook time: 6 minutes | Serves 6

1 large clove garlic, crushed
1 teaspoon coarse salt
1 teaspoon paprika
½ teaspoon cayenne pepper
2 teaspoons lemon juice
2 tablespoons plus 1 teaspoon olive oil, divided
2 pounds (907 g) large shrimp, peeled and deveined
8 wedges lemon, for garnish

1. Preheat the grill to medium heat.
2. Stir together the garlic, salt, paprika, cayenne pepper, lemon juice, and 2 tablespoons of olive oil in a small bowl until a paste forms. Add the shrimp and toss until well coated.
3. Grease the grill grates lightly with remaining 1 teaspoon of olive oil.
4. Grill the shrimp for 4 to 6 minutes, flipping the shrimp halfway through, or until the shrimp is totally pink and opaque.
5. Garnish the shrimp with lemon wedges and serve hot.

Per Serving

calories: 163 | fat: 5.8g | protein: 25.2g | carbs: 2.8g | fiber: 0.4g | sodium: 585mg

Cod with Parsley Pistou

Prep time: 15 minutes | Cook time: 10 minutes | Serves 4

1 cup packed roughly chopped fresh flat-leaf Italian parsley
Zest and juice of 1 lemon
1 to 2 small garlic cloves, minced
1 teaspoon salt
½ teaspoon freshly ground black pepper
1 cup extra-virgin olive oil, divided
1 pound (454 g) cod fillets, cut into 4 equal-sized pieces

1. Make the pistou: Place the parsley, lemon zest and juice, garlic, salt, and pepper in a food processor until finely chopped. With the food processor running, slowly drizzle in ¾ cup of olive oil until a thick sauce forms. Set aside.
2. Heat the remaining ¼ cup of olive oil in a large skillet over medium-high heat.
3. Add the cod fillets, cover, and cook each side for 4 to 5 minutes, until browned and cooked through.
4. Remove the cod fillets from the heat to a plate and top each with generous spoonfuls of the prepared pistou. Serve immediately.

Per Serving calories: 580 | fat: 54.6g | protein: 21.1g | carbs: 2.8g | fiber: 1.0g | sodium: 651mg

Fried Cod Fillets

Prep time: 5 minutes | Cook time: 10 minutes | Serves 4

½ cup all-purpose flour
1 teaspoon garlic powder
1 teaspoon salt
4 (4- to 5-ounce / 113- to 142-g) cod fillets
1 tablespoon extra-virgin olive oil

1. Mix together the flour, garlic powder, and salt in a shallow dish. Dredge each piece of fish in the seasoned flour until they are evenly coated.
2. Heat the olive oil in a medium skillet over medium-high heat. Once hot, add the cod fillets and fry for 6 to 8 minutes, flipping the fish halfway through, or until the fish is opaque and flakes easily.
3. Remove from the heat and serve on plates.

Per Serving calories: 333 | fat: 18.8g | protein: 21.2g | carbs: 20.0g | fiber: 5.7g | sodium: 870mg

Mediterranean Braised Cod with Vegetables

Prep time: 10 minutes | Cook time: 18 minutes | Serves 2

1 tablespoon olive oil
½ medium onion, minced
2 garlic cloves, minced
1 teaspoon oregano
1 (15-ounce / 425-g) can artichoke hearts in water, drained and halved
1 (15-ounce / 425-g) can diced tomatoes with basil
¼ cup pitted Greek olives, drained
10 ounces (284 g) wild cod
Salt and freshly ground black pepper, to taste

1. In a skillet, heat the olive oil over medium-high heat.
2. Sauté the onion for about 5 minutes, stirring occasionally, or until tender. Stir in the garlic and oregano and cook for 30 seconds more until fragrant.
3. Add the artichoke hearts, tomatoes, and olives and stir to combine. Top with the cod. Cover and cook for 10 minutes, or until the fish flakes easily with a fork and juices run clean. Sprinkle with the salt and pepper. Serve warm.

Per Serving calories: 332 | fat: 10.5g | protein: 29.2g | carbs: 30.7g | fiber: 8.0g | sodium: 1906mg

Lemon-Parsley Swordfish

Prep time: 10 minutes | Cook time: 17 to 20 minutes | Serves 4

1 cup fresh Italian parsley	2 cloves garlic
¼ cup lemon juice	½ teaspoon salt
¼ cup extra-virgin olive oil	4 swordfish steaks
¼ cup fresh thyme	Olive oil spray

1. Preheat the oven to 450°F (235°C). Grease a large baking dish generously with olive oil spray.
2. Place the parsley, lemon juice, olive oil, thyme, garlic, and salt in a food processor and pulse until smoothly blended.
3. Arrange the swordfish steaks in the greased baking dish and spoon the parsley mixture over the top.
4. Bake in the preheated oven for 17 to 20 minutes until flaky.
5. Divide the fish among four plates and serve hot.

Per Serving

calories: 396 | fat: 21.7g | protein: 44.2g | carbs: 2.9g | fiber: 1.0g | sodium: 494mg

Baked Salmon with Tarragon Mustard Sauce

Prep time: 5 minutes | Cook time: 12 minutes | Serves 4

1¼ pounds (567 g) salmon fillet (skin on or removed), cut into 4 equal pieces	2 tablespoons chopped fresh tarragon
¼ cup Dijon mustard	½ teaspoon salt
¼ cup avocado oil mayonnaise	¼ teaspoon freshly ground black pepper
Zest and juice of ½ lemon	4 tablespoons extra-virgin olive oil, for serving

1. Preheat the oven to 425°F (220°C). Line a baking sheet with parchment paper. Arrange the salmon pieces on the prepared baking sheet, skin-side down.
2. Stir together the mustard, avocado oil mayonnaise, lemon zest and juice, tarragon, salt, and pepper in a small bowl. Spoon the mustard mixture over the salmon.
3. Bake for 10 to 12 minutes, or until the top is golden and salmon is opaque in the center.
4. Divide the salmon among four plates and drizzle each top with 1 tablespoon of olive oil before serving.

Per Serving

calories: 386 | fat: 27.7g | protein: 29.3g | carbs: 3.8g | fiber: 1.0g | sodium: 632mg

Baked Lemon Salmon

Prep time: 5 minutes | Cook time: 20 minutes | Serves 4

¼ teaspoon dried thyme	½ teaspoon freshly ground black pepper
Zest and juice of ½ lemon	1 pound (454 g) salmon fillet
¼ teaspoon salt	Nonstick cooking spray

1. Preheat the oven to 425°F (220°C). Coat a baking sheet with nonstick cooking spray.
2. Mix together the thyme, lemon zest and juice, salt, and pepper in a small bowl and stir to incorporate.
3. Arrange the salmon, skin-side down, on the coated baking sheet. Spoon the thyme mixture over the salmon and spread it all over.
4. Bake in the preheated oven for about 15 to 20 minutes, or until the fish flakes apart easily. Serve warm.

Per Serving calories: 162 | fat: 7.0g | protein: 23.1g | carbs: 1.0g | fiber: 0g | sodium: 166mg

Glazed Broiled Salmon

Prep time: 5 minutes | Cook time: 5 to 10 minutes | Serves 4

4 (4-ounce / 113-g) salmon fillets	1 teaspoon coconut aminos
	1 teaspoon rice vinegar
3 tablespoons miso paste	
2 tablespoons raw honey	

1. Preheat the broiler to High. Line a baking dish with aluminum foil and add the salmon fillets.
2. Whisk together the miso paste, honey, coconut aminos, and vinegar in a small bowl. Pour the glaze over the fillets and spread it evenly with a brush.
3. Broil for about 5 minutes, or until the salmon is browned on top and opaque. Brush any remaining glaze over the salmon and broil for an additional 5 minutes if needed. The cooking time depends on the thickness of the salmon.
4. Let the salmon cool for 5 minutes before serving.

Per Serving

calories: 263 | fat: 8.9g | protein: 30.2g | carbs: 12.8g | fiber: 0.7g | sodium: 716mg

Baked Salmon with Basil and Tomato

Prep time: 10 minutes | Cook time: 20 minutes | Serves 2

2 (6-ounce / 170-g) boneless salmon fillets	1 tablespoon olive oil
	2 tablespoons grated Parmesan cheese
1 tablespoon dried basil	
1 tomato, thinly sliced	Nonstick cooking spray

1. Preheat the oven to 375°F (190°C). Line a baking sheet with a piece of aluminum foil and mist with nonstick cooking spray.
2. Arrange the salmon fillets onto the aluminum foil and scatter with basil. Place the tomato slices on top and drizzle with olive oil. Top with the grated Parmesan cheese.
3. Bake for about 20 minutes, or until the flesh is opaque and it flakes apart easily.
4. Remove from the oven and serve on a plate.

Per Serving

calories: 403 | fat: 26.5g | protein: 36.3g | carbs: 3.8g | fiber: 0.1g | sodium: 179mg

Honey-Mustard Roasted Salmon

Prep time: 5 minutes | Cook time: 15 to 20 minutes | Serves 4

2 tablespoons whole-grain mustard	¼ teaspoon freshly ground black pepper
2 garlic cloves, minced	1 pound (454 g) salmon fillet
1 tablespoon honey	Nonstick cooking spray
¼ teaspoon salt	

1. Preheat the oven to 425°F (220°C). Coat a baking sheet with nonstick cooking spray.
2. Stir together the mustard, garlic, honey, salt, and pepper in a small bowl.
3. Arrange the salmon fillet, skin-side down, on the coated baking sheet. Spread the mustard mixture evenly over the salmon fillet.
4. Roast in the preheated oven for 15 to 20 minutes, or until it flakes apart easily and reaches an internal temperature of 145°F (63°C).Serve hot.

Per Serving

calories: 185 | fat: 7.0g | protein: 23.2g | carbs: 5.8g | fiber: 0g | sodium: 311mg

Baked Fish with Pistachio Crust

Prep time: 10 minutes | Cook time: 15 to 20 minutes | Serves 4

½ cup extra-virgin olive oil, divided	½ cup ground flaxseed
1 pound (454 g) flaky white fish (such as cod, haddock, or halibut), skin removed	Zest and juice of 1 lemon, divided
½ cup shelled finely chopped pistachios	1 teaspoon ground cumin
	1 teaspoon ground allspice
	½ teaspoon salt
	¼ teaspoon freshly ground black pepper

1. Preheat the oven to 400°F (205°C).
2. Line a baking sheet with parchment paper or aluminum foil and drizzle 2 tablespoons of olive oil over the sheet, spreading to evenly coat the bottom.
3. Cut the fish into 4 equal pieces and place on the prepared baking sheet. In a small bowl, combine the pistachios, flaxseed, lemon zest, cumin, allspice, salt, and pepper. Drizzle in ¼ cup of olive oil and stir well.
4. Divide the nut mixture evenly on top of the fish pieces. Drizzle the lemon juice and remaining 2 tablespoons of olive oil over the fish and bake until cooked through, 15 to 20 minutes, depending on the thickness of the fish.
5. Cool for 5 minutes before serving.

Per Serving

calories: 509 | fat: 41.0g | protein: 26.0g | carbs: 9.0g | fiber: 6.0g | sodium: 331mg

Sole Piccata with Capers

Prep time: 10 minutes | Cook time: 17 minutes | Serves 4

1 teaspoon extra-virgin olive oil	2 tablespoons all-purpose flour
4 (5-ounce / 142-g) sole fillets, patted dry	2 cups low-sodium chicken broth
3 tablespoons almond butter	Juice and zest of ½ lemon
2 teaspoons minced garlic	2 tablespoons capers

1. Place a large skillet over medium-high heat and add the olive oil.
2. Sear the sole fillets until the fish flakes easily when tested with a fork, about 4 minutes on each side. Transfer the fish to a plate and set aside.
3. Return the skillet to the stove and add the butter.
4. Sauté the garlic until translucent, about 3 minutes.
5. Whisk in the flour to make a thick paste and cook, stirring constantly, until the mixture is golden brown, about 2 minutes.
6. Whisk in the chicken broth, lemon juice and zest.
7. Cook for about 4 minutes until the sauce is thickened.
8. Stir in the capers and serve the sauce over the fish.

Per Serving

calories: 271 | fat:13.0g | protein: 30.0g | carbs: 7.0g | fiber: 0g | sodium: 413mg

Haddock with Cucumber Sauce

Prep time: 10 minutes | Cook time: 10 minutes | Serves 4

¼ cup plain Greek yogurt	1 teaspoon honey
½ scallion, white and green parts, finely chopped	Sea salt and freshly ground black pepper, to taste
½ English cucumber, grated, liquid squeezed out	4 (5-ounce / 142-g) haddock fillets, patted dry
2 tbsp chopped fresh mint	Nonstick cooking spray

1. In a small bowl, stir together the yogurt, cucumber, scallion, mint, honey, and a pinch of salt. Set aside.
2. Season the fillets lightly with salt and pepper.
3. Place a large skillet over medium-high heat and spray lightly with cooking spray.
4. Cook the haddock, turning once, until it is just cooked through, about 5 minutes per side.
5. Remove the fish from the heat and transfer to plates.
6. Serve topped with the cucumber sauce.

Per Serving

calories: 164 | fat: 2.0g | protein: 27.0g | carbs: 4.0g | fiber: 0g | sodium: 104mg

Crispy Herb Crusted Halibut

Prep time: 10 minutes | Cook time: 20 minutes | Serves 4

4 (5-ounce / 142-g) halibut fillets, patted dry	1 tablespoon chopped fresh parsley
Extra-virgin olive oil, for brushing	1 teaspoon chopped fresh basil
½ cup coarsely ground unsalted pistachios	1 teaspoon chopped fresh thyme
Pinch freshly ground black pepper	Pinch sea salt

1. Preheat the oven to 350°F (180°C). Line a baking sheet with parchment paper.
2. Place the fillets on the baking sheet and brush them generously with olive oil.
3. In a small bowl, stir together the pistachios, parsley, basil, thyme, salt, and pepper.
4. Spoon the nut mixture evenly on the fish, spreading it out so the tops of the fillets are covered.
5. Bake in the preheated oven until it flakes when pressed with a fork, about 20 minutes. Serve immediately.

Per Serving

calories: 262 | fat: 11.0g | protein: 32.0g | carbs: 4.0g | fiber: 2.0g | sodium: 77mg

Dill Baked Sea Bass

Prep time: 10 minutes | Cook time: 10 to 15 minutes | Serves 6

¼ cup olive oil	1 garlic clove, minced
2 pounds (907 g) sea bass	¼ cup dry white wine
Sea salt and freshly ground pepper, to taste	3 teaspoons fresh dill
	2 teaspoons fresh thyme

1. Preheat the oven to 425°F (220°C).
2. Brush the bottom of a roasting pan with the olive oil. Place the fish in the pan and brush the fish with oil.
3. Season the fish with sea salt and freshly ground pepper. Combine the remaining and pour over the fish.
4. Bake in the preheated oven for 10 to 15 minutes, depending on the size of the fish. Serve hot.

Per Serving calories: 224 | fat: 12.1g | protein: 28.1g | carbs: 0.9g | fiber: 0.3g | sodium: 104mg

Pesto Shrimp over Zoodles

Prep time: 15 minutes | Cook time: 10 minutes | Serves 4

1 pound (454 g) fresh shrimp, peeled and deveined
Salt and freshly ground black pepper, to taste
2 tablespoons extra-virgin olive oil
½ small onion, slivered
8 ounces (227 g) store-bought jarred pesto
¾ cup crumbled goat or feta cheese, plus additional for serving
2 large zucchini, spiralized, for serving
¼ cup chopped flat-leaf Italian parsley, for garnish

1. In a bowl, season the shrimp with salt and pepper. Set aside.
2. In a large skillet, heat the olive oil over medium-high heat. Sauté the onion until just golden, 5 to 6 minutes.
3. Reduce the heat to low and add the pesto and cheese, whisking to combine and melt the cheese. Bring to a low simmer and add the shrimp. Reduce the heat back to low and cover. Cook until the shrimp is cooked through and pink, about 3 to 4 minutes.
4. Serve the shrimp warm over zoodles, garnishing with chopped parsley and additional crumbled cheese.

Per Serving

calories: 491 | fat: 35.0g | protein: 29.0g | carbs: 15.0g | fiber: 4.0g | sodium: 870mg

Salt and Pepper Calamari and Scallops

Prep time: 5 minutes | Cook time: 10 minutes | Serves 4

8 ounces (227 g) calamari steaks, cut into ½-inch-thick rings
8 ounces (227 g) sea scallops
1½ teaspoons salt, divided
1 teaspoon garlic powder
1 teaspoon freshly ground black pepper
⅓ cup extra-virgin olive oil
2 tablespoons almond butter

1. Place the calamari and scallops on several layers of paper towels and pat dry. Sprinkle with 1 teaspoon of salt and allow to sit for 15 minutes at room temperature.
2. Pat dry with additional paper towels. Sprinkle with pepper and garlic powder.
3. In a deep medium skillet, heat the olive oil and butter over medium-high heat. When the oil is hot but not smoking, add the scallops and calamari in a single layer to the skillet and sprinkle with the remaining ½ teaspoon of salt. Cook for 2 to 4 minutes on each side, depending on the size of the scallops, until just golden but still slightly opaque in center.
4. Using a slotted spoon, remove from the skillet and transfer to a serving platter. Allow the cooking oil to cool slightly and drizzle over the seafood before serving.

Per Serving

Calories: 309 | fat: 25.0g | protein: 18.0g | carbs: 3.0g | fiber: 0g | sodium: 928mg

Baked Cod with Vegetables

Prep time: 15 minutes | Cook time: 25 minutes | Serves 2

1 pound (454 g) thick cod fillet, cut into 4 even portions
¼ teaspoon onion powder (optional)
¼ teaspoon paprika
3 tablespoons extra-virgin olive oil
4 medium scallions
½ cup fresh chopped basil, divided
3 tablespoons minced garlic (optional)
2 teaspoons salt
2 teaspoons freshly ground black pepper
¼ teaspoon dry marjoram (optional)
6 sun-dried tomato slices
½ cup dry white wine
½ cup crumbled feta cheese
1 (15-ounce / 425-g) can oil-packed artichoke hearts, drained
1 lemon, sliced
1 cup pitted kalamata olives
1 teaspoon capers (optional)
4 small red potatoes, quartered

1. Preheat the oven to 375°F (190°C).
2. Season the fish with paprika and onion powder (if desired).
3. Heat an ovenproof skillet over medium heat and sear the top side of the cod for about 1 minute until golden. Set aside.
4. Heat the olive oil in the same skillet over medium heat. Add the scallions, ¼ cup of basil, garlic (if desired), salt, pepper, marjoram (if desired), tomato slices, and white wine and stir to combine. Bring to a boil and remove from heat.
5. Evenly spread the sauce on the bottom of skillet. Place the cod on top of the tomato basil sauce and scatter with feta cheese. Place the artichokes in the skillet and top with the lemon slices.
6. Scatter with the olives, capers (if desired), and the remaining ¼ cup of basil. Remove from the heat and transfer to the preheated oven. Bake for 15 to 20 minutes, or until it flakes easily with a fork.
7. Meanwhile, place the quartered potatoes on a baking sheet or wrapped in aluminum foil. Bake in the oven for 15 minutes until fork-tender.
8. Cool for 5 minutes before serving.

Per Serving

calories: 1168 | fat: 60.0g | protein: 63.8g | carbs: 94.0g | fiber: 13.0g | sodium: 4620mg

Slow Cooker Salmon in Foil

Prep time: 5 minutes | Cook time: 2 hours | Serves 2

2 (6-ounce / 170-g) salmon fillets
1 tablespoon olive oil
2 cloves garlic, minced
½ tablespoon lime juice
1 teaspoon finely chopped fresh parsley
¼ teaspoon black pepper

1. Spread a length of foil onto a work surface and place the salmon fillets in the middle. Mix together the olive oil, garlic, lime juice, parsley, and black pepper in a small bowl. Brush the mixture over the fillets. Fold the foil over and crimp the sides to make a packet.
2. Place the packet into the slow cooker, cover, and cook on High for 2 hours, or until the fish flakes easily with a fork.
3. Serve hot.

Per Serving calories: 446 | fat: 20.7g | protein: 65.4g | carbs: 1.5g | fiber: 0.2g | sodium: 240mg

Dill Chutney Salmon

Prep time: 5 minutes | Cook time: 3 minutes | Serves 2

Chutney:
¼ cup fresh dill
¼ cup extra virgin olive oil
Juice from ½ lemon
Sea salt, to taste
¼ teaspoon paprika

Fish:
2 cups water
2 salmon fillets
Juice from ½ lemon
Salt and freshly ground pepper to taste

1. Pulse all the chutney in a food processor until creamy. Set aside. Add the water and steamer basket to the Instant Pot. Place salmon fillets, skin-side down, on the steamer basket. Drizzle the lemon juice over salmon and sprinkle with the paprika. Secure the lid. Select the Manual mode and set the cooking time for 3 minutes at High Pressure.
2. Once cooking is complete, do a quick pressure release. Carefully open the lid. Season the fillets with pepper and salt to taste. Serve topped with the dill chutney.

Per Serving calories: 636 | fat: 41.1g | protein: 65.3g | carbs: 1.9g | fiber: 0.2g | sodium: 477mg

Garlic-Butter Parmesan Salmon and Asparagus

Prep time: 10 minutes | Cook time: 15 minutes | Serves 2

2 (6-ounce / 170-g) salmon fillets, skin on and patted dry
Pink Himalayan salt
Freshly ground black pepper, to taste
1 pound (454 g) fresh asparagus, ends snapped off
3 tbsp almond butter
2 garlic cloves, minced
¼ cup grated Parmesan cheese

1. Preheat the oven to 400ºF (205ºC). Line a baking sheet with aluminum foil. Season both sides of the salmon fillets with salt and pepper. Put the salmon in the middle of the baking sheet and arrange the asparagus around the salmon.
2. Heat the almond butter in a small saucepan over medium heat. Add the minced garlic and cook for about 3 minutes, or until the garlic just begins to brown. Drizzle the garlic-butter sauce over the salmon and asparagus and scatter the Parmesan cheese on top. Bake in the preheated oven for about 12 minutes, or until the salmon is cooked through and the asparagus is crisp-tender.
3. You can switch the oven to broil at the end of cooking time for about 3 minutes to get a nice char on the asparagus.
4. Let cool for 5 minutes before serving.

Per Serving calories: 435 | fat: 26.1g | protein: 42.3g | carbs: 10.0g | fiber: 5.0g | sodium: 503mg

Grilled Lemon Pesto Salmon

Prep time: 5 minutes | Cook time: 6 to 10 minutes | Serves 2

10 ounces (283 g) salmon fillet (1 large piece or 2 smaller ones)
Salt and freshly ground black pepper, to taste
2 tbsp prepared pesto sauce
1 large fresh lemon, sliced
Cooking spray

1. preheat the grill to medium-high heat. Spray the grill grates with cooking spray. Season the salmon with salt and black pepper. Spread the pesto sauce on top.
2. Make a bed of fresh lemon slices about the same size as the salmon fillet on the hot grill, and place the salmon on top of the lemon slices. Put any additional lemon slices on top of the salmon. Grill the salmon for 6 to 10 minutes, or until the fish is opaque and flakes apart easily. Serve hot.

Per Serving calories: 316 | fat: 21.1g | protein: 29.0g | carbs: 1.0g | fiber: 0g | sodium: 175mg

Lemon Rosemary Roasted Branzino

Prep time: 15 minutes | Cook time: 30 minutes | Serves 2

4 tablespoons extra-virgin olive oil, divided
2 (8-ounce / 227-g) branzino fillets, preferably at least 1 inch thick
1 garlic clove, minced
1 bunch scallions (white part only), thinly sliced
10 to 12 small cherry tomatoes, halved
1 large carrot, cut into ¼-inch rounds
½ cup dry white wine
2 tablespoons paprika
2 teaspoons kosher salt
½ tablespoon ground chili pepper
2 rosemary sprigs or 1 tablespoon dried rosemary
1 small lemon, thinly sliced
½ cup sliced pitted kalamata olives

1. Heat a large ovenproof skillet over high heat until hot, about 2 minutes. Add 1 tablespoon of olive oil and heat for 10 to 15 seconds until it shimmers.
2. Add the branzino fillets, skin-side up, and sear for 2 minutes. Flip the fillets and cook for an additional 2 minutes. Set aside. Swirl 2 tablespoons of olive oil around the skillet to coat evenly.
3. Add the garlic, scallions, tomatoes, and carrot, and sauté for 5 minutes, or until softened.
4. Add the wine, stirring until all are well combined. Carefully place the fish over the sauce.
5. Preheat the oven to 450ºF (235ºC).
6. Brush the fillets with the remaining 1 tablespoon of olive oil and season with paprika, salt, and chili pepper. Top each fillet with a rosemary sprig and lemon slices. Scatter the olives over fish and around the skillet.
7. Roast for about 10 minutes until the lemon slices are browned. Serve hot.

Per Serving calories: 724 | fat: 43.0g | protein: 57.7g | carbs: 25.0g | fiber: 10.0g | sodium: 2950mg

Breaded Shrimp

Prep time: 10 minutes | Cook time: 4 to 6 minutes | Serves 4

2 large eggs
1 tablespoon water
2 cups seasoned Italian bread crumbs
1 teaspoon salt
1 cup flour
1 pound (454 g) large shrimp (21 to 25), peeled and deveined
Extra-virgin olive oil, as needed

1. In a small bowl, beat the eggs with the water, then transfer to a shallow dish. Add the bread crumbs and salt to a separate shallow dish, then mix well.
2. Place the flour into a third shallow dish.
3. Coat the shrimp in the flour, then the beaten egg, and finally the bread crumbs. Place on a plate and repeat with all of the shrimp. Heat a skillet over high heat. Pour in enough olive oil to coat the bottom of the skillet. Cook the shrimp in the hot skillet for 2 to 3 minutes on each side. Remove and drain on a paper towel. Serve warm.

Per Serving
calories: 714 | fat: 34.0g | protein: 37.0g | carbs: 63.0g | fiber: 3.0g | sodium: 1727mg

Roasted Trout Stuffed with Veggies

Prep time: 10 minutes | Cook time: 25 minutes | Serves 2

2 (8-ounce / 227-g) whole trout fillets, dressed (cleaned but with bones and skin intact)	1 small onion, thinly sliced
1 tablespoon extra-virgin olive oil	½ red bell pepper, seeded and thinly sliced
¼ teaspoon salt	1 poblano pepper, seeded and thinly sliced
⅛ teaspoon freshly ground black pepper	2 or 3 shiitake mushrooms, sliced
	1 lemon, sliced
	Nonstick cooking spray

1. Preheat the oven to 425ºF (220ºC). Spray a baking sheet with nonstick cooking spray. Rub both trout fillets, inside and out, with the olive oil. Season with salt and pepper.
2. Mix together the onion, bell pepper, poblano pepper, and mushrooms in a large bowl. Stuff half of this mixture into the cavity of each fillet. Top the mixture with 2 or 3 lemon slices inside each fillet.
3. Place the fish on the prepared baking sheet side by side. Roast in the preheated oven for 25 minutes, or until the fish is cooked through and the vegetables are tender.
4. Remove from the oven and serve on a plate.

Per Serving

calories: 453 | fat: 22.1g | protein: 49.0g | carbs: 13.8g | fiber: 3.0g | sodium: 356mg

Lemony Trout with Caramelized Shallots

Prep time: 10 minutes | Cook time: 20 minutes | Serves 2

Shallots:	2 (4-ounce / 113-g) trout
1 teaspoon almond butter	fillets
2 shallots, thinly sliced Dash salt	3 tablespoons capers
	¼ cup freshly squeezed
Trout:	lemon juice
1 tablespoon plus 1 teaspoon almond butter, divided	¼ teaspoon salt
	Dash freshly ground black pepper
	1 lemon, thinly sliced

Make the Shallots

1. In a large skillet over medium heat, cook the butter, shallots, and salt for 20 minutes, stirring every 5 minutes, or until the shallots are wilted and caramelized. Make the Trout Meanwhile, in another large skillet over medium heat, heat 1 teaspoon of almond butter.
2. Add the trout fillets and cook each side for 3 minutes, or until flaky. Transfer to a plate and set aside.
3. In the skillet used for the trout, stir in the capers, lemon juice, salt, and pepper, then bring to a simmer. Whisk in the remaining 1 tablespoon of almond butter. Spoon the sauce over the fish.
4. Garnish the fish with the lemon slices and caramelized shallots before serving.

Per Serving

calories: 344 | fat: 18.4g | protein: 21.1g | carbs: 14.7g | fiber: 5.0g | sodium: 1090mg

Tomato Tuna Melts

Prep time: 5 minutes | Cook time: 3 to 4 minutes | Serves 2

1 (5-ounce / 142-g) can chunk light tuna packed in water, drained	2 teaspoons freshly squeezed lemon juice
2 tablespoons plain Greek yogurt	Pinch cayenne pepper
	1 large tomato, cut into ¾-inch-thick rounds
2 tablespoons finely chopped celery	½ cup shredded Cheddar cheese
1 tablespoon finely chopped red onion	

1. Preheat the broiler to High. Stir together the tuna, yogurt, celery, red onion, lemon juice, and cayenne pepper in a medium bowl. Place the tomato rounds on a baking sheet. Top each with some tuna salad and Cheddar cheese.
2. Broil for 3 to 4 minutes until the cheese is melted and bubbly. Cool for 5 minutes before serving.

Per Serving

calories: 244 | fat: 10.0g | protein: 30.1g | carbs: 6.9g | fiber: 1.0g | sodium: 445mg

Mackerel and Green Bean Salad

Prep time: 10 minutes | Cook time: 10 minutes | Serves 2

2 cups green beans	1 avocado, sliced
1 tablespoon avocado oil	2 tablespoons lemon juice
2 mackerel fillets	2 tablespoons olive oil
4 cups mixed salad greens	1 teaspoon Dijon mustard
2 hard-boiled eggs, sliced	Salt and black pepper, to taste

1. Cook the green beans in a medium saucepan of boiling water for about 3 minutes until crisp-tender. Drain and set aside.
2. Melt the avocado oil in a pan over medium heat. Add the mackerel fillets and cook each side for 4 minutes.
3. Divide the greens between two salad bowls. Top with the mackerel, sliced egg, and avocado slices.
4. In another bowl, whisk together the lemon juice, olive oil, mustard, salt, and pepper, and drizzle over the salad. Add the cooked green beans and toss to combine, then serve.

Per Serving calories: 737 | fat: 57.3g | protein: 34.2g | carbs: 22.1g | fiber: 13.4g | sodium: 398mg

Hazelnut Crusted Sea Bass

Prep time: 10 minutes | Cook time: 15 minutes | Serves 2

2 tablespoons almond butter	⅓ cup roasted hazelnuts
2 sea bass fillets	A pinch of cayenne pepper

1. Preheat the oven to 425ºF (220ºC). Line a baking dish with waxed paper. Brush the almond butter over the fillets.
2. Pulse the hazelnuts and cayenne in a food processor.
3. Coat the sea bass with the hazelnut mixture, then transfer to the baking dish. Bake in the preheated oven for about 15 minutes. Cool for 5 minutes before serving.

Per Serving calories: 468 | fat: 30.8g | protein: 40.0g | carbs: 8.8g | fiber: 4.1g | sodium: 90mg

Garlic Shrimp with Arugula Pesto

Prep time: 20 minutes | Cook time: 5 minutes | Serves 2

3 cups lightly packed arugula	Salt and freshly ground black pepper, to taste
½ cup lightly packed basil leaves	1 (10-ounce / 283-g) package zucchini noodles
¼ cup walnuts	8 ounces (227 g) cooked, shelled shrimp
3 tablespoons olive oil	
3 medium garlic cloves	2 Roma tomatoes, diced
2 tablespoons grated Parmesan cheese	
1 tablespoon freshly squeezed lemon juice	

1. Process the arugula, basil, walnuts, olive oil, garlic, Parmesan cheese, and lemon juice in a food processor until smooth, scraping down the sides as needed. Season with salt and pepper to taste.
2. Heat a skillet over medium heat. Add the pesto, zucchini noodles, and cooked shrimp. Toss to combine the sauce over the noodles and shrimp, and cook until heated through. Taste and season with more salt and pepper as needed. Serve topped with the diced tomatoes.

Per Serving calories: 435 | fat: 30.2g | protein: 33.0g | carbs: 15.1g | fiber: 5.0g | sodium: 413mg

Baked Oysters with Vegetables

Prep time: 30 minutes | Cook time: 15 to 17 minutes | Serves 2

2 cups coarse salt, for holding the oysters	¼ cup finely chopped red bell pepper
1 dozen fresh oysters, scrubbed	1 garlic clove, minced
1 tablespoon almond butter	1 tablespoon finely chopped fresh parsley
¼ cup finely chopped scallions, both white and green parts	Zest and juice of ½ lemon
	Pinch salt
½ cup finely chopped artichoke hearts	Freshly ground black pepper, to taste

1. Pour the salt into a baking dish and spread to evenly fill the bottom of the dish.
2. Prepare a clean work surface to shuck the oysters. Using a shucking knife, insert the blade at the joint of the shell, where it hinges open and shut. Firmly apply pressure to pop the blade in, and work the knife around the shell to open. Discard the empty half of the shell. Using the knife, gently loosen the oyster, and remove any shell particles. Set the oysters in their shells on the salt, being careful not to spill the juices. Preheat the oven to 425°F (220°C).
3. Heat the almond butter in a large skillet over medium heat. Add the scallions, artichoke hearts, and bell pepper, and cook for 5 to 7 minutes. Add the garlic and cook for 1 minute more. Remove from the heat and stir in the parsley, lemon zest and juice, and season to taste with salt and pepper. Divide the vegetable mixture evenly among the oysters. Bake in the preheated oven for 10 to 12 minutes, or until the vegetables are lightly browned. Serve warm.

Per Serving calories: 135 | fat: 7.2g | protein: 6.0g | carbs: 10.7g | fiber: 2.0g | sodium: 280mg

Steamed Trout with Lemon Herb Crust

Prep time: 10 minutes | Cook time: 15 minutes | Serves 2

3 tablespoons olive oil	¼ tbsp dried ground thyme
3 garlic cloves, chopped	1 teaspoon sea salt
2 tbsp fresh lemon juice	1 pound (454 g) fresh trout (2 pieces)
1 tbsp chopped fresh mint	
1 tbsp chopped fresh parsley	2 cups fish stock

1. Stir together the olive oil, garlic, lemon juice, mint, parsley, thyme, and salt in a small bowl. Brush the marinade onto the fish. Insert a trivet in the Instant Pot. Pour in the fish stock and place the fish on the trivet.
2. Secure the lid. Select the Steam mode and set the cooking time for 15 minutes at High Pressure. Once cooking is complete, do a quick pressure release. Carefully open the lid. Serve warm.

Per Serving
calories: 477 | fat: 29.6g | protein: 51.7g | carbs: 3.6g | fiber: 0.2g | sodium: 2011mg

Shrimp and Pea Paella

Prep time: 20 minutes | Cook time: 60 minutes | Serves 2

2 tablespoons olive oil	1¼ cups low-sodium chicken stock
1 garlic clove, minced	
½ large onion, minced	8 ounces (227 g) large raw shrimp
1 cup diced tomato	1 cup frozen peas
½ cup short-grain rice	¼ cup jarred roasted red peppers, cut into strips
½ teaspoon sweet paprika	
½ cup dry white wine	Salt, to taste

1. Heat the olive oil in a large skillet over medium-high heat.
2. Add the garlic and onion and sauté for 3 minutes, or until the onion is softened. Add the tomato, rice, and paprika and stir for 3 minutes to toast the rice.
3. Add the wine and chicken stock and stir to combine. Bring the mixture to a boil.
4. Cover and reduce the heat to medium-low, and simmer for 45 minutes, or until the rice is just about tender and most of the liquid has been absorbed.
5. Add the shrimp, peas, and roasted red peppers. Cover and cook for an additional 5 minutes. Season with salt to taste and serve.

Per Serving calories: 646 | fat: 27.1g | protein: 42.0g | carbs: 59.7g | fiber: 7.0g | sodium: 687mg

Steamed Bass

Prep time: 10 minutes | Cook time: 8 minutes | Serves 4

1½ cups water	2 turnips, chopped
1 lemon, sliced	2 pinches salt
4 sea bass fillets	1 pinch ground black pepper
4 sprigs thyme	2 teaspoons olive oil
1 white onion, cut into thin rings	

1. Add water and set a rack into the pot.
2. Line a parchment paper to the bottom of the steamer basket. Place lemon slices in a single layer on the rack.
3. Arrange fillets on the top of the lemons, cover with onion and thyme sprigs. Top with turnip slices.
4. Drizzle pepper, salt, and olive oil over the mixture. Put steamer basket onto the rack. Seal lid and cook on Low pressure for 8 minutes. Release the pressure quickly.
5. Serve over the delicate onion rings and thinly turnips.

Per Serving
calories: 177 | fat: 4.9g | protein: 24.7g | carbs: 7.8g | fiber: 2.0g | sodium: 209mg

Steamed Cod

Prep time: 15 minutes | Cook time: 7 minutes | Serves 4

1 pound (454 g) cherry tomatoes, halved	2 cups water
1 bunch fresh thyme sprigs	1 cup white rice
4 fillets cod	1 cup Kalamata olives
1 teaspoon olive oil	2 tablespoons pickled capers
1 clove garlic, pressed	1 tablespoon olive oil
3 pinches salt	1 pinch ground black pepper

1. Line a parchment paper on the basket of your instant pot. Place about half the tomatoes in a single layer on the paper. Sprinkle with thyme, reserving some for garnish.
2. Arrange cod fillets on top. Sprinkle with a little bit of olive oil. Spread the garlic, pepper, salt, and remaining tomatoes over the fish. In the pot, mix rice and water.
3. Lay a trivet over the rice and water. Lower steamer basket onto the trivet. Seal the lid, and cook for 7 minutes on Low Pressure. Release the pressure quickly.
4. Remove the steamer basket and trivet from the pot. Use a fork to fluff rice. Plate the fish fillets and apply a garnish of olives, reserved thyme, pepper, remaining olive oil, and capers. Serve with rice.

Per Serving calories: 352 | fat: 9.1g | protein: 22.2g | carbs: 44.7g | fiber: 3.9g | sodium: 827mg

Catfish and Shrimp Jambalaya

Prep time: 20 minutes | Cook time: 4 hours 45 minutes | Serves

4 ounces (113 g) catfish (cut into 1-inch cubes)	1 cup canned diced tomatoes
4 ounces (113 g) shrimp (peeled and deveined)	1 cup uncooked long-grain white rice
1 tablespoon olive oil	½ tablespoon Cajun seasoning
2 bacon slices, chopped	¼ teaspoon dried thyme
1¼ cups vegetable broth	¼ teaspoon cayenne pepper
¾ cup sliced celery stalk	½ teaspoon dried oregano
¼ teaspoon minced garlic	Salt and freshly ground black pepper, to taste
½ cup chopped onion	

1. Select the Sauté function on your Instant Pot and add the oil into it.
2. Put the onion, garlic, celery, and bacon to the pot and cook for 10 minutes.
3. Add all the remaining to the pot except seafood.
4. Stir well, then secure the cooker lid.
5. Select the Slow Cook function on a medium mode.
6. Keep the pressure release handle on venting position. Cook for 4 hours.
7. Once done, remove the lid and add the seafood to the gravy.
8. Secure the lid again, keep the pressure handle in the venting position.
9. Cook for another 45 minutes then serve.

Per Serving calories: 437 | fat: 13.1g | protein: 21.3g | carbs: 56.7g | fiber: 2.6g | sodium: 502mg

Salmon and Potato Casserole

Prep time: 20 minutes | Cook time: 8 hours | Serves 4

½ tablespoon olive oil	3 tablespoons flour
8 ounces (227 g) cream of mushroom soup	1 (1-pound / 454-g) can salmon (drained and flaked)
¼ cup water	½ cup chopped scallion
3 medium potatoes (peeled and sliced)	¼ teaspoon ground nutmeg
	Salt and freshly ground black pepper, to taste

1. Pour mushroom soup and water in a separate bowl and mix them well.
2. Add the olive oil to the Instant Pot and grease it lightly.
3. Place half of the potatoes in the pot and sprinkle salt, pepper, and half of the flour over it.
4. Now add a layer of half of the salmon over potatoes, then a layer of half of the scallions.
5. Repeat these layers and pour mushroom soup mix on top.
6. Top it with nutmeg evenly.
7. Secure the lid and set its pressure release handle to the venting position.
8. Select the Slow Cook function with Medium heat on your Instant Pot.
9. Let it cook for 8 hours then serve.

Per Serving
calories: 388 | fat: 11.6g | protein: 34.6g | carbs: 37.2g | fiber: 4.4g | sodium: 842mg

Salmon and Tomato Curry

Prep time: 10 minutes | Cook time: 12 minutes | Serves 8

3 pounds (1.4 kg) salmon fillets (cut into pieces)	4 teaspoons ground coriander
2 tablespoons olive oil	2 small yellow onions, chopped
2 Serrano peppers, chopped	2 teaspoons red chili powder
1 teaspoon ground turmeric	4 garlic cloves, minced
4 tablespoons curry powder	4 cups unsweetened coconut milk
4 teaspoons ground cumin	2½ cups tomatoes, chopped
4 curry leaves	2 tablespoons fresh lemon juice
	Fresh cilantro leaves to garnish

1. Put the oil and curry leaves to the insert of the Instant Pot. Select the Sauté function to cook for 30 secs.
2. Add the garlic and onions to the pot, cook for 5 minutes.
3. Stir in all the spices and cook for another 1 minute.
4. Put the fish, Serrano pepper, coconut milk, and tomatoes while cooking.
5. Cover and lock the lid. Seal the pressure release valve.
6. Select the Manual function at Low Pressure for 5 minutes.
7. After the beep, do a Natural release to release all the steam.
8. Remove the lid and squeeze in lemon juice.
9. Garnish with fresh cilantro leaves and serve.

Per Serving
calories: 551 | fat: 40.6g | protein: 38.9g | carbs: 10.6g | fiber: 3.2g | sodium: 778mg

Lemony Salmon

Prep time: 10 minutes | Cook time: 3 minutes | Serves 3

1 cup water	1 teaspoon fresh lemon
3 lemon slices	juice
1 (5-ounce / 142-g) salmon	Salt and ground black
fillet	pepper, to taste
	Fresh cilantro to garnish

1. Add the water to the Instant pot and place a trivet inside.
2. In a shallow bowl, place the salmon fillet. Sprinkle salt and pepper over it.
3. Squeeze some lemon juice on top then place a lemon slice over the salmon fillet.
4. Cover the lid and lock it. Set its pressure release handle to Sealing position.
5. Use Steam function on your cooker for 3 minutes to cook.
6. After the beep, do a Quick release and release the pressure.
7. Remove the lid, then serve with the lemon slice and fresh cilantro on top.

Per Serving

calories: 161 | fat: 5.0g | protein: 26.6g | carbs: 0.7g | fiber: 0.2g | sodium: 119mg

Spicy Cumin Salmon

Prep time: 10 minutes | Cook time: 2 minutes | Serves 8

2 cups water	2 teaspoons ground cumin
2 garlic cloves, minced	Salt and freshly grated black
2 teaspoons powdered	pepper, to taste
stevia	2 pounds (907 g) salmon
8 lemon slices	fillet, cut into 8 pieces
2 tablespoons red chili	
powder	

1. Pour two cups of water in the insert of the Instant Pot. Set the trivet in it.
2. In a separate bowl, add all the except the lemon slices and mix them well.
3. Pour this mixture over the salmon fillets and rub it all over it.
4. Place the salmon slices over the trivet in a single layer.
5. Top each fillet with a lemon slice.
6. Secure the lid and select Steam function for 2 minutes.
7. After the beep, do a Quick release and then remove the lid.
8. Serve immediately.

Per Serving

calories: 151 | fat: 4.7g | protein: 23.3g | carbs: 3.1g | fiber: 1.0g | sodium: 117mg

Sardines and Plum Tomato Curry

Prep time: 10 minutes | Cook time: 8 hours 2 minutes | Serves 4

1 tablespoon olive oil	1 garlic clove, minced
1 pound (454 g) fresh	½ cup tomato purée
sardines, cubed	Salt and ground black
2 plum tomatoes, chopped finely	pepper, to taste
½ large onion, sliced	

1. Select the Sauté function on your Instant pot then add the oil and sardines to it. Let it sauté for 2 minutes then add all the remaining.
2. Cover the lid and select Slow Cook function for 8 hours.
3. Remove the lid and stir the cooked curry. Serve warm.

Per Serving

calories: 292 | fat: 16.5g | protein: 28.9g | carbs: 6.0g | fiber: 1.3g | sodium: 398mg

Rosemary Salmon with Feta Cheese

Prep time: 5 minutes | Cook time: 3 minutes | Serves 6

1½ pounds (680 g) salmon	½ teaspoon dried oregano
fillets	3 tablespoons fresh lemon
1½ cups water	juice
¼ cup olive oil	Salt and freshly ground
1½ garlic cloves, minced	black pepper, to taste
1½ tablespoons feta cheese,	3 fresh rosemary sprigs
crumbled	3 lemon slices

1. Take a large bowl and add the garlic, feta cheese, salt, pepper, lemon juice, and oregano. Whisk well all the .
2. Add the water to the Instant pot then place the steamer trivet in it.
3. Arrange the salmon fillets over the trivet in a single layer.
4. Pour the cheese mixture over these fillets.
5. Place a lemon slice and a rosemary sprig over each fillet.
6. Secure the lid.
7. Select the Steam function on your cooker and set 3 mins cooking time.
8. After it is done, carefully do a Quick release. Remove the lid.
9. Serve hot.

Per Serving

calories: 229 | fat: 14.0g | protein: 23.4g | carbs: 1.3g | fiber: 0.2g | sodium: 88mg

Mahi-Mahi Meal

Prep time: 15 minutes | Cook time: 7 minutes | Serves 4

1½ cups water	4 garlic cloves, minced
4 (4-ounce / 113-g) mahi-	4 tablespoons fresh lime
mahi fillets	juice
Salt and freshly ground	4 tablespoons erythritol
black pepper, to taste	2 teaspoons red pepper
	flakes, crushed

1. Sprinkle some salt and pepper over Mahi-Mahi fillets for seasoning. In a separate bowl add all the remaining & mix well.
2. Add the water to the Instant pot and place the trivet in it.
3. Arrange the seasoned fillets over the trivet in a single layer.
4. Pour the prepared sauce on top of each fillet.
5. Cover and secure the lid.
6. Set the Steam function on your cooker for 5 minutes.
7. Once it beeps, do a quick release then remove the lid.
8. Serve the steaming hot Mahi-Mahi and enjoy.

Per Serving calories: 228 | fat: 1.4g | protein: 38.0g | carbs: 14.2g | fiber: 0.1g | sodium: 182mg

Rosemary Cod with Cherry Tomato

Prep time: 20 minutes | Cook time: 5 minutes | Serves 6

1½ pounds (680 g) cherry	3 garlic cloves, minced
tomatoes, halved	2 tablespoons olive oil
2½ tbsp fresh rosemary,	Salt and freshly ground
chopped 6 (4-ounce / 113-	black pepper, to taste
g) cod fillets	

1. Add the olive oil, half of the tomatoes and rosemary to the insert of the Instant Pot. Place the cod fillets over these tomatoes. Then add more tomatoes to the pot.
2. Add the garlic to the pot. Then secure the lid.
3. Select the Manual function with High Pressure for 5 minutes. After the beep, use the quick release to discharge all the steam. Serve cod fillets with tomatoes and sprinkle a pinch of salt and pepper on top.

Per Serving calories: 143 | fat: 5.2g | protein: 18.8g | carbs: 5.0g | fiber: 1.5g | sodium: 358mg

Cod Curry

Prep time: 5 minutes | Cook time: 12 minutes | Serves 8

3 pounds (1.4 kg) cod fillets, cut into bite-sized pieces	4 teaspoons ground cumin
2 tablespoons olive oil	4 teaspoons ground coriander
4 curry leaves	2 teaspoons red chili powder
4 medium onions, chopped	1 teaspoon ground turmeric
2 tablespoons fresh ginger, grated finely	4 cups unsweetened coconut milk
4 garlic cloves, minced	2½ cups tomatoes, chopped
4 tablespoons curry powder	2 Serrano peppers, seeded and chopped
	2 tbsp fresh lemon juice

1. Add the oil to the Instant Pot and select Sauté function for cooking. Add the curry leaves and cook for 30 seconds. Stir the onion, garlic, and ginger into the pot and cook 5 minutes. Add all the spices to the mixture and cook for another 1½ minutes. Hit Cancel then add the coconut milk, Serrano pepper, tomatoes, and fish to the pot.
2. Secure the lid and select the Manual settings with Low Pressure and 5 minutes cooking time. After the beep, do a Quick release and remove the lid. Drizzle lemon juice over the curry then stir. Serve immediately.

Per Serving

calories: 424 | fat: 29.1g | protein: 30.2g | carbs: 14.4g | fiber: 3.8g | sodium: 559mg

Shrimps with Northern Beans

Prep time: 10 minutes | Cook time: 25 minutes | Serves 3

1½ tablespoons olive oil	½ teaspoon cayenne pepper
1 medium onion, chopped	½ pound (227 g) great northern beans, rinsed, soaked, and drained
½ small green bell pepper, seeded and chopped	
½ celery stalk, chopped	1 cup chicken broth
1 garlic clove, minced	1 bay leaf
1 tablespoon fresh parsley, chopped	½ pound (227 g) medium shrimp, peeled and deveined
½ teaspoon red pepper flakes, crushed	

1. Select the Sauté function on your Instant pot, then add the oil, onion, celery, bell pepper and cook for 5 minutes.
2. Now add the parsley, garlic, spices, and bay leaf to the pot and cook for another 2 minutes. Pour in the chicken broth then add the beans to it. Secure the cooker lid.
3. Select the Manual function for 15 minutes with medium pressure. After the beep, do a Natural release for 10 minutes and remove the lid. Add the shrimp to the beans and cook them together on the Manual function for 2 minutes at High Pressure. Do a Quick release, keep it aside for 10 minutes, then remove the lid. Serve hot.

Per Serving calories: 405 | fat: 9.1g | protein: 29.1g | carbs: 53.1g | fiber: 16.4g | sodium: 702mg

Shrimp and Potato Curry

Prep time: 5 minutes | Cook time: 9 minutes | Serves 8

2 tablespoons olive oil	6 medium tomatoes, chopped
1½ medium onions, chopped	2 pounds (907 g) medium shrimp, peeled and deveined
1½ teaspoons ground cumin	1½ tablespoons fresh lemon juice
2 teaspoons red chili powder	Salt, to taste
2 teaspoons ground turmeric	½ cup fresh cilantro, chopped
3 medium white rose potatoes, diced	

1. Select the Sauté function on your Instant Pot. Add the oil and onions then cook for 2 minutes.
2. Add the tomatoes, potatoes, cilantro, lemon juice and all the spices into the pot and secure the lid.
3. Select the Manual function at medium pressure for 5 minutes. Do a natural release then remove the lid. Stir shrimp into the pot. Secure the lid again then set the Manual function with High Pressure for 2 minutes.
4. After the beep, use Natural release and let it stand for 10 minutes. Remove the lid and serve hot.

Per Serving

calories: 197 | fat: 5.0g | protein: 18.1g | carbs: 20.3g | fiber: 3.9g | sodium: 700mg

Salmon and Mushroom Hash with Pesto

Prep time: 15 minutes | Cook time: 20 minutes | Serves 6

Pesto:	**Hash:**
¼ cup extra-virgin olive oil	2 tablespoons extra-virgin olive oil
1 bunch fresh basil	
Juice and zest of 1 lemon	6 cups mixed mushrooms (brown, white, shiitake, cremini, portobello, etc.), sliced
⅓ cup water	
¼ teaspoon salt, plus additional as needed	
	1 pound (454 g) wild salmon, cubed

1. Make the pesto: Pulse the olive oil, basil, juice and zest, water, and salt in a blender or food processor until smoothly blended. Set aside.
2. Heat the olive oil in a large skillet over medium heat.
3. Stir-fry the mushrooms for 6 to 8 minutes, or until they begin to exude their juices.
4. Add the salmon and cook each side for 5 to 6 minutes until cooked through.
5. Fold in the prepared pesto and stir well. Taste and add additional salt as needed. Serve warm.

Per Serving

calories: 264 | fat: 14.7g | protein: 7.0g | carbs: 30.9g | fiber: 4.0g | sodium: 480mg

Mussels with Onions

Prep time: 10 minutes | Cook time: 7 minutes | Serves 8

2 tablespoons olive oil
2 medium yellow onions, chopped
1 teaspoon dried rosemary, crushed
2 garlic cloves, minced
2 cups chicken broth
4 pounds (1.8 kg) mussels, cleaned and debearded
¼ cup fresh lemon juice
Salt and ground black pepper as needed

1. Put the oil to the Instant Pot and select the Sauté function for cooking. Add the onions and cook for 5 minutes with occasional stirring.
2. Add the rosemary and garlic to the pot. Stir and cook for 1 minute. Pour the chicken broth and lemon juice into the cooker, sprinkle some salt and black pepper over it.
3. Place the trivet inside the cooker and arrange the mussels over it.
4. Select the Manual function at Low Pressure for 1 minute.
5. Secure the lid and let the mussels cook.
6. After the beep, do a Quick release then remove the lid.
7. Serve the mussels with its steaming hot soup in a bowl.

Per Serving calories: 249 | fat: 8.8g | protein: 28.5g | carbs: 11.9g | fiber: 0.5g | sodium: 844mg

Crispy Tilapia with Mango Salsa

Prep time: 5 minutes | Cook time: 10 minutes | Serves 2

Salsa:
1 cup chopped mango
2 tablespoons chopped fresh cilantro
2 tablespoons chopped red onion
2 tablespoons freshly squeezed lime juice
½ jalapeño pepper, seeded and minced
Pinch salt
Tilapia:
1 tablespoon paprika
1 teaspoon onion powder
½ teaspoon dried thyme
½ teaspoon freshly ground black pepper
¼ teaspoon cayenne pepper
½ teaspoon garlic powder
¼ teaspoon salt
½ pound (227 g) boneless tilapia fillets
2 teaspoons extra-virgin olive oil
1 lime, cut into wedges, for serving

1. Make the salsa: Place the mango, cilantro, onion, lime juice, jalapeño, and salt in a medium bowl and toss to combine. Set aside.
2. Make the tilapia: Stir together the paprika, onion powder, thyme, black pepper, cayenne pepper, garlic powder, and salt in a small bowl until well mixed. Rub both sides of fillets generously with the mixture.
3. Heat the olive oil in a large skillet over medium heat.
4. Add the fish fillets and cook each side for 3 to 5 minutes until golden brown and cooked through.
5. Divide the fillets among two plates and spoon half of the prepared salsa onto each fillet. Serve the fish alongside the lime wedges.

Per Serving
calories: 239 | fat: 7.8g | protein: 25.0g | carbs: 21.9g | fiber: 4.0g | sodium: 416mg

Mediterranean Grilled Sea Bass

Prep time: 20 minutes | Cook time: 20 minutes | Serves 6

¼ teaspoon onion powder
¼ teaspoon garlic powder
¼ teaspoon paprika
Lemon pepper and sea salt to taste
2 pounds (907 g) sea bass
3 tablespoons extra-virgin olive oil, divided
2 large cloves garlic, chopped
1 tablespoon chopped Italian flat leaf parsley

1. Preheat the grill to high heat.
2. Place the onion powder, garlic powder, paprika, lemon pepper, and sea salt in a large bowl and stir to combine.
3. Dredge the fish in the spice mixture, turning until well coated.
4. Heat 2 tablespoon of olive oil in a small skillet. Add the garlic and parsley and cook for 1 to 2 minutes, stirring occasionally. Remove the skillet from the heat and set aside. Brush the grill grates lightly with remaining 1 tablespoon olive oil.
5. Grill the fish for about 7 minutes. Flip the fish and drizzle with the garlic mixture and cook for an additional 7 minutes, or until the fish flakes when pressed lightly with a fork. Serve hot.

Per Serving calories: 200 | fat: 10.3g | protein: 26.9g | carbs: 0.6g | fiber: 0.1g | sodium: 105mg

Spiced Citrus Sole

Prep time: 10 minutes | Cook time: 10 minutes | Serves 4

1 teaspoon garlic powder
1 teaspoon chili powder
½ teaspoon lemon zest
½ teaspoon lime zest
¼ teaspoon smoked paprika
¼ teaspoon freshly ground black pepper Pinch sea salt
4 (6-ounce / 170-g) sole fillets, patted dry
1 tablespoon extra-virgin olive oil
2 teaspoons freshly squeezed lime juice

1. Preheat the oven to 450°F (235°C). Line a baking sheet with aluminum foil and set aside.
2. Mix together the garlic powder, chili powder, lemon zest, lime zest, paprika, pepper, and salt in a small bowl until well combined.
3. Arrange the sole fillets on the prepared baking sheet and rub the spice mixture all over the fillets until well coated. Drizzle the olive oil and lime juice over the fillets.
4. Bake in the preheated oven for about 8 minutes until flaky.
5. Remove from the heat to a plate and serve.

Per Serving
calories: 183 | fat: 5.0g | protein: 32.1g | carbs: 0g | fiber: 0g | sodium: 136mg

Asian-Inspired Tuna Lettuce Wraps

Prep time: 10 minutes | Cook time: 0 minutes | Serves 2

⅓ cup almond butter
1 tablespoon freshly squeezed lemon juice
1 teaspoon low-sodium soy sauce
1 teaspoon curry powder
½ teaspoon sriracha, or to taste

½ cup canned water chestnuts, drained and chopped
2 (2.6-ounce / 74-g) package tuna packed in water, drained
2 large butter lettuce leaves

1. Stir together the almond butter, lemon juice, soy sauce, curry powder, sriracha in a medium bowl until well mixed. Add the water chestnuts and tuna and stir until well incorporated.
2. Place 2 butter lettuce leaves on a flat work surface, spoon half of the tuna mixture onto each leaf and roll up into a wrap. Serve immediately.

Per Serving

calories: 270 | fat: 13.9g | protein: 19.1g | carbs: 18.5g | fiber: 3.0g | sodium: 626mg

Braised Branzino with Wine Sauce

Prep time: 15 minutes | Cook time: 15 minutes | Serves 2 to 3

Sauce:
¾ cup dry white wine
2 tablespoons white wine vinegar
2 tablespoons cornstarch
1 tablespoon honey
Fish:
1 large branzino, butterflied and patted dry
2 tablespoons onion powder

2 tablespoons paprika
½ tablespoon salt
6 tablespoons extra-virgin olive oil, divided
4 garlic cloves, thinly sliced
4 scallions, both green and white parts, thinly sliced
1 large tomato, cut into ¼-inch cubes
4 kalamata olives, pitted and chopped

1. Make the sauce: Mix together the white wine, vinegar, cornstarch, and honey in a bowl and keep stirring until the honey has dissolved. Set aside.
2. Make the fish: Place the fish on a clean work surface, skin-side down. Sprinkle the onion powder, paprika, and salt to season. Drizzle 2 tablespoons of olive oil all over the fish.
3. Heat 2 tablespoons of olive oil in a large skillet over high heat until it shimmers.
4. Add the fish, skin-side up, to the skillet and brown for about 2 minutes. Carefully flip the fish and cook for another 3 minutes. Remove from the heat to a plate and set aside.
5. Add the remaining 2 tablespoons olive oil to the skillet and swirl to coat. Stir in the garlic cloves, scallions, tomato, and kalamata olives and saut é for 5 minutes. Pour in the prepared sauce and stir to combine.
6. Return the fish (skin-side down) to the skillet, flipping to coat in the sauce. Reduce the heat to medium-low, and cook for an additional 5 minutes until cooked through.
7. Using a slotted spoon, transfer the fish to a plate and serve warm.

Per Serving calories: 1059 | fat: 71.9g | protein: 46.2g | carbs: 55.8g | fiber: 5.1g | sodium: 2807mg

Garlic Skillet Salmon

Prep time: 5 minutes | Cook time: 14 to 16 minutes | Serves 4

1 tablespoon extra-virgin olive oil
2 garlic cloves, minced
1 teaspoon smoked paprika
1½ cups grape or cherry tomatoes, quartered
1 (12-ounce / 340-g) jar roasted red peppers, drained and chopped

1 tablespoon water
¼ teaspoon freshly ground black pepper
¼ teaspoon kosher or sea salt
1 pound (454 g) salmon fillets, skin removed and cut into 8 pieces
1 tablespoon freshly squeezed lemon juice

1. In a large skillet over medium heat, heat the oil. Add the garlic and smoked paprika and cook for 1 minute, stirring often. Add the tomatoes, roasted peppers, water, black pepper, and salt. Turn up the heat to medium-high, bring to a simmer, and cook for 3 minutes, stirring occasionally and smashing the tomatoes with a wooden spoon toward the end of the cooking time.
2. Add the salmon to the skillet, and spoon some of the sauce over the top. Cover and cook for 10 to 12 minutes, or until the salmon is cooked through and just starts to flake.
3. Remove the skillet from the heat, and drizzle lemon juice over the top of the fish. Stir the sauce, then break up the salmon into chunks with a fork. Serve hot.

Per Serving

calories: 255 | fat: 11.7g | protein: 24.2g | carbs: 5.9g | fiber: 1.2g | sodium: 809mg

Baked Halibut Steaks with Vegetables

Prep time: 15 minutes | Cook time: 20 minutes | Serves 4

2 teaspoon olive oil, divided
1 clove garlic, peeled and minced
½ cup minced onion
1 cup diced zucchini
2 cups diced fresh tomatoes

2 tablespoons chopped fresh basil
¼ teaspoon salt
¼ teaspoon ground black pepper
4 (6-ounce / 170-g) halibut steaks
⅓ cup crumbled feta cheese

1. Preheat oven to 450°F (235°C). Coat a shallow baking dish lightly with 1 teaspoon of olive oil.
2. In a medium saucepan, heat the remaining 1 teaspoon of olive oil.
3. Add the garlic, onion, and zucchini and mix well. Cook for 5 minutes, stirring occasionally, or until the zucchini is softened.
4. Remove the saucepan from the heat and stir in the tomatoes, basil, salt, and pepper.
5. Place the halibut steaks in the coated baking dish in a single layer. Spread the zucchini mixture evenly over the steaks. Scatter the top with feta cheese.
6. Bake in the preheated oven for about 15 minutes, or until the fish flakes when pressed lightly with a fork. Serve hot.

Per Serving

calories: 258 | fat: 7.6g | protein: 38.6g | carbs: 6.5g | fiber: 1.2g | sodium: 384mg

Spicy Haddock Stew

Prep time: 15 minutes | Cook time: 35 minutes | Serves 6

¼ cup coconut oil
1 tablespoon minced garlic
1 onion, chopped
2 celery stalks, chopped
½ fennel bulb, thinly sliced
1 carrot, diced
1 sweet potato, diced
1 (15-ounce / 425-g) can low-sodium diced tomatoes
1 cup coconut milk
1 cup low-sodium chicken broth
¼ teaspoon red pepper flakes
12 ounces (340 g) haddock, cut into 1-inch chunks
2 tablespoons chopped fresh cilantro, for garnish

1. In a large saucepan, heat the coconut oil over medium-high heat.
2. Add the garlic, onion, and celery and sauté for about 4 minutes, stirring occasionally, or until they are tender.
3. Stir in the fennel bulb, carrot, and sweet potato and sauté for 4 minutes more.
4. Add the diced tomatoes, coconut milk, chicken broth, and red pepper flakes and stir to incorporate, then bring the mixture to a boil.
5. Once it starts to boil, reduce the heat to low, and bring to a simmer for about 15 minutes, or until the vegetables are fork-tender.
6. Add the haddock chunks and continue simmering for about 10 minutes, or until the fish is cooked through.
7. Sprinkle the cilantro on top for garnish before serving.

Per Serving

calories: 276 | fat: 20.9g | protein: 14.2g | carbs: 6.8g | fiber: 3.0g | sodium: 226mg

Canned Sardine Donburi (Rice Bowl)

Prep time: 10 minutes | Cook time: 40 to 50 minutes | Serves 4 to 6

4 cups water
2 cups brown rice, rinsed well
½ teaspoon salt
3 (4-ounce / 113-g) cans sardines packed in water, drained
3 scallions, sliced thin
1-inch piece fresh ginger, grated
4 tablespoons sesame oil

1. Place the water, brown rice, and salt to a large saucepan and stir to combine. Allow the mixture to boil over high heat.
2. Once boiling, reduce the heat to low, and cook covered for 45 to 50 minutes, or until the rice is tender.
3. Meanwhile, roughly mash the sardines with a fork in a medium bowl.
4. When the rice is done, stir in the mashed sardines, scallions, and ginger.
5. Divide the mixture into four bowls. Top each bowl with a drizzle of sesame oil. Serve warm.

Per Serving

calories: 603 | fat: 23.6g | protein: 25.2g | carbs: 73.8g | fiber: 4.0g | sodium: 498mg

Orange Flavored Scallops

Prep time: 10 minutes | Cook time: 10 minutes | Serves 4

2 pounds (907 g) sea scallops, patted dry
Sea salt and freshly ground black pepper, to taste
2 tablespoons extra-virgin olive oil
1 tablespoon minced garlic
¼ cup freshly squeezed orange juice
1 teaspoon orange zest
2 teaspoons chopped fresh thyme, for garnish

1. In a bowl, lightly season the scallops with salt and pepper. Set aside.
2. Heat the olive oil in a large skillet over medium-high heat until it shimmers.
3. Add the garlic and sauté for about 3 minutes, or until fragrant.
4. Stir in the seasoned scallops and sear each side for about 4 minutes, or until the scallops are browned.
5. Remove the scallops from the heat to a plate and set aside.
6. Add the orange juice and zest to the skillet, scraping up brown bits from bottom of skillet.
7. Drizzle the sauce over the scallops and garnish with the thyme before serving.

Per Serving

calories: 266 | fat: 7.6g | protein: 38.1g | carbs: 7.9g | fiber: 0g | sodium: 360mg

Peppercorn-Seared Tuna Steaks

Prep time: 5 minutes | Cook time: 10 minutes | Serves 2

2 (5-ounce / 142-g) ahi tuna steaks
1 teaspoon kosher salt
¼ teaspoon cayenne pepper
2 tablespoons olive oil
1 teaspoon whole peppercorns

1. On a plate, Season the tuna steaks on both sides with salt and cayenne pepper.
2. In a skillet, heat the olive oil over medium-high heat until it shimmers.
3. Add the peppercorns and cook for about 5 minutes, or until they soften and pop.
4. Carefully put the tuna steaks in the skillet and sear for 1 to 2 minutes per side, depending on the thickness of the tuna steaks, or until the fish is cooked to the desired level of doneness.
5. Cool for 5 minutes before serving.

Per Serving

calories: 260 | fat: 14.3g | protein: 33.4g | carbs: 0.2g | fiber: 0.1g | sodium: 1033mg

Instant Pot Poached Salmon

Prep time: 10 minutes | Cook time: 3 minutes | Serves 4

1 lemon, sliced ¼ inch thick
4 (6-ounce / 170-g) skinless salmon fillets, 1½ inches thick
½ teaspoon salt
¼ teaspoon pepper
½ cup water

1. Layer the lemon slices in the bottom of the Instant Pot.
2. Season the salmon with salt and pepper, then arrange the salmon (skin-side down) on top of the lemon slices. Pour in the water. Secure the lid. Select the Manual mode and set the cooking time for 3 minutes at High Pressure.
3. Once cooking is complete, do a quick pressure release. Carefully open the lid. Serve warm.

Per Serving calories: 350 | fat: 23.0g | protein: 35.0g | carbs: 0g | fiber: 0g | sodium: 390mg

Seared Salmon with Lemon Cream Sauce

Prep time: 10 minutes | Cook time: 20 minutes | Serves 4

4 (5-ounce / 142-g) salmon fillets	Juice and zest of 1 lemon
Sea salt and freshly ground black pepper, to taste	1 teaspoon chopped fresh thyme
1 tablespoon extra-virgin olive oil	½ cup fat-free sour cream
½ cup low-sodium vegetable broth	1 teaspoon honey
	1 tablespoon chopped fresh chives

1. Preheat the oven to 400ºF (205ºC).
2. Season the salmon lightly on both sides with salt and pepper. Place a large ovenproof skillet over medium-high heat and add the olive oil.
3. Sear the salmon fillets on both sides until golden, about 3 minutes per side. Transfer the salmon to a baking dish and bake in the preheated oven until just cooked through, about 10 minutes.
4. Meanwhile, whisk together the vegetable broth, lemon juice and zest, and thyme in a small saucepan over medium-high heat until the liquid reduces by about one-quarter, about 5 minutes.
5. Whisk in the sour cream and honey.
6. Stir in the chives and serve the sauce over the salmon.

Per Serving calories: 310 | fat: 18.0g | protein: 29.0g | carbs: 6.0g | fiber: 0g | sodium: 129mg

Tuna and Zucchini Patties

Prep time: 10 minutes | Cook time: 12 minutes | Serves 4

3 slices whole-wheat sandwich bread, toasted	1 teaspoon lemon zest
2 (5-ounce / 142-g) cans tuna in olive oil, drained	¼ teaspoon freshly ground black pepper
1 cup shredded zucchini	¼ teaspoon kosher or sea salt
1 large egg, lightly beaten	1 tablespoon extra-virgin olive oil
¼ cup diced red bell pepper	Salad greens or 4 whole-wheat rolls, for serving (optional)
1 tablespoon dried oregano	

1. Crumble the toast into bread crumbs with your fingers (or use a knife to cut into ¼-inch cubes) until you have 1 cup of loosely packed crumbs. Pour the crumbs into a large bowl. Add the tuna, zucchini, beaten egg, bell pepper, oregano, lemon zest, black pepper, and salt. Mix well with a fork. With your hands, form the mixture into four (½-cup-size) patties. Place them on a plate, and press each patty flat to about ¾-inch thick.
2. In a large skillet over medium-high heat, heat the oil until it's very hot, about 2 minutes.
3. Add the patties to the hot oil, then reduce the heat down to medium. Cook the patties for 5 minutes, flip with a spatula, and cook for an additional 5 minutes. Serve the patties on salad greens or whole-wheat rolls, if desired.

Per Serving

calories: 757 | fat: 72.0g | protein: 5.0g | carbs: 26.0g | fiber: 4.0g | sodium: 418mg

Salmon Baked in Foil

Prep time: 5 minutes | Cook time: 25 minutes | Serves 4

2 cups cherry tomatoes	1 teaspoon oregano
3 tbsp extra-virgin olive oil	½ teaspoon salt
3 tablespoons lemon juice	4 (5-ounce / 142-g) salmon fillets
3 tablespoons almond butter	

1. Preheat the oven to 400ºF (205ºC).
2. Cut the tomatoes in half and put them in a bowl.
3. Add the olive oil, lemon juice, butter, oregano, and salt to the tomatoes and gently toss to combine.
4. Cut 4 pieces of foil, about 12-by-12 inches each.
5. Place the salmon fillets in the middle of each piece of foil.
6. Divide the tomato mixture evenly over the 4 pieces of salmon. Bring the ends of the foil together and seal to form a closed pocket.
7. Place the 4 pockets on a baking sheet. Bake in the preheated oven for 25 minutes.
8. Remove from the oven and serve on a plate.

Per Serving

calories: 410 | fat: 32.0g | protein: 30.0g | carbs: 4.0g | fiber: 1.0g | sodium: 370mg

Mediterranean Cod Stew

Prep time: 10 minutes | Cook time: 20 minutes | Serves 6

2 tablespoons extra-virgin olive oil	1 cup sliced olives, green or black
2 cups chopped onion	⅓ cup dry red wine
2 garlic cloves, minced	¼ teaspoon kosher or sea salt
¾ teaspoon smoked paprika	
1 (14.5-ounce / 411-g) can diced tomatoes, undrained	¼ teaspoon freshly ground black pepper
1 (12-ounce / 340-g) jar roasted red peppers, drained and chopped	1½ pounds (680 g) cod fillets, cut into 1-inch pieces
	3 cups sliced mushrooms

1. In a large stockpot over medium heat, heat the oil. Add the onion and cook for 4 minutes, stirring occasionally. Add the garlic and smoked paprika and cook for 1 minute, stirring often. Mix in the tomatoes with their juices, roasted peppers, olives, wine, pepper, and salt, and turn the heat to medium-high. Bring the mixture to a boil. Add the cod fillets and mushrooms, and reduce the heat to medium.
2. Cover and cook for about 10 minutes, stirring a few times, until the cod is cooked through and flakes easily, and serve.

Per Serving calories: 167 | fat: 5.0g | protein: 19.0g | carbs: 11.0g | fiber: 5.0g | sodium: 846mg

Balsamic-Honey Glazed Salmon

Prep time: 2 minutes | Cook time: 8 minutes | Serves 4

½ cup balsamic vinegar	Sea salt and freshly ground pepper, to taste
1 tablespoon honey	
4 (8-ounce / 227-g) salmon fillets	1 tablespoon olive oil

1. Heat a skillet over medium-high heat. Combine the vinegar and honey in a small bowl.
2. Season the salmon fillets with the sea salt and freshly ground pepper; brush with the honey-balsamic glaze.
3. Add olive oil to the skillet, and sear the salmon fillets, cooking for 3 to 4 minutes on each side until lightly browned and medium rare in the center.
4. Let sit for 5 minutes before serving.

Per Serving calories: 454 | fat: 17.3g | protein: 65.3g | carbs: 9.7g | fiber: 0g | sodium: 246mg

Teriyaki Salmon

Prep time: 10 minutes | Cook time: 8 minutes | Serves 4

4 (8-ounce / 227-g) thick salmon fillets.	4 teaspoons sesame seeds
1 cup soy sauce	2 cloves garlic, minced
2 cups water	2 tablespoons freshly grated ginger
½ cup mirin	4 tablespoons brown sugar
2 tablespoons sesame oil	1 tablespoon corn starch
	4 green onions, minced

1. Add the soy sauce, sesame oil, sesame seeds, mirin, ginger, water, garlic, green onions, and brown sugar to a small bowl. Mix them well. In a shallow dish place the salmon fillets and pour half of the prepared mixture over the fillets. Let it marinate for 30 minutes in a refrigerator.
2. Pour 1 cup of water into the insert of your Instant pot and place trivet inside it. Arrange the marinated salmon fillets over the trivet and secure the lid.
3. Select the Manual settings with High Pressure and 8 minutes cooking time. Meanwhile, take a skillet and add the remaining marinade mixture in it.
4. Let it cook for 2 minutes, then add the corn starch mixed with water. Stir well and cook for 1 minute.
5. Check the pressure cooker, do a Quick release if it is done.
6. Transfer the fillets to a serving platter and pour the sesame mixture over it. Garnish with chopped green chilies then serve hot.

Per Serving calories: 622 | fat: 28.6g | protein: 51.3g | carbs: 29.6g | fiber: 2.0g | sodium: 1086mg

Coconut Tangy Cod Curry

Prep time: 5 minutes | Cook time: 3 minutes | Serves 6

1 (28-ounce / 794-g) can coconut milk	2 teaspoons ground turmeric
Juice of 2 lemons	2 teaspoons ground ginger
2 tablespoons red curry paste	1 teaspoon sea salt
2 teaspoons fish sauce	1 teaspoon white pepper
2 teaspoons honey	2 pounds (907 g) codfish, cut into 1-inch cubes
4 teaspoons Sriracha	½ cup chopped fresh
4 cloves garlic, minced	cilantro, for garnish
	4 lime wedges, for garnish

1. Add all the , except the cod cubes and garnish, to a large bowl and whisk them well. Arrange the cod cube at the base of the Instant Pot and pour the coconut milk mixture over it. Secure the lid and hit the Manual key, select High Pressure with 3 minutes cooking time.
2. After the beep, do a Quick release then remove the lid.
3. Garnish with fresh cilantro and lemon wedges then serve.

Per Serving calories: 396 | fat: 29.1g | protein: 26.6g | carbs: 11.4g | fiber: 2.0g | sodium: 1024mg

Shrimps with Broccoli

Prep time: 5 minutes | Cook time: 10 minutes | Serves 2

2 teaspoons vegetable oil	¼ cup water
2 tablespoons corn starch	¼ cup sliced carrots
1 cup broccoli florets	3 tablespoons rice vinegar
¼ cup chicken broth	2 teaspoons sesame oil
8 ounces (227 g) large shrimp, peeled and deveined	1 tablespoon chili garlic sauce
¼ cup soy sauce	Coriander leaves to garnish
	Boiled rice or noodles, for serving

1. Add 1 tablespoon of corn starch and shrimp to a bowl. Mix them well then set it aside.
2. In a small bowl, mix the remaining corn starch, chicken broth, carrots, chili garlic sauce, rice vinegar and soy sauce together. Keep the mixture aside.
3. Select the Sauté function on your Instant pot, add the sesame oil and broccoli florets to the pot and sauté for 5 minutes. Add the water to the broccoli, cover the lid and cook for 5 minutes. Stir in shrimp and vegetable oil to the broccoli, sauté it for 5 minutes. Garnish with coriander leaves on top. Serve with rice or noodles.

Per Serving calories: 300 | fat: 16.5g | protein: 19.6g | carbs: 17.1g | fiber: 2.2g | sodium: 1241mg

Shrimp and Spaghetti Squash Bowls

Prep time: 5 minutes | Cook time: 25 minutes | Serves 4

½ cup dry white wine	1 (28-ounce / 794-g) can crushed tomatoes
¼ teaspoon crushed red pepper flakes	2 cloves garlic, minced
1 large shallot, finely chopped	2½ pounds (1.1 kg) spaghetti squash
1 pound (454 g) jumbo shrimp, peeled and deveined	1 teaspoon olive oil
	Salt and pepper, to taste
	Parsley leaves (garnish)

1. At first, sprinkle some salt and pepper over the shrimp and keep them in a refrigerator until further use.
2. Hit the Sauté function on your Instant Pot, then add the olive oil and red pepper flakes into it. Sauté for 1 minute.
3. Add the shallot and cook for 3 minutes. Then add the garlic, cook for 1 minute.
4. Add the dry wine, tomatoes, and whole spaghetti squash in the pot. Select Manual settings with medium pressure for 20 minutes. After the beep, do a Natural release. Remove the lid and the spaghetti squash.
5. Cut squash in half, remove its seed and stab with a fork to form spaghetti strands out of it. Keep them aside.
6. Select the Sauté function on your instant pot again, stir in shrimp. Mix well the shrimp with sauce.
7. To serve, top the spaghetti squash with shrimp and sauce. Garnish it with parsley.

Per Serving calories: 222 | fat: 4.4g | protein: 19.3g | carbs: 30.1g | fiber: 8.5g | sodium: 974mg

Scallop Teriyaki

Prep time: 5 minutes | Cook time: 5 minutes | Serves 6

2 pounds (907 g) jumbo sea scallops	1 cup coconut aminos
2 tablespoons olive oil	1 teaspoon ground ginger
6 tbsp pure maple syrup	1 teaspoon garlic powder
	1 teaspoon sea salt

1. Add the olive oil to the Instant pot and heat it on the Sauté settings of your pot. Add the scallops to the pot and cook for a minute from each side.
2. Stir in all the remaining in the pot and mix them well. Secure the lid and select the Steam function to cook for 3 minutes. After the beep, do a Quick release then remove the lid. Serve hot.

Per Serving calories: 228 | fat: 5.3g | protein: 23.4g | carbs: 21.4g | fiber: 0.5g | sodium: 3664mg

Shrimp and Tomato Creole

Prep time: 20 minutes | Cook time: 7 hours 10 minutes | Serves 4

1 pound (454 g) shrimp (peeled and deveined)	1 (8-ounce / 227-g) can tomato sauce
1 tablespoon olive oil	½ teaspoon minced garlic
1 (28-ounce / 794-g) can crush whole tomatoes	¼ teaspoon ground black pepper
1 cup celery stalk (sliced)	1 tbsp Worcestershire sauce
¾ cup chopped white onion	4 drops hot pepper sauce
½ cup green bell pepper (chopped)	Salt, to taste
	White rice for serving

1. Put the oil to the Instant Pot along with all the except the shrimp. Secure the cooker lid and keep the pressure handle valve turned to the venting position.
2. Select the Slow Cook function on your cooker and set it on medium heat. Let the mixture cook for 6 hours.
3. Remove the lid afterwards and add the shrimp to the pot.
4. Stir and let the shrimp cook for another 1 hour on Slow Cook function. Keep the lid covered with pressure release handle in the venting position. To serve, pour the juicy shrimp creole over steaming white rice.

Per Serving calories: 231 | fat: 4.8g | protein: 27.6g | carbs: 23.8g | fiber: 6.1g | sodium: 646mg

Mahi-Mahi and Tomato Bowls

Prep time: 5 minutes | Cook time: 14 minutes | Serves 3

3 (4-ounce / 113-g) mahi-mahi fillets	1 tablespoon fresh lemon juice
1½ tablespoons olive oil	Salt and freshly ground black pepper, to taste
½ yellow onion, sliced	
½ teaspoon dried oregano	1 (14-ounce / 397-g) can sugar-free diced tomatoes

1. Add the olive oil to the Instant Pot. Select the Sauté function on it. Add all the ingredient to the pot except the fillets. Cook them for 10 minutes. Press the Cancel key, then add the mahi-mahi fillets to the sauce.
2. Cover the fillets with sauce by using a spoon.
3. Secure the lid and set the Manual function at High Pressure for 4 minutes. After the beep, do a Quick release then remove the lid. Serve the fillets with their sauce, poured on top.

Per Serving calories: 265 | fat: 8.6g | protein: 39.1g | carbs: 7.0g | fiber: 3.1g | sodium: 393mg

Alfredo Tuscan Shrimp with Penne

Prep time: 5 minutes | Cook time: 5 minutes | Serves 3

1 pound (454 g) shrimp	1 cup sun-dried tomatoes
1 jar alfredo sauce	1 box penne pasta
1½ cups fresh spinach	1½ tbsp Tuscan seasoning
	3 cups water

1. Add the water and pasta to a pot over a medium heat, boil until it cooks completely. Then strain the pasta and keep it aside. Select the Sauté function on your Instant Pot and add the tomatoes, shrimp, Tuscan seasoning, and alfredo sauce into it.
2. Stir and cook until shrimp turn pink in color.
3. Now add the spinach leaves to the pot and cook for 5 mins.
4. Add the pasta to the pot and stir well.
5. Serve hot.

Per Serving

calories: 1361 | fat: 70.1g | protein: 55.9g | carbs: 134.4g | fiber: 19.4g | sodium: 933mg

Tuna with Shirataki Noodles

Prep time: 5 minutes | Cook time: 4 minutes | Serves 2

½ can tuna, drained	1 (14-ounce / 397-g) can cream mushroom soup
8 ounces (227 g) Shirataki noodles	2 ounces (57 g) shredded Cheddar cheese
½ cup frozen peas	1½ cups water

1. Add the water with noodles to the base of your Instant Pot.
2. Place the tuna and peas over it. Then pour the mushroom soup on top.
3. Secure the lid and cook with the Manual function at High Pressure for 4 minutes.
4. After the beep, do a Quick release then remove the lid.
5. Stir in shredded cheese to the tuna mix.
6. Serve warm.

Per Serving

calories: 362 | fat: 11.1g | protein: 19.5g | carbs: 46.5g | fiber: 1.5g | sodium: 645mg

Grits with Shrimp

Prep time: 5 minutes | Cook time: 15 minutes | Serves 8

1 tablespoon oil	24 ounces (680 g) tail-on shrimp
2 cups quick grits	
12 ounces (340 g) Parmesan cheese, shredded	2 tbsp Old Bay seasoning
	A pinch of ground black pepper
2 cups heavy cream	4 cups water

1. Add a tablespoon of oil to the Instant Pot. Select the Sauté function for cooking.
2. Add the shrimp to the oil and drizzle old bay seasoning over it.
3. Cook the shrimp for 3-4 mins while stirring then set them aside.
4. Now add the water, cream, and quick grits to the pot. Select the Manual function for 3 minutes at High Pressure.
5. After the beep, do a Quick release then remove the lid.
6. Add the shredded cheese to the grits then stir well.
7. Take a serving bowl, first pour in the creamy grits mixture then top it with shrimp.
8. Sprinkle black pepper on top then serve hot.

Per Serving

calories: 528 | fat: 38.6g | protein: 30.7g | carbs: 15.2g | fiber: 0.7g | sodium: 1249mg

Fennel Poached Cod with Tomatoes

Prep time: 10 minutes | Cook time: 20 minutes | Serves 4

1 tablespoon olive oil	2 cups chicken broth
1 cup thinly sliced fennel	½ cup white wine
½ cup thinly sliced onion	Juice and zest of 1 orange
1 tablespoon minced garlic	1 pinch red pepper flakes
1 (15-ounce / 425-g) can diced tomatoes	1 bay leaf
	1 pound (454 g) cod

1. Heat the olive oil in a large skillet. Add the onion and fennel and cook for 6 minutes, stirring occasionally, or until translucent. Add the garlic and cook for 1 minute more. Add the tomatoes, chicken broth, wine, orange juice and zest, red pepper flakes, and bay leaf, and simmer for 5 minutes to meld the flavors.
2. Carefully add the cod in a single layer, cover, and simmer for 6 to 7 minutes. Transfer fish to a serving dish, ladle the remaining sauce over the fish, and serve.

Per Serving calories: 336 | fat: 12.5g | protein: 45.1g | carbs:11.0g | fiber: 3.3g | sodium: 982mg

Fish Tacos (Italian)

Preparation Time: 40 minutes Cooking Time: 15 minutes Servings: 8

1cup flour	2tablespoons corn flour
1 teaspoon baking powder	1 egg
1/2 teaspoon of salt	
1 cup of beer	1/2 cup of yogurt
1/2 cup of mayonnaise 1 lime, juice	1 jalapeño pepper, minced 1 c. Finely chopped capers 1/2 teaspoon dried oregano 1/2 teaspoon ground cumin 1/2 teaspoon dried dill
1 teaspoon ground cayenne pepper 1 liter of oil for frying 1/2 medium cabbage, finely shredded	1 pound of cod fillets, 2-3 ounces each 8 corn tortillas

1. Prepare beer dough: combine flour, corn flour, baking powder and salt in a large bowl. Mix the egg and the beer and stir in the flour mixture quickly.
2. To make a white sauce: combine yogurt and mayonnaise in a medium bowl. Gradually add fresh lime juice until it is slightly fluid — season with jalapeño, capers, oregano, cumin, dill, and cayenne pepper.
3. Heat the oil in a frying pan.
4. Lightly sprinkle the fish with flour. Dip it in the beer batter and fry until crispy and golden brown. Drain on kitchen paper. Heat the tortillas. Place the fried fish in a tortilla and garnish with grated cabbage and white sauce.

Nutrition: 409 calories 18.8 g of fat 43 grams of carbohydrates 17.3 g of protein 54 mg cholesterol 407 mg of sodium.

Grilled Tilapia with Mango Salsa (Spanish)

Preparation Time: 45 minutes Cooking Time: 10 minutes Servings: 2

1/3 cup extra virgin olive oil	1 tablespoon chopped fresh parsley 1 clove of garlic, minced
1 tablespoon lemon juice	
1 teaspoon dried basil	1teaspoon ground black pepper 1/2 teaspoon salt
2tilapia fillets (1 oz. each)	1large ripe mango, peeled, pitted and diced 1/2 red pepper, diced
2tablespoons chopped red onion	1 tablespoon chopped fresh coriander 1 jalapeño pepper, seeded and minced 2 tablespoons lime juice
1 tablespoon lemon juice salt and pepper to taste	

1. Mix extra virgin olive oil, 1 tablespoon lemon juice, parsley, garlic, basil, 1 teaspoon pepper, and 1/2 teaspoon salt in a bowl, then pour into a resealable plastic bag. Add the tilapia fillets, cover with the marinade, remove excess air, and close the bag. Marinate in the fridge for 1 hour.
2. Prepare the mango salsa by combining the mango, red pepper, red onion, coriander, and jalapeño pepper in a bowl. Add the lime juice and 1 tablespoon lemon juice and mix well. Season with salt and pepper and keep until serving.
3. Preheat a grill over medium heat and lightly oil.
4. Remove the tilapia from the marinade and remove the excess. Discard the rest of the marinade. Grill the fillets until the fish is no longer translucent in the middle and flake easily with the fork for 3 to 4 minutes on each side, depending on the thickness of the fillets. Serve the tilapia topped with mango salsa.

Nutrition: 634 calories 40.2 grams of fat 33.4 g carbohydrates 36.3 g of protein 62 mg cholesterol 697 mg of sodium.

Salmon with Lemon & Dill (Spanish)

Prep Time: 15 minutes Cooking Time: 2 hours Servings: 4

Cooking spray	1 teaspoon olive oil 2 lb. salmon
1 tablespoon fresh dill, chopped Salt and pepper to taste	1 clove garlic, minced 1 lemon, sliced

1. Spray your slow cooker with oil.
2. Brush both sides of salmon with olive oil.
3. Season the salmon with salt, pepper, dill and garlic.
4. Add to the slow cooker.
5. Put the lemon slices on top.
6. Cover the pot and cook on high for 2 hours.

Nutrition: Calories 313 Fat 15.2g Sodium 102mg Carbohydrate 0.7g Fiber 0.1g Protein 44.2g Sugars 0g

Asparagus Smoked Salmon (Spanish)

Preparation Time: 15 minutes Cooking time: 5 hours Servings: 6

1 tablespoon extra-virgin olive oil 6 large eggs	1cup heavy (whipping) cream
2teaspoons chopped fresh dill, plus additional for garnish	½ teaspoon kosher salt
¼ teaspoon freshly ground black pepper	11/2 cups shredded Havarti or Monterey Jack cheese 12 ounces asparagus, trimmed and sliced
6 ounces smoked salmon, flaked	

1. Brush butter into a cooker
2. Whisk in the heavy cream with eggs, dill, salt, and pepper.
3. Stir in the cheese and asparagus.
4. Gently fold in the salmon and then pour the mixture into the prepared insert.
5. Cover and cook on low or 3 hours on high.
6. Serve warm, garnished with additional fresh dill.

Nutrition: Calories 388 Fat 19 Carbs 1.0 Protein 21

One-Pot Seafood Chowder (Greek)

Prep Time: 10 minutes Cooking Time: 10 minutes Servings: 3

3 cans coconut milk	1 tablespoon garlic, minced Salt and pepper to taste
3 cans clams, chopped 2 cans shrimps, canned	1 package fresh shrimps, shelled and deveined 1 can corn, drained
4 large potatoes, diced	2carrots, peeled and chopped 2 celery stalks, chopped

1. Place all in a pot and give a good stir to mix everything.
2. Close the lid and turn on the heat to medium.
3. Bring to a boil and allow to simmer for 10 minutes.
4. Place in individual containers.
5. Put a label and store in the fridge.
6. Allow to warm at room temperature before heating in the microwave oven.

Nutrition: Calories: 532; Carbs: 92.5g; Protein: 25.3g; Fat: 6.7g

Cedar Planked Salmon (Greek)

Prep Time: 15 minutes Cooking Time: 20 minutes Servings: 6

2untreated cedar boards 1/3 cup of vegetable oil 1/3 cup soy sauce	1/4 cup chopped green onions 1 1/2 tablespoon rice vinegar 1 teaspoon sesame oil
1 teaspoon finely chopped garlic	1 tbsp grated fresh ginger root 2 skinless salmon fillets

1. Soak the cedar boards in hot water for at least 1 hour. Enjoy longer if you have time.
2. Combine vegetable oil, rice vinegar, sesame oil, soy sauce, green onions, ginger, and garlic in a shallow dish. Place the salmon fillets in the marinade and turn them over to coat them. Cover and marinate for a minimum of 15 minutes or a maximum of one hour.
3. Preheat an outside grill over medium heat. Place the shelves on the rack. The boards are ready when they start to smoke a little.
4. Place the salmon fillets on the shelves and discard the marinade — cover and grill for about 20 minutes. The fish is cooked if you can peel it with a fork.

Nutrition: 678 calories 45.8 g fat 1.7 g carbohydrates 61.3 g of protein 179 mg cholesterol 981 mg of sodium

Broiled Tilapia Parmesan (Spanish)

Preparation Time: 5 minutes Cooking Time: 10 minutes Servings: 8

1/2 cup Parmesan cheese 1/4 cup butter, soft	3 tablespoons mayonnaise
2 tablespoons fresh lemon juice 1/4 teaspoon dried basil	1/4 teaspoon ground black pepper 1/8 teaspoon onion powder
1/8 teaspoon celery salt 2 pounds Tilapia fillets	

1. Preheat the grill on your oven. Grease a drip tray or grill pan with aluminum foil.
2. Combine parmesan, butter, mayonnaise, and lemon juice in a small bowl. Season with dried basil, pepper, onion powder, and celery salt mixed well and set aside.
3. Place the fillets in a single layer on the prepared dish. Grill a few centimeters from the heat for 2 to 3 minutes, turn the fillets and grill for a few minutes. Remove the fillets from the oven and cover with the Parmesan cheese mixture on top. Grill for another 2 minutes or until the garnish is golden brown and fish flakes easily with a fork. Be careful not to overcook the fish.

Nutrition: 224 calories 12.8 g of fat 0.8 g carbohydrates 25.4 g of protein 63 mg cholesterol 220 mg of sodium.

Seafood Linguine (Italian)

Preparation Time: 45 minutes Cooking Time: 20 minutes Servings: 8

1 packet of linguine pasta	½ cup chopped red onion 3 teaspoons garlic powder 1/4 cup olive oil
3 cups milk	2 teaspoons chopped fresh parsley 1/2 cup chopped green pepper
1/2 cup chopped red pepper 1/2 cup broccoli florets	1/2 cup sliced carrots
1 cup chopped fresh mushrooms 1 cup canned shrimp	1 cup crabmeat, drained 1-pound scallops

1. Bring a large pot of lightly salted water to a boil. Add linguini and cook for 6 to 8 minutes, or until al dente. Drain.
2. Meanwhile, fry the red onion and garlic in olive oil in an electric frying pan or large frying pan. Add the milk when the onion is transparent. Boil until bubbles form on the edges of the pan. Add parsley, green and chopped red pepper, broccoli, carrots, mushrooms, shrimps, crab, and scallops and stir until well absorbed.
3. Remove 1/2 cup of milk from the mixture and place it in a small bowl with the flour. Stir until smooth. Return to the pan with seafood and vegetables. Let the mixture thicken. Season with salt and pepper.
4. Pour the fish sauce over the cooked and drained linguini noodles. Serve hot.

Nutrition: 418 calories 11 g of fat 52 grams of carbohydrates 28.2 g of protein 69 mg of cholesterol 242 mg of sodium.

Salmon with Caper Sauce (Italian)

Preparation Time: 5 minutes Cooking time: 45 minutes
Servings: 4

1/2 cup dry white wine 1/2 cup water	1yellow onion, thin sliced 1/2 teaspoon salt
1/4 teaspoon black pepper 4 salmon steaks	2tablespoons butter
2 tablespoons flour 1 cup chicken broth	2 teaspoons lemon juice 3 tablespoons capers

1. Combine wine, water, onion, salt and black pepper in a crock pot; cover and cook on high 20 minutes.
2. Add salmon steaks; cover and cook on high until salmon is tender or about 20 minutes.
3. To make the sauce, in a small skillet, melt butter over medium flame. Stir in flour and cook for 1 minute.
4. Pour in chicken broth and lemon juice; whisk for 1 to 2 minutes. Add capers; serve the sauce with salmon.

Nutrition: Calories: 234 Fat: 15 g Carbs: 2 g Protein: 12 g

Herbed Salmon Loaf with Sauce (Italian)

Preparation Time: 5 minutes Cooking time: 5 hours Servings: 4

For the Salmon Meatloaf: 1cup fresh bread crumbs	1 can (7 1/2 ounce) salmon, drained 1/4 cup scallions, chopped
1/3 cup whole milk 1 egg	1 tablespoon fresh lemon juice 1 teaspoon dried rosemary
1 teaspoon ground coriander 1/2 teaspoon fenugreek	1 teaspoon mustard seed 1/2 teaspoon salt
1/4 teaspoon white pepper 1/2 cup cucumber, chopped Salt, to taste	1/2 cup reduced-fat plain yogurt 1/2 teaspoon dill weed

1. Line your crock pot with a foil.
2. Mix all for the salmon meatloaf until everything is well incorporated; form into loaf and place in the crock pot.
3. Cover with a suitable lid and cook on low heat setting 5 hours.
4. Combine all of the for the sauce; whisk to combine.
5. Serve your meatloaf with prepared sauce.

Nutrition: Calories: 145 Fat: 11 g Carbs: 2 g Protein: 11 g

Grilled Salmon (Spanish)

Prep Time: 15 minutes Cooking Time: 16 minutes Servings: 6

1 1/2 pounds salmon fillet Pepper to taste	Garlic powder to taste 1/3 cup soy sauce
1/3 cup of brown sugar 1/3 cup of water	1/4 cup vegetable oil

1. Season the salmon fillets with lemon pepper, salt, and garlic powder.
2. Mix the soy sauce, brown sugar, water, and vegetable oil in a small bowl until the sugar is dissolved. Place the fish in a big resealable plastic bag with the soy sauce mixture, seal, and let marinate for at least 2 hours.
3. Preheat the grill on medium heat.
4. Lightly oil the grill. Place the salmon on the preheated grill and discard the marinade. Cook salmon 6 to 8 minutes per side or until the fish flakes easily with a fork.

Nutrition: 318 calories 20.1 grams of fat 13.2 g carbohydrates 20.5 g of protein 56 mg cholesterol 1092 mg of sodium

Warm Caper Tapenade on Cod (Greek)

Preparation Time: 10 minutes Cooking Time: 30 minutes
Servings: 4

¼ cup chopped cured olives	¼ teaspoon freshly ground pepper
1 ½ teaspoon chopped fresh oregano 1 cup halved cherry tomatoes	1 lb. cod fillet
1 tablespoon capers, rinsed and chopped 1 tablespoon minced shallot	1 teaspoon balsamic vinegar
3 teaspoon extra virgin olive oil, divided	

1. Grease baking sheet with cooking spray and preheat oven to 450 F.
2. Place cod on prepared baking sheet. Rub with 2 teaspoon oil and season with pepper.
3. Roast in oven for 15 to 20 minutes or until cod is flaky.
4. While waiting for cod to cook, on medium fire, place a small fry pan and heat 1 teaspoon oil.
5. Sauté shallots for a minute.
6. Add tomatoes and cook for two minutes or until soft.
7. Add capers and olives. Sauté for another minute.
8. Add vinegar and oregano. Turn off fire and stir to mix well.
9. Evenly divide cod into 4 serving and place on a plate.
10. 1 To serve, top cod with Caper-Olive-Tomato Tapenade and enjoy.

Nutrition: Calories: 107; Fat: 2.9g; Protein: 17.6g; Carbs: 2.0g

Berries and Grilled Calamari (Spanish)

Preparation Time: 10 minutes Cooking Time: 5 minutes
Servings: 4

¼ cup dried cranberries	¼ cup extra virgin olive oil
¼ cup olive oil	¼ cup sliced almonds
½ lemon, juiced	¾ cup blueberries
1½ pounds calamari tube, cleaned 1 granny smith apple, sliced thinly 1 tablespoon fresh lemon juice Freshly grated pepper to taste Sea salt to taste	2tablespoons apple cider vinegar 6 cups fresh spinach

1. In a small bowl, make the vinaigrette by mixing well the tablespoon of lemon juice, apple cider vinegar, and extra virgin olive oil. Season with pepper and salt to taste. Set aside.
2. Turn on the grill to medium fire and let the grates heat up for a minute or two.
3. In a large bowl, add olive oil and the calamari tube. Season calamari generously with pepper and salt.
4. Place seasoned and oiled calamari onto heated grate and grill until cooked or opaque. This is around two minutes per side.
5. As you wait for the calamari to cook, you can combine almonds, cranberries, blueberries, spinach, and the thinly sliced apple in a large salad bowl. Toss to mix.
6. Remove cooked calamari from grill and transfer on a chopping board. Cut into ¼-inch thick rings and throw into the salad bowl.
7. Drizzle with vinaigrette and toss well to coat salad.
8. Serve and enjoy!

Nutrition: Calories: 567; Fat: 24.5g; Protein: 54.8g; Carbs: 30.6g

Scallops in Wine 'n Olive Oil (Greek)

Preparation Time: 10 minutes Cooking Time: 8 minutes
Servings: 4

¼ teaspoon salt	½ cup dry white wine
1 ½ lbs. large sea scallops	1 ½ teaspoon chopped fresh tarragon 2 tablespoon olive oil

Black pepper – optional

1. On medium high fire, place a large nonstick fry pan and heat oil.
2. Add scallops and fry for 3 minutes per side or until edges are lightly browned. Transfer to a serving plate.
3. On same pan, add salt, tarragon and wine while scraping pan to loosen browned bits.
4. Turn off fire.
5. Pour sauce over scallops and serve.

Nutrition: Calories: 205.2; Fat: 8 g; Protein: 28.6 g; Carbohydrates: 4.7 g

Seafood Stew Cioppino (Italian)

Preparation Time: 10 minutes Cooking Time: 40 minutes
Servings: 6

¼ cup Italian parsley, chopped	¼ teaspoon dried basil
¼ teaspoon dried thyme	½ cup dry white wine like pinot grigio
½ lb. King crab legs, cut at each joint	½ onion, chopped
½ teaspoon red pepper flakes (adjust to desired spiciness) 1 28-oz can crush tomatoes	1 lb. mahi mahi, cut into ½-inch cubes 1 lb. raw shrimp
1 tablespoon olive oil 2 bay leaves	2 cups clam juice
50 live clams, washed 6 cloves garlic, minced Pepper and salt to taste	

1. On medium fire, place a stockpot and heat oil.
2. Add onion and for 4 minutes sauté until soft.
3. Add bay leaves, thyme, basil, red pepper flakes and garlic. Cook for a minute while stirring a bit.
4. Add clam juice and tomatoes. Once simmering, place fire to medium low and cook for 20 minutes uncovered.
5. Add white wine and clams. Cover and cook for 5 minutes or until clams have slightly opened.
6. Stir pot then add fish pieces, crab legs and shrimps. Do not stir soup to maintain the fish's shape. Cook while covered for 4 minutes or until clams are fully opened; fish and shrimps are opaque and cooked.
7. Season with pepper and salt to taste.
8. Transfer Cioppino to serving bowls and garnish with parsley before serving.

Nutrition: Calories: 371; Carbs: 15.5 g; Protein: 62 g; Fat: 6.8 g

Garlic Roasted Shrimp with Zucchini Pasta (Italian)

Prep Time: 10 minutes Cooking Time: 10 minutes Servings: 2

2 medium-sized zucchinis, cut into thin strips or spaghetti noodles Salt and pepper to taste 2 tablespoon ghee, melted	1 lemon, zested and juiced 2 garlic cloves, minced 2 tablespoon olive oil 8 ounces shrimps, cleaned and deveined

1. Preheat the oven to 4000F.
2. In a mixing bowl, mix all except the zucchini noodles. Toss to coat the shrimp.
3. Bake for 10 minutes until the shrimps turn pink.
4. Add the zucchini pasta then toss.

Nutrition: Calories: 299; Fat: 23.2g; Protein: 14.3g; Carbs: 10.9g

Dijon Mustard and Lime Marinated Shrimp (Italian)

Prep Time: 10 minutes Cooking Time: 10 minutes Servings: 8

½ cup fresh lime juice, plus lime zest as garnish	½ cup rice vinegar
½ teaspoon hot sauce 1 bay leaf	1 cup water
1 lb. uncooked shrimp, peeled and deveined 1 medium red onion, chopped 2 tablespoon Dijon mustard 3 whole cloves	2 tablespoon capers

1. Mix hot sauce, mustard, capers, lime juice and onion in a shallow baking dish and set aside.
2. Bring to a boil in a large saucepan bay leaf, cloves, vinegar and water.
3. Once boiling, add shrimps and cook for a minute while stirring continuously.
4. Drain shrimps and pour shrimps into onion mixture.
5. For an hour, refrigerate while covered the shrimps.
6. Then serve shrimps cold and garnished with lime zest.

Nutrition: Calories: 232.2; Protein: 17.8g; Fat: 3g; Carbs: 15g

Dill Relish on White Sea Bass (Greek)

Prep Time: 10 minutes Cooking Time: 12 minutes Servings: 4

1 ½ tablespoon chopped white onion 1 ½ teaspoon chopped fresh dill	1 lemon, quartered
1 teaspoon Dijon mustard 1 teaspoon lemon juice	1 teaspoon pickled baby capers, drained 4 pieces of 4-oz white sea bass fillets

1. Preheat oven to 375oF.
2. Mix lemon juice, mustard, dill, capers and onions in a small bowl.
3. Prepare four aluminum foil squares and place 1 fillet per foil.
4. Squeeze a lemon wedge per fish.
5. Evenly divide into 4 the dill spread and drizzle over fillet.
6. Close the foil over the fish securely and pop in the oven.
7. Bake for 10 to 12 minutes or until fish is cooked through.
8. Remove from foil and transfer to a serving platter, serve and enjoy.

Nutrition: Calories: 115; Protein: 7g; Fat: 1g; Carbs: 12g

Sweet Potatoes Oven Fried (Spanish)

Preparation time: 10 minutes Cooking time: 30 minutes
Servings: 7

1 small garlic clove, minced	1 tablespoon fresh parsley, chopped finely
1 teaspoon grated orange rind	
¼ teaspoon pepper	¼ teaspoon salt
1 tablespoon olive oil	4 medium sweet potatoes, peeled and sliced to ¼-inch thickness

1. In a large bowl mix well pepper, salt, olive oil and sweet potatoes.
2. In a greased baking sheet, in a single layer arrange sweet potatoes.
3. Pop in a preheated 400oF oven and bake for 15 minutes, turnover potato slices and return to oven. Bake for another 15 minutes or until tender.
4. Meanwhile, mix well in a small bowl garlic, orange rind and parsley, sprinkle over cooked potato slices and serve.
5. You can store baked sweet potatoes in a lidded container and just microwave whenever you want to eat it. Do consume within 3 days.

Nutrition: Calories: 176; Carbs: 36.6g; Protein: 2.5g; Fat: 2.5g

Tasty Avocado Sauce over Zoodles (Italian)

Preparation time: 10 minutes Cooking time: 10 minutes
Servings: 2

1zucchini peeled and spiralized into noodles 4 tablespoon pine nuts	2tablespoon lemon juice
1 avocado peeled and pitted	1 1/4 cup basil
12 sliced cherry tomatoes	
1/3 cup water	
Pepper and salt to taste	

1. Make the sauce in a blender by adding pine nuts, lemon juice, avocado, water, and basil. Pulse until smooth and creamy. Season with pepper and salt to taste. Mix well.
2. Place zoodles in salad bowl. Pour over avocado sauce and toss well to coat.
3. Add cherry tomatoes, serve, and enjoy.

Nutrition: Calories: 313; Protein: 6.8g; Carbs: 18.7g; Fat: 26.8g

Tomato Basil Cauliflower Rice (Spanish)

Preparation time: 5 minutes Cooking time: 10 minutes Servings: 4

Salt and pepper to taste	¼ cup tomato paste
Dried parsley for garnish	
½ teaspoon garlic, minced	½ teaspoon onion powder
½ teaspoon marjoram	1 ½ teaspoon dried basil 1 teaspoon dried oregano
1 large head of cauliflower 1 teaspoon oil	

1. Cut the cauliflower into florets and place in the food processor.
2. Pulse until it has a coarse consistency similar with rice. Set aside.
3. In a skillet, heat the oil and sauté the garlic and onion for three minutes. Add the rest of the . Cook for 8 minutes.

Nutrition: Calories: 106; Carbs: 15.1g; Protein: 3.3g; Fat: 5.0g

Vegan Sesame Tofu and Eggplants (Greek)

Preparation time: 10 minutes Cooking time: 20 minutes
Servings: 4

5 tablespoons olive oil	1-pound firm tofu, sliced 3 tablespoons rice vinegar
2 teaspoons Swerve sweetener 2 whole eggplants, sliced	¼ cup soy sauce
Salt and pepper to taste	4 tablespoons toasted sesame oil
¼ cup sesame seeds	1 cup fresh cilantro, chopped

1. Heat the oil in a pan for 2 minutes.
2. Pan fry the tofu for 3 minutes on each side.
3. Stir in the rice vinegar, sweetener, eggplants, and soy sauce. Season with salt and pepper to taste.
4. Cover and cook for 5 minutes on medium fire. Stir and continue cooking for another 5 minutes.
5. Toss in the sesame oil, sesame seeds, and cilantro.
6. Serve and enjoy.

Nutrition: Calories: 616; Carbs: 27.4g; Protein: 23.9g; Fat: 49.2g

Easy Seafood French Stew (Italian)

Preparation Time: 10 minutes Cooking Time: 45 minutes
Servings: 12

Pepper and Salt	1/2 lb. littleneck clams 1/2 lb. mussels
1lb. shrimp, peeled and deveined 1 large lobster	2lbs. assorted small whole fresh fish, scaled and cleaned 2 tablespoon parsleys, finely chopped
2tablespoon garlic, chopped 1 cup fennel, julienned	Juice and zest of one orange
3cups tomatoes, peeled, seeded, and chopped 1 cup leeks, julienned	Pinch of Saffron Stew
1 cup white wine Water	1 lb. fish bones 2 sprigs thyme
8 peppercorns	1 bay leaf
3 cloves garlic Salt and pepper	1/2 cup chopped celery 1/2 cup chopped onion 2 tablespoon olive oil

1. Do the stew: Heat oil in a large saucepan. Sauté the celery and onions for 3 minutes. Season with pepper and salt. Stir in the garlic and cook for about a minute. Add the thyme, peppercorns, and bay leaves. Stir in the wine, water and fish bones. Let it boil then before reducing to a simmer. Take the pan off the fire and strain broth into another container.
2. For the Bouillabaisse: Bring the strained broth to a simmer and stir in the parsley, leeks, orange juice, orange zest, garlic, fennel, tomatoes and saffron. Sprinkle with pepper and salt. Stir in the lobsters and fish. Let it simmer for eight minutes before stirring in the clams, mussels and shrimps. For six minutes, allow to cook while covered before seasoning again with pepper and salt.
3. Assemble in a shallow dish all the seafood and pour the broth over it.

Nutrition: Calories: 348; Carbs: 20.0g; Protein: 31.8g; Fat: 15.2g

Creamy Bacon-Fish Chowder (Greek)

Preparation Time: 10 minutes Cooking Time: 30 minutes
Servings: 8

1 1/2 lbs. cod	1 1/2 teaspoon dried thyme
	1 large onion, chopped
1 medium carrot, coarsely chopped	1 tablespoon butter, cut into small pieces 1 teaspoon salt, divided
31/2 cups baking potato, peeled and cubed 3 slices uncooked bacon	3/4 teaspoon freshly ground black pepper, divided 4 1/2 cups water
4bay leaves	4 cups 2% reduced-fat milk

1. In a large skillet, add the water and bay leaves and let it simmer. Add the fish. Cover and let it simmer some more until the flesh flakes easily with fork. Remove the fish from the skillet and cut into large pieces. Set aside the cooking liquid.
2. Place Dutch oven in medium heat and cook the bacon until crisp. Remove the bacon and reserve the bacon drippings. Crush the bacon and set aside.
3. Stir potato, onion and carrot in the pan with the bacon drippings, cook over medium heat for 10 minutes. Add the cooking liquid, bay leaves, 1/2 teaspoon salt, 1/4 teaspoon pepper and thyme, let it boil. Lower the heat and let simmer for 10 minutes. Add the milk and butter, simmer until the potatoes becomes tender, but do not boil. Add the fish, 1/2 teaspoon salt, 1/2 teaspoon pepper. Remove the bay leaves.
4. Serve sprinkled with the crushed bacon.

Nutrition: Calories: 400; Carbs: 34.5g; Protein: 20.8g; Fat: 19.7g

Crisped Coco-Shrimp with Mango Dip (Italian)

Preparation Time: 10 minutes Cooking Time: 20 minutes
Servings: 4

1 cup shredded coconut	1 lb. raw shrimp, peeled and deveined 2 egg whites
4 tablespoon tapioca starch Pepper and salt to taste Mango Dip	1 cup mango, chopped
1 jalapeño, thinly minced 1 teaspoon lime juice	1/3 cup coconut milk 3 teaspoon raw honey

1. Preheat oven to 400oF.
2. Ready a pan with wire rack on top.
3. In a medium bowl, add tapioca starch and season with pepper and salt.
4. In a second medium bowl, add egg whites and whisk.
5. In a third medium bowl, add coconut.
6. To ready shrimps, dip first in tapioca starch, then egg whites, and then coconut. Place dredged shrimp on wire rack. Repeat until all shrimps are covered.
7. Pop shrimps in the oven and roast for 10 minutes per side.
8. Meanwhile make the dip by adding all in a blender. Puree until smooth and creamy. Transfer to a dipping bowl.
9. Once shrimps are golden brown, serve with mango dip.

Nutrition: Calories: 294.2; Protein: 26.6g; Fat: 7g; Carbs: 31.2g

Cucumber-Basil Salsa on Halibut Pouches(Spanish)

Preparation Time: 10 minutes Cooking Time: 17 minutes
Servings: 4

1lime, thinly sliced into 8 pieces	2cups mustard greens, stems removed 2 teaspoon olive oil
4 – 5 radishes trimmed and quartered 4 4-oz skinless halibut filets	4 large fresh basil leaves
Cayenne pepper to taste – optional Pepper and salt to taste	Salsa
1 ½ cups diced cucumber	1½ finely chopped fresh basil leaves
Pepper and salt to taste	2 teaspoon fresh lime juice

1. Preheat oven to 400oF.
1. 2.Prepareparchmentpapersbymaking4piecesof15x12-inch rectangles. Lengthwise, fold in half and unfold pieces on the table.
2. Season halibut fillets with pepper, salt and cayenne—if using cayenne.
3. Just to the right of the fold going lengthwise, place ½ cup of mustard greens. Add a basil leaf on center of mustard greens and topped with 1 lime slice. Around the greens, layer ¼ of the radishes. Drizzle with ½ teaspoon of oil, season with pepper and salt. Top it with a slice of halibut fillet.
4. Just as you would make a calzone, fold parchment paper over your filling and crimp the edges of the parchment paper beginning from one end to the other end. To seal the end of the crimped parchment paper, pinch it.
5. Repeat process to remaining until you have 4 pieces of parchment papers filled with halibut and greens.
6. Place pouches in a baking pan and bake in the oven until halibut is flaky, around 15 to 17 minutes.
7. While waiting for halibut pouches to cook, make your salsa by mixing all salsa in a medium bowl.
8. Once halibut is cooked, remove from oven and make a tear on top. Be careful of the steam as it is very hot. Equally divide salsa and spoon ¼ of salsa on top of halibut through the slit you have created.

Nutrition: Calories: 335.4; Protein: 20.2g; Fat: 16.3g; Carbs: 22.1g

Fresh and No-Cook Oysters (Spanish)

Preparation Time: 10 minutes
Cooking Time: 5 minutes Servings: 4

1lemons	24 medium oysters tabasco sauce

1. If you are a newbie when it comes to eating oysters, then I suggest that you blanch the oysters before eating.
2. For some, eating oysters raw is a great way to enjoy this dish because of the consistency and juiciness of raw oysters. Plus, adding lemon juice prior to eating the raw oysters cooks it a bit. So, to blanch oysters, bring a big pot of water to a rolling boil. Add oysters in batches of 6-10 pieces. Leave on boiling pot of water between 3-5 minutes and remove oysters right away. To eat oysters, squeeze lemon juice on oyster on shell, add tabasco as desired and eat.

Nutrition: Calories: 247; Protein: 29g; Fat: 7g; Carbs: 17g

Simple Cod Piccata (Italian)

Preparation Time: 10 minutes Cooking Time: 15 minutes
Servings: 3

¼ cup capers, drained	½ teaspoon salt
¾ cup chicken stock 1/3 cup almond flour	1-pound cod fillets, patted dry
2tablespoon fresh parsley, chopped 2 tablespoon grapeseed oil	3tablespoon extra-virgin oil 3 tablespoon lemon juice

1. In a bowl, combine the almond flour and salt.
2. Dredge the fish in the almond flour to coat. Set aside.
3. Heat a little bit of olive oil to coat a large skillet. Heat the skillet over medium high heat. Add grapeseed oil. Cook the cod for 3 minutes on each side to brown. Remove from the plate and place on a paper towel- lined plate.
4. In a saucepan, mix together the chicken stock, capers and lemon juice. Simmer to reduce the sauce to half. Add the remaining grapeseed oil.
5. Drizzle the fried cod with the sauce and sprinkle with parsley.

Nutrition: Calories: 277.1; Fat: 28.3 g; Protein: 1.9 g; Carbs: 3.7 g

Yummy Salmon Panzanella (Italian)

Preparation Time: 10 minutes Cooking Time: 10 minutes
Servings: 4

¼ cup thinly sliced fresh basil	¼ cup thinly sliced red onion
¼ teaspoon freshly ground pepper, divided	½ teaspoon salt
1lb. center cut salmon, skinned and cut into 4 equal portions 1 medium cucumber, peeled, seeded, and cut into 1-inch slices 1 tablespoon capers, rinsed and chopped	2large tomatoes, cut into 1-inch pieces
2thick slices day old whole grain bread, sliced into 1-inch cubes 3 tablespoon extra-virgin olive oil	3tablespoon red wine vinegar
8 Kalamata olives, pitted and chopped	

1. Grease grill grate and preheat grill to high.
2. In a large bowl, whisk 1/8 teaspoon pepper, capers, vinegar, and olives. Add oil and whisk well.
3. Stir in basil, onion, cucumber, tomatoes, and bread.
4. Season both sides of salmon with remaining pepper and salt.
5. Grill on high for 4 minutes per side.
6. Into 4 plates, evenly divide salad, top with grilled salmon, and serve.

Nutrition: Calories: 383; Fat: 20.6g; Protein: 34.8g; Carbs: 13.6g

Vegetarian Coconut Curry (Spanish)

Preparation time: 10 minutes Cooking time: 30 minutes
Servings: 4

4 tablespoons coconut oil 1 medium onion, chopped 1 teaspoon minced garlic 1 teaspoon minced ginger 1 cup broccoli florets	2 cups fresh spinach leaves 2 teaspoons fish sauce
1 tablespoon garam masala	½ cup coconut milk Salt and pepper to taste

1. Heat oil in a pot.
2. Sauté the onion and garlic until fragrant, around 3 minutes.
3. Stir in the rest of the , except for spinach leaves.
4. Season with salt and pepper to taste.
5. Cover and cook on medium fire for 5 minutes.
6. Stir and add spinach leaves. Cover and cook for another 2 minutes.
7. Turn off fire and let it sit for two more minutes before serving.

Nutrition: Calories: 210; Carbs: 6.5g; Protein: 2.1g; Fat: 20.9g

Healthy Poached Trout (Greek)

Preparation Time: 10 minutes Cooking Time: 10 minutes
Servings: 2

18-oz boneless, skin on trout fillet 2 cups chicken broth or water	2leeks, halved
6-8 slices lemon	salt and pepper to taste

1. On medium fire, place a large nonstick skillet and arrange leeks and lemons on pan in a layer. Cover with soup stock or water and bring to a simmer.
2. Meanwhile, season trout on both sides with pepper and salt. Place trout on simmering pan of water. Cover and cook until trout are flaky, around 8 minutes.
3. In a serving platter, spoon leek and lemons on bottom of plate, top with trout and spoon sauce into plate. Serve and enjoy.

Nutritional Information: Calories: 360.2; Protein: 13.8g; Fat: 7.5g; Carbs: 51.5g

Leftover Salmon Salad Power Bowls (Greek)

Preparation Time: 10 minutes Cooking Time: 10 minutes
Servings: 1

½ cup raspberries	½ cup zucchini, sliced 1 lemon, juice squeezed
1 tablespoon balsamic glaze 2 sprigs of thyme, chopped 2 tablespoon olive oil	4 cups seasonal greens
4 ounces leftover grilled salmon Salt and pepper to taste	

1. Heat oil in a skillet over medium flame and sauté the zucchini. Season with salt and pepper to taste.
2. In a mixing bowl, mix all together.
3. Toss to combine everything.
4. Sprinkle with nut cheese.

Nutrition: Calories: 450.3; Fat: 35.5 g; Protein: 23.4g; Carbs: 9.3 g

Lemon-Garlic Baked Halibut (Spanish)

Prep Time: 10 minutes Cooking Time: 15 minutes Servings: 2

1 large garlic clove, minced	1tablespoon chopped flat leaf parsley 1 teaspoon olive oil
25-oz boneless, skin-on halibut fillets 2 tbsp lemon zest	Juice of ½ lemon, divided Salt and pepper to taste

1. Grease a baking dish with cooking spray and preheat oven to 400oF.
2. Place halibut with skin touching the dish and drizzle with olive oil.
3. Season with pepper and salt.
4. Pop into the oven and bake until flaky around 12-15 minutes.
5. Remove from oven and drizzle with remaining lemon juice, serve and enjoy with a side of salad greens.

Nutrition: Calories: 315.3; Protein: 14.1g; Fat: 10.5g; Carbs: 36.6g

Smoked Trout Tartine (Italian)

Preparation Time: 10 minutes

Cooking Time: 0 minutes Servings: 4

½ 15-oz can cannellini beans	½ cup diced roasted red peppers
3/4 lb. smoked trout, flaked into bite-sized pieces 1 stalk celery, finely chopped	1 tablespoon extra-virgin olive oil 1 teaspoon chopped fresh dill
1teaspoon Dijon mustard	2tablespoon capers, rinsed and drained
2 tablespoon freshly squeezed lemon juice 2 teaspoon minced onion Pinch of sugar	4 large whole grain breads, toasted Dill sprigs – for garnish

1. Mix sugar, mustard, olive oil and lemon juice in a big bowl.
2. Add the rest of the except for toasted bread.
3. Toss to mix well.
4. Evenly divide fish mixture on top of bread slices and garnish with dill sprigs.
5. Serve and enjoy.

Nutrition: Calories: 348.1; Protein: 28.2 g; Fat: 10.1g; Carbs: 36.1g

Steamed Mussels Thai Style (Spanish)

Prep Time: 10 minutes Cooking Time: 15 minutes Servings: 4

¼ cup minced shallots	½ teaspoon Madras curry 1 cup dry white wine
1 small bay leaf	1 tbsp chopped fresh basil
1tablespoon chopped fresh cilantro	2lbs. mussel, cleaned and debearded 2 tablespoon butters
4 medium garlic cloves, minced	1 tbsp chopped fresh mint

1. In a large heavy bottomed pot, on medium high fire add to pot the curry powder, bay leaf, wine plus the minced garlic and shallots. Bring to a boil and simmer for 3 minutes.
2. Add the cleaned mussels, stir, cover, and cook for 3 minutes.
3. Stir mussels again, cover, and cook for another 2 or 3 minutes. Cooking is done when majority of shells have opened.
4. With a slotted spoon, transfer cooked mussels in a large bowl. Discard any unopened mussels.
5. Continue heating pot with sauce. Add butter and the chopped herbs.
6. Season with pepper and salt to taste.
7. Once good, pour over mussels, serve and enjoy.

Nutrition: Calories: 407.2; Protein: 43.4g; Fat: 21.2g; Carbs: 10.8g

Easy Broiled Lobster Tails (Spanish)

Prep Time: 10 minutes Cooking Time: 10 minutes Servings: 2

1 6-oz frozen lobster tails 1 tablespoon olive oil	1teaspoon lemon pepper seasoning

1. Preheat oven broiler.
2. With kitchen scissors, cut thawed lobster tails in half lengthwise.
3. Brush with oil the exposed lobster meat. Season with lemon pepper.
4. Place lobster tails in baking sheet with exposed meat facing up.
5. Place on top broiler rack and broil for 10 minutes until lobster meat is lightly browned on the sides and center meat is opaque. Serve and enjoy.

Nutrition: Calories: 175.6; Protein: 3g; Fat: 10g; Carbs: 18.4g 10.16

Easy Fish Curry (Spanish)

Preparation Time: 10 minutes Cooking Time: 20 minutes Servings: 4

Juice of half a lime	A handful of coriander leaves
½ pound white fish cut into large strips Salt and pepper to taste	1tomatoes, chopped
½ cup coconut milk 15 curry leaves	1teaspoon turmeric, ground 2 teaspoon curry powder
2tablespoon gingers, grated 3 cloves garlic, sliced 2tablespoon coconut oil	1onion, chopped

1. Heat oil in a medium saucepan. Sauté the onion over medium heat until translucent.
2. Add the ginger and garlic and cook for a minute before adding the curry powder, curry leaves and turmeric. Continue cooking for a minute before adding the coconut milk.
3. Add the chopped tomatoes and simmer for 5 minutes or until the tomatoes are soft.
4. Add the fish and season with salt and pepper to taste. Cook for 8 mins before adding the lime juice and coriander leaves.
5. Serve warm.

Nutrition: Calories: 213; Fat: 14.7g; Protein: 12.3g; Carbs: 10.5g

Ginger Scallion Sauce over Seared Ahi (Spanish)

Preparation Time: 10 minutes Cooking Time: 6 minutes Servings: 4

1 bunch scallions, bottoms removed, finely chopped 1 tablespoon rice wine vinegar	1tablespoon. Bragg's liquid amino 16-oz ahi tuna steaks
2tablespoons. fresh ginger, peeled and grated 3 tbsp. coconut oil, melted	Pepper and salt to taste

1. In a small bowl mix together vinegar, 2 tablespoons. oil, soy sauce, ginger and scallions. Put aside.
2. On medium fire, place a large saucepan and heat remaining oil. Once oil is hot and starts to smoke, sear tuna until deeply browned or for two minutes per side.
3. Place seared tuna on a serving platter and let it stand for 5 minutes before slicing into 1-inch-thick strips.
4. Drizzle ginger-scallion mixture over seared tuna, serve and enjoy.

Nutrition: Calories: 247; Protein: 29g; Fat: 1g; Carbs: 8g

Baked Cod Fillets with Ghee Sauce (Greek)

Preparation Time: 10 minutes Cooking Time: 15 minutes
Servings: 2

Pepper and salt to taste	2 tbsp minced parsley
1 lemon, sliced into ¼-inch thick circles	4 garlic cloves, crushed, peeled, and minced
¼ cup melted ghee 4 Cod fillets	1 lemon, juiced and zested

1. Bring oven to 425oF.
2. Mix parsley, lemon juice, lemon zest, garlic, and melted ghee in a small bowl. Mix well and then season with pepper and salt to taste.
3. Prepare a large baking dish by greasing it with cooking spray.
4. Evenly lay the cod fillets on the greased dish. Season generously with pepper and salt.
5. Pour the bowl of garlic-ghee sauce from step 2 on top of cod fillets. Top the cod fillets with the thinly sliced lemon.
6. Pop in the preheated oven and bake until flaky, around 13 to 15 minutes. Remove from oven, transfer to dishes, serve, and enjoy.

Nutrition: Calories: 200; Fat: 12g; Protein: 21g; Carbs: 2g

Thyme and Lemon on Baked Salmon (Italian)

Preparation Time: 10 minutes Cooking Time: 25 minutes
Servings: 2

1 32-oz salmon fillet 1 lemon, sliced thinly 1 tablespoon capers	1 tablespoon fresh thyme 1 Olive oil for drizzling Pepper and salt to taste

1. In a foil line baking sheet, place a parchment paper on top.
2. Place salmon with skin side down on parchment paper.
3. Season generously with pepper and salt.
4. Place capers on top of fillet. Cover with thinly sliced lemon.
5. Garnish with thyme.
6. Pop in cold oven and bake for 25 minutes at 400oF settings.
7. Serve right away and enjoy.

Nutrition: Calories: 684.4; Protein: 94.3g; Fat: 32.7g; Carbs: 4.3g

Healthy Carrot & Shrimp (Spanish)

Preparation Time: 10 minutes Cooking Time: 6 minutes
Servings 4

1 lb. shrimp, peeled and deveined 1 tbsp. chives, chopped	1 onion, chopped 1 tbsp. olive oil 1 cup fish stock
1 cup carrots, sliced Pepper	Salt

1. Add oil into the inner pot of instant pot and set the pot on sauté mode.
2. Add onion and sauté for 2 minutes.
3. Add shrimp and stir well.
4. Add remaining and stir well.
5. Cover the pot with lid and cook on high for 4 minutes.
6. Once done, release pressure using quick release. Remove lid.
7. Serve and enjoy.

Nutrition: Calories 197 Fat 5.9 g Carbohydrates 7 g Sugar 2.5 g Protein 27.7 g Cholesterol 239 mg

Tasty Tuna Scaloppine (Italian)

Preparation Time: 10 minutes Cooking Time: 10 minutes
Servings: 4

¼ cup chopped almonds	¼ cup fresh tangerine juice
½ teaspoon fennel seeds	½ teaspoon ground black pepper, divided
½ teaspoon salt	1 tablespoon extra-virgin olive oil 2 tablespoon chopped fresh mint 2 tbsp chopped red onion
46-ozsushi-gradeYellowfin tunasteaks,eachsplitinhalf horizontally	Cooking spray

1. In a small bowl mix fennel seed, olive oil, mint, onion, tangerine juice, almonds, ¼ teaspoon pepper and ¼ teaspoon salt. Combine thoroughly.
2. Season fish with remaining salt and pepper.
3. On medium high fire, place a large nonstick pan and grease with cooking spray. Pan fry fish in two batches cooking each side for a minute.
4. Fish is best served with a side of salad greens or a half cup of cooked brown rice.

Nutrition: Calories: 405; Protein: 27.5g; Fat: 11.9g; Carbs: 27.5

Orange Rosemary Seared Salmon (Spanish)

Prep Time: 10 minutes Cooking Time: 10 minutes Servings: 4

½ cup chicken stock	1 cup fresh orange juice 1
2 garlic cloves, minced	tablespoon coconut oil
1tablespoon tapioca starch	2tbsp fresh lemon juice
2 tbsp fresh rosemary, minced 2 tbsp orange zest	4 salmon fillets, skins removed Salt and pepper to taste

1. Season the salmon fillet on both sides.
2. In a skillet, heat coconut oil over medium high heat. Cook the salmon fillets for 5 minutes on each side. Set aside.
3. In a mixing bowl, combine the orange juice, chicken stock, lemon juice and orange zest.
4. In the skillet, sauté the garlic and rosemary for 2 minutes and pour the orange juice mixture. Bring to a boil. Lower the heat to medium low and simmer. Season with salt and pepper to taste.
5. Pour the sauce all over the salmon fillet then serve.

Nutrition: Calories: 493; Fat: 17.9g; Protein: 66.7g; Carbs: 12.8g

Salmon with Potatoes (Spanish)

Prep Time: 10 minutes Cooking Time: 15 minutes Servings 4

1 1/2 lbs. Salmon fillets, boneless and cubed	1cup fish stock 2 tbsp. olive oil
2tbsp. parsley, chopped 1 tsp. garlic, minced Salt	1 lb. baby potatoes, halved Pepper

1. Add oil into the inner pot of instant pot and set the pot on sauté mode.
2. Add garlic and sauté for 2 minutes.
3. Add remaining and stir well.
4. Cover the pot with lid and cook on high for 13 minutes.
5. Once done, release pressure using quick release. Remove lid.
6. Serve and enjoy.

Nutrition: Calories 362 Fat 18.1 g Carbohydrates 14.5 g Sugar 0 g Protein 37.3g Cholesterol 76 mg

Fish Stew (Greek)

Prep Time: 15 minutes Cooking Time: 1 hour and 24 minutes
Servings: 2

1 lb. white fish	1 tablespoon lime juice 1 onion, sliced
2 cloves garlic, sliced 1 red pepper, sliced	1 jalapeno pepper, sliced 1 teaspoon paprika
2 cups chicken broth	2 cups tomatoes, chopped Salt and pepper to taste 2 oz. coconut milk

1. Marinate the fish in lime juice for 10 minutes.
2. Pour the olive oil into a pan over medium heat.
3. Add the onion, garlic and peppers.
4. Cook for 4 minutes.
5. Add the rest of the except the coconut milk.
6. Cover the pot.
7. Cook on low for 1 hour.
8. Stir in the coconut milk and simmer for 10 minutes

Nutrition: Calories 323 Fat 28.6g Sodium 490mg Carbohydrate 1.1g Protein 9.3g Fiber 3.2g Sugars 6.2g

Minty-Cucumber Yogurt Topped Grilled Fish(Greek)

Prep Time: 10 minutes Cooking Time: 2 minutes Servings: 4

¼ cup 2% plain Greek yogurt	¼ teaspoon + 1/8 teaspoon salt
¼ teaspoon black pepper	½ green onion, finely chopped
½ teaspoon dried oregano	1 tablespoon finely chopped fresh mint leaves
3 tablespoons finely chopped English cucumber	Cooking oil as needed
4 5-oz cod fillets	

1. Brush grill grate with oil and preheat grill to high.
2. Season cod fillets on both sides with pepper, ¼ teaspoon salt and oregano.
3. Grill cod for 3 minutes per side or until cooked to desired doneness.
4. Mix thoroughly 1/8 teaspoon salt, onion, mint, cucumber and yogurt in a small bowl. Serve cod with a dollop of the dressing. This dish can be paired with salad greens or brown rice.

Nutrition: Calories: 253.5; Protein: 25.5g; Fat: 1g; Carbs: 5g

Soy-Ginger Braised Squid (Spanish)

Prep Time: 5 minutes Cooking Time: 8 hours Servings: 6

18-ounce wild-caught squid, cut into rings 2 scallions, chopped	2 bay leaves
1 tablespoon grated ginger	1 bulb. of garlic, peeled & minced
½ cup swerve sweetener	¼ cup soy sauce
¼ cup oyster sauce	¼ cup avocado oil
¼ cup white wine	

1. Plug in a 6-quart slow cooker, add all the and stir until mixed.
2. Shut with lid and cook for 8 hours at low heat setting or until cooked through.
3. Serve straightaway.

Nutrition: Calories: 154 Fat: 13 g Protein: 15 g Carbs: 3.4 g Fiber: 17 g Sugar: 1.9 g

Sea Bass in Coconut Cream Sauce (Spanish)

Prep Time: 5 minutes Cooking Time: 1 hour Servings: 3

18-ounce wild-caught sea bass 5 jalapeno peppers	4 stalks of bock Choy
2 stalks of scallions, sliced 1 tablespoon grated ginger 11/2 teaspoon salt	1 tablespoon fish sauce, unsweetened 2 cups coconut cream

1. Stir together all the except for bok choy and fish in a bowl and add this mixture in a 6-quarts slow cooker.
2. Plug in the slow cooker, then add fish, top with bok choy and shut with lid.
3. Cook sea bass for 1 hour and 30 minutes or until cooked.
4. Serve straightaway.

Nutrition: Calories: 315 Fat: 17 g Protein: 15 g Carbs: 2.4 g Fiber: 17 g Sugar: 3.2 g

Cod Chowder (Spanish)

Prep time: 20 minutes Cooking time: 3 hours Servings: 6

yellow onion 10 oz. cod	3 oz. bacon, sliced 1 teaspoon sage 5 oz. potatoes
1 carrot, grated	5 cups water
1 tablespoon almond milk	1 teaspoon ground coriander
	1 teaspoon salt

1. Peel the onion and chop it.
2. Put the chopped onion and grated carrot in the slow cooker bowl. Add the sage, almond milk, ground coriander, and water. After this, chop the cod into the 6 pieces.
3. Add the fish in the slow cooker bowl too. Then chop the sliced bacon and peel the potatoes.
4. Cut the potatoes into the cubes.
5. Add the in the slow cooker bowl and close the slow cooker lid.
6. Cook the chowder for 3 hours on HIGH. Ladle the prepared cod chowder in the serving bowls.
7. Sprinkle the dish with the chopped parsley if desired. Enjoy!

Nutrition: Calories 108 Fat 4.5 Fiber 2, Carbs 3.02 Protein 10

Avocado Peach Salsa on Grilled Swordfish (Greek)

Prep Time: 15 minutes Cooking Time: 12 minutes Servings: 2

1 garlic clove, minced	1 tablespoon apple cider vinegar
1 lemon juice	
1 teaspoon honey	2 swordfish fillets (around 4oz each) Pinch cayenne pepper
1 tablespoon coconut oil	
Pinch of pepper & salt Salsa	¼ red onion, finely chopped
½ cup cilantro, finely chopped	1 garlic clove, minced
1 avocado, halved and diced	
2 peaches, seeded and diced	Salt to taste
Juice of 1 lime	

1. In a shallow dish, mix all swordfish marinade except fillet. Mix well then add fillets to marinate. Place in refrigerator for at least an hour.
2. Meanwhile create salsa by mixing all salsa in a medium bowl. Put in the refrigerator to cool.
3. Preheat grill and grill fish on medium fire after marinating until cooked around 4 minutes per side.
4. Place each cooked fillet on one serving plate, top with half of salsa, serve and enjoy.

Nutrition: Calories: 416; Carbohydrates: 21g; Protein: 30g; Fat: 23.5g

Honey Garlic Shrimp (Italian)

Preparation Time: 10 minutes Cooking Time: 5 minutes
Servings 4

1 lb. shrimp, peeled and deveined 1/4 cup honey	1 tbsp. garlic, minced 1 tbsp. ginger, minced 1 tbsp. olive oil
1/4 cup fish stock Pepper	Salt

1. Add shrimp into the large bowl. Add remaining over shrimp and toss well.
2. Transfer shrimp into the instant pot and stir well.
3. Cover the pot with lid and cook on high for 5 minutes.
4. Once done, release pressure using quick release. Remove lid.
5. Serve and enjoy.

Nutrition: Calories 240 Fat 5.6 g Carbohydrates 20.9 g Sugar 17.5 g Protein 26.5 g Cholesterol 239 mg

Simple Lemon Clams (Italian)

Preparation Time: 10 minutes Cooking Time: 10 minutes
Servings 4

1 lb. clams, clean	1 tbsp. fresh lemon juice 1 lemon zest, grated
1 onion, chopped 1/2 cup fish stock Pepper	Salt

1. Add all into the inner pot of instant pot and stir well.
2. Cover the pot with lid and cook on high for 10 minutes.
3. Once done, release pressure using quick release. Remove lid.
4. Serve and enjoy.

Nutrition: Calories 76 Fat 0.6 g Carbohydrates 16.4 g Sugar 5.4 g Protein 1.8 g Cholesterol 0 mg

Coconut Salsa on Chipotle Fish Tacos (Italian)

Preparation Time: 10 minutes Cooking Time: 10 minutes
Servings: 4

¼ cup chopped fresh cilantro	½ cup seeded and finely chopped plum tomato 1 cup peeled and finely chopped mango
1 lime cut into wedges	1 tablespoon chipotle Chile powder
1/3 cup finely chopped red onion	10 tablespoon fresh lime juice, divided 4 6-oz boneless, skinless cod fillets
5 tbsp dried unsweetened shredded coconut 8 pcs of 6-inch tortillas, heated	1 tablespoon safflower oil

1. Whisk well Chile powder, oil, and 4 tablespoon lime juice in a glass baking dish. Add cod and marinate for 12 – 15 minutes. Turning once halfway through the marinating time.
2. Make the salsa by mixing coconut, 6 tablespoon lime juice, cilantro, onions, tomatoes and mangoes in a medium bowl. Set aside.
3. On high, heat a grill pan. Place cod and grill for four minutes per side turning only once.
4. Once cooked, slice cod into large flakes and evenly divide onto tortilla.
5. Evenly divide salsa on top of cod and serve with a side of lime wedges.

Nutrition: Calories: 477; Protein: 35.0g; Fat: 12.4g; Carbs: 57.4g

.Baked Cod Crusted with Herbs (Greek)

Preparation Time: 5 minutes Cooking Time: 10 minutes
Servings: 4

¼ cup honey	¼ teaspoon salt
½ cup panko	½ teaspoon pepper
1 tablespoon extra-virgin olive oil 1 tablespoon lemon juice	1 teaspoon dried basil
1 teaspoon dried parsley 1 teaspoon rosemary	4 pieces of 4-oz cod fillets

1. With olive oil, grease a 9 x 13-inch baking pan and preheat oven to 375oF.
2. In a zip top bag mix panko, rosemary, salt, pepper, parsley and basil.
3. Evenly spread cod fillets in prepped dish and drizzle with lemon juice.
4. Then brush the fillets with honey on all sides. Discard remaining honey if any.
5. Then evenly divide the panko mixture on top of cod fillets.
6. Pop in the oven and bake for ten minutes or until fish is cooked.
7. Serve and enjoy.

Nutrition: Calories: 137; Protein: 5g; Fat: 2g; Carbs: 21g

.Tuna in Potatoes (Spanish)

Prep time: 16 minutes Cooking time: 4 hours Servings: 8

4 large potatoes 8oz. tuna, canned	1/2 cup cream cheese 4oz. Cheddar cheese 1 garlic clove
1 teaspoon onion powder	1 teaspoon ground black pepper 1 teaspoon dried dill
1/2 teaspoon salt	

1. Wash the potatoes carefully and cut them into the halves.
2. Wrap the potatoes in the foil and place in the slow cooker. Close the slow cooker lid and cook the potatoes on HIGH for 2 hours.
3. Meanwhile, peel the garlic clove and mince it. Combine the minced garlic clove with the cream cheese, tuna, salt, ground black pepper, onion powder, and dill.
4. Then shred Cheddar cheese and add it to the mixture.
5. Mix it carefully until homogenous.
6. When the time is over – remove the potatoes from the slow cooker and discard the foil only from the flat surface of the potatoes.
7. Then take the fork and mash the flesh of the potato halves gently. Add the tuna mixture in the potato halves and return them back in the slow cooker.
8. Cook the potatoes for 2 hours more on HIGH. Enjoy!

Nutrition: Calories 247, Fat 5.9, Fiber 4, Carbs 3.31, Protein 14

.Shrimp Scampi (Italian)

Preparation Time: 15 minutes Cooking Time: 3 hours Servings: 4

1/4 cup chicken bone broth	Salt and pepper to taste
1/2 cup white cooking wine	1 tablespoon garlic, minced
2 tablespoons olive oil	2 tablespoons parsley, chopped 1 tablespoon lemon juice
2 tablespoons butter	
1 lb. shrimp, peeled and deveined	

1. Mix all the in your slow cooker.
2. Cover the pot.
3. Cook on low for 3 hours.

Nutrition: Calories 256 Fat 14.7 g Sodium 466 mg Carbohydrate 2.1 g Fiber 0.1g Protein 23.3 g Sugars 2 g

Shrimp & Sausage Gumbo (Italian)

Preparation Time: 15 minutes Cooking Time: 1 hour and 15 minutes Servings: 4

2tablespoons olive oil	2lb. chicken thigh fillet, sliced into cubes 2cloves garlic, crushed and minced 1onion, sliced
2stalks celery, chopped 1green bell pepper, chopped 1teaspoon Cajun seasoning Salt to taste	2cups beef broth
28oz. canned crushed tomatoes 4oz. sausage 1lb. shrimp, peeled & deveined	2tablespoons butter

1. Pour the olive oil in a pan over medium heat.
2. Cook the garlic and chicken for 5 minutes.
3. Add the onion, celery and bell pepper.
4. Cook until tender.
5. Season with the Cajun seasoning and salt.
6. Cook for 2 minutes.
7. Stir in the sausage, broth and tomatoes.
8. Cover and cook on low for 1 hour.
9. Add the butter and shrimp in the last 10 minutes of cooking.

Nutrition: Calories 467 Fat 33 g Sodium 1274 mg Potassium 658 mg Carbohydrate 5 g Fiber 2 g Protein 33 g Sugars 5 g

.Cajun Garlic Shrimp Noodle Bowl (Italian)

Preparation Time: 10 minutes Cooking Time: 15 minutes Servings: 2

½ tsp salt 1 onion, sliced 1teaspoon garlic granules 1 teaspoon onion powder 1 teaspoon paprika	1 red pepper, sliced 1 tbsp butter 2large zucchinis, cut into noodle strips
20 jumbo shrimps, shells removed and deveined 3 cloves garlic, minced A dash of cayenne pepper A dash of red pepper flakes	3 tablespoon ghee

1. Prepare the Cajun seasoning by mixing the onion powder, garlic granules, pepper flakes, cayenne pepper, paprika and salt. Toss in the shrimp to coat in the seasoning.
2. In a skillet, heat the ghee and sauté the garlic. Add in the red pepper and onions and continue sautéing for 4 minutes.
3. Add the Cajun shrimp and cook until opaque. Set aside.
4. In another pan, heat the butter and sauté the zucchini noodles for three minutes.
5. Assemble by the placing the Cajun shrimps on top of the zucchini noodles.

Nutrition: Calories: 712; Fat: 30.0g; Protein: 97.8g; Carbs: 20.2g

.Crazy Saganaki Shrimp (Greek)

Prep Time: 10 minutes Cooking Time: 10 minutes Servings: 4

¼ teaspoon salt	½ cup Chardonnay
½ cup crumbled Greek feta cheese	1 medium bulb. fennel, cored and finely chopped
1 tbsp extra-virgin olive oil 1 small Chile pepper, seeded and minced	12 jumbo shrimps, peeled and deveined with tails left on 2 tbsp lemon juice, divided
5 scallions sliced thinly Pepper to taste	

1. In medium bowl, mix salt, lemon juice and shrimp.
2. On medium fire, place a saganaki pan (or large nonstick saucepan) and heat oil.
3. Sauté Chile pepper, scallions, and fennel for 4 minutes or until starting to brown and is already soft.
4. Add wine and sauté for another minute.
5. Place shrimps on top of fennel, cover and cook for 4 minutes or until shrimps are pink.
6. Remove just the shrimp and transfer to a plate.
7. Add pepper, feta and 1 tablespoon lemon juice to pan and cook for a minute or until cheese begins to melt.
8. To serve, place cheese and fennel mixture on a serving plate and top with shrimps.

Nutrition: Calories: 310; Protein: 49.7g; Fat: 6.8g; Carbs: 8.4g

.Shrimp Boil (Spanish)

Preparation Time: 15 minutes Cooking Time: 4 hours Servings: 4

11/2 lb. potatoes, sliced into wedges 2cloves garlic, peeled	2ears corn
1lb. sausage, sliced 1/4cup Old Bay seasoning tbsp lemon juice 2cups water	2lb. shrimp, peeled

1. Put the potatoes in your slow cooker. Add the garlic, corn and sausage in layers.
2. Season with the Old Bay seasoning.
3. Drizzle lemon juice on top.
4. Pour in the water.
5. Do not mix.
6. Cover the pot.
7. Cook on high for 4 hours.
8. Add the shrimp on top.
9. Cook for 15 minutes.

Nutrition: Calories 585 Fat 25.1g Sodium 2242mg Potassium 1166mg Carbohydrate 3.7g Fiber 4.9g Protein 53.8g Sugars 3.9g

.Soup And Stew Spinach Soup (Spanish)

Prep Time: 10 minutes Cooking Time: 21 minutes Serving: 6

14 oz frozen spinach 1 large onion	1 carrot
4 cups water	3-4 tbsp olive oil 1/4 cup white rice
1-2 cloves garlic, crushed	

1. Cook oil in a cooking pot, stir in onion and carrot and sauté together for a few minutes, until just softened. Add chopped garlic and rice and stir for a minute. Remove from heat.
2. Add in the chopped spinach along with about 2 cups of hot water and season with salt and pepper. Bring back to a boil, then reduce the heat and simmer for around 30 minutes.

Nutrition: 291 Calories 16g Fat 7g Protein

.Spinach and Feta Cheese Soup (Greek)

Preparation Time: 8 minutes Cooking Time: 24 minutes
Serving: 4

14 oz frozen spinach oz feta cheese	1large onion or 4-5 scallions
2-3 tbsp light cream 3-4 tbsp olive oil	1-2 cloves garlic
4 cups water	

1. Cook oil in a cooking pot, add the onion and spinach and sauté together for a few minutes, until just softened. Add garlic and stir for a minute. Remove from heat. Fill 2 cups of hot water and season with salt and pepper.
2. Bring back to the boil, then reduce the heat and simmer for around 30 minutes. Blend soup in a blender. Crumble the cheese with a fork. Stir in the crumbled feta cheese and the cream. Serve hot.

Nutrition: 251 Calories 13g Fat 5g Protein

.Basil Broccoli Soup (Greek)

Preparation Time: 10 minutes Cooking Time: 15 minutes
Servings: 6

1 lb. broccoli florets	1 tsp chili powder 1 tsp dried basil
6 cups vegetable stock 1 onion, chopped	2 leeks, chopped Pepper
Salt	1 tbsp olive oil

1. Add oil into the inner pot of the instant pot and set the pot on sauté mode. Add onion and leek and sauté for 5 minutes.
2. Add the rest of the and stir well. Seal pot with lid and cook on high for 10 minutes.
3. Once done, allow to release pressure naturally for 10 minutes, then release remaining using quick release. Remove lid.
4. Blend soup using an immersion blender until smooth. Serve and enjoy.

Nutrition: Calories 79 Fat 2.9 g Carbohydrates 12.1 g Protein 3.2 g

Chapter 9
Fruits and Desserts

Rice Pudding with Roasted Orange

Prep time: 10 minutes | Cook time: 19 to 20 minutes | Serves 6

2 medium oranges	1 cup orange juice
2 teaspoons extra-virgin olive oil	1 cup uncooked instant brown rice
⅛ teaspoon kosher salt	¼ cup honey
2 large eggs	½ tbsp ground cinnamon
2 cups unsweetened almond milk	1 teaspoon vanilla extract
	Cooking spray

1. Preheat the oven to 450°F (235°C). Spritz a large, rimmed baking sheet with cooking spray. Set aside.
2. Slice the unpeeled oranges into ¼-inch rounds. Brush with the oil and sprinkle with salt. Place the slices on the baking sheet and roast for 4 minutes. Flip the slices and roast for 4 more minutes, or until they begin to brown. Remove from the oven and set aside.
3. Crack the eggs into a medium bowl. In a medium saucepan, whisk together the milk, orange juice, rice, honey and cinnamon. Bring to a boil over medium-high heat, stirring constantly. Reduce the heat to medium- low and simmer for 10 minutes, stirring occasionally.
4. Using a measuring cup, scoop out ½ cup of the hot rice mixture and whisk it into the eggs. While constantly stirring the mixture in the pan, slowly pour the egg mixture back into the saucepan.
5. Cook on low heat for 1 to 2 minutes, or until thickened, stirring constantly. Remove from the heat and stir in the vanilla. Let the pudding stand for a few minutes for the rice to soften. The rice will be cooked but slightly chewy. For softer rice, let stand for another half hour. Top with the roasted oranges. Serve warm or at room temperature.

Per Serving

calories: 204 | fat: 6.0g | protein: 5.0g | carbs: 34.0g | fiber: 1.0g | sodium: 148mg

Crispy Sesame Cookies

Prep time: 5 minutes | Cook time: 8 to 10 minutes | Serves 14 to 16

1 cup hulled sesame seeds	8 tablespoons almond butter
1 cup sugar	2 large eggs
	1¼ cups flour

1. Preheat the oven to 350°F (180°C).
2. Toast the sesame seeds on a baking sheet for 3 minutes. Set aside and let cool. Using a mixer, whisk together the sugar and butter. Add the eggs one at a time until well blended. Add the flour and toasted sesame seeds and mix until well blended. Drop spoonfuls of cookie dough onto a baking sheet and form them into round balls, about 1-inch in diameter, similar to a walnut.
3. Put in the oven and bake for 5 to 7 minutes, or until golden brown. Let the cookies cool for 5 minutes before serving.

Per Serving calories: 218 | fat: 12.0g | protein: 4.0g | carbs: 25.0g | fiber: 2.0g | sodium: 58mg

Cherry Walnut Brownies

Prep time: 10 minutes | Cook time: 20 minutes | Serves 9

2 large eggs	⅓ cup unsweetened dark chocolate cocoa powder
½ cup 2% plain Greek yogurt	¼ teaspoon baking powder
½ cup sugar ⅓ cup honey	¼ teaspoon salt
¼ cup extra-virgin olive oil	⅓ cup chopped walnuts
1 teaspoon vanilla extract	9 fresh cherries, stemmed and pitted
½ cup whole-wheat pastry flour	Cooking spray

1. Preheat the oven to 375°F (190°C) and set the rack in the middle of the oven. Spritz a square baking pan with cooking spray. In a large bowl, whisk together the eggs, yogurt, sugar, honey, oil and vanilla.
2. In a medium bowl, stir together the flour, cocoa powder, baking powder and salt. Add the flour mixture to the egg mixture and whisk until all the dry are incorporated. Fold in the walnuts.
3. Pour the batter into the prepared pan. Push the cherries into the batter, three to a row in three rows, so one will be at the center of each brownie once you cut them into squares. Bake the brownies for 20 minutes, or until just set. Remove from the oven and place on a rack to cool for 5 minutes. Cut into nine squares and serve.

Per Serving

calories: 154 | fat: 6.0g | protein: 3.0g | carbs: 24.0g | fiber: 2.0g | sodium: 125mg

Watermelon and Blueberry Salad

Prep time: 5 minutes | Cook time: 0 minutes | Serves 6 to 8

1 medium watermelon	2 tablespoons lemon juice
1 cup fresh blueberries	2 tablespoons finely chopped fresh mint leaves
⅓ cup honey	

1. Cut the watermelon into 1-inch cubes. Put them in a bowl.
2. Evenly distribute the blueberries over the watermelon.
3. In a separate bowl, whisk together the honey, lemon juice and mint. Drizzle the mint dressing over the watermelon and blueberries. Serve cold.

Per Serving calories: 238 | fat: 1.0g | protein: 4.0g | carbs: 61.0g | fiber: 3.0g | sodium: 11mg

Mint Banana Chocolate Sorbet

Prep time: 4 hours 5 minutes | Cook time: 0 minutes | Serves 1

1 frozen banana	2 to 3 tbsp dark chocolate chips (60% cocoa or higher)
1 tablespoon almond butter	
2 tbsp minced fresh mint	2 to 3 tbsp goji (optional)

1. Put the banana, butter, and mint in a food processor. Pulse to purée until creamy and smooth.
2. Add the chocolate and goji, then pulse for several more times to combine well. Pour the mixture in a bowl or a ramekin, then freeze for at least 4 hours before serving chilled.

Per Serving calories: 213 | fat: 9.8g | protein: 3.1g | carbs: 2.9g | fiber: 4.0g | sodium: 155mg

Pecan and Carrot Cake

Prep time: 15 minutes | Cook time: 45 minutes | Serves 12

½ cup coconut oil, at room temperature, plus more for greasing the baking dish
2 teaspoons pure vanilla extract
¼ cup pure maple syrup 6 eggs
½ cup coconut flour
1 teaspoon baking powder
1 teaspoon baking soda
½ teaspoon ground nutmeg
1 teaspoon ground cinnamon
⅛ teaspoon sea salt
½ cup chopped pecans
3 cups finely grated carrots

1. Preheat the oven to 350ºF (180ºC). Grease a 13-by-9-inch baking dish with coconut oil.
2. Combine the vanilla extract, maple syrup, and ½ cup of coconut oil in a large bowl. Stir to mix well.
3. Break the eggs in the bowl and whisk to combine well. Set aside. Combine the coconut flour, baking powder, baking soda, nutmeg, cinnamon, and salt in a separate bowl. Stir to mix well. Make a well in the center of the flour mixture, then pour the egg mixture into the well. Stir to combine well. Add the pecans and carrots to the bowl and toss to mix well. Pour the mixture in the single layer on the baking dish. Bake in the preheated oven for 45 minutes or until puffed and the cake spring back when lightly press with your fingers. Remove the cake from the oven. Allow to cool for at least 15 minutes, then serve.

Per Serving calories: 255 | fat: 21.2g | protein: 5.1g | carbs: 12.8g | fiber: 2.0g | sodium: 202mg

Raspberry Yogurt Basted Cantaloupe

Prep time: 15 minutes | Cook time: 0 minutes | Serves 6

2 cups fresh raspberries, mashed
1 cup plain coconut yogurt
½ teaspoon vanilla extract
1 cantaloupe, peeled and sliced
½ cup toasted coconut flakes

1. Combine the mashed raspberries with yogurt and vanilla extract in a small bowl. Stir to mix well.
2. Place the cantaloupe slices on a platter, then top with raspberry mixture and spread with toasted coconut.
3. Serve immediately.

Per Serving calories: 75 | fat: 4.1g | protein: 1.2g | carbs: 10.9g | fiber: 6.0g | sodium: 36mg

Apple Compote

Prep time: 15 minutes | Cook time: 10 minutes | Serves 4

6 apples, peeled, cored, and chopped
¼ cup raw honey
1 teaspoon ground cinnamon
¼ cup apple juice
Sea salt, to taste

1. Put all the in a stockpot. Stir to mix well, then cook over medium-high heat for 10 minutes or until the apples are glazed by honey and lightly saucy. Stir constantly. Serve immediately.

Per Serving calories: 246 | fat: 0.9g | protein: 1.2g | carbs: 66.3g | fiber: 9.0g | sodium: 62mg

Spiced Sweet Pecans

Prep time: 4 minutes | Cook time: 17 minutes | Serves 4

1 cup pecan halves
3 tablespoons almond butter
1 teaspoon ground cinnamon
½ teaspoon ground nutmeg
¼ cup raw honey
¼ teaspoon sea salt

1. Preheat the oven to 350ºF (180ºC). Line a baking sheet with parchment paper.
2. Combine all the in a bowl. Stir to mix well, then spread the mixture in the single layer on the baking sheet with a spatula. Bake in the preheated oven for 16 minutes or until the pecan halves are well browned.
3. Serve immediately.

Per Serving calories: 324 | fat: 29.8g | protein: 3.2g | carbs: 13.9g | fiber: 4.0g | sodium: 180mg

Greek Yogurt Affogato with Pistachios

Prep time: 5 minutes | Cook time: 0 minutes | Serves 4

24 ounces (680 g) vanilla Greek yogurt
2 teaspoons sugar
4 shots hot espresso
4 tablespoons chopped unsalted pistachios
4 tablespoons dark chocolate chips

1. Spoon the yogurt into four bowls or tall glasses.
2. Mix ½ teaspoon of sugar into each of the espresso shots.
3. Pour one shot of the hot espresso over each bowl of yogurt.
4. Top each bowl with 1 tablespoon of the pistachios and 1 tablespoon of the chocolate chips and serve.

Per Serving calories: 190 | fat: 6.0g | protein: 20.0g | carbs: 14.0g | fiber: 1.0g | sodium: 99mg

Grilled Peaches with Whipped Ricotta

Prep time: 5 minutes | Cook time: 14 to 22 minutes | Serves 4

4 peaches, halved and pitted
2 teaspoons extra-virgin olive oil
¾ cup whole-milk Ricotta cheese
1 tablespoon honey
¼ teaspoon freshly grated nutmeg
4 sprigs mint
Cooking spray

1. Spritz a grill pan with cooking spray. Heat the grill pan to medium heat.
2. Place a large, empty bowl in the refrigerator to chill.
3. Brush the peaches all over with the oil. Place half of the peaches, cut-side down, on the grill pan and cook for 3 to 5 minutes, or until grill marks appear.
4. Using tongs, turn the peaches over. Cover the grill pan with aluminum foil and cook for 4 to 6 minutes, or until the peaches are easily pierced with a sharp knife. Set aside to cool. Repeat with the remaining peaches.
5. Remove the bowl from the refrigerator and add the Ricotta. Using an electric beater, beat the Ricotta on high for 2 minutes. Add the honey and nutmeg and beat for 1 more minute. Divide the cooled peaches among 4 serving bowls. Top with the Ricotta mixture and a sprig of mint and serve.

Per Serving calories: 176 | fat: 8.0g | protein: 8.0g | carbs: 20.0g | fiber: 3.0g | sodium: 63mg

Peanut Butter and Chocolate Balls

Prep time: 45 minutes | Cook time: 0 minutes | Serves 15 balls

¾ cup creamy peanut butter
¼ cup unsweetened cocoa powder
2 tablespoons softened almond butter
½ teaspoon vanilla extract
1¾ cups maple syrup

1. Line a baking sheet with parchment paper.
2. Combine all the in a bowl. Stir to mix well.
3. Divide the mixture into 15 parts and shape each part into a 1-inch ball. Arrange the balls on the baking sheet and refrigerate for at least 30 minutes, then serve chilled.

Per Serving (1 ball)

calories: 146 | fat: 8.1g | protein: 4.2g | carbs: 16.9g | fiber: 1.0g | sodium: 70mg

Honey Baked Cinnamon Apples

Prep time: 5 minutes | Cook time: 20 minutes | Serves 2

1 teaspoon extra-virgin olive oil
4 firm apples, peeled, cored, and sliced
½ teaspoon salt
1½ teaspoons ground cinnamon, divided
2 tablespoons unsweetened almond milk
2 tablespoons honey

1. Preheat the oven to 375ºF (190ºC). Coat a small casserole dish with the olive oil.
2. Toss the apple slices with the salt and ½ teaspoon of the cinnamon in a medium bowl. Spread the apples in the prepared casserole dish and bake in the preheated oven for 20 minutes. Meanwhile, in a small saucepan, heat the milk, honey, and remaining 1 teaspoon of cinnamon over medium heat, stirring frequently. When it reaches a simmer, remove the pan from the heat and cover to keep warm. Divide the apple slices between 2 plates and pour the sauce over the apples. Serve warm.

Per Serving

calories: 310 | fat: 3.4g | protein: 1.7g | carbs: 68.5g | fiber: 12.6g | sodium: 593mg

Strawberries with Balsamic Vinegar

Prep time: 5 minutes | Cook time: 0 minutes | Serves 2

2 cups strawberries, hulled and sliced
2 tablespoons sugar
2 tbsp balsamic vinegar

1. Place the sliced strawberries in a bowl, sprinkle with the sugar, and drizzle lightly with the balsamic vinegar.
2. Toss to combine well and allow to sit for about 10 minutes before serving.

Per Serving calories: 92 | fat: 0.4g | protein: 1.0g | carbs: 21.7g | fiber: 2.9g | sodium: 5mg

Frozen Mango Raspberry Delight

Prep time: 5 minutes | Cook time: 0 minutes | Serves 2

3 cups frozen raspberries
1 mango, peeled and pitted
1 peach, peeled and pitted
1 teaspoon honey

1. Place all the into a blender and purée, adding some water as needed.
2. Put in the freezer for 10 minutes to firm up if desired. Serve chilled or at room temperature.

Per Serving

calories: 276 | fat: 2.1g | protein: 4.5g | carbs: 60.3g | fiber: 17.5g | sodium: 4mg

Grilled Stone Fruit with Honey

Prep time: 8 minutes | Cook time: 6 minutes | Serves 2

3 apricots, halved and pitted
2 plums, halved and pitted
2 peaches, halved and pitted
½ cup low-fat ricotta cheese
2 tablespoons honey
Cooking spray

1. Preheat the grill to medium heat. Spray the grill grates with cooking spray.
2. Arrange the fruit, cut side down, on the grill, and cook for 2 to 3 minutes per side, or until lightly charred and softened.
3. Serve warm with a sprinkle of cheese and a drizzle of honey.

Per Serving

calories: 298 | fat: 7.8g | protein: 11.9g | carbs: 45.2g | fiber: 4.3g | sodium: 259mg

Mascarpone Baked Pears

Prep time: 10 minutes | Cook time: 20 minutes | Serves 2

2 ripe pears, peeled
1 tablespoon plus 2 teaspoons honey, divided
1 teaspoon vanilla, divided
¼ teaspoon ground coriander
¼ teaspoon ginger
¼ cup minced walnuts
¼ cup mascarpone cheese
Pinch salt
Cooking spray

1. Preheat the oven to 350ºF (180ºC). Spray a small baking dish with cooking spray.
2. Slice the pears in half lengthwise. Using a spoon, scoop out the core from each piece. Put the pears, cut side up, in the baking dish.
3. Whisk together 1 tablespoon of honey, ½ teaspoon of vanilla, ginger, and coriander in a small bowl. Pour this mixture evenly over the pear halves.
4. Scatter the walnuts over the pear halves.
5. Bake in the preheated oven for 20 minutes, or until the pears are golden and you're able to pierce them easily with a knife.
6. Meanwhile, combine the mascarpone cheese with the remaining 2 teaspoons of honey, ½ teaspoon of vanilla, and a pinch of salt. Stir to combine well.
7. Divide the mascarpone among the warm pear halves and serve.

Per Serving

calories: 308 | fat: 16.0g | protein: 4.1g | carbs: 42.7g | fiber: 6.0g | sodium: 88mg

Mixed Berry Crisp

Prep time: 15 minutes | Cook time: 30 minutes | Serves 2

1½ cups frozen mixed berries, thawed
1 tablespoon coconut sugar
1 tablespoon almond butter
¼ cup oats
¼ cup pecans

1. Preheat the oven to 350ºF (180ºC). Divide the mixed berries between 2 ramekins Place the coconut sugar, almond butter, oats, and pecans in a food processor, and pulse a few times, until the mixture resembles damp sand.
2. Divide the crumble topping over the mixed berries.
3. Put the ramekins on a sheet pan and bake for 30 minutes, or until the top is golden and the berries are bubbling.
4. Serve warm.

Per Serving calories: 268 | fat: 17.0g | protein: 4.1g | carbs: 26.8g | fiber: 6.0g | sodium: 44mg

Orange Mug Cakes

Prep time: 10 minutes | Cook time: 3 minutes | Serves 2

6 tablespoons flour
2 tablespoons sugar
1 teaspoon orange zest
½ teaspoon baking powder
Pinch salt
1 egg
2 tablespoons olive oil
2 tablespoons unsweetened almond milk
2 tablespoons freshly squeezed orange juice
½ teaspoon orange extract
½ teaspoon vanilla extract

1. Combine the flour, sugar, orange zest, baking powder, and salt in a small bowl. In another bowl, whisk together the egg, olive oil, milk, orange juice, orange extract, and vanilla extract. Add the dry to the wet and stir to incorporate. The batter will be thick.
2. Divide the mixture into two small mugs. Microwave each mug separately. The small ones should take about 60 seconds, and one large mug should take about 90 seconds, but microwaves can vary. Cool for 5 minutes before serving.

Per Serving calories: 303 | fat: 16.9g | protein: 6.0g | carbs: 32.5g | fiber: 1.0g | sodium: 118mg

Fruit and Nut Chocolate Bark

Prep time: 15 minutes | Cook time: 2 minutes | Serves 2

2 tablespoons chopped nuts
3 ounces (85 g) dark chocolate chips
¼ cup chopped dried fruit (blueberries, apricots, figs, prunes, or any combination of those)

1. Line a sheet pan with parchment paper and set aside.
2. Add the nuts to a skillet over medium-high heat and toast for 60 seconds, or just fragrant. Set aside to cool.
3. Put the chocolate chips in a microwave-safe glass bowl and microwave on High for 1 minute.
4. Stir the chocolate and allow any unmelted chips to warm and melt. If desired, heat for an additional 20 to 30 seconds. Transfer the chocolate to the prepared sheet pan. Scatter the dried fruit and toasted nuts over the chocolate evenly and gently pat in so they stick.
5. Place the sheet pan in the refrigerator for at least 1 hour to let the chocolate harden. When ready, break into pieces and serve.

Per Serving calories: 285 | fat: 16.1g | protein: 4.0g | carbs: 38.7g | fiber: 2.0g | sodium: 2mg

Crunchy Almond Cookies

Prep time: 5 minutes | Cook time: 5 to 7 minutes | Serves 4 to 6

½ cup sugar
8 tablespoons almond butter
1 large egg
1½ cups all-purpose flour
1 cup ground almonds

1. Preheat the oven to 375°F (190°C). Line a baking sheet with parchment paper.
2. Using a mixer, whisk together the sugar and butter. Add the egg and mix until combined. Alternately add the flour and ground almonds, ½ cup at a time, while the mixer is on slow.
3. Drop 1 tablespoon of the dough on the prepared baking sheet, keeping the cookies at least 2 inches apart.
4. Put the baking sheet in the oven and bake for about 5 to 7 minutes, or until the cookies start to turn brown around the edges.
5. Let cool for 5 minutes before serving.

Per Serving
calories: 604 | fat: 36.0g | protein: 11.0g | carbs: 63.0g | fiber: 4.0g | sodium: 181mg

Walnut and Date Balls

Prep time: 5 minutes | Cook time: 8 to 10 minutes | Serves 6 to 8

1 cup walnuts
1 cup unsweetened shredded coconut
14 medjool dates, pitted
8 tablespoons almond butter

1. Preheat the oven to 350°F (180°C).
2. Put the walnuts on a baking sheet and toast in the oven for 5 minutes.
3. Put the shredded coconut on a clean baking sheet. Toast for about 3 to 5 minutes, or until it turns golden brown. Once done, remove it from the oven and put it in a shallow bowl.
4. In a food processor, process the toasted walnuts until they have a medium chop. Transfer the chopped walnuts into a medium bowl.
5. Add the dates and butter to the food processor and blend until the dates become a thick paste. Pour the chopped walnuts into the food processor with the dates and pulse just until the mixture is combined, about 5 to 7 pulses.
6. Remove the mixture from the food processor and scrape it into a large bowl.
7. To make the balls, spoon 1 to 2 tablespoons of the date mixture into the palm of your hand and roll around between your hands until you form a ball. Put the ball on a clean, lined baking sheet. Repeat until all the mixture is formed into balls.
8. Roll each ball in the toasted coconut until the outside of the ball is coated. Put the ball back on the baking sheet and repeat.
9. Put all the balls into the refrigerator for 20 minutes before serving. Store any leftovers in the refrigerator in an airtight container.

Per Serving
calories: 489 | fat: 35.0g | protein: 5.0g | carbs: 48.0g | fiber: 7.0g | sodium: 114mg

Banana, Cranberry, and Oat Bars

Prep time: 15 minutes | Cook time: 40 minutes | Makes 16 bars

2 tablespoon extra-virgin olive oil
2 medium ripe bananas, mashed
½ cup almond butter
½ cup maple syrup
⅓ cup dried cranberries
1½ cups old-fashioned rolled oats
¼ cup oat flour
¼ cup ground flaxseed
¼ teaspoon ground cloves
½ cup shredded coconut
½ teaspoon ground cinnamon
1 teaspoon vanilla extract

1. Preheat the oven to 400°F (205°C). Line a 8-inch square pan with parchment paper, then grease with olive oil.
2. Combine the mashed bananas, almond butter, and maple syrup in a bowl. Stir to mix well.
3. Mix in the remaining and stir to mix well until thick and sticky.
4. Spread the mixture evenly on the square pan with a spatula, then bake in the preheated oven for 40 minutes or until a toothpick inserted in the center comes out clean.
5. Remove them from the oven and slice into 16 bars to serve.

Per Serving calories: 145 | fat: 7.2g | protein: 3.1g | carbs: 18.9g | fiber: 2.0g | sodium: 3mg

Berry and Rhubarb Cobbler

Prep time: 15 minutes | Cook time: 35 minutes | Serves 8

Cobbler:
1 cup fresh raspberries
2 cups fresh blueberries
1 cup sliced (½-inch) rhubarb pieces
1 tablespoon arrowroot powder
¼ cup unsweetened apple juice
2 tablespoons melted coconut oil
¼ cup raw honey

Topping:
1 cup almond flour
1 tablespoon arrowroot powder
½ cup shredded coconut
¼ cup raw honey
½ cup coconut oil

Make the Cobbler
1. Preheat the oven to 350ºF (180ºC). Grease a baking dish with melted coconut oil.
2. Combine the for the cobbler in a large bowl. Stir to mix well.
3. Spread the mixture in the single layer on the baking dish. Set aside.

Make the Topping
4. Combine the almond flour, arrowroot powder, and coconut in a bowl. Stir to mix well.
5. Fold in the honey and coconut oil. Stir with a fork until the mixture crumbled.
6. Spread the topping over the cobbler, then bake in the preheated oven for 35 minutes or until frothy and golden brown.
7. Serve immediately.

Per Serving
calories: 305 | fat: 22.1g | protein: 3.2g | carbs: 29.8g | fiber: 4.0g | sodium: 3mg

Citrus Cranberry and Quinoa Energy Bites

Prep time: 25 minutes | Cook time: 0 minutes | Makes 12 bites

2 tablespoons almond butter
2 tablespoons maple syrup
¾ cup cooked quinoa
1 tablespoon dried cranberries
1 tablespoon chia seeds
¼ cup ground almonds
¼ cup sesame seeds, toasted
Zest of 1 orange
½ teaspoon vanilla extract

1. Line a baking sheet with parchment paper.
2. Combine the butter and maple syrup in a bowl. Stir to mix well.
3. Fold in the remaining and stir until the mixture holds together and smooth.
4. Divide the mixture into 12 equal parts, then shape each part into a ball.
5. Arrange the balls on the baking sheet, then refrigerate for at least 15 minutes.
6. Serve chilled.

Per Serving (1 bite)
calories: 110 | fat: 10.8g | protein: 3.1g | carbs: 4.9g | fiber: 3.0g | sodium: 211mg

Chocolate, Almond, and Cherry Clusters

Prep time: 15 minutes | Cook time: 3 minutes | Makes 10 clusters

1 cup dark chocolate (60% cocoa or higher), chopped
1 tablespoon coconut oil
½ cup dried cherries
1 cup roasted salted almonds

1. Line a baking sheet with parchment paper.
2. Melt the chocolate and coconut oil in a saucepan for 3 minutes. Stir constantly.
3. Turn off the heat and mix in the cherries and almonds.
4. Drop the mixture on the baking sheet with a spoon. Place the sheet in the refrigerator and chill for at least 1 hour or until firm.
5. Serve chilled.

Per Serving
calories: 197 | fat: 13.2g | protein: 4.1g | carbs: 17.8g | fiber: 4.0g | sodium: 57mg

Chocolate and Avocado Mousse

Prep time: 40 minutes | Cook time: 5 minutes | Serves 4 to 6

8 ounces (227 g) dark chocolate (60% cocoa or higher), chopped
¼ cup unsweetened coconut milk
2 tablespoons coconut oil
2 ripe avocados, deseeded
¼ cup raw honey
Sea salt, to taste

1. Put the chocolate in a saucepan. Pour in the coconut milk and add the coconut oil.
2. Cook for 3 minutes or until the chocolate and coconut oil melt. Stir constantly.
3. Put the avocado in a food processor, then drizzle with honey and melted chocolate. Pulse to combine until smooth.
4. Pour the mixture in a serving bowl, then sprinkle with salt. Refrigerate to chill for 30 minutes and serve.

Per Serving
calories: 654 | fat: 46.8g | protein: 7.2g | carbs: 55.9g | fiber: 9.0g | sodium: 112mg

Coconut Blueberries with Brown Rice

Prep time: 55 minutes | Cook time: 10 minutes | Serves 4

1 cup fresh blueberries
2 cups unsweetened coconut milk
1 teaspoon ground ginger
¼ cup maple syrup
Sea salt, to taste
2 cups cooked brown rice

1. Put all the , except for the brown rice, in a pot. Stir to combine well.
2. Cook over medium-high heat for 7 minutes or until the blueberries are tender.
3. Pour in the brown rice and cook for 3 more minute or until the rice is soft. Stir constantly.
4. Serve immediately.

Per Serving
calories: 470 | fat: 24.8g | protein: 6.2g | carbs: 60.1g | fiber: 5.0g | sodium: 75mg

Blueberry and Oat Crisp

Prep time: 15 minutes | Cook time: 20 minutes | Serves 4

2 tablespoons coconut oil, melted, plus more for greasing	¼ cup maple syrup
	1 cup gluten-free rolled oats
4 cups fresh blueberries	½ cup chopped pecans
Juice of ½ lemon	½ teaspoon ground cinnamon
2 teaspoons lemon zest	Sea salt, to taste

1. Preheat the oven to 350°F (180°C). Grease a baking sheet with coconut oil.
2. Combine the blueberries, lemon juice and zest, and maple syrup in a bowl. Stir to mix well, then spread the mixture on the baking sheet.
3. Combine the remaining in a small bowl. Stir to mix well. Pour the mixture over the blueberries mixture.
4. Bake in the preheated oven for 20 minutes or until the oats are golden brown.
5. Serve immediately with spoons.

Per Serving

calories: 496 | fat: 32.9g | protein: 5.1g | carbs: 50.8g | fiber: 7.0g | sodium: 41mg

Glazed Pears with Hazelnuts

Prep time: 10 minutes | Cook time: 20 minutes | Serves 4

4 pears, peeled, cored, and quartered lengthwise	1 tablespoon grated fresh ginger
1 cup apple juice	½ cup pure maple syrup
	¼ cup chopped hazelnuts

1. Put the pears in a pot, then pour in the apple juice. Bring to a boil over medium-high heat, then reduce the heat to medium-low. Stir constantly.
2. Cover and simmer for an additional 15 minutes or until the pears are tender.
3. Meanwhile, combine the ginger and maple syrup in a saucepan. Bring to a boil over medium-high heat. Stir frequently. Turn off the heat and transfer the syrup to a small bowl and let sit until ready to use.
4. Transfer the pears in a large serving bowl with a slotted spoon, then top the pears with syrup.
5. Spread the hazelnuts over the pears and serve immediately.

Per Serving

calories: 287 | fat: 3.1g | protein: 2.2g | carbs: 66.9g | fiber: 7.0g | sodium: 8mg

Apple and Berries Ambrosia

Prep time: 15 minutes | Cook time: 0 minutes | Serves 4

2 cups unsweetened coconut milk, chilled	1 apple, peeled, cored, and chopped
2 tablespoons raw honey	2 cups fresh raspberries
	2 cups fresh blueberries

1. Spoon the chilled milk in a large bowl, then mix in the honey. Stir to mix well.
2. Then mix in the remaining . Stir to coat the fruits well and serve immediately.

Per Serving calories: 386 | fat: 21.1g | protein: 4.2g | carbs: 45.9g | fiber: 11.0g | sodium: 16mg

Lemony Blackberry Granita

Prep time: 10 minutes | Cook time: 0 minutes | Serves 4

1 pound (454 g) fresh blackberries	½ cup raw honey
	½ cup water
1 teaspoon chopped fresh thyme	
¼ cup freshly squeezed lemon juice	

1. Put all the in a food processor, then pulse to purée.
2. Pour the mixture through a sieve into a baking dish. Discard the seeds remain in the sieve.
3. Put the baking dish in the freezer for 2 hours. Remove the dish from the refrigerator and stir to break any frozen parts.
4. Return the dish back to the freezer for an hour, then stir to break any frozen parts again.
5. Return the dish to the freezer for 4 hours until the granita is completely frozen.
6. Remove it from the freezer and mash to serve.

Per Serving

calories: 183 | fat: 1.1g | protein: 2.2g | carbs: 45.9g | fiber: 6.0g | sodium: 6mg

Lemony Tea and Chia Pudding

Prep time: 30 minutes | Cook time: 0 minutes | Serves 3 to 4

2 teaspoons matcha green tea powder (optional)	1 to 2 dates
	2 cups unsweetened coconut milk
2 tablespoons ground chia seeds	Zest and juice of 1 lime

1. Put all the in a food processor and pulse until creamy and smooth.
2. Pour the mixture in a bowl, then wrap in plastic. Store in the refrigerator for at least 20 minutes, then serve chilled.

Per Serving

calories: 225 | fat: 20.1g | protein: 3.2g | carbs: 5.9g | fiber: 5.0g | sodium: 314mg

Sweet Spiced Pumpkin Pudding

Prep time: 2 hours 10 minutes | Cook time: 0 minutes | Serves 6

1 cup pure pumpkin purée	½ teaspoon ground ginger
2 cups unsweetened coconut milk	Pinch cloves
	¼ cup pure maple syrup
1 teaspoon ground cinnamon	2 tablespoons chopped pecans, for garnish
¼ teaspoon ground nutmeg	

1. Combine all the , except for the chopped pecans, in a large bowl. Stir to mix well.
2. Wrap the bowl in plastic and refrigerate for at least 2 hours.
3. Remove the bowl from the refrigerator and discard the plastic. Spread the pudding with pecans and serve chilled.

Per Serving

calories: 249 | fat: 21.1g | protein: 2.8g | carbs: 17.2g | fiber: 3.0g | sodium: 46mg

Mango and Coconut Frozen Pie

Prep time: 1 hour 10 minutes | Cook time: 0 minutes | Serves 8

Crust:	Filling:
1 cup cashews	2 large mangoes, peeled and chopped
½ cup rolled oats	½ cup unsweetened shredded coconut
1 cup soft pitted dates	½ cup water
1 cup unsweetened coconut milk	

1. Combine the for the crust in a food processor. Pulse to combine well.
2. Pour the mixture in an 8-inch springform pan, then press to coat the bottom. Set aside.
3. Combine the for the filling in the food processor, then pulse to purée until smooth.
4. Pour the filling over the crust, then use a spatula to spread the filling evenly. Put the pan in the freeze for 30 minutes.
5. Remove the pan from the freezer and allow to sit for 15 minutes under room temperature before serving.

Per Serving (1 slice)

calories: 426 | fat: 28.2g | protein: 8.1g | carbs: 14.9g | fiber: 6.0g | sodium: 174mg

Mini Nuts and Fruits Crumble

Prep time: 15 minutes | Cook time: 15 minutes | Serves 6

Topping:	Filling:
¼ cup coarsely chopped hazelnuts	6 fresh figs, quartered
1 cup coarsely chopped walnuts	2 nectarines, pitted and sliced
1 teaspoon ground cinnamon	1 cup fresh blueberries
Sea salt, to taste	2 teaspoons lemon zest
1 tablespoon melted coconut oil	½ cup raw honey
	1 teaspoon vanilla extract

Make the Topping

1. Combine the for the topping in a bowl. Stir to mix well. Set aside until ready to use.

Make the Filling:

2. Preheat the oven to 375°F (190°C).
3. Combine the for the fillings in a bowl. Stir to mix well.
4. Divide the filling in six ramekins, then divide and top with nut topping.
5. Bake in the preheated oven for 15 minutes or until the topping is lightly browned and the filling is frothy.
6. Serve immediately.

Per Serving

calories: 336 | fat: 18.8g | protein: 6.3g | carbs: 41.9g | fiber: 6.0g | sodium: 31mg

Cozy Superfood Hot Chocolate

Prep time: 5 minutes | Cook time: 8 minutes | Serves 2

2 cups unsweetened almond milk	1 teaspoon ground cinnamon
1 tablespoon avocado oil	1 teaspoon ground ginger
1 tablespoon collagen protein powder	1 teaspoon vanilla extract
2 teaspoons coconut sugar	½ teaspoon ground turmeric
2 tablespoons cocoa powder	Dash salt
	Dash cayenne pepper (optional)

1. In a small saucepan over medium heat, warm the almond milk and avocado oil for about 7 minutes, stirring frequently.
2. Fold in the protein powder, which will only properly dissolve in a heated liquid.
3. Stir in the coconut sugar and cocoa powder until melted and dissolved.
1. Carefully transfer the warm liquid into a blender, along with the cinnamon, ginger, vanilla, turmeric, salt, and cayenne pepper (if desired). Blend for 15 seconds until frothy.
4. Serve immediately.

Per Serving

calories: 217 | fat: 11.0g | protein: 11.2g | carbs: 14.8g | fiber: 6.0g | sodium: 202mg

Chapter 10
Sauces, Dips, and Dressings

Creamy Cucumber Dip

Prep time: 10 minutes | Cook time: 0 minutes | Serves 6

1 medium cucumber, peeled and grated

¼ teaspoon salt

1 cup plain Greek yogurt

2 garlic cloves, minced

1 tablespoon extra-virgin olive oil

1 tablespoon freshly squeezed lemon juice

¼ teaspoon freshly ground black pepper

1. Place the grated cucumber in a colander set over a bowl and season with salt. Allow the cucumber to stand for 10 minutes. Using your hands, squeeze out as much liquid from the cucumber as possible. Transfer the grated cucumber to a medium bowl.
2. Add the yogurt, garlic, olive oil, lemon juice, and pepper to the bowl and stir until well blended.
3. Cover the bowl with plastic wrap and refrigerate for at least 2 hours to blend the flavors. Serve chilled.

Per Serving (¼ cup)

calories: 47 | fat: 2.8g | protein: 4.2g | carbs: 2.7g | fiber: 0g | sodium: 103mg

Italian Dressing

Prep time: 5 minutes | Cook time: 0 minutes | Serves 12

½ cup extra-virgin olive oil

¼ cup red wine vinegar

1 teaspoon dried Italian seasoning

1 teaspoon Dijon mustard

¼ teaspoon salt

¼ teaspoon freshly ground black pepper

1 garlic clove, minced

1. Place all the in a mason jar and cover. Shake vigorously for 1 minute until completely mixed.
2. Store in the refrigerator for up to 1 week.

Per Serving (1 tablespoon)

calories: 80 | fat: 8.6g | protein: 0g | carbs: 0g | fiber: 0g | sodium: 51mg

Ranch-Style Cauliflower Dressing

Prep time: 10 minutes | Cook time: 0 minutes | Serves 8

2 cups frozen cauliflower, thawed

½ cup unsweetened plain almond milk

2 tablespoons apple cider vinegar

2 tbsp extra-virgin olive oil

1 garlic clove, peeled

2 teaspoons finely chopped fresh parsley

2 teaspoons finely chopped scallions (both white and green parts)

1 teaspoon finely chopped fresh dill

½ teaspoon onion powder

½ teaspoon Dijon mustard

½ teaspoon salt

¼ teaspoon freshly ground black pepper

1. Place all the in a blender and pulse until creamy and smooth.
2. Serve immediately, or transfer to an airtight container to refrigerate for up to 3 days.

Per Serving (2 tablespoons)

calories: 41 | fat: 3.6g | protein: 1.0g | carbs: 1.9g | fiber: 1.1g | sodium: 148mg

Asian-Inspired Vinaigrette

Prep time: 5 minutes | Cook time: 0 minutes | Serves 2

¼ cup extra-virgin olive oil

3 tablespoons apple cider vinegar

1 garlic clove, minced

1 tablespoon peeled and grated fresh ginger

1 tablespoon chopped fresh cilantro

1 tablespoon freshly squeezed lime juice

½ teaspoon sriracha

1. Add all the in a small bowl and stir to mix well.
2. Serve immediately, or store covered in the refrigerator and shake before using.

Per Serving

calories: 251 | fat: 26.8g | protein: 0g | carbs: 1.8g | fiber: 0.7g | sodium: 3mg

Not Old Bay Seasoning

Prep time: 10 minutes | Cook time: 0 minutes | Makes about ½ cup

3 tablespoons sweet paprika

1 tablespoon mustard seeds

2 tablespoons celery seeds

2 teaspoons freshly ground black pepper

1½ teaspoons cayenne pepper

1 teaspoon red pepper flakes

½ teaspoon ground ginger

½ teaspoon ground nutmeg

½ teaspoon ground cinnamon

¼ teaspoon ground cloves

1. Mix together all the in an airtight container until well combined.
2. You can store it in a cool, dry, and dark place for up to 3 months.

Per Serving (1 tablespoon)

calories: 26 | fat: 1.9g | protein: 1.1g | carbs: 3.6g | fiber: 2.1g | sodium: 3mg

Tzatziki

Prep time: 15 minutes | Cook time: 0 minutes | Serves 4 to 6

½ English cucumber, finely chopped

1 teaspoon salt, divided

1 cup plain Greek yogurt

8 tablespoons olive oil, divided

1 garlic clove, finely minced

1 to 2 tablespoons chopped fresh dill

1 teaspoon red wine vinegar

½ teaspoon freshly ground black pepper

1. In a food processor, pulse the cucumber until puréed. Place the cucumber on several layers of paper towels lining the bottom of a colander and sprinkle with ½ teaspoon of salt. Allow to drain for 10 to 15 minutes. Using your hands, squeeze out any remaining liquid.
2. In a medium bowl, whisk together the cucumber, yogurt, 6 tablespoons of olive oil, garlic, dill, vinegar, remaining ½ teaspoon of salt, and pepper until very smooth.
3. Drizzle with the remaining 2 tablespoons of olive oil. Serve immediately or refrigerate until ready to serve.

Per Serving calories: 286 | fat: 29.0g | protein: 3.0g | carbs: 5.0g | fiber: 0g | sodium: 615mg

Harissa Sauce

Prep time: 10 minutes | Cook time: 20 minutes | Makes 3 to 4 cups

1 large red bell pepper, deseeded, cored, and cut into chunks	2 tablespoons tomato paste
1 yellow onion, cut into thick rings	1 tablespoon tamari
4 garlic cloves, peeled	1 teaspoon ground cumin
1 cup vegetable broth	1 tablespoon Hungarian paprika

1. Preheat the oven to 450°F (235°C). Line a baking sheet with parchment paper.
2. Place the bell pepper on the prepared baking sheet, flesh-side up, and space out the onion and garlic around the pepper.
3. Roast in the preheated oven for 20 minutes. Transfer to a blender.
4. Add the vegetable broth, tomato paste, tamari, cumin, and paprika. Purée until smooth. Served chilled or warm.

Per Serving (¼ cup)

calories: 15 | fat: 1.0g | protein: 1.0g | carbs: 3.0g | fiber: 1.0g | sodium: 201mg

Pineapple Salsa

Prep time: 10 minutes | Cook time: 0 minutes | Serves 6 to 8

1 pound (454 g) fresh or thawed frozen pineapple, finely diced, juices reserved	1 bunch cilantro or mint, leaves only, chopped
1 white or red onion, finely diced	1 jalapeño, minced (optional)
	Salt, to taste

1. Stir together the pineapple with its juice, onion, cilantro, and jalapeño (if desired) in a medium bowl. Season with salt to taste and serve.
2. The salsa can be refrigerated in an airtight container for up to 2 days.

Per Serving

calories: 55 | fat: 0.1g | protein: 0.9g | carbs: 12.7g | fiber: 1.8g | sodium: 20mg

Creamy Grapefruit and Tarragon Dressing

Prep time: 5 minutes | Cook time: 0 minutes | Serves 4 to 6

½ cup avocado oil mayonnaise	½ teaspoon salt
2 tablespoons Dijon mustard	Zest and juice of ½ grapefruit
1 teaspoon dried tarragon or 1 tablespoon chopped fresh tarragon	¼ teaspoon freshly ground black pepper
	1 to 2 tablespoons water (optional)

1. In a large mason jar with a lid, combine the mayonnaise, Dijon, tarragon, grapefruit zest and juice, salt, and pepper and whisk well with a fork until smooth and creamy. If a thinner dressing is preferred, thin out with water.
2. Serve immediately or refrigerate until ready to serve.

Per Serving

calories: 86 | fat: 7.0g | protein: 1.0g | carbs: 6.0g | fiber: 0g | sodium: 390mg

Vinaigrette

Prep time: 5 minutes | Cook time: 0 minutes | Makes 1 cup

½ cup extra-virgin olive oil	½ teaspoon salt
¼ cup red wine vinegar	½ teaspoon freshly ground black pepper
1 tablespoon Dijon mustard	
1 teaspoon dried rosemary	

1. In a cup or a mansion jar with a lid, combine the olive oil, vinegar, mustard, rosemary, salt, and pepper and shake until well combined.
2. Serve chilled or at room temperature.

Per Serving

calories: 124 | fat: 14.0g | protein: 0g | carbs: 1.0g | fiber: 0g | sodium: 170mg

Ginger Teriyaki Sauce

Prep time: 5 minutes | Cook time: 0 minutes | Serves 2

¼ cup pineapple juice	1 tablespoon grated fresh ginger
¼ cup low-sodium soy sauce	
2 tablespoons packed coconut sugar	1 tablespoon arrowroot powder or cornstarch
	1 teaspoon garlic powder

1. Whisk the pineapple juice, soy sauce, coconut sugar, ginger, arrowroot powder, and garlic powder together in a small bowl.
2. Store in an airtight container in the fridge for up to 5 days.

Per Serving

calories: 37 | fat: 0.1g | protein: 1.1g | carbs: 12.0g | fiber: 0g | sodium: 881mg

Aioli

Prep time: 5 minutes | Cook time: 0 minutes | Makes ½ cup

½ cup plain Greek yogurt	½ teaspoon hot sauce
2 teaspoons Dijon mustard	¼ teaspoon raw honey
	Pinch salt

1. In a small bowl, whisk together the yogurt, mustard, hot sauce, honey, and salt.
2. Serve immediately or refrigerate in an airtight container for up to 3 days.

Per Serving calories: 47 | fat: 2.5g | protein: 2.1g | carbs: 3.5g | fiber: 0g | sodium: 231mg

Parsley Vinaigrette

Prep time: 5 minutes | Cook time: 0 minutes | Makes about ½ cup

½ cup lightly packed fresh parsley, finely chopped	3 tablespoons red wine vinegar
⅓ cup extra-virgin olive oil	1 garlic clove, minced
	¼ teaspoon salt, plus additional as needed

1. Place all the in a mason jar and cover. Shake vigorously for 1 minute until completely mixed.
2. Taste and add additional salt as needed.
3. Serve immediately or serve chilled.

Per Serving (1 tablespoon)

calories: 92 | fat: 10.9g | protein: 0g | carbs: 0g | fiber: 0g | sodium: 75mg

Hot Pepper Sauce

Prep time: 10 minutes | Cook time: 20 minutes | Makes 4 cups

1 red hot fresh chiles, deseeded	½ small yellow onion, roughly chopped
2 dried chiles	2 cups water
2 garlic cloves, peeled	2 cups white vinegar

1. Place all the except the vinegar in a medium saucepan over medium heat. Allow to simmer for 20 minutes until softened. Transfer the mixture to a food processor or blender. Stir in the vinegar and pulse until very smooth. Serve immediately or transfer to a sealed container and refrigerate for up to 3 months.

Per Serving (2 tablespoons) calories: 20 | fat: 1.2g | protein: 0.6g | carbs: 4.4g | fiber: 0.6g | sodium: 12mg

Lemon-Tahini Sauce

Prep time: 10 minutes | Cook time: 0 minutes | Makes 1 cup

½ cup tahini	½ tbsp salt, plus more as needed
1 garlic clove, minced	½ cup warm water, plus more as needed
Juice and zest of 1 lemon	

1. Combine the tahini and garlic in a small bowl.
2. Add the lemon juice and zest and salt to the bowl and stir to mix well. Fold in the warm water and whisk until well combined and creamy. Feel free to add more warm water if you like a thinner consistency. Taste and add more salt as needed. Store the sauce in a sealed container in the refrigerator for up to 5 days.

Per Serving (¼ cup)
calories: 179 | fat: 15.5g | protein: 5.1g | carbs: 6.8g | fiber: 3.0g | sodium: 324mg

Peri-Peri Sauce

Prep time: 10 minutes | Cook time: 5 minutes | Serves 4

1 tomato, chopped	2 tablespoons extra-virgin olive oil
1 red onion, chopped	
1 red bell pepper, deseeded and chopped	Juice of 1 lemon
	1 tablespoon dried oregano
1 red chile, deseeded and chopped	1 tablespoon smoked paprika
4 garlic cloves, minced	1 teaspoon sea salt

1. Process all the in a food processor or a blender until smooth. Transfer the mixture to a small saucepan over medium-high heat and bring to a boil, stirring often.
2. Reduce the heat to medium and allow to simmer for 5 minutes until heated through. You can store the sauce in an airtight container in the refrigerator for up to 5 days.

Per Serving calories: 98 | fat: 6.5g | protein: 1.0g | carbs: 7.8g | fiber: 3.0g | sodium: 295mg

Garlic Lemon-Tahini Dressing

Prep time: 5 minutes | Cook time: 0 minutes | Serves 8 to 10

½ cup tahini	1 garlic clove, finely minced
¼ cup extra-virgin olive oil	¼ cup freshly squeezed lemon juice
2 teaspoons salt	

1. In a glass mason jar with a lid, combine the tahini, olive oil, lemon juice, garlic, and salt. Cover and shake well until combined and creamy.
2. Store in the refrigerator for up to 2 weeks.

Per Serving
calories: 121 | fat: 12.0g | protein: 2.0g | carbs: 3.0g | fiber: 1.0g | sodium: 479mg

Peanut Sauce with Honey

Prep time: 5 minutes | Cook time: 0 minutes | Serves 4

¼ cup peanut butter	1 tablespoon low-sodium soy sauce
1 tablespoon peeled and grated fresh ginger	1 garlic clove, minced
1 tablespoon honey	Juice of 1 lime
	Pinch red pepper flakes

1. Whisk together all the in a small bowl until well incorporated. Transfer to an airtight container and refrigerate for up to 5 days.

Per Serving calories: 117 | fat: 7.6g | protein: 4.1g | carbs: 8.8g | fiber: 1.0g | sodium: 136mg

Cilantro-Tomato Salsa

Prep time: 10 minutes | Cook time: 0 minutes | Serves 6

2 or 3 medium, ripe tomatoes, diced	¼ cup minced fresh cilantro
	Juice of 1 lime
1 serrano pepper, seeded and minced	¼ teaspoon salt, plus more as needed
½ red onion, minced	

1. Place the tomatoes, serrano pepper, onion, cilantro, lime juice, and salt in a small bowl and mix well. Taste and add additional salt, if needed. Store in an airtight container in the refrigerator for up to 3 days.

Per Serving (¼ cup) calories: 17 | fat: 0g | protein: 1.0g | carbs: 3.9g | fiber: 1.0g | sodium: 83mg

Cheesy Pea Pesto

Prep time: 5 minutes | Cook time: 0 minutes | Serves 4

½ cup fresh green peas	¼ cup pine nuts
½ cup grated Parmesan cheese	¼ cup fresh basil leaves
	2 garlic cloves, minced
¼ cup extra-virgin olive oil	¼ teaspoon sea salt

1. Add all the to a food processor or blender and pulse until the nuts are chopped finely.
2. Transfer to an airtight container and refrigerate for up to 2 days. You can also store it in ice cube trays in the freezer for up to 6 months.

Per Serving calories: 247 | fat: 22.8g | protein: 7.1g | carbs: 4.8g | fiber: 1.0g | sodium: 337mg

Guacamole

Prep time: 10 minutes | Cook time: 0 minutes | Serves 6

2 large avocados	2 tablespoons freshly squeezed lime juice
¼ white onion, finely diced	
1 small, firm tomato, finely diced	¼ teaspoon salt
¼ cup finely chopped fresh cilantro	Freshly ground black pepper, to taste

1. Slice the avocados in half and remove the pits. Using a large spoon to scoop out the flesh and add to a medium bowl.
2. Mash the avocado flesh with the back of a fork, or until a uniform consistency is achieved. Add the onion, tomato, cilantro, lime juice, salt, and pepper to the bowl and stir to combine.
3. Serve immediately, or transfer to an airtight container and refrigerate until chilled.

Per Serving (¼ cup)
calories: 81 | fat: 6.8g | protein: 1.1g | carbs: 5.7g | fiber: 3.0g | sodium: 83mg

Lemon-Dill Cashew Dip

Prep time: 10 minutes | Cook time: 0 minutes | Makes 1 cup

¾ cup cashews, soaked in water for at least 4 hours and drained well	Juice and zest of 1 lemon
	2 tbsp chopped fresh dill
	¼ teaspoon salt, plus more as needed
¼ cup water	

1. Put the cashews, water, lemon juice and zest in a blender and blend until smooth.
2. Add the dill and salt to the blender and blend again.
3. Taste and adjust the seasoning, if needed.
4. Transfer to an airtight container and refrigerate for at least 1 hour to blend the flavors. Serve chilled.

Per Serving (1 tablespoon)

calories: 37 | fat: 2.9g | protein: 1.1g | carbs: 1.9g | fiber: 0g | sodium: 36mg

Homemade Blackened Seasoning

Prep time: 10 minutes | Cook time: 0 minutes | Makes about ½ cup

2 tablespoons smoked paprika	1 teaspoon dried dill
2 tablespoons garlic powder	1 teaspoon freshly ground black pepper
2 tablespoons onion powder	½ tbsp ground mustard
1 tablespoon sweet paprika	¼ teaspoon celery seeds

1. Add all the to a small bowl and mix well.
2. Serve immediately, or transfer to an airtight container and store in a cool, dry and dark place for up to 3 months.

Per Serving (1 tablespoon)

calories: 22 | fat: 0.9g | protein: 1.0g | carbs: 4.7g | fiber: 1.0g | sodium: 2mg

Basil Pesto

Prep time: 5 minutes | Cook time: 0 minutes | Makes 1 cup

2 cups packed fresh basil leaves	⅓ cup pine nuts
3 garlic cloves, peeled	Kosher salt and freshly ground black pepper, to taste
½ cup freshly grated Parmesan cheese	
½ cup extra-virgin olive oil	

1. Place all the , except for the salt and pepper, in a food processor. Pulse a few times until smoothly pur é ed. Season with salt and pepper to taste.
2. Store in an airtight container in the fridge for up to 2 weeks.

Per Serving

calories: 100 | fat: 10.2g | protein: 2.2g | carbs: 1.2g | fiber: 0g | sodium: 72mg

Orange-Garlic Dressing

Prep time: 5 minutes | Cook time: 0 minutes | Serves 2

¼ cup extra-virgin olive oil	1 teaspoon garlic powder
1 orange, zested	½ teaspoon salt
2 tablespoons freshly squeezed orange juice	¼ teaspoon Dijon mustard
¾ teaspoon za'atar seasoning	Freshly ground black pepper, to taste

1.Whisk together all in a bowl until well combined. Serve immediately or refrigerate until ready to serve.

Per Serving calories: 287 | fat: 26.7g | protein: 1.2g | carbs: 12.0g | fiber: 2.1g | sodium: 592mg

Creamy Cider Yogurt Dressing

Prep time: 5 minutes | Cook time: 0 minutes | Serves 2

1 cup plain, unsweetened, full-fat Greek yogurt	½ teaspoon dried parsley
½ cup extra-virgin olive oil	½ teaspoon kosher salt
½ lemon, juiced	¼ teaspoon garlic powder
1 tablespoon chopped fresh oregano	¼ teaspoon freshly ground black pepper
1 tablespoon apple cider vinegar	

1. In a large bowl, whisk all to combine.
2. Serve chilled or at room temperature.

Per Serving calories: 407 | fat: 40.7g | protein: 8.3g | carbs: 3.8g | fiber: 0.5g | sodium: 382mg

Lentil-Tahini Dip

Prep time: 10 minutes | Cook time: 15 minutes | Makes 3 cups

1 cup dried green or brown lentils, rinsed	⅓ cup tahini
	1 garlic clove
2½ cups water, divided	½ teaspoon salt, plus more as needed

1. Add the lentils and 2 cups of water to a medium saucepan and bring to a boil over high heat.
2. Once it starts to boil, reduce the heat to low, and then cook for 14 minutes, stirring occasionally, or the lentils become tender but still hold their shape. You can drain any excess liquid.
3. Transfer the lentils to a food processor, along with the remaining water, tahini, garlic, and salt and process until smooth and creamy.
4. Taste and adjust the seasoning if needed. Serve immediately.

Per Serving (¼ cup)

calories: 100 | fat: 3.9g | protein: 5.1g | carbs: 10.7g | fiber: 6.0g | sodium: 106mg

Basic French Vinaigrette

Prep time: 5 minutes | Cook time: 0 minutes | Serves 2

3 tablespoons apple cider vinegar	½ teaspoon dried thyme
2 tablespoons minced shallot (or 1 tablespoon minced red onion)	1 teaspoon Dijon mustard
	¼ cup olive oil
1 tablespoon balsamic vinegar	Salt and black pepper, to taste

1. Stir together the apple cider vinegar, shallot, and balsamic vinegar in a medium jar with a tight-fitting lid. Allow to sit for 5 minutes.
2. Stir in the mustard and thyme. Whisk in the olive oil in a slow, steady stream and season to taste with salt and pepper.
3. Store in an airtight container in the fridge for up to 5 days.

Per Serving

calories: 256 | fat: 27.1g | protein: 0.3g | carbs: 3.4g | fiber: 0.4g | sodium: 207mg

.Cranberry and Pistachio Biscotti (Italian)

Prep time: 15 minutes Cooking time: 35 minutes Servings: 36

¼ cup light olive oil	¾ cup white sugar
1tsps. vanilla extract	½ tsp. almond extract 2 eggs
1 ¾ cup all-purpose flour	¼ tsp. salt
1 tsp. baking powder	½ cup dried cranberries 1 ½ cup pistachio nuts

1. Preheat the oven to 150°C.
2. Combine the oil and sugar in a large bowl until a homogeneous mixture is obtained. Stir in the vanilla and almond extract and add the eggs. Combine the flour, salt, and baking powder; gradually add to the egg mixture— mix the cranberries and nuts by hand.
3. Divide the dough in half—form 2 12x2-inch logs on a parchment baking sheet. The dough can be sticky, wet hands with cold water to make it easier to handle the dough.
4. Bake in the preheated oven for 35 minutes or until the blocks are golden brown. Pull out from the oven and let cool for 10 minutes. Then, reduce the oven heat to 275°F (135ºC).
5. Cut diagonally into ¾ inch-thick slices. Place on the sides of the baking sheet covered with parchment bake for 8 10 minutes.

Nutrition: Calories: 92 Fat: 4.3 g. Protein: 2.1 g.

.Rhubarb Strawberry Crunch (Greek)

Prep time: 15 minutes Cooking time: 45 minutes Servings: 18

1 cup of white sugar	3 tbsps. all-purpose flour
3 cups fresh strawberries, sliced 3 cups rhubarb, cut into cubes	1 ½ cup flour
1 cup packed brown sugar 1 cup butter	1 cup oatmeal

1. Preheat the oven to 190°C.
2. Combine the white sugar, 3 tbsps. of flour, strawberries, and rhubarb in a large bowl.
3. Place the mixture in a 9x13-inch baking dish.
4. Mix 1 ½ cups of flour, brown sugar, butter, and oats until a crumbly texture is obtained. You may want to use a blender for this.
5. Crumble the mixture of rhubarb and strawberry.
6. Bake for 45 minutes.

Nutrition: Calories: 253 Fat: 10.8 g. Protein: 2.3 g.

.Vanilla Cream (Italian)

Preparation time: 2 hours Cooking time: 10 minutes Servings: 4

1 cup almond milk	1cup coconut cream 2 cups coconut sugar
2tbsps. cinnamon powder 1 tsp. vanilla extract	

1. Heat a pan with the almond milk over medium heat, add the rest of the , whisk, and cook for 10 minutes more.
2. Divide the mix into bowls, cool down, and keep in the fridge for 2 hours before serving.

Nutrition: Calories: 254 Fat: 7.5 g. Protein: 9.5 g.

.Cocoa Almond Pudding (Spanish)

Preparation time: 10 minutes Cooking time: 10 minutes Servings: 4

2 tbsps. coconut sugar 3 tbsps. coconut flour 2 tbsps. cocoa powder 2 cups almond milk	2eggs, whisked
½ tsp. vanilla extract	

1. Fill the milk in a pan, add the cocoa and the other, whisk, simmer over medium heat for 10 minutes, pour into small cups, and serve cold.

Nutrition: Calories: 385 Fat: 31.7 g. Protein: 7.3 g.

.Nutmeg Cream (Greek)

Preparation time: 10 minutes Cooking time: 0 minutes Servings: 6

2cups almond milk	1 tsp. nutmeg, ground 2 tsps. vanilla extract 4 tsps. coconut sugar
1cup walnuts, chopped	

1. In a bowl, combine the milk with the nutmeg and the other, whisk well, divide into small cups and serve cold.

Nutrition: Calories: 243 Fat: 12.4 g. Protein: 9.7 g.

.Vanilla Avocado Cream (Greek)

Preparation time: 70 minutes Cooking time: 0 minutes Servings: 4

1cups coconut cream	2 avocados, peeled, pitted, and mashed 2 tbsps. coconut sugar
1tsp. vanilla extract	

1. Blend the cream with the avocados and the other , pulse well, divide into cups and keep in the fridge for 1 hour before serving.

Nutrition: Calories: 532 Fat: 48.2 g. Protein: 5.2 g.

.Ice Cream Sandwich Dessert (Italian)

Prep time: 20 minutesCooking time: 0 minute Servings: 12

22 ice cream sandwiches	16 oz. container frozen whipped topping, thawed 1 (12 oz.) jar caramel ice cream
1½ cups salted peanuts	

1. Cut a sandwich with ice in 2. Place a whole sandwich and a half sandwich on a short side of a 9x13-inch baking dish. Repeat this until the bottom is covered. Alternate the full sandwich, and the half sandwich.
2. Spread half of the whipped topping. Pour the caramel over it. Sprinkle with half the peanuts. Do layers with the rest of the ice cream sandwiches, whipped cream, and peanuts.
3. Cover and freeze for up to 2 months. Remove from the freezer 20 minutes before serving. Cut into squares.

Nutrition: Calories: 559 Fat: 28.8 g. Protein: 10 g.

.Chocolate Matcha Balls (Greek)

Preparation Time: 10 minutes Cooking Time: 5 minutes
Servings: 15

1tbsp unsweetened cocoa powder 3 tbsp oats, gluten-free	½ cup pine nuts
½ cup almonds	1cup dates, pitted
2tbsp matcha powder	

1. Add oats, pine nuts, almonds, and dates into a food processor and process until well combined.
2. Place matcha powder in a small dish.
3. Make small balls from mixture and coat with matcha powder.
4. Enjoy or store in refrigerator until ready to eat.

Nutrition: Calories 88, Fat 4.9g, Carbohydrates 11.3g, Sugar 7.8g, Protein 1.9g, Cholesterol 0mg

.Blueberries Bowls (Greek)

Preparation time: 10 minutes Cooking time: 0 minutes
Servings: 4

1 tsp. vanilla extract 2 cups blueberries	1 tsp. coconut sugar 8 oz. Greek yogurt

1. Mix strawberries with the vanilla and the other , toss and serve cold.

Nutrition: Calories: 343 Fat: 13.4 g. Protein: 5.5 g.

Brownies (Greek)

Preparation time: 10 minutes Cooking time: 25 minutes
Servings: 8

1 cup pecans, chopped 3 tbsps. coconut sugar 2 tbsps. cocoa powder 3 eggs, whisked	cup avocado oil
½ tsp. baking powder 2 tsps. vanilla extract Cooking spray	

1. In your food processor, combine the pecans with the coconut sugar and the other except for the cooking spray and pulse well.
2. Grease a square pan with the cooking spray, add the brownies mix, spread, introduce in the oven, bake at 350°F for 25 minutes, leave aside to cool down, slice, and serve.

Nutrition: Calories: 370 Fat: 14.3 g. Protein: 5.6 g.

.Raspberries Cream Cheese Bowls (Italian)

Preparation time: 10 minutes Cooking time: 25 minutes
Servings: 4

1tbsps. almond flour 1 cup coconut cream 3 cups raspberries	1 cup coconut sugar 8 oz. cream cheese

1. In a bowl, the flour with the cream and the other , whisk, transfer to a round pan, cook at 360°F for 25 minutes, divide into bowls and serve.

Nutrition: Calories: 429 Fat: 36.3 g. Protein: 7.8 g.

.Minty Coconut Cream (Spanish)

Preparation Time: 4 minutes Cooking Time: 0 minutes
Servings: 2

1banana, peeled	2cups coconut flesh, shredded 3 tablespoons mint, chopped
1and ½ cups coconut water 2 tablespoons stevia	½ avocado, pitted and peeled

1. In a blender, combine the coconut with the banana and the rest of the , pulse well, divide into cups and serve cold.

Nutrition: Calories 193; Fat 5.4 g; Fiber 3.4 g; Carbs 7.6 g; Protein 3 g

.Almond Honey Ricotta Spread (Greek)

Preparation time: 7 minutes Cooking time: 0 minutes Servings: 3

½ cup whole milk Ricotta	¼ cup orange zest
¼ cup almonds, sliced 1/8 tsp. almond extract	½ tsp. honey
1Peaches, sliced Hone to drizzle Bread of your choice	

1. Take a medium bowl, and combine the almonds, almond extract, and Ricotta.
2. Once you have stirred it well, place it in a bowl to serve.
3. Sprinkle with the sliced almonds and drizzle some honey on the Ricotta.
4. Extent 1 tbsp. the spread to your choice of bread, top it with some honey and sliced peaches.

Nutrition: Calories: 199 Protein: 8.5 g. Fat: 12 g.

.Apricot Energy Bites (Greek)

Prep time: 16 minutes Cooking time: 0 minute Servings: 10

1cup unsalted raw cashew nuts	¼ tsp. ground ginger
½ cup dried apricots	2¾ tbsp. unsweetened coconut, shredded 2 tbsps. dates, chopped
1 tsp. orange zest 1 tsp. lemon zest	¼ tsp. cinnamon Salt to taste

1. Grind the apricots, coconut, dates, and cashew nuts in a food processor.
2. Pulse until a crumbly mixture has formed.
3. Add the spices, salt, and citrus zest to the mixture.
4. Pulse it again to mix well.
5. Process the batter on HIGH till it sticks together.
6. Take a dish or a tray and line it with parchment paper.
7. Shape the balls in your palm, make around 20 balls.
8. Keep in the refrigerator. Serve as needed.

Nutrition: Calories: 102 Protein: 2 g. Fat: 6 g.

.Cranberry Orange Cookies (Italian)

Preparation time: 20 minutes Cooking time: 16 minutes
Servings: 24

1 cup soft butter 1 cup white sugar	½ cup brown sugar 1 egg
1tsp. orange peel, grated 2 tbsps. orange juice	2½ cups flour
½ tsp. baking powder	½ tsp. salt
2 cups cranberries, chopped	½ cup walnuts, chopped (optional) For the icing:
½ tsp. orange peel, grated 3 tbsps. orange juice	1½ cup confectioner's sugar

1. Preheat the oven to 190°C.
2. Blend the butter, white sugar, and brown sugar. Beat the egg until everything is well mixed. Mix 1 tsp. orange zest and 2 tbsps. of orange juice. Mix the flour, baking powder, and salt; stir in the orange mixture.
3. Mix the cranberries and, if used, the nuts until well distributed. Place the dough with a spoon on ungreased baking trays.
4. Bake in the preheated oven for 12–14 minutes. Cool on racks.
5. In a small bowl, mix icing . Spread over cooled cookies.

Nutrition: Calories: 110 Fat: 4.8 g. Protein: 1.1 g.

.Rhubarb Cream (Greek)

Preparation time: 10 minutes Cooking time: 14 minutes
Servings: 4

1/3 cup cream cheese	½ cup coconut cream
1lbs. rhubarb, roughly chopped 3 tbsps. coconut sugar	

1. Blend the cream cheese with the cream and the other well.
2. Divide into small cups, introduce in the oven, and bake at 350°F for 14 minutes.
3. Serve cold.

Nutrition: Calories: 360 Fat: 14.3 g. Protein: 5.2 g.

.Dipped Sprouts (Italian)

Preparation time: 12 minutes Cooking time: 10 minutes
Servings: 2

16 oz. Brussels sprouts 4 tbsps. honey	6 tbsps. raisins and nuts, crushed

1. Boil water in a pot.
2. Add the sprouts, and cook for 10 minutes until soft.
3. Glaze the sprouts in the honey and coat well. Add the nuts and raisins.

Nutrition: Calories: 221 Fat: 15.1 g. Protein: 5.3 g.

.Healthy & Quick Energy Bites (Italian)

Preparation Time: 10 minutes Cooking Time: 0 minutes
Servings: 20

2 cups cashew nuts	¼ tsp cinnamon 1 tsp lemon zest
4 tbsp dates, chopped	1/3 cup unsweetened shredded coconut
¾ cup dried apricots	

1. Line baking tray with parchment paper and set aside.
2. Add all in a food processor and process until the mixture is crumbly and well combined.
3. Make small balls from mixture and place on a prepared baking tray.
4. Serve and enjoy.

Nutrition: Calories 100, Fat 7.5g, Carbohydrates 7.2g, Sugar 2.8g, Protein 2.4g, Cholesterol 0mg

.Creamy Yogurt Banana Bowls (Greek)

Preparation Time: 10 minutes Cooking Time: 0 minutes
Servings: 4

2 bananas, sliced	½ tsp ground nutmeg 3 tbsp flaxseed meal
¼ cup creamy peanut butter	
4 cups Greek yogurt	

1. Divide Greek yogurt between 4 serving bowls and top with sliced bananas.
2. Add peanut butter in microwave-safe bowl and microwave for 30 seconds.
3. Drizzle 1 tablespoon of melted peanut butter on each bowl on top of the sliced bananas.
4. Sprinkle cinnamon and flax meal on top and serve.

Nutrition: Calories 351, Fat 13.1g, Carbohydrates 35.6g, Sugar 26.1g, Protein 19.6g, Cholesterol 15mg

.Watermelon Cream (Italian)

Preparation Time: 15 minutes Cooking Time: 0 minutes
Servings: 2

1-pound watermelon, peeled and chopped 1 teaspoon vanilla extract	1 cup heavy cream 1 teaspoon lime juice 2 tablespoons stevia

1. In a blender, combine the watermelon with the cream and the rest of the , pulse well, divide into cups and keep in the fridge for 15 minutes before serving.

Nutrition: Calories 122; Fat 5.7 g; Fiber 3.2 g; Carbs 5.3 g; Protein 0.4 g

.Mango Bowls (Spanish)

Prep time: 10 minutes Cooking time: 0 minutes Servings: 4

2cups mango, peeled & cubed 1 tsp. chia seeds	1 cup coconut cream 1 tsp. vanilla extract 1 tbsp. mint, chopped

1. Mix the mango with the cream and the other , toss, divide into smaller bowls and keep in the fridge for 10 minutes before serving.

Nutrition: Calories: 238 Fat: 16.6 g. Protein: 3.3 g.

.Chocolate Mousse (Greek)

Prep Time: 10 minutes Cooking Time: 6 minutes Servings: 5

4 egg yolks	½ tsp vanilla
½ cup unsweetened almond milk 1 cup whipping cream	¼ cup cocoa powder
¼ cup water	½ cup Swerve 1/8 tsp salt

1. Add egg yolks to a large bowl and whisk until well beaten.
2. In a sauccpan, add swerve, cocoa powder, and water and whisk until well combined.
3. Add almond milk and cream to the saucepan and whisk until well mix.
4. Once saucepan mixtures are heated up then turn off the heat.
5. Add vanilla and salt and stir well.
6. Add a tablespoon of chocolate mixture into the eggs and whisk until well combined.
7. Slowly pour remaining chocolate to the eggs and whisk until well combined.
8. Pour batter into the ramekins.
9. Pour 1 ½ cups of water into the instant pot then place a trivet in the pot.
10. Place ramekins on a trivet.
11. Seal pot with lid and select manual and set timer for 6 minutes.
12. Release pressure using quick release method than open the lid.
13. Carefully remove ramekins from the instant pot and let them cool completely.
14. Serve and enjoy.

Nutrition: Calories 128, Fat 11.9g, Carbohydrates 4g, Sugar 0.2g, Protein 3.6g, Cholesterol 194mg

.Pistachio Balls (Italian)

Preparation Time: 10 minutes Cooking Time: 5 minutes Servings: 16

½ cup pistachios, unsalted 1 cup dates, pitted	½ tsp ground fennel seeds
½ cup raisins Pinch of pepper	

1. Add all into the food processor and process until well combined.
2. Make small balls and place onto the baking tray.
3. Serve and enjoy.

Nutrition: Calories 55, Fat 0.9g, Carbohydrates 12.5g, Sugar 9.9g, Protein 0.8g, Cholesterol 0mg

.Chocolate Covered Strawberries (Greek)

Preparation time: 15 minutes Cooking time: 0 minute Servings: 24

16 oz. milk chocolate chips 2 tbsps. shortening	1 lb. fresh strawberries with leaves

1. In a bain-marie, melt the chocolate and shortening, occasionally stirring until smooth. Pierce the tops of the strawberries with toothpicks and immerse them in the chocolate mixture.
2. Turn the strawberries and put the toothpick in Styrofoam so that the chocolate cools.

Nutrition: Calories: 115 Fat: 7.3 g. Protein: 1.4 g.

.Almonds and Oats Pudding (Greek)

Preparation Time: 10 minutes Cooking Time: 15 minutes Servings: 4

1 tablespoon lemon juice	1 and ½ cups almond milk 1
Zest of 1 lime	teaspoon almond extract
½ cup oats	2 tablespoons stevia
½ cup silver almonds, chopped	

1. In a pan, combine the almond milk with the lime zest and the other , whisk, bring to a simmer and cook over medium heat for 15 minutes.
2. Divide the mix into bowls and serve cold.

Nutrition: Calories 174 Fat 12.1 Fiber 3.2 Carbs 3.9 Protein 4.8

.Chocolate Cups (Greek)

Preparation Time: 2 hours Cooking Time: 0 minutes Servings: 6

½ cup avocado oil	1 cup, chocolate, melted
1 teaspoon matcha powder 3 tablespoons stevia	

1. In a bowl, mix the chocolate with the oil and the rest of the , whisk really well, divide into cups and keep in the freezer for 2 hours before serving.

Nutrition: Calories 174 Fat 9.1 Fiber 2.2 Carbs 3.9 Protein 2.8

.Peach Sorbet (Spanish)

Preparation Time: 2 hours Cooking Time: 10 minutes Servings: 4

2 cups apple juice 1 cup stevia	2 tablespoons lemon zest, grated
2 pounds peaches, pitted and quartered	

1. Heat up a pan over medium heat, add the apple juice and the rest of the , simmer for 10 minutes, transfer to a blender, pulse, divide into cups and keep in the freezer for 2 hours before serving.

Nutrition: Calories 182; Fat 5.4 g; Fiber 3.4 g; Carbs 12 g; Protein 5.4 g

.Cranberries and Pears Pie (Italian)

Preparation Time: 10 minutes Cooking Time: 40 minutes Servings: 4

1 cup cranberries	2 cups pears, cubed A
1 cup rolled oats	drizzle of olive oil 1 cup stevia
1/3 cup almond flour	¼ avocado oil

1. In a bowl, mix the cranberries with the pears and the other except the olive oil and the oats, and stir well.
2. Grease a cake pan with a drizzle of olive oil, pour the pears mix inside, sprinkle the oats all over and bake at 350° F for 40 minutes.
3. Cool the mix down, and serve.

Nutrition: Calories 172; Fat 3.4 g; Fiber 4.3 g; Carbs 11.5 g; Protein 4.5 g

.Chia and Berries Smoothie Bowl (Spanish)

Preparation Time: 5 minutes Cooking Time: 0 minutes
Servings: 2

1 and ½ cup almond milk 1 cup blackberries	¼ cup strawberries, chopped
1 and ½ tablespoons chia seeds 1 teaspoon cinnamon powder	

1. In a blender, combine the blackberries with the strawberries and the rest of the , pulse well, divide into small bowls and serve cold.

Nutrition: Calories 182; Fat 3.4 g; Fiber 3.4 g; Carbs 8 g; Protein 3 g

.Jasmine Rice Pudding with Cranberries (Greek)

Preparation Time: 5 minutes Cooking Time: 15 minutes
Servings 4

1 cup apple juice	1 heaping tablespoon honey 1/3 cup granulated sugar
1 ½ cups jasmine rice 1 cup water	1/4 teaspoon ground cinnamon 1/4 teaspoon ground cloves
1/3 teaspoon ground cardamom 1 teaspoon vanilla extract	3 eggs, well-beaten 1/2 cup cranberries

1. Thoroughly combine the apple juice, honey, sugar, jasmine rice, water, and spices in the inner pot of your Instant Pot.
2. Secure the lid. Choose the "Manual" mode and cook for 4 minutes at High pressure. Once cooking is complete, use a natural pressure release for 5 minutes; carefully remove the lid.
3. Press the "Sauté" button and fold in the eggs. Cook on "Less" mode until heated through.
4. Ladle into individual bowls and top with dried cranberries. Enjoy!

Nutrition:402 Calories; 3.6g Fat; 81.1g Carbs; 8.9g Protein; 22.3g Sugars; 2.2g Fiber

.Apple Couscous Pudding (Greek)

Prep Time: 10 minutes Cooking Time: 25 minutes Servings: 4

½ cup couscous	½ cups milk
¼ cup apple, cored and chopped 1 tbsp. stevia	½ tsp. rose water
1 tbsp. orange zest, grated	

1. Heat up a pan with the milk over medium heat, add the couscous and the rest of the , whisk, simmer for 25 minutes, divide into bowls and serve.

Nutrition: Calories 150, Fat: 4.5g, Fiber: 5.5g, Carbs: 7.5g, Protein: 4g

.Orange and Almond Cupcakes (Greek)

Preparation Time: 5 minutes Cooking Time: 20 minutes
Servings: 9

Cupcakes:	1orange extract
2tablespoons olive oil	2 tablespoons ghee, at room temperature 3 eggs, beaten
2 ounces Greek yogurt 2 cups cake flour	A pinch of salt
1tablespoon grated orange rind 1/2 cup brown sugar 2ounces cream cheese	1/2 cup almonds, chopped Cream Cheese Frosting: 1 tablespoon whipping cream
1/2 cup butter, at room temperature 1 ½ cups confectioners' sugar, sifted 1/3 teaspoon vanilla	A pinch of salt

1. Mix the orange extract, olive oil, ghee, eggs, and Greek yogurt until well combined.
2. Thoroughly combine the cake flour, salt, orange rind, and brown sugar in a separate mixing bowl. Add the egg/yogurt mixture to the flour mixture. Stir in the chopped almonds and mix again.
3. Place parchment baking liners on the bottom of a muffin tin. Pour the batter into the muffin tin.
4. Place 1 cup of water and metal trivet in the inner pot of your Instant Pot. Lower the prepared muffin tin onto the trivet.
5. Secure the lid. Choose the "Manual" mode and cook for 11 minutes at High pressure. Once cooking is complete, use a quick pressure release; carefully remove the lid. Transfer to wire racks.
6. Meanwhile, make the frosting by mixing all until creamy. Frost your cupcakes and enjoy!

Nutrition:392 Calories; 18.7g Fat; 50.1g Carbohydrates; 5.9g Protein; 25.2g Sugars; 0.7g Fiber

.Strawberry Angel Food Dessert (Italian)

Preparation time: 15 minutes Cooking time: 0 minutes
Servings: 18

1angel cake (10-inch)	2packages softened cream cheese 1 cup of white sugar
1 (8 oz.) container frozen fluff, thawed 1 l. fresh strawberries, sliced	1 jar strawberry icing

1. Crumble the cake in a 9x13-inch dish.
2. Beat the cream cheese and sugar in a medium bowl until the mixture is light and fluffy. Stir in the whipped topping. Crush the cake with your hands, and spread the cream cheese mixture over the cake.
3. Combine the strawberries and the frosting in a bowl until the strawberries are well covered. Spread over the layer of cream cheese. Cool until ready to serve.

Nutrition: Calories: 261 Fat: 11 g. Protein: 3.2 g.

.Hazelnut Cookies (Greek)

Preparation time: 8 minutes Cooking time: 21 minutes
Servings: 5

1 ¼ cups hazelnut meal 6 tbsps. flour	1tbsp. brown sugar
2tbsps. powdered sugar	½ tsp. kosher salt
½ lemon zest	½ lemon juice
½ tsp. vanilla	¼ cup extra-virgin olive oil

1. Heat the oven at 375ºF.
2. Take a bowl, add the hazelnut meal, brown sugar, flour, half of the powdered sugar, lemon zest, and salt. Next, whisk it well.
3. Whisk the olive oil and vanilla.
4. Once the dough is crumbly, shape them into cookies and line them on the baking sheet.
5. Bake it until the edges are lightly brown, for 20 minutes.
6. Take it out on a cooling rack. Let it sit to cool.
7. Meanwhile, take a small bowl, add the lemon juice and the remaining powdered sugar.
8. Drizzle the syrup over the cookies before serving.

Nutrition: Calories: 276 Protein: 3.6 g. Fat: 21.2 g.

.Fruit Pizza (Italian)

Preparation time: 30 minutes Cooking time: 0 minute
Servings: 8

1 (18 oz.) package sugar cookie dough	1(8 oz.) package cream cheese, softened 1 (8 oz.) frozen filling, defrosted
2cups freshly cut strawberries or another fruit of your preference	½ cup of white sugar 1 pinch of salt
1tbsp. corn flour	2tbsps. lemon juice
½ cup orange juice	¼ cup water
½ tsp. orange zest	

1. Preheat the oven to 175°C. Slice the cookie dough, then place it on a greased pizza pan. Press the dough flat into the mold. Bake for 10–12 minutes. Let it cool.
2. Soften the cream cheese in a large bowl and then stir in the whipped topping. Spread over the cooled crust.
3. Start with strawberries cut in half. Place them in a circle around the outer edge. Continue with the fruit of your choice by going to the center. If you use bananas, immerse them in lemon juice. Then make a sauce with a spoon on the fruit.
4. Combine the sugar, salt, corn flour, orange juice, lemon juice, and water in a pan. Boil and stir over medium heat. Boil for 1–2 minutes until thick. Remove from heat and add the grated orange zest. Place on the fruit.
5. Allow it to cool for 2 hours, cut into quarters, and serve.

Nutrition: Calories: 535 Fat: 30 g. Protein: 5.5 g.

.Good Sweet (Italian)

Preparation time: 10 minutes Cooking time: 10 minutes
Servings: 2

¼ tsp. tomatoes, chopped	¼ tsp. cucumber, chopped 2 tbsps. honey
Other veggies/beans (optional)	

1. Whisk all the well except for the honey.
2. In a bowl, toss to coat with honey as smoothly as possible.

Nutrition: Calories: 187 Fat: 15.6 g. Protein: 2 g.

.Bananas Foster (Greek)

Prep time: 5 minutes Cooking time: 6 minutes Servings: 4

2/3 cup dark brown sugar	¼ cup butter 3 ½ tbsp. rum
1 ½ tsp. vanilla extract	½ tsp. ground cinnamon
3 bananas, peeled and cut lengthwise and broad	¼ cup nuts, coarsely chopped Vanilla ice cream

1. Melt the butter in a deep-frying pan over medium heat. Stir in the sugar, rum, vanilla, and cinnamon.
2. When the mixture starts to bubble, place the bananas and nuts in the pan. Bake until the bananas are hot, 1–2 minutes. Serve immediately with vanilla ice cream.

Nutrition: Calories: 534 Fat: 23.8 g. Protein: 4.6 g.

.A Taste of Dessert (Italian)

Preparation time: 15 minutes
Cooking time: 0 minutes Servings: 2

1 tbsp. cilantro	1 tbsp. green onion
1 mango, peeled, seeded, and chopped	¼ cup bell pepper, chopped 2 tbsps. honey

1. Incorporate all.
2. Serve when all of them are well combined.

Nutrition: Calories: 21 Fat: 0.1 g. Protein: 0.3 g.

.Honey Carrots

Preparation time: 5 minutes Cooking time: 15 minutes
Servings: 2

16 oz. baby carrots	¼ cup brown sugar

1. Boil carrots with water in a large pot.
2. Drain after 15 minutes, and steam for 2 minutes.
3. Stir in the sugar, and serve when mixed well.

Nutrition: Calories: 402 Fat: 23.3 g. Protein: 1.4 g.

.Fresh Cherry Treat (Greek)

Preparation time: 10 minutes Cooking time: 10 minutes
Servings: 2

1 tbsp. honey	1 tbsp. almonds, crushed 12 oz. cherries

1. Preheat the oven to 350ºF, and bake the cherries for 5 minutes.
2. Coat them with the honey, and serve with almonds on top.

Nutrition: Calories: 448 Fat: 36.4 g. Protein: 3.5 g.

.Key Lime Pie (Italian)

Preparation time: 15 minutes Cooking time: 8 minutes
Servings: 8

1 (9-inch) Prepared Graham Cracker crust 3 cups sweetened condensed milk	½ cup sour cream
¾ cup lime juice	1tbsp. lime zest, grated

1. Preheat the oven to 175°C.
2. Combine the condensed milk, sour cream, lime juice, and lime zest in a medium bowl. Mix well and pour into the graham cracker crust.
3. Bake in the preheated oven for 5–8 minutes.
4. Cool the cake well before serving. Decorate with lime slices and whipped cream if desired.

Nutrition: Calories: 553 Fat: 20.5 g. Protein: 10.9 g.

.Lemon Cream (Greek)

Preparation Time: 1 hour Cooking Time: 10 minutes Servings: 6

1eggs, whisked	¼ cup stevia
10 tbsps. avocado oil 1 cup heavy cream Juice of 2 lemons	Zest of 2 lemons, grated

1. In a pan, combine the cream with the lemon juice and the other , whisk well, cook for 10 minutes, divide into cups, and keep in the fridge for 1 hour before Servings.

Nutrition: Calories 200, Fat: 8.5g, Fiber: 4.5g, Carbs: 8.6g, Protein: 4.5g

.Blueberries Stew (Spanish)

Preparation Time: 10 minutes Cooking Time: 10 minutes
Servings: 4

2cups blueberries	3tbsps. stevia
½ cups pure apple juice 1 tsp. vanilla extract	

1. In a pan, combine the blueberries with stevia and the other, bring to a simmer and cook over medium-low heat for 10 minutes.
2. Divide into cups and serve cold.

Nutrition: Calories 192, Fat: 5.4g, Fiber: 3.4g, Carbs: 9.4g, Protein: 4.5g

.Mandarin Cream (Spanish)

Preparation Time: 20 minutes Cooking Time: 0 minutes
Servings: 8

2 mandarins, peeled and cut into segments Juice of 2 mandarins	2 tbsps. stevia
4 eggs, whisked	¾ cup stevia
¾ cup almonds, ground	

1. In a blender, combine the mandarins with the juice and the other , whisk well, divide into cups and keep in the fridge for 20 minutes before Servings.

Nutrition: Calories 106, Fat: 3.4g, Fiber: 0g, Carbs: 2.4g, Protein: 4g

.Vanilla Cake (Italian)

Preparation Time: 10 minutes Cooking Time: 25 minutes
Servings: 10

3 cups almond flour	3 tsps. baking powder cup olive oil
1 and ½ cup almond milk 1 and 2/3 cup stevia	cups water
1 tbsp. lime juice Tsps. vanilla extract Cooking spray	

1. In a bowl, mix the almond flour with the baking powder, the oil, and the rest of the except the cooking spray and whisk well.
2. Pour the mix into a cake pan greased with the cooking spray, introduce in the oven, and bake at 370F for 25 minutes.
3. Leave the cake to cool down, cut and serve!

Nutrition: Calories 200, Fat: 7.6g, Fiber: 2.5g, Carbs: 5.5g, Protein: 4.5g

.Orange Cake (Greek)

Preparation Time: 20 minutes Cooking Time: 60 minutes
Servings: 8

4 oranges	1/3 cup water
½ cup Erythritol	½ tsp. ground cinnamon 4 eggs, beaten
3 tbsps. stevia powder 10 oz. Phyllo pastry	½ tsp. baking powder
½ cup Plain yogurt 3 tbsps. olive oil	

1. Squeeze the juice from 1 orange and pour it in the saucepan.
2. Add water, squeezed oranges, water, ground cinnamon, and Erythritol. Bring the liquid to boil.
3. Simmer the liquid for 5 minutes over the medium heat. When the time is over, cool it.
4. Grease the baking mold with 1 tbsp. of olive oil. Chop the phyllo dough and place it in the baking mold.
5. Slice ½ of orange for decorating the cake. Slice it. Squeeze juice from remaining oranges.
6. Then mix up together, squeeze orange juice, Plain yogurt, baking powder, stevia powder, and eggs. Add remaining olive oil
7. Mix up the mixture with the help of the hand mixer.
8. Pour the liquid over the chopped Phyllo dough. Stir to distribute evenly.
9. Top the cake with sliced orange (that one which you leave for decorating).
10. Bake the dessert for 50 minutes at 370F.
11. Pour the baked cake with cooled orange juice syrup. Leave it for 10 minutes to let the cake soaks the syrup.
12. Cut it into servings.

Nutrition: Calories 237, Fat: 4.4 g, Fiber: 1.4 g, Carbs: 36.9 g, Protein: 1.9 g

.Cocoa Brownies (Greek)

Preparation Time: 10 minutes Cooking Time: 20 minutes
Servings: 8

30 ounces canned lentils, rinsed and drained 1 tablespoon honey	1 banana, peeled and chopped
½ teaspoon baking soda	4 tablespoons almond butter 2 tablespoons cocoa powder Cooking spray

1. In a food processor, combine the lentils with the honey and the other except the cooking spray and pulse well.
2. Pour this into a pan greased with cooking spray, spread evenly, introduce in the oven at 375° F and bake for 20 minutes.
3. Cut the brownies and serve cold.

Nutrition: Calories 200; Fat 4.5 g; Fiber 2.4 g; Carbs 8.7 g; Protein 4.3 g

.Chocolate Chip Banana Dessert (Italian)

Preparation time: 20 minutes Cooking time: 20 minutes
Servings: 24

2/3 cup white sugar 3/4 cup butter	2/3 cup brown sugar 1 egg, beaten slightly 1 tsp. vanilla extract 1 cup banana puree
13/4 cup flour	2tsps. baking powder
½ tsp. salt	1 cup semi-sweet chocolate chips

1. Preheat the oven to 175°C. Grease and bake a 10x15-inch baking pan.
2. Beat the butter, white sugar, and brown sugar in a large bowl until light.
3. Beat the egg and vanilla.
4. Fold in the banana puree: mix baking powder, flour, and salt in another bowl.
5. Mix the flour mixture into the butter mixture. Stir in the chocolate chips. Spread in the pan.
6. Bake for 20 minutes.
7. Cool before cutting into squares.

Nutrition: Calories: 174 Fat: 8.2 g. Protein: 1.7 g.

.Milky Peachy Dessert (Italian)

Preparation time: 15 minutes Cooking time: 10 minutes
Servings: 2

1 fresh peach, peeled and sliced 1 tsp. brown sugar	1 tbsp. milk

1. Prepare a baking dish with a layer of peaches and toss in the milk.
2. Top the peaches with sugar, and bake at 350°F for 5 minutes.

Nutrition: Calories: 366 Fat: 22.5 g. Protein: 1.9 g.

.Citrus Sections (Greek)

Preparation time: 20 minutes Cooking time: 5 minutes
Servings: 2

1 grapefruit, peeled and sectioned	½ cup pineapple, chunks
1 small orange, sectioned into chunks	½ tbsp. brown sugar,
½ tsp. butter, low fat and unsalted, melted	

1. Preheat an oven tray at 350ºF.
2. Set the fruits on the tray, top with the brown sugar mixed with the butter, and bake for 5 minutes.
3. Transfer to a platter.

Nutrition: Calories: 279 Fat: 5.9 g. Protein: 2.2 g.

.Mediterranean Watermelon Salad (Greek)

Preparation time: 4 minutes Cooking time: 0 minutes Servings: 4

1 cup watermelon, peeled and cubed 2 apples, cored and cubed	1tbsp. coconut cream
2bananas, cut into chunks	

1. Incorporate watermelon with the apples and the other , toss and serve.

Nutrition: Calories: 131 Fat: 1.3 g. Protein: 1.3 g.

.Fruit Dessert Nachos (Italian)

Preparation time: 9 minutes Cooking time: 13 minutes
Servings: 3

1tbsp. sugar	A pinch of ground cinnamon 1 ½ whole wheat tortillas
¼ cup light cream cheese, softened 1 cup assorted melon, chopped	2½ tbsp. light dairy sour cream
½ tsp. orange peel, finely shredded 1 tbsp. orange juice plus 30 g.	Cooking spray

1. Preheat the oven at 425ºF.
2. Grease a large baking sheet with cooking spray.
3. Take a small bowl, combine the cinnamon and half of the sugar.
4. Take the tortillas and lightly coat them with cooking spray. Sprinkle each side with the sugar mix.
5. Cut the tortillas to make 8 wedges and place them on the baking sheet.
6. Bake the tortillas until they turn lightly browned, for 7–8 minutes. Turn once halfway.
7. Meanwhile, take a small-sized bowl and mix the sour cream, cream cheese, 30 g. orange juice, orange peel, and the remaining sugar. Once smooth, set it aside.
8. Take a medium bowl and combine melon and the remaining orange juice.
9. Serve by adding a spoon of melon mix on each tortilla wedge and 1 spoon of cream cheese mixture.

Nutrition: Calories: 121 Protein: 5.3 g. Fat: 5.2 g.

.Decadent Croissant Bread Pudding (Italian)

Preparation Time: 5 minutes Cooking Time: 15 minutes
Servings: 6

1/2 cup double cream 6 tablespoons honey 1/4 cup rum, divided 2 eggs, whisked	1 teaspoon cinnamon A pinch of salt
A pinch of grated nutmeg 1 teaspoon vanilla essence	8 croissants, torn into pieces
1 cup pistachios, toasted and chopped	

1. Spritz a baking pan with cooking spray and set it aside.
2. In a mixing bowl, whisk the eggs, double cream, honey, rum, cinnamon, salt, nutmeg, and vanilla; whisk until everything is well incorporated.
3. Place the croissants in the prepared baking dish. Pour the custard over your croissants. Fold in the pistachios and press with a wide spatula.
4. Add 1 cup of water and metal rack to the inner pot of your Instant Pot. Lower the baking dish onto the rack.
5. Secure the lid. Choose the "Manual" mode and cook for 12 minutes at High pressure. Once cooking is complete, use a quick pressure release; carefully remove the lid.
6. Serve at room temperature or cold. Bon appétit!

Nutrition:513 Calories; 27.9g Fat; 50.3g Carbohydrates; 12.5g Protein; 25.7g Sugars; 3.8g Fiber

.Poached Apples with Greek Yogurt and Granola(Greek)

Preparation Time: 5 minutes Cooking Time: 15 minutes
Servings: 4

4 medium-sized apples, peeled 1/2 cup brown sugar	1 vanilla bean
1 cinnamon stick	1/2 cup cranberry juice 1 cup water
1/2 cup 2% Greek yogurt	
1/2 cup granola	

1. Secure the lid. Choose the "Manual" mode and cook for 5 minutes at High pressure. Once cooking is complete, use a natural pressure release for 5 minutes; carefully remove the lid. Reserve poached apples.
2. Press the "Sauté" button and let the sauce simmer on "Less" mode until it has thickened.
3. Place the apples in serving bowls. Add the syrup and top each apple with granola and Greek yogurt. Enjoy!

Nutrition:247 Calories; 3.1g Fat; 52.6g Carbohydrates; 3.5g Protein; 40g Sugars; 5.3g Fiber

.Ricotta Ramekins (Italian)

Preparation Time: 10 minutes Cooking Time: 1 hour Servings: 4

6 eggs, whisked	½ pounds ricotta cheese, soft
½ pound stevia	1 tsp. vanilla extract
½ tsp. baking powder	
Cooking spray	

1. In a bowl, mix the eggs with the ricotta and the other except the cooking spray and whisk well.
2. Grease 4 ramekins with the cooking spray, pour the ricotta cream in each and bake at 360F for 1 hour.
3. Serve cold.

Nutrition: Calories 180, Fat: 5.3g, Fiber: 5.4g, Carbs: 11.5g, Protein: 4g

.Papaya Cream (Spanish)

Preparation Time: 10 minutes Cooking Time: 0 minutes
Servings: 2

1cup papaya, peeled and chopped 1 cup heavy cream	1 tbsp. stevia
½ tsp. vanilla extract	

1. In a blender, combine the cream with the papaya and the other , pulse well, divide into cups and serve cold.

Nutrition: Calories 182, Fat: 3.1g, Fiber: 2.3g, Carbs: 3.5g, Protein: 2g

.Orange Butterscotch Pudding (Greek)

Preparation Time: 10 minutes Cooking Time: 15 minutes
Servings: 4

4 caramels	2 eggs, well-beaten
1/4 cup freshly squeezed orange juice 1/3 cup sugar	1 cup cake flour
1/2 teaspoon baking powder 1/4 cup milk	1 stick butter, melted
1/2 teaspoon vanilla essence Sauce:	1/2 cup golden syrup 2 teaspoons corn flour 1 cup boiling water

1. Melt the butter and milk in the microwave. Whisk in the eggs, vanilla, and sugar. After that, stir in the flour, baking powder, and orange juice.
2. Lastly, add the caramels and stir until everything is well combined and melted.
3. Divide between the four jars. Add 1 ½ cups of water and a metal trivet to the bottom of the Instant Pot. Lower the jars onto the trivet.
4. To make the sauce, whisk the boiling water, corn flour, and golden syrup until everything is well combined. Pour the sauce into each jar.
5. Secure the lid. Choose the "Steam" mode and cook for 15 minutes under High pressure. Once cooking is complete, use a natural pressure release; carefully remove the lid. Enjoy!

Nutrition: Calories 565; Fat 25.9g; Carbohydrates 79.6g; Protein 6.4g; Sugars 51.5g

.Honey Yogurt with Berries (Greek)

Preparation time: 12 minutes Cooking time: 0 minute
Servings: 2

4 oz. hulled halved strawberries 1/6 cup Greek yogurt	½ cup blueberries
½ cup raspberries 1 tsp. honey	½ tbsp. balsamic vinegar

1. Take a large bowl and toss the berries with balsamic vinegar.
2. Set it aside for 8–10 minutes.
3. Meanwhile, mix the honey and yogurt in a bowl.
4. Serve it by topping the berries with honey yogurt.

Nutrition: Calories: 111 Protein: 4.6 g. Fat: 3 g.

.Carrot Spread (Greek)

Preparation Time: 10 minutes Cooking Time: 10 minutes
Servings: 4

¼ cup veggie stock	A pinch of salt and black pepper 1 teaspoon onion powder
½ teaspoon garlic powder	½ teaspoon oregano, dried 1-pound carrots, sliced
½ cup coconut cream	

1. In your instant pot, combine all the except the cream, put the lid on and cook on High for 10 minutes.
2. Release the pressure naturally for 10 minutes, transfer the carrots mix to food processor, add the cream, pulse well, divide into bowls and serve cold.

Nutrition: Calories 124, Fat 1g, Fiber 2g, Carbohydrates 5g, Protein 8g

Caramelized Apples with Yogurt (Italian)

Preparation time: 14 minutes Cooking time: 9 minutes
Servings: 4

½ cup Greek yogurt	2 tbsps. toasted, chopped walnuts
¼ cup heavy cream 21 g. sugar	½ tbsp. honey
1 tbsp. unsalted butter 1 apple	A pinch of ground cinnamon

1. Take a bowl and add the yogurt, honey, and cream. Next, beat it with a hand blender or a whisk. Beat it until the mixture forms peaks and has thickened.
2. Place a large skillet on medium heat and warm the butter.
3. Add 21 g. sugar and the apples into the pan and mix it well.
4. Cook the apples for 5–7 minutes while occasionally stirring, so it doesn't stick.
5. Once the apples soften, sprinkle the cinnamon and the remaining sugar on them.
6. Cook for 2 more minutes before removing from the heat.
7. Wait for the apples to appear warm.
8. Serve the whipped yogurt topped with apples and almonds.

Nutrition: Calories: 315 Protein: 6.4 g. Fat: 22 g.

.Ricotta Brulee (Greek)

Preparation time: 7 minutes Cooking time: 14 minutes
Servings: 4

Fresh raspberries	1 cup whole milk Ricotta cheese 1 tbsp. granulated sugar
½ tsp. lemon zest, finely grated 1 tbsp. honey	

1. Take a large bowl, stir in the lemon zest, ricotta, and honey.
2. Combine the well.
3. Place 4 ramekins and divide the batter among them.
4. Add the sugar on top if you don't have a kitchen torch.
5. Add all of the ramekins to a baking sheet and place them on the oven rack.
6. Keep the rack on the highest level and turn on the broiler.
7. Once the Ricotta is golden-brown and starts to bubble, turn off the oven.
8. Top with the raspberries once it has cooled down. Serve it cold.

Nutrition: Calories: 254 Protein: 12.8 g. Fat: 14.7 g.

CHAPTER 11: DINNER

.Salad Skewers (Greek)

Preparation Time: 10 minutes Cooking Time: 0 minutes Servings: 1

1wooden skewers, soaked in water for 30 minutes before use. 8 large black olives.	8 cherry tomatoes.
1 yellow pepper, cut into eight squares.	½ red onion, chopped in half and separated into eight pieces. 3.5-oz. (about 10cm) cucumber, cut into four slices and halved. oz. feta, cut into 8 cubes.
For the dressing:	1 tbsp. extra-virgin olive oil. 1 tsp. balsamic vinegar.
Juice of ½ lemon.	Few leaves basil, finely chopped (or ½ tsp dried mixed herbs to replace basil and oregano).
A right amount of salt and freshly ground black pepper. Few leaves oregano, finely chopped.	½ clove garlic, peeled and crushed.

1. Thread each skewer in the order with salad olive, tomato, yellow pepper, red onion, cucumber, feta, basil, olive, yellow pepper, red ointment, cucumber, feta.
2. Put all the ingredients of the dressing in a small bowl and blend well together. Pour over the spoils.

Nutrition: Calories: 315 g. Fat: 30 g. Protein: 56 g. Carbs: 45 g. Cholesterol: 230 mg. Sugar: 0 g.

.Turkey With Cauliflower Couscous (Italian)

Preparation Time: 20 minutes Cooking Time: 50 minutes Servings: 1

3 oz. turkey.	1-oz. cauliflower. 2 oz. red onion.
1 tsp. fresh ginger. 1 pepper Bird's Eye. 1 clove of garlic. oz. dried tomatoes. 0.3-oz. parsley. ¼ fresh lemon juice.	3 tbsps. extra virgin olive oil. 2 tsps. turmeric. Dried sage to taste. 1 tbsp. capers.

1. Blend the raw cauliflower tops and cook them in a tsp. of extra virgin olive oil, garlic, red onion, chili pepper, ginger, and a tsp. of turmeric.
2. Leave to flavor on the fire for a minute, then add the chopped sun-dried tomatoes and 5 g of parsley. Season the turkey slice with a tsp. of extra virgin olive oil, the dried sage, and cook it in another tsp. of extra virgin olive oil. Once ready, season with a tbsp. of capers, ¼ of lemon juice, 5 g of parsley, a tbsp. of water and add the cauliflower.

Nutrition: Calories: 120 g. Fat: 10 g. Protein: 56 g. Carbs: 45 g. Cholesterol: 230 mg. Sugar: 0 g.

.Parmesan Honey Pork Loin Roast (Italian)

Preparation time: 10 minutes Cooking time: 5 hours Servings: 8

3 lbs. pork loin	2/3 cup grated parmesan cheese
½ cup honey	3 tbsps. soy sauce 1 tbsp. oregano
1 tbsp. basil	2 tbsps. garlic, chopped 2 tbsps. olive oil
½ tsp. salt	2 tbsps. cornstarch
¼ cup chicken broth	Olive oil or nonstick cooking spray

1. Spray your slow cooker with olive oil or nonstick cooking spray.
2. Place the pork loin in the slow cooker.
3. In a small mixing bowl, combine the cheese, honey, soy sauce, oregano, basil, garlic, olive oil, and salt. Stir with a fork to mix well, then pour over the pork loin.
4. Cook on low for 5–6 hours.
5. Remove the pork loin and put it on a serving platter.
6. Pour the juices from the slow cooker into a small saucepan.
7. Create a slurry by mixing the cornstarch into the chicken broth and whisking until smooth.
8. Bring the contents of the saucepan to a boil, then whisk in the slurry and let simmer until thickened. Pour over the pork loin and serve.

Nutrition: Calories: 449 g. Fat: 15 g. Protein: 55 g.

.Fried Whole Tilapia (Spanish)

Preparation Time: 10 minutes Cooking Time: 25 minutes Servings: 2

10-oz. tilapia. 2 tbsps. oil.	5 garlic cloves, mince.
4 large onions, chopped. 2 tbsps. red chili powder. 1 tsp. turmeric powder.	1 tsp. cumin powder.
1 tsp. coriander powder. Salt to taste.	Black pepper to taste. 2 tbsps. soy sauce.
2 tbsps. fish sauce.	

1. Take the tilapia fish and clean it well without taking off the skin. You need to fry it whole, so you have to be careful about cleaning the gut inside.
2. Cut few slits on the skin so the seasoning gets inside well.
3. Marinate the fish with fish sauce, soy sauce, red chili powder, cumin powder, turmeric powder, coriander powder, salt, and pepper.
4. Coat half of the onions in the same mixture too.
5. Let them marinate for 1 hour.
6. In a skillet heat the oil. Fry the fish for 8 minutes on each side.
7. Transfer the fish to a serving plate.
8. Fry the marinated onions until they become crispy.
9. Add the remaining raw onions on top and serve hot.

Nutrition: Calories: 368 g. Fats: 30.1 g. Carbs: 9.2 g. Proteins: 16.6 g.

Mediterranean Pearl Couscous (Italian)

Preparation Time: 4 minutes Cooking Time: 10 minutes
Servings: 6

For the Lemon Dill Vinaigrette: 1 large lemon, juice of	1/3 cup Extra virgin olive oil 1 tsp dill weed
1tsp garlic powder Salt and pepper	For the Israeli Couscous:
2cups Pearl Couscous, Israeli Couscous Extra virgin olive oil	2 cups grape tomatoes, halved
1/3 cup finely chopped red onions 1/2 English cucumber	15 oz. can chickpeas
14 oz. can good quality artichoke hearts 1/2 cup Kalamata olives	15–20 fresh basil leaves 3 oz. fresh baby mozzarella or feta cheese

1. Make the lemon-dill vinaigrette, scourge lemon juice, olive oil, dill weed, garlic powder, salt and pepper then keep aside
2. In a medium-sized heavy pot, heat two tbsp. of olive oil
3. Sauté the couscous in the olive oil briefly until golden brown, then add cups of boiling water (or follow the instructed on the package), and cook according to package.
4. Once done, drain in a colander, set aside in a bowl and allow to cool
5. In a large mixing bowl, combine the extra virgin olive oil, grape tomatoes, red onions, cucumber, chickpeas, artichoke hearts, and Kalamata olives
6. Then add in the couscous and the basil, mix together gently
7. Now, give the lemon-dill vinaigrette a quick whisk and add to the couscous salad, mix to combine
8. Taste and adjust salt, if needed
9. Distribute among the containers, store for 2-3 days
10. To Serve: Add in the mozzarella cheese, garnish with more fresh basil and enjoy!

Nutrition: Calories: 393 Fat: 13g Protein: 13g

.Italian Style Ground Beef (Italian)

Preparation Time: 10 minutes Cooking Time: 20 minutes
Servings: 4

2 lbs. ground beef Salt	2eggs, lightly beaten 1/4 tsp dried basil
3tbsp olive oil 1/2 tsp dried sage	11/2 tsp dried parsley 1 tsp oregano
2tsp thyme	1 tsp rosemary Pepper

1. Pour 1 1/2 cups of water into the instant pot then place the trivet in the pool.
2. Spray loaf pan with cooking spray.
3. Add all ingredients into the mixing bowl and mix until well combined.
4. Transfer meat mixture into the prepared loaf pan and place loaf pan on top of the trivet in the pot.
5. Seal pot with lid and cook on high for 35 minutes.
6. Once done, allow to release pressure naturally for 10 minutes then release remaining using quick release. Remove lid.
7. Serve and enjoy.

Nutrition: Calories 365 Fat 18 g Carbohydrates 0.7 g Sugar 0.1 g Protein 47.8 g Cholesterol 190 mg

.Mediterranean Tuna Noodle Casserole (Italian)

Preparation time: 15 minutes Cooking time: 40 minutes
Servings: 5

10 oz. dried egg noodles	9 oz. halved frozen artichoke hearts 6 oz. drained olive oil-packed tuna 4 sliced scallions
1 lb. small red potatoes, sliced 1/4-inch thick 2 cup milk	3/4 cup Parmesan cheese, finely grated
3/4 cup drained capers	1/2 cup flat-leaf parsley, finely chopped
1/2 cup black olives, sliced	1/4 cup flour
4 tbsps. unsalted butter	2 tsps. Kosher salt, divided 2 tbsps. olive oil
Pepper to taste	

1. Place a grill in the middle of the oven and heat to 400°F. Lightly coat a 2-quart baking tray with oil. Set aside.
2. Bring a large pan of salt and water to a boil. Add the noodles and cook for 2 minutes less than recommended in the package directions. Strain noodles. Season immediately with olive oil so that they don't pile up. Set aside.
3. Fill the pan with water again and bring to a boil. Add the potato slices and cook for 4 minutes. Drain well, then bring them back to the pan.
4. Heat the butter in a small saucepan over medium heat, while the noodles and potatoes are cooking. When it melts and expands, add the flour and cook for 5 minutes mixing constantly, until the sauce thickens slightly for 5 minutes. Add 1 tsp. salt and pepper to taste.
5. Add the egg noodles to the potato pan, then pour the sauce over it. Add and mix the remaining 1 tsp. salt, capers, olive oil, tuna, artichoke hearts, shallots, parsley, and 1/2 cup of Parmesan cheese. Taste and season with more salt as needed.
6. Transfer to the baking tray and distribute it in a uniform layer. Season with the remaining 1/4 cup of Parmesan and bake, uncovered, for 25 min.

Nutrition: Calories: 457 Protein: 37 g. Fat: 21 g.

.Artichoke Petals Bites (Spanish)

Preparation Time: 10 minutes Cooking Time: 10 minutes
Servings: 8

8 oz. artichoke petals, boiled, drained, without salt.	1/2 cup almond flour.
4 oz. Parmesan, grated.	2 tbsps. almond butter, melted.

1. In the mixing bowl, mix up together almond flour and grated Parmesan.
2. Preheat the oven to 355° F.
3. Dip the artichoke petals in the almond butter and then coat in the almond flour mixture.
4. Place them in the tray.
5. Transfer the tray to the preheated oven and cook the petals for 10 minutes.
6. Chill the cooked petal bites a little before serving.

Nutrition: Calories: 140 g. Fat: 6.4 g. Fiber: 7.6 g. Carbs: 14.6 g. Protein: 10 g.

.African Chicken Curry (Greek)

Prep Time: 10 minutes Cooking Time: 30 minutes Servings: 4

1 lb. whole chicken. ½ onion.
½ cup coconut milk. ½ bay leaf.
1 ½ tsps. olive oil. ½ cup peeled tomatoes. 1
 tsp. curry powder. tsp. salt.
½ lemon, juiced. 1 clove garlic.

1. Keep the skin of the chicken.
2. Cut your chicken into 8 pieces. It looks good when you keep the size not too small or not too big.
3. Discard the skin of the onion and garlic and mince the garlic and dice the onion.
4. Cut the tomato wedges.
5. Now in a pot add the olive oil and heat over medium heat.
6. Add the garlic and fry until it becomes brown.
7. Add the diced onion and caramelize it.
8. Add the bay leaf, and chicken pieces.
9. Fry the chicken pieces until they are golden.
10. Add the curry powder, coconut milk, and salt.
11. Cover and cook for 10 minutes on high heat.
12. Lower the heat to medium-low and add the lemon juice.
13. Add the tomato wedges and coconut milk.
14. Cook for another 10 minutes.
15. Serve hot with rice or tortilla.

Nutrition: Calories: 354 g. Fats: 10 g. Proteins: 18 g. Carbs: 17 g.

.Prawn Arrabbiata (Greek)

Preparation Time: 10 minutes Cooking Time: 40 minutes Servings: 1

Raw or cooked prawns (Ideally king prawns). oz. buckwheat pasta. 1 tbsp. extra-virgin olive oil. For the arrabbiata sauce:
Red onion, finely chopped. 1 garlic clove, finely chopped. 1.2-oz. celery, finely chopped.
1 Bird's eye chili, finely chopped. 1 tsp. dried mixed herbs. 1tsp. extra-virgin olive oil. 2tbsps. white wine (optional). 14-oz. tinned chopped tomatoes.
1 tbsp. chopped parsley.

1. Firstly, fry the onion, garlic, celery, and chili over medium-low heat and dry herbs in the oil for 1–2 minutes. Switch the flame to medium, then add the wine and cook for 1 minute. Add the tomatoes and leave the sauce to cook for 20–30 minutes over medium-low heat until it has a nice rich consistency. If you feel the sauce becomes too thick, add some water.
2. While the sauce is cooking, boil a pan of water, and cook the pasta as directed by the packet. Drain, toss with the olive oil when cooked to your liking, and keep in the pan until needed.
3. Add the raw prawns to the sauce and cook for another 3–4 minutes until they have turned pink and opaque, then attach the parsley and serve. If you use cooked prawns add the parsley, bring the sauce to a boil and eat.
4. Add the cooked pasta to the sauce, blend well, and then serve gently.

Nutrition: Calories: 185 g. Fat: 30 g. Protein: 56 g. Carbs: 45 g. Cholesterol: 230 mg. Sugar: 0 g.

.Creamy Strawberry & Cherry Smoothie (Greek)

Prep Time: 10 minutes Cooking Time: 15 minutes Servings: 1

1½ oz. strawberries. oz. frozen pitted cherries.
1 tbsp. plain full-fat yogurt.
 oz. unsweetened soya milk.

1. Place the ingredients into a blender then process until smooth. Serve and enjoy.

Nutrition: Calories: 132 g. Fat: 30 g. Protein: 56 g. Carbs: 45 g. Cholesterol: 230 mg. Sugar: 0 g.

.Spicy Chicken Shawarma (Greek)

Preparation time: 15 minutes Cooking time: 6 minutes Servings: 4

1 lb. chicken breast 4(6-inch) halved pitas
½ cup plum tomato, chopped ½ cup cucumber, chopped
¼ cup red onion, chopped 5tbsps. plain low-fat Greek-style yogurt, divided 2 tbsps. lemon juice, divided
2 tbsps. parsley, finely chopped 2 tbsps. extra-virgin olive oil 1tbsp. tahini
½ tsp. salt ½ tsp. crushed red pepper
¼ tsp. ground cumin ¼ tsp. ground ginger
1/8 tsp. ground coriander

1. Combine the parsley, salt, red pepper, ginger, cumin, coriander, 1 tbsp. yogurt, 1 tbsp. juice, and 2 cloves of garlic. Add the chicken, stir to coat. Preheat the oil in a nonstick pan over medium-high heat. Add the chicken mixture to the pan and cook for 6 minutes.
2. In the meantime, combine the remaining 1 tbsp. lemon juice, the remaining ¼ cup of yogurt, the remaining 1 clove of garlic, and the tahini, mixing well. Put 1 ½ tsp. the tahini mixture inside each half of the pita, divide the chicken between the pita halves. Fill each half of the pita with 1 tbsp. cucumber, 1 tbsp. tomato, and 1 ½ tsp. onion.

Nutrition: Calories: 440 Protein: 37 g. Fat: 19 g.

.Chicken Sausage and Peppers (Spanish)

Preparation time: 10 minutes Cooking time: 20 minutes Servings: 6

1tbsps. extra-virgin olive oil 1 red bell pepper
6 Italian chicken sausage links 1 onion
1 green bell pepper 3 garlic cloves, minced
½ cup dry white wine ½ tsp. sea salt
¼ tsp. freshly ground black pepper Pinch red pepper flakes

1. Heat the olive oil in a skillet at medium-high heat.
2. Add the sausages and cook for 5–7 minutes, turning occasionally, until browned, and they reach an internal temperature of 165°F. With tongs, remove the sausage from the pan and set it aside on a platter, tented with aluminum foil to keep warm.
3. Put the skillet back to heat and add the onion, red bell pepper, and green bell pepper. Cook them for 5–7 minutes.
4. Cook the garlic for 30 seconds, stirring constantly.
5. Stir in the wine, sea salt, pepper, and red pepper flakes. Scrape and fold in any browned bits from the bottom. Simmer for 4 minutes more. Spoon the peppers over the sausages and serve.

Nutrition: Calories: 173 Protein: 22 g. Fat: 5 g.

.Chicken Merlot with Mushrooms (Spanish)

Prep Time: 10 minutes Cooking Time: 40 minutes Servings: 2

6 boneless, skinless chicken breasts, cubed. 3 cups mushrooms, sliced.

1 large red onion, chopped. 2 cloves garlic, minced.

¾ cup chicken broth.

1 (6 oz.) can tomato paste.

¼ cup Merlot.

3 tbsps. chia seeds.

2 tbsps. basil, chopped finely. 2 tsps. sugar.

Salt and pepper to taste.

1 (10 oz.) package buckwheat ramen noodles, cooked.

2 tbsps. Parmesan, shaved.

1. Rinse chicken; set aside.
2. Add mushrooms, onion, and garlic to the crockpot and mix.
3. Place chicken cubes on top of the vegetables and do not mix.
4. In a large bowl, combine broth, tomato paste, wine, chia seeds, basil, sugar, salt, and pepper. Pour over the chicken.
5. Cover and cook on low for 7–8 hours or on high for 3 ½–4 hours.
6. To serve, spoon chicken, mushroom mixture, and sauce over hot cooked buckwheat ramen noodles. Top with shaved Parmesan.

Nutrition: Calories: 213 g. Fat: 10 g. Protein: 56 g. Carbs: 45 g. Cholesterol: 230 mg. Sugar: 0 g.

.Coated Cauliflower Head (Spanish)

Preparation Time: 10 minutes Cooking Time: 40 minutes Servings: 6

2-lb. cauliflower head. 3 tbsps. olive oil.

1 tbsp. butter softened. 1 tsp. ground coriander. 1 tsp. salt.

1 egg, whisked.

1 tsp. dried cilantro. 1 tsp. dried oregano. 1 tsp. Tahini paste.

1. Trim cauliflower head if needed.
2. Preheat oven to 350° F.
3. In the mixing bowl, mix up together olive oil, softened butter, ground coriander, salt, whisked egg, dried cilantro, dried oregano, and tahini paste.
4. Then brush the cauliflower head with this mixture generously and transfer it to the tray.
5. Bake the cauliflower head for 40 minutes.
6. Brush it with the remaining oil mixture every 10 minutes.

Nutrition: Calories: 131 g. Fat: 10.3 g. Fiber: 4 g. Carbs: 8.4 g. Protein: 4.1 g.

.Garlic Herb Grilled Chicken Breast (Greek)

Prep Time: 7 minutes Cooking Time: 20 minutes Servings: 4

1 ¼ lb. chicken breasts, skinless and boneless. 2 tsps. olive oil.

1 tbsp. garlic & herb seasoning blend. Salt. Pepper.

1. Pat dries the chicken breasts, coat it with olive oil, and season it with salt and pepper on both sides.
2. Season the chicken with garlic and herb seasoning or any other seasoning of your choice.
3. Turn the grill on and oil the grate.
4. Place the chicken on the hot grate and let it grill till the sides turn white.
5. Flip them over and let them cook again.
6. When the internal temperature is about 160° F, it is most likely cooked.
7. Set aside for 15 minutes. Chop into pieces.

Nutrition: Calories: 187 g. Fats: 6 g. Protein: 32 g. Carbs: 5 g.

.Stuffed Beef Loin in Sticky Sauce (Italian)

Preparation Time: 15 minutes Cooking Time: 6 minutes Servings: 4

1 tbsp. Erythritol.

1 tbsp. lemon juice.

½ tsp. tomato sauce.

¼ tsp. dried rosemary. 9 oz. beef loin.

½ cup of water.

3 oz. celery root, grated. 3 oz. bacon, sliced.

1 tbsp. walnuts, chopped. 2 tsps. butter.

¾ tsps. garlic, diced.

1tbsp. olive oil. 1 tsp. salt.

1. Cut the beef loin into the layer and spread it with the dried rosemary, butter, and salt.
2. Then place over the beef loin: grated celery root, sliced bacon, walnuts, and diced garlic.
3. Roll the beef loin and brush it with olive oil.
4. Secure the meat with the help of the toothpicks.
5. Place it in the tray and add a ½ cup of water.
6. Cook the meat in the preheated to 365° F oven for 40 minutes.
7. Meanwhile, make the sticky sauce: mix up together Erythritol, lemon juice, 4 tbsps. of water, and butter.
8. Preheat the mixture until it starts to boil.
9. Then add tomato sauce and whisk it well.
10. Bring the sauce to boil and remove from the heat.
11. When the beef loin is cooked, remove it from the oven and brush it with the cooked sticky sauce very generously.
12. Slice the beef roll and sprinkle with the remaining sauce.

Nutrition: Calories: 248 g. Fat: 17.5 g. Fiber: 0.5 g. Carbs: 2.2 g. Protein:20.7 g.

.Olive Feta Beef (Greek)

Preparation Time: 10 minutes Cooking Time: 6 hours Servings: 8

1lbs. beef stew meat, cut into half-inch pieces. 1 cup olives, pitted, and cut in half.

30 oz. can tomato, diced.

½ cup feta cheese, crumbled.

¼ tsp. pepper.

½ tsp. salt.

1. Add all ingredients into the crockpot and stir well.
2. Cover and cook on high for 6 hours.
3. Season with pepper and salt.
4. Stir well and serve.

Nutrition: Calories: 370 g. Fat: 12 g. Fiber: 1 g. Carbs: 10 g. Protein: 50 g.

.Excellent Beef Meal (Spanish)

Prep Time: 15 minutes Cooking Time: 7 hours 4 minutes Servings: 6

1 tbsp. vegetable oil 2 lb. beef stew meat 1 can artichoke hearts 1 onion

4 garlic cloves

1 can diced tomatoes with juice 1/2 C.

1 container beef broth 1 can tomato sauce

Kalamata olives, pitted 1 tsp. dried oregano

1 tsp. dried basil

1 tsp. dried parsley 1 bay leaf, crumbled

1/2 tsp. ground cumin

1. In a skillet, heat the oil over medium-high heat and cook the beef for about 2 minutes per side.
2. Transfer the beef into a slow cooker and top with artichoke hearts, followed by the onion and garlic.
3. Place the remaining ingredients on top.
4. Set the slow cooker on "Low" and cook, covered for about 7 hours.

Nutrition: Calories: 410; Carbohydrates: 0.9g; Protein: 53.1g; Fat: 14.2g; Sugar: 6.7g; Sodium: 1116mg; Fiber: 6.4g

245

.Osso Bucco (Spanish)

Preparation time: 30 minutes Cooking time: 8 hours Servings: 2–4

beef shanks or veal shanks 1 tsp. sea salt
½ tsp. ground black pepper
3 tbsps. whole wheat flour
1–2 tbsps. olive oil

2 medium onions, diced 2 medium carrots, diced
4 garlic cloves, minced
2 celery stalks, diced

1 (14 oz.) can diced tomatoes 2 tsps.
½ cup beef or vegetable dried thyme leaves stock

1. Season the shanks on both sides, then dip in the flour to coat.
2. Heat a large skillet over high heat. Add the olive oil. When the oil is hot, add the shanks and brown evenly on both sides. When browned, transfer to the slow cooker.
3. Pour the stock into the skillet and let simmer for 3–5 minutes while stirring to deglaze the pan.
4. Add the rest of the ingredients to the slow cooker and pour the stock from the skillet over the top.
5. Click slow cooker to low and cook for 8 hours.
6. Serve the Osso Bucco over quinoa, brown rice, or even cauliflower rice.

Nutrition: Calories: 589 Fat: 21.3 g. Protein: 74.7g.

.Spanish Meatballs (Spanish)

Preparation time: 20 minutes Cooking time: 5 hours Servings: 6

1 lb. ground turkey 1 lb. ground pork 2 eggs
1 (20 oz.) can tomatoes, diced

¾ cup sweet onion, minced, divided
¼ cup plus 1 tbsp. breadcrumbs 3 tbsps.

1½ tsp. paprika (sweet or hot) 2 tbsps. olive oil
fresh parsley, chopped 1 ½ tsp. cumin

1. Spray the slow cooker with olive oil.
2. In a mixing bowl, mix the ground meat, eggs, about half of the onions, the breadcrumbs, and the spices.
3. Wash your hands and mix until everything is well combined. Shape into meatballs.
4. Mix 2 tbsps. of olive oil over medium heat. When the skillet and oil are hot, add the meatballs and brown on all sides. When they are done, transfer them to the slow cooker.
5. Add the rest of the onions and the tomatoes to the skillet and allow them to cook for a few minutes, scraping the brown bits from the meatballs up to add flavor.
6. Pour the tomatoes over the meatballs in the slow cooker and cook on low for 5 hours.

Nutrition: Calories: 372 Fat: 21.7 g. Protein: 28.5g.

.Lamb Shanks with Red Wine (Greek)

Preparation time: 20 minutes Cooking time: 5 hours Servings: 4

1tbsps. olive oil 2 tbsps. flour
4 lamb shanks, trimmed 1 onion, chopped

2garlic cloves, crushed 2/3 cup red wine
3cups tomato sauce

1. Heat a skillet over high heat. Add the olive oil.
2. Season the lamb shanks, then roll in the flour. Shake off excess flour and place the shanks in the skillet to brown on all sides.
3. Spray the slow cooker with olive oil and place the browned shanks in the slow cooker.
4. Add the crushed garlic to the red wine. Mix with the tomato sauce and then, pour the mixture over the lamb shanks and cook on low for 5–6 hours.

Nutrition: Calories: 354 Fat: 12 g. Protein: 42 g.

.Chicken and Tzatziki Pitas (Greek)

Preparation Time: 10 minutes Cooking Time: 0 minutes Servings: 8

2pita breads
10 oz chicken fillet, grilled 1 cup lettuce, chopped

8 teaspoons tzatziki sauce

1. Cut every pita bread on the halves to get 8 pita pockets.
2. Then fill every pita pocket with chopped lettuce and sprinkle greens with tzatziki sauce.
3. Chop chicken fillet and add it in the pita pockets too.

Nutrition: calories 106, fat 3.8, fiber 0.2, carbs 6.1, protein 11

.Lime Chicken with Black Beans (Spanish)

Preparation Time: 15 minutes Cooking Time: 30 minutes Servings: 8

8 chicken thighs (boneless and skinless) 3 tablespoons lime juice
1 cup black beans

1 cup canned tomatoes
4 teaspoons garlic powder

1. Marinate the chicken in a mixture of lime juice and garlic powder.
2. Add the chicken to the Instant Pot.
3. Pour the tomatoes on top of the chicken.
4. Seal the pot.
5. Set it to manual.
6. Cook at high pressure for 10 minutes.
7. Release the pressure naturally.
8. Stir in the black beans.
9. Press sauté to simmer until black beans are cooked.

Nutrition: Calories 370; Total Fat 11.2g; Saturated Fat 3.1g; Cholesterol 130mg; Sodium 128mg; Total Carbohydrate 17.5g; Dietary Fiber 4.1g; Total Sugars 1.5g; Protein 47.9g; Potassium 790mg

.Flavorful Beef Bourguignon (Spanish)

Preparation Time: 10 minutes Cooking Time: 20 minutes Servings: 4

11/2 lbs. beef chuck roast, cut into chunks 2/3 cup beef stock
2tbsp fresh thyme 1 bay leaf

1 tsp garlic, minced
8 oz mushrooms, sliced 2 tbsp tomato paste

2/3 cup dry red wine 1 onion, sliced
4 carrots, cut into chunks 1 tbsp olive oil

Pepper Salt

1. Add oil into the instant pot and set the pot on sauté mode.
2. Add meat and sauté until brown. Add onion and sauté until softened.
3. Add remaining ingredient and stir well.
4. Seal pot with lid and cook on high for 12 minutes.
5. Once done, allow to release pressure naturally. Remove lid.
6. Stir well and serve.

Nutrition: Calories 744 Fat 51.3 g Carbohydrates 14.5 g Sugar 6.5 g Protein 48.1g Cholesterol 175 mg

.Cauliflower Tomato Beef (Spanish)

Preparation Time: 10 minutes Cooking Time: 25 minutes Servings: 2

1/2 lb. beef stew meat, chopped 1 tsp paprika	1 celery stalk, chopped 1 tbsp balsamic vinegar
1/4 cup grape tomatoes, chopped 1 onion, chopped	1/4 cup cauliflower, chopped 1 tbsp olive oil
Pepper Salt	

1. Add oil into the instant pot and set the pot on sauté mode.
2. Add meat and sauté for 5 minutes.
3. Add remaining ingredients and stir well.
4. Seal pot with lid and cook on high for 20 minutes.
5. Once done, allow to release pressure naturally. Remove lid.
6. Stir and serve.

Nutrition: Calories 306 Fat 14.3 g Carbohydrates 7.6 g Sugar 3.5 g Protein 35.7 g Cholesterol 101 mg

.Dinner Party Brisket (Italian)

Preparation Time: 15 minutes Cooking Time: 11 hours 5 minutes Servings: 8

1 fresh beef brisket, trimmed	3 tsp. dried Italian seasoning, crushed and divided
1 can diced tomatoes with basil, garlic and oregano with juice 1/2 C. olives, pitted	1 tsp. lemon peel, grated finely
Pinch salt and freshly ground black pepper, to taste 1/2 C. low-sodium beef broth	2 medium fennel bulbs, trimmed, cored and cut into wedges 2 tbsp. all-purpose flour
1/4 C. cold water	

1. Season the brisket with 1 tsp. of the Italian seasoning.
2. In a bowl, add the remaining Italian seasoning, tomatoes with juice, olives, lemon peel, salt, black pepper and broth and mix well.
3. In a slow cooker, place the brisket and top with fennel, followed by the tomato mixture.
4. Set the slow cooker on "Low" and cook, covered for about 10-11 hours.
5. Uncover the slow cooker and with a slotted spoon, transfer the brisket and vegetables onto a platter.
6. With a piece of foil, cover the meat to keep warm.
7. Skim off the fat from the top of cooking liquid.
8. In a small pan, add about 2 C. of the cooking liquid over medium heat.
9. In a small bowl, dissolve the flour in water.
1. 10.Inthepanofcookingliquid,addtheflourmixture,stirring continuously.
10. Cook for about 2-3 minutes or until desired thickness of sauce, stirring continuously.
11. Cut the brisket into desired sized slices and serve with the topping of gravy.

Nutrition: Calories: 367; Carbohydrates: 8.g; Protein: 53.3g; Fat: 12.3g; Sugar: 1.5g; Sodium: 266mg; Fiber: 2.8g

.Sunday Dinner Brisket (Spanish)

Preparation Time: 10 minutes Cooking Time: 8 hours 10 minutes Servings: 6

2 1/2 lb. beef brisket, trimmed	Salt and freshly ground black pepper, to taste 2 tsp. olive oil
2 medium onions, chopped 2 large garlic cloves, sliced 1 tbsp. Herbs de Provence	1 (15-oz.) can diced tomatoes, drained 2 tsp. Dijon mustard
1 C. dry red wine	

1. Season the brisket with salt and black pepper evenly.
2. In a non-stick skillet, heat the oil over medium heat and cook the brisket for about 4-5 minutes per side.
3. Transfer the brisket into a slow cooker.
4. Add the remaining ingredients and stir to combine.
5. Set the slow cooker on "Low" and cook, covered for about 8 hours.
6. Uncover the slow cooker and with a slotted spoon, transfer the brisket onto a platter.
7. Cut the brisket into desired sized slices and serve with the topping of pan sauce.

Nutrition: Calories: 427; Carbohydrates: 7.7g; Protein: 58.5g; Fat: 193.6g; Sugar: 3.7g; Sodium: 178mg; Fiber: 1.7g

.Leg of Lamb with Rosemary and Garlic (Greek)

Preparation time: 15 minutes Cooking time: 8 hours Servings: 4–6

3–4-lb. leg of lamb	4 garlic cloves, sliced thin
5–8 sprigs of fresh rosemary, more if desired 2 tbsps. olive oil	1 lemon, halved
¼ cup flour	

1. Put a skillet over high heat and pour the olive oil.
2. When the olive oil is hot, add the leg of lamb and sear on both sides until brown.
3. Spray the slow cooker with olive oil and then transfer the lamb to the slow cooker.
4. Squeeze the lemon over the meat and then place it in the pot next to the lamb.
5. Take a sharp knife, make small incisions in the meat, and then stuff the holes you created with rosemary and garlic.
6. Place any remaining rosemary and garlic on top of the roast.
7. Cook on low for 8 hours.

Nutrition: Calories: 557 Fat: 39 g. Protein: 46 g.

.Lemon Honey Lamb Shoulder (Spanish)

Preparation time: 10 minutes Cooking time: 8 hours Servings: 4

3 garlic cloves, thinly sliced	1 tbsp. fresh rosemary, chopped 1 tsp. lemon zest, grated
½ tsp. each salt and pepper	4–5-lb. boneless lamb shoulder roast 3 tbsps. lemon juice
1 tbsp. honey	6 shallots, quartered
2 tsps. cornstarch 2 tsps. Olive oil	

1. Stir the garlic, rosemary, lemon zest, salt, and pepper.
2. Rub the spice mixture into the lamb shoulder. Make sure to coat the whole roast.
3. Spray the slow cooker with olive oil and add the lamb.
4. Mix the honey and lemon juice and then pour over the meat.
5. Arrange the shallots beside the meat in the slow cooker.
6. Cook on low for 8 hours.
7. Serve. You can make a gravy by transferring the juice from the slow cooker to a medium saucepan. Thoroughly mix the cornstarch into a bit of water until smooth. Then mix into the juice and bring to a simmer. Simmer until mixture thickens.

Nutrition: Calories: 240 Fat: 11 g. Protein: 31 g.

.Lemony Trout with Caramelized Shallots (Greek)

Preparation time: 10 minutes Cooking time: 20 minutes Servings: 2

For the shallots:	1tsp. almond butter
2shallots, thinly sliced Dash salt	For the trout:
1tbsp. almond butter	2(4 oz./113 g.) trout fillets
3tbsps. capers	¼ cup freshly squeezed lemon juice
¼ tsp. salt	Dash freshly grounds black pepper 1 lemon, thinly sliced

1. For the shallots:
1. Place a skillet over medium heat, cook the butter, shallots, and salt for 20 minutes, stirring every 5 minutes.
2. For the trout:
3. Meanwhile, in another large skillet over medium heat, heat 1 tsp. almond butter.
4. Add the trout fillets and cook each side for 3 minutes, or until flaky. Transfer to a plate and set aside.
5. In the skillet used for the trout, stir in the capers, lemon juice, salt, and pepper, then bring to a simmer. Whisk in the remaining 1 tbsp. almond butter. Spoon the sauce over the fish.
6. Garnish the fish with lemon slices and caramelized shallots before serving.

Nutrition: Calories: 344 Fat: 18 g. Protein: 21 g.

.Butternut Squash Risotto (Italian)

Preparation Time: 10 minutes Cooking Time: 15 minutes Servings: 4

3 tbsps. butter.	2 tbsps. minced sage.
¼ tsp. black pepper, ground.	1 tsp. salt.
1 tsp. minced rosemary.	
½ cup dry sherry.	4 cups riced cauliflower.
½ cup butternut squash, cooked and mashed.	½ cup parmesan cheese, grated.
½ cup mascarpone cheese.	1tsp. minced garlic.
1/8 tsp. grated nutmeg.	

1. Melt your butter inside of a large frying pan turned to a medium level of heat.
2. Add your rosemary, your sage, and the garlic. Cook this for about 1 minute or until this mixture begins to become fragrant.
3. Add in the cauliflower rice, pepper and salt, and the mashed squash. Cook this for 3 minutes. You will know it is ready for the next step when cauliflower is starting to soften up for you.
4. Add in your sherry and cook this for an additional 6 minutes, or until the majority of the liquid is absorbed into the rice, or when the cauliflower is much softer.
5. Stir in the mascarpone cheese, the parmesan cheese, as well as the nutmeg (grated).
6. Cook all of this on a medium heat level, being sure to stir it occasionally and do this until the cheese has melted and the risotto has gotten creamy. This will take around 4–5 minutes.
7. Taste the risotto and add more pepper and salt to season if you wish.
8. Remove your pan from the burner and garnish your risotto with more of the herbs as well as some grated parmesan.
9. Serve and enjoy

Nutrition: Calories: 337 g. Fats: 25 g. Carbs: 9 g. Protein: 8 g.

.Fall-Apart Tender Beef (Spanish)

Preparation Time: 10 minutes Cooking Time: 11 hours Serving: 12

4 lb. boneless beef chuck roast, trimmed 2 large onions, sliced into thin strips	4 celery stalks, sliced 4 garlic cloves, minced 1 1/2 C. catsup
1C. BBQ sauce 1/4 C. molasses	1/4 C. apple cider vinegar
2tbsp. prepared yellow mustard 1/4 tsp. red chili powder	Fresh ground black pepper, to taste

1. In a slow cooker, place all the ingredients and stir to combine.
2. Set the slow cooker on "Low" and cook, covered for about 8-10 hours.
3. Uncover the slow cooker and with 2 forks, shred the meat.
4. Stir the meat with pan sauce.
5. Set the slow cooker on "Low" and cook, covered for about 1 hour.
6. Serve hot.

Nutrition: Calories: 454; Carbohydrates: 43.4g; Protein: 48.3g; Fat: 10g; Sugar: 35.5g; Sodium: 1000mg; Fiber: 1.2g

.Cheesy Broccoli Soup (Greek)

Preparation Time: 5 minutes Cooking Time: 30 minutes Servings: 6

1lbs. broccoli, chopped. Salt to taste.	5 cups vegetable broth.
¼ cup shredded cheddar cheese. 1 tbsp. olive oil.	¼ cup lemon juice.
2 garlic cloves, mince. 1 white onion, chopped. Pepper to taste.	

1. Heat the olive oil in a pan with medium heat.
2. Fry the onion for 1 minute and then add the garlic. Fry until the garlic becomes golden in color.
3. Toss in the broccoli and stir for 3 minutes.
4. Pour in the vegetable broth.
5. Add salt, pepper and mix well.
6. Cook for 20 minutes or until your broccoli is perfectly cooked through.
7. Take off the heat and let it cool down a bit.
8. Add to a blender, and blend it until your soup is perfectly smooth.
9. Transfer the soup into the pot again and heat it over medium heat.
10. Add lemon juice, cheddar cheese, and check if it needs more seasoning.
11. Serve hot with more cheese on top.

Nutrition: Calories: 97 g. Fats: 3.6 g. Carbs: 13.4 g. Proteins: 5 g.

.Balsamic Beef (Spanish)

Preparation time: 5 minutes Cooking time: 8 hours Servings: 8–10

1lbs. boneless chuck roast 1 tbsp. olive oil	For the rub:
1 tsp. garlic powder	½ tsp. onion powder 1 tsp. sea salt
½ tsp. black pepper For the sauce:	½ cup balsamic vinegar 2 tbsps. honey
1 tbsp. honey mustard 1 cup beef broth	1 tbsp. tapioca

1. Incorporate all the ingredients for the rub.
2. In a separate bowl, mix the balsamic vinegar, honey, and honey mustard, and beef broth.
3. Coat the roast in olive oil, then rub in the spices from the rub mix.
4. Place the roast in the slow cooker and then pour the sauce over the top.
5. Select slow cooker to LOW and cook for 8 hours.
6. If you want to thicken, pour the liquid into a saucepan and heat it to boiling on the stovetop. Stir in the flour until smooth and let simmer until the sauce thickens.

Nutrition: Calories: 306 Fat: 19 g. Protein: 25 g.

.Slow-Cooked Beef Bourguignon (Greek)

Preparation time: 5 minutes Cooking time: 6–8 hours Servings: 6–8

1 tbsp. extra-virgin olive oil 6 oz. bacon	3 lbs. beef brisket 1 large carrot
1large white onion 6 garlic cloves	½ tsp. coarse salt
½ tsp. pepper	2tbsps. whole-wheat flour 12 small pearl onions
3cups red wine 2 cups beef stock	2 tbsps. tomato paste 1 beef bouillon cube 1 tsp. fresh thyme
2 tbsps. fresh parsley 2 bay leaves	2 tbsps. butter
1lb. mushrooms	

1. Preheat a skillet over medium-high heat, pour olive oil. When the oil has heated, cook the bacon until it is crisp, then place it in your slow cooker. Save the bacon fat in the skillet.
2. Dry the beef with a paper towel and cook it in the same skillet with the bacon fat until all sides have the same brown coloring.
3. Transfer to the slow cooker.
4. Add the onions and carrots to the slow cooker and season with salt and pepper. Stir to combine the ingredients and make sure everything is seasoned.
5. Pour the red wine into the skillet and simmer for 4–5 minutes to deglaze the pan, then whisk in the flour, stirring until smooth.
6. When the liquid has thickened, pour it into the slow cooker and stir to coat everything with the wine mixture. Add the tomato paste, bouillon cube, thyme, parsley, 4 cloves of garlic, and bay leaf.
7. Set your slow cooker to high and cook for 6 hours, or set it to low and cook for 8 hours.
8. Before serving, melt the butter in a skillet over medium heat. When the oil is hot, add the remaining 2 cloves of garlic and cook for about 1 minute before adding the mushrooms.
9. Cook the mushrooms until soft, then add to the slow cooker and mix to combine.
10. Serve with mashed potatoes, rice, or noodles.

Nutrition: Calories: 672 Fat: 32 g. Protein: 56 g.

.Healthy Chickpea Burger (Spanish)

Preparation Time: 15 minutes Cooking Time: 10 minutes Servings: 2

1 cup chickpeas, boiled. 1 tbsp. tomato puree.	1tsp. soy sauce.
A pinch of paprika.	A pinch of white pepper. 1 onion, diced.
Salt to taste.	2lettuce leaves.
½ cup bell pepper, sliced. 1 tsp. olive oil.	1avocado, sliced.
2burger buns to serve.	

1. Mash the chickpeas and combine with bell pepper, salt, pepper, paprika, soy sauce, and tomato puree.
2. Use your hands to make patties.
3. Fry the patties golden brown with oil.
4. Assemble the burgers with lettuce, onion, avocado, and enjoy.

Nutrition: Calories: 254 g. Fat: 12 g. Protein: 9 g. Carbs: 7.8 g.

.Cajun Shrimp (Spanish)

Prep Time: 10 minutes Cooking Time: 5 minutes Servings: 2

16 tiger shrimp.	2 tbsps. corn starch.
1 tsp. cayenne pepper.	1tsp. old bay seasoning. 1 tsp. olive oil.
Salt. Pepper.	

1. Rinse the shrimp. Pat dry.
2. In a bowl, combine corn starch, cayenne pepper, old bay seasoning, salt, pepper. Stir.
3. In a bowl, add the shrimp. Drizzle olive oil over shrimp to lightly coat.
4. Dip the shrimp in seasoning, shake off any excess.
5. Preheat fryer to 375° F. Lightly spray cook basket with non-stick keto cooking spray.
6. Transfer to the fryer. Cook 5 minutes; shake after 2 minutes, until cooked thoroughly.
7. Serve on a platter.

Nutrition: Calories: 127 g. Fat: 10 g. Carbs: 3 g. Protein: 7 g.

.Sesame-Crusted Mahi-Mahi (Greek)

Preparation Time: 5 minutes Cooking Time: 13 minutes Servings: 4

1tbsps. Dijon mustard.	1 tbsp. sour cream, low-fat.
½ cup sesame seeds. 2 tbsps. olive oil.	1 lemon, wedged.
4 (4 oz. each) mahi-mahi or sole filets.	

1. Rinse filets and pat dry. In a bowl, mix sour cream and mustard. Spread this mixture on all sides of the fish. Roll in sesame seeds to coat.
2. Heat olive oil in a large skillet over medium heat. Pan-fry fish, turning once, for 5–8 minutes or until fish flakes when tested with fork and sesame seeds are toasted. Serve immediately with lemon wedges.

Nutrition: Calories: 282 g. Fat: 17 g. Protein: 18 g. Carbs: 5 g.

.Country Chicken (Spanish)

Preparation Time: 10 minutes Cooking Time: 15 minutes Servings: 2

¾ lbs. chicken tenders, fresh, boneless skinless.	½ cup almond meal.
½ cup almond flour. Pepper.	1tsp. rosemary, dried. Salt. 2eggs, beaten.

1. Rinse the chicken tenders, pat dry.
2. In a medium bowl, pour in almond flour.
3. In a medium bowl, beat the eggs.
4. In a separate bowl, pour in an almond meal. Season with rosemary, salt, pepper.
5. Take the chicken pieces and toast in flour, then egg, then almond meal. Set on a tray.
6. Place the tray in the freezer for 5 minutes.
7. Preheat fryer to 350° F. Lightly spray cook basket with non-stick cooking spray.
8. Cook tenders for 10 minutes. After the timer runs out, set the temperature to 390° F, cook for 5 more minutes until golden brown.
9. Serve on a platter. Side with preferred dipping sauce.

Nutrition: Calories: 480 g. Fat: 36 g. Carbs: 13 g. Protein: 26 g.

.Mahi-Mahi Tacos with Avocado and FreshCabbage (Italian)

Preparation Time: 5 minutes Cooking Time: 15 minutes Servings: 4

1 lb. mahi-mahi. Salt.	Pepper.
1 tsp. olive oil. 1 avocado.	4 corn tortillas.
2 cups cabbage, shredded. 2 quartered limes	

1. Season fish with salt and pepper.
2. Set a pan over medium-high heat. Add in oil and heat. Once the oil is hot, sauté fish for about 3–4 minutes on each side. Slice or flake fish into 1-oz. pieces.
3. Slice avocado in half. Remove seed and, using a spoon, remove the flesh from the skin. Slice the avocado halves into ½ thick slices.
4. In a small pan, warm corn tortillas; cook for about 1 minute on each side.
5. Place one-fourth of Mahi-mahi of each tortilla, top with avocado and cabbage. Serve with lime wedges.

Nutrition: Calories: 251 g. Fat: 9 g. Protein: 25 g. Carbs: 21 g.

.Deliciously Simple Beef (Spanish)

Preparation Time: 10 minutes
Cooking Time: 10 hours Servings: 4

1 large onion, sliced thinly	1tsp. dried oregano
1/4 C. extra-virgin olive oil 1 tbsp. garlic, minced	
Salt and freshly ground black pepper, to taste 2 tbsp. fresh lemon juice	2lb. beef chuck roast, cut into bite-sized pieces

1. In a slow cooker, place all the ingredients except for beef cubes and stir to combine.
2. Add the beef cubes and stir to combine.
3. Set the slow cooker on "Low" and cook, covered for about 8-10 hours.
4. Serve hot.

Nutrition: Calories: 553; Carbohydrates: 4.6g; Protein: 62.8g; Fat: 30.3g; Sugar: 18g; Sodium: 124mg; Fiber: 1g

.Tuna and Kale (Greek)

Preparation Time: 5 minutes Cooking Time: 20 minutes Servings: 4

1-lb. tuna fillets, boneless, skinless, and cubed. 2 tbsps. olive oil.	1cup kale, torn. ½ cup cherry tomatoes, cubed. 1 yellow onion, chopped

1. Heat up a pan with the oil over medium heat, add the onion and sauté for 5 minutes.
2. Add the tuna and the other ingredients, toss, cook everything for 15 minutes more, divide between plates and serve.

Nutrition: Calories: 251 g. Fat: 4 g. Protein: 56 g. Carbs: 45 g. Cholesterol: 230 mg. Sugar: 0 g.

.Country Chicken Breasts (Spanish)

Preparation Time: 10 minutes Cooking Time: 45 minutes Servings: 2

2 medium green apples, diced. 1 small red onion, finely diced.	1small green bell pepper, chopped. 3 cloves garlic, minced.
2tbsps. dried currants. 1 tbsp. curry powder. 1 tsp. turmeric.	1 tsp. ground ginger.
¼ tsp. chili pepper flakes.	1 can (14 ½ oz.) diced tomatoes.
6 skinless, boneless chicken breasts, halved.	½ cup chicken broth.
1 cup long-grain white rice.	1-lb. large raw shrimp, shelled and deveined. Salt and pepper to taste.
Chopped parsley.	1/3 cup slivered almonds.

1. Rinse chicken, pat dry, and set aside.
2. In a large crockpot, combine apples, onion, bell pepper, garlic, currants, curry powder, turmeric, ginger, and chili pepper flakes. Stir in tomatoes.
3. Arrange chicken, overlapping pieces slightly, on top of tomato mixture.
4. Pour in broth and do not mix or stir.
5. Cover and cook for 6–7 hours on low.
6. Preheat oven to 200° F.
7. Carefully transfer chicken to an oven-safe plate, cover lightly, and keep warm in the oven.
8. Stir rice into the remaining liquid. Increase cooker heat setting to high; cover and cook, stirring once or twice, until rice is almost tender to bite, 30–35 minutes. Stir in shrimp, cover, and cook until shrimp are opaque in center, about 10 more minutes.
9. Meanwhile, toast almonds in a small pan over medium heat until golden brown, 5–8 minutes, stirring occasionally. Set aside.
10. To serve, season the rice mixture to taste with salt and pepper. Mound in a warm serving dish and arrange chicken on top. Sprinkle with parsley and almonds.

Nutrition: Calories: 155 g. Fat: 5 g. Protein: 56 g. Carbs: 45 g. Cholesterol: 230 mg. Sugar: 0 g.

.Greek Lamb Chop (Greek)

Preparation time: 10 minutes
Cooking time: 8 minutes Servings: 8

8 trimmed lamb loin chops 2 tbsps. lemon juice	1 tbsp. dried oregano 1 tbsp. garlic, minced
½ tsp. salt	¼ tsp. black pepper Cooking spray

1. Preheat the broiler.
2. Combine oregano, garlic, lemon juice, salt, and pepper and rub on both sides of the lamb. Place the lamb on a broiler pan coated with cooking spray and cook for 4 minutes on each side.

Nutrition: Calories: 457 Protein: 49 g. Fat: 20 g.

.Beef Cabbage Stew (Spanish)

Preparation Time: 30 minutes Cooking Time: 2 hours Servings: 8

1lbs. beef stew meat. 1 cube beef bouillon. 8-oz. tomato sauce.	¼ cup chopped celery. 2 bay leaves.
8-oz. plum tomatoes, chopped. 1 cup hot chicken broth.	Salt and pepper to taste. 1 cabbage.
1 tsp. Greek seasoning. 4 onions, chopped.	

1. Cut off the stem of the cabbage. Separate the leaves carefully. Wash well and rinse off. Set aside for now.
2. Fry the beef in a large pan over medium-low heat for about 8–10 minutes or until you get a brown color.
1. 3.Into the pan, pour inof the chicken broth.
3. Add the beef bouillon, and mix well.
4. Add the black pepper, salt and mix again.
5. Add the lid and cook on medium-low heat for about 1 hour.
6. Take off the heat and transfer the mix into a bowl.
7. Spread the cabbage leaves on a flat surface.
8. Fill the middle using the beef mixture. Use a generous portion of filling, it will give your stew a better taste.
9. Wrap the cabbage leaves tightly. Use a kitchen thread to tie it. Finish it with the remaining leaves and filling.
10. In a pot heat the oil over fry the onion for 1 minute.
11. Add the remaining chicken broth.
12. Add in the celery and tomato sauce and cook for another 10 minutes.
13. Add the Greek seasonings, and mix well. Bring to boil and then carefully add the wrapped cabbage.
14. Cover and cook for another 10 minutes.
15. Serve hot.

Nutrition: Calories: 372 g. Fats: 22.7 g. Carbs: 9 g. Protein: 31.8 g.

.Lamb with String Beans (Spanish)

Preparation time: 10 minutes
Cooking time: 1 hour Servings: 6

¼ cup extra-virgin olive oil 6 lamb chops	1 tsp. sea salt
½ tsp. black pepper 2 tbsps. tomato paste 1 ½ cups hot water	1lb. green beans 1 onion
2tomatoes	

1. In a skillet at medium-high heat, pour 2 tbsps. of olive oil.
2. Season the lamb chops with ½ tsp. sea salt and 1/8 tsp. pepper. Cook the lamb in the hot oil for 4 minutes. Transfer the meat to a platter and set it aside.
3. Put back to the heat then put the 2 tbsps. of olive oil. Heat until it shimmers.
4. Blend the tomato paste and the hot water. Mix to the hot skillet along with the green beans, onion, tomatoes, and the remaining ½ tsp. sea salt and ¼ tsp. pepper. Bring to a simmer.
5. Return the lamb chops to the pan. Bring to boil and reduce the heat to medium-low. Simmer for 45 minutes until the beans are soft, adding additional water as needed to adjust the thickness of the sauce.

Nutrition: Calories: 439 Protein: 50 g. Fat: 22 g.

.Chicken Piccata (Italian)

Preparation time: 10 minutes Cooking time: 10 minutes
Servings: 6

½ cup whole-wheat flour	½ tsp. sea salt
1/8 tsp. freshly ground black pepper 1 ½ lb. boneless	3 tbsps. extra-virgin olive oil
½ cup dry white wine 1 lemon juice	1 cup unsalted chicken broth 1 lemon zest
¼ cup capers, drained and rinsed	¼ cup fresh parsley leaves, chopped

1. In a shallow dish, whisk the flour, sea salt, and pepper. Dredge the chicken in the flour and tap off any excess.
2. Heat the olive oil in a pan over medium-high heat.
3. Add the chicken and cook for 4 minutes. Remove the chicken from the pan and set aside, tented with aluminum foil to keep warm.
4. Return to the heat and mix the broth, wine, lemon juice, and lemon zest, and capers. Simmer for 3–4 minutes, stirring. Remove the skillet from the heat and return the chicken to the pan. Turn to coat. Stir in the parsley and serve.

Nutrition: Calories: 153 Protein: 8 g. Fat: 9 g.

.One-Pan Tuscan Chicken (Italian)

Preparation time: 10 minutes Cooking time: 25 minutes
Servings: 6

¼ cup extra-virgin olive oil, divided 1 lb. boneless chicken	1 onion
1 red bell pepper 3 garlic cloves	½ cup dry white wine 2 (14 oz.) can tomatoes
1 (14 oz.) can white beans	1 tbsp. dried Italian seasoning
½ tsp. sea salt	1/8 tsp. freshly ground black pepper 1/8 tsp. red pepper flakes
¼ cup fresh basil leaves, chopped	

1. In a huge skillet over medium-high heat, preheat 2 tbsps. of olive oil.
2. Add the chicken and cook for 6 minutes, stirring. Take out the chicken and set it aside on a platter, tented with aluminum foil to keep warm.
3. Return the skillet to heat and heat the remaining 2 tbsps. of olive oil.
4. Add the onion and red bell pepper. Cook for 5 minutes.
5. Cook the garlic for 30 seconds.
6. Stir in the wine. Cook for 1 minute, stirring.
7. Add the crushed and chopped tomatoes, white beans, Italian seasoning, sea salt, pepper, and red pepper flakes. Bring to a simmer and reduce the heat to medium. Cook for 5 minutes, stirring occasionally.
8. Take the chicken and any juices that have collected back to the skillet. Cook for 1–2 minutes. Pull out from the heat and stir in the basil before serving.

Nutrition: Calories: 271 Protein: 14 g. Fat: 0.1 g.

.Chicken Kapama (Spanish)

Preparation time: 10 minutes Cooking time: 90 minutes
Servings: 4

1 (32 oz.) can tomatoes, chopped	¼ cup dry white wine 2 tbsps. tomato paste
3 tbsps. extra-virgin olive oil	¼ tsp. red pepper flakes 1 tsp. ground allspice
½ tsp. dried oregano 2 whole cloves	1 cinnamon stick
½ tsp. sea salt	1/8 tsp. black pepper
4 boneless, skinless chicken breast halves	

1. In a pot over medium-high heat, mix the tomatoes, wine, tomato paste, olive oil, red pepper flakes, allspice, oregano, cloves, cinnamon stick, sea salt, and pepper. Bring to a simmer, stirring occasionally. Adjust the heat to medium-low and simmer for 30 minutes, stirring occasionally. Remove and discard the whole cloves and cinnamon stick from the sauce and let the sauce cool.
2. Preheat the oven to 350°F.
3. Place the chicken in a 9-by-13-inch baking dish. Drizzle sauce over the chicken and cover the pan with aluminum foil. Bake for 45 minutes.

Nutrition: Calories: 220 Protein: 8 g. Fat: 14 g.

.Spinach and Feta-Stuffed Chicken Breasts (Greek)

Preparation time: 10 minutes Cooking time: 45 minutes
Servings: 4

2tbsps. extra-virgin olive oil 1 lb. fresh baby spinach	3garlic cloves, minced 1 lemon zest
½ tsp. sea salt	1/8 tsp. freshly ground black pepper
½ cup Feta cheese, crumbled 4 chicken breast halves	

1. Preheat the oven to 350°F.
2. Preheat the oil and skillet over medium-high heat.
3. Cook the spinach for 3–4 minutes.
4. Cook the garlic, lemon zest, sea salt, and pepper.
5. Cool slightly and mix in the cheese.
6. Spread the spinach and cheese mixture in an even layer over the chicken pieces and roll the breast around the filling.
7. Hold closed with toothpicks or butcher's twine.
8. Place the breasts in a 9-by-13-inch baking dish and bake for 30–40 minutes.
9. Take away from the oven and let rest for 5 minutes before slicing and serving.

Nutrition: Calories: 263 Protein: 17 g. Fat: 20 g.

.Steamed Trout with Lemon Herb Crust (Spanish)

Preparation time: 10 minutes Cooking time: 15 minutes Servings: 2

3 tbsps. olive oil	3 garlic cloves, chopped 2 tbsps. fresh lemon juice
1 tbsp. fresh mint, chopped	1 tbsp. fresh parsley, chopped
¼ tsp. dried ground thyme 1 tsp. sea salt	1lb. (454 g.) fresh trout (2 pieces) 2 cups fish stock

1. Blend the olive oil, garlic, lemon juice, mint, parsley, thyme, and salt. Brush the marinade onto the fish.
2. Insert a trivet in the electric pressure cooker. Fill in the fish stock and place the fish on the trivet.
3. Secure the lid. Select the STEAM mode and set the cooking time for 15 minutes at high pressure.
4. Once cooking is complete, do a quick pressure release. Carefully open the lid. Serve warm.

Nutrition: Calories: 477 Fat: 30 g. Protein: 52 g.

.Roasted Trout Stuffed with Veggies (Greek)

Preparation time: 10 minutes Cooking time: 25 minutes Servings: 2

1(8 oz.) whole trout fillets 1 tbsp. extra-virgin olive oil	¼ tsp. salt
1/8 tsp. black pepper	1 poblano pepper
½ red bell pepper	1small onion, thinly sliced
Cooking spray	2–3 shiitake mushrooms, sliced 1 lemon, sliced

1. Set the oven to 425°F (220°C). Coat the baking sheet with nonstick cooking spray.
2. Rub both trout fillets, inside and out, with olive oil. Season with salt and pepper.
3. Mix the onion, bell pepper, poblano pepper, and mushrooms in a large bowl. Stuff half of this mix into the cavity of each fillet. Top the mixture with 2–3 lemon slices inside each fillet.
4. Place the fish on the prepared baking sheet side by side. Roast in the preheated oven for 25 minutes.
5. Pull out from the oven and serve on a plate.

Nutrition: Calories: 453 Fat: 22 g. Protein: 49 g.

.Mediterranean Rice and Sausage (Italian)

Preparation time: 15 minutes Cooking time: 8 hours Servings: 6

1½ lb. Italian sausage, crumbled 1 medium onion, chopped	2tbsps. steak sauce
2 cups long-grain rice, uncooked	1 (14 oz.) can diced tomatoes with juice
½ cup water	1medium green pepper, diced Olive oil or nonstick cooking spray

1. Spray your slow cooker with olive oil or nonstick cooking spray.
2. Add the sausage, onion, and steak sauce to the slow cooker.
3. Cook on low for 8–10 hours.
4. After 8 hours, add the rice, tomatoes, water, and green pepper. Stir to combine thoroughly.
5. Cook for 20–25 minutes.

Nutrition: Calories: 650 Fat: 36 g. Protein: 22 g.

.Veal Pot Roast (Spanish)

Preparation time: 20 minutes Cooking time: 5 hours Servings: 6–8

1tbsps. olive oil Salt and pepper	2lbs. boneless veal roast 4 medium carrots, peeled
2 parsnips, peeled and halved	2 white turnips, peeled and quartered 10 garlic cloves, peeled
2 sprigs of fresh thyme	1 orange, scrubbed and zested 1 cup chicken or veal stock

1. Heat a large skillet over medium-high heat.
2. Coat veal roast all over with olive oil, then season with salt and pepper.
3. When the skillet is hot, add the veal roast and sear on all sides.
4. Once the veal roast is cooked on all sides, transfer it to the slow cooker.
5. Toss the carrots, parsnips, turnips, and garlic into the skillet. Stir and cook for 5 minutes—not all the way through, just to get some of the brown bits from the veal and give them a bit of color.
6. Transfer the vegetables to the slow cooker, placing them all around the meat.
7. Top the veal roast with the thyme and the zest from the orange. Slice orange in half and squeeze the juice over the top of the meat.
8. Add the chicken stock, then cook the veal roast on LOW for 5 hours.

Nutrition: Calories: 426 Fat: 12.8 g. Protein: 48.8 g.

.Slow Cooker Salmon in Foil (Italian)

Preparation time: 5 minutes Cooking time: 2 hours Servings: 2

1(6 oz./170 g.) salmon fillets	2 garlic cloves, minced
1 tbsp. olive oil	
½ tbsp. lime juice	1 tsp. fresh parsley, finely chopped
¼ tsp. black pepper	

1. Spread a length of foil onto a work surface and place the salmon fillets in the middle.
2. Blend the olive oil, garlic, lime juice, parsley, and black pepper. Brush the mixture over the fillets. Fold the foil over and crimp the sides to make a packet.
3. Place the packet into the slow cooker, cover, and cook on HIGH for 2 hours. Serve hot.

Nutrition: Calories: 446 Fat: 21 g. Protein: 65 g.

.Chicken Gyros with Tzatziki (Italian)

Preparation time: 10 minutes Cooking time: 80 minutes Servings: 6

1lb. ground chicken breast 1 onion	2tbsps. dried rosemary 1 tbsp. dried marjoram 6 garlic cloves, minced
½ tsp. sea salt	¼ tsp. freshly ground black pepper Tzatziki Sauce

1. Preheat the oven to 350°F.
2. In a stand mixer, blend the chicken, onion, rosemary, marjoram, garlic, sea salt, and pepper.
3. Press the mixture into a loaf pan. Bake for 1 hour. Pull out from the oven and set it aside for 20 minutes before slicing.
4. Slice the gyro and spoon the tzatziki sauce over the top.

Nutrition: Calories: 289 Protein: 50 g. Fat: 1 g.

.Chicken with Kale and Chili Salsa (Italian)

Preparation Time: 5 minutes Cooking Time: 45 minutes
Servings: 1

3 oz. buckwheat.	1 tsp. chopped fresh ginger. Juice of ½ lemon, divided. 2 tsps. ground turmeric.
3oz. kale, chopped. oz. red onion, sliced.	4oz. skinless, boneless chicken breast. 1 tbsp. extra-virgin olive oil.
1 tomato.	1 handful parsley.
1 bird's eye chili, chopped.	

1. Start with the salsa: Remove the eye out of the tomato and finely chop it, making sure to keep as much of the liquid as you can. Mix it with chili, parsley, and lemon juice. You could add everything to a blender for different results.
2. Heat your oven to 220° F. Marinate the chicken with a little oil, 1 tsp. of turmeric, and lemon juice. Let it rest for 5–10 mins.
3. Heat a pan over medium heat until it is hot then add marinated chicken and allow it to cook for a minute on both sides (until it is pale gold). Transfer the chicken to the oven if the pan is not ovenproof, place it in a baking tray and bake for 8–10 minutes or until it is cooked through. Take the chicken out of the oven, cover with foil, and let it rest for 5 minutes before you serve.
4. Meanwhile, in a steamer, steam the kale for about 5 minutes.
5. In a little oil, fry the ginger and red onions until they are soft but not colored, and then add in the cooked kale and fry it for a minute.
6. Cook the buckwheat in accordance with the packet directions with the remaining turmeric. Serve alongside the vegetables, salsa, and chicken.

Nutrition: Calories: 134.8 g. Fat: 30 g. Protein: 56 g. Carbs: 45 g. Cholesterol: 230 mg. Sugar: 0 g.

.Dijon and Herb Pork Tenderloin (Spanish)

Preparation time: 10 minutes Cooking time: 30 minutes
Servings: 6

½ cup fresh Italian parsley leaves 3 tbsps. fresh rosemary leaves	1tbsps. fresh thyme leaves 3 tbsps. Dijon mustard
1 tbsp. extra-virgin olive oil	½ tsp. sea salt
4 garlic cloves, minced	
¼ tsp. freshly ground black pepper 1 (1 ½ lb.) pork tenderloin	

1. Preheat the oven to 400°F.
2. In a blender, pulse the parsley, rosemary, thyme, mustard, olive oil, garlic, sea salt, and pepper. Spread the mixture evenly over the pork and place it on a rimmed baking sheet.
3. Bake for 20 minutes. Remove from the oven and set it aside for 10 minutes before slicing and serving.

Nutrition: Calories: 393 Protein: 74 g. Fat: 12 g.

.Eggplant Casserole (Italian)

Preparation time: 10 minutes Cooking time: 45 minutes
Servings: 8

5 tbsps. extra-virgin olive oil 1 eggplant	1 onion
1 green bell pepper 1 lb. ground turkey	3 garlic cloves, minced 2 tbsps. tomato paste
1(14 oz.) can tomatoes, chopped 1 tbsp. Italian seasoning	2tsps. Worcestershire sauce 1 tsp. dried oregano
½ tsp. ground cinnamon	1cup unsweetened nonfat plain Greek yogurt 1 egg, beaten
¼ tsp. freshly ground black pepper	¼ tsp. ground nutmeg
¼ cup Parmesan cheese, grated	2tbsps. fresh parsley leaves, chopped

1. Preheat the oven to 400°F.
2. Preheat a skillet over medium-high heat, pour 3 tbsps. of olive oil.
3. Add the eggplant slices and brown for 3–4 minutes per side. Transfer to paper towels to drain.
4. Return to the heat and pour the remaining 2 tbsps. of olive oil. Add the onion and green bell pepper. Cook for 5 minutes. Remove from the pan and set them aside.
5. Put back to the heat and add the turkey. Cook for 5 mins.
6. Cook the garlic.
7. Stir in the tomato paste, tomatoes, Italian seasoning, Worcestershire sauce, oregano, and cinnamon. Return the onion and bell pepper to the pan. Cook for 5 mins, stirring.
8. Scourge the yogurt, egg, pepper, nutmeg, and cheese.
9. In a 9-by-13-inch baking dish, spread half the meat mixture. Layer with half of the eggplant. Add the remaining meat mixture and the remaining eggplant. Spread with the yogurt mixture. Bake for about 20 minutes.
10. Garnish with the parsley and serve.

Nutrition: Calories: 338 Protein: 28 g. Fat: 20 g.

.Greek Meatballs (Greek)

Preparation time: 20 minutes Cooking time: 25 minutes
Servings: 4

2 whole-wheat bread slices 1 ¼ lb. ground turkey	1egg
¼ cup seasoned whole-wheat bread crumbs 3 garlic cloves, minced	¼ red onion, grated
¼ cup fresh Italian parsley leaves, chopped 2 tbsps. fresh mint leaves, chopped	2tbsps. fresh oregano leaves, chopped
½ tsp. sea salt	¼ tsp. freshly ground black pepper

1. Preheat the oven to 350°F.
2. Prepare a baking sheet with foil.
3. Run the bread underwater to wet it, and squeeze out any excess. Tear the wet bread into small pieces and place it in a medium bowl.
4. Add the turkey, egg, bread crumbs, garlic, red onion, parsley, mint, oregano, sea salt, and pepper. Mix well. Form the mixture into ¼-cup- size balls. Place the meatballs on the prepared sheet and bake for 25 minutes.

Nutrition: Calories: 350 Protein: 42 g. Fat: 18 g.

.Steak with Red Wine–Mushroom Sauce (Italian)

Preparation time: 10 minutes Cooking time: 20 minutes
Servings: 4

For the marinade and steak 1 cup dry red wine	3 garlic cloves, minced
2 tbsps. extra-virgin olive oil	1tsp. Dijon mustard
1 tbsp. low-sodium soy sauce 1 tbsp. dried thyme	
2tbsps. extra-virgin olive oil 1 ½ lb. skirt steak	For the mushroom sauce
2 tbsps. extra-virgin olive oil 1 lb. cremini mushrooms	½ tsp. sea salt
1tsp. dried thyme 1/8 tsp. black pepper	2garlic cloves, minced 1 cup dry red wine

For the marinade and steak:

1. In a small bowl, whisk the wine, garlic, olive oil, soy sauce, thyme, and mustard. Pour into a resealable bag and add the steak. Refrigerate the steak to marinate for 4–8 hours. Remove the steak from the marinade and pat it dry with paper towels.
2. In a big skillet over medium-high heat, warm up olive oil.
3. Cook the steak for 4 minutes per side. Pull out steak from the skillet and put it on a plate tented with aluminum foil to keep warm, while you prepare the mushroom sauce.
4. When the mushroom sauce is ready, slice the steak against the grain into

½-inch-thick slices. For the mushroom sauce:

1. Preheat the skillet over medium-high heat, heat the olive oil.
2. Add the mushrooms, sea salt, thyme, and pepper. Cook for 6 minutes.
3. Cook the garlic for 30 seconds.
4. Stir in the wine, and use the side of a wooden spoon to scrape and fold in any browned bits from the bottom of the skillet. Cook for 4 minutes. Serve the mushrooms spooned over the steak.

Nutrition: Calories: 405 Protein: 33 g. Fat: 22 g.

.Dijon Fish Fillets (Greek)

Preparation Time: 15 minutes Cooking Time: 3 minutes
Servings: 2

2 white fish fillets Salt	1 tbsp Dijon mustard 1 cup of water Pepper

1. Pour water into the instant pot and place trivet in the pot.
2. Brush fish fillets with mustard and season with pepper and salt and place on top of the trivet.
3. Seal pot with lid and cook on high for 3 minutes.
4. Once done, release pressure using quick release. Remove lid.
5. Serve and enjoy.

Nutrition: Calories 270 Fat 11.9 g Carbohydrates 0.5 g Sugar 0.1 g Protein 38 g Cholesterol 119 mg

.Quinoa Protein Bars (Spanish)

Preparation Time: 15 minutes Cooking Time: 40 minutes
Servings: 16

½ cup almonds, chopped.	½ cup chocolate chips.
½ cup coconut oil, melted.	½ cup flaxseed, ground.
½ cup honey.	½ tsp. salt.
1cup quinoa, dry.	2¼ cups quick oats. 3 large egg whites.

1. Preheat oven to 325° F
2. On the bottom of a clean, dry baking sheet evenly spread oats, quinoa, and almonds.
3. Bake for about 15 minutes or until lightly brown. You may want to stir the items in the cookie sheet every few minutes to ensure nothing burns.
4. Remove grains and nuts from the oven and allow to cool completely, but don't turn off the oven.
5. Whisk the egg whites in a bowl and beat the coconut oil and honey into them.
6. Combine flaxseed, chocolate chips, and salt into the cooled grains and nuts, and then pour that mixture into the mixing bowl, coating everything completely.
7. Line your baking sheet with parchment paper and spread the mixture evenly onto it, pressing it into one even layer. You may want to shape the sides of the mass, depending on whether or not it reaches the edges of your baking sheet without thinning out too much.
8. Bake for 30 minutes, then remove from the oven.
9. Let cool for one hour before slicing into evenly-shaped bars, then cool completely.
10. Enjoy!

Nutrition: Calories: 269 g. Carbs: 30 g. Fats: 15 g. Protein: 6 g.

.Marinated Tuna Steak (Spanish)

Preparation Time: 6 minutes Cooking Time: 18 minutes
Servings: 4

Olive oil (2 tbsp.) Orange juice (.25 cup) Soy sauce (.25 cup) Lemon juice (1 tbsp.) Fresh parsley (2 tbsp.) Garlic clove (1)	Ground black pepper (.5 tsp.) Fresh oregano (.5 tsp.)
Tuna steaks (4 - 4 oz. Steaks)	

1. Mince the garlic and chop the oregano and parsley.
3. In a glass container, mix the pepper, oregano, garlic, parsley, lemon juice, soy sauce, olive oil, and orange juice.
4. Warm the grill using the high heat setting. Grease the grate with oil.
5. Add to tuna steaks and cook for five to six minutes. Turn and baste with the marinated sauce.
6. Cook another five minutes or until it's the way you like it. Discard the remaining marinade.

Nutrition: Calories: 200 Protein: 27.4g Fat: 7.9g

.Garlic and Shrimp Pasta (Italian)

Preparation Time: 4 minutes Cooking Time: 16 minutes
Servings: 4

6 ounces whole wheat spaghetti	12 ounces raw shrimp, peeled and deveined, cut into 1-inch pieces 1 bunch asparagus, trimmed
1 large bell pepper, thinly sliced 1 cup fresh peas	3 garlic cloves, chopped
1 and ¼ teaspoons kosher salt	½ and ½ cups non-fat plain yogurt 3 tablespoon lemon juice
1 tablespoon extra-virgin olive oil	½ teaspoon fresh ground black pepper
¼ cup pine nuts, toasted	

1. Take a large sized pot and bring water to a boil
2. Add your spaghetti and cook them for about minutes less than the directed package instruction
3. Add shrimp, bell pepper, asparagus and cook for about 2-4 minutes until the shrimp are tender
4. Drain the pasta and the contents well
5. Take a large bowl and mash garlic until a paste form
6. Whisk in yogurt, parsley, oil, pepper and lemon juice into the garlic paste
7. Add pasta mix and toss well
8. Serve by sprinkling some pine nuts!

Nutrition: Calories: 406 Fat: 22g Protein: 26g

.Paprika Butter Shrimps (Spanish)

Preparation Time: 6 minutes Cooking Time: 31 minutes
Servings: 2

¼ tablespoon smoked paprika 1/8 cup sour cream	½ pound tiger shrimps 1/8 cup butter
Salt and black pepper, to taste	

1. Prep the oven to 390F and grease a baking dish.
2. Mix all the ingredients in a large bowl and transfer into the baking dish.
3. Situate in the oven and bake for about 15 minutes.
4. Place paprika shrimp in a dish and set aside to cool for meal prepping. Divide it in 2 containers and cover the lid. Refrigerate for 1-2 days and reheat in microwave before serving.

Nutrition: Calories: 330 Protein: 32.6g Fat: 21.5g

.Rosemary Baked Chicken Drumsticks (Spanish)

Preparation time: 5 minutes Cooking time: 1 hour Servings: 6

1tbsps. fresh rosemary leaves, chopped 1 tsp. garlic powder	½ tsp. sea salt
1/8 tsp. freshly ground black pepper 1 lemon zest	12 chicken drumsticks

1. Preheat the oven to 350°F.
2. Blend the rosemary, garlic powder, sea salt, pepper, and lemon zest.
3. Place the drumsticks in a 9-by-13-inch baking dish and sprinkle with the rosemary mixture. Bake for 1 hour.

Nutrition: Calories: 163 Protein: 26 g. Fat: 6 g.

.Mediterranean Avocado Salmon Salad (Greek)

Preparation Time: 6 minutes Cooking Time: 10 minutes
Servings: 4

1 lb. skinless salmon fillets Marinade/Dressing:	3 tbsp. olive oil
2 tbsp. lemon juice fresh, squeezed 1 tbsp. red wine vinegar, optional 1 tbsp. fresh chopped parsley	2 tsp garlic minced 1 tsp dried oregano 1 tsp salt
Cracked pepper, to taste Salad:	4 cups Romaine (or Cos) lettuce leaves 1 large cucumber
2 Roma tomatoes	1 red onion
1avocado	1/2 cup feta cheese
1/3 cup pitted Kalamata olives	

1. Scourge the olive oil, lemon juice, red wine vinegar, chopped parsley, garlic minced, oregano, salt and pepper
2. Fill out half of the marinade into a large, shallow dish, refrigerate the remaining marinade to use as the dressing
3. Coat the salmon in the rest of the marinade
4. Place a skillet pan or grill over medium-high, add 1 tbsp oil and sear salmon on both sides until crispy and cooked through
5. Allow the salmon to cool
6. Distribute the salmon among the containers, store in the fridge for 2-3 days
7. To Serve: Prep the salad by putting the romaine lettuce, cucumber, Roma tomatoes, red onion, avocado, feta cheese, and olives in a bowl. Reheat the salmon in the microwave for 30seconds to 1 minute or until heated through.
8. Slice the salmon and arrange over salad. Drizzle the salad with the remaining untouched dressing, serve with lemon wedges.

Nutrition: Calories:411 Fat: 27g Protein: 28g

.Chicken with Onions, Potatoes, Figs, and Carrots(Greek)

Preparation time: 5 minutes Cooking time: 45 minutes Servings: 4

2 cups fingerling potatoes, halved 4 fresh figs, quartered	2 carrots, julienned
2 tbsps. extra-virgin olive oil	¼ tsp. freshly ground black pepper 4 chicken leg-thigh quarters
1 tsp. sea salt, divided	
2 tbsps. fresh parsley leaves, chopped	

1. Preheat the oven to 425°F.
2. In a small bowl, toss the potatoes, figs, and carrots with the olive oil, ½ tsp. sea salt, and pepper. Spread in a 9-by-13-inch baking dish.
3. Rub the chicken with the remaining ½ tsp. sea salt.
4. Place it on top of the vegetables.
5. Bake for 35–45 minutes.
6. Sprinkle with the parsley and serve.

Nutrition: Calories: 429 Protein: 52 g. Fat: 12 g.

.Skillet Braised Cod with Asparagus and Potatoes(Spanish)

Preparation time: 20 minutes Cooking time: 20 minutes
Servings: 4

4 skinless cod fillets 1 lb. asparagus	12 oz. halved small purple potatoes
½ lemon zest, finely grated	½ lemon juice
½ cup white wine	¼ cup torn fresh basil leaves 1 ½ tbsp. olive oil
1 tbsp. capers	3 garlic cloves, sliced
½ tsp. salt	¼ tsp. pepper

1. Take a large and tall pan on the sides and heat the oil over medium- high.
2. Season the cod abundantly with salt and pepper and put in the pan, with the hot oil, for 1 minute. Carefully flip for 1 more minute and after transferring the cod to a plate. Set aside.
3. Add the lemon zest, capers, and garlic to the pan and mix to coat with the remaining oil in the pan, and cook for 1 minute. Add the wine and deglaze the pan. Add the lemon juice, potatoes, ½ tsp. salt, ¼ tsp. pepper and 2 cups of water and bring to a boil, reduce the heat, and simmer until potatoes are tender, for 10–12 minutes.
4. Mix the asparagus and cook for 2 minutes. Bring back the cod filets and any juices accumulated in the pan. Cook until the asparagus are tender, for 3 minutes.
5. Divide the cod fillets into shallow bowls and add the potatoes and asparagus. Mix the basil in the broth left in the pan and pour over the cod.

Nutrition: Calories: 461 Protein: 40 g. Fat: 16 g.

.Savory Vegetable Pancakes (Greek)

Preparation time: 10 minutes Cooking time: 40 minutes
Servings: 7

8 peeled carrots	2 garlic cloves
1 zucchini	1 bunch green onions
½ bunch parsley	1 recipe pancake batter 3 tbsps. of olive oil Salt to taste

1. Grate chop the zucchini and carrots using the grater. Finely chop the onions, mince the garlic and roughly chop the parsley.
2. Prepare the pancakes with your favorite recipe or buy them in the store, but use ¼ cup of liquid less than required, zucchini will add a large amount of liquid to the mix. Fold the vegetables in the prepared pancake batter.
3. Heat a pan over medium-high heat and brush it gently with the olive oil. Use a 1/3 measuring cup to scoop the batter on the heated pan. Cook for 3–4 minutes, until the outer edge has set, then turn over. Cook for another 2 minutes and remove from the heat.
4. Season the pancakes with plenty of salt. Serve with butter, sour cream, or even a salted jam.

Nutrition: Calories: 291 Protein: 24 g. Fat: 10 g.

.Niçoise-inspired Salad with Sardines (Spanish)

Preparation Time: 9 minutes Cooking Time: 16 minutes
Servings: 4

4 eggs	12 ounces baby red potatoes (about 12 potatoes) 6 ounces green beans, halved
4 cups baby spinach leaves or mixed greens	1 bunch radishes, quartered (about 1 1/3 cups) 1 cup cherry tomatoes
20 Kalamata or Niçoise olives (about 1/3 cup)	3 (3.75-ounce) cans skinless, boneless sardines packed in olive oil, drained
8 tablespoons Dijon Red Wine Vinaigrette	

1. Situate the eggs in a saucepan and cover with water. Bring the water to a boil. Once the water starts to boil, close then turn the heat off. Set a timer for minutes.
2. Once the timer goes off, strain the hot water and run cold water over the eggs to cool. Peel the eggs when cool and cut in half.
3. Poke each potato a few times using fork. Place them on a microwave- safe plate and microwave on high for 4 to 5 minutes, until the potatoes are tender. Let cool and cut in half.
4. Place green beans on a microwave-safe plate and microwave on high for 1½ to 2 minutes, until the beans are crisp-tender. Cool.
5. Place 1 egg, ½ cup of green beans, 6 potato halves, 1 cup of spinach, 1/3 cup of radishes, ¼ cup of tomatoes, olives, and 3 sardines in each of 4 containers. Pour 2 tablespoons of vinaigrette into each of 4 sauce containers.

Nutrition: Calories: 450 Fat: 32g Protein: 21g

.Broiled Chili Calamari (Spanish)

Preparation Time: 9 minutes Cooking Time: 8 minutes
Servings: 4

2 tablespoons extra virgin olive oil 1 teaspoon chili powder	½ teaspoon ground cumin Zest of 1 lime
Juice of 1 lime Dash of sea salt	1and ½ pounds squid, cleaned and split open, with tentacles cut into ½ inch rounds
2tablespoons cilantro, chopped	2 tablespoons red bell pepper, minced

1. Take a medium bowl and stir in olive oil, chili powder, cumin, lime zest, sea salt, lime juice and pepper
2. Add squid and let it marinade and stir to coat, coat and let it refrigerate for 1 hour
3. Pre-heat your oven to broil
4. Arrange squid on a baking sheet, broil for 8 minutes turn once until tender
5. Garnish the broiled calamari with cilantro and red bell pepper
6. Serve and enjoy!

Nutrition: Calories: 159 Fat: 13g Protein: 3g

.Salmon with Corn Pepper Salsa (Greek)

Preparation Time: 9 minutes   Cooking Time: 12 minutes
Servings: 2

1garlic clove, grated	1/2 teaspoon mild chili powder 1/2 teaspoon ground coriander teaspoon ground cumin
2limes – 1, zest and juice; 1 cut into wedges 2 teaspoons rapeseed oil	2 wild salmon fillets
1 ear of corn on the cob	
1 avocado, cored, peeled, and finely chopped 1 red pepper, deseeded and finely chopped	1 red chili, halved and deseeded
1/2 a pack of finely chopped coriander	

1. Boil the corn in water for about 6-8 minutes until tender.
2. Drain and cut off the kernels.
3. In a bowl, combine garlic, spices, 1 tablespoon of lime juice, and oil; mix well to prepare spice rub.
4. Coat the salmon with the rub.
5. Add the zest to the corn and give it a gentle stir.
6. Heat a frying pan over medium heat.
7. Cook salmon for 4 minutes on both sides.
8. Serve the cooked salmon with salsa and lime wedges.
9. Enjoy!

Nutrition: Calories: 949 Fat: 57.4g Protein: 76.8g

.Garlic-Butter Parmesan Salmon and Asparagus(Greek)

Preparation time: 10 minutes   Cooking time: 15 minutes
Servings: 2

2 (6 oz./170 g.) salmon fillets, skin on and patted dry Pink Himalayan salt	Freshly ground black pepper, to taste
1lb. (454 g) fresh asparagus, ends snapped off 3 tbsps. almond butter	2garlic cloves, minced
¼ cup Parmesan cheese, grated	

1. Preheat the oven to 400ºF (205ºC). Line a baking sheet with aluminum foil.
2. Season both sides of the salmon fillets.
3. Place the salmon in the middle of the baking sheet and arrange the asparagus around the salmon.
4. Heat the almond butter in a small saucepan over medium heat.
5. Cook the minced garlic.
6. Drizzle the garlic-butter sauce over the salmon and asparagus and scatter the Parmesan cheese on top.
7. Bake in the preheated oven for 12 minutes. You can switch the oven to broil at the end of cooking time for 3 minutes to get a nice char on the asparagus.
8. Let cool for 5 minutes before serving.

Nutrition: Calories: 435 Fat: 26 g. Protein: 42 g.

.Seafood Paella (Italian)

Preparation Time: 9 minutes   Cooking Time: 41 minutes
Servings: 4

4 small lobster tails (6-12 oz. each)	1large yellow onion 2 cups Spanish rice 4 garlic cloves
3 tbsp. Extra Virgin Olive Oil	
2large pinches of Spanish saffron threads 1 tsp. Sweet Spanish paprika	1 tsp. cayenne pepper
1/2 tsp. Aleppo pepper flakes 2 large Roma tomatoes	6 oz. French green beans
1lb. prawns or large shrimp	
1/4 cup chopped fresh parsley	

1. Using big pot, add 3 cups of water and bring it to a rolling boil
2. Add in the lobster tails and allow boil briefly, about 1-minutes or until pink, remove from heat
3. Using tongs situate the lobster tails to a plate and do not discard the lobster cooking water
4. Allow the lobster is cool, then remove the shell and cut into large chunks.
5. Using a deep pan or skillet over medium-high heat, add 3 tbsp olive oil
6. Add the chopped onions, sauté the onions for 2 minutes and then add the rice, and cook for 3 more minutes, stirring regularly
7. Then add in the lobster cooking water and the chopped garlic and, stir in the saffron and its soaking liquid, cayenne pepper, Aleppo pepper, paprika, and salt
8. Gently stir in the chopped tomatoes and green beans, bring to a boil and allow it to slightly reduce, then cover and cook over low heat for 20 minutes
9. Once done, uncover and spread the shrimp over the rice, push it into the rice slightly, add in a little water, if needed
10. Close and cook for 18 minutes
11. Then add in the cooked lobster chunks
12. Once the lobster is warmed through, remove from heat allow the dish to cool completely
13. Distribute among the containers, store for 2 days
14. To Serve: Reheat in the microwave for 1-2 minutes or until heated through. Garnish with parsley and enjoy!

Nutrition: Calories: 536 Fat: 26g Protein:50g

.Tuscan Beef Stew (Spanish)

Preparation time: 10 minutes Cooking time: 4 hours Servings: 8

1lbs. beef stew meat 4 carrots	2 (14 ½ oz.) cans tomatoes
1 medium onion	1 package McCormick® Slow Cookers Hearty Beef Stew Seasoning
1 tsp. rosemary leaves 8 slices Italian bread	
½ cup water	½ cup dry red wine

1. Place the cubed beef in the slow cooker along with the carrots, diced tomatoes, and onion wedges.
2. Mix the seasoning package in ½ cup of water and stir well, making sure no lumps are remaining.
3. Add the red wine to the water and stir slightly. Add the rosemary leaves to the water-and-wine mixture and then pour over the meat, stirring to ensure the meat is completely covered.
4. Turn the slow cooker to LOW and cook for 8 hours, or cook for 4 hours on HIGH.
5. Serve with toasted Italian bread.

Nutrition: Calories: 329 Fat: 15 g. Protein: 25.6 g.

.Dill Chutney Salmon (Greek)

Preparation time: 5 minutes Cooking time: 3 minutes Servings: 2

For the chutney:	¼ cup fresh dill
¼ cup extra-virgin olive oil	½ lemon juice Sea salt, to taste
For the fish:	1cups water
2 salmon fillets	½ lemon juice
¼ tsp. paprika	Salt and freshly ground pepper to taste

1. Pulse all the chutney ingredients in a food processor until creamy. Set it aside.
2. Add the water and steamer basket to the electric pressure cooker. Place the salmon fillets, skin-side down, on the steamer basket. Drizzle the lemon juice over the salmon and sprinkle with the paprika.
3. Secure the lid. Select the MANUAL mode and set the cooking time for 3 minutes at high pressure.
4. Once cooking is complete, do a quick pressure release. Carefully open the lid.
5. Season the fillets with pepper and salt to taste. Serve topped with the dill chutney.

Nutrition: Calories: 636 Fat: 41 g. Protein: 65 g.

.Lemon Rosemary Roasted Branzino (Greek)

Preparation time: 15 minutes Cooking time: 20 minutes Servings: 2

4 tbsps. extra-virgin olive oil, divided 2 (8 oz.) Branzino fillets	1garlic clove, minced 1 bunch scallions
10–12 small cherry tomatoes, halved 1 large carrot, cut into ¼-inch rounds	½ cup dry white wine 2 tbsps. paprika
2tsps. kosher salt	½ tbsp. ground chili pepper
2 rosemary sprigs or 1 tbsp. dried rosemary 1 small lemon, thinly sliced	½ cup Kalamata olives, pitted, sliced

1. Heat a large ovenproof skillet over high heat until hot, for 2 minutes. Add 1 tbsp. olive oil and heat.
2. Add the Branzino fillets, skin-side up, and sear for 2 minutes. Flip the fillets and cook. Set them aside.
3. Swirl 2 tbsps. of olive oil around the skillet to coat evenly.
4. Add the garlic, scallions, tomatoes, and carrot, and sauté for 5 minutes.
5. Add the wine, stirring until all ingredients are well combined. Carefully place the fish over the sauce.
6. Preheat the oven to 450°F (235°C).
7. Brush the fillets with the remaining 1 tbsp. olive oil and season with paprika, salt, and chili pepper. Top each fillet with a rosemary sprig and lemon slices. Scatter the olives over fish and around the skillet.
8. Roast for about 10 minutes until the lemon slices are browned. Serve hot.

Nutrition: Calories: 724 Fat: 43 g. Protein: 57 g.

.Grilled Lemon Pesto Salmon (Italian)

Preparation time: 5 minutes Cooking time: 10 minutes Servings: 2

10 oz. (283 g.) salmon fillet 2 tbsps. prepared pesto sauce	1 large fresh lemon, sliced Cooking spray

1. Preheat the grill to medium-high heat. Spray the grill grates with cooking spray.
2. Season the salmon well. Spread the pesto sauce on top.
3. Make a bed of fresh lemon slices about the same size as the salmon fillet on the hot grill, and place the salmon on top of the lemon slices. Put any additional lemon slices on top of the salmon.
4. Grill the salmon for 10 minutes.
5. Serve hot.

Nutrition: Calories: 316 Fat: 21 g. Protein: 29 g.

Baked Salmon Salad with Creamy Mint Dressing (Greek)

Preparation Time: 20 minutes Cooking Time: 20 minutes Servings: 1

1salmon fillet. Mixed salad leaves.	2radishes, trimmed and thinly sliced. oz. young spinach leaves.
5 cm piece cucumber, cut into chunks.	1 small handful of parsley, roughly chopped. 2 spring onions, trimmed and sliced.
For the dressing:	1 tbsp. natural yogurt.
1tsp. low-fat mayonnaise.	2leaves mint, finely chopped. 1 tbsp. rice vinegar.

Salt and freshly ground black pepper.

1. Firstly, you heat the oven to 200° C (Gas 6).
2. Place the salmon filet on a baking tray and bake for 16–18 minutes until you have just cooked. Remove, and set aside from the oven. The salmon in the salad is equally nice and hot or cold. If your salmon has skin, cook the skin side down and remove the salmon from the skin after cooking, use a slice of fish. When cooked, it should slide away easily.
3. Mix the mayonnaise, yogurt, rice wine vinegar, mint leaves, and salt and pepper in a small dish and let it stand for at least 5 minutes for aromas to evolve.
4. Place on a serving plate the salad leaves and spinach, and top with the radishes, the cucumber, the spring onions, and the parsley. Flake the cooked salmon over the salad and sprinkle over the dressing.

Nutrition: Calories: 340 g. Fat: 30 g. Protein: 56 g. Carbs: 0 g. Cholesterol: 230 mg. Sugar: 0 g.

.Lamb, Butternut Squash and Date Tagine (Greek)

Prep Time: 15 minutes Cooking Time: 40 minutes Servings: 4 to 6

2 tbsps. olive oil.	2cm ginger, grated. 1 red onion, sliced.
3garlic cloves, grated or crushed. 1 tsp. chili flake (or to taste).	1cinnamon stick.
2tsps. cumin seeds.	2 tsps. ground turmeric.
½ tsp. salt.	Lamb neck fillet, cut into 2 cm chunks. Medjool dates, pitted and chopped.
14 oz. tin chopped tomatoes, plus ½ can of water.	oz. butternut squash, cut into 1 cm cubes.
Two tbsp. fresh coriander (plus extra for garnish). Buckwheat, couscous, flatbreads, or rice to serve.	14 oz. tin chickpeas, drained.

1. Preheat the oven until 140° C.
2. Sprinkle about 2 tbsps. of olive oil in a large oven-proof casserole dish or cast-iron pot. Put the sliced onion and cook on a gentle heat until the onions softened but not brown, with the lid on for about 5 minutes.
3. Add chili, cumin, cinnamon, and turmeric to the grated garlic and ginger. Remove well and cook the lid off for one more minute. If it gets too dry, add a drop of water.
4. Add pieces of lamb. In the onions and spices, stir well to coat the meat and then add salt, chopped dates, and tomatoes, plus about half a can of water (100–200ml).
5. Bring the tagine to a boil, then put the lid on and put it for 1 hour and 15 minutes in your preheated oven.
6. Add the chopped butternut squash and drained chickpeas 30 minutes before the end of the cooking time. Stir all together, bring the lid back on and go back to the oven for the remaining 30 minutes of cooking.
7. Remove from the oven when the tagine is finished and stir through the chopped coriander. Serve with couscous, buckwheat, flatbreads, or basmati rice.

Nutrition: Calories: 404 g. Fat: 30 g. Protein: 56 g. Carbs: 30 g. Cholesterol: 230 mg. Sugar: 0 g.

.Italian Shredded Pork Stew (Italian)

Preparation time: 20 minutes Cooking time: 8 hours Servings: 8

2 medium sweet potatoes 2 cups fresh kale, chopped	4 garlic cloves, minced
1 2 ½–3 ½ lb. boneless pork shoulder butt roast 1 (14 oz.) can of cannellini beans	1 large onion, chopped 1 ½ tsp. Italian seasoning
½ tsp. salt	½ tsp. pepper
3 (14 ½ oz.) cans of chicken broth Sour cream (optional)	Nonstick cooking spray or olive oil

1. Coat the slow cooker with nonstick cooking spray or olive oil.
2. Place the cubed sweet potatoes, kale, garlic, and onion into the slow cooker.
3. Add the pork shoulder on top of the potatoes.
4. Add the beans, Italian seasoning, salt, and pepper.
5. Pour the chicken broth over the meat.
6. Cook on low for 8 hours.
7. Serve with sour cream, if desired.

Nutrition: Calories: 283 Fat: 13 g. Protein: 24 g.

.Italian Beef Casserole (Italian)

Prep Time: 10 minutes Cooking Time: 1 hour 30 minutes Servings: 6

1 lb. lean stew beef, cut into chunks. 3 tsps. paprika.	4 oz. black olives, sliced. 7 oz. can tomato, chopped. 1 tbsp. tomato puree.
¼ tsp. garlic powder.	2 tsps. herb de Provence. 2 cups beef stock.
2 tbsps. olive oil.	

1. Preheat the oven to 350° F.
2. Heat oil in a pan over medium heat.
3. Add meat to the pan and cook until brown.
4. Add stock, olives, tomatoes, tomato puree, garlic powder, herb de Provence, and paprika. Stir well and bring to boil.
5. Transfer the meat mixture to the casserole dish.
6. Cover and cook in preheated oven for 1 ½ hour.
7. Serve and enjoy.

Nutrition: Calories: 100 g. Fat: 7 g. Fiber: 2 g. Carbs: 8 g. Protein: 6g.

.Moroccan Fish (Greek)

Prep Time: 9 minutes Cooking Time: 76 minutes Servings: 12

Garbanzo beans (15 oz. Can) Red bell peppers (2) Garlic (1 clove)	Large carrot (1) Vegetable oil (1 tbsp.) Onion (1) Tomatoes (3 chopped/14.5 oz can) Olives (4 chopped)
Chopped fresh parsley (.25 cup) Ground cumin (.25 cup) Paprika (3 tbsp.) Salt (to your liking) Tilapia fillets (5 lb.)	Chicken bouillon granules (2 tbsp.) Cayenne pepper (1 tsp.)

1. Drain and rinse the beans. Thinly slice the carrot and onion. Mince the garlic and chop the olives. Throw away the seeds from the peppers and cut them into strips.
2. Warm the oil in a frying pan using the medium temperature setting. Toss in the onion and garlic. Simmer them for approximately five minutes.
3. Fold in the bell peppers, beans, tomatoes, carrots, and olives.
4. Continue sautéing them for about five additional minutes.
5. Sprinkle the veggies with the cumin, parsley, salt, chicken bouillon, paprika, and cayenne.
6. Stir thoroughly and place the fish on top of the veggies.
7. Pour in water to cover the veggies.
8. Lower the heat setting and cover the pan to slowly cook until the fish is flaky (about 40 min.

Nutrition: Calories: 268 Protein: 42g Fat: 5g

.Mediterranean Lamb (Spanish)

Prep Time: 10 minutes Cooking Time: 35 minutes Servings: 4

2 ½ lbs. lamb shoulder, cut into chunks. 1 bay leaf.	1cup vegetable stock. 10 oz. prunes, soaked. 1 tsp. garlic, minced. 2 tbsp. honey.
1 tsp. ground ginger.	
2onions, sliced.	1 tsp. ground cumin.
1 tsp. ground turmeric.	¼ tsp. cinnamon.
3 oz. almonds sliced. Pepper.	Salt.

1. Add all ingredients into the inner pot of the Instant Pot and stir well.
2. Seal pot with lid and cook on high for 35 minutes.
3. Once done, allow to release pressure naturally. Remove lid.
4. Serve and enjoy.

Nutrition: Calories: 870 g. Fat: 34 g. Fiber: 4 g. Carbs: 30 g. Protein: 86 g.

.Artichoke, Chicken, and Capers (Spanish)

Preparation Time: 10 minutes Cooking Time: 55 minutes
Servings: 2

6 boneless, skinless chicken breasts. 2 cups mushrooms, sliced.	1 (14 ½ oz.) can diced tomatoes.
1 (8 or 9 oz.) package frozen artichokes. 1 cup chicken broth.	¼ cup dry white wine.
1 medium yellow onion, diced.	½ cup Kalamata olives, sliced.
¼ cup capers, drained. 3 tbsps. chia seeds.	3 tsps. curry powader. 1 tsp. turmeric.
¾ tsps. dried lovage. Salt and pepper to taste.	3 cups hot cooked buckwheat.

1. Rinse chicken & set aside.
2. In a large bowl, combine mushrooms, tomatoes (with juice), frozen artichoke hearts, chicken broth, white wine, onion, olives, and capers.
3. Stir in chia seeds, curry powder, turmeric, lovage, salt, and pepper.
4. Pour half the mixture into your crockpot, add the chicken, and pour the remainder of the sauce over top.
5. Cover and cook on low for 7–8 hours or on High for 3 ½ to 4 hours.
6. Serve with hot cooked buckwheat.

Nutrition: Calories: 473 g. Protein: 20 g. Fat: 3 garbs: 15 g.

.Fragrant Asian Hotpot (Spanish)

Preparation Time: 15 minutes Cooking Time: 45 minutes
Servings: 2

1 tsp. tomato purée.	1-star anise, crushed (or ¼ tsp. ground anise). Small handful parsley, stalks finely chopped. Juice of ½ lime.
Small handful coriander, stalks finely chopped. 500 ml chicken stock, fresh or made with one cube.	½ carrot, peeled and cut. Beansprouts.
Broccoli, cut into small florets. 1 tbsp. good-quality miso paste. oz. raw tiger prawns. oz. firm tofu, chopped.	oz. rice noodles that are cooked according to packet instructions. Cooked water chestnuts, drained. Little Sushi ginger, chopped.

1. In a large saucepan, put the tomato purée, star anise, parsley stalks, coriander stalks, lime juice, and chicken stock and bring to boil for 10 minutes.
2. Stir in the carrot, broccoli, prawns, tofu, noodles, and water chestnuts, and cook gently until the prawns are cooked. Take it from heat and stir in the ginger sushi and the paste miso.
3. Serve sprinkled with peregrine leaves and coriander.

Nutrition: Calories: 185 g. Fat: 30 g. Protein: 56 g. Carbs: 45 g. Cholesterol: 230 mg. Sugar: 0 g.

.Asian King Prawn Stir Fry with Buck wheat Noodles (Italian)

Preparation Time: 10 minutes Cooking Time: 20 minutes
Servings: 1

oz. shelled raw king prawns, deveined. 2 tsps. tamaris.	oz. soba (buckwheat noodles). 2 tsps. extra virgin olive oil.
1 garlic clove, finely chopped.	1 bird's eye chili, finely chopped. 1 tsp. finely chopped fresh ginger. oz. celery, trimmed and sliced.
Red onions, sliced. Green beans, chopped.	oz. kale, roughly chopped. Little lovage or celery leaves. Chicken stock.

1. Heat a frying pan over a high flame, then cook the prawns for 2–3 minutes in 1 tsp. tamari and 1 tsp. oil. Place the prawns onto a tray. Wipe the pan out with paper from the kitchen, as you will be using it again.
2. Cook the noodles for 5–8 minutes in boiling water, or as directed on the packet. Drain and put away.
3. Meanwhile, over medium-high heat, fry the garlic, chili, and ginger, red onion, celery, beans, and kale in the remaining oil for 2–3 minutes. Add the stock and boil, then cook for 2–3 minutes until the vegetables are cooked but crunchy.
4. Add the prawns, noodles, and leaves of lovage/celery to the pan, bring back to the boil, then remove and eat.

Nutrition: Calories: 185 g. Fat: 30 g. Protein: 56 g. Carbs: 20 g. Cholesterol: 230 mg. Sugar: 0 g.

.Turkey Burgers with Mango Salsa (Greek)

Preparation time: 15 minutes Cooking time: 10 minutes
Servings: 6

1½ lb. ground turkey breast 1 tsp. sea salt, divided	¼ tsp. freshly ground black pepper 2 tbsps. extra-virgin olive oil
2mangos, peeled, pitted, and cubed	½ red onion, finely chopped 1 lime juice
1garlic clove, minced	½ jalapeño pepper, seeded and finely minced 2 tbsps. fresh cilantro leaves, chopped

1. Form the turkey breast into 4 patties and season with ½ tsp. sea salt and pepper.
2. In a nonstick skillet over medium-high heat, heat the olive oil until it shimmers.
3. Add the turkey patties and cook for 5 minutes per side until browned.
4. While the patties cook, mix the mango, red onion, lime juice, garlic, jalapeño, cilantro, and remaining ½ tsp. sea salt in a small bowl. Spoon the salsa over the turkey patties and serve.

Nutrition: Calories: 384 Protein: 3 g. Fat: 16 g.

.Herb-Roasted Turkey Breast (Greek)

Preparation time: 15 minutes Cooking time: 90 minutes
Servings: 6

1tbsps. extra-virgin olive oil	1 lemon zest
4 garlic cloves, minced	
1 tbsp. fresh thyme leaves	1tbsp. fresh rosemary leaves
2tbsps. fresh Italian parsley leaves 1 tsp. ground mustard	1 tsp. sea salt
¼ tsp. black pepper	1 (6 lbs.) bone-in, skin-on turkey breast
1 cup dry white wine	

1. Preheat the oven to 325°F.
2. Scourge the olive oil, garlic, lemon zest, thyme, rosemary, parsley, mustard, sea salt, and pepper. Layout the herb mixture evenly over the surface of the turkey breast, and loosen the skin, and rub underneath as well. Place the turkey breast in a roasting pan on a rack, skin-side up.
3. Pour the wine into the pan. Roast for 1–1 ½ hour. Take out from the oven and rest for 20 minutes, tented with aluminum foil to keep it warm, before carving.

Nutrition: Calories: 392 Protein: 84 g. Fat: 6 g.

.Halibut with Lemon-Fennel Salad (Greek)

Preparation time: 15 minutes Cooking time: 5 minutes Servings: 4

4 halibut fillets	2 cups fennel bulb, thinly sliced
¼ cup red onion, thinly vertically sliced 2 tbsps. lemon juice	1 tbsp. thyme leaves
1 tbsp. flat-leaf parsley, chopped	5 tsps. extra-virgin olive oil, divided 1 tsp. coriander
½ tsp. salt	½ tsp. cumin
¼ tsp. ground black pepper	
2 garlic cloves, minced	

1. Combine the coriander, cumin, salt, and black pepper in a small bowl. Combine 2 tsps. of olive oil, garlic, and 1 ½ tsp. spice mixture in another small bowl, evenly rub the garlic mixture on the halibut. Heat 1 tsp. oil in a large nonstick pan over medium-high heat. Cook the halibut to the pan for 5 minutes.
2. Combine the remaining 2 tsps. of oil, ¾ tsp. the spice mixture, the fennel bulb, onion, lemon juice, thyme leaves, and parsley in a bowl, mix well to coat and serve salad with halibut.

Nutrition: Calories: 427 Protein: 39 g. Fat: 20 g.

.Cabbage Roll Casserole with Veal (Spanish)

Prep time: 5 minutes Cooking time: 4–8 hours Servings: 6

1 lb. raw ground veal 1 head of cabbage	1 medium green pepper
1medium onion, chopped 1 (15 oz.) can of tomatoes	2(15 oz.) cans of tomato sauce 1 tsp. garlic, minced
1 tbsp. Worcestershire sauce	½ tsp. salt
1 tbsp. beef bouillon	
½ tsp. pepper	1 cup uncooked brown rice

1. Place all the ingredients into your slow cooker.
2. Stir well to combine.
3. Set your slow cooker to high and cook for 4 hours, or cook for 8 hours on LOW.

Nutrition: Calories: 335 Fat: 18 g. Protein: 22.9 g.

.Baked Cod with Vegetables (Greek)

Preparation time: 15 minutes Cooking time: 25 minutes
Servings: 2

1 lb. (454 g.) thick cod fillet, cut into 4 even portions	¼ tsp. onion powder (optional)
¼ tsp. paprika	3 tbsps. extra-virgin olive oil
	4 medium scallions
½ cup fresh basil, chopped, divided 3 tbsps. garlic, minced (optional)	2 tsps. salt
2 tsps. freshly ground black pepper	¼ tsp. dry marjoram (optional)
½ cup dry white wine	6 sun-dried tomato slices
	½ cup Feta cheese, crumbled
1 (15 oz./425 g.) can oil-packed artichoke hearts, drained 1 lemon, sliced	1 cup pitted Kalamata olive
	1 tsp. capers (optional)
4 small red potatoes, quartered	

1. Set the oven to 375°F (190°C).
2. Season the fish with paprika and onion powder (if desired).
3. Heat an ovenproof skillet over medium heat and sear the top side of the cod for 1 minute until golden. Set it aside.
4. Heat the olive oil in the same skillet over medium heat. Add the scallions, ¼ cup of basil, garlic (if desired), salt, pepper, marjoram (if desired), tomato slices, and white wine, and stir to combine. Boil, then removes from heat.
5. Evenly spread the sauce on the bottom of the skillet. Place the cod on top of the tomato basil sauce and scatter with Feta cheese. Place the artichokes in the skillet and top with the lemon slices.
6. Scatter with the olives, capers (if desired), and the remaining ¼ cup of basil. Pull out from the heat and transfer to the preheated oven. Bake for 15–20 minutes.
7. Meanwhile, place the quartered potatoes on a baking sheet or wrapped in aluminum foil. Bake in the oven for 15 minutes.
8. Cool for 5 minutes before serving.

Nutrition: Calories: 1168 Fat: 60 g. Protein: 64 g.

.Acquapazza Snapper (Greek)

Prep time: 10 minutes Cooking time: 35 minutes Servings: 4

1 ½ lb. cut into 4 pieces red snapper fillets 1 ½ ripe tomatoes, coarsely chopped	3 cups water
2 tbsps. olive oil	1tbsp. thyme leaves, chopped 1 tbsp. oregano leaves, chopped
¼ tsp. red pepper flakes 3 garlic cloves, minced Salt to taste	

1. Heat the oil in a casserole large enough to hold all 4 pieces of snapper fillets in a single layer over medium heat. Cook the garlic and red pepper flakes.
2. Add the water, tomatoes, thyme, oregano, and simmer. Cover, reduce over medium-low heat and simmer for 15 min. Remove the lid and continue to simmer for another 10 min so that the liquid decreases slightly, pressing occasionally on the tomatoes. Taste and season with salt as needed.
3. Put the snapper fillets in the casserole with the skin facing down, if there is skin. Season with the salt, and cook for 8–10 min.
4. Place the snapper fillets on 4 large, shallow bowls and put the broth around it. Serve immediately.

Nutrition: Calories: 501 Protein: 52 g. Fat: 26 g.

.Mediterranean Beef Stew (Greek)

Prep time: 25 minutes Cooking time: 8 hours Servings: 6

1 tbsp. olive oil	8 oz. sliced mushrooms 1 onion
2 lbs. chuck roast 1 cup beef stock	1(14 ½ oz.) can tomatoes with juice
½ cup tomato sauce	¼ cup balsamic vinegar 1 can of black olives
½ cup garlic cloves	2tbsps. fresh rosemary 2 tbsps. fresh parsley
1 tbsp. capers	

1. Heat a skillet over high heat. Add 1 tbsp. olive oil. Once heated, cook the cubed roast.
2. Once cooked, stir the rest of the olive oil (if needed), then toss in the onions and mushrooms. When they have softened, transfer to the slow cooker.
3. Add the beef stock to the skillet to deglaze the pan, then pour it over the meat in the slow cooker.
4. Mix the rest of the ingredients to the slow cooker to coat.
5. Set the temperature on your slow cooker to low and cook for 8 hours.

Nutrition: Calories: 471 Fat: 23.4 g. Protein: 47.1g.

.Slow-Cooked Daube Provencal (Spanish)

Preparation time: 15 minutes Cooking time: 4–8 hours Servings: 8–10

1 tbsp. olive oil	10 garlic cloves, minced
2 lbs. boneless chuck roast 1 ½ tsp. salt	½ tsp. black pepper 1 cup dry red wine
2 cups carrots, chopped 1 ½ cups onion, chopped	½ cup beef broth
1 (14 oz.) can diced tomatoes 1 tbsp. tomato paste	1tsp. fresh rosemary, chopped 1 tsp. fresh thyme, chopped
½ tsp. orange zest, grated	½ tsp. ground cinnamon
¼ tsp. ground cloves 1 bay leaf	

1. Preheat a skillet and then add the olive oil. Cook the minced garlic and onions.
2. Add the cubed meat, salt, and pepper and cook until the meat has browned.
3. Transfer the meat to the slow cooker.
4. Put beef broth to the skillet and let simmer for about 3 minutes to deglaze the pan, then pour into slow cooker over the meat.
5. Add the rest of the ingredients to the slow cooker and stir well to combine.
6. Set your slow cooker to low and cook for 8 hours, or set it to high and cook for 4 hours.
7. Serve with a side of egg noodles, rice, or some crusty Italian bread.

Nutrition: Calories: 547 Fat: 30.5 g. Protein: 45.2g.

CHAPTER 12: SNACK AND APPETIZER

.Garlic Parmesan Artichokes (Greek)

Preparation time: 9 minutes Cooking time: 10 minutes
Servings: 4

4 artichokes, wash, trim, and cut top	½ cup vegetable broth
¼ cup Parmesan cheese, grated 1 tbsp. olive oil	2 tsps. garlic, minced Salt

1. Pour the broth into the electric pressure cooker, then place the steamer rack in the pot.
2. Place the artichoke steam side down on the steamer rack into the pot.
3. Sprinkle the garlic and grated cheese on top of artichokes and season with salt. Drizzle the oil over artichokes.
4. Seal pot with the lid and cook on high for 10 minutes.
5. Once done, release pressure using quick release. Remove the lid.
6. Serve and enjoy.

Nutrition: Calories: 132 Fat: 5.2 g. Protein: 7.9 g.

.Manchego Crackers (Spanish)

Preparation time: 55 minutes Cooking time: 15 minutes
Servings: 4

4 tbsps. butter, at room temperature 1 cup Manchego cheese	1 cup almond flour 1 tsp. salt, divided
¼ tsp. black pepper 1 large egg	

1. Scourge butter and shredded cheese using an electric mixer.
2. Mix the almond flour with ½ tsp. salt and pepper. Mix the almond flour mixture to the cheese, constantly mixing to form a ball.
3. Put it onto plastic wrap and roll into a cylinder log about 1 ½-inch thick. Wrap tightly and refrigerate for at least 1 hour.
4. Preheat the oven to 350°F. Prepare 2 baking sheets with parchment paper.
5. For egg wash, blend egg and remaining ½ tsp. salt.
6. Slice the refrigerated dough into small rounds, about ¼-inch thick, and place on the lined baking sheets.
7. Top the crackers with egg wash and bake for 15 minutes. Pull out from the oven and situate in a wire rack.
8. Serve.

Nutrition: Calories: 243 Fat: 23 g. Protein: 8 g.

.Greek Deviled Eggs (Greek)

Preparation time: 45 minutes Cooking time: 15 minutes
Servings: 4

4 large hardboiled eggs	2 tbsps. roasted garlic aioli
½ cup Feta cheese	8 pitted Kalamata olives
2 tbsps. sun-dried tomatoes, chopped 1 tbsp. red onion, minced	½ tsp. dried dill
¼ tsp. black pepper	

1. Slice the hardboiled eggs in half lengthwise, remove the yolks, and place the yolks in a medium bowl.
2. Reserve the egg white halves and set them aside.
3. Smash the yolks well with a fork.
4. Add the aioli, Feta cheese, olives, sun-dried tomatoes, onion, dill, and pepper and stir to combine until smooth and creamy.
5. Spoon the filling into each egg white half and chill for 30 minutes, or up to 24 hours, covered.

Nutrition: Calories: 147 Fat: 11 g. Protein: 9 g.

.Burrata Caprese Stack (Greek)

Preparation time: 5 minutes Cooking time: 0 minutes Servings: 4

1 large organic tomato	½ tsp. salt
¼ tsp. black pepper	1(4 oz.) ball of Burrata cheese 8 fresh basil leaves
2tbsps. extra-virgin olive oil	
1 tbsp. red wine	

1. Slice the tomato into 4 thick slices, removing any tough center core, and sprinkle with salt and pepper. Place the tomatoes, seasoned-side up, on a plate.
2. On a separate rimmed plate, slice the Burrata cheese into 4 thick slices and place 1 slice on top of each tomato slice. Top each with 2 basil leaves and pour any reserved Burrata cream from the rimmed plate over the top.
3. Drizzle with olive oil and vinegar and serve with a fork and knife.

Nutrition: Calories: 153 Fat: 13 g. Protein: 7 g.

.Citrus-Marinated Olives (Greek)

Preparation time: 10 minutes + 4 hours Cooking time: 0 minute Servings: 4

2 cups mixed green olives with pits	¼ cup red wine vinegar
¼ cup extra-virgin olive oil	4 garlic cloves, finely minced 1 orange zest and juice
1tsp. red pepper flakes 2 bay leaves	½ tsp. ground cumin
½ tsp. ground allspice	

1. In a jar, mix the olives, vinegar, oil, garlic, orange zest and juice, red pepper flakes, bay leaves, cumin, and allspice.
2. Cover and chill for 4 hours, tossing again before serving.

Nutrition: Calories: 133 Fat: 14 g. Protein: 1 g.

.Zucchini-Ricotta Fritters with Lemon-GarlicAioli (Italian)

Preparation time: 30 minutes Cooking time: 25 minutes
Servings: 4

1 large zucchini	1 tsp. salt, divided
½ cup whole-milk Ricotta cheese 2 scallions	1large egg
2garlic cloves	2 tbsps. fresh mint (optional) 2 tsps. grated lemon zest
¼ tsp. freshly ground black pepper	½ cup almond flour 1 tsp. baking powder
8 tbsps. extra-virgin olive oil	
8 tbsps. roasted garlic aioli	

1. Place the shredded zucchini in a colander or on several layers of paper towels. Sprinkle with ½ tsp. salt and let sit for 10 minutes. Using another layer of paper towel, press down on the zucchini to release any excess moisture and pat dry.
2. In a large bowl, combine the drained zucchini, Ricotta, scallions, egg, garlic, mint (if using), lemon zest, the remaining ½ tsp. salt, and pepper and stir well.
3. Blend the almond flour and baking powder. Mix in flour mixture into the zucchini mixture and let rest for 10 minutes.
4. In a large skillet, working in 4 batches, fry the fritters. For each batch of 4, heat 2 tbsps. of olive oil over medium-high heat. Add 1 heaping tbsp. zucchini batter per fritter, pressing down with the back of a spoon to form 2–3-inch fritters. Cover and let fry 2 minutes before flipping. Fry another 2–3 minutes, covered.
5. Repeat for the remaining 3 batches, using 2 tbsps. of olive oil for each batch.
6. Serve with aioli.

Nutrition: Calories: 448 Fat: 42 g. Protein: 8 g.

.Zucchini Feta Roulades (Italian)

Preparation Time: 10 minutes Cooking Time: 10 minutes
Servings: 6

½ cup feta	1garlic clove, minced
2tablespoons fresh basil, minced 1 tbsp capers, minced	1/8 teaspoon salt
1/8 teaspoon red pepper flakes 1 tablespoon lemon juice	2 medium zucchinis
12 toothpicks	

1. Preheat the air fryer to 360°F. (If using a grill attachment, make sure it is inside the air fryer during preheating.) In a small bowl, mix the feta, garlic, basil, capers, salt, red pepper flakes, and lemon juice.
2. Slice the zucchini into 1/8-inch strips lengthwise. (Each zucchini should yield around 6 strips.) Spread 1 tablespoon of the cheese filling onto each slice of zucchini, then roll it up and locked it with a toothpick through the middle.
3. Place the zucchini roulades into the air fryer basket in a one layer, individually. Bake or grill in the air fryer for 10 minutes. Remove the zucchini roulades from the air fryer and gently remove the toothpicks before serving.

Nutrition 46 Calories 3g Fat 6g Carbohydrates 3g Protein

.Garlic-Roasted Tomatoes and Olives (Greek)

Preparation Time: 5 minutes Cooking Time: 20 minutes
Servings: 6

2 cups cherry tomatoes	4 garlic cloves, roughly chopped
½ red onion, roughly chopped 1 cup black olives	1 cup green olives
1 tablespoon fresh basil, minced	1 tablespoon fresh oregano, minced 2 tablespoons olive oil
¼ to ½ teaspoon salt	

1. Preheat the air fryer to 380°F. In a large bowl, incorporate all of the ingredients and toss together so that the tomatoes and olives are coated well with the olive oil and herbs.
2. Pour the mixture into the air fryer basket, and roast for 10 minutes. Stir the mixture well, then continue roasting for an additional 10 minutes. Remove from the air fryer, transfer to a serving bowl, and enjoy.

Nutrition 109 Calories 10g Fat 5g Carbohydrates 1g Protein

.Tuna Croquettes (Italian)

Preparation time: 40 minutes Cooking time: 25 minutes
Servings: 12

6 tbsps. extra-virgin olive oil, plus 1–2 cups 5 tbsps. almond flour, plus 1 cup, divided	1 ¼ cups heavy cream
1(4 oz.) can olive oil-packed yellowfin tuna 1 tbsp. red onion, chopped	2tsps. capers, minced
½ tsp. dried dill	¼ tsp. freshly ground black pepper 2 large eggs
1 cup panko breadcrumbs	

1. In a large skillet, heat 6 tbsps. of olive oil over medium-low heat. Add 5 tbsps. of almond flour and cook, constantly stirring, until it forms a smooth paste and the flour browns slightly, 2–3 minutes.
2. Increase the heat to medium-high and gradually add the heavy cream, constantly whisking for 5 minutes.
3. Pull out from heat and stir in the tuna, red onion, capers, dill, and pepper.
4. Pour into an 8-inch square baking dish that is well coated with olive oil and allow it to cool to room temperature. Cover and chill for 4 hours.
5. To form the croquettes, set out 3 bowls. In one, beat together the eggs. In another, add the remaining almond flour. In the third, add the panko. Line a baking sheet with parchment paper.
6. Put 1 tbsp. cold prepared dough into the flour mixture and roll to coat. Shake off excess and, using your hands, roll into an oval.
7. Dip the croquette into the beaten egg, then lightly coat in panko. Set on a lined baking sheet and repeat with the remaining dough.
8. In a small saucepan, heat 1–2 cups of olive oil over medium-high heat.
9. Once the oil is heated, fry the croquettes 3 or 4 at a time.

Nutrition: Calories: 245 Fat: 22 g. Protein: 6 g.

.Smoked Salmon Crudités (Spanish)

Preparation time: 10 minutes
Cooking time: 0 minute Servings: 4

6 oz. smoked wild salmon 2 tbsps. roasted garlic aioli 1 tbsp. Dijon mustard	1 tbsp. scallions, chopped 2 tsps. capers, chopped
½ tsp. dried dill	4 endive spears or hearts of romaine
½ English cucumber	

1. Cut the smoked salmon.
2. Add the aioli, Dijon, scallions, capers, and dill and mix well.
3. Top endive spears and cucumber rounds with a spoonful of smoked salmon mixture and enjoy chilled.

Nutrition: Calories: 92 Fat: 5 g. Protein: 9 g.

.Olive Tapenade with Anchovies (Greek)

Preparation time: 70 minutes Cooking time: 0 minute
Servings: 4

1cups Kalamata olives, pitted 2 anchovy fillets	2 tsps. capers
1 garlic clove	1 egg yolk, cooked 1 tsp. Dijon mustard
¼ cup extra-virgin olive oil	

1. Wash the olives in cold water and drain well.
2. In a food processor, mix the drained olives, anchovies, capers, garlic, egg yolk, and Dijon.
3. With the food processor running, slowly stream in the olive oil.
4. Wrap and refrigerate for at least 1 hour.
5. Serve with seedy crackers.

Nutrition: Calories: 179 Fat: 19 g. Protein: 2 g.

.Smoked Mackerel Pâté (Spanish)

Preparation Time: 10 minutes Cooking Time: 0 minute
Servings: 4

4 ounces olive oil-packed wild-caught mackerel 2 ounces goat cheese	Zest and juice of 1 lemon
2 tablespoons chopped fresh parsley 2 tablespoons chopped fresh arugula 1 tablespoon extra-virgin olive oil	2 teaspoons chopped capers
1 to 2 teaspoons fresh horseradish (optional)	Crackers, cucumber rounds, endive spears, or celery, for serving (optional)

1. In a food processor, blender, or large bowl with immersion blender, combine the mackerel, goat cheese, lemon zest and juice, parsley, arugula, olive oil, capers, and horseradish (if using). Process or blend until smooth and creamy.
2. Serve with crackers, cucumber rounds, endive spears, or celery. Seal covered in the refrigerator for up to 1 week.

Nutrition 118 Calories 8g Fat g Carbohydrates 9g Protein

.Medi Fat Bombs (Greek)

Preparation Time: 4 hours and 15 minutes Cooking Time: 0
minute Servings: 6

1 cup crumbled goat cheese	12 pitted Kalamata olives, finely chopped
4 tablespoons jarred pesto	
½ cup finely chopped walnuts	1tablespoon chopped fresh rosemary

1. In a medium bowl, scourge the goat cheese, pesto, and olives and mix well using a fork. Freeze for 4 hours to toughen.
2. With your hands, create the mixture into 6 balls, about ¾-inch diameter. The mixture will be sticky.
3. In a small bowl, place the walnuts and rosemary and roll the goat cheese balls in the nut mixture to coat. Store the fat bombs in the refrigerator for up to 1 week or in the freezer for up to 1 month.

Nutrition 166 Calories 15g Fat 1g Carbohydrates 5g Protein

.Baked Clams Oreganata (Spanish)

Preparation Time: 30 minutes Cooking Time: 13 minutes
Serving: 10

Cherrystone clams (30)	Onions (1 oz, chopped fine)
Olive oil (2 Fl oz)	Garlic (1 tsp, finely chopped) Lemon juice (1 Fl oz)
Fresh breadcrumbs (10 oz)	White pepper (1/8 tsp)
Parsley (1 tbsp, chopped)	Parmesan cheese (1/3 cup)
Oregano (3/4 tsp, dried)	Paprika (as needed) Lemon wedges (10)

1. Open the clams. Place the juice in a bowl.
2. Take out the clams from the shell. Situate them in a strainer over the bowl of juice. Let them drain 15 minutes in the refrigerator. Save the 30 best half-shells.
3. Cut the clams into small pieces.
4. Cook the oil in a sauté pan. Add the onion and garlic. Sauté about 1 minute, but do not brown.
5. Pour in half of the clam juice, then reduce it over high heat by three- fourths.
6. Remove from the heat and add the crumbs, parsley, lemon juice, white pepper, and oregano. Mix gently to avoid making the crumbs pasty.
7. If necessary, adjust the seasonings.
8. Once the mixture has cooled. Mix in the chopped clams.
9. Place the mixture in the 30 clamshells. Sprinkle with parmesan cheese and (very lightly) with paprika.
10. Place on a sheet pan and refrigerate until needed.
11. For each order, bake 3 clams in a hot oven (450 F) until they are hot and the top brown.
12. Garnish with a lemon wedge.

Nutrition: 180 Calories 8g Fat 10g Protein

.Pumpkin Oatmeal with Spices (Italian)

Preparation Time: 10 minutes Cooking Time: 13 minutes
Servings: 6

1cups oatmeal	1 cup of coconut milk 1 cup milk
1 teaspoon Pumpkin pie spices 2 tablespoons pumpkin puree 1 tablespoon Honey	½ teaspoon butter

1. Pour coconut milk and milk in the saucepan. Add butter and bring the liquid to boil. Add oatmeal, stir well with the help of a spoon and close the lid.
2. Simmer the oatmeal for 7 minutes over the medium heat. Meanwhile, mix up together honey, pumpkin pie spices, and pumpkin puree. When the oatmeal is cooked, add pumpkin puree mixture and stir well. Transfer the cooked breakfast in the serving plates.

Nutrition 232 Calories 12.5g Fat 3.8g Carbohydrates 5.9g Protein

.Goat Cheese and Garlic Crostini (Italian)

Preparation Time: 3 minutes Cooking Time: 5 minutes
Servings: 4

1whole wheat baguette	¼ cup olive oil
2garlic cloves, minced 4 ounces goat cheese	2tablespoons fresh basil, minced

1. Preheat the air fryer to 380°F. Cut the baguette into ½-inch-thick slices. In a small bowl, incorporate together the olive oil and garlic, then brush it over one side of each slice of bread.
2. Place the olive-oil-coated bread in a single layer in the air fryer basket and bake for 5 minutes. In the meantime, combine together the goat cheese and basil. Remove the toast from the air fryer, then spread a thin layer of the goat cheese mixture over on each piece and serve.

Nutrition 365 Calories 21g Fat 10g Carbohydrates 12g Protein

.White Bean Hummus (Greek)

Preparation time: 11 minutes Cooking time: 40 minutes
Servings: 12

2/3 cup dried white beans	2garlic cloves, peeled and crushed
¼ cup olive oil	1 tbsp. lemon juice
½ tsp. salt	

1. Place the beans and garlic in the electric pressure cooker and stir well. Add enough cold water to cover the ingredients. Cover, set steam release to SEALING, select the MANUAL button, and time to 30 minutes.
2. Once the timer stops, release the pressure for 20 minutes. Select CANCEL and open the lid. Use a fork to check that beans are tender. Drain off the excess water and transfer the beans to a food processor.
3. Add the oil, lemon juice, and salt to the processor and pulse until the mixture is smooth with some small chunks. Pour into a container and refrigerate for at least 4 hours. Serve cold or at room temperature.

Nutrition: Calories: 57 Fat: 5 g. Protein: 1 g.

.Kidney Bean Dip with Cilantro, Cumin, and Lime(Spanish)

Preparation time: 13 minutes Cooking time: 51 minutes
Servings: 16

1 cup dried kidney beans 4 cups water	3 garlic cloves
¼ cup cilantro	¼ cup extra-virgin olive oil 1 tbsp. lime juice
2 tsps. lime zest, grated 1 tsp. ground cumin	½ tsp. salt

1. Place the beans, water, garlic, and 2 tbsps. of cilantro in the electric pressure cooker. Close the lid, select steam release to SEALING, click on the BEAN button, and cook for 30 minutes.
2. When the timer alarms, let the pressure release naturally for 20 minutes. Press the CANCEL button, open the lid, and check that the beans are tender. Drain off the extra water and transfer the beans to a medium bowl. Gently mash the beans with a potato masher. Add the oil, lime juice, lime zest, cumin, salt, and the remaining 2 tbsps. of cilantro and stir to combine. Serve warm or at room temperature.

Nutrition: Calories: 65 Fat: 3 g. Protein: 2 g.

.Crispy Green Bean Fries with Lemon-YogurtSauce (Greek)

Preparation Time: 5 minutes Cooking Time: 5 minutes
Servings: 4

For the green beans 1 egg 1tablespoon whole wheat flour	2 tablespoons water ¼ teaspoon paprika
½ teaspoon garlic powder	½ teaspoon salt
¼ cup whole wheat bread crumbs	½ pound whole green beans For the lemon-yogurt sauce
½ cup nonfat plain Greek yogurt 1 tablespoon lemon juice	¼ teaspoon salt
1/8 teaspoon cayenne pepper	

1. To make the green beans
2. Preheat the air fryer to 380°F.
3. In a medium shallow bowl, combine together the egg and water until frothy. In a separate medium shallow bowl, whisk together the flour, paprika, garlic powder, and salt, then mix in the bread crumbs.
4. Spread the bottom of the air fryer with cooking spray. Dip each green bean into the egg mixture, then into the bread crumb mixture, coating the outside with the crumbs. Situate the green beans in a single layer in the bottom of the air fryer basket.
5. Fry in the air fryer for 5 minutes, or until the breading is golden brown.
6. To make the lemon-yogurt sauce
7. Incorporate the yogurt, lemon juice, salt, and cayenne. Serve the green bean fries alongside the lemon-yogurt sauce as a snack or appetizer.

Nutrition 88 Calories 2g Fat 10g Carbohydrates 7g Protein

.Homemade Sea Salt Pita Chips (Spanish)

Preparation Time: 2 minutes Cooking Time: 8 minutes
Servings: 2

1whole wheat pitas 1 tablespoon olive oil	½ teaspoon kosher salt

1. Preheat the air fryer to 360°F. Cut each pita into 8 wedges. In a medium bowl, mix the pita wedges, olive oil, and salt until the wedges are coated and the olive oil and salt are evenly distributed.
2. Place the pita wedges into the air fryer basket in an even layer and fry for 6 to 8 minutes.
3. Season with additional salt, if desired. Serve alone or with a favorite dip.

Nutrition 230 Calories 8g Fat 11g Carbohydrates 6g Protein

.Rosemary-Roasted Red Potatoes (Greek)

Preparation Time: 5 minutes Cooking Time: 20 minutes
Servings: 6

1-pound red potatoes, quartered	¼ cup olive oil
½ teaspoon kosher salt	¼ teaspoon black pepper 1 garlic clove, minced
4 rosemary sprigs	

1. Preheat the air fryer to 360°F.
2. In a large bowl, toss in the potatoes with the olive oil, salt, pepper, and garlic until well coated. Fill the air fryer basket with potatoes and top with the sprigs of rosemary.
3. Roast for 10 minutes, then stir or toss the potatoes and roast for 10 minutes more. Remove the rosemary sprigs and serve the potatoes. Season well.

Nutrition 133 Calories 9g Fat 5g Carbohydrates 1g Protein

.Summer Tomato Salad (Greek)

Preparation Time: 20 minutes Cooking Time: 0 minutes
Servings: 4

1 cucumber, sliced	¼ cup sun dried tomatoes 1 lb. Tomatoes, cubed
½ cup black olives 1 red onion, sliced	1 tablespoon balsamic vinegar
¼ cup parsley, fresh & chopped 2 tablespoons olive oil	

1. Mix all of your vegetables together. For dressing, mix all your seasoning, olive oil and vinegar. Toss with your salad and serve fresh.

Nutrition: 126 Calories 2.1g Protein 9.2g Fat

.Cheese Beet Salad (Italian)

Preparation Time: 15 minutes Cooking Time: 0 minutes
Servings: 4

6 red beets	3 ounces feta cheese
2 tablespoons olive oil	2 tablespoons balsamic vinegar

1. Combine everything together, and then serve.

Nutrition: 230 Calories 7.3g Protein 12g Fat

.Cauliflower and Cherry Tomato Salad (Greek)

Preparation Time: 15 minutes Cooking Time: 0 minutes
Servings: 4

1head cauliflower	2tablespoons parsley
2 cups cherry tomatoes, halved 2 tablespoons lemon juice, fresh 2 tablespoons pine nuts	

1. Blend lemon juice, cherry tomatoes, cauliflower and parsley then season. Garnish with pine nuts, and mix well before serving.

Nutrition: 64 Calories 2.8g Protein 3.3g Fat

.Veggie Shish Kebabs (Spanish)

Preparation Time: 10 minutes Cooking Time: 0 minute
Serving: 3

Cherry tomatoes (9)	Olive oil (1 tsp.) Zucchini
Mozzarella balls (9 low-fat)	(3, sliced) Dash of pepper
Basil leaves (9)	
For Serving:	Whole Wheat Bread (6 slices)

1. Stab 1 cherry tomato, low-fat mozzarella ball, zucchini, and basil leaf onto each skewer.
2. Place skewers on a plate and drizzle with olive oil. Finish with a sprinkle of pepper.
3. Set your bread to toast. Serve 2 bread slices with 3 kebobs.

Nutrition: 349 Calories 5.7g Fat 15g Protein

.Crispy Falafel (Greek)

Preparation Time: 20 minutes Cooking Time: 8 minutes
Serving: 3

Chickpeas (1 cup, drained and rinsed)	Parsley (½ cup, chopped with stems removed) Cilantro (1/3 cup, chopped with stems removed) Dill (¼ cup, chopped with stems removed) Cloves garlic (4, minced)
Sesame seeds (1 tbsp., toasted) Coriander (½ tbsp.)	Black pepper (½ tbsp.) Cumin (½ tbsp.) Baking powder (½ tsp.) Cayenne (½ tsp.)

1. Thoroughly dry your chickpeas with a paper towel.
2. Place the parsley, cilantro, and dill in a food processor.
3. Mix chickpeas, garlic, coriander, black pepper, cumin, baking powder, and cayenne.
4. Place the mixture to an airtight container and chill for about an hour.
5. Take out from the refrigerator and mix the baking powder and sesame seeds.
6. Scoop the mixture into a pan with 3 inches of olive oil over medium heat to create patties. Keep in mind as you create the patties that you are aiming to make 12 with the mixture.
7. Let the falafel patties fry for 1-2 minutes on each side.
8. Once your falafel patties are nicely browned, transfer them to a plate lined with paper towels to finish crisping.
9. Dip, dunk, fill, and enjoy!

Nutrition: 328 Calories 10.8g Fat 24g Protein

.Herb-Marinated Feta and Artichokes (Greek)

Preparation Time: 10 minutes, plus 4 hours inactive time
Cooking Time: 10 minutes Servings: 2

4 ounces traditional Greek feta, cut into ½-inch cubes	4 ounces drained artichoke hearts, quartered lengthwise 1/3 cup extra-virgin olive oil
Zest and juice of 1 lemon	2 tablespoons roughly chopped fresh rosemary 2 tablespoons roughly chopped fresh parsley
½ teaspoon black peppercorns	

1. In a glass bowl combine the feta and artichoke hearts. Add the olive oil, lemon zest and juice, rosemary, parsley, and peppercorns and toss gently to coat, being sure not to crumble the feta.
2. Cool for 4 hours, or up to 4 days. Take out of the refrigerator 30 minutes before serving.

Nutrition 235 Calories 23g Fat 1g Carbohydrates 4g Protein

.Roasted Garlic Hummus (Greek)

Prep time: 9 minutes Cooking time: 33 minutes Servings: 4

1 cup dried chickpeas 4 cups water	1 tbsp., plus ¼ cup extra-virgin olive oil, divided 1/3 cup tahini
1 tsp. ground cumin	½ tsp. onion powder 3/4 tsp. salt
½ tsp. ground black pepper 1/3 cup lemon juice	3 tbsps. roasted garlic, mashed 2 tbsps. fresh parsley, chopped

1. Put the chickpeas, water, and 1 tbsp. oil in the electric pressure cooker. Cover, press steam release to sealing, set the manual button, and time to 30 minutes.
2. When the timer beeps, quick-release the pressure. Select the cancel button and open it. Strain, reserving the cooking liquid.
3. Place the chickpeas, the remaining ¼ cup of oil, tahini, cumin, onion powder, salt, pepper, lemon juice, and roasted garlic in a food processor and process until creamy. Top with parsley. Serve at room temperature.

Nutrition: Calories: 104 Fat: 6 g. Protein: 4 g.

.Salmon-Stuffed Cucumbers (Spanish)

Prep time: 10 minutes Cooking time: 0 minute Servings: 4

2 large cucumbers, peeled 1 (4 oz.) can of red salmon	1 medium avocado, very ripe 1 tbsp. extra-virgin olive oil 1 lime zest and juice
3 tbsps. fresh cilantro, chopped	½ tsp. salt
¼ tsp. black pepper	

1. Slice the cucumber into 1-inch-thick segments, and using a spoon, scrape seeds out of the center of each piece and stand up on a plate.
2. Mix the salmon, avocado, olive oil, lime zest and juice, cilantro, salt, and pepper in a medium bowl.
3. Spoon the salmon mixture into the center of each cucumber segment and serve chilled.

Nutrition: Calories: 159 Fat: 11 g. Protein: 9 g.

.Potato Salad (Italian)

Preparation time: 9 minutes Cooking time: 13 minutes
Servings: 6

2lbs. golden potatoes 3 tbsps. olive oil	3tbsps. lemon juice, fresh 1 tbsp. olive brine
¼ tsp. sea salt, fine	½ cup olives, sliced 1 cup celery, sliced 2 tbsps. oregano
2 tbsps. mint leaves	

1. Boil the potatoes in a saucepan before turning the heat down to medium-low. Cook for 15 more minutes. Get a small bowl and whisk the oil, lemon juice, olive brine, and salt together.
2. Drain the potatoes using a colander and transfer them to a serving bowl. Pour in 3 tbsps. of dressing over the potatoes, mix well with the oregano, and serve with the remaining dressing.

Nutrition: Calories: 175 Protein: 3 g. Fat: 7 g.

.Baked Spanakopita Dip (Spanish)

Preparation Time: 10 minutes Cooking Time: 15 minutes
Servings: 2

Olive oil cooking spray	3 tablespoons olive oil, divided
2 tablespoons minced white onion 2 garlic cloves, minced	4 cups fresh spinach
4 ounces cream cheese, softened 4 ounces feta cheese, divided Zest of 1 lemon	¼ teaspoon ground nutmeg 1 teaspoon dried dill
½ teaspoon salt	Pita chips, carrot sticks, or sliced bread for serving (optional)

1. Preheat the air fryer to 360°F. Coat the inside of a 6-inch ramekin or baking dish with olive oil cooking spray.
2. Using skillet over medium heat, cook 1 tablespoon of the olive oil. Add the onion, then cook for 1 minute. Add in the garlic and cook, stirring for 1 minute more.
3. Lower heat and combine the spinach and water. Cook until the spinach has wilted. Remove the skillet from the heat. In a medium bowl, scourge the cream cheese, 2 ounces of the feta, and the rest of olive oil, lemon zest, nutmeg, dill, and salt. Mix until just combined.
4. Add the vegetables to the cheese base and stir until combined. Pour the dip mixture into the prepared ramekin and top with the remaining 2 ounces of feta cheese.
5. Place the dip into the air fryer basket and cook for 10 minutes, or until heated through and bubbling. Serve with pita chips, carrot sticks, or sliced bread.

Nutrition 550 Calories 52g Fat 21g Carbohydrates 14g Protein

.Roasted Pearl Onion Dip (Greek)

Preparation Time: 5 minutes Cooking Time: 12 minutes plus 1 hour to chill Servings: 4

2cups peeled pearl onions 3 garlic cloves	3tablespoons olive oil, divided
½ teaspoon salt	1 cup nonfat plain Greek yogurt 1 tablespoon lemon juice
¼ teaspoon black pepper	1/8 teaspoon red pepper flakes
Pita chips, vegetables, or toasted bread for serving (optional)	

1. Preheat the air fryer to 360°F. In a large bowl, combine the pearl onions and garlic with 2 tablespoons of the olive oil until the onions are well coated.
2. Pour the garlic-and-onion mixture into the air fryer basket and roast for 12 minutes. Place the garlic and onions to a food processor. Pulse the vegetables several times, until the onions are minced but still have some chunks.
3. Toss in the garlic and onions and the remaining 1 tablespoon of olive oil, along with the salt, yogurt, lemon juice, black pepper, and red pepper flakes. Chill for 1 hour before serving with pita chips, vegetables, or toasted bread.

Nutrition 150 Calories 10g Fat 6g Carbohydrates 7g Protein

.Spiced Salmon Crudités (Spanish)

Preparation Time: 10 minutes Cooking Time: 15 minutes Servings: 4

6 ounces smoked wild salmon	2 tablespoons Roasted Garlic Aioli 1 tablespoon Dijon mustard
1 tablespoon chopped scallions, green parts only 2 teaspoons chopped capers	½ teaspoon dried dill
4 endive spears or hearts of romaine	½ English cucumber, cut into ¼-inch-thick rounds

1. Roughly cut the smoked salmon and transfer in a small bowl. Add the aioli, Dijon, scallions, capers, and dill and mix well. Top endive spears and cucumber rounds with a spoonful of smoked salmon mixture and enjoy chilled.

Nutrition 92 Calories 5g Fat 1g Carbohydrates 9g Protein

.All-Spiced Olives (Italian)

Preparation Time: 4 hours and 10 minutes Cooking Time: 0 minute Servings: 2

2 cups mixed green olives with pits	¼ cup red wine vinegar
¼ cup extra-virgin olive oil	4 garlic cloves, finely minced Zest and juice of 1 large orange 1 teaspoon red pepper flakes
2 bay leaves	½ teaspoon ground cumin
½ teaspoon ground allspice	

1. Incorporate the olives, vinegar, oil, garlic, orange zest and juice, red pepper flakes, bay leaves, cumin, and allspice and mix well. Seal and chill for 4 hours or up to a week to allow the olives to marinate, tossing again before serving.

Nutrition 133 Calories 14g Fat 2g Carbohydrates 1g Protein

.Vegetable Fritters (Italian)

Preparation Time: 15 minutes Cooking Time: 6 minutes Serving: 5

Egg (3, beaten) Milk (8 Fl oz)	Whole wheat flour (8 oz) Baking powder (1 tbsp) Salt (½ tsp)
Maple syrup (1/2 oz) Vegetables:	Carrot (12 oz,)
Baby lima beans (12 oz) Asparagus (12 oz)	Celery (12 oz)
Turnip (12 oz) Cauliflower (12 oz)	Eggplant (12 oz) Zucchini (12 oz)
Parsnips (12 oz)	

1. Combine the eggs and milk.
2. Mix the flour, baking powder, salt, and maple syrup. Stir in to the milk and eggs and mix until smooth.
3. Set aside the batter for several hours in a refrigerator.
4. Stir the cold, cooked vegetable into the batter.
5. Drop with a No. 24 scoop into deep fat at 350 F. Toss the content from the scoop carefully in the hot oil. Fry until golden brown.
6. Drain well and serve.

Nutrition: 140 Calories 6g Fat 4g Protein

.Avocado and Turkey Mix Panini (Italian)

Preparation Time: 5 minutes Cooking Time: 8 minutes Servings: 2

2 red peppers, roasted and sliced into strips	¼ lb. thinly sliced mesquite smoked turkey breast 1 cup whole fresh spinach leaves, divided
2 slices provolone cheese 1 tbsp olive oil, divided 2 ciabatta rolls	¼ cup mayonnaise
½ ripe avocado	

1. In a bowl, mash thoroughly together mayonnaise and avocado. Then preheat Panini press.
2. Chop the bread rolls in half and spread olive oil on the insides of the bread. Then fill it with filling, layering them as you go: provolone, turkey breast, roasted red pepper, spinach leaves and spread avocado mixture and cover with the other bread slice.
3. Place sandwich in the Panini press and grill for 5 to 8 minutes until cheese has melted and bread is crisped and ridged.

Nutrition 546 Calories 34.8g Fat 31.9g Carbohydrates 27.8g Protein

270

.Cucumber, Chicken and Mango Wrap (Greek)

Preparation Time: 5 minutes Cooking Time: 20 minutes
Serving: 1

½ of a medium cucumber cut lengthwise	½ of ripe mango
1tbsp salad dressing of choice 1 whole wheat tortilla wrap	1-inch-thick slice of chicken breast around 6-inch in length 2 tbsp oil for frying
2tbsp whole wheat flour 2 to 4 lettuce leaves	Salt and pepper to taste

1. Slice a chicken breast into 1-inch strips and just cook a total of 6-inch strips. That would be like two strips of chicken. Store remaining chicken for future use.
2. Season chicken with pepper and salt. Dredge in whole wheat flour.
3. On medium fire, place a small and nonstick fry pan and heat oil. Once oil is hot, add chicken strips and fry until golden brown around 5 minutes per side.
4. While chicken is cooking, place tortilla wraps in oven and cook for 3 to 5 minutes. Then set aside and transfer in a plate.
5. Slice cucumber lengthwise, use only ½ of it and store remaining cucumber. Peel cucumber cut into quarter and remove pith. Place the two slices of cucumber on the tortilla wrap, 1-inch away from the edge.
6. Slice mango and store the other half with seed. Peel the mango without seed, slice into strips and place on top of the cucumber on the tortilla wrap.
7. Once chicken is cooked, place chicken beside the cucumber in a line.
8. Add cucumber leaf, drizzle with salad dressing of choice.
9. Roll the tortilla wrap, serve and enjoy.

Nutrition 434 Calories 10g Fat 65g Carbohydrates 21g Protein

Raisin Rice Pilaf (Italian)

Preparation time: 13 minutes Cooking time: 8 minutes
Servings: 5

1 tbsp. olive oil 1 tsp. cumin	1cup onion, chopped
½ cup carrot, shredded	½ tsp. cinnamon
2cups instant brown rice 1	1 cup golden raisins
¾ cup orange juice	
¼ cup water	½ cup pistachios, shelled
Fresh chives, chopped for garnish	

1. Place a medium saucepan over medium-high heat before adding in the oil. Add in the onion, and stir often, so it doesn't burn. Cook for 5 minutes, and then add in the cumin, cinnamon, and carrot. Cook for another minute.
2. Add in the orange juice, water, and rice. Boil before covering the saucepan. Turn the heat down to medium-low and then allow it to simmer for 6–7 minutes.
3. Stir in the pistachios, chives, and raisins. Serve warm.

Nutrition: Calories: 320 Protein: 6 g. Fat: 7 g.

.Tuna Tartare (Spanish)

Preparation Time: 15 minutes Cooking Time: 0 minute
Serving: 8

Sashimi quality tuna (26.5 g, well-trimmed) Shallots (1 oz, minced)	Parsley (2 tbsp, chopped)
Fresh tarragon (2 tbsp, chopped) Lime juice (2 tbsp)	Dijon-style mustard (1 Fl oz) Olive oil (2 Fl oz)

1. Use a knife to mince the tuna.
2. Mixed the rest of the ingredients with the chopped tuna.
3. Use a ring mold to make a beautifully presented tuna tartare.
4. Season to taste with pepper and salt.

Nutrition 200 Calories 12g Fat 21g Protein

.Goat Cheese–Mackerel Pâté (Italian)

Preparation time: 10 minutes Cooking time: 0 minute
Servings: 4

4 oz. olive oil-packed wild-caught mackerel 2 oz. goat cheese	1lemon zest and juice
2tbsps. fresh parsley, chopped 2 tbsps. fresh arugula, chopped 1 tbsp. extra-virgin olive oil	2 tsps. capers, chopped
2 tsps. fresh horseradish (optional)	

1. In a food processor, blender, or large bowl with an immersion blender, combine the mackerel, goat cheese, lemon zest and juice, parsley, arugula, olive oil, capers, and horseradish (if using). Process or blend until smooth and creamy.
2. Serve with crackers, cucumber rounds, endive spears, or celery.

Nutrition: Calories: 118 Fat: 8 g. Protein: 9 g.

.Taste of the Mediterranean Fat Bombs (Greek)

Preparation time: 15 minutes + 4 hours Cooking time: 0 minute Servings: 6

1 cup goat cheese, crumbled	12 pitted Kalamata olives
4 tbsps. jarred pesto	
½ cup walnuts, finely chopped 1 tbsp. fresh rosemary, chopped	

1. Mix the goat cheese, pesto, and olives. Cool for 4 hours to harden.
2. Make 6 balls from the mixture, about ¾-inch diameter. The mixture will be sticky.
3. Place the walnuts and rosemary in a small bowl and roll the goat cheese balls in the nut mixture to coat.

Nutrition: Calories: 166 Fat: 15 g. Protein: 5 g.

.Cream of Cauliflower Gazpacho (Spanish)

Preparation time: 15 minutes Cooking time: 25 minutes
Servings: 6

1 cup raw almonds	½ tsp. salt
½ cup, plus 1 tbsp. extra-virgin olive oil 1 small white onion	1small head cauliflower 2 garlic cloves
2cups chicken stock	1 tbsp. red wine vinegar
¼ tsp. freshly ground black pepper	

1. Boil the almonds in the water for 1 minute. Drain in a colander and run under cold water. Pat dry. Discard the skins.
2. In a food processor or blender, blend the almonds and salt. With the processor running, drizzle in ½ cup extra-virgin olive oil, scraping down the sides as needed. Set the almond paste aside.
3. In a stockpot, cook the remaining 1 tbsp. olive oil over medium-high heat. Sauté onion for 4 minutes. Add the cauliflower florets and sauté for another 3–4 minutes. Cook the garlic for 1 minute more.
4. Add 2 cups of stock and bring to a boil. Cover, reduce the heat to medium-low and simmer the vegetables until tender, 8–10 minutes. Pull out from the heat and allow to cool slightly.
5. Blend the vinegar and pepper with an immersion blender. With the blender running, add the almond paste and blend until smooth, adding extra stock if the soup is too thick.
6. Serve warm, or chill in the refrigerator for at least 4–6 hours to serve a cold gazpacho.

Nutrition: Calories: 505 Fat: 45 g. Protein: 10 g.

.Red Pepper Hummus (Greek)

Preparation time: 7 minutes Cooking time: 34 minutes
Servings: 4

1 cup dried chickpeas 4 cups water	1 tbsp., plus ¼ cup extra-virgin olive oil, divided
½ cup roasted red pepper, chopped, divided 1/3 cup tahini	1tsp. ground cumin 3/4 tsp. salt
½ tsp. ground black pepper	¼ tsp. smoked paprika 1/3 cup lemon juice
½ tsp. garlic, minced	

1. Put chickpeas, water, and 1 tbsp. oil in the electric pressure cooker. Seal put steam release to sealing, select the manual button, and time to 30 minutes.
2. When the timer rings, quick-release the pressure. Click the cancel button and open it. Drain and next set aside the cooking liquid.
3. Process the chickpeas, 1/3 cup roasted red pepper, the remaining ¼ cup of oil, tahini, cumin, salt, black pepper, paprika, lemon juice, and garlic using a food processor. Serve, garnished with reserved roasted red pepper on top.

Nutrition: Calories: 96 Fat: 8 g. Protein: 2 g.

.Cod Cakes (Greek)

Preparation Time: 25 minutes Cooking Time: 30 minutes
Serving: 12

Cod (12 oz, cooked)	White pepper (to taste)
Turnip's puree (12 oz.)	Ground ginger (pinch)
Whole eggs (2 ½ oz, beaten) Egg yolk (1 yolk, beaten) Salt (to taste)	Standard Breading Procedure:
Whole wheat flour Egg wash Breadcrumbs Tomatoes sauce	

1. Shred the fish.
2. Combine with the turnips, egg, and egg yolk.
3. Season with salt, pepper, and ground ginger.
4. Divide the mixture into 2 ½ oz portions. Shape the mixture into a ball and then slightly flatten the mixture cakes.
5. Place the mixture through the Standard Breading Procedure.
6. Deep-fry at 350 F until golden brown.
7. Serve 2 cakes per portion. Accompany with tomato sauce.

Nutrition: 280 Calories 6g Fat 23g Protein

.Avocado Gazpacho (Spanish)

Preparation time: 15 minutes Cooking time: 0 minute
Servings: 4

1cups chopped tomatoes 2 large ripe avocados
1 large cucumber
1 medium bell pepper
1cup plain whole-milk Greek yogurt
¼ cup extra-virgin olive oil
¼ cup fresh cilantro, chopped
¼ cup scallions, chopped 2 tbsps. red wine vinegar 2 limes or
1 lemon juice
½–1 tsp. salt
¼ tsp. black pepper

1. If using an immersion blender in a blender or a large bowl, combine the tomatoes, avocados, cucumber, bell pepper, yogurt, olive oil, cilantro, scallions, vinegar, and lime juice. Blend until smooth. If using a stand blender, you may need to blend in 2–3 batches.
2. Season with salt and pepper and blend to combine the flavors.
3. Chill for 2 hours before serving. Serve cold.

Nutrition: Calories: 392 Fat: 32 g. Protein: 6 g.

.Tuscan Kale Salad with Anchovies (Greek)

Preparation time: 45 minutes Cooking time: 0 minute
Servings: 4

1large bunch lacinato kale	¼ cup pine nuts, toasted 1 cup Parmesan cheese
¼ cup extra-virgin olive oil 8 anchovy fillets	2–3 tbsps. lemon juice
2tsps. red pepper flakes (optional)	

Nutrition: Calories: 337 Fat: 25 g. Protein: 16 g.

.Pitted Olives and Anchovies (Greek)

Preparation Time: 1 hour and 10 minutes Cooking Time: 0 minute Servings: 2

1cups pitted Kalamata olives or other black olives	2 teaspoons chopped capers
2 anchovy fillets, chopped	1 garlic clove, finely minced
1 teaspoon Dijon mustard	1 cooked egg yolk
Seedy Crackers, Versatile Sandwich Round, or vegetables, for serving (optional)	¼ cup extra-virgin olive oil

1. Wash the olives in cold water and strain well. In a food processor, blender, or a large jar (if using an immersion blender) place the drained olives, anchovies, capers, garlic, egg yolk, and Dijon. Process until it forms a thick paste. While running, gradually stream in the olive oil.
2. Handover to a small bowl, cover, and refrigerate at least 1 hour to let the flavors develop. Serve with Seedy Crackers, atop a Versatile Sandwich Round, or with your favorite crunchy vegetables.

Nutrition 179 Calories 19g Fat 2g Carbohydrates 2g Protein

.Cheese Crackers (Italian)

Preparation Time: 1 hour and 15 minutes Cooking Time: 15 minutes Servings: 20

4 tablespoons butter, at room temperature 1 cup finely shredded Manchego cheese 1 cup almond flour ¼ teaspoon freshly ground black pepper 1 large egg	1 teaspoon salt, divided

1. Using an electric mixer, scourge together the butter and shredded cheese until well combined and smooth. Incorporate the almond flour with ½ teaspoon salt and pepper. Gradually put the almond flour mixture to the cheese, mixing constantly until the dough just comes together to form a ball.
2. Situate a piece of parchment or plastic wrap and roll into a cylinder log about 1½ inches thick. Seal tightly then freezes for at least 1 hour. Preheat the oven to 350°F. Put parchment paper or silicone baking mats into 2 baking sheets.
3. To make the egg wash, scourge together the egg and remaining ½ teaspoon salt. Slice the refrigerated dough into small rounds, about ¼ inch thick, and place on the lined baking sheets.
4. Egg washes the tops of the crackers and bake until the crackers are golden and crispy. Situate on a wire rack to cool.
5. Serve warm or, once fully cooled, store in an airtight container in the refrigerator for up to 1 week.

Nutrition 243 Calories 23g Fat 1g Carbohydrates 8g Protein

.Cheesy Caprese Stack (Spanish)

Preparation Time: 5 minutes Cooking Time: 0 minute Servings: 4

1 large organic tomato, preferably heirloom	½ teaspoon salt
¼ teaspoon freshly ground black pepper 1 (4-ounce) ball burrata cheese	8 fresh basil leaves, thinly sliced
2 tablespoons extra-virgin olive oil	1 tablespoon red wine or balsamic vinegar

1. Slice the tomato into 4 thick slices, removing any tough center core and sprinkle with salt and pepper. Place the tomatoes, seasoned-side up, on a plate. On a separate rimmed plate, slice the burrata into 4 thick slices and place one slice on top of each tomato slice. Top each with one- quarter of the basil and pour any reserved burrata cream from the rimmed plate over top.
2. Dash with olive oil and vinegar and serve with a fork and knife.

Nutrition 153 Calories 13g Fat 1g Carbohydrates 7g Protein

.Guaca Egg Scramble (Greek)

Preparation Time: 8 minutes Cooking Time: 15 minutes Servings: 4

4 eggs, beaten	1 white onion, diced
1 tablespoon avocado oil 1 avocado, finely chopped	½ teaspoon chili flakes
1 oz Cheddar cheese, shredded	½ teaspoon salt
1 tablespoon fresh parsley	

1. Pour avocado oil in the skillet and bring it to boil. Then add diced onion and roast it until it is light brown. Meanwhile, mix up together chili flakes, beaten eggs, and salt.
2. Fill the egg mixture over the cooked onion and cook the mixture for 1 minute over the medium heat. After this, scramble the eggs well with the help of the fork or spatula. Cook the eggs until they are solid but soft.
3. After this, add chopped avocado and shredded cheese. Stir the scramble well and transfer in the serving plates. Sprinkle the meal with fresh parsley.

Nutrition 236 Calories 20g Fat 4g Carbohydrates8.6g Protein

.Medi Deviled Eggs (Greek)

Prep Time: 45 minutes Cooking Time: 15 minutes Servings: 4

4 large hardboiled eggs	2 tablespoons Roasted Garlic Aioli
½ cup finely crumbled feta cheese	8 pitted Kalamata olives, finely chopped
2 tablespoons chopped sun-dried tomatoes 1 tablespoon minced red onion	½ teaspoon dried dill
	¼ teaspoon freshly ground black pepper

1. Chop the hardboiled eggs in half lengthwise, remove the yolks, and place the yolks in a medium bowl. Reserve the egg white halves and set aside. Smash the yolks well with a fork. Add the aioli, feta, olives, sun- dried tomatoes, onion, dill, and pepper and stir to combine until smooth and creamy.
2. Spoon the filling into each egg white half and chill for 30 minutes, or up to 24 hours, covered.

Nutrition 147 Calories 11g Fat 6g Carbohydrates 9g Protein

.Vegetarian Quinoa Pilaf (Italian)

Prep time: 9 minutes Cooking time: 35 minutes Servings: 1

3 tbsps. extra-virgin olive oil	2 Portobello mushrooms, sliced
1 medium red onion, finely chopped 1 tbsp. garlic, minced	1(16 oz.) can diced tomatoes, with juice 2 cups water
2tsps. salt	1 tbsp. dried oregano 1 tbsp. turmeric
1 tsp. paprika	1 tsp. ground black pepper 2 cups red or yellow quinoa
½ cup fresh parsley, chopped	

1. In a large, 3-quart pot, cook the extra-virgin olive oil over medium heat. Cook the Portobello mushrooms.
2. Cook the red onion and garlic, stir for 5 minutes.
3. Add the tomatoes with juice, water, salt, oregano, turmeric, paprika, and black pepper. Stir, and simmer for 5 minutes.
4. Add the red quinoa to the pot, and stir. Cover, reduce heat to low and cook for 20 minutes.
5. Remove from heat, fluff with a fork, cover, and let sit for 10 mins.
6. Spoon the quinoa onto a plate, sprinkle with parsley, and serve warm.

Nutrition: Calories: 305 Fat: 8 g. Protein: 4 g.

.Five-Ingredient Falafel with Garlic-Yogurt Sauce(Italian)

Prep Time: 5 minutes Cooking Time: 15 minutes Servings: 4

For the falafel	1(15-ounce) can chickpeas, drained and rinsed
½ cup fresh parsley	2garlic cloves, minced
½ tablespoon ground cumin	1 tablespoon whole wheat flour Salt
For the garlic-yogurt sauce	1 cup nonfat plain Greek yogurt 1 garlic clove, minced
1 tablespoon chopped fresh dill 2 tbsp lemon juice	

1. To make the falafel
2. Preheat the air fryer to 360°F. Put the chickpeas into a food processor. Pulse until mostly chopped, then add the parsley, garlic, and cumin and pulse for another minutes, until the ingredients turn into a dough.
3. Add the flour. Pulse a few more times until combined. The dough will have texture, but the chickpeas should be pulsed into small bits. Using clean hands, roll the dough into 8 balls of equal size, then pat the balls down a bit so they are about ½-thick disks.
4. Put the basket of the air fryer with olive oil cooking spray, then place the falafel patties in the basket in a single layer, making sure they don't touch each other. Fry in the air fryer for 15 minutes.
5. To make the garlic-yogurt sauce
6. Mix the yogurt, garlic, dill, and lemon juice. Once the falafel is done cooking and nicely browned on all sides, remove them from the air fryer and season with salt. Serve hot side it dipping sauce.

Nutrition 151 Calories 2g Fat 10g Carbohydrates 12g Protein

.Lemon Shrimp with Garlic Olive Oil (Greek)

Preparation Time: 5 minutes Cooking Time: 6 minutes Servings: 4

1-pound medium shrimp, cleaned and deveined	¼ cup plus 2 tablespoons olive oil, divided Juice of ½ lemon
3garlic cloves, minced and divided	½ teaspoon salt
¼ teaspoon red pepper flakes	Lemon wedges, for serving (optional) Marinara sauce, for dipping (optional)

1. Preheat the air fryer to 380°F. Toss in the shrimp with 2 tablespoons of the olive oil, lemon juice, 1/3 of minced garlic, salt, and red pepper flakes and coat well.
2. In a small ramekin, combine the remaining ¼ cup of olive oil and the remaining minced garlic. Tear off a 12-by-12-inch sheet of aluminum foil. Place the shrimp into the center of the foil, then fold the sides up and crimp the edges so that it forms an aluminum foil bowl that is open on top. Place this packet into the air fryer basket.
3. Roast the shrimp for 4 minutes, then open the air fryer and place the ramekin with oil and garlic in the basket beside the shrimp packet. Cook for 2 more minutes. Transfer the shrimp on a serving plate or platter with the ramekin of garlic olive oil on the side for dipping. You may also serve with lemon wedges and marinara sauce, if desired.

Nutrition 264 Calories 21g Fat 10g Carbohydrates 16g Protein

.Cheesy Beet Salad (Spanish)

Preparation time: 10 minutes Cooking time: 1 hour Servings: 4

3beets	3 tbsps. olive oil
¼ cup lime juice	8 slices goat cheese 1/3 cup walnuts
1 tbsp. chives	

1. In a roasting pan, combine the beets with the oil, salt, and pepper, toss and bake at 400°F for 1 hour.
2. Cool the beets down, transfer them to a bowl, add the rest of the ingredients, toss and serve as a side salad.

Nutrition: Calories: 156 Fat: 4.2 g. Protein: 4 g.

.Rosemary Beets (Greek)

Preparation time: 10 minutes Cooking time: 20 minutes Servings: 4

4 medium beets	1/3 cup balsamic vinegar 1 tsp. rosemary, chopped 1 garlic clove, minced
½ tsp. Italian seasoning 1 tbsp. olive oil	

1. Place a pan with the oil over medium heat, add the beets and the rest of the ingredients, toss, and cook for 20 minutes.
2. Divide the mix between plates and serve.

Nutrition: Calories: 165 Fat: 3.4 g. Protein: 2.3 g.

.Roasted and Curried Cauliflower (Italian)

Preparation time: 8 minutes Cooking time: 50 minutes
Servings: 6

1 lime juice	1 medium cauliflower head
	1 tsp. cayenne pepper
1 tsp. sea salt	1 tsp. smoked paprika
1½ cups full-fat Greek yogurt	½ tsp. black pepper
2tbsps. yellow curry powder	1 clove garlic
2 tsps. lime zest	
1tbsp. cilantro	½ cup pine nuts
¼ cup olive oil	¼ cup sun-dried tomatoes
2tbsps. Feta cheese, crumbled	

1. Prepare a baking sheet with parchment paper and preheat the oven to 375°F.
2. Mix well the lime zest, curry, black pepper, yogurt, paprika, sea salt, and lime in a bowl. Rub all over the cauliflower.
3. Place the cauliflower on the prepared pan and put it in the oven. Bake for 45 minutes.
4. Meanwhile, make the topping ingredients by pulsing sun-dried tomatoes, half of the pine nuts, and garlic in a food processor. Process until chunky.
5. Transfer the mixture to a bowl and fold in the remaining topping ingredients.
6. Once the cauliflower is done, remove it from the oven and let it cool enough to handle. Break into bite-sized pieces and drizzle topping ingredients over it.
7. Serve and enjoy.

Nutrition: Calories: 384 Protein: 15 g. Fat: 30 g.

.Classic Hummus (Greek)

Preparation time: 8 minutes Cooking time: 30 minutes
Servings: 6

1 cup dried chickpeas 4 cups water	1 tbsp., plus ¼ cup extra-virgin olive oil 1/3 cup tahini
1½ tsp. ground cumin 3/4 tsp. salt	½ tsp. ground black pepper
½ tsp. ground coriander	1 tsp. garlic, minced
1/3 cup lemon juice	

1. Put the chickpeas, water, and 1 tbsp. oil in the electric pressure cooker. Close, select steam release to sealing, click on manual, and time to 30 minutes.
2. When the timer rings, quick-release the pressure. Press the cancel button and open the lid. Drain, reserving the cooking liquid.
3. Blend chickpeas, the remaining ¼ cup of oil, tahini, cumin, salt, pepper, coriander, lemon juice, and garlic in a food processor. Serve.

Nutrition: Calories: 152 Fat: 12 g. Protein: 4 g.

.Cheese-Cauliflower Fritters (Greek)

Preparation Time: 10 minutes Cooking Time: 10 minutes
Servings: 2

1 cup cauliflower, shredded	1 tablespoon wheat flour, whole grain 1 oz Parmesan, grated
1 egg, beaten	
½ teaspoon ground black pepper 1 tablespoon canola oil	

1. In the mixing bowl mix up together shredded cauliflower and egg. Add wheat flour, grated Parmesan, and ground black pepper. Stir the mixture with the help of the fork until it is homogenous and smooth.
2. Pour canola oil in the skillet and bring it to boil. Make the fritters from the cauliflower mixture with the help of the fingertips or use spoon and transfer in the hot oil. Roast the fritters for 4 minutes from each side over the medium-low heat.

Nutrition 167 Calories 12.3g Fat 1.5g Carbohydrates 8.8g Protein

.Baked Cinnamon Oatmeal (Greek)

Preparation Time: 10 minutes Cooking Time: 25 minutes
Servings: 4

1 cup oatmeal 1/3 cup milk	1 pear, chopped
1 teaspoon vanilla extract 1 tablespoon Splenda	1 teaspoon butter
½ teaspoon ground cinnamon 1 egg, beaten	

1. In the big bowl mix up together oatmeal, milk, egg, vanilla extract, Splenda, and ground cinnamon. Melt butter and add it in the oatmeal mixture. Then add chopped pear and stir it well.
2. Transfer the oatmeal mixture in the casserole mold and flatten gently. Cover it with the foil and secure edges. Bake the oatmeal for 25 minutes at 350F.

Nutrition 151 Calories 3.9g Fat 3.3g Carbohydrates 4.9g Protein

.Easy and Healthy Baked Vegetables (Italian)

Preparation time: 9 minutes Cooking time: 75 minutes
Servings: 6

2 lbs. Brussels sprouts, trimmed 3 lbs. butternut squash	1 lb. pork breakfast sausage
	1 tbsp. fat from fried sausage

1. Grease a 9-inch baking pan and preheat the oven to 350°F.
2. With medium-high heat, put a nonstick saucepan and cook sausage. Break up the sausages and cook until browned.
3. In a greased pan, mix browned sausage, squash, sprouts, sea salt, and fat. Toss to mix well. Pop into the oven and cook for 1 hour.
4. Remove from oven and serve warm.

Nutrition: Calories: 364 Protein: 19 g. Fat: 17 g.

.Morning Tostadas (Spanish)

Prep Time: 15 minutes Cooking Time: 6 minutes Servings: 6

½ white onion, diced 1 tomato, chopped	1 cucumber, chopped
1 tablespoon fresh cilantro, chopped	½ jalapeno pepper, chopped 1 tablespoon lime juice
6 corn tortillas	1tablespoon canola oil
2oz Cheddar cheese, shredded	½ cup white beans, canned, drained 6 eggs
½ teaspoon butter	½ teaspoon Sea salt

1. Make Pico de Galo: in the salad bowl combine together diced white onion, tomato, cucumber, fresh cilantro, and jalapeno pepper. Then add lime juice and a ½ tablespoon of canola oil. Mix up the mixture well. Pico de Galo is cooked.
2. After this, preheat the oven to 390F. Line the tray with baking paper. Arrange the corn tortillas on the baking paper and brush with remaining canola oil from both sides. Bake the tortillas until they start to be crunchy. Chill the cooked crunchy tortillas well. Meanwhile, toss the butter in the skillet.
3. Crack the eggs in the melted butter and sprinkle them with sea salt. Fry the eggs until the egg whites become white (cooked). Approximately for 3-5 minutes over the medium heat. After this, mash the beans until you get puree texture. Spread the bean puree on the corn tortillas.
4. Add fried eggs. Then top the eggs with Pico de Galo and shredded Cheddar cheese.

Nutrition 246 Calories 11g Fat 4.7g Carbohydrates 13.7g Protein

.Cheese Omelet (Italian)

Prep Time: 5 minutes Cooking Time: 10 minutes Servings: 2

1 tablespoon cream cheese	¼ teaspoon paprika
2 eggs, beaten	
½ teaspoon dried oregano	¼ teaspoon dried dill 1 oz Parmesan, grated 1 teaspoon coconut oil

1. Mix up together cream cheese with eggs, dried oregano, and dill. Pour coconut oil in the skillet and heat it up until it will coat all the skillet.
2. Then fill the skillet with the egg mixture and flatten it. Add grated Parmesan and close the lid. Cook omelet for 10 minutes over the low heat. Then transfer the cooked omelet in the serving plate and sprinkle with paprika.

Nutrition 148 Calories 11.5g Fat 0.3g Carbohydrates10.6g Protein

.Fruity Pizza (Italian)

Prep Time: 10 minutes Cooking Time: 0 minute Servings: 2

1 tablespoon fresh cilantro, chopped	9 oz watermelon slice
1 tbsp Pomegranate sauce	2 oz Feta cheese, crumbled

1. Place the watermelon slice in the plate and sprinkle with crumbled Feta cheese. Add fresh cilantro. After this, sprinkle the pizza with Pomegranate juice generously. Cut the pizza into the servings.

Nutrition 143 Calories 6.2g Fat 0.6g Carbohydrates 5.1g Protein

.Herb and Ham Muffins (Greek)

Preparation Time: 10 minutes Cooking Time: 15 minutes Servings: 4

3 oz ham, chopped 4 eggs, beaten	2 tablespoons coconut flour
½ teaspoon dried oregano	¼ teaspoon dried cilantro Cooking spray

1. Spray the muffin's molds with cooking spray from inside. In the bowl mix up together beaten eggs, coconut flour, dried oregano, cilantro, and ham. When the liquid is homogenous, pour it in the prepared muffin molds.
2. Bake the muffins for 15 minutes at 360F. Chill the cooked meal well and only after this remove from the molds.

Nutrition 128 Calories 7.2g Fat 2.9g Carbohydrates10.1g Protein

.Morning Sprouts Pizza (Greek)

Preparation Time: 15 minutes Cooking Time: 20 minutes Servings: 6

½ cup wheat flour, whole grain 2 tablespoons butter, softened	¼ teaspoon baking powder
¾ teaspoon salt	5 oz chicken fillet, boiled
2 oz Cheddar cheese, shredded 1 teaspoon tomato sauce	1 oz bean sprouts

1. Make the pizza crust: mix up together wheat flour, butter, baking powder, and salt. Knead the soft and non-sticky dough. Add more wheat flour if needed. Leave the dough for 10 minutes to chill. Then place the dough on the baking paper. Cover it with the second baking paper sheet.
2. Roll up the dough with the help of the rolling pin to get the round pizza crust. After this, remove the upper baking paper sheet. Transfer the pizza crust in the tray.
3. Spread the crust with tomato sauce. Then shred the chicken fillet and arrange it over the pizza crust. Add shredded Cheddar cheese. Bake pizza for 20 minutes at 355F. Then top the cooked pizza with bean sprouts and slice into the servings.

Nutrition 157 Calories 8.8g Fat 0.3g Carbohydrates 10.5g Protein

.Chia and Nut Porridge (Greek)

Preparation Time: 10 minutes Cooking Time: 30 minutes Servings: 4

3 cups organic almond milk	1 teaspoon vanilla extract 1 tablespoon honey
1 1/3 cup chia seeds, dried	
¼ teaspoon ground cardamom	

1. Pour almond milk in the saucepan and bring it to boil. Then chill the almond milk to the room temperature (or appx. For 10-15 minutes). Add vanilla extract, honey, and ground cardamom. Stir well. After this, add chia seeds and stir again. Close the lid and let chia seeds soak the liquid for 20-25 minutes. Transfer the cooked porridge into the serving ramekins.

Nutrition 150 Calories 7.3g Fat 6.1g Carbohydrates 3.7g Protein

.Chocolate Oatmeal (Greek)

Preparation Time: 10 minutes Cooking Time: 15 minutes
Servings: 2

1 ½ cup oatmeal	1 tablespoon cocoa powder
½ cup heavy cream	¼ cup of water
1teaspoon vanilla extract 1 tablespoon butter	2tablespoons Splenda

1. Mix up together oatmeal with cocoa powder and Splenda. Transfer the mixture in the saucepan. Add vanilla extract, water, and heavy cream. Stir it gently with the help of the spatula.
2. Close the lid and cook it for 10-15 minutes over the medium-low heat. Remove the cooked cocoa oatmeal from the heat and add butter. Stir it well.

Nutrition 230 Calories 10.6g Fat 3.5g Carbohydrates 4.6g Protein

.Cinnamon Roll Oats (Spanish)

Preparation Time: 7 minutes Cooking Time: 10 minutes
Servings: 4

½ cup rolled oats 1 cup milk	1 teaspoon vanilla extract
1teaspoon ground cinnamon 2 teaspoon honeys	2tablespoons Plain yogurt 1 teaspoon butter

1. Transfer milk in the saucepan and bring it to boil. Add rolled oats and stir well. Close the lid and simmer the oats for 5 minutes over the medium heat. The cooked oats will absorb all milk.
2. Then add butter and stir the oats well. In the separated bowl, whisk together Plain yogurt with honey, cinnamon, and vanilla extract. Transfer the cooked oats in the serving bowls. Top the oats with the yogurt mixture in the shape of the wheel.

Nutrition 243 Calories 20.2g Fat 1g Carbohydrates 13.3g Protein

.Crunchy Kale Chips (Italian)

Preparation time: 11 minutes Cooking time: 2 hours Servings: 8

2 tbsps. filtered water	½ tsp. sea salt
1tbsp. raw honey	2tbsps. nutritional yeast 1 lemon, juiced
1cup sweet potato 1 cup fresh cashews	2bunches of green curly kale

1. Prepare a baking sheet by covering it with unbleached parchment paper. Preheat the oven to 350 F.
2. In a large mixing bowl, place the kale.
3. In a food processor, process the remaining ingredients until smooth. Pour over the kale.
4. With your hands, coat the kale with marinade.
5. Evenly spread the kale onto parchment paper and pop in the oven. Dehydrate for 2 hours and turn leaves after the first hour of baking.
6. Remove from the oven; let it cool completely before serving.

Nutrition: Calories: 209 Protein: 7 g. Fat: 15.9 g.

.Zucchini Lasagna (Greek)

Preparation time: 13 minutes Cooking time: 45 minutes
Servings: 4

2 zucchinis, trimmed	1 cup Mozzarella, shredded
½ cup tomato sauce 1 onion, chopped	1 tbsp. olive oil
½ cup potato, boiled, mashed 1 tsp. Italian seasonings	¼ cup tomato sauce 1 tsp. butter softened

1. Heat the olive oil in a skillet.
2. Add the onion and roast it until light brown.
3. Meanwhile, slice the zucchini lengthwise.
4. Grease the casserole mold with butter from inside.
5. Put ½ part of sliced zucchini in the casserole mold to get the layer.
6. Then add the layer of cooked onion and a ½ cup of Mozzarella cheese.
7. After this, make the layer from the remaining zucchini.
8. Top the vegetables with a layer of mashed potatoes and Mozzarella.
9. Pour the tomato sauce over the cheese and cover the surface of the mold with foil. Secure the edges.
10. Bake the lasagna for 30 minutes at 365°F.
11. Then discard the foil and cook lasagna for 10 minutes more.

Nutrition: Calories: 103 Fat: 6.3 g. Protein: 4.1 g.

.Quinoa with Banana and Cinnamon (Greek)

Preparation Time: 10 minutes Cooking Time: 12 minutes
Servings: 4

1cup quinoa	2cup milk
1teaspoon vanilla extract 1 teaspoon honey	2bananas, sliced
¼ teaspoon ground cinnamon	

1. Pour milk in the saucepan and add quinoa. Close the lid and cook it over the medium heat for 12 minutes or until quinoa will absorb all liquid. Then chill the quinoa for 10-15 minutes and place in the serving mason jars.
2. Add honey, vanilla extract, and ground cinnamon. Stir well. Top quinoa with banana and stirs it before serving.

Nutrition 279 Calories 5.3g Fat 4.6g Carbohydrates 10.7g Protein

.Balsamic Eggplant Mix (Greek)

Preparation time: 10 minutes Cooking time: 20 minutes
Servings: 6

1/3 cup chicken stock	2 tbsps. balsamic vinegar 1 tbsp. lime juice
2 large eggplants	1tbsp. rosemary
¼ cup cilantro	2tbsps. olive oil

1. In a roasting pan, combine the eggplants with the stock, vinegar, and the rest of the ingredients. Put the pan in the oven and bake at 390°F for 20 minutes.
2. Divide the mix between plates and serve.

Nutrition: Calories: 201 Fat: 4.5 g. Protein: 3 g.

.Egg Casserole (Greek)

Prep Time: 10 minutes Cooking Time: 28 minutes Servings: 4

2 eggs, beaten	1 red bell pepper, chopped
	1 chili pepper, chopped
½ red onion, diced	1 teaspoon canola oil
½ teaspoon salt	1 teaspoon paprika
1 tbsp fresh cilantro, chopped 1 garlic clove, diced	1 teaspoon butter, softened
¼ teaspoon chili flakes	

1. Brush the casserole mold with canola oil and pour beaten eggs inside. After this, toss the butter in the skillet and melt it over the medium heat. Add chili pepper and red bell pepper.
2. After this, add red onion and cook the vegetables for 7-8 minutes over the medium heat. Stir them from time to time. Transfer the vegetables in the casserole mold.
3. Add salt, paprika, cilantro, diced garlic, and chili flakes. Stir mildly with the help of a spatula to get a homogenous mixture. Bake the casserole for 20 minutes at 355F in the oven. Then chill the meal well and cut into servings. Transfer the casserole in the serving plates with the help of the spatula.

Nutrition 68 Calories 4.5g Fat 1g Carbohydrates 3.4g Protein

.Zucchini-Cheese Fritters with Aioli (Greek)

Preparation Time: 10 minutes, plus 20 minutes rest time Cooking Time: 25 minutes Servings: 4

1 large or 2 small/medium zucchini 1 teaspoon salt, divided	½ cup whole-milk ricotta cheese 2 scallions
1large egg	2garlic cloves, finely minced
2 tablespoons chopped fresh mint (optional) 2 teaspoons grated lemon zest	¼ teaspoon freshly ground black pepper
½ cup almond flour	1 teaspoon baking powder
8 tablespoons extra-virgin olive oil	8 tablespoons Roasted Garlic Aioli or avocado oil mayonnaise

1. Situate the shredded zucchini in a colander or on several layers of paper towels. Sprinkle with ½ teaspoon salt and let sit for 10 minutes.
2. Using another layer of paper towel press down on the zucchini to release any excess moisture and pat dry. Incorporate the drained zucchini, ricotta, scallions, egg, garlic, mint (if using), lemon zest, remaining ½ teaspoon salt, and pepper.
3. Scourge together the almond flour and baking powder. Fold in the flour mixture into the zucchini mixture and let rest for 10 minutes. In a large skillet, working in four batches, fry the fritters.
4. For each batch of four, heat 2 tablespoons olive oil over medium-high heat. Add 1 heaping tablespoon of zucchini batter per fritter, pressing down with the back of a spoon to form 2- to 3-inch fritters. Cover and let fry 2 minutes before flipping. Fry another 2 to 3 minutes, covered, or until crispy and golden and cooked through. You may need to reduce heat to medium to prevent burning. Remove from the pan and keep warm.
5. Repeat for the remaining three batches, using 2 tablespoons of the olive oil for each batch. Serve fritters warm with aioli.

Nutrition 448 Calories 42g Fat 2g Carbohydrates 8g Protein

.Cucumbers Filled with Salmon (Italian)

Preparation Time: 10 minutes Cooking Time: 0 minute Servings: 4

2 large cucumbers, peeled 1 (4-ounce) can red salmon	1 medium very ripe avocado
1 tablespoon extra-virgin olive oil Zest and juice of 1 lime	3 tablespoons chopped fresh cilantro
½ teaspoon salt	¼ teaspoon freshly ground black pepper

1. Slice the cucumber into 1-inch-thick segments and using a spoon, scrape seeds out of center of each segment and stand up on a plate. In a medium bowl, mix the salmon, avocado, olive oil, lime zest and juice, cilantro, salt, and pepper and mix until creamy.
2. Scoop the salmon mixture into the center of each cucumber segment and serve chilled.

Nutrition 159 Calories 11g Fat 3g Carbohydrates 9g Protein

.Mini Crab Cakes (Greek)

Preparation Time: 10 minutes Cooking Time: 10 minutes Servings: 6

8 ounces lump crab meat	2 tablespoons diced red bell pepper
1 scallion, white parts and green parts, diced 1 garlic clove, minced	1 tablespoon capers, minced
1 tablespoon nonfat plain Greek yogurt 1 egg, beaten	¼ cup whole wheat bread crumbs
¼ teaspoon salt	1 tablespoon olive oil
1 lemon, cut into wedges	

1. Preheat the air fryer to 360°F. In a medium bowl, mix the crab, bell pepper, scallion, garlic, and capers until combined. Add the yogurt and egg. Stir until incorporated. Mix in the bread crumbs and salt.
2. Portion this mixture into 6 equal parts and pat out into patties. Place the crab cakes inside the air fryer basket on single layer, separately. Grease the tops of each patty with a bit of olive oil. Bake for 10 minutes.
3. Pull out the crab cakes from the air fryer and serve with lemon wedges on the side.

Nutrition 87 Calories 4g Fat 6g Carbohydrates 9g Protein

.Wrapped Plums (Spanish)

Preparation time: 10 minutes Cooking time: 0 minutes Servings: 8

4 plums, quartered	2 ounces prosciutto, cut into 16 pieces 1 tablespoon chives, chopped
A pinch red pepper flakes, crushed	

1. Wrap each plum quarter in a prosciutto slice, arrange them all on a platter, sprinkle the chives and pepper flakes all over, and serve.

Nutrition: Calories: 30 Fat:1 g Fiber:0 g Carbohydrates: 4 g Protein: 2 g

.Tomato Cream Cheese Spread (Italian)

Preparation time: 10 minutes Cooking time: 0 minutes
Servings: 6

12 ounces cream cheese, soft 2 garlic cloves, minced	2 tablespoons lime juice
2tablespoons red onion, chopped 1 big tomato, cubed	¼ cup homemade mayonnaise Salt and black pepper to taste

1. In your blender, mix the cream cheese with the tomato and the rest of the ingredients, pulse well, divide into small cups and serve cold.

Nutrition: Calories:204Fat:6.7gFiber:1.4gCarbohydrates:7.3g
Protein:4.5 g

Italian Fries (Italian)

Preparation time: 10 minutes Cooking time: 10 minutes
Servings: 4

2tablespoons canola oil 1 tablespoon dried dill	1 tablespoon Italian seasoning 1 teaspoon turmeric
1/3 cup baby red potatoes ½ teaspoon sea salt	½ teaspoon dried rosemary

1. Cut the red potatoes into wedges and transfer them to the big bowl.
2. After this, sprinkle the vegetables with Italian seasoning, canola oil, turmeric, sea salt, dried rosemary, and dried dill.
3. Shake the potato wedges carefully.
4. Line the baking tray with baking paper.
5. Place the potatoes wedges in the tray. Flatten it well to make one layer.
6. Preheat the oven to 375 °F.
7. Place the tray with potatoes in the oven and bake for 40 minutes. Stir the potatoes with the help of the spatula from time to time.
8. The potato fries are cooked when they have crunchy edges.

Nutrition: Calories: 122 Fat:11.6 gFiber:0.5 g Carbohydrates: 4.5 g Protein: 0.6g

Appendix 1   Measurement Conversion Chart

VOLUME EQUIVALENTS(DRY)

US STANDARD	METRIC (APPROXIMATE)
1/8 teaspoon	0.5 mL
1/4 teaspoon	1 mL
1/2 teaspoon	2 mL
3/4 teaspoon	4 mL
1 teaspoon	5 mL
1 tablespoon	15 mL
1/4 cup	59 mL
1/2 cup	118 mL
3/4 cup	177 mL
1 cup	235 mL
2 cups	475 mL
3 cups	700 mL
4 cups	1 L

VOLUME EQUIVALENTS(LIQUID)

US STANDARD	US STANDARD (OUNCES)	METRIC (APPROXIMATE)
2 tablespoons	1 fl.oz.	30 mL
1/4 cup	2 fl.oz.	60 mL
1/2 cup	4 fl.oz.	120 mL
1 cup	8 fl.oz.	240 mL
1 1/2 cup	12 fl.oz.	355 mL
2 cups or 1 pint	16 fl.oz.	475 mL
4 cups or 1 quart	32 fl.oz.	1 L
1 gallon	128 fl.oz.	4 L

TEMPERATURES EQUIVALENTS

FAHRENHEIT(F)	CELSIUS(C) (APPROXIMATE)
225 °F	107 °C
250 °F	120 °C
275 °F	135 °C
300 °F	150 °C
325 °F	160 °C
350 °F	180 °C
375 °F	190 °C
400 °F	205 °C
425 °F	220 °C
450 °F	235 °C
475 °F	245 °C
500 °F	260 °C

WEIGHT EQUIVALENTS

US STANDARD	METRIC (APPROXIMATE)
1 ounce	28 g
2 ounces	57 g
5 ounces	142 g
10 ounces	284 g
15 ounces	425 g
16 ounces (1 pound)	455 g
1.5 pounds	680 g
2 pounds	907 g

Appendix 2   Dirty Dozen and Clean Fifteen

The Environmental Working Group (EWG) is a nonprofit, nonpartisan organization dedicated to protecting human health and the environment Its mission is to empower people to live healthier lives in a healthier environment. This organization publishes an annual list of the twelve kinds of produce, in sequence, that have the highest amount of pesticide residue-the Dirty Dozen-as well as a list of the fifteen kinds ofproduce that have the least amount of pesticide residue-the Clean Fifteen.

THE DIRTY DOZEN	THE CLEAN FIFTEEN
• The 2016 Dirty Dozen includes the following produce. These are considered among the year's most important produce to buy organic:	• The least critical to buy organically are the Clean Fifteen list. The following are on the 2016 list:

Strawberries	Spinach	Avocados	Papayas
Apples	Tomatoes	Corn	Kiw
Nectarines	Bell peppers	Pineapples	Eggplant
Peaches	Cherry tomatoes	Cabbage	Honeydew
Celery	Cucumbers	Sweet peas	Grapefruit
Grapes	Kale/collard greens	Onions	Cantaloupe
Cherries	Hot peppers	Asparagus	Cauliflower
		Mangos	

• *The Dirty Dozen list contains two additional itemskale/collard greens and hot peppers-because they tend to contain trace levels of highly hazardous pesticides.*	• *Some of the sweet corn sold in the United States are made from genetically engineered (GE) seedstock. Buy organic varieties of these crops to avoid GE produce.*

Appendix 3   Index

I

J

K

L

M

S

W

Y

Z

Leave a Review

As an independent author with a small marketing budget, reviews are my livelihood on this platform. If you enjoyed this book, I'd appreciate it if you could leave your honest feedback.

I read EVERY single review because I love the feedback from MY readers!

Thank you for staying with me

Made in the USA
Monee, IL
24 April 2022

95300360R00168